Making Whiteness

GRACE ELIZABETH HALE

Making Whiteness

THE CULTURE OF SEGREGATION
IN THE SOUTH, 1890–1940

Pantheon Books   New York

Permissions Acknowledgments appear on pages 409-10.

Library of Congress Cataloging-in-Publication Data

Hale, Grace Elizabeth.
    Making whiteness : the culture of segregation in the South,
1890-1940 / Grace Elizabeth Hale.
        p.   cm.
    Includes bibliographical references and index.
    ISBN 0-679-44263-4
    1. Southern states—Race relations.   2. Southern states—
Social conditions—1865–1945.   3. Afro-Americans—
Segregation—Southern states—History.   4. Whites—
Southern states—Race identity.   I. Title.
F215.H18   1998
305.8'00973—dc21   97-40906
                                                            CIP

Random House Web Address: http://www.randomhouse.com

Book design by Suvi Asch

Printed in the United States of America

9 8 7 6 5 4 3 2

For Jessica Bruce Hunt
and Margaret Lawson Hall,
for our history

Table of Contents

Preface

CENTRAL TO THE MEANING of whiteness is a broad, collective American silence. The denial of white as a racial identity, the denial that whiteness has a history, allows the quiet, the blankness, to stand as the norm. This erasure enables many to fuse their absence of racial being with the nation, making whiteness their unspoken but deepest sense of what it means to be an American. And despite, and paradoxically because of, their treasured and cultivated distinctiveness, southern whites are central to this nationalism of denial.

On the brink of the civil rights movement, white southerners imagined themselves linked across the fissures of locality, gender and class differences, and political and religious loyalties. As important, they understood their collectivity as moral, as an integral part of a strong and modern American world. The racial identities crafted in that space and time between Reconstruction and World War II have grounded those of our own national present. This book is about how some southerners created a common whiteness to solve the problems of the post–Civil War era and built their collectivity on not just a convention or a policy but on segregation as a culture.

I have tried here, against the deepest currents of late twentieth-century life, to write of racial making, not racial meaning. Segregation—the nation's broadest twentieth-century enactment of the difference between blacks and whites—is the product of human choice and decision, of power and fear, of longing, even of love and hate. At the level of culture, I have traced the origins and contours of modern southern whiteness, the ways in which segregation presented a profound cultural problem, even as, in the late 1890s, it offered a practical political and social solution. My goal has been to illuminate who white southerners imagined they were and the stories and images that enabled them to make their collectiveness powerful and persuasive and true.

Certainly, identities are slippery, ambiguous, and individual things. I am not suggesting that local differences did not interact with and sharply focus southern white racial thinking. I am not arguing that all classes and genders participated equally in this project of racial making. But I think that the commonalities are important, that the most pervasive characteristics of southern whiteness have been the most powerful. Why does this abstraction of the world into black and white continue to color our own imaginings? Why does the culture of segregation, despite the very real successes of the civil rights movement, still seduce and ensnare us all? An understanding of what has made whiteness a cohesive and national as well as regional category seems to me necessary in any effort to find a future beyond it, to find a twenty-first-century American collectivity outside whiteness's racial denial that will actually include us all. Our differences are emphasized everywhere—from academic scholarship to the consumer marketplace. When will we try honestly, with and not against history, to create a new commonality? The implication of "making whiteness," of course, is that whiteness can be unmade, so that other, more democratic grounds of coherence can be established and lived.

Making Whiteness

Producing the Ground of Difference

The discovery of personal whiteness among the world's peoples is a very modern thing—a nineteenth and twentieth century matter indeed.

W. E. B. DU BOIS[1]

To BE AMERICAN is to be both black and white.[2] Yet to be a modern American has also meant to deny this mixing, our deep biracial genesis. Racial segregation colors even our language, and thinking beyond its construction is not easy. To trace the creation of whiteness as a modern racial identity, we must leave assumed, habitual ways of racial knowing behind.

The cultural history of the American South between 1890 and 1940 provides the chiaroscuro necessary to make the invisible visible, to give whiteness a color. The ways in which the South has served national imaginings have, after all, doubled the ways in which blackness has served American whiteness. The South has been, to use the language of our racial orderings, the darkness that has made the American nation lose its color. Replicating the contradictions of whiteness itself both everywhere present and nowhere visible, the region has been both founding family member and military foe, both too black and more white, both less fragmented and more segregated, both a place apart, outside the flow of time, and an essential part of the national whole.

Long before they conceived of such regional differences, early Americans linked skin color to the origins of peoples, using it to distinguish various nationalities and ethnicities of Africans, Native Americans, and Europeans. Nevertheless, racial identity before the nineteenth century was not an overarching or absolute category. Europeans enslaved Africans and regarded them as inferior because they were pagans, without nationality or culture, and because, unlike those other "savages," they could not readily escape to their own people. The existence of free blacks as well as black slaveholders made the antebellum dynamic of power one of slave versus citizen, dependent versus independent, rather than white versus black. Slaves could in principle become free, although their freedom was often circumscribed. Antebellum society grounded racialized difference in the law, in the legal status of a human being as a person or as chattel. Other categories like gender, ethnicity, class, locality, and religion also shaped citizenship status. Nonslave women as well as "free" male apprentices and landless agricultural laborers, for instance, possessed only limited rights.

Arguing that the link between antebellum slave status and the modern dominant social connotation of blackness in American culture is not straightforward or isomorphic should not diminish the horrific, nor mitigate the crime of slavery. It is to note that slaves occupied the brutally exploited bottom of a premodern social hierarchy. It is to make use for our present of the insights gained by an understanding of American social reality, in which, until the 1850s, slave status was a political difference enacted through the law rather than a naturalized, embodied identity existing outside it. Slavery, in other words, founded and fixed the meaning of blackness more than any transparent and transhistorical meaning of black skin founded the category of slavery.

Before the Civil War, however, Americans from both regions began transforming the meaning of race. Outside the South, the maturation of free black communities, the rise of abolitionism, the enforcement of the Fugitive Slave Law, and the making of increasingly distinct middle and working classes increased consciousness of racial difference. Rising defensiveness about slavery and the regional identity undergirded by human bondage created a parallel development inside the region. Slaveholders searched for ways both to legitimate their system of unfree labor in a Western world in which revolutionary thinking denied the morality of such hierarchies of men, and to assert a unified regional identity—a collectivity across the class divides between slaveholders and nonslaveholders—against a mounting northern antagonism. Scientific explanations of the world, particularly natural scientists' new biological theories of race and separate creationism, added weight to racialist thinking even as they contradicted older religious defenses of paternalistic stewardship over dependents.

The Civil War greatly magnified these trends, making whiteness a more important category, a way to assert a new collectivity, the Confederacy, across lines of class and gender that divided free southerners. The old antebellum category of inclusion and power, citizenship, although defined most centrally against the figure of the slave, proved a weak identity in a new "nation" and possessed class and gender hierarchies of its own. But the need for free southerners to secure some measure of slave loyalty mitigated the potential excesses of narrowly racial arguments. By 1863, Lincoln's Emancipation Proclamation had made the freeing of the slave, that opposite of the citizen, the symbolic goal of the northern armies. And Union victory delegitimated that nascent nationalist collectivity, the Confederacy. The Reconstruction amendments extended national citizenship to the freedpeople and specifically gave the freedmen its most fundamental expression, the right to vote. By the end of Reconstruction, all southern men possessed the same legal rights in the newly reunited nation. But what would citizenship mean in a world without slaves?

From Appomattox through the end of the nineteenth century, Americans of both regions shattered the old hierarchical structures of power, imagined as organic and divinely inspired, and used the fragments to erect more binary orderings, imagined as natural and physically grounded. Racial identity had never been completely subsumed within the citizen-versus-slave dialectic, but Reconstruction severed these linkages completely. The ex-Confederates, the "Southerners," called any people who did not support them politically "Black Republicans"—the freedpeople certainly but also transplanted white northerners and white southern unionists as well. Regional antagonisms—the northern conquerors versus the defeated South—retarded the development of an overarching conception of collective white identity even as biological theories of racial worth gained ground. For a brief time, at least, many northerners saw the freedpeople as both dependents and allies against their former enemies, the ex-Confederates. And the former enemies found themselves locked in yet another contest, over who would control the labor and the votes of the ex-slaves. The freedpeople sought pragmatic local alliances where they could find them and worked to retain and expand their freedom and citizenship, their control over themselves and their hope of belonging to what would become a new American whole. But by the 1880s these political conflicts, as well as the economic trends toward centralization, standardization, urbanization, and mechanization, accelerated and permanently institutionalized by the war, meant that American collective identity itself was now anything but clear.[3]

The overlapping of the aftermath of the Civil War and the fate of the ex-slaves with these economic changes destabilized the categories of power during the 1880s and 1890s. The question of what structure of social ordering would replace the familiar hierarchies of both North and South made this a period of volatility and uncertainty. Hierarchical structures founded in the personalized social relations of specific localities lost their authority in an increasingly mobile and rapidly changing society. How would people know who they were within this spinning abstraction, the newly economically integrated, industrialized nation-state?

To make order within the seeming fragmentation of their world, some Americans elaborated spatial mediations of modernity—ways of attaching identities to physical moorings, from bodies to buildings to larger geographies like region and nation. They produced new grounds of difference to mediate the ruptures of modernity. In effect, they translated the specific and individualized linkages between identity, place, and power that had reigned in an earlier, smaller world into connections between categories of people and imagined spaces that moved far beyond local boundaries.[4]

Serving as a catalyst for this growing sense of both a fragmented and an increasingly abstract society, the Civil War violently, convulsively produced the need to narrate new foundations. The war and Reconstruction had definitively shifted the location of citizenship from the individual states to the national level, a centralization of government power made readily visible by the circulation of the first national currency and the emancipation of the slaves. American nationalism—our modern sense of ourselves as a national community—as well as American imperialism, marked a newly narrowed and deepened opposition between Americans and non-Americans, manifest especially in the Spanish-American War. The defeat of the last independent Indian nations as well as the official closing of the frontier with the 1890 census gave this rising nationalism a contiguous and continental geography.

Spurred by the ongoing revolution in transportation, the economy boomed to fill in the continent, creating a marketplace both wide and deep, the first national mass market. The reconstitution of the southern economy—sharecropping organized more narrowly toward the market as opposed to the wider balancing of household and market production that characterized antebellum plantations and farms—eased the complete incorporation of the South into this increasingly national economy. These changes, in turn, operated dialectically with another spatial ordering of identity. The founding geography of the northern middle class was the split between work and home and the extension of the older gendering of the male public and the female private to these changing and more concretely embodied spheres. The conservation movement and the construction of national parks undergirded other geographical elaborations of power, ensuring that nature as embodied in wilderness would continue to exist in opposition to culture—what the people had made. Parks literally marked the ground as important, as the move to towns and cities detached many from the land as both a site of work and a more localized identity.[5]

Yet it was racial identity that became the paramount spatial mediation of modernity within the newly reunited nation. Not self-evidently more meaningful, not more real or natural than other markings, race nevertheless became the crucial means of ordering the newly enlarged meaning of America. This happened because former Confederates, a growing working class, embattled farmers, western settlers, a defensive northeastern elite, women's rights advocates, an increasingly powerful scientific community, and others, simultaneously but for different reasons, found race useful in creating new collective identities to replace older, more individual, and local groundings of self. As important, these mass racial meanings were made and marked at a time when technological change made the cheap production of visual imagery possible and the development of a mass market provided a financial incentive—selling through advertising—to circulate the imagery.

Historians have called this convergence of economic and cultural change consumer culture, the creation of a mass market for everything from chewing tobacco to sporting events to movies. Consumer culture has become a way of designating not just the increasing importance of buying—including what and how a person eats and dresses and relaxes— but also consumption's centrality to how she understands and locates her very self. The invention of photography and motion pictures and changes in lithography, engraving, and printing as well as the construction of museums, expositions, department stores, and amusement parks emphasized visibility, the act of looking and the authority of the eye—the spectacle. The desire to mark racial difference as a mass identity, as white versus "colored," converged with the means to create and circulate the spectacle. And spectacle, the power of looking, was different from narrative, the power of telling. A picture, a representation, could convey contradictions and evoke oppositions like white racial supremacy, white racial innocence, and white racial dependency more easily and persuasively than a carefully plotted story.[6]

It is important to place southern segregation, then, within this contradictory historical context of representational fluidity and spatial grounding. Geographically separating peoples as a way of making and fixing absolute racial difference occurred across the nation. By the early twentieth century, segregation laws and more localized conventions affected Native Americans, Asian Americans, and African Americans, and the separation has remained visible in our very language. But "the people who think of themselves as white"—a naming James Baldwin crafted to render visible this process of racial making—also produced their own mass cultural identity across divisions of class, gender, region, and religion and rendered its whiteness invisible at the same time. Focusing on the visible, they attempted to control both the geographical and representational mobility of nonwhites. African Americans were clearly inferior in the South because they occupied inferior spaces like Jim Crow cars, often literally marked as colored, and across the nation because they appeared at fairs, in advertisements, and in movies as visibly inferior characters. Yet whites made modern racial meaning not just by creating boundaries but also by crossing them. Containing the mobility of others allowed whites to put on blackface, to play with and project upon darkness, to let whiteness float free. These transgressions characterized and broadened modern whiteness, increasing its invisibility and its power.[7]

By the early twentieth century, whites were constructing modern racial identity: a mass cultural rather than a localized, socially embodied, particularized self, an absolute division that dissolved any range of racially mixed subjectivities, a natural and embodied but not strictly biological or legal category, a way to mediate the fragmentation of modernity and still enjoy its freedom. And racial separation, what W. E. B. Du Bois famously called "the problem of the color line," became the founding metaphor as well as policy of modern American life. But the whiteness that some Americans made through segregation was always contingent, always fragile, always uncertain.

Positing an absolute boundary and the freedom to cross only in one direction, segregation remained vulnerable at its muddled middle, where mixed-race people moved through mixed spaces, from railroad cars to movies to department stores, neither public nor private, neither black nor white.[8]

And nowhere was this ambiguous middle, the contradictory, simultaneous need for race to be visible—blackness—and invisible—whiteness—more apparent than in the South. Southern whites constructed their racial identities on two interlocking planes: within a regional dynamic of ex-Confederates versus ex-slaves and within a national dynamic of the South, understood as white, versus the nation. The demands and desires of southern African Americans as well as the needs of America, as both a state and an identity, shaped the contours of modern southern whiteness. This doubled dynamic deepened the shadings of southern racial identities, making them more starkly apparent than, even as they were vitally important to, American whiteness in general. As culture, southern segregation made a new collective white identity across lines of gender and class and a new regional distinctiveness. Yet paradoxically, the southern whiteness that segregation created provided a cultural foundation for the very "natural" racial differences white southerners had hoped to protect and a route back into the nation. Grounding the modern whiteness that in turn grounded national reconciliation, the specifically southern culture of segregation became doubly important for the nation, as racial narratives and spectacles utilized southern settings and reworked southern history and as southern blacks in growing numbers began to migrate out of the region.

Like other Americans seeking social order, white southerners chose geographic anchors, whether the imagined spaces evoked by narratives or the physical spaces recaptured through spectacle, literally to ground their racial identity within the mobility of modernity. The particular narratives and spectacles they created and used, of course, grew out of the specific social history of the region. Under circumstances where the legal bifurcations of slave versus free status no longer operated, elite whites in the Reconstruction era remained dependent on their ex-slaves. But how would they control the labor of African Americans within the post–Civil War reality of an at least presumptive free labor and in which the state tools of law and punishment remained semi-hostile and partially outside of their political control? And this problem of how to ground a social order in a South without economic and political autonomy did not diminish with the end of Reconstruction. White southerners created their modern sense of themselves as different, externally, from the rest of Americans and different, internally, from African Americans, at the level of culture. This book tries to show how, in detail and in the actual event, they crafted their modern racial and regional identity and how that making served the rest of the nation.

I wish to avoid the mistakes of past white liberalisms that have reinscribed racist limits on the democratic imagination by painting African Americans as consigned by white exclusion to cultural pathology. Nor do I wish to present whites as victims of the very racial divisions in which they have continually invested. Toni Morrison in her novel *Jazz* inverts William Faulkner's *Absalom, Absalom!* and rejects the tragedy of a founding racial flaw and the resulting impasse of history that figures the past as barricade—as dense, suffocating, and unbearable. Instead, she sings history's possibility and the ways in which love, both intimate and otherwise, can heal wounds and propel us forward. By doing so, she exposes the greater and desperate rejection of American reality behind claims linking pathology to blackness. That whites have been unable within the culture of segregation to think about race without the blackfaced minstrel or the happy slave merely means that they have once again projected their own concoction of guilt and nostalgia, their own cultural damage, onto a dark ground. They are not racism's victims. The disproportionate numbers of African Americans living in poverty amid the plenty of late twentieth-century American capitalism exposes the idiocy of any competing alienations. The cost of the investment in whiteness has been borne overwhelmingly by African Americans.

Nevertheless, it is necessary to highlight the collective cost, the damage segregation has done to the collective ability to conjure our broadest cross-racial connectedness, and to acknowledge the resulting poverty of the attempts to imagine an inclusive America. That both whites and blacks, or more broadly all people of all colors, cannot truly embrace the range of North American humanity as their own, as their imagined community, is the collective cost. Making whiteness American culture, the nation has forgone other possibilities. The hybridity that could have been our greatest strength has been made into a means of playing across the color line, with its rotting distance of voyeurism and partisanship, a confirmation of social and psychological division.[9]

American history in its broadest sense—what has happened, how we have represented to ourselves what has happened, and how we will continue in this intersecting of making and telling—is vitally important here. If we understand the past as always having been only white and black, what will be the catalyst that makes the future different? The epiphany that erases the bloody divisions? The revelation that makes tomorrow, any time, whole? If we cannot imagine less racially binary pasts or raceless futures, who will? If we cannot craft a dance of time to do more than deepen and elaborate racial difference—and set the hued fragments in motion until the jig reveals the pattern and the colors blur—who will make this time? Integration, created from within our history now, is our only future.

CHAPTER ONE

No Easy Place or Time

THE BLACK SIDE OF SEGREGATION

> *Around us the history of the land has centered for thrice*
> *a hundred years . . . Actively we have woven ourselves with the very*
> *warp and woof of this nation . . . Would America have been*
> *America without her Negro people?*
>
> W. E. B. DU BOIS[1]

> *For, while the tale of how we suffer, and how we are delighted,*
> *and how we may triumph is never new, it always must be heard.*
> *There isn't any other tale to tell, it's the only*
> *light we've got in all this darkness.*
>
> JAMES BALDWIN[2]

How can we narrate the founding moment of emancipation, the achievement at long last by four million people of the ownership of their own mid-nineteenth-century selves?[3] Freedom has so many other, more metaphorical uses in the late twentieth century, small meanings indeed in the shadow of this grand liberation, that the act of historical imagining fails. In the beginning, there was joy, certainly, and rapture. The slaves had used biblical stories to prophesy the defeat of the white South for at least half a century, and when the great transformation came, they were as likely to attribute their liberty to their own actions, from praying to fleeing to fighting, as to the Union armies. As a former slave insisted years later, "God planned dem slave prayers to free us like he did the Israelites, and dey did." But magnanimous in the moment, they were willing to share the credit, and to name a Moses too: "Well, I s'pose that God sent Abe Lincoln to 'liver us." The time the stories foretold had come.[4]

When Union troops conquered Richmond, Virginia, in 1865, white and black northern soldiers reported that the ex-slaves ran in the streets singing: "Slavery chain done broke at last; slavery chain done broke at last—I's goin' praise God till I die." The chaplain of the Twenty-eighth U.S. Colored Troops, Garland H. White, was among the liberators. Returning to the place where he had been a slave before he ran away to Ohio, White made a speech "amid the shouts of ten thousand voices, and proclaimed for the first time in that city freedom to all mankind." When other soldiers opened the cells of the slave market, he could not continue speaking. "I became so over-come with tears, that I could not stand up under the pressure of such full-ness of joy in my own heart." After such public celebration came a more private freedom as White embraced his mother, ending their twenty-year separation. A slave on a plantation near Appomattox Courthouse, Fannie Berry, learned of the defeat of the Confederacy a week after Richmond fell. Years later she insisted, "Never was no time like 'em befo' or since. Niggers shoutin' an' clappin' hands an' singin'! Chillun runnin' all over de place beatin' tins an' yellin'. Everybody happy. Sho' did some celebratin'."[5]

But emancipation, as the former slaves knew, was not simply a govern-ment proclamation or a spontaneous celebration. They had stretched that chain to make it break. Throughout the war, slaves fled their masters. Rec-ognizing the moral and military advantages of supporting their actions, in 1863 Lincoln declared the slaves in the rebelling states free. For many, as in Richmond, liberation came with the arrival of the Union armies, or as with Fannie Berry, with an unintended word from her owner. For others, word came, as one ex-slave remembered, "way after freedom" when "de Guv-ment man" came to the plantations. Years later Sarah Ford recalled, "Dat one time Massa Charley can't open he mouth, 'cause de captain tell him to shut up, dat he'd do de talkin'." As another woman later remembered her first thoughts on hearing the news, "De soul buyers can neber take my two chillen lef' me; no, neber can take 'em from me no mo'." The freedpeople had long imagined emancipation, and they wove the worldly specificities of seeing owners mastered and holding families tight with the more transcen-dent liberties of possessing their selves.[6]

And the freeing of the slaves performed a double collective duty as well. For the freedpeople, it fulfilled the sacred prophecy that lay at the center of slave culture, that distinct translation of African ways into an American con-text shaped also by European settlers and American Indian peoples. But emancipation also had the potential to free the rest of America from the systematic violations of humanity that had paradoxically grounded and betrayed the democratic promise of the new nation. From the earliest colonization, European Americans had created a system of bondage less "peculiar" than brutal and had asserted the difference, the absence of the people they enslaved, by the late seventeenth century almost solely of African descent, from the very category of humanity. The naked power of this exclusion, over time, erased differences between slaves of many different African ethnic and tribal affiliations, creating the context for a common slave culture. And the slaves filled this context with the wiliness and wisdom that assured their survival and their sense of grace. Emancipation confirmed the core values of this slave culture: the intimate relation of humans and God, the sense of fluidity between past, present, and future, and the always possible transformations that these communions conjured against the bounded thinking of slave owners. Within the larger American context, however, most white Americans had equated blackness with bondage. With freedom, African American identity became unhinged for the first time collectively from the taint of slavery, from its dialectical place as the antithesis of citizenship. Finally, African Americans had the agency to shape the meaning of their collectivity within the larger world. Selves, not slaves, they shouted: "we are free; we are free!"[7]

A Necessary Space

The abolition of slavery, then, transformed the grounding of both the relatively unified culture slaves had developed within the interstices of the southern slave system and the larger American culture of which slavery had been such a constituent part. Emancipation changed everything with its infinite promise, made anything possible and nothing certain. The freedpeople had seen the powerful signs: masters laid low and weeping with hardship, seemingly powerful white men returning broken or worse from war, and armed black men in the United States Army. They had witnessed federal officials giving them the lands of former Confederates, former owners paying them for their labor, white northerners freely offering them schooling, and black churches meeting independently of white control.

And overshadowing all these miracles, many ex-slaves had made lost families whole.[8]

But who would they be, collectively, now that the oppressive context within and despite which they had made their own meaning had been destroyed? Would they be southerners, in a remaking of that regional identity into some post-Confederate amalgamation that finally acknowledged both their agency and their historical and cultural centrality? Would they be Americans, enacting with northerners white and black the radical promise of abolitionism, a nation of equality for all God's children, men and women of every hue? General O. O. Howard, head of the Freedmen's Bureau, reported that while visiting Atlanta's Walton Springs School for freedpeople in the 1860s, he asked the class what they would most like to say to their fellow youth in the North. In what became a powerful folk motto, young Richard R. Wright replied, "Tell them, General, we're rising." Their optimism was not foolhardy—the ground had shaken with miracles, and victory, despite cynical historical hindsight, was entirely possible. What would this freedom mean?[9]

Despite their social existence as property, slaves had managed to carve love and even joy from the block of their oppression. "Slave music, slave religion, slave folk beliefs—the entire sacred world of the black slave," in the historian Lawrence Levine's words, had created a *necessary space* between the slaves and their owners and were the means of preventing legal slavery from becoming spiritual slavery." The freedpeople now wanted both to cross and to preserve this space, to bring what they had created under slavery into freedom, to weld their strengths with literacy and mobility, the golden fruits that they had been denied.[10]

But whites had filled this "necessary space" with images of their own devising, and although the specific contours of the characters African Americans were cast to play varied after emancipation, the narrow number of positions remained. These white-crafted representations of slave and ex-slave identity were not, especially in the antebellum South, created in isolation. Instead, in a dangerous dialectic, slaves constructed masks of simplemindedness and sycophancy, loyalty and laziness to play to their owners' fantasies and desires while securing very material benefits—more food and movement, less work and control—in return. The African American anthropologist and novelist Zora Neale Hurston aptly described a process still at work when she was collecting folklore in the South in the 1930s:

The Negro offers a feather-bed resistance . . . The theory behind our tactics: "The white man is always trying to know into somebody else's business. All right, I'll set something outside the door of my mind for him to play with and handle. He can read my writing but he sho' can't read my mind. I'll put this play toy in his hand, and he will seize it and go away. Then I'll say my say and sing my song."[11]

The problem was that these "play things," these masks, what the novelist and African American critic Ralph Ellison later called the "darky act," became the reality of black existence for most white Americans. Southern whites in particular missed the performance, and usually confused slave and ex-slave masks with black selves, an absurdity never more evident than in their ante- and postbellum assertions that they alone understood "their Negroes." Northern whites could fall prey to the same delusions, the most influential of which was surely Harriet Beecher Stowe's 1853 novel *Uncle Tom's Cabin*. In a dizzying circularity, both southern and northern novelists wrote slaves' fictive selves as "real" characters into their own literary fictions. The minstrel show, a northern invention, became the most original and successful popular art form in America by self-consciously dramatizing the dialectic of exchange, both African Americans' conscious and whites' often unconscious real-life performances, on the stage. While neither the slaves nor the freedpeople had many opportunities to craft their own literary and dramatic characters—and the narratives of escaped slaves like Frederick Douglass and Harriet Jacobs were the key exceptions—representations of slaves filled American popular culture immediately before and after emancipation. In a process that will be explored more fully in later chapters, African Americans were never the first folks to create slave or free images for themselves within either the southern regional context or the larger American culture of which the South was a distinct but vital part. White translations of slaves' and freedpeople's identities, perversions of the very masks African Americans had originally made, filled that "necessary space" from a different direction. That distance so necessary for survival, the space of contact between the larger American culture and the folkways of slavery, had become a means of cultural control. Yet before emancipation, southern whites' absolute power over the very bodies of slaves proved much more relevant to black liberation.[12]

The Civil War, then, shattered the isolated context, itself a product of southern white oppression, within which the former slaves had created their

culture and could assume a relatively unself-conscious unity. Although
African Americans greatly influenced the cultural ways of southern white
folks, slave status offered the majority no other options, except escape, than
the world of the quarters. The ex-slaves entered freedom with a cultural
ᵧ heritage that was their greatest asset collectively but that, in the larger world
of free Americans, might also be their greatest impediment. American
culture already associated dark skin with bondage, the very opposite of self-
determination, the value that sat at the symbolic center of American identity. Would skin color cease to suggest these meanings now that slavery had
been abolished? That "necessary space," so essential to past survival and yet
so filled by white fantasy, now blocked the route to the cultural self-
determination that would allow the freedpeople to retain aspects of their
slave heritage while finding a place of agency within the American whole.
Would the freedpeople be able to replace the masks, whites' blackface perversions of subjectivities slaves had created for their own protection, with
their own unmediated creations, with the myriad possibilities of their new
free selves?[13]

"Tell them we are rising." Freedom may not be an easy place or time,
but it is the only time and place to be.

The Double Self

As emancipation broadened the context of African American life, the freedpeople reunited families, reveled in their newfound mobility, and sought literacy. They would read and write and vote and legislate and work and pray
their way into the full measure of their liberty. Yet many former slaves
became self-conscious for the first time about their forms of speech, styles of
worship, and other traditions. They learned more than reading and writing
from their northern white teachers. Some of these teachers' sense of the
freedpeople's backwardness, recorded in detail in their letters home, must
have seeped into their packed classrooms as well. These idealistic educators, however, saw this difference of their charges not as proof of natural
inferiority but as an opportunity, a mere environmental obstacle in their
mission to educate "all men equally as members of the same great com-
monwealth." As one white woman teacher phrased the dilemma, "they
need so much instruction." Slavery had rendered the freedpeople illiterate

and primitive, the northern teachers believed, and the Yankee schoolhouse would make them whole and establish "one common civilization" across the land. Many freedpeople at least partially accepted this route to inclusion and looked to the future. Americans did not act like slaves.[14]

Yet the field of freedom was crowded, and such cultural transactions still seemed less than pressing as Reconstruction dissolved into a formless recapitulation of the war. The freedpeople made huge strides in building schools and churches, buying farms, and even starting businesses, and yet many remained agricultural laborers in situations that did not differ enough from slavery. Former Confederates fought the freedpeople's voting, office-holding, and landownership in a fury of terrorist violence that left many of America's newest citizens dead. And white Republican allies often proved politically corrupt, their betrayals sealing the fate of federal support for the radical reconstruction of southern life. Reconstruction ended officially in 1877, and the former Confederates regained control of the South. The freedpeople entered the post-Reconstruction era determined to hold onto their conception of freedom as literacy, mobility, and economic and political self-determination.[15]

They also remained self-conscious about the cultural heritage of slavery. A black scholar attempting to write an article in 1899 about the games of slave children reported his difficulties collecting information: "The natural tendency of the day is to forget the black history of the past; and so the younger generation seldom speak of the days of yore, with all their lights and shadows." In 1919, a resident of one of the Sea Islands off South Carolina still insisted to a white collector of folklore, "Dere is not'in de matter wid us but bad grammar." And Hurston had found self-consciousness about telling traditional tales and singing the old songs for outsiders persisting into the 1930s. Certainly, the patronizing attitudes toward the folk traditions of slavery expressed by southern and northern whites, from amateur travelers to professional educators and anthropologists, as well as the educational and civic programs of the rising class of African American leaders and reformers, made many self-conscious about the slave past. Yet this very circumspection, a reworking of the old dance of masks and selves perfected under slavery, was proof of the very thing it denied, the enduring legacy of their shared history.[16]

In the late nineteenth century, as they were beaten and cheated and eventually legislated out of politics, the freedpeople turned to other, less limited avenues for the enactment of their liberty—to advancement in the

church, in business, in the arts, and in education. And despite white southern violence and repression, as a contributor to the *Colored American Magazine* noted, "the Negro race was gaining success along many lines." Yet
advancement seemed only to antagonize whites. "Impediments became
more numerous" and white crimes more vile. Many contributors to a volume of Atlanta University's sociological studies, educated blacks from across
the country, expressed the view that "the Negro's ignorance, superstition,
vice and poverty do not disturb and unnerve his enemies so much as his *&*
rapid strides upward and onward." A northern correspondent wrote, "I
sometimes think it is the progress rather than our lack of progress that is
causing the continued friction between the races." Charles Chesnutt, a
well-respected African American writer at the turn of the century, believed
that disenfranchisement was an attempt by white southerners to "forestall
the development of the wealthy and educated negro, whom the South
seems to anticipate as a greater menace than the ignorant ex-slave." As one
of black writer Frances Harper's fictional characters expressed this common
conception, "in some sections, as colored men increase in wealth and intelligence, there will be an increase in race rivalry."[17]

This commentary on turn-of-the-century race relations signified two
important new developments. First, the coming together of those rising ex-
slaves, antebellum southern free blacks, and the small African American
communities of the North had produced a growing group of educated and
economically successful African Americans, a new black middle class. And
second, the beginning of the stream of migration north as well as the more
specific movement of black intellectuals and educators between colleges in
the South like Atlanta, Howard, and Fisk Universities and northern educational institutions were creating an increasingly national conception of
African American collectivity. As an ex-slave and a prominent abolitionist,
Frederick Douglass already possessed strong ties to both regions before the
Civil War, and he pioneered this newly national orientation.[18]

But the reconciliation of northern and southern whites, rippling out-
ward from the compromise of 1877 that had ended Reconstruction, drove
the nationalization of black consciousness as well. Educated African Americans understood that whites across the nation increasingly framed their own
collectivity across class and gender divisions, in both particularly southern
and more generally national varieties, as a racialized commonality of whiteness. W. E. B. Du Bois, a versatile black writer, academic, and activist who
would become one of America's greatest twentieth-century intellectuals,

had edited the Atlanta University sociological studies. As he so aptly claimed, looking back at the turn of the century from the early 1920s, "The discovery of personal whiteness among the world's peoples is a very modern thing, a nineteenth and twentieth century matter indeed." This expanding sense of a national, race-wide black collectivity, then, arose in conjunction with whites' increasingly racialized thinking and paradoxically at the same moment that class, gender, and even regional gaps between African Americans grew ever wider. As the very concept of race leadership thrust "spokespersons" for the race to the fore, the cultural diversity of African Americans across the nation had never been greater.[19]

And whites responded to this increasing diversity and this rising black middle class with fear, violent reprisals, and state legislation—their floundering attempts to build a new racial order. Whites created the culture of segregation in large part to counter black success, to make a myth of absolute racial difference, to stop the rising. For the antebellum inferiority of African Americans, despite the rise of scientific racism in the 1850s, had been more a matter of their slave status than their strictly racial identity. The freedpeople, free blacks in the North, and their white allies hoped that with slavery abolished, the racial identity of the former slaves would lose these marks of bondage, would no longer connote for whites the antithesis of agency. Only historical hindsight has made this hope seem quixotic. While important, completely racialized ideologies like the theories of the white southerner E. A. Pollard did not dominate the thinking of whites, even the former Confederates, until after the Civil War and Reconstruction. Racial essentialism, the conception of sets of personal characteristics as biologically determined racial identities, grew in popularity among whites in tandem with the rise of the new black middle class and its increasing visibility, especially in cities. Making these "New Negroes" invisible in the North, where black populations were predominantly urban, small, and already fairly separated from white communities, was relatively easy to achieve. But in the South, slavery had scattered the black population across the region and the vast majority still lived there—in 1910 approximately 90 percent of African Americans were southerners. White efforts there to erase the visibility of middle-class blacks, to see the world as a minstrel show writ large and all African Americans as its narrow range of characters, proved more difficult. Making and perpetuating the myth of absolute racial difference in this region, the division of the world into absolute blackness and whiteness, required the creation of racial segregation as the central metaphor of the

new regional culture. In important respects, the "New Negro," the name
some educated African Americans of the generation born in freedom chose
for themselves, forced white southerners to create a "New South."[20]

As the diversity of freedom erased the old easy unity, African Americans
constructed new conceptions of their connectedness to counter white control and the increasingly segregated racial order. If whites would see racial
identity as the coin of African American exclusion, African Americans
would view their racial identities as the source of their communion and
strength. They created modern conceptions of the meaning of blackness,
then, within this doubled dialectic. By the dawning of the twentieth century
in the South and by the 1910s across the nation, racial essentialism dominated white thinking, dividing the world into black and white. The force
of this external pressure, from violations of civil rights to violence, made
African American unity a necessity despite growing internal diversity. Yet
middle-class-dominated racial leadership covered important contradictions
of class and gender. Many middle-class blacks possessed a patronizing sense
of superiority to the black working class, an elitist attitude of color snobbery,
and a desperate desire to distance themselves from the history and folk
culture of slavery. Rural and urban black workers often wondered who
exactly these race leaders were leading and where their own material needs
and their own voices fit into middle-class plans for racial uplift. Within
middle-class families, many African American men demanded that women
sacrifice their own desires for greater agency to help create the patriarchal
families, following white models, that were considered central to respectability. As a result, African American women often felt they must choose whether
to work toward easing racial or gendered burdens.[21]

And these internal conflicts within the race were compounded by the
contradictions that the expanding culture of segregation, the whiteness of
Americanness, wedged within the very self. Du Bois described this plight of
African Americans in his 1903 book *The Souls of Black Folk*:

> It is a peculiar sensation, this double consciousness, this sense of always
> looking at one's self through the eyes of others, of measuring one's soul by
> the tape of a world that looks on in amused contempt and pity. One ever
> feels his two-ness, — an American, a Negro; two souls, two thoughts, two
> unreconciled strivings; two warring ideals in one dark body, whose dogged
> strength alone keeps it from being torn asunder.

What would be the solution to this fragmentation, to "this longing . . . to merge [the] double self into a better and truer self," to free black identity within the segregated order?[22]

In 1896, the larger American society, increasingly self-consciously white, signaled its refusal to consider racial mixing—as personal heritage, as the riders in railroad cars, as the truest expression of American culture—in the U.S. Supreme Court's ruling in *Plessy v. Ferguson*. Homer Plessy, a very light-skinned, racially mixed man, had made a planned attempt to challenge Louisiana's 1890 law requiring segregated streetcars. His lawyer, Albion Tourgee, a northern white Reconstruction official and popular novelist, had argued the case on the grounds that the government did not have the right to determine the racial identities of its citizens. But the Supreme Court decided against Plessy, proclaiming "separate but equal" facilities constitutional and upholding Louisiana's law. As important as the ruling was the Court's reasoning: its insistence that racial differences lay outside the law, beyond and before any act of human agency. The law, the Court decided, could only reflect the sense of racial difference that was a part of human nature itself. Plessy could not be both black and white. He could follow law and custom, the "one drop rule," and despite his predominantly white ancestry choose "For Colored." Or, in an option the Court in no way promoted, he could deny his African American heritage and by "passing" choose "For White." How he could merge his "double self," how he could deal with his specific embodiment of a not always so literal biracial cultural heritage the Court did not say. The *Plessy* decision fully denied what the African American writer Albert Murray later called the "incontestably mulatto" nature of American culture and set this lie at the very center of modern society.[23]

As Du Bois, who seemed so often to fill the role of the intellectual prophet of the Zeitgeist, so famously predicted, the "problem of the twentieth century" would be "the color line." If whites no longer owned African American bodies, they had new, more flexible means of maintaining a different power. If there were more opportunities for African Americans, the "necessary space" was fragmented and the channels of white co-optation and commercialization of black disguises, as well as other African American cultural productions, were well entrenched. Reform-minded whites across the nation saw their own fantasies about blackness as biological realities, and found no difficulty in justifying their sense of superiority racially and, especially in the South, encoding their racial essentialism in local and state law. For African Americans, the end result was not a new slavery, but the loss of their newly acquired citizenship and the devastating fact that segregation made either side of the Court's color line a self-conscious space, an uneasy place or time to be.[24]

Making Blackness

If our commonality must be blackness, if whites will only see us racially, then whose blackness will we be? As the twentieth century opened, both Booker T. Washington and the black nationalists offered their versions of a racialized commonality. Washington, then the most powerful black man in America, refigured the old slavery dance of masks and selves. A public accommodationist, he implicitly endorsed, in his industrial education programs, playing the role of the white folks' black folks as the surest route to racial progress. Black nationalists like Henry McNeal Turner and Marcus Garvey countered with a militant message of migration to Africa. Complete racial segregation, they argued, was the only route to political and economic self-determination and by implication cultural agency. Africa in the future was the only place and time to craft a black-authored blackness, to leave the racial dialectic of America permanently behind.[25]

If ever there was a master of minstrel performance, it was Booker T. Washington. "Born a slave" on a plantation in Franklin County, Virginia, Washington was never exactly sure of the specifics of his origins. But Washington, whose unparalleled Horatio Alger brand of American optimism served up such homilies as the civilizing benefits of slavery, did not dwell on the tragedy of such uncertain beginnings. Cracking a joke that lacked only a rendering in dialect to fit it for the stage, Washington opened his 1901 best-selling autobiography: "I suspect I must have been born somewhere and at some time." In reality, Washington was the son of a slave woman and a white man. And although he only knew slavery as a child—he was six or seven when the Civil War ended—his literal embodiment of the link between slavery and freedom, black and white, poverty and success, illiteracy and articulation, made him the "race leader" acknowledged at the turn of the century by both blacks and whites. The title of his own story, its allegorical conflation of individual and racial progress transcendently clear, described his educational programs as well: *Up From Slavery.*[26]

Booker T. Washington wrote the slaves' old means of survival, the weaving of a mask of acquiescence and dissembling in front of whites, into the new era. In his 1909 *The Story of the Negro: The Rise of the Race from Slavery*, Washington provided an example of his kind of modern accommodation. While traveling through South Carolina, he met a black man who "was very anxious to reach the railway train and had only a few minutes in which to do so. He hailed, naturally enough, the first hackman he saw, who happened to be a white man. The white man told him that it was not his custom to carry Negroes in his carriage. The coloured man, not in the least disturbed, at once replied: 'That's all right, we will fix that; you get in the carriage and I'll take the front seat and drive you.' " Reaching the station on time, the black man got out, paid the white man the fare, and caught his train: "Both were satisfied and the colour line was preserved." Yet Washington told the tale to illustrate "the ability of the Negro to avoid the rocks and shoals . . . and still manage to get what he wants." "Few white people," Washington insisted, "realize what the Negro has to do, to what extent he has been compelled to go out of his way, to avoid causing trouble and prevent friction." Even African Americans' skills in accommodating white whims and local conventions of segregation, in Washington's telling, could be proof that they were far from inferior to whites.[27]

And the elaboration of the troubles to which especially southern blacks must go to appease whites also revealed the very performative nature of segregation. If whites wanted the world to be a minstrel show, Booker T. Washington, like black entertainers before and after him, would point out the masquerade. In this sense Washington's reputed telling of "darky" jokes for white audiences simply added another layer to the performance. If a black man must play the white man's black man, then the "king" of the race could go one further and play the white man's black man's white man as well.[28]

Booker T. Washington was a complicated man. His own racially mixed identity, his writings, and his staggering accomplishments rebuked whites' illusions of absolute racial difference and black inferiority even as his accommodationist stance, moralism, and program of industrial education offered no resistance to the expansion of segregation. In a period of growing disenfranchisement, the "race leader's" own denouncement of black political involvement proved fatal. Yet despite his public criticism of higher education for African Americans and his facile advice for southern blacks "to cast down your bucket where you are" and remain in the rural South, Washington offered important behind-the-scenes support for African American colleges and universities. His 1901 invitation to meet with President Theodore Roosevelt at the White House became for African Americans across the nation a powerful symbol that they were rising. The "Story of the Negro" was not his racial inferiority, but "simply the story of the man who is farthest down." Washington argued not for racial essentialism but environmentalism— gradually African Americans would become culturally and economically middle-class, and this progress would lead to white acceptance and national inclusion.[29]

But if, in Du Bois's words, the Negro "would not bleach his Negro soul in a flood of white Americanism, for he knows that Negro blood has a message for the world," then instead Booker T. Washington would have him sell that soul cheaply for food and toothbrushes and have that lesson be one of masking and dissemblance. Washington rose to power on his "Atlanta Compromise" speech at the Cotton States Exposition in 1895, the year that Frederick Douglass died, and his power was always as much the result of his backing by rich northern white philanthropists and his translation of their support into a political machine based at his own Tuskegee Institute as African American support. When the Atlanta race riot of 1906 violently proved that acceptance of segregation and even middle-class status provided no safety, many blacks questioned the wisdom of Washington's methods. This new "darky act" replicated the doubled self of slavery and conceded public control over the meaning of black collective identity to whites. How and when would the selves be merged, the space between be crossed?[30]

A growing group of African Americans, building on mid-nineteenth-century proponents of colonization and nationhood like Alexander Nap and Martin Delaney, insisted that the only chance for self-determination of any kind lay in emigration to Africa. An American Methodist Episcopal bishop in the South, Henry McNeal Turner, responded to the increased white violence that black progress had provoked by stating his position with none of Washington's political subtlety. "Hell is an improvement upon the United States where the Negro is concerned," he claimed, and "God is a Negro." African Americans who advocated emigration hoped to forge a black-directed racial separation in contrast to Washington's acceptance of white's racially figured control.[31]

Yet nationalist thinking among African Americans reached its lowest point in the years between the Civil War and World War II as many embraced emancipation's promise of inclusion in their nation despite whites' expansive racial essentialism. Turner attracted relatively little support in his attempt to revive the religiously inflected antebellum nationalism that had spurred settlement in Liberia. The new black middle class, the only freed people with the resources to go, had little interest in "Back to Africa" appeals. Most blacks proved unwilling to accept his belief that there was "no manhood future in the United States for the Negro," and that here he might "eke out an existence for generations to come, but he can never be a *man*—full symmetrical and undwarfed." Yet Turner never retreated: "The colored man who will stand up and in one breath say that the Negroid race does not want social equality and in the next predict a great future in the face of all that proscription of which the colored man is the victim, is either an ignoramus, or is an advocate of the perpetual servility and degradation of his race variety." Despite this indirect attack on Booker T. Washington, however, Turner conceded more to rising white racism than Washington ever did. He called slavery a "heaven permitted if not divinely sanctioned manual laboring school" that gave African Americans the chance to "have direct contact with the mightiest race that ever trod the face of the globe." And he enjoyed the support of the most radically racist southern whites who preached not separation, but the very end of black life in America.[32]

The black nationalist call for emigration to Africa would not become a mass movement until the black Jamaican-born Marcus Garvey brought his Universal Negro Improvement Association to Harlem in 1916. UNIA's slogan, "Africa for the Africans, at home and abroad," attracted the support of many working-class and poor blacks in northern cities in the early 1920s. In Garvey's words, a trip to Europe and a reading of Washington's *Up From Slavery* made him aware of his destiny as a race leader: "I asked, 'Where is the Black man's government?' 'Where is his king and his kingdom?' 'Where is his president, his country, and his ambassador, his army, his navy, his men of big affairs?' I could not find them, and then I declared, 'I will help to make them.' " Garvey saw before him "a new world of *Black* men, not peons, serfs, dogs and slaves, but a nation of sturdy men making impress upon civilization and causing a new light to dawn upon the human race."[33]

Before he could "embrace the purpose of all black humanity," however, Garvey confessed that he had to find that racial community. He remembered his own childhood with its freedom from racial thinking and his early difficulties convincing Jamaicans of the existence of their racial commonality: "But nobody wanted to be a Negro . . . Men and women as black as I, and even more so, had believed themselves white while under the West Indian order of society . . . , the 'black whites' of Jamaica." There was, he found, no seemingly transparent blackness within his native "Colored-Black-White" society.[34]

Among the many blacks who had migrated to Harlem by the 1920s, from the American South as well as the West Indies, Garvey found his audience. Facing an increasingly hegemonic white form of racial essentialism, unpunished white violence, and an expansive and legally mandated separation, northern blacks embraced Garvey and UNIA's brand of nationalist Pan-Africanism, a global collectivity of all current and former African peoples. Garvey had found a way to unite Turner's "God is a Negro" with a nonaccommodationist updating of Washington's school of self-help. But the corruption-induced failure of Garvey's most ambitious project, the Black Star shipping line, as well as harassment by the federal government resulted in Garvey's imprisonment and eventual deportation and the collapse of UNIA by the late 1920s. The project of building a black nation in Africa attracted little support with the charismatic leader gone. As Garvey had argued, "the Negro's greatest enemy," the barrier to a black-directed separatism and migration from America, was the African American, the double self.[35]

The majority of blacks still lived in the South in the 1920s, and for them the North, despite letters home full of hardship from family and friends who had already migrated, continued to serve as the land of promise. When late nineteenth-century attempts to establish African American settlements in Africa failed, black southerners with emigration dreams chose Kansas and Oklahoma instead. Movement out of the South gained momentum slowly. A small first wave of middle-class blacks like the journalists Ida B. Wells and J. Max Barber left Memphis and Atlanta respectively under threat of death. Other educated men and women who could afford the cost of relocation left to escape the more general oppressiveness of southern life. By the second decade of the twentieth century, expanding northeastern and midwestern cities offered better jobs at exponentially better pay and relatively little public racial segregation, a seeming utopia for African Americans still laboring in southern rural poverty. "I do feel so fine . . . with the aid of God I am making very good I make $75 per month . . . I don't have to work hard," one migrant to Philadelphia wrote in a letter published in the black-owned *Chicago Defender*. "Don't have to mister every little white boy comes along . . . I can ride in the electric street and steam cars any where I can get a seat . . . And if you are first in a place shopping you don't have to wait until the white folks get through trading . . . The kids are in school every day." Migration to the North became more possible for working-class African Americans as relatives and friends who had made the journey offered places to stay and job connections to more recent arrivals and the Great War created an urban labor shortage. The great migration did occur, but the flow of people crossed not the ocean but the nation.[36]

In addition to the soaring financial obstacles, the contradictions of nationalist Pan-Africanism in particular and the African American's ambiguous relationship to Africa in general surely blunted the appeal of Back to Africa movements as well. Zora Neale Hurston's interview with Cudjo Lewis or Kossola-O-Lo-Loo-Ay, reported to be "the last Negro alive that came over on a slave ship," became the exception that proved the rule. African Americans no longer had any direct experience with the continent from which whites had forced them in chains. As the poet Countee Cullen asked, his rhythm soaked with ambiguity and desire, "One three centuries removed/ From the scenes his fathers loved/ Spicy grove and banyan trees,/ What is Africa to me?" A conception of a shared racial identity provided the foundation of Pan-Africanist nationalism. Yet when nationalists like Turner and Garvey looked at the African continent they saw only absence and the contributions that a returning diaspora, having learned "civilization" and "manhood" from the Anglo-Saxons, would bring. Only New World blacks in the early twentieth century imagined Africa as a unified racial motherland, a conceptualization that with a flip of the moral valuation they shared with noncolored Westerners. Africa in this sense was an invention, a black translation of white racialist thinking, a view inseparable from the history of their racialized oppression in America, which had rendered diverse peoples into an African American whole. Only from outside the complex and overlapping tribal and colonial identities of early twentieth-century Africans could people conflate geographical and racial categories, using a continent to ground the fantasy of a single black racial self. Constructing a black America in Africa would not merge the double vision, only change its poles. The African American in Africa would remain both a Negro—in this conflation of race and place—and a non-African, an American.[37]

Most black intellectuals in the late nineteenth and early twentieth century fell somewhere between the poles of Booker T. Washington's accommodationism, with its acceptance of a white-constructed racial separation, and the nationalism and Pan-Africanism of Garvey, with its assertion that blacks must separate themselves. Most refused to concede, as did Washington, or promote, as did Garvey, the predominantly white-crafted myth of absolute racial difference. Seeking some degree of integration, many African Americans sought a greater recognition of their contributions to and citizenship within the nation of their birth. As Du Bois so plaintively phrased this dilemma, "would America have been America without her Negro people?" But Du Bois like many intellectuals coupled this integrationist stance with a romantic racialism that founded a mystical black communion in Africa: "The spell of Africa is upon me. The ancient witchery of her medicine is burning my drowsy, dreamy blood. This is not a country, it is a world—a universe of itself and for itself, a thing Different, Immense, Menacing, Alluring. It is a great black bosom where the Spirit longs to die. It is a life so burning. . . ." Whites made the color line the central metaphor of modern life, and African Americans were determined to weight their side with positive value, to turn a mark of shame into their own "vast family of human beings," their "wonderful possibilities of culture," their gifts of spirituality and song. As Du Bois attempted to narrate the contradiction in his 1897 address before the American Negro Academy, "We are Americans, not only by birth and by citizenship, but by our political ideals, our language, our religion. Farther than that our Americanism does not go. At that point, we are Negroes, members of a vast historic race that from the very dawn of creation has slept, but half awakening in the dark forests of the African fatherland."[38]

Du Bois would spend an intellectual lifetime mining this middle ground, seeking both to refute and assert the reality of racial difference and the ambiguous relationship of Africanness and Americanness. And many others shared his shifting double vision. It was possible, even necessary, to be both an integrationist and a racial essentialist. White racially figured oppression had created a context within which a black collective racial self became the basis for political and cultural solidarity. The making of white racial identity made its opposite, blackness, as well. And few African Americans after the heyday of the Washington machine were willing ever again to concede so publicly this representational power to white Americans.

Paradoxically, then, this muddled middle offered the only escape from the racial dialectic, the opposition of whiteness and blackness, that whites had set in motion in crafting their own racial commonality. Washington's accommodation left the dialectic publicly untouched even if he worked more privately to undermine it. Black nationalist Pan-Africanism cast the African American as a more benevolent white man in Africa, bringing civilization to, in the familial metaphors then popular, their slower siblings who had remained at home. Only an existential search for a ground of merging, an "ever striving," offered any cultural liberation, some relief from playing the whites' blacks or the blacks' whites. Du Bois as well as any single figure embodied the internal divisions among African Americans, the ambiguities, the impossible necessity of a space between whites' perceptions of black versus white. And his story of making the individual connection between his middle-class intellectual present, his free black northern past, and the rural southern black reality as he taught a one-room school in the Tennessee mountains served as a model of the needed consciousness. An educational exchange, a sense of the narrowing of the distance between himself and his charges—poorly fed and poorly educated and yet rich in the folk traditions unknown to Du Bois—pervaded his 1903 autobiographical essay "Of the Meaning of Progress." There was no transparent unity of blackness, no transcendent African American communion. Only with an historical understanding of the making of blackness could freedom ring.[39]

"Of My Womanhood"

It was symptomatic of the difficult position of black women that Frances Harper too had written of the forging of a connection between educated African Americans and rural southern blacks, rather than any already existing racial union, in her 1892 novel *Iola LeRoy*. Yet Harper's translation into fiction of her own experiences and theories about racial leadership received much less attention from both whites and blacks than Du Bois's own autobiographical musings in *Souls* and his more theoretical elaborations in another 1903 essay, "The Talented Tenth." Harper had been born in 1825 to free black parents in Baltimore. Her heroine Iola's travels through the South, her discovery of the traditions of the rural freedpeople, paralleled Harper's own movement through the Reconstruction era region. Like Du Bois, Harper wrote the story of an educated person's journey into the black folk as a parable about the relationship of the new black middle class to the black masses. Certainly Du Bois was a better writer, but his academic credentials hardly outweighed Harper's long career, beginning in 1854, as an abolitionist, suffragist, temperance activist, and well-known lecturer. When Washington and Du Bois were both still children, Harper had argued for the rights of the freedpeople, supporting Frederick Douglass in his break from his former allies Elizabeth Cady Stanton and Susan B. Anthony over suffrage. As some white suffragists pressed for opposition to the Fifteenth Amendment if it did not extend the vote to women, Harper agreed with Douglass that some southern blacks simply had to have the vote: "When it is a question of race we let the lesser question of sex go. But the white women go all for sex, letting race occupy a minor position."[40]

And in the late nineteenth century, it seemed, black men went all for sex as well. If neither the accommodationists nor the nationalists could escape the cultural operation of the color line, they had little to offer the gendered concerns of black women either. The majority of black men, working-class and middle-class, trying to live a little dignity somewhere between these poles of white- or black-directed separation, fared little better. Many men expected to assert in the domestic realm the manly superiority they were too often denied in the larger world. Often these gendered tensions literally paled in comparison to white men's sexual predations. Suggesting, coercing, and raping with little fear of legal retribution, white men exploited black women of all classes. And both white men and women, rich and poor, exploited African American women economically, paying them pitifully for the deadening chores of domestic work. Southern whites especially tended to see African American women in the mask of mammy or jezebel, in a racialized transcription of that old feminine dualism, the mother or the whore. But many black men, too, conceived a limited role for women. Middle-class men in particular expected black families to conform to white-influenced norms of domestic life. Women would be the mothers of the race and maintain the black home as the ground of racial progress, of middle-class morality and respectability. But educated African American women, steeped in the antebellum blend of abolitionism and suffrage and propelled forward by their religious and educational activism during and since Reconstruction, saw a much larger field for their efforts. As Harper announced at the 1893 World Congress of Representative Women in Chicago, they were standing on "the threshold of woman's era."[41]

Despite or perhaps because of the increasingly violent racism of whites, both in the South and across the nation, middle-class black women made good on Harper's challenge. At the turn of the century, these women published works of fiction and nonfiction, founded journals, made speeches, formed suffrage and racial uplift organizations, and worked for urban renewal and temperance. By 1896 they had created their first national organization, the National Association of Colored Women. A decade before Du Bois, the writer and educator Anna Julia Cooper predicted the centrality of racial identity to modern American life: "The colored man's inheritance and apportionment is still the sombre crux, the perplexing *cul de sac* of the nation." Yet while black middle-class men experienced a contradiction between their own manly superiority and whites' sense of black racial inferiority, women knew a doubled oppression of the doubled self. And segregated transportation often provided both the anecdotes and the metaphors for describing their dilemma.[42]

The activist, lecturer, and writer Mary Church Terrell, in remembering her first consideration of "the Race Problem," told of an incident in which the contradictions of gender and racial conventions overwhelmed her childhood self. On a train trip with her father through Tennessee, which at that time had no legally mandated segregation, little Mary sat alone in the first-class car while her father went to the smoker for a light. When the conductor tried to move her to "the coach 'where I belonged,' " her father returned with a white friend and intervened, causing "a scene which no one who saw it could ever forget." At home later, little Mary became distraught trying to assure her mother of her ladylike behavior—her clean hands, her neatly ribboned braids, her perfect dress. The only answer her mother could give was that railroad conductors were "sometimes unkind."[43]

Cooper too used an account of a train journey to describe the "less civilized sections of our country," her native South, "where women have been forcibly ejected from cars, thrown out of seats, their garments rudely torn, their persons wantonly and cruelly injured." "America," she slyly asserted, "is large and must for some time yet endure its out-of-the-way jungles of barbarism as Africa its uncultivated tracts of marsh and malaria." Their treatment of women of color, Cooper implied, demonstrated that whites were just not as superior as they wanted to think. After a swaggering, tobacco-stained white man ordered her into the smoking car, Cooper looked out the window and saw a teenage chain gang, feet bound to heavy blocks, working on a farm. She made a note to herself to start a "Society for the Prevention of Cruelty to Human Beings." The train stopped, and she examined the small station: "I see two dingy little rooms with 'FOR LADIES' swinging over one and 'FOR COLORED PEOPLE' over the other while wondering under which head I come." Almost thirty years before Du Bois used such a train trip to illuminate the material and cultural oppression of the culture of segregation, Cooper, the daughter of a slave mother and the white man who owned her, used such a journey to argue for her own special insight. African American women had long ago learned to see clearly despite the blur.[44]

And this keen perspective enabled many black women intellectuals to escape the gender essentialism, the translation of female inferiority into an assertion of moral superiority, that pervaded the thinking of many of their fellow white reformers. Cooper told the story of a "color ripple" among "the advanced ladies," "a cream-colored" woman's application to the typing classes of the Wimodaughsis women's club. The earnest secretary was a Kentucky native, "who really would like to help elevate the colored people (in her own way of course and as long as they understood their places)." But this potential student created quite a problem: "indeed, she had not calculated that there were any wives, mothers, daughters, and sisters, except white ones; she is really convinced that Whimodaughsis would sound just as well, and then it need mean just *white mothers, daughters, and sisters.*" Nothing, Cooper joked, would be lost from dropping wives who had after all already been daughters. And although this incident ended in a principled stand by white suffragist Anna Shaw, the group's president, black women were well aware that national women's organizations often traded away African American inclusion for southern white women's support.[45]

Even in the interracial organizations that became active in the 1920s, black women faced white women's blindness to racial questions. As the writer and reformer Alice Dunbar-Nelson remembered a 1928 meeting of the Interracial Council of the Federal Council of Church Women, "it was the colored women . . . who kept the discussions on a frank and open plan; who struggled hardest to prevent the conference from degenerating into a sentimental mutual admiration society, who insisted that all is not right and perfect in this country of ours." The absurd conjunction of white racism and female moralizing made black women activists dubious of any claims to feminine superiority. Harper "was not sure that women are naturally so much better than men that they will clear the stream [of political life] by virtue of their womanhood." Women should have the vote not because of any moral influence but because "no nation can gain its full measure of enlightenment and happiness if one half of it is free and the other half is fettered." Race and sex both, then—"the grand and holy purpose of uplifting the human race"—did not require its disciples to chose between the fetters.[46]

African American clubwomen and reformers did not blame black men, however, even as they worked to reconfigure middle-class conceptions of responsible womanhood. As Cooper insisted, "We are the heirs of a past which was not our fathers' molding." But just as whites could not "*quite* put themselves in the dark man's place, neither should the dark man be wholly expected fully and adequately to reproduce the exact voice of the Black Woman." In Cooper's most famous phrasing, "Only the Black Woman can say 'when and where I enter, in the quiet, undisputed dignity of my womanhood, without violence and without suing or special patronage, then and there the whole *Negro race enters with me.*' " If we are race mothers, then from the ambiguity of our being—both and neither, ladies and colored, black and American—we will bear the race.[47]

"I, Too, Sing America"

By the 1910s and 1920s, the urban North had become the promised land for African American migrants from the South not because it presented a time or place of racial ease but because it held out the promise of racial agency. And Harlem was the mecca of this swelling migration, "the greatest Negro City in the world." As the African American academic Alain Locke wrote in his 1925 anthology *The New Negro*, "in Harlem, Negro life is seizing upon its first chances to group expression and self-determination. It is—or promises at least to be—a race capital." In the 1910s, African Americans had captured in mass this recently rural but rapidly modernizing neighborhood of housing, businesses, and amusements in Manhattan. Yet it was not just the place but the time—New York in the 1920s became the center of what would be the nation's global hegemony, its creative conflation of commercial and aesthetic power. The physical and artistic movement of African Americans into Manhattan helped make New York City the modern heart of America. Locke and others called the new collective cultural self-consciousness that resulted "The Negro Renaissance."[48]

Signaling the new era, on July 28, 1917, "the colored citizens of all greater New York" staged the first black mass demonstration in the history of the nation, the Silent Protest Parade. In East St. Louis at the beginning of

July, whites had assaulted, shot, and burned alive hundreds of African Americans in what could only be described as a massacre. Organized by Du Bois and James Weldon Johnson, leaders of the young National Association for the Advancement of Colored People, ten thousand blacks marched down Fifth Avenue to protest the carnage, in a startling silence punctuated by the staccato of muffled drums. Children wearing white headed the procession, followed by women too in white and men in black. Placards broke the quiet, asking "Mothers, Do Lynchers Go to Heaven?" and "Mr. President, Why Not Make America Safe for Democracy?" Before the man who carried the American flag, other marchers stretched a banner reading "Your Hands Are Full of Blood." The New York mayor shut down traffic, and whites seeped silently out of buildings and sidestreets to gawk. Black New Yorkers had made the modern cityscape itself their stage. And their silence and symmetry only dramatized the powerful counterpoise of restraint and rage.[49]

Black Boy Scouts passed out pamphlets, reprinted in the press, that gave reasons for the protest that went beyond the riots:

> We march because the growing consciousness and solidarity of race, coupled with sorrow and discrimination, have made us one, a union that may never be dissolved . . . We march because we are thoroughly opposed to Jim Crow cars, Segregation, Discrimination, Disenfranchisement, Lynching, and the host of evils that are forced upon us . . . We march because we want our children to live in a better land . . .

The Harlem Renaissance took up this opening performance of conscious self-creation. Locke's words in 1925 became a manifesto after the fact for a cultural movement already in progress. "The Old Negro," he asserted, "had long been more of a myth than a man." "A historical fiction" shaped of "innocent sentimentalism" and "deliberate reactionism," "the Old Negro"—"'aunties,' 'uncles,' and 'mammies'"—was gone. "Hitherto it must be admitted that American Negroes have been a race more in name than in fact, . . . [sharing] a common condition rather than a common consciousness." In Harlem, "what began in terms of segregation becomes more and more, as its elements mix and react, the laboratory of a great race-welding." For the first time, collectively and continually, blacks would challenge whites' directorship of the play of racial identity. With white dresses, black suits, dark skins, and drums, African Americans had staged their own national cultural coming of age.[50]

Only Harlem was big and bold enough to hold all the contradictions. For the self-conscious attempt to create a New Negro image bore the strains of both its mostly middle-class parentage and the white racial fantasies it was created to deny. Choosing cultural production as the ground of future racial inclusion, educated African Americans in Harlem believed, as Johnson phrased it, that "a people that has produced great art and literature has never been looked upon as distinctly inferior." Renaissance thinking reconfigured Washington's optimism about the end result of "race progress" and yet gave the process a cosmopolitan, modernist air. In place of cotton the buckets would bring up instead poems, novels, and paintings, a new spirituality, a new song. The Renaissance proclaimed an apolitical politics conducted outside the patterns of government power, and an independent, even militant art of inclusion often backed by and directed at white patrons. It sought integration from inside its segregated haven above 125th Street and outside the strongest ground of white racial power, the American South. Renaissance artists worshipped the folk and yet embraced Western ideals of high culture. They ignored the explosive genius of a more working-class scene of popular musical and dramatic performance, an earlier collective expression that had not fewer contradictions, just less self-consciousness and more commercial savvy, than their own.[51]

Perhaps most importantly, however, Renaissance thinkers celebrated black distinctiveness and yet exposed racial difference as a product of historical development and white fantasy. They researched and wrote black history while illuminating the fallacy of white-authored histories that ignored the interracial past. They created, in Johnson's phrase, a "cultural capital" and yet demanded an inclusive nation. "I, too, sing America," wrote the poet Langston Hughes. "I am the darker brother./ They send me to eat in the kitchen/ When company comes./ But I laugh,/ And eat well,/ And grow strong./ Tomorrow/ I'll sit at the table/ When company comes/ Nobody'll dare/ say to me,/ 'Eat in the kitchen'/ Then./ Besides, they'll see how beautiful I am/ And be ashamed,—/ I, too, am America." In 1920s New York, African American writers, historians, artists, and musicians proclaimed both the blackness of Americanness—in Johnson's words, "our sweat is in its fruitful soil"—and the Americanness of blackness, their right to their own individual and collective self-determination.[52]

And one of the most crucial forms of this cultural freedom was the right to draw from both sides of the color line whites had erected, to stake out the muddled middle and claim a "miscegenated" style. African American minstrel showmen like Bert Williams had staked out a territory of subtle subversion before the 1920s. His signature song, "Nobody," played to blackface characterizations crafted by whites but ended with a sly self-assertion that "until I get somethin' from somebody, sometime, I'll never do nothin' for nobody, no time." To act "blackface," African American performers had to look at "darkies" through white people's eyes—they had in effect to play whites. Blues singers like Bessie Smith and Ma Rainey seized the white fantasy of sexually available black women and made their own sexuality the source of their self-assertion and creative power. Black musicians, composers, and singers as diverse as Duke Ellington, Ethel Waters, and James P. Johnson drew from European, black folk, and black and white popular traditions, and their black and white styles were most often encouraged by black only, not white crossover, audiences. Given the popular context of minstrelsy, African American performers and musicians' creation of "miscegenated" styles paradoxically subverted white spectators' expectations and declared black freedom to match white methods and survey the full measure of musical sources. "Miscegenated" style self-consciously and publicly claimed the white American trademark of appropriation, often much less conscious of its racially figured thefts, for African Americans as well.[53]

African American writers used the figure of the mixed-race character "passing" as white to stage this space between white figurations of sharp racial difference. Frances Harper had mapped this ground from the opposite direction in *Iola Leroy*, her 1892 novel in which a southern "white" girl discovers she is black when her dead father's relatives sell her into slavery. White writers often used the tragic mulatta or mulatto story to illustrate a racially figured, hereditary degeneration, the biological and moral evils of miscegenation. But Harlem Renaissance writers made the crossing of the deepening color line, the movement from black to white, into a genre that exposed the modern ambiguities of both individual and collective racial identities. Nella Larsen's 1929 novel *Passing* recounts the loneliness and emotional damage of the racially mixed Claire Kendry, who has passed from poverty into wealth and social position by concealing her race and marrying white. Larsen's story, in its nuanced characterizations of black middle-class social relations, moves well beyond the tragic mulatta trope. She pairs Claire with the respectable Irene Redfield, a light-skinned woman who has chosen instead to live black. But Larsen's middle-class, mixed-race characters find no solace in black or white. The threat of Claire's affair with Irene's husband and her tentative attempt to pass back ends in murder: an increasingly self-righteous Irene simply pushes the black "white" woman out of a high city window. In *Quicksand*, not ostensibly a novel of passing, Larsen had earlier plumbed these ambiguities of black middle-class life in a tale of another educated racially mixed figure, Helga Crane. Surrender to religious devotion and a marriage to a small-town black southern preacher—a sort of passing as "southern black"—concludes almost as bleakly in another falling, this time into endless childbirth and despair. For Larsen, there was no easy place or time on either side of the line.[54]

Narratives of passing did increase the readership for serious African American fiction—the racial crossing within the stories paradoxically created a mixing within, an integration of, the audience. And African American authors were able to use this space between to lecture these readers between, to escape the cultural dynamic of segregation and its minstrel play. While much black fiction as well as nonfiction in the early twentieth century affected a kind of whiteface, a placing of black characters within narratives of American self-making and success, passing stories challenged not only the color values but the very racial categories. And James Weldon Johnson established a newly introspective tone, an often intellectually dispassionate self-probing, in his pioneering *Autobiography of an Ex-Colored Man*, a passing novel of 1912 not widely read until its Renaissance reprinting in 1927. As his narrator, the illegitimate son of a wealthy southern white man and his black servant, baldly states at the outset, "I know that I am playing with fire, and I feel the thrill which accompanies that most fascinating pastime; and, back of it all, I think I find a sort of savage and diabolical desire to gather up all the little tragedies of my life, and turn them into a practical joke on society."[55]

Both the narrator and Johnson, who first published the novel anonymously, knew well the absurdity and the danger. As he tells his story, Johnson's ex-colored man revisits the variety of turn-of-the-century black life: his birth in the small-town South, a northern upbringing, a term at Atlanta University, young adulthood among the black middle class of a small Florida city, and the bohemian world of nighttime New York. But instead of racial commonality his journeys yield racial illusions. Whites, he argues, possess less a "natural" than an "acquired antipathy" to "Negroes as a race." And all the myriad possibilities of African American life find unity only in his witnessing of a lynching, in the "shame of being identified with a people that could with impunity be treated like animals," a collective blackness born of white might. Like Larsen, Johnson writes neither side as salvation. His ex-colored man "would neither disclaim the black race nor claim the white race": "I would change my name, raise a mustache, and let the world take me for what it would." And he ends his tale in equal measures of personal love and historical regret. Telling black truth as a counter to white racial imaginings would never be enough to challenge the categories of segregation. "Black," "white"—there could be no redemption, only denial, in having to choose.[56]

Passing and mimicking and masking—the creation with more or less self-consciousness of a "miscegenated" style—became by the late 1920s the ultimate resistance to the racial polarities whites set at the center of modern American life. For segregation, as metaphor and as law, depended upon a myth of absolute racial difference, a translation of the body into collective meaning, into culture. Any public staging by African Americans of a space between black and white subverted the fantasies of absolute division that founded an expansive whiteness. Black activists and artists would continually reconfigure the mix of their miscegenated appropriations. Zora Neale Hurston in the 1930s and 1940s would use the academic discipline of anthropology to cleanse black folklore of the lingering traces of minstrelsy and Uncle Remus and transform it into brilliant fiction. A decade later, Ralph Ellison would place the invisible black man at the center of both American national mythology and Western modernism. And the civil rights movement, in a more activist revisitation of the cultural politics of the Harlem Renaissance, would convey both a militant integrationism and a separatism of black beauty and black power.[57]

Yet in Ralph Ellison's famous phrasing that has become in our own time more true for the nation as a whole, "whatever the efficiency of segregation as a socio-political arrangement, it has been far from absolute at the level of *culture*. Southern whites cannot walk, talk, sing, conceive of laws or justice, think of sex, love, the family or freedom without responding to the presence of Negroes." For African Americans, however, this corresponding depth of racial obsession occurred only with passing. In literature or in life, to "pass" as white, the "black" subject had to think always of a racial identity essentialized as other. While in many contexts—to purchase shoes, to keep a job, or protect a life—African Americans had to consider white belief and behavior, only in passing did they have to immerse themselves in whiteness.

Yet the very meaning of this whiteness, germinated in denial, in the racial opposition of black versus white, was nonblackness. In passing, African Americans had in effect to live whites' obsession with blackness. The tragic mulatto trope, in the strange permutations that coat the career of race in America, revealed what Ellison called "the joke" at the heart of American identity, that whites, in their "not-blackness," were simply passing too.[58]

CHAPTER TWO

Lost Causes and Reclaimed Spaces

"HISTORY" AS THE AUTOBIOGRAPHY
OF SOUTHERN WHITENESS

*Partly in one of the old Southern States and partly in the yet vaguer
land of Memory . . . They were subjected to the greatest humiliation of
modern times: their slaves were put over them—they reconquered their
section and preserved the civilization of the Anglo Saxons.*

THOMAS NELSON PAGE[1]

*And what petty precision to quibble about locations in space or chronology,
who to care or insist* Now come, old man, tell the truth: did you see this?
were you really there? . . . *This War ain't over. Hit just started good . . .
A dream is not a very safe thing to be near.*

WILLIAM FAULKNER[2]

I N THE LATE nineteenth-century South, history seemed more the cousin
of prophecy than the sibling of science. "The undead past," Robert Penn
Warren's later phrase for the twisted temporality of his region, still lived
because white southerners' historical imaginations became the cards in
which they read their racial future. The deep uncertainty of life in turn-of-
the-century America—the rise of political and economic conflicts on the
heels of war, emancipation, the Reconstruction amendments, and the fight
for women's rights—sent many across the nation backward into imaginary
pasts for the regrounding of authority. But the looking behind was most pronounced in the old slaveholding states that had fought against the bonds of
national union to retain their human property. The history of this region
before the Civil War quickly lost the steeped resonances and complicated
flavorings of flowing time to become instead a flat and simplistic mantra, in

Allen Tate's approving figuration, "a vast body of concrete fact to which [the white southerner] must be loyal." Named the "Old South," the antebellum past provided white southerners, particularly a modern middle class in the process of formation, with perhaps their most abundant postwar resource, a strangely other time and space within which first to deny and escape the present and then to reconstruct the foundations of racial difference. Stories of the Old South, the Civil War, and Reconstruction permeated the popular fiction as well as amateur and professional histories and autobiographical writing of the nation and the region. They became the origin narratives that absolved white southerners of moral obligation to the freedpeople and blurred white class and gender differences while legitimating segregation as the only possible southern future. But one white southerner conspicuously refused this method of crafting the future by first remaking the past.[3]

September 1884 was still summer in the Deep South. Train cars often held the heat. True, a slight breeze could be expected to ripple through the rough comfort of this faster-than-horses means of travel, but moist crowds often overwhelmed mere air's feeble rush. Traveling across Alabama the white southern journalist and writer George Washington Cable, already nationally known for his short stories collected in 1879 as *Old Creole Days* and his 1880 novel *The Grandissimes*, enjoyed the relative comfort of his almost empty first-class coach. His restless survey of the other cars, however, turned up a different one, a stinking and suffocating scene, an image that would inspire his courageous stand in the late 1880s and early 1890s against the beginnings of segregation as culture:

> At rather late bed-time there came upon the train a young mother and her little daughter of three or four years. They were neatly and tastefully dressed in cool, fresh muslins, and as the train went on its way they sat together very still and quiet. At the next station there came aboard a most melancholy and revolting company. In filthy rags, with vile odors and the clanking of shackles and chains, nine penitentiary convicts chained to one chain, and ten more chained to another, dragged laboriously into the compartment of the car where in one corner sat this mother and child, and packed it full, and the train moved on. The keeper of the convicts told me he should take them in that car two hundred miles that night . . .

My seat was not in that car, and I stayed in it but a moment. It stank insufferably.

George Washington Cable looked at his region and saw a different future.[4]

When Cable published his pioneering defense of African American civil rights, "The Freedman's Case in Equity," in *Century Magazine* in 1885, segregation was not fully established in the South. Despite the federal abandonment of Reconstruction, the form that postbellum southern race relations would take remained uncertain. While white southerners experimented with segregation by custom and in a few places also by law, Cable believed that many whites, "the silent South," preferred a social order erected upon more flexible and individual lines of "dress, behavior, character or aspirations" rather than race. Cable cited just one detailed example, his earlier epiphany on the train, to support his contention that southern whites were violating their moral duty toward the freedpeople. Although as secretary of a New Orleans grand jury Cable had elsewhere described the convict lease system as a reinscription of slavery, here he skimmed over the black convicts' sufferings to rest his gaze upon the fashionable female pair. Not until he had recounted his return to the clean-smelling comfort of his own coach did he mention what had caused this unlikely grouping of convicts with a middle-class mother and child "in that foul hole." The white conductor had "distinctly refused them admission elsewhere because they were of African blood." And Cable only found it an even greater wrong that had the child been white and had the woman been her guardian and "as black as the mouth of the coal-pit to which her loathsome fellow-passengers were being carried in chains," the conductor would have allowed the pair to sit anywhere. For this white writer, the juxtaposition of the well-dressed and well-mannered African Americans against what he saw as the unwashed and unlettered black masses on an early Jim Crow car made visible the arbitrariness and absurdity of the infant color line.[5]

Throughout his writings on "the Negro Question," Cable would return again and again to this trope, the figure of the middle-class black, knowable by the visible signs of clothing, behavior, and an implied though not often directly expressed lightness of skin color, forced to endure "hopeless excommunication from the civil rewards of gentility," "marked off . . . as a menial," "not by railings and partitions merely" but also by "the most uncomfortable, uncleanest, and unsafest place" and by the advertisement of glaring signs.

This expansive, extremely varied, and thus (Cable insisted) arbitrary group-ing of all blacks together in one place and all whites together in another went against not just the American Constitution but more importantly the very morality of the South's own traditional class-based gentility. Two years before the racially mixed Homer Adolph Plessy set out deliberately to chal-lenge Louisiana's new segregated railroad car law and six years before the U.S. Supreme Court in deciding his case sanctioned "separate but equal" as the measure of racial order across the land, Cable had already moved beyond white pretense to the heart of what was at stake no matter the actual conditions of the separate facilities provided: "as if permanent ignominious distinction, on account of ancestry, made in public, by strangers and in the enjoyment of common public rights were not an insult or an injury unless joined to some bodily discomfort." "The core of the colored man's griev-ance," Cable insisted despite his belief that blacks formed "an inferior race," was "that the individual, in matters of right that do not justly go by race, [was] treated, whether man or child, without regard to person, dress, behav-ior, character or aspirations, in public and by law, as though African tinc-ture, much or little, were itself stupidity, squalor and vice."[6]

Henry Grady, a Georgian nationally known as the spokesman for the New South, argued in his fierce 1885 rejoinder to Cable, "In Plain Black and White," that no other "matters of right" came before race. Yet Cable had described the root of the New South dilemma, that "intelligence, char-acter, and property" did not belong exclusively to white southerners. Race and class, Cable realized on that 1884 Alabama train ride, had with emanci-pation become seriously unhinged. At stake were the very social categories of difference that secured white elite male power. And the problem was only aggravated by the visibly widespread fact of miscegenation, particularly in Cable's home of New Orleans, no matter white denial. But "no portion of white men's blood . . . unless it washes out the very memory of African tinc-ture," the "one drop" definition, could absolve a person of being publicly set apart by the expansion of the color line. Since almost-white people were assigned to colored cars, "the race line," Cable insisted in perhaps his most damning critique, was "not a race line at all." Far from preventing social equality, an absolute color line would cause it by erasing all class differences within the two "racial" groups, destroying "more reasonable and mutually agreeable self-assortments" and forcing together all blacks and all whites as alike. But if the color line did not stop miscegenation and did nothing to clarify social confusion, what was its purpose? "The entire essence of the offense, any and everywhere the race line is insisted on," Cable concluded, was "the apparition of the colored man or woman as his or her own master." The salvage of "masterhood," not the specters of racial amalgamation and social chaos, required the publicly visible separation of the races. If individual white men could no longer be masters, then the white community collectively would, by custom and when necessary by law, name the space if not the content of servitude.[7]

"The Negro Question" for Cable, then, was really a series of quandaries facing southern and northern whites at the century's end. How could white southerners make the moral mistake of judgment by a category easily proven arbitrary rather than the more equitable standard of individual achievement? How could northern whites allow this collective erasure of the freedpeople's rising after the financial and human costs of war? As Cable bluntly demanded, "then tell us, gentlemen, which are you really for; the color line, or the line of character, intelligence, and property . . . ?" Far from calling for the end of distinctions between people, Grady's threatened declension into the darkness of chaos and horror, Cable demanded the elevation of flexible and visibly ascertainable divisions of class over some white southerner's immoral racial fictions. Integration in public or "civic" places was possible precisely because class divisions, Cable's public "self-assortments of people," would persist.[8]

Cable's liberal prescriptions for the structure of the modern southern social order did not of course become reality, and the elevation of class over race would not have replaced the coming nadir of American race relations with a peacefully "self-assorted" utopia. By 1885, in fact, many white middle-class northerners were already anxious about the confusion of appearances and their failure to match knowable class identities. In an increasingly urban and consumption-oriented culture the appearance of "dress, behavior, character, or aspiration" could prove as untrustworthy in delineating class status as Cable found the racial absolutes of the new segregation. Cable had even hinted at his own fear of class uncertainty in his *Century Magazine* rebuttal of Henry Grady's attack: "nobody wants to see the civil rewards of decency in dress and behavior usurped by the common herd of clowns and regamuffins." The rise of racial thinking and white supremacist ideology throughout late nineteenth-century American culture had in part been an attempt to ground this feared mutability of identity in the seeming concreteness of blood, science, and the body. The modernity of racial "science," then, could satisfy forward-looking white northerners while backward-facing white southerners could find assurance in resurrected and reconditioned pro-slavery polemics. As important, a new racial order could slow the national growth of class solidarity among workers and farmers and redirect the fight for women's rights. Whiteness rather than more specifically conceived rights as workers or as women bound potential rebels at least partially to a white male elite. Certainly, the vast majority of white southerners, less well educated and connected than Cable, would not have agreed with the class bias of his alternative social order.[9]

Still, Cable was unique among southern whites in his broad perception that the color line would have tremendous cultural as well as economic, political, and psychological implications. The effort required to make a fiction into a truth would shape the development of twentieth-century southern culture, projecting a screen of common racial identity and white supremacy over the myriad varieties of class, gender, and locality. And the first boundary to become permeable in the reinscription of race, uncoupled from slavery, as the single most important social category of southern life was the orderly division of time into past, present, and future. Tales of past white southern glory became the legitimating narratives of origin for the culture of segregation. In these stories, the antebellum past seemed both to flow into the present and simultaneously to recede from it. Not just the work of the white South's own Confederate memorial organizations, the Lost Cause widened into a narration of the sectional and racial dynamics of the nation, the place to remake the relationship of South to North and white to black. Reimagining the recent past, southern whites celebrated a plantation pastoral of racial harmony and a noble war of principle and valor, while making Reconstruction the fall that made segregation the only possible future. The present with its mixed-race, middle-class figures on the train simply disappeared from view.[10]

Cable was not entirely immune to the widespread tendency to ground the future in a looking backward, proclaiming his authority to speak as a Confederate veteran and the son and grandson of slaveholders. He even tried to turn the national surge of respect for the southern soldier to his advantage, claiming Robert E. Lee as the symbol of the "Silent South" that intended to uphold its moral obligation to African Americans. *Plessy v. Ferguson*, too, the 1896 Supreme Court decision that gave federal sanction to segregation as policy, followed this "path of anachronism" and turned to cases decided before the Reconstruction amendments to justify "separate but equal" doctrine. The Lost Cause celebrations and publications of white southern patriotic associations gave the past-in-the-present a popular base, and regional and dialect fiction circulated in the new national magazines fed a less sectional audience. Professional histories and memoirs and auto-biography, on the other hand, brought the present into the past by basing interpretations of antebellum days on postbellum experiences. "History" was the first battlefield in the creation of modern southern whiteness. W. E. B. Du Bois stood "virtually alone," in his words, in his 1935 recognition of the achievements of Reconstruction; in his view the false history of the ante-bellum South, the war, and especially the federal occupation of the region had "led the world to embrace and worship the color bar as social salvation." In Lost Cause stories of white southern glory and Reconstruction horror, this confused interpenetration of past and present locked the "integration" of the plantation garden firmly away in an Old South destroyed by Yankee "aggression" and black "betrayal." "History" provided moral absolution and grounding for the culture of segregation.[11]

Yet the figure of the middle-class, mixed-race train passenger remained. Cable's staging of the color line's arbitrary confusions of race and class found expression and expansion in the later work of African American writ-ers for whom the Old South represented not a lost pastoral utopia but the cold truth of human bondage. Placing the reader with his mulatto character Dr. William Miller on his return by railroad from New York to North Car-olina, Charles W. Chesnutt, in his 1901 novel *The Marrow of Tradition*, gives an account of the indignities of Jim Crow travel that echoes Cable's detailed descriptions in *The Negro Question*. And like Cable, Chesnutt emphasizes that the injury is less the inferior facilities than the evil of being "branded and tagged and set apart from the rest of mankind upon the public high-ways, like an unclean thing": "Lest a white man should forget that he was white—not a very likely contingency,—these cars would keep him con-stantly admonished of the fact; should a colored person endeavor, for a moment, to lose sight of his disability, these staring signs would remind him continually that between him and the rest of mankind not of his own color, there was by law a great gulf fixed."[12]

In the first four decades of the twentieth century, W. E. B. Du Bois also used the trope often, shaping it into an image that defined a racial identity even as it pointed to the very constructedness of blackness. Imagining from their well-appointed living room a stylish and respectable black family enduring the indignities of Jim Crow railway travel, he explained in his 1920 genre-blurring *Darkwater* why the middle-class southerners he was visiting never journeyed north or west to forget the indignities of the color line. Later, in a 1923 article, Du Bois answered the question of how blackness could be both superior and the salvation of humanity if race in fact had no existence in nature: "I recognized it [racial identity] easily and with full legal sanction: the black man is a person who must ride 'Jim Crow' in Georgia." In his 1925 article in *The Nation* on Georgia and his 1940 autobiography *Dusk of Dawn*, Du Bois refined the image of the middle-class African American in a Jim Crow car into a complex definition of the very meaning of race in America.[13]

Yet the late summer on the railroad soon faded to fall. Charles Chesnutt had ended his 1901 novel with the admonition that "there's time enough, but none to spare" in creating a less racist life. Cable, too, could not help giving one last warning in his 1918 novel *Lovers of Louisiana*. In reply to a Creole's claim that the race issue is "the deadest queztion in Ammerica," a visiting Scottish banker voices the by then southern expatriate Cable's alienation: "it isn't dead, it's merely 'possuming . . . Ye may crrack its bones and yet never a whimper yet 'tis but 'possuming. Lorrd! Ye can't *neglect* it to death; the neglect of all America can't kill it. It's in the womb o' the future and bigger than Asia, Africa, and Ammerica combined. Ye'll do well to be friendly wi' its friends and trreat it kindly while it's young and trractable." But white southerners ignored the deeper ramifications of their train rides in the present to ramble instead, relieved of the sense of impending crisis, in the "distant" timelessness of the past. Origin stories of southern whiteness — from regional and national fiction to amateur and professional histories — narrated an Old South in which the coming of age of the race issue could be denied because this bastard child of the Civil War had not even been born. As the literary critic Richard Gray has argued, "nostalgia could run riot, distance could give a romantic blur to everything, while if any gap was perceived between ideal and reality, word and thing . . . it could be equated with the gap between past and present; once things were perfect, the argument went, and if they do not seem so now, then the war is entirely to blame." History, a sense of the distance between the past and the present, became not only a time but a cultural space in which to craft a new southern order. The segregation of time — the whiteness of Civil War valor, the blackness of Reconstruction — paralleled and founded and deepened the segregation of space, providing the foundations of the southern future.[14]

The culture of segregation, then, erased Cable's, Chesnutt's, and Du Bois's marginal figures, hiding their racial and class contradictions from view under the whiteface of passing or the blackface performance of inferiority mandated by Jim Crow. Another image of the southern black, occupying an altogether different time and space, appeared in the narratives of origins white southerners told to both enable and legitimate their new segregated social order. If "even the moonlight was richer and mellower 'before the war,'" as the then much more representative white southerner Thomas Nelson Page wrote, then certainly no mixed-race, middle-class figures walked the simplified geography of the plantation. As the old ex-slave and stable boss implied in answer to an unruly and disobedient black stable boy in another of Page's stories, even "freedom" for the loyal black was better back then, when everyone had a place. The "before the war" Negro as slave required no railings, partitions, signs, or inferior accommodations to deny his subjecthood. In the founding stories of southern whiteness, what W. E. B. Du Bois called "the fairy tale of a beautiful Southern slave civilization" replaced the hot complications of southern railroad travel. And there was never any doubt about the "darky's" color.[15]

Race in the Garden

In sharp contrast to the figure of the middle-class mulatto on the train, by the opening of the twentieth century the radically different image of the comic and contented slave had become one of the most popular figures in American culture. Blacked-up white men had long before pioneered the commodification of black images and continued to impersonate African Americans on booming minstrel stages across the nation. White children played with "darky" figured toys and squealed in delight at Uncle Remus's tales of Brer Rabbit's adventures. White southern editorialists asked both the region and the nation to honor the ex-slaves with monuments, pensions, and old age homes. White southern fiction and memoirs flowed off the presses with tales of the loyal and lifelong relationships of black slaves or servants and white owners or employers. And advertisers seized upon the image's connotations of servitude to sell everything from pancake mix to stove polish. As the writer and ex-Reconstruction official Albion Tourgee had stated in 1888, the ex-slave was already one of the most popular figures in American culture. While Dixie may have long ago lost the war, the nation had become, in Tourgee's phrase, "distinctly Confederate in sympathy." The white South, its regional autobiography fixed in a plantation romance peopled with "happy darkies," noble masters, and doting mistresses, had won the peace.[16]

Though minstrelsy originated as early as the 1840s in the North, the boom in Old South nostalgia and sentimentality as opposed to comic caricature began after the close of Reconstruction. The historian Paul M. Gaston has argued that writers, particularly in the newly expanding national magazines, staged "a national love feast for the Old South." Joel Chandler Harris created his African American storyteller Uncle Remus in the late 1870s in the *Atlanta Constitution*, but this most famous "Uncle" reached a wider audience in 1880 with the publication of Harris's first book. Seeking to distinguish himself from "the intolerable misrepresentations of the minstrel stage," in *Uncle Remus: His Songs and His Sayings* Harris claimed to record the legends of the ex-slaves "without embellishment and without exaggeration" and "to give to the whole a genuine flavor of the old plantation." Thomas Nelson Page launched his own slave character "marse Chan" in *Century Magazine* in 1884, bringing alive "Old Massa and Mistis" and "Meh Lady" along with their worshipful black retainers. Page's *In Ole Virginia; or Marse Chan and Other Stories* told of a loyal old slave distraught over the death of his Confederate soldier master and initiated a genre that would culminate over fifty years later in David O. Selznick's 1939 film version of Margaret Mitchell's *Gone With the Wind.* The slave body had been emancipated, but representations of slavery had never been more popular or profitable.[17]

Although the plantation with its happy slaves, the narrative parallel of the pro-slavery argument, had been eulogized since the antebellum period, not until the federal government had repudiated Reconstruction and repealed the Civil Rights Acts did the plantation past become for many whites a time and space of pleasure and escape, the "Old" South. Left alone with the freedpeople fighting to retain their citizenship, many white southerners turned wistfully away from present conflicts to a past named "old" and therefore distant, a time that northern minstrel shows had established as infinitely entertaining. Nostalgic celebrations of a golden age of racial innocence deflected present white southerners' hardships and hid rising racial violence and new forms of bondage like convict labor and peonage under a haze of moonlight and magnolias. The passage of time only multiplied the possibilities, detaching any "historical" narration from the pesky details of everyday life and crafting "those old plantation days" into a golden age of perfect race, class, and gender harmony. The minister in one of Thomas Nelson Page's novels tells a northern visitor to this "vague region partly in one of the old Southern States and partly in the yet vaguer land of Memory" that he has evidence proving "that the Garden of Eden was situated not very far" from the site of the Red Rock plantation and "certainly within the limits of the State."[18]

But the historians C. Vann Woodward and Paul M. Gaston have found more than a romantic false consciousness at stake. The Old South enabled the New South, providing an interpretation of the past that satisfied white southern sectionalism while allowing a rising white middle class to pursue industrial development and urban professionalism on a northern model. In Woodward's famous phrasing, "the bitter mixture of recantation and heresy could never have been swallowed so readily had it not been dissolved in the syrup of romanticism." And as many of the crafters of the plantation pastorale came from a rising southern white middle class as did the builders of factories. While Thomas Nelson Page had been born on a plantation near Richmond, the fatherless Joel Chandler Harris grew up with his seamstress mother to become a journalist, and the historian most responsible for promoting the image of the plantation pastorale, Ulrich B. Phillips, had been born in 1877 into a family of small farmers. By the turn of the century, middle-class white southerners from towns and small cities dominated the Confederate memorial organizations—the United Confederate Veterans, the United Daughters of the Confederacy, and the United Sons of the Confederacy—and filled the pages of their official organ *The Confederate Veteran* with sentimental paeans to the old plantations their ancestors had seldom known. Old South nostalgia, the funhouse mirror of New South progress, culturally anchored the authority of a rising white southern middle class while paradoxically transforming the region into the northeastern-centered economy's developing market of choice.[19]

While Woodward and Gaston have traced the importance of Old South–New South interdependence for the economic development of the South, the plantation romance as entertainment and escape played a specific role in the creation of a new southern racial order as well. The passage of time did more than free the white southern historical imagination from the burdens of recorded events and conflicting memories. Distance also provided whites with an opportunity to conflate individual and regional childhoods. By the 1880s and especially the 1890s the destruction of the antebellum dream in war converged with the lost childhoods of the chroniclers. Only as children had writers like Joel Chandler Harris, Thomas Nelson Page, and the myriad other depicters of those happy prewar days experienced plantations or slaves. Individual desire for childhood innocence converged with a regional longing for racial harmony. The making of modern southern whiteness began, then, within a time and space imagined as a racially innocent plantation pastorale, where whites and blacks loved and depended upon each other. Since it was never the individual or the race's intention to leave this "integrated" utopia, a rising white middle class absorbing an old elite and its professed values could celebrate the master-slave relationship unencumbered by the paternalistic moral obligations whose past existence they loudly praised. The external forces of "Yankee aggression" and "black betrayal" shaped their present life outside the garden, white adulthood after the fall.[20]

Joel Chandler Harris's *Uncle Remus*, one of the first and most popular collections of stories about plantation life, ran through repeated editions from its 1880 publication well into the twentieth century. The *Atlanta Constitution* editor's first book initiated a literary boom of sentimental old black characters set vaguely between slavery and freedom, and he wrote twenty-eight more novels and short story collections himself, most featuring Uncle Remus or other slave characters like the mammy figure Aunt Minervy Ann or the escaped slave Mingo. Born in 1848, the illegitimate son of a young white woman of middling means and an itinerant Irish laborer who soon deserted his child, Harris grew up with his mother's surname in the small town of Eatonton, Georgia. Too young to serve in the Confederate army, Harris spent the war as a printer's apprentice for the newspaper *The Countryman*, published in the 1860s on a middle Georgia plantation. Afterward, he used this training to become a journalist. Harris was the second most popular southern writer, after his friend Mark Twain, in the nation by the turn of the century. He crafted some of the most complicated and sympathetic white-authored black characters of his time; nevertheless his work contributed to the pitting by whites of an "integrated" plantation pastorale against current racial conflict as justification for a segregated future.[21]

In the relationship of the old ex-slave Uncle Remus and the white "Little Boy," extended over several volumes, Harris skillfully mixes the remembered regional past and white southern childhood. The slave/ex-slave character, in Harris's writings, becomes the repository of the white historical narrative. In a post-Reconstruction present, the black man tells the white child about the times "way back yander." Rarely does this present intrude on the past. Yet Harris's remembered black voices often recite allegorical African tales that shed a subversive light on slavery. This borrowing places Remus somewhat closer to black subjectivity than the blackface caricature of the stage and other white fiction. Still, the potential black voice of Remus's folktales is limited by the frame. Little Boy and to a lesser extent his mother Miss Sally embody a curiously timeless plantation life. Little Boy inhabits a world where a loyal ex-slave has "little or nothing to do"; his most onerous tasks include entertaining a white boy, pulling a fat yam out of the fire, "twisting and waxing some shoe-thread," and lighting his pipe while whites comfortably provide his room and board. The African American folktales in which the wily Brer Rabbit outsmarts his stronger enemy Brer Fox, often in those most intimate of activities, eating and courting, are subversive in their way; but the blackfaced context—the southern white writer's rendition in dialect of "authentic" slave lore—blunts their power.[22]

Still, Uncle Remus has downright dignity in comparison to later slave/-ex-slave characters invented by whites. When Little Boy corrects his storytelling, the mask of even this white-figured black character cracks: "A frown gathered on his usually serene brow as he turned his gaze upon the child—a frown in which both scorn and indignation were visible. Then all at once he seemed to regain control of himself. The frown was chased away by a look of Christian resignation." Yet religion aside, Uncle Remus, however cautiously, speaks his mind, ignoring the racial hierarchy, making the disrespect a matter of age rather than race, and enlisting Miss Sally and past generations of the white family on his side. "Bles grashus! ef chilluns ain't gittin' so dey knows mo'n old folks, en dey'll spute longer you en spute longer you, ceppin der ma call um . . . en den I'll set by de chimbly-cornder en git som peace er mine. W'en ole Miss wuz livin', hit 'uz mo'n enny her chilluns 'ud dast ter do ter come sputin' longer me . . ." Harris mutes Remus's outspokenness by having him address "some imaginary person" rather than the child. His days of respect, too, occur in that vague plantation past when Remus was a slave. And reconciliation, of course, happens after Little Boy begins to cry. In what became a much more sentimental trope in later versions of the plantation romance, the Civil War as memory provides the staging of reunion: " 'I 'clar to goodness,' he said, reaching out and taking the little boy tenderly by the hand, 'ef you ain't de ve'y spit en image er old Miss w'en I bring 'er de las news er de war." Unlike the dialogues of minstrel skits and songs and the work of contemporary writers like Thomas Nelson Page, Harris's literary blackface demonstrated a measure of respect for his black character creations. "To all who have any knowledge of the negro," Harris wrote, "the Plantation darkey, as he was, is a very attractive figure. It is a silly trick of the clowns to give him over to burlesque," or, he might have added, to flat and sappy sentimentality.[23]

Literary critics and folklorists have often separated the Uncle Remus books into the Harris-created frame and the African American folktale content. This segregation of the Remus tales, however, has erased the ambivalence present in the Remus character as well. Certainly Remus's actions prove more muted than Brer Rabbit's antics, like this animal character's whiteface mimicry of southern whites' demands for polite and subservient address in the popular tar-baby story. Yet Uncle Remus bears the marks of Harris's own racial confusions, of his coming of age in a period when southern race relations were in often violent transition between the professed paternalism of the plantation and the separation of segregation, of Harris's own difficulty in performing the white southern ritual of denying the blackness within himself. Uncle Remus—animal tales, character, and frame— was larger than blackface; like the region despite the growing denial of segregation, he was both black and white. Harris perfected dialect as the linguistic equivalent of blackface pain. But this mask served so well to mark off blackness that it partially shielded the black resistance that had slipped into Remus through the slaves and ex-slaves Harris met and used as models. Blacks' own resistance to the racial categories imagined by whites occasionally survived, whether further concealed in animal stories or not, the editing hand of Harris, and these moments provide a fascinating glimpse of black subjectivity.[24]

Thus, while Remus can only sing about "gemmun" jumping Jim Crow wearing the additional mask of Brer Rabbit, his own performative subversions come through in the "sayings" that record his own deeds. In "The Fourth of July," Uncle Remus begins by complaining about the troubles stirred up by city blacks: "Show me a Mobile nigger an' I'll show you a nigger dat's marked for de chain-gang." In Remus's ventriloquism of white attitudes toward urban African Americans, Harris moves the limiting action of the Little Boy frame into these non-animal and thus less distant stories. Yet Harris also created a scene in which the ambiguity of Remus's comments on the recent and still-contentious Reconstruction past remained unresolved. The scene itself, in which white folks gather in the aftermath of Reconstruction to celebrate their American patriotism, provides an ironic and performative context. The contentless forms with which southern whites demonstrated their national allegiance, then, threw doubt upon the black man's own enactment of southern white loyalty: "I speck I'm ez fon' er deze Nunited States ez de nex' man w'at knows dat de Buro is busted up." Remus speaks to a tripled white audience: the white men in the saying, the boy in the storytelling frame, and the reading public in the late nineteenth century. Despite the layers of white interpretation, whether Remus is for or against either the newly reunited nation or the Freedmen's Bureau remains impossible to fix.[25]

Yet Harris always managed to close off the glimmers of black resistance that appeared in Remus outside his animal tales. As in the episode with Little Boy, Harris slips back from his move toward black subjectivity into the white safety of blackface, quickly closing the crack. Remus ends "his saying" by asserting his mastery against the "Mobile black," "one er deze yer slick-lookin' niggers, wid a bee-gum hat an' a brass watch ez big ez de head uv a beer-bar'l," a white refraction of Cable's, Chesnutt's, and later Du Bois's middle-class "New Negro" on the train. This city "nigger" has provoked Remus, who brags that he "spatter de nigger's eyeballs on de groun', and w'en he riz his count'nence look fresh like beef-haslett." Despite the intended minstrel comedy, Uncle Remus earns his subjectivity by performing the Ku Klux Klan's violent Reconstruction role in policing "uppity" blacks. He becomes a man, then, in the same way that disenfranchised white southern men reclaimed their own diminished manhood. Harris crafted a dialect-speaking black character who nevertheless retains traces of the subjectivity of the white author's African American sources, including most importantly the ability to imitate and slyly ridicule whites themselves. With the exception of Mark Twain, Joel Chandler Harris's work presented a racial complexity missing in his white contemporaries' one-dimensional depictions of black identity as equal to either the masks blacks had long presented southern whites or the minstrel stereotypes crafted by northerners.[26]

Harris's celebration of a past racial unity extended the Old South romance and yet also undermined the power of its racial categories. Occasionally, plantation "integration" reached an extreme within which blacks and whites became almost interchangeable. In *Uncle Remus*, Harris included among his "legends of the old plantation" an Uncle Remus story entitled "Why the Negro is Black." Little Boy's discovery that the old man's palms are "as white as his own" prompts a reply that suggests both the constructedness and recent origins of racial difference. "Dey wuz a time w'en all de w'ite folks 'uz black," Uncle Remus begins, "blacker den me, kaze I done bin yer

so long dat I bin sorter bleach out." Having subversively claimed more
whiteness than some whites, Remus continues with a little touch of warning: "Fokes dunner w'at bin yit, let 'lone w'at qwineter be. Niggers is niggers
now, but de time wuz w'en we'uz all niggers tergedder." Who will be "niggers" in the future, Remus suggests, no one now knows, but this story like
many of his more allegorical animal tales implies that blackness and whiteness are more performative and constructed than essential and eternal. People then got along about the same as today, he continues, until the discovery
of a pond with water that would wash the skin white. Arriving at the water
first, one group lost all their color. A huge crowd that reached the pond next
became "merlatters," "de Injun en de Chinee." The last to arrive, of course,
could only dabble their hands and feet in the remaining puddle. Blacks are
"niggers," Remus implies, not because they are innately inferior but
because they came, to the pond or over the Atlantic or even to freedom, too
late. Once Remus even directly addresses the arbitrariness and interchange-
ability of racial identity. When Little Boy asks whether the man in another
tale Remus has begun is white or black, he replies: "I'm des tellin' you de
tale, en you kin take en take de man en w'itewash 'im, er you kin black 'im
up des ez you please. Dat's de way I looks at it."[27]

Far from "irrelevant," as the historian Wayne Mixon has claimed, racial
identities swirl everywhere in the Uncle Remus volumes. Blackness and
whiteness, like slavery and freedom in Harris's own boyhood, become
detached from the very black and white bodies from which they were supposed to be inseparable. Publicly, Harris the journalist wrote moderately
against the late nineteenth-century extreme of white racism, penning editorials in the *Atlanta Constitution* on the advantages of education for the
freedpeople and the evils of lynching. Yet Harris let slip Remus's troubling
racial permutations in his own private writings as well, signing letters to his
own children "Uncle Remus" and using a sexualized metaphor to describe
his own insertion of African American folklore into white American literature: "I probably did my best when I got North American literature in the
family way with the Tar-Baby." How a white man could impregnate a white
woman with a mulatto child, he never made clear. In 1907 he even suggested in a letter to Andrew Carnegie that his highest ambition was "to
smooth over and sooth [*sic*], and finally dissipate all ill feelings between the
races . . . [with] such gentle and sure policies of persuasion with respect to
the negro question, which is also the white man's question, that honest peo-

ple cannot resist them." Certainly one way for a white author to perform such a service was to imagine himself as a black man. A fellow white southern journalist and author, Walter Hines Page, remarked, "I have Mr. Harris' own word for it, that he can think in the negro dialect." In crafting Remus, Harris claimed to have made "a human syndicate . . . of three or four old darkies." He had also created a black self.[28]

Yet in capturing the racial uncertainties of the 1870s and 1880s and white longing for a now gone and mostly imagined intimacy with blacks, Harris did more to cement the old ex-slave stereotype's popularity with turn-of-the-century white audiences, to erase the middle-class and often mixed-race figure on the train with the old plantation-bound ex-slave, than any other author. No matter how much this "before-the-war Negro" asserted his subjecthood, he moved within a framework of stories that inscribed the past—even in terms of white children's respect for a black man—as better way back then. As an even more ancient Remus tells the son of the first Little Boy, "dem wuz laughin' times, an' it look like dez ain't never comin' back." What time Harris or Remus is referring to—the before-the-plantation of the animal stories, the before-the-war of the plantation, or the after-the-war period called Reconstruction just before the storytelling begins—remains unclear within the tale. But white southerners, including at times even Harris, were constantly mistaking black masks for black selves. The nostalgia the Remus character fed did not leave much room for such subtlety. Other white southerners simply lifted the most sentimental aspects of the Uncle Remus shell right off the layered and partially stolen and decidedly biracial meat around which it had for protection grown. Perhaps they relied upon the various illustrations of the black storyteller that publishers inserted in the volumes and that Harris rarely liked. The Remus stories, as the literary critic Bernard Wolfe observes, proved an exceptionally public and popular "monument" to white southerners' racial ambivalence, to both fear and desire.[29]

White southerners, increasingly joined by their northern contemporaries as the nineteenth century closed, countered blacks' demands for freedom by memorializing the loyal ex-slave. Unlike the multidimensional Uncle Remus, this "before-the-war Negro" knew a much more simplified "place" corresponding to a vague and flat time. Thomas Nelson Page praised the "integrated" race relations of the antebellum South as much as the moonlight and wrote stories peopled with happy darkies and loving masters. Almost fifty years later, Margaret Mitchell's *Gone With the Wind* eulogized ex-slaves like Pork and Mammy who despite emancipation refused to leave their mistresses and masters.[30]

Having encountered Uncle Remus in Harris's and others' fictions, white southerners then attempted to construct this ex-slave in fact. A well-ordered plantation past, imagined free of slave resistance, flowed into the present figure of the loyal ex-slave, and this imagined character, in turn, justified the often violent treatment of African Americans who desired more than white "love." The "Old Negro," in the white journalist Ray Stannard Baker's 1906 phrase, needed to be singled out not just in fiction and song but in "life." Imaginatively sited at the center of the plantation romance, he needed a location squarely within the southern community as well.[31]

The major Confederate memorial organizations—the United Daughters of the Confederacy (UDC), the United Confederate Veterans (UCV), and the Sons of Confederate Veterans—included African Americans willing to play the role of loyal ex-slave in Confederate celebrations. In the pages of *Confederate Veteran* and in local chapter meetings the merits of erecting "monuments to faithful slaves" across the region were argued as early as the late nineteenth century. In 1923, the UDC even asked Congress to authorize the construction of a "mammy" memorial in the nation's capital. The site would honor black women who had nursed southern whites in that elided time before and after emancipation. Other suggested plans called for the erection of a statue to honor "the faithful old slaves who remained loyal and true to their owners in the dark days of the sixties and on through the infamous reconstruction period," a memorial to express the "inextinguishable gratitude" that remained "smoldering in the souls of those who owned them." In North Carolina, whites actually erected a monument to Uncle Tom, whose northern abolitionist origins were forgotten in praise of the "old Negro's" loyalty, patient suffering, and love.[32]

But whites intended the slave memorial to work for the present as much as honor the past. The ex-slaveholders needed "to leave a mark," to "tell future generations that the white men of the South were the negro's best friends then and that the men of the South are the negro's best friends today." An opponent of the memorial work who desired instead the building of a home for aged and destitute ex-Confederate women inadvertently highlighted the reason other whites advocated its construction: "The negro of this generation would not appreciate any monument not smacking of social equality." All the more reason, then, to set up a magnificent marker to the "old time" African American who knew his or her place.[33]

Similar white anxieties over "New Negroes" more like Cable's train passengers than Harris's Uncle Remus sparked calls for pensions and old age homes for ex-slaves. Southern whites began "honoring" these "Old Negroes" by hosting dinners and announcing holidays. A correspondent in the *Confederate Veteran* clarified his call for federal government-funded pensions by providing an image of the African American who would deserve such treatment: "the old, polite *ante-bellum darky* [who] still stands with his hat off and says with a grin of expectancy, 'At your service, Mass William.' Especially, in the interest of this class I am writing." Some whites suggested that federal assistance be provided to help ex-slaves purchase lands upon which to live in the rural South. A *Confederate Veteran* article noted that the one-time expenditure would amount to less than one-third of what the federal government spent annually for Union veterans' pensions and would help "the Southern people, white as well as black." Specifically, Sumner A. Cunningham, the editor and owner of the *Veteran*, insisted that such assistance would aid whites who "maintained these old black people . . . any how" and "would induce many darkies to remove from dingy suburbs of cities and towns to the open and healthier atmosphere of the country." The *Confederate Veteran* did not need to inform its readership that rural blacks were more available for agricultural work than urban blacks and often more dependent in general upon whites. Ironically, the official organ of Confederate memorial organizations even made a reference to the Reconstruction promise of "forty acres and a mule" in support of its plan. Of course, white paternalism would gain systematic and federal sanction as whites would be appointed to select land for purchase and the recipients of funds would not be able to sell the land for ten years. To reward slavelike blacks, who were more imagined than real, some southern whites offered to give them as dependents the land they had been denied as citizens. Uncle Remus, these whites sensed, did not try to ride first class on the train.[34]

A convergence of praise for slavelike behavior and the ex-slaves, the seepage of the imagined past into the present, filled both amateur and professional histories of slavery that poured forth in the years between the 1890s and the 1918 publication of Ulrich B. Phillips's *American Negro Slavery*. Mildred L. Rutherford, a white woman from Georgia, became perhaps the best-known amateur historian in the early twentieth century for her extensive writings and speeches, her historical journal, published from 1923 to 1927, and her promotion of historical work among the UDC as that organization's Historian General from 1911 to 1916. Condemning present-day educated African Americans, Rutherford insisted that "slavery was no disgrace to the owner or the owned." Blacks had arrived in America "savage," "without thought of clothes," "bowing down to fetishes," and "sometimes cannibals." Slavery not only Christianized the slaves but made them "the happiest set of people on the face of the globe—free from care or thought of food, clothes, home, or religious privileges." Insisting that "slaveholders felt a personal responsibility," Rutherford then made that familiar move of the imagined past into the present that became central to modern southern whiteness. Although she had been but a schoolgirl when the Civil War ended, she shifted into the first person: "We never called them slaves; they were our people, our negroes, part of our very homes." The only thing wrong about slavery for Rutherford, making the familiar slave-as-a-burden argument, was the great obligation the institution placed upon whites. In a passage in which her logic defied gravity, she insisted that "the negro was the free man and the slaveholder was the slave." More polemical and less complicated and entertaining, Rutherford nevertheless joined Harris in the larger muting of the hard facts of human bondage. In race relations as in the rest of regional life, Rutherford advocated "preserving the best of the 'Old South'—modernized to meet the present."[35]

For Rutherford, "the truths of Southern history" were the very essence of white southern identity. To take a less absolute view risked "los[ing] out in all things Southern." Even more influential among an expansive urban and educated white middle class across the region were professional historians. Trained at the University of Georgia and Columbia University, Rutherford's fellow Georgia native Ulrich B. Phillips added extensive documentation and translated a similar dismissal of the evils of slavery into the rationalized, nonpartisan discourse of an increasingly professionalized academia. Much like Rutherford and as Page before her had suggested in his fiction, Phillips stressed that slavery burdened white southerners more than blacks as larger, inflexible expenditures on slaves limited regional economic development. In a 1904 article, "The Plantation as a Civilizing Factor," Phillips added the weight of professional scholarship to the argument often presented in fiction and amateur histories that slavery, in Page's words, had been the salvation of blacks arriving from Africa as "savages." Far from wrong, the institution for Phillips functioned both as a "training school" and a family in which "mutual requirements, concessions and understandings [produced] reciprocal codes of conventional morality." The way to improve the economic situation of the present South, the historian argued, was to convince the freed people to work for their former owners, "the most substantial, practical, and valuable friends . . . [blacks] have ever had." W. E. B. Du Bois, however, in his 1918 review of Phillips's lauded *American Negro Slavery*, found it difficult to credit the "friendship" of a scholar who refused to recognize the humanity of African Americans.[36]

Yet despite Phillips's careful distinctions in his correspondence between the amateur and professional practice of history, his historical interpretations relied upon the same strange slippages of time, the movement from the imagined past to the present and back again, that marked most white southern writing on the "Old South" from the 1890s through the 1930s. He compared the plantation in its efficient staple production as a structure of agricultural labor organization to the "modern factory" and its ordering of industry. He also both admitted in his publications and suggested in private correspondence that his accounts of plantation life drew heavily upon his "own observations in post-bellum times." To a cotton factor with whom he corresponded, Phillips wrote that his historical work confirmed the white southern businessman's and planter's own views of race relations: "It will be a great pleasure to discuss these things with you personally and a delight to visit your plantations." Again, relying on his own postwar travels, in *American Negro Slavery* he disputed accounts that slaves were worked until early death to repay their master's large investments: "anyone who has had experience with negro labor may reasonably be skeptical when told that healthy, well-fed negroes, whether slave or free, can by any routine insistence of the employer be driven beyond the point at which fatigue begins to be injurious." Bondage, having turned wild Africans into happy slaves, Phillips claimed, "had completed its work and was already an anachronism [in labor control] when the Civil War and reconstruction overthrew it." It was impossible to determine just how many of his observations about the plantation as "the best resource for agricultural progress and racial sympathy in the present and near future" rested upon the historical records he consulted as opposed to the scenes he witnessed and the tales of old plantation days, themselves inflected through the tropes of plantation fiction, that he heard while guided by his early twentieth-century hosts.[37]

The professionalization of the practice of history did not keep the plantation romance from sliding into the professor's commentary on the contemporary condition either. However much Phillips emphasized the distinction between the plantation systems before and after slavery, his conception of the plantation's function in using African American workers rested upon the persistence into the present of the imagined submissiveness of the slave. In Phillips's arguments, the plantation as ideal was not lost. Divorced from slavery as its form of labor control, it remained in the present and could continue growing contented, free "darkies" as well as cotton far into the future. In the concluding paragraph of his "masterpiece" on American slavery, however, nostalgia completely triumphed over argument. Admitting the Old South's "injustice, oppression, brutality and heartburning," he asked:

> but where in the struggling world are these absent? There were also gentleness, kindhearted friendship, and mutual loyalty to a degree hard for him to believe who regards the system with a theorist's eye and a partisan squint. For him on the other hand who has known the considerate and cordial, courteous and charming men and women, white and black, which that picturesque life in its best phases produced, it is impossible to agree that its basis and its operation were wholly evil.

The imagined past and Phillips's own childhood memories converged here and entered the present. For all his scholarly objectivity, Phillips sounded a lot like Page, who in proclaiming the perfection of the white southern elite admitted that they "were the product of a system of which it is the fashion nowadays to have only words of condemnation." By providing a more nuanced and documented account, the historian did not so much revise the romance as reempower it.[38]

Both northern and southern white contemporaries overwhelmingly considered Phillips nonsectional and objective. The *Baltimore Sun's* reviewer perhaps said more than he intended, praising the book as a "fair and impartial account," "as interesting as a romance." Another historian of the economics of slavery, Phillip Alexander Bruce, wrote Phillips that "most works relating to this subject are disfigured and warped by biased opinion . . . They are either too northern or too southern—but . . . you have struck exactly the right key." Ironically, Universal Pictures Corporation asked him in 1926 to provide them with illustrations and details of slave markets and slave weddings for use in a movie version of Harriet Beecher Stowe's *Uncle Tom's Cabin*. Thus the plantation romance came to color in twentieth-century awareness the very antebellum abolitionist narrative whose popularity exacerbated sectional tensions and helped cause the war. The white southerner who dedicated, despite his publisher's objections, his second book, *The History of Transportation in the Eastern Cotton Belt to 1860,* "to the dominant classes of the south," had become the nation's expert on slavery. In the early twentieth century, then, not just fiction but also the professional practice of history had taken on what Tourgee had prophetically described in 1888 as a tone of "Confederate sympathy."[39]

Yet white writing about history did more than provide, as the historian John David Smith has characterized it, "a historical rationale for the continued repression of blacks." It also suggested the forms available for the racial future. Academic historians joined with amateur historians, antiquarians, Confederate memorialists, novelists, and short story writers to create a broad historical narrative that despite idiosyncrasies and differences of detail praised a romanticized past of racial "integration." And the more perfect this past became, the more free of racial and class conflict, the more plantation narratives helped destroy the possibility of an integrated future. The proslavery perspective, loosely defined as both direct defenses of as well as apologies for the institution of human bondage, linked an intimate racial mixing of blacks and whites with the distant plantation pastorale of a simpler age.[40]

Perhaps the least romantic of the plantation's chroniclers, U. B. Phillips modernized the genre, making it palatable for educated and urban middle-class whites across the nation. "The lives of the whites and blacks were partly segregate, partly intertwined," Phillips wrote in *American Negro Slavery,* using a phrase that although less vivid echoed the image of fingers on a hand in Booker T. Washington's famous 1895 "Atlanta Compromise" speech. "If any special link were needed, the children supplied it." "White children," he insisted, in the frequent convergence of nostalgia for both a lost way of life and a lost childhood that broadly marked white southern writing on the Old South, "hardly [knew] their mothers from their mammies or their uncles by blood from their 'uncles' by courtesy." However much the "uncles" detested the title Phillips claimed offered praise rather than insult, the professional historian betrayed his own romanticism even more strongly when he claimed that "white youths found something to envy in the freedom of their [black] fellows' feet from the cramping weight of shoes and the freedom of their mind from the restraints of school." Erasing the existence of human beings as property in a sanitized language of friends and fellows, Phillips, in this passage on racial mixing, borrowed another popular trope from the plantation romance and buried the very institution that brought whites and blacks together in a flurry of the foods and activities of an idealized rural childhood. He did not even consider that those young slave boys might have envied their masters as well.[41]

This pattern of alternating mixture and separation, Phillips argued, marked adult amusements and religious activities as well as childhood games. Whites and blacks responded to the same "rampant emotionalism" of Baptist "protracted meetings" and Methodist camp revivals. For whites, "the plantations were homes to which, as they were fond of singing, their hearts turned ever and the negroes . . . were an element in the home itself." "Separation," Phillips argued, "was no more than rudimentary. They [slaves] were always within the social mind and conscience of the whites, as the whites in turn were within the mind and conscience of the blacks." "Relations on both sides were felt to be based on pleasurable responsibility," the professional historian argued, with "adjustments and readjustments . . . mutually made." In an article published in the same year as *American Negro Slavery*, Phillips insisted that a "spirit of camaraderie," not "race alienation" pervaded race relations in the past, in an implicit comparison to the present: "The grouping of persons of the two races in the intimate relationship of possession tended strongly to counteract that antipathy which all races feel toward each other. The possession was not wholly of the slave by the master, but also of the master by the slave." In his idealization of the harmonious racial mixing on the antebellum plantation, Phillips echoed the very paeans to slavery of the amateur historians for whom he had so little respect.[42]

"Integration" then became the mode of race relations that elite and middle-class white southerners associated with a past both distant and yet vaguely present in the figure of the storytelling ex-slave. Still, white southerners had to create a narrative structure that covered both the garden and the fall, a fable that allowed them to leave these African Americans for whom they had professed their fondness and almost love out of the new southern future. For an explanation of how they lost their plantation pastorale, their regional and racial childhood, whites followed the beat of a Confederate drummer boy and the soft bags of Yankee businessmen and Bureau officials on to other stories, of the "War Between the States" and "the hell that [was] called Reconstruction." Though the most dedicated members of Confederate Memorial organizations refused to utter the term, in the interpretations that dominated American popular culture by the early twentieth century, the war became increasingly "civil" indeed, its muted violence an extension of the plantation utopia's romanticization of slavery.[43]

A "Civil" War

Contemporary historians, whether amateur or professional, however, found it difficult to discuss the American Civil War without offering their interpretations of its causes. The task of crafting a less political and thus more conciliatory war narrative fell to others, most often the writers of fiction and participants in Confederate celebrations but occasionally also the purveyors of fact. The Union and Confederate veterans who penned *Century Magazine*'s extremely popular 1884–1887 series "Battles and Leaders of the Civil War" buried political questions in often vivid if sanitized accounts of crucial engagements. The editors had demanded this approach, asking contributors to avoid the "official report style" and provide instead, "as it were in fatigue dress, such facts as you would be likely to state if you should set out to tell the story of the battle to your own family about the fireside." Although memoirs and letters of white southerners described such "fireside chats" as often fiercely partisan, in the *Century* series a muted violence became the ground for sectional reconciliation. According to the historian Gaines M. Foster, local and regional Confederate celebrations—periodic reunions of veterans accompanied by parades, speeches, and the dedication of monuments—allowed white southerners "to distance themselves from the issues of the war without repudiating the veterans." The reconciliation that had begun between former military foes reached a peak after the Spanish-American War as white southern soldiers fought valiantly for the federal army. White northerners and southerners came to view the Civil War as "a glorious time to be celebrated" rather than "a tragic failure" to be condemned. By 1912 a Confederate veteran called the northern soldiers he had once fought "our friends the enemy."[44]

The "civilized" war, then, became a space both for sectional reconciliation and for the creation of modern southern whiteness. Recent historians have created a nuanced and complex historiography of national reunion, examining the gendered, class, and racial foundations upon which white southern and northern men and women began to figure their rejoining. David Roediger has argued that despite the potential of emancipation to liberate white workers from their own racially figured identities as "free laborers" by destroying slavery as the model of depravity, northern labor activists had difficulty embracing African Americans in the pursuit of postwar labor goals. David Montgomery has outlined the centrality of "a code of manly behavior usually cast in ethnic and racial terms" to labor organizing after the war. Broadening this gendered interpretation, Nina Silber has argued that a common celebration of white masculine valor provided the ground of sectional reconciliation by the late nineteenth century for more middle-class and elite white men as well. And LeeAnn Whites has added that the domestication of the meaning of the war, a recasting of Confederate war aims as the defense of southern homes, not southern slavery, provided the ground for acceptance of reunion in the South. The momentary and always partial unity of blacks and the northern whites against white southerners fell, then, in the face of a threatened white masculinity and the imperialist adventures needed for its reclamation. And white women too sought greater rights within a common racial identity, as southern demands for white women's suffrage to ensure white supremacy meshed with northern claims that white women should vote before ignorant Irishmen. Sectional reconciliation within a common whiteness, then, provided a common grounding for late nineteenth-century activism, from the suffrage and labor movements to progressive reform and the expansion of American imperialism.[45]

But national white reunion, particularly as figured in white southern stories of plantations, war, and Reconstruction, provided crucial legitimation for the new culture of segregation, an adoption and expansion in the South of a racial ordering already in force in parts of the urban North, as well. Although Confederate memorialists wove tales of contented bonds-people and appearances by "loyal" ex-slaves into their celebrations, past or present race relations were marginal to these ritualized sanitations of what had been a horrifyingly violent war. Tales of the plantation had narrated the utopian racial past. Accounts of the "dark days of Reconstruction" would found the expansion of segregation as the modern and orderly racial future. The "civilization" of the war, then, provided the crucial link between the antebellum plantation ideal and the postbellum era, shifting the location of the tragedy for both southern and northern whites from the war itself and their sectional animosity to Reconstruction and the setting of blacks over southern whites. Confederate celebrations made a simplified view of the war the dividing line between a romanticized and thus unusable past and present disorder. Current white southern racial problems, the argument went, had nothing to do with that increasingly faultless and distant plantation ideal. Monuments in myriad southern cities and towns emphasized that the wartime valor of both white men and women rather than actual ownership of a plantation granted whites an exalted place within the community. Requiring only that an ancestor had fought for the cause, membership criteria of organizations like the Sons, Daughters, and Children of the Confederacy, too, suggested that participation in the war effort superseded class status in determining "Southernness." White war stories erased the bread riots and desertion of poorer recruits, denying class tensions between whites in both the past and the present. The "civil" war became not just the paradoxical space of national reconciliation but also the moment that counted, when the distant plantation past and the postbellum South met, the touchstone of modern "classless" southern whiteness.[46]

Despite Confederate organizations' emphasis on genealogy, and the accounts of aristocratic ancestors that gave context to the plantation pastorale, the "civilization" of the war created a strange aura of fatherlessness that both aided sectional reconciliation and perpetuated the celebration of an imagined past of racial integration. The tendency to mute the causes of the war first displayed in the *Century* series "Battles and Leaders of the Civil War" found public reenactment in reunions of Union and Confederate veterans like the fiftieth anniversary of the Battle of Gettysburg. Within the South, white men and women emphasized that the region had not caused the war, that the Confederacy had not lacked "bravery, gallantry, or patriotism" or loyalty to the Constitution and thus had no reason to feel shame.[47]

Indeed, if any entity filled this absence of authorship it was that distantly abstract founding father, the U.S. Constitution, patriarch of the feuding brother sections. Correspondents to the *Confederate Veteran* as well as the professional historian U. B. Phillips emphasized the region's constitutional right to leave the Union. But if the Constitution had fathered the conflict it had also fathered the nation. Thus even the most fanatically "Confederate" southern whites' interpretations of the war provided grounding for reconciliation. White writers extended the family metaphors—used in the antebellum chapter of the plantation romance to mute the harshness of slavery—to blunt the horrors of the war as well.[48]

Lovers as well as soldiers, then, as the historian Nina Silber has argued, played crucial roles in the staging of sectional reconciliation. Romantic love proved as viable as a common experience of violence and display of courage in muting white sectional and class tensions. Often, as in Harris's 1880 Remus tale "A Story of War" and Thomas Dixon's 1905 novel *The Clansman*, both violence and love worked together to stage a regional reconciliation. But in fiction and memoirs, the conflict that would destroy the Old South utopia also ironically provided the grounds for the most spectacular display of its "values." Glossing over the inherent drama of emancipation, the plantation romance staged in its stead a postwar wedding of the once-fighting sides. Most often the trope married a southern white woman, usually the sister or widow of a dashing Confederate soldier, and the former Union officer she has somehow met and come to love. As war swept across the region, the power of the plantation as imagined ideal to deny racial conflict extended to sectional fighting as well.[49]

If the soldier reunions transformed the legacy of the battles from southern defeat to national martial valor, the plantation romance reclaimed the homefront as well. Figuring the war through the white-imagined character of the loyal ex-slave, southern whites integrated and reclaimed this space as plantation triumph rather than Confederate defeat. Narrations of the "civil" war provided southern whites with a reservoir of imagined racial integration performing under the most stressful of conditions. Often serving as the one character not defined by wartime activities, the ex-slave brought together in white memory the past, present, and future as an imagined and exaggerated loyalty spanned the war's divide. One of the first of these extensions of the plantation romance into the period of the Civil War appeared in Harris's first Uncle Remus collection in 1880. The very title, "A Story of the War," set the conciliatory tone, as Harris refused to become involved in sectional arguments about whether "Civil War" or "War Between the States" more accurately named the four years of fighting. Harris wrote a sectional romance and reunion into the plantation ideal by marrying a wounded northern officer into the antebellum "family black and white."[50]

Yet like most Uncle Remus tales, this war story's simplicity is deceptive. Harris begins by introducing the character of Theodosia Huntingdon, the sister of the northern officer, to poke fun at white northerners' ignorance and sense of the South as "remote and semi-barbarous" and the freedpeople as quaintly "picturesque." As the story progresses, Remus recalls running the plantation during the war. When the Yankees came the old black slave saved all the livestock and provisions in the swamp. He also stood armed with an ax beside his mistress, helping her to save the silver. While all of these activities quickly became standard in white southern accounts of the war, Harris gives Remus an agency missing in most white writers' accounts of the loyal ex-slave. Remus did not just save the white folks' property. Armed with a rifle, he also saved his master, "Mars Jeems," the son of Remus's mistress, the white man who called the storyteller "Daddy."[51]

Yet Harris constructed a form of black subjectivity, even armed black masculine assertion, that aided southern whites. Remus storms around in the tale's Reconstruction era present, fuming to Theodosia, John, and his southern white folks about the worthlessness of the new "sunshine niggers." When he finally settles into his "story of the war," he tells Theodosia how he shot her brother John as the northerner sat in a tree preparing to shoot at "Mars Jeems." "Do you mean to say," the northern woman interjects, "that you shot the Union soldier, when you knew he was fighting for your freedom?" Harris's Remus is not, like the slave characters in most white southern stories, unaware of what was at stake in the war: "Co'se, I know all about dat, en it sorter made cole chills run up my back." But even the armed and capable Remus has to declare his loyalty: "w'en I see dat man take aim, en Mars Jeems gwine home ter Old Miss en Miss Sally, I des disremembered all 'bout freedom en lammed aloose." Trading a shot for freedom for an act of sectional reconciliation, Remus brought the injured Yankee, Theodosia's brother John, home to nurse him. John later married Sally, joining the "Old Negro" and southern and northern whites together in a new happy family, a template for the new Union. When Theodosia presses in conclusion that Remus cost her brother an arm, Remus answers that he has given him "Miss Sally" and himself, and "En ef dem ain't nuff fer enny man den I done los de way." Harris's narrative gives the old ex-slave the agency to create reconciliation — he was skilled and resourceful enough to protect the wealth and the Confederate and Yankee soldiers, saving the warring sections from themselves. But having this place in the new national family came at a price. Remus not only extended his servitude to northern whites but his shot confirmed what southern whites so desperately wanted to believe, that their slaves, the "old Negroes," loved them even more than freedom.[52]

Yet when Harris drew from his own life to expand the theme of sectional reconciliation, he lost the complicated layerings of racial performance that resulted from his acts of "love and theft," and thus the fleeting subjectivity visible behind the black and white masks. Narrating the war from the home front perspective of the white boy Joe Maxwell, a double for his own childhood self in his 1892 autobiographical novel *On the Planta-*

tion: A Story of a Georgia Boy's Adventures During the War, Harris presents a curiously sanitized, nonviolent, and at times nostalgic picture of his life as a printer's apprentice on a large plantation in middle Georgia. In fact, with the exception of the drilling of a boy's school militia, a scene more of playing war than actually training for the conflict, the Civil War makes no appearance at all until the second half of the novel. In the figure of Joe Maxwell, Harris conflates a boy's coming of age with that of the nation, bringing a powerful personal nostalgia to bear on the "civilization" of the war. Yet the boy Maxwell, in the story virtually parentless, seems fathered less by the fighting than by his life on the plantation. Though Harris elsewhere wrote racing tales of wartime adventure, here he stamps the story of his own life into a bland ballad of regional reconciliation. Rotten individuals alone cause the rare miseries of a single runaway slave, Mink, and the few nonslaveholding Confederate soldiers who desert the army to feed their families. As Joe gets his closest glimpse of the conflict, watching the passing Union army with less fear than fascination from atop the plantation fence, Harris presents his moral: "It was an imposing array as to numbers, but not so as to appearance. For once and for all . . . the glamour and romance of war were dispelled." The plantation feels real to the young Joe while the Civil War "was surely a dream."[53]

The autobiographical novel, in fact, is less a story of a boy's Civil War adventures than Harris's most uncomplicated celebration of the plantation utopia and its ability even on the edge of destruction to solve all class and racial conflict. In the end, the farmer-soldiers' families are fed, and Mink works happily as a tenant on the plantation. What happens to the plantation idyll in the aftermath of Confederate defeat, other than that Mink eventually buys his own farm, Harris only vaguely suggests: "It can not be spun out here and now so as to show the great changes that have been wrought—the healing of the wounds of war; the lifting up of a section from ruin and poverty to prosperity; the molding of the beauty, the courage, the energy, and the strength of the old civilization into the new; the gradual uplifting of a lowly race." No section bears responsibility, and as Joe Maxwell grows and prospers, "the old plantation days still lived in his dreams."

Most disturbing is Harris's interpretation of the meaning, or meaninglessness, of the slaves' new freedom. The "older negroes" remain on the plantation in Harris's narrative out of loyalty and affection for their owners. Only "the younger ones, especially those who, by reason of their fieldwork, had not been on familiar terms with their master and mistress, had followed the federal army." The insertion of an anecdote that Harris uncharacteristically authenticates in a footnote completes the erasure of emancipation as the event that destroyed the plantation ideal. After watching the Union troops marching by, Joe returns home to find a strange old black couple, the woman "shivering and moaning" and the man dead. The pitiful pair "had followed the army for many a weary mile on the road to freedom," only to find it "in a fence corner" and "in the humble cabin" where the old woman too soon dies, cared for, of course, by the good white folks. That "the old things had passed away and everything was new" meant simply that the now ex-slaves could die among strangers. Dramatizing the meaninglessness of emancipation became as common a trope in white southern writing as having the slaves help hide the silver.[54]

Here Harris narrated reconciliation at the cost of even the limited subjectivity often apparent in Remus. This shift from the complex layerings of racial performance often present in his Remus books toward a sentimental blackface, a tone increasingly common in other plantation fiction, in popular song, and on the minstrel stage as well, promoted a movement toward racial violence rather than its resistance. Thomas Dixon's best-selling novel *The Clansman* (1905) transformed Harris's sacrifice of black subjectivity in the name of national reunion, the fictional parallel of the nation's repudiation of black citizenship, into the destruction of black bodies as well. In *The Clansman*, blacks lose not just their freedom to leave their white folks but their very lives. And D. W. Griffith's *Birth of a Nation*, the 1915 motion picture version of Dixon's novel, only makes the translation of regional reconciliation into a race war in which whites reunite to dominate and even kill blacks even more clear. This new national family excluded African Americans entirely. But replacing the loyal "Old Negro" with the black beast rapist required that something more than a "civil" war bear responsibility for the fall from plantation grace. By the early twentieth century many white northerners agreed with white southerners in rating Reconstruction as a greater tragedy than the war. The Civil War killed only people. By the early twentieth century, Reconstruction had become for most southern whites the monster that slew the golden age.[55]

The "Old Negro" lived on, however, in white southerners' fiction and memoirs, past the Reconstruction days of the "sunshine niggers" and into life after the plantation. Playing a relic of a "lost civilization" rather than a subject in the present, the aging ex-slaves crept out of their cozy cabin usually supplied by the white folks to spin their tales of happier times. Southern whites still, in the words of Harris's Uncle Remus, "ain't know nothin' 'tall 'bout dem ole times," but stories of an integrated flat fantasy land replaced the layerings of white- and black-shaped folk memories of America and Africa. In *Confederate Veteran* stories and other regionalist writing, African Americans not only hid the silver during the war. They also kept the white folks' genealogy and even their very memories after it. The white southern journalist Clarence Cason recounted in his 1935 memoir a meeting with an old black woman who minded an entire white community's heritage along with its old Episcopal church and cemetery, keeping the history along with the graves. While Cason read regret into her voice, a story of her "neglect" by "her white people" who had moved off to new southern towns and northern cities to leave her alone, the longing for the past seemed entirely his own.[56]

In the twentieth century, the ex-slave as a bearer of white antebellum memory lived on in the modernized figures of a Pullman porter or, even more commonly, a mammy. By the 1930s, having fashioned a common whiteness out of the racial absolutes of the color line, southern whites with aristocratic pretensions and middle-class presents formed black figures as the conduits of white difference, translating class into race. "The Negroes," Cason claimed he believed as a child, were "the most reliable touchstones" of white class position, and thus as a boy on a train trip to Atlanta he "so wanted [the porter] to know that I belonged to the 'nice people.'" "What I desired," he recounted thirty years later, "was not an air of servitude and abasement; it was rather a sense of companionship, unforced and unembarrassed on both sides. My innermost knowledge told me that he and I were parts of the same civilization." Cason admitted that white "southerners of a certain type lik[ed] to imagine that special bonds exist[ed] between them and the Negro descendants of the plantation economy" and that this link was "largely sentimental." Still, the longing came through the narration of his lost childhood. What Cason desired was the very racial reunion that the plantation romance, with the exception of the figure of the "black mammy," locked so distantly away.[57]

"The Hell That Is Called Reconstruction"

The "civilized" war with its homefront hardships had provided the ultimate opportunity for the plantation pastorale to demonstrate its biracial grace. White southerners from Harris and Rutherford to Cason felt that the racial ease of the plantation past had been lost. But this fall required a different story, an evil to serve as the hinge between romance and present-day reality and to absolve white southerners of their own paternalistic promises. How could southern whites in the late nineteenth century demand separation from the very people they concurrently claimed a special knowledge of and concern for in a recently imagined past? The answer lay in the blacking up of Reconstruction, read backward from the late nineteenth-century turmoil of financial panic, farmers' and workers' and women's protests, and the shocking visibility of the middle-class "new Negro" on the train. Reconstruction in fiction, white southern memoir, and history became as peopled as the plantation romance with flat and caricatured blacks. The "darky" had become the easily manipulated tool of corrupt and scheming and often northern whites, granted either a dumb and petted loyalty or a beastlike agency to steal and rape and kill. White southerners made Reconstruction the first black space of their new culture of segregation, the grounding for the abandonment of the blacks they had claimed to love.

White northerners needed this story as well. They grasped it to explain their repudiation of their own occupation and their reconciliation with their former enemies after so much bloodshed. Sectional reconciliation required more than common martial valor and North-South marriage. And sectional unity was more than ever necessary as the foundation of a global projection of American power, surging triumphantly from the victory in the Spanish-American war. Both the expansion of segregation in the nation and the expansion of American control outside the continent's boundaries meant that "little brown brothers" would be exiled from Harris's gentle image of a new national family where blacks would simply become the "free" dependents of both northern and southern whites. Many African Americans had already rejected this place behind rather than at the table anyhow, and their attempts publicly to assert their self-mastery had spurred white southerners' demands for racial separation. The mass immigration of Eastern Europeans to northeastern and midwestern American cities at the turn of the century also shaped northern whites' conceptions of racial and ethnic identities and raised fears there of both the possibility and the impossibility of assimilation. An increasingly, problematically, and therefore self-consciously "Anglo-Saxon" nation did not want more new states full of nonwhites demanding citizenship rights. National and sectional desires merged. What powerful whites in the North and South needed was a good race war, safely in the past where white middle-class property and white middle-class lives would not be destroyed. What they needed were "the dark days of Reconstruction."[58]

One white southerner, Edward Alfred Pollard, a journalist in Richmond during the Civil War, had proposed this reconfiguration of the national conflict from sectional to racial war as early as 1866. Pollard was as much an enigma in the sixties as Cable had been in the late eighties and early nineties, with one crucial difference. Pollard foretold the future. It had been wrong, Pollard claimed, to fight for slavery as a form of property or labor system. Instead, the "true ground of defence," the "true cause of the war," should have been race, a fight for slavery as "a barrier against a contention and war of races." And this conflict, "this new cause—or rather the true question of the war— . . . the supremacy of the white race," was yet to be won. "WHITE," Pollard asserted, was in 1868 a new call to arms and "the winning word." "Let us never be done repeating it." And Pollard also pioneered the use of Reconstruction to absolve the white South of any moral responsibility for this cause "regained." Fiercely partisan and with war wounds still fresh, Pollard of course blamed the North for the postwar horror, but he added another crucial actor to the picture. "The black thread of the Negro has been spun throughout the scheme of Reconstruction," and Pollard insisted that this almost unspeakable oppression not only justified all past conflict but, he implied, any future fighting as well.[59]

By the late nineteenth century, white southerners had returned to Pollard's conception of racial warfare as they crafted a way of remembering the past that legitimated segregation, that allowed them to push their "beloved darkies" out of the regional future. Reconstruction as the world turned upside down in the aftermath of total war and defeat became instead a flattened time of black over white. The participation of many southern whites alongside Freedmen's Bureau officials and northern soldiers and the genuine reforms of Reconstruction governments disappeared under the increasingly ritualistic accounts of "carpetbaggers" come South to swindle and steal and their traitorous southern allies the "scalawags." The first Ku Klux Klan and other similar organizations, terrorist arms of the Democratic Party that attacked both white and black Republicans and worked to reestablish Democratic rule, emerged reborn now as the avenging angels of Anglo-Saxon "civilization." Differences over the degree of northern responsibility and black betrayal existed, but in white southern fiction, autobiography, and history, Pollard's "black thread of the Negro" had become whiteness's unifying song. As even so enlightened a white southerner as the temperance and suffrage activist Belle Kearney recalled in 1900, "Anarchy triumphed, grinning, red-handed." U. B. Phillips simply named the era "the hell that is called Reconstruction."[60]

Emancipation, the central event of the period, appeared in white southern stories as a great opportunity to take a timely accounting of the black race. As with the plantation romance, imagined past and present flowed together, and white southerners split their black characters into loyal versus betraying "free darkies" much as they divided contemporary African Americans into "Old" and "New Negroes." In most accounts, not Lincoln and the Union armies but the master himself freed the slaves. In Page's *Red Rock: A Chronicle of Reconstruction*, published in 1898 and popular in both the North and the South, after Lincoln's announcement of emancipation, a Confederate army surgeon and slaveholder offers his "old body-servant" freedom and the money to make a new home in Philadelphia. The "loyal" slave of course rejects the offer, suggesting he would never want such a foreign state as Philadelphia or as freedom. After the war this doctor assembles his slaves and informs them of their new status. Those blacks who agree to work and yield as before to his mastery may stay, and most, especially "the older ones," remain in their "homes." Most pointedly, the doctor exiles as now an "outsider" a "swaggering" black man who, manipulated by a scalawag, has been preaching blacks' rights.[61]

In her autobiography, *A Slaveholder's Daughter* (1900), Belle Kearney recalls an almost identical "nonfictional" scene in which her father assembled and freed his slaves. Yet Kearney goes even further, claiming in a way that became common that the reactions whites wanted blacks to have were written on the very faces of the freedpeople themselves: "There was no wild shout of joy or other demonstration of gladness. The deepest gloom prevailed in their ranks and an expression of mournful bewilderment settled upon their dusky faces. They did not understand that strange, sweet word—freedom. Poor things!" In a trope that became as common as slaves hiding the silver, whites narrated emancipation as meaning nothing to African

Americans but confusion and pain. Blacks who left "their white folks" wandered blindly down roads littered with the too old and too young, abandoned not by southern whites but by their new northern friends and fellow ex-slaves. In *Gabriel Tolliver: A Story of Reconstruction* (1902), Joel Chandler Harris even compares freedom to the "rare" antebellum selling of slaves, the irrevocable loss of family and home. In these stories of Reconstruction, bewildered black characters enact white feelings of loss and turn-of-the-century longings for interracial intimacy in a flat and formulaic dance.[62]

For southern whites, however, emancipation meant a transference of responsibility for southern blacks to northern whites, the simple shifting of black dependency from one group of whites to another. It never occurred to white southerners that African Americans had earned the right to self-mastery. Many accounts like Kearney's complained that the poor and defeated slaveholders then had to spend meager resources tending elderly and infirm ex-slaves. "Disloyal" ex-slaves, however, those blacks who left "their whites," became the northern soldiers' and government officials' problem. In William Faulkner's short story "Raid," an ex-mistress says of the former slaves, "But we cannot be responsible. The Yankees brought it on themselves; let them pay the price." And although her daughter retorts that "those negroes are not Yankees," her efforts to save them fail, overwhelmed by the federal soldiers' callous unconcern. While whites might write their own martyrdom in supporting blacks, they laid the moral responsibility as well as the social disorder of the "hell" of Reconstruction at the feet of their northern conquerors. In both fictional and nonfictional white southern accounts of Reconstruction, northern whites learned what a difficult responsibility stewardship of an "inferior race" could be.[63]

If "niggers" and "Yankees" stood united in destroying the plantation pastorale, the white southerner Thomas Dixon's feat and the source of his great popularity was to separate them. In *The Leopard's Spots* and *The Clansman*, Dixon, born in North Carolina in 1864, transformed more completely than other white writers the complex class, race, and sectional alliances and conflicts of the Reconstruction era into Pollard's race war. His rabidly racist and awkwardly written novels twisted the ignorant and easily corruptible black voters of other accounts into lustful and violent beasts. Dixon quoted a review of *The Leopard's Spots* approvingly in a letter to a friend:

> No other book yet printed has given such a graphic presentation of the
> Southern view of the Negro Problem . . . the book will slow up sectional

prejudices. It will be read with more than passing interest in the North . . .
It is the best apology for lynching, it is the finest protest against the mistakes of reconstruction— The South has been silent when books like this
might have made their position clearer.[64]

With *The Clansman* in particular, the romanticization of Civil War violence reached into Reconstruction and wrapped itself around the Ku Klux
Klan, the very terrorist organization that twenty years earlier had been the
extensive subject of Congressional investigation. In fact, Dixon claimed
that in reading "the US report on the Ku Klux conspiracy" while research-
ing the novel, he found the actions of his own uncle, Colonel Durham of
Shelby, North Carolina, described "on almost every page." In his second
book about the recent history of the South, a few evil white northern
extremists unleash black barbarity from the bonds of white control. Desiring
not just self-mastery but white domination, not just equality but sex with
white women, the freedpeople in this Reconstruction fiction no longer
wander blindly but run rampaging through the land. Black mobility is transformed from a vague threat to an apocalyptic force. And D. W. Griffith's
monumental film adaptation, *Birth of a Nation*, brought the thrillingly new
power of film spectacle to bear on the theme of Reconstruction as race war.
In these extremely popular portrayals of Reconstruction, both the white
South and the white North have slipped free from any last traces of moral
obligation to the ex-slaves. The fall from plantation grace, the loss of racial
ease that make segregation the only possible future, have been African
Americans' fault all along. Beastlike blacks have destroyed the Old South's
racial paradise and the North's idealistic if misguided attempt to lift up an
"inferior race." In *Birth of a Nation*, blacks at last stand virtually alone
responsible for the "hell" of Reconstruction, and its repudiation creates not
just national reconciliation but the birth of the new Anglo-Saxon nation as
well. The black beast rapist, unlike the blurred figure of the slave/ex-slave,
could have no place in twentieth-century southern life.[65]
    Dixon made his ride to the rescue for white masculine as well as racial
supremacy in part because middle-class white women had found space
within the narratives of war and Reconstruction to write their own expanding agency. Sectional reconciliation—a concurrent depoliticization and
racialization of the conflict—opened up greater possibilities for white
middle-class women to use the Confederate tradition for their own empowerment. Donning their male ancestors' Confederate jackets, speaking at

Confederate Memorial Days, and writing their own white southern history, white women crafted wartime memories that stressed their own valor and accomplishments, their own status as "Southerners," as whites as central in the maintenance of white supremacy as their men. Male and female novelists seeking sales pitched to white women's own wartime heroism. Page, ever mindful of the public pulse, had his male characters continually praise the superior homefront efforts of white women. The amateur historian and UDC officer Mildred Rutherford claimed that "it was harder to live after the war than it was to face bullets on battlefields," and that the women succeeded far better than their men in "adjust[ing] themselves to the new order of things": "some men never did get adjusted, and some women have never been reconstructed." And Rutherford along with other UDC women crafted a decisive "Battle of the Handkerchiefs" to compete with men's accounts of better-known Civil War battles. In *Gone With the Wind* (1936), that most popular fictional portrayal of the Old South, the war, and Reconstruction, Margaret Mitchell crafts a heroine, Scarlett O'Hara, who not only saves her family's plantation Tara in those "dark days," but supports her ex-slaves and her menfolks as well.[66]

If southern whites imagined Reconstruction as the first black space, however, Reconstruction historiography became the first clearly white space within the culture of segregation. While white amateur historians and writers of autobiography usually included accounts of slaves who remained loyal to "their white folks" in "those darkest days," professional historians left even this blackfaced agency out of their accounts of federal occupation of the region. The Dunning school, as the first scholarly interpretation of Reconstruction became known, denounced "negro rule" and "negro government" and yet ignored African American actions and desires. John W. Burgess, a Confederate veteran turned professor, described Reconstruction as the rule "of the uncivilized Negroes over the whites of the South"; he then ignored the African American elected officials who actually participated in government. In the work of Burgess, fellow Columbia University professor William A. Dunning, and their students, the historian Eric Foner has argued, in the most recent reinterpretation of Reconstruction, "blacks appeared either as passive victims of white manipulation or as an unthinking people whose 'animal natures' threatened the stability of civilized society." A white southerner and a professor at the University of Georgia, E. Merton Coulter, describing Reconstruction as a "diabolical" time "to be remembered, shuddered at, and execrated," sounded surprisingly like Thomas

Dixon despite his claims to scholarly objectivity. Reconstruction appeared in professional histories through 1940 as it did in white southern fiction and memoir, as the "blackest" page of American history and a backdrop for creation of the darky–beast dichotomy. As Phillips had accomplished for the plantation pastorale, the Dunning school added a glaze of academic style and documentation to white southerners' stories of "the dark days of Reconstruction," making the origins of the modern South's culture of segregation paradoxically both the white North's fault and that much more palpable to the rest of the nation.[67]

African American historians, largely ignored by whites, vigorously countered these accounts of Reconstruction as more racist fantasy than scientific truth. In an explicit denunciation of the Dunning school, W. E. B. Du Bois published in 1935 his *Black Reconstruction in America, 1860–1880* and foregrounded the emancipated slaves as the central actors in the immediate postwar period. No matter how much whites, North and South, continued in the 1930s to celebrate the "Old Negro," the blurred figure of the slave/ex-slave, they proved incapable, Du Bois insisted, of crediting the basic humanity of less fictional African Americans and thus would disagree with the very premise with which he began his book. In his conclusion, "The Propaganda of History," Du Bois made more clear the connections between the blacking up of Reconstruction and modern American whiteness. The history of Reconstruction, he argued, was "a field devastated by passion and belief" in which whites used history for "pleasure and amusement, for inflating their national ego." "What is the object of writing the history of Reconstruction?" DuBois asked. He answered: "to paint the South a martyr to inescapable fate, to make the North the magnanimous emancipator, and to ridicule the Negro as the impossible joke . . . this may be fine romance but it is not science . . . It has . . . led the world to worship the color bar as social salvation."[68]

Du Bois understood that white southern racial identity formed an increasingly crucial part of modern nationalism. American whiteness, he argued, would have no moral "historical" foundation without the rewriting of Reconstruction, without the denial of white northerners' brief concern for the freedpeople and at least partial admission of the nation's debt for slavery. Sectional reconciliation in a common whiteness, projected backward from the late nineteenth and early twentieth century onto the Reconstruction era, needed a race war to bury the hostilities of a civil war and buttress the nation's new imperialistic expansion. White accounts simply

ignored the evidence, erasing the interracial alliances, more representative
government, progressive reforms, and the joyous exploration of freedom
that marked the period. Reconstruction became a cautionary tale about the
dangers of mixing politics, economics, and race. More generous than his
white counterparts, however, Du Bois declined to create white southern
monsters to replace their black beast rapists: "One reads the truer deeper
facts of Reconstruction with a great despair. It is at once so simple and
human, and yet so futile. There is no villain, no idiot, no saint. There are
just men." And, he might have added, women.[69]

In the early 1940s, when he composed the short stories that would eventually make up the novel *Go Down, Moses*, William Faulkner attempted to
reach back beyond the plantation romance and fictions of Reconstruction
to recapture the biracial legacy of the antebellum South, the values of
courage and honor and honesty that had been created by blacks and whites
together. Lucas Beauchamp, his countenance "the composite tintype face
of ten thousand undefeated Confederated soldiers," rises above the racial
"battleground" of his southernness, his identity "a vessel, durable, ancestry-
less, nonconductive, in which toxin and its anti stalemated one another," a
"composite of the two races which made him" and a better man because of
it. More than any other white-crafted slave/ex-slave character, Faulkner's
Beauchamp presents, in Cable's phrase, "the apparition of the colored man
or woman as his or her own master."

    And yet even Faulkner could not write Lucas Beauchamp free of the
plantation pastorale. A nagging sense that white male mastery was better in
that idyllic past, despite what that slave society would do to the black man
who had become its heir, pervades the novel. Opportunities to assert patriarchal power were rare in a turn-of-the-century world of doomed wilderness,
the last bear, and increasing racial conflict. Outside of fiction, the freedmen
desired not a vanished form of male mastery, despite Faulkner's insistence
in his characterization of Beauchamp, but status as modern free men. The
integration of the old plantation, lingering in the hunt, could not be risked
in a different time and place where middle-class, well-dressed, and light-
skinned "blacks," appearing without past or present white masters, rode visibly on trains.

    But segregation had many flaws, cutting white men off from imagined
masculine communion with black men like Lucas and providing a com-

mon ground of whiteness for refiguring the claims of white farmers and workers and women. The beautiful tragedy of Go Down, Moses is that Faulkner attempted to rework an imagined antebellum white mastery in the figure of a racially mixed, emancipated, and thus racially innocent ex-slave. But the old black man could not become an old white man in that new southern world.[70]

More successful was Margaret Mitchell's refiguration of antebellum white male mastery in the figure of a white woman. Scarlett O'Hara, alone of the "before-the-war" whites of the middle Georgia plantation district in which Mitchell sets her heroine's beloved plantation Tara, not only survives the war and Reconstruction with her plantation intact, but protects and supports her loyal ex-slaves and war-damaged menfolks too, and even prospers. Scarlett succeeds because she shifts easily between playing the man and playing the woman, seducing a future husband for needed cash one day and running her own business to earn her money the next. But a comparable racial play—a shifting between black and white identities—had not appeared in white southern writing since Harris's Uncle Remus. Faulkner's Beauchamp always plays the white. The fluidity and ambiguity of racial performance that characterized Uncle Remus no longer seemed possible. The white South had firmly recast its past and its present in black and white. Yet the disorder of Faulkner's Go Down, Moses—his plotted fragmentation of stories, chronologies, and even identities themselves—more clearly matches the twentieth-century South than does Mitchell's clear and linear narrative with its flat and stereotypical white-figured black characters. The unifying plot of Gone With the Wind summarizes, completes, and makes archetypal white stories of plantations, wars, and reconstructions, mirroring the lie of segregation, that race is absolute and knowable and eternal, of the culture from which it came.[71]

Not the freedpeople, then, but the white South, became a part of the modern American nation. What the journalist Ben Robertson claimed in 1941 was true of most white southerners by the early twentieth century: "I even find that I have a queer way of translating the Confederacy straight into the present United States." In his The Mind of the South (1941), another white southern journalist, W. J. Cash, noted how southern whiteness sustained both regional distinctiveness and national unity. The "history" of the plantation pastorale, the "civilization" of the war, and the blacking up of Reconstruction narrated away both southern and national moral obligations to African Americans, providing a cultural foundation for the expansion of both segregation at home and the American empire abroad. If the imagined southern past sentimentalized and sanitized slaves' forced contributions to southern society, fictions of Reconstruction acknowledged and allowed no place for African Americans at all. Allen Tate had mourned the difference of history for the "modern [white] Southerner," its existence as a "vast body of concrete fact to which he must be loyal" in vain. The southern white too, like the "Northern industrialist" Tate criticized, used history as "a source of mechanical formulas," a place of conjuring for spiriting oneself back to some better past way of life. What in the North compared to "the society of abstractions" in the modern South, the arbitrariness of the color line with what Cable had described as its falsely unifying racial fictions, a middle-class, segregated present passing as the transparent offspring of an aristo-cratic, integrated, and nonexistent past?[72]

CHAPTER THREE

Domestic Reconstruction

WHITE HOMES, "BLACK MAMMIES,"
AND "NEW WOMEN"

*Many southerners look back wistfully to the faithful, simple, ignorant, obedient,
cheerful, old plantation Negro and deplore his disappearance. They want the
New South, but the Old Negro. That Negro is disappearing forever along with
the old feudalism and the old-time exclusively agricultural life. A new Negro
is not less inevitable than a new white man and a new South.*

RAY STANNARD BAKER[1]

*Soon Mammy would be with her—Ellen's Mammy, her Mammy . . . Her eyes
lighted up at the sight of Scarlett, her white teeth gleamed as she set down the
buckets, and Scarlett ran to her, laying her head on the broad, sagging breasts which
had held so many heads, black and white. Here was something of stability,
thought Scarlett, something of the old life that was unchanging.*

MARGARET MITCHELL[2]

O N THE NIGHT of November 14, 1912, an expectant crowd packed the
ballroom of the New Willard Hotel in Washington, D.C. A large woman,
her gray hair piled high, her long skirt reminiscent of the style popular half
a century before, rose from her table and climbed the speakers' platform.
The chattering laughter of renewed friendships stopped, and the audience
focused its attention on the featured speaker. Mildred Lewis Rutherford was
not nervous. As the new Historian General of the United Daughters of the
Confederacy, a group she would lead in that office and then in the office of
honorary President until her death in 1928, the sixty-one-year-old speaker
faced her audience in the smiling confidence of almost fifty years of white
women's efforts to rebuild their region's homes and history. And "Miss Mil-
lie," as everyone called her, could claim her own significant share of this
activism. A resident of Athens, Georgia, nearly all her life, Rutherford was
well known in the community as the director of the Lucy Cobb Institute, an

elite female academy there, and across the region as a tireless campaigner for temperance and health reform and against suffrage.[3]

Yet, resplendent in the costume of the Old South, Rutherford argued in the nation's capital against the transformation of her region into anything new. Her well-received speech, "The South in the Building of the Nation," replayed the by then familiar chorus of Lost Cause reassurance, that the Old South was more than the southern past and indeed lived on as a very template for the southern future: "There is no new South. The South of today is the South of yesterday remade to fit the new order of things. And the men of today and the women of today are readjusting themselves to the old South remade." But Mildred Rutherford added an important innovation to this familiar narrative of southern postwar origins. Moving beyond a celebration of white women's wartime role as managers of the home front and their Job-like perseverance as rebuilders in the face of Reconstruction's poverty and northern domination, she loudly proclaimed a continuing power in the present: "Now you say, 'What can we do?' What can we do? Anything in the world we wish to do. If there is a power that is placed in any hands, it is the power that is placed in the Southern woman in her home! That power is great enough to direct legislative bodies and that, too, without demanding the ballot!" As the collectors of southern history, the keepers of southern culture, the "Daughters, yes, Daughters of Confederate heroes" were vital to ensuring that remaking never again became reconstructing, that traditional race and gender roles were not altered but "remade." Not just Mildred Rutherford, but (she implied) all southern white women had found their stage.[4]

What the midwestern journalist Ray Stannard Baker had neglected to mention as he "followed the color line" in 1908, then, was that the New South also required a new white woman. And no matter how much Rutherford thought she was reconstructing the Old South in general and the role of the "lady" in particular, her very speech before hundreds in that packed ballroom in the nation's capital placed her, anti-suffrage views and all, within the maelstrom of southern cultural change. Narratives of the Civil War and Reconstruction and, increasingly, professional historians' interpretations as well had locked what elite and middle-class whites perceived as the easy racial mixing of the antebellum past away in a space destroyed by "Yankee aggression" and African-American "betrayal." In the narratives of both amateur and professional historians, this "integration," admittedly an interaction of the races that preserved rather than denied hierarchy, was the white southern answer to the "race problem." White southerners, however, did not live in a world of their own choosing, as their historical narratives insisted. Northern whites and southern blacks had created a time and place in which segregation served as the only possible preserver of white supremacy, as the foundation of the new southern racial order. Yet segregation, elite and middle-class white southerners' Lost Cause stories implied, was a departure from the integration of their old southern world.[5]

Southern whites, then, stressed the continuity of white supremacy, a perspective perhaps most famously summarized by U. B. Phillips in his 1928 American Historical Association paper "The Central Theme of Southern History": "the southerner is American with a difference . . . that the South shall be and remain a white man's country." Yet the spaces within the emerging culture of segregation were, despite the *Confederate Veteran's* masthead objection to even the terms "Lost Cause" and "New South," very different places from the old plantation households that had dominated antebellum southern life. Profound differences existed between the relatively self-sufficient agrarianism of the Old South and the more urban and consumer-oriented domesticity of the new. White southern men and women of the rising middle class, however, insisted on conflating the plantation household and the post-Reconstruction white home in order to ground their own cultural authority within the power—which by the late nineteenth century had grown to mythical proportions—of the plantation-based planter class. And images of integrated domesticity were central to this fiction of continuity as African American servants, symbolized and idealized most frequently as mammy, replaced slaves. Though the integration of the white home was itself questionable—with the spread of indoor plumbing in the twentieth century, for example, many whites kept their outhouses for their servants to use—the increasing segregation of the rest of southern society made the white home increasingly seem like an island of racial mixing in a sea of separation.[6]

Mildred Rutherford, however, was right about the source of southern white women's power. And in her assumption that the "home" was a static geographic as well as symbolic place, she participated in the conflation of new middle-class home and old plantation household that helped ground the white middle class's new racial order. The Lost Cause had for whites locked integration firmly away in a pastoral idyll destroyed by "Yankee" aggression and black betrayal. But it was the white home as both site and symbol that would, by linking the southern past and present, by collapsing the very important differences between the postbellum white home and the antebellum household, help make segregation the future. For the fiction of continuity also obscured the very real interdependence of whites and blacks in a haze of sentimental nostalgia. The white home served as a major site in the production of racial identity precisely because there this racial interdependence was both visible and denied.

The central symbolic figure in this conflation, the star of the cherished story of unchanged race and gender relations, was the "black mammy." The South, the narrator of southerner Frances Newman's 1928 novel *Dead Lovers Are Faithful Lovers* proclaims, trusted "the virtue of any custom which had happened to coincide with its own youth." More pointedly, Newman might have stated that the matching that white southerners demanded had more to do with the sentimental images created in the present than those experiences lived in the past. And the mammy symbol increasingly focused all the evasions, confusions, and contradictions of a white supremacist ideology of domesticity. While white middle-class men sometimes created their own mammy stories, men had many sites beyond the white home, from farm fields to polling places, and a broader group of African American laborers within which to ground their own race and class authority. White middle-class women, however, were the most frequent authors of mammy lore. Based in the new white home, imaginatively as well as physically supported by the domestic labor of African American women, white southern "ladies" exerted a powerful influence on an emerging culture of segregation and the meaning of whiteness in this new southern world. And they played their important role even while and perhaps because many like Rutherford loudly insisted that nothing had changed.[7]

The Passing of the Plantation Household

The shift from the plantation household to the white home was already well under way by 1890. Despite Rutherford's claims of "an Old South remade," the fiction of continuity that she helped create, these changes occurred within a profound transformation of both the southern economy and geography. Slavery with its fixed labor costs made a type of relative self-sufficiency both feasible and profitable on many southern agricultural units. The plantation household in this sense referred not to the white-columned "Big House" of legend but, more specifically, to the economic unit engaged in the production with slave labor of crops like cotton and sugar for the market and goods like food, clothing, soap, and other products for household use. Certainly the sale of cash crops entailed involvement in a market, in this case an international one, but most southern households were relatively isolated from commercial activities in daily life in comparison to northerners of equal wealth. The Civil War accelerated the destruction of these households by disrupting the rhythms of home production as Confederates allocated crucial resources—free men, slave men, mules, food, and other supplies—to the war effort and slaves began taking advantage of northern lines to emancipate themselves. By 1880 most ex-slaves and many white farmers did not have the resources to pursue subsistence and wealthier whites had no need to make what they could more easily and often as cheaply buy. For all classes of southerners, domestic spaces increasingly became places of consumption rather than production. The general store and, after the 1890s, the mail-order catalog spread a new world of goods across the region.[8]

Most white southerners were well aware that by the late nineteenth century, the material experience of their domestic lives had dramatically changed. Rebecca Latimer Felton, a journalist, suffragist, temperance crusader, and, in 1922, the first woman to be a U.S. Senator, pithily described the shift from self-sufficiency and home production to increasing consumption as the "rise of paper sack supplies." Celebrating those antebellum days when "everything to eat and to wear that could be grown at home was diligently cultivated," Felton mourned the loss of "those affluent households with always something good to cook inside, and no stint anywhere in big-house or negro cabin." Certainly Felton's fable of antebellum abundance would have looked very different to the actual residents of the quarters. Yet in a manner sure to appeal to her white women farmer fans, Felton contrasted those productive Edenlike households with the consuming postbellum home: "The present generation lives in paper sack supplies. They buy everything in paper sacks from a goober-pea to a small sack of meal." By mentioning the purchase of a peanut, Felton stressed that even the poorest Georgians bought goods for their homes rather than made them. She even pled guilty herself, asserting that "tickled with a hoe," her own land could produce the peaches she was currently purchasing.[9]

Despite the blistered fact that hoeing has always been hard work, other white women described this material shift in the spaces of white domesticity even more nostalgically than Felton. Mary I. Stanton, a teacher and founder of the El Paso Public Library and a Texas business college, wrote an article in the 1930s recalling her childhood on a northern Georgia farm in the 1870s. Idealizing this household's near self-sufficiency, she compared the "artistry" of her mother's handwoven counterpanes and coverlets and the wonder of watching the itinerant cobbler making the family's shoes out of their own leather to "the cheap, garish output of factories." Claiming that then "little for the family had to be bought at the village store," she located the roots of the shift from production to consumption in her 1870s child-hood, and lamented this shift. While Stanton acknowledged that farm pro-duction required a little more exertion than Felton's "tickling," she told a tragic tale of the creep of the "readymade Sunday suit" and the assault of store-bought "dress-good," the loss of a way of life rather than a few pennies on purchased peaches.[10]

Southern whites also noted the changing geography of their world, often measured as a move from the country to town, that was both a cause and an effect of this shift from production to consumption. Suburban growth ringed southern cities, providing thinner versions of the outer gar-ments northern cities too were acquiring as the century turned. And south-ern town booster publications from the late nineteenth and early twentieth centuries provide an architectural picture of this shift from the household to the home, including photographs of "plentiful" and "comfortable" newer dwellings among the pictures of antebellum residences. The opening speaker at an 1893 convention of southern governors specifically "extend[ed] a cordial and pressing invitation to home-seekers to come and cast their for-tunes with the South": "the South is bounding forward now. It is the field in which the immediate future will unfold the most marvelous development of the century. Here new homes are to grow, like spring flowers coming up out of the 'winter of our discontent,' and are to multiply with increasing rapidity as the years go by." If the boosters exaggerated the charm of living in small southern towns and larger cities from Arkansas to Alabama, they did mark the changing geography as elite and middling southern whites joined poorer whites and African Americans in the great move, between 1880 and 1910, to town.[11]

Yet this shift from the plantation household as an economically pro-ductive unit toward an alternative form of white southern economic and domestic life had crucial cultural implications as well. Despite the heavy ideological load the concept of home has borne within American society, historians have used the term to refer to domestic spaces relatively divorced, both geographically and symbolically, from the resources and practices of economic production and public interaction. The transformation of the household into the home, they have argued, has been a significant part of northern middle-class formation beginning as early as the opening of the nineteenth century. In the three decades before the Civil War, this emerging northern middle class constructed itself against images of an indolent, slave-dependent, household-centered white South. And representations of slaves as well as slaveholders helped legitimate this new class and its increasingly hegemonic culture.

The existence of southern slavery greatly eased the splitting of what mid-nineteenth-century labor republicans had conceived as the producing classes. A growing economic divide between those men and few women who continued to own the means of production, including the emerging professions, and those who increasingly, permanently, did not, shaped more distinct working and middle classes. While sentimental middle-class anti-slavery advocates mourned the plight of Harriet Beecher Stowe's hugely popular Uncle Tom, wage laborers found humor in blackfaced minstrels' mocking of a stereotyped slave life. For most northerners, however, working for wages seemed significantly better than its readily apparent alternative, slavery. Workers at least retained some semblance of control over their domestic arrangements. And a republican belief in the unity of the producing classes, crystallized in the Republican Party's slogan "Free Soil, Free Labor, Free Men," covered a growing economic and cultural divide through the Civil War years. That crucial collective identity as producers did not break down until the Reconstruction period, allowing the new northern middle class to gain hegemony even as wage laborers' rising class consciousness led them to begin significant worker organizing.[12]

While middle-class formation in the North occurred in opposition to images of lazy white planters and inferior—whether sentimentally or humorously—black slaves, gender was also a central organizing principle of the new culture. The historian Mary Ryan has described the emergence of middle-class family-centered domesticity out of the publicly active female voluntary organizations of the 1830s and 1840s. Leaving their households, women developed new social relations and values in associations that they later used in constructing the child-centered, middle-class home. And women constructed these new domestic spaces as refuges from the frenzied pace of male market life. What economic activity remained within the middle-class house—food and clothing preparation and the cleaning of furnishings and clothing—disappeared from view through a process the historian Jeanne Boydston has called "the pastoralization of housework." Even when, increasingly as the nineteenth century closed, middle-class women and not their dwindling numbers of servants performed these tasks, middle-class northerners saw housework as part of women's nature, their influence, and even their leisure, but not their labor. And yet middle-class women exercised a relatively significant degree of control over the changing spaces and activities of the home. In the dialectic of economic, spatial, and cultural changes that brought the new northern middle class to hegemony within post–Civil War America, women's home-building efforts were as significant as men's more market-directed activities.[13]

Yet middle-class development in the South, while not unaffected by the values of a nationally hegemonic northern middle-class culture, occurred within an entirely different historical context. The war accelerated the destruction of the household as the South's most significant economic unit, a process that continued through the early 1890s. And as in the North, white women would play a central role in the formation of the new cultural values through their activities outside the household—in this case wartime nursing and charitable organizing and postbellum memorial associations. Yet white southerners experienced Confederate defeat and Reconstruction as the sharp and sudden destruction rather than the more gradual dismantling of rural households that had occurred elsewhere. And this sense of profound loss made white women like Rutherford determined, well into the twentieth century, to see their actions in terms of reconstructing an old social structure rather than building a new one. But white women working to preserve traditional gender roles conceived as continuous with antebellum social relations contradicted the very meaning of those antebellum roles. No matter the rhetoric or desire, white women could not go back to the Old South through work or will. The plantation household could not be remade, and white women could not consciously act to re-create a gender role, the "southern lady," that depended on passivity, male protection, and a life on a pedestal.[14]

Despite the contradiction of a willed passivity, the earlier loss of slave labor, and the growing place of consumption within late nineteenth-century domestic life, white southern women could, drawing on northern middle-class images of home as a pastoral, Edenlike refuge wrapped in gardens and steeped in sentimentality, turn their plantation households into homes. Their conflation, however, ignored the profoundly different economic, social, and political contexts within which southern white women practiced their white supremacist domesticity. Yet the image of the white home with its "air of plantation authenticity" brought the Lost Cause's fiction of continuity out of an imagined past and into the present. As the historian John C. Cell has argued, segregation as the new southern order absolutely depended upon a representation of continuity between old and new. In their creation of the white home as a central symbolic site in the New South, women of a rising white southern middle class were key creators of the new racial order, segregation as culture.[15]

An emerging southern middle class, then, created the culture of segregation in part by fusing the northern middle-class antebellum precedent of posing the "home" as a symbolic counterweight to the expanding role of the market with a white southern sense of the inviolability of white supremacy. To the segregation of home and work, middle-class southern whites added, drawing upon the traditions of an antebellum nonslaveholding class, the segregation of white and black. Yet making the home a central symbolic site, an echo of an antebellum elite's plantation-centered world, also helped ground the new middle class's cultural authority in an indigenous even if romanticized source of power. As Ellen Glasgow revealed in her lament about the loss of a southern aristocratic culture, "even before the First World War, elegiac airs were played out in Richmond, and the lament for the dead was already succeeded by the regimental bands of the living. Few qualities were more admired in the South than a native gift, however crude, for getting somewhere. Imponderables might be respected, but possessions were envied." And writer and temperance and suffragist activist Belle Kearney, who described a small antebellum middle class that "carried on the concerns of commerce and the trades incident to a vast agricultural area, and were the men of affairs in its churches and municipalities," also found a significant change at the turn of the century, a new regime in which "the upper and middle classes have become amalgamated." Though the white southern writer William Alexander Percy disagreed and described an aristocratic southern culture surviving into the twentieth century in the Mississippi delta, he ended his "recollections of a planter's son" with a celebration of the local graveyard in a chapter entitled "Home." There, alone in what Percy called "this refuge with its feel of home," he felt close to his own people. By the late 1930s, even Percy implied that the planter class world view was long buried.[16]

Whiteness Makes a Home

Providing for most whites more comfort than the town cemetery, the white home was a more domestic and female-centered space than the antebellum plantation household. White male-directed economic production continued to move outside the white family's living spaces and landscapes as did the African American wage workers who had replaced the slaves. The crucial exception, however, was the black female domestic worker. Thus even as segregation increasingly became policy in the late nineteenth-century South, the white home continued as a site of racial mixing through the employment of African American domestic labor. The white home became a central site for the production and reproduction of racial identity precisely because it remained a space of integration within an increasingly segregated world.[17]

And whites writing about their southern childhoods often recounted the home-centered scenes in which their racial epiphanies occurred. In her autobiographical *Killers of the Dream*, written throughout the 1940s and published in 1949, Lillian Smith claims to tell not her own particular story but the experiences "most white southerners born at the turn of the century share with each other." The white home, Smith argues, was the site where white children learned racial difference, where the culture of segregation began: "We were given no formal instruction in these difficult matters but we learned our lessons well. We learned the intricate systems of taboos, of renunciations and compensations, of manners, voice modulations, words, feelings, along with our prayers, our toilet habits, and our games." For her, the "dance" of white superiority and black inferiority, "the drama of the South," occurred most memorably and painfully when her parents adopted a little white girl found "in the colored section of our town."[18]

The tragedy began when a friend of Smith's mother, driving to her washwoman's house, found the girl swinging on the front gate of a "shack." Assuming that the "sick-looking colored folks" who recently moved into the "pigsty" had kidnapped the child, the woman called a meeting of her club to decide what to do, "for the child was very white indeed." Later, getting no satisfactory answers from the "strange Negroes," a group of white women returned with the town marshall and took the child away from her tearful adopted family. The club had decided that "Janie" would live with the Smiths, and she and Lillian, the same size and age, became quick and fast friends, sharing a bed, dresses, and toys. The Smith family eventually discovered, however, that looks could be deceiving, that color was not transparent despite the seemingly stark contrast of black and white. Investigating Smith's new sister's background, the club found that Janie's light skin covered a mixed racial ancestry. Mrs. Smith struggled to convince a stubborn little Lillian that her new sister was not white: "She is a little colored girl . . . a colored girl cannot live in our home . . . You have always known that white and colored people do not live together." Over thirty years later Smith remembered that she "felt compelled to believe they were right. It was the only way my world could be held together. And slowly, it began to seep through me: I was white . . . It was bad to be together. Though you ate with your nurse when you were little, it was bad to eat with a colored person after that . . . It was bad."[19]

Of that generation for which Smith claimed to speak, Katharine Lumpkin too eventually came to criticize the white identities created by the culture of segregation in which she and Smith grew to adulthood. Lumpkin recalled the white home as the site of "the making of a Southerner," and in her autobiography by that title she recounts how she learned the meaning of race within her home:

> We can be certain that from the time I could sit in my high chair at table or play about the parlor floor while others conversed, my ears saturated with words and phrases at all times intimately familiar to Southern ears and in those years of harsh excitement carrying a special urgency: "white supremacy," . . . "inferiority," "good darkey," "bad darkey," "keep them in their place." As time passed, I myself would learn to speak these words perhaps with special emphasis . . . even before I had the understanding to grasp all they stood for. Of course I did come to comprehend. When I did, it was a sharp awakening.[20]

Instead of her mother, however, the agent of her racial making in this case was Lumpkin's father.[21]

On a summer morning as a child Lumpkin overheard someone being beaten in the kitchen before breakfast: "Our little black cook, a woman small in stature though full grown, was receiving a severe thrashing. I could see her writhing under the blows of the master of the house. I could see her

face distorted with fear and agony and his with stern rage . . . I could hear
her screams . . . Having seen and heard, I chose the better part of stuffing my
fists in my ears and creeping away on trembling legs." Yet Lumpkin remembers knowing, even as a young child, that despite the acceptance of the
event by her mother, older siblings, and neighbors, "it was not the custom
for Southern white gentlemen to thrash their cooks, not by the early 1900s."
In writing about the event forty years later, Lumpkin in shame cannot name
as father the man responsible for inflicting this horrible pain on the cook,
blows that in Lumpkin's memory also fell upon her own developing consciousness. The central moment in the making of a white southerner, the
primal scene of the culture of segregation, then, was one of learning the
meaning of race: "The inevitable had happened and what is bound to come
to a Southern child chanced to come to me this way. Thereafter, I was fully
aware of myself as white, and of Negroes as Negroes. Thenceforth, I began
to be self-conscious about the many signs and symbols of my race position
that had been battering against my consciousness since virtual infancy."
Knowing race, the small girl knew her place within southern society.[22]

But women who were writing their autobiographies even as Smith and
Lumpkin were learning to talk, who were born in the midst of the destruction of the old southern world view rather than within the New South's culture of segregation, also described childhood as the crucial period when
whites learned racial difference. Born in 1863, the white suffragist and temperance activist Belle Kearney recalled a much more ambiguous awakening
of racial understanding within her own Reconstruction era childhood.
Hearing "nothing discussed but Republicans" and hearing them called
"black," she began to wonder "what sort of creatures they could be": "Gradually my cranium cast out its terrifying myths, and reached an adjustment
so far as that Republicans looked like other men, but should never be spoken to, and must be shunned like the pox." Racial identity, then, far from
being transparently determined from the color of human skin, seemed to
have regional and ideological components as well. Kearney wrote even
more frankly, "It is doubtful if there is a natural race prejudice; that is, if
white and black children were reared together from the cradle as equals
whether they would feel any antagonism of stock." Within her 1900 memoir
A Slaveholder's Daughter, she uses her understanding of the constructedness of racial difference to support the extension and solidification of the
culture of segregation. Black children, she argues, must be prevented from
contaminating white children with "their deadly immoral trail."[23]

Ellen Glasgow, whose birth in 1873 placed her closer to Kearney's than to Smith's and Lumpkin's generation, wrote much more ambiguously about the whiteness created by segregation than these other southern white women. Yet she too described a transformative racial event that occurred on the pavement in front of her Richmond home in her early childhood: "I am standing, with my hand in my mammy's, watching the struggles of an old Negro, Uncle Henry, as he is brought out from his cellar and put into the wagon from the almshouse." Later Glasgow was told that the white men were taking the older black man because he was poor and crazy and old and would die if "left in his cellar." Then, however, she saw only that he struggled and cried, "that the tears roll[ed] down his blue, wrinkled cheeks into his toothless mouth," that he screamed "Don't put me in," and that he did not want to go. Still, she remembers that, mimicking a group of little white boys, she mocked his cries until her mammy made her stop. Though the mammy could command the white child, as a black woman she was as unable as that child, as "Henry" himself, to stop the humiliating capture. Glasgow recalls this incident as a lesson in her own powerlessness in her memoir *The Woman Within*, written in the early 1940s. And yet unlike the "mammy" and the "uncle," Glasgow could still grow up. The rest of her autobiography as well as her many novels suggest that Glasgow, unlike Uncle Henry and even her mammy, could make her voice count.[24]

As Glasgow's story most clearly revealed, the figure of the mammy haunted these scenes of racial learning, hovering within but never directly responsible for the painful instruction, because she most visibly integrated the white home. Lillian Smith remembered the "old nurse" who cared for her through a long illness and gave her "refuge when a little sister took my place as the baby of the family, who soothed, fed me, delighted me with her smiles and games, let me fall asleep on her deep warm breast." White children, Smith insisted, had two mothers. Lumpkin's family moved often, and a stream of black workers filled the often rented homes of her childhood: "If I knew their names I at once forgot them, contenting myself with 'Sally' or 'Jim,' or if they were old, perhaps 'Uncle' or 'Auntie'—generic terms we were wont to use for Negroes whose names we did not know." Yet if she did not experience her own special relationship with an African American woman, she filled in the gaps of her own disadvantaged childhood with her father's postbellum memories of his own plantation mammy, "Aunt Winnie." Growing up during the Civil War and Reconstruction, Kearney too could not celebrate her own special mammy. Instead she praised the generic black mammy and located her within those happy prewar days as the help-meet of the plantation mistress, the one who "relieved" the white woman of the "actual drudgery of child-worry."[25]

Remembering My Old Mammy

But most white men and women were more sentimental than Lumpkin and Kearney and less critical than Lumpkin and Smith. Mammies circulated throughout the popular currents of southern culture in both written and visual forms. As the historian Cheryl Thurber has revealed, a mammy craze swept the region and indeed the nation between the 1890s and the 1920s. Mammies appeared in books, magazines, and films, in advertisements, on menus, in the names and iconography of restaurants and cookbooks, and as the shape of commodities from salt shakers to cookie jars. A 1924 New York shop window even advertised "a fascinating new style for women, an auda-ciously colored scarf, 'the Paris version of mammy's old Southern ban-danna.'" In the South, the movement reached some unusual extremes. In 1911 in Athens, Georgia, a group of white men and an African American educator appealed for subscriptions to fund the "Black Mammy Memorial Institute," not "a shaft of stone—cold and speechless—but a living monu-ment where the sons and daughters of these distinctive Southern characters may be trained in the arts and industries that made the 'old Black Mammy' valuable and worthy of the tender memory of the South." By 1923, in the culmination of an ex-slave memorial movement that swept the South, the United Daughters of the Confederacy even demanded that a monument to the mammy be erected within the nation's capital.[26]

But as the twentieth century opened, the actual domestic worker had little connection to the mammy figure that white southerners increasingly celebrated beyond the fact that black women regularly performed domestic work in the homes of white families. In the mammy stories written more often by southern white women than by white men and circulated widely in magazines, memoirs, and autobiographies between 1890 and 1940, pre- and postwar images fused and mammy became the crucial nurturer, protector, and teacher of white children. In a poem by Howard Weeden, a white woman artist from Huntsville, Alabama, well known for her romanticized

paintings of and verses about mammies, a white child describes the importance of this mythical black woman:

> Me and Mammy know a child
>> About my size and age
> Who, Mammy says, won't go to heaven
>> 'Cause she's so grown and wise.
>
> She answers "Yes" and "No" just so
>> When folks speak to her,
> And laughs at Mammy and at me
>> When I say "Ma'am" and "Sir."
>
> And Mammy says the reason why
>> This child's in such a plight
> Is 'cause she's had no Mammy dear
>> To raise her sweet and right;
>
> To stand between her and the world,
>> With all its old sad noise,
> And give her baby heart a chance
>> To keep its baby joys.
>
> Then Mammy draws me close to her
>> And says: "The lord be praised,
> Here's what I calls a decent chile,
>> 'Cause hit's been Mammy-raised."[27]

Representative of an entire genre, this poem offers a portrait of the black
woman domestic worker from the perspective of the white child who loved
her. Stories of mammies as the protectors of white children filled white
southerners' recollections of both pre- and postwar childhoods. Mammy
was a white child's best friend, a secure refuge against the world. In a less
characteristic tribute to a mammy written by a white man, "Captain" James
Dinkins recalled, "Oftentimes as a child, when I felt that an injustice had
been done me, my black mammy would take me in her arms to her house,
and many times I have sobbed myself to sleep with my head on her dear old

fat shoulder." To be "mammy-raised" was to experience mammy's powerful protection from the pain of growing up.[28]

And mammy did more than protect and nurture white children. As Weeden's poem makes clear, the black woman taught the white child manners as well. Mammies became important signifiers of membership in the southern white middle class, that amalgamation of ex-planters, prewar middling southerners, and rising shopkeepers, farmers, and businessmen developing its own class consciousness. Manners distinguished better-off white southerners from the "crackers" that Mildred Rutherford often humorously described. The female academy was the social teacher of last resort, according to "Mannie Brown That School Girl," a story Rutherford wrote for the girls at the Lucy Cobb Institute where she was principal. This story, in which other children make fun of Mannie's misbehavior, bluntly conveys the message that children should know their manners before they arrive at school. Another white southern woman wrote more bluntly: "They [white children] frequently received almost their entire training from these . . . colored potentates until they had passed into the hands of their school teachers . . . They [mammies] had to teach them [white children] their manners."[29]

Most importantly, manners, through the time-blurred figure of the mammy, linked the turn-of-the-century emerging southern middle class to the cultural authority of the old planter elite. Julia Porcher Wickham, celebrating a specific mammy named Louisa, claimed that these African American women "were extremely aristocratic in their ideas, and it was difficult for 'skim milk' to masquerade as cream with them. 'Who dat young gentleman what come here las' night?' one of them would ask. 'He ain't none of our white folks.' She had seen the difference at once, and didn't want any 'po' white trash,' as she would have expressed it, coming around her young mistress." Though the white woman writing here mourned a late nineteenth-century mammy who had died in 1906, the teaching of manners by mammies in the Old South was also described in early twentieth-century memoirs by white southerners. Rebecca Latimer Felton recalls her own 1830s and 1840s childhood in her 1919 memoir *Country Life in Georgia in the Days of My Youth*. Her mammy Agnes, she claims, nursed and loved her from the moment of her birth; their "strong affection" lasted until the black woman died. Agnes, like those postbellum aristocratic mammies Wickham described, was no ordinary slave—she belonged to "the F.F.V. colored, in old Virginia." But what Felton remembers most about Mammy Agnes is their trip to a neighbor's wedding:

To start out as I had done with my best bib and Tucker, traveling in fine style with a pair of matched horses and a driver, with the comfortable feeling that I was going to a big wedding, and then to be brought home in some sort of disgrace, because I ate under a table, out of a scrap bucket, with all the indignation that Mammy was capable of expressing by words and looks and gestures, I was given a lesson as to table manners and wedding feasts that always remained with me.[30]

Stories of both pre- and postwar mammies teaching the manners that signified class circulated interchangeably in the early twentieth century. Mammy embodied the fiction of continuity between the Old South and the new southern world, anchoring the emerging white middle class within a romanticized conception of the antebellum plantation elite.[31]

But mammies rooted the new southern world within the paternalistic race relations of the antebellum South as well. Whites described postwar mammies naming themselves "befo' da war nigger," "white folks niggers," and "an echo of my white folks" and calling their white charges "my chile." Much more than a servant, "her big motherly heart embraced the little white babies placed within her care with all the love that only a real southern 'mammy' could give." "White children" provided financial support for aging mammies and flocked from around the world to her bedside, carried her coffin, buried her body, and erected her tombstone. For those adults who could not memorialize their own childhood mammies, white southerners erected monuments to unnamed faithful slaves in general and mammies of all times in particular. And mammies, whites claimed, reciprocated and more privately remembered their white children as well, keeping photographs of their "white folks" in their places of retirement, sometimes "comfortable houses" in those very white folks' yards.[32]

In perhaps the most famous memorial to a specific mammy, William Faulkner dedicated his Go Down, Moses "To Mammy/ Caroline Barr/ Mississippi/ (1840–1940)/ Who was born in slavery and who gave my family a fidelity without stint or calculation of recompense and to my childhood an immeasurable devotion and love." Yet Faulkner's remembrance of his mammy captured all the ambiguities and contradictions of white southern mammy worship. Despite his stories to the contrary, Caroline Barr was never owned by any of his ancestors, and Faulkner performed the same conflation of the Old South and the new as did other less famous white southerners. He also managed to ignore the African American Falkners, the ex-slaves of his

family and their descendants, who did live scattered all around him in Oxford. Working for the family as a domestic servant, however, Barr did care
for Faulkner and his brothers as children. She also worked for Faulkner and
his wife Estelle and lived and died in a little house behind the writer's
estate, Rowan Oak. And Faulkner, in a ritual repeated by many white southerners across the region, placed a stone on her grave that read "Mammy" —
"Her white children bless her."[33]

Some mammies, whites implied, went beyond "love" for individual
whites to support white supremacy itself. A Mammy Easter, a *Confederate
Veteran* article claimed, subscribed to and read with interest this Lost Cause
magazine, which often praised slavery. Mammies even became important
sources of white family history, remembering both the genealogies and
events that proved postwar whites' antebellum greatness. He wrote "My Old
Black Mammy" for the *Confederate Veteran*, "Captain" James Dinkins
explained, because "my own experience and that of my father and family
and friends was so closely associated with the negroes, and those experiences so satisfactory and pleasant, I feel impelled by every sense of duty,
appreciation, and love for my dear old black mammy as well as for many of
the other negroes, old and young, to record such facts as I can." The black
woman as domestic symbol, then, not only crossed the chasm between the
Old South and the New, she transgressed the color line as well, making the
white home an island of integration, however limited, within an increasingly segregated world.[34]

Yet mammies were broad signifiers of whiteness as well as nurturers,
protectors, and teachers of manners to middle-class children. Though the
image of the white home occupied by the black mammy was a white
middle-class construction, black woman domestics worked in the houses of
white families of all classes. As Arthur Raper discovered in the 1930s, the cotton mill wage scale, though low, was "high enough to enable many white
mothers to hire Negro domestic help, while they themselves worked in the
mills." He found this situation deplorable for what it implied about African
American wage scales and "the Negro's consequent plane of living." For
white mill workers, however, employing black women as domestics permitted access both to the amount of money white women could earn in the
mill above the black woman's low wage and, perhaps as important, to the
racial power the culture of segregation's white supremacy lodged within
whiteness itself. Women who lived on small farms that their husbands
owned or rented also had access to black domestic labor. Racial identity

within the culture of segregation depended in more ways than one upon the symbolic power of the mammy—being white meant having black help.[35]

In the stories whites told about "mammy," however, these African American women were rarely responsible for setting in motion events that taught white children the power of their racial identity. White children in their own autobiographical recollections learned difference through recognizing as "other" someone other than "mammy." And this recognition occurred under the direction of other whites. For Lillian Smith, her mother served as the catalyst in a chain of events in which a racially ambiguous child signified the meaning of race. For Katharine Lumpkin, the moment came when her father beat an African American woman serving as the family's cook. And Ellen Glasgow's transformation into a white child occurred when she witnessed outside her house a group of white men taking a black man against his will to the almshouse.

But a short story, "Little White Girl," published in 1931 by Sara Haardt, both captures well the image of the white home as the space within which whites learned racial difference and provides a powerful exception to the white southern genre of the mammy story. Haardt's tale recounts the common theme of an integrated childhood, of the twinning of white and black childhood playmates. Susie Tarleton and Pinky—her last name is not given—make up and name their own game, the Penny-Poppy Show: "Pinky was Aunt Hester's little girl, born the month before Susie, and they played on the same pallet spread under the big oak tree when they were babies, for Aunt Hester was Susie's mammy as well." But a visiting white girl who has recently moved into a neighboring house tells Susie that whites outgrow playing with black children and encourages Susie to treat Pinky as a servant. When Susie mimics the other white child's actions, Pinky's "face hardened into a mask of sober deference . . . In the short space it had taken her to walk into the house and back, she had become a little colored girl who knew her place." Susie's discovery of the meaning of her own racial identity, however, occurs only after the other white girl has gone, and Susie calls Pinky to resume their play. When Pinky does not come, Susie approaches the domestic servants' quarters in the back yard of her own home and overhears Aunt Hester, called "Mammy" not by the white child in Haardt's tale but by her own daughter, forbidding Pinky ever again to play with the white mistress. Though they live on the grounds of the white home, Aunt Hester struggles to protect her daughter from the pain of becoming the material upon which Susie practices her own racial identity. And in her concern for her own child, this fictional mammy teaches the "little white girl" the painful reality of segregation as culture. Insisting that Hester is the "mammy" only of her own child, Haardt's story provides a rare example of black domestic agency in white southern writing.[36]

The southern African American writer Zora Neale Hurston described even more explicitly this battle of black women working as domestic servants to extract their own families from the racial lessons taught within the white home. In *Their Eyes Were Watching God,* though Janie's grandmother retains the name "Nanny" given her by her white charges and continues her domestic work, she changes her own living arrangements for the sake of her granddaughter: "Ah done the best Ah kin by you. Ah raked and scraped and bought dis lil piece of land so you wouldn't have to stay in de white folks' yard . . . Ah wanted you to look upon yo'self." Although whites seldom noticed, the racial dramas enacted within the spaces of the white home shaped black as well as white children.[37]

But with the exceptions of Haardt, Smith, and Lumpkin, most whites did not so self-consciously or critically discuss the role of black women within southern homes. One of the few white southerners to protest the sentimentalization that even critics like Lillian Smith bestowed upon African American women working as domestics, William Alexander Percy fell into the opposite stereotype and painted mammy as a jezebel too: "The gentle, devoted creature who is your baby's nurse can carve her boy-friend from ear to ear at midnight and by seven a.m. will be changing the baby's diaper while she sings 'Hear the Lambs a-calling.' " For most middle-class white southerners, however, mammy was their black mother and they her children, and she taught them to be themselves, an identity as white that gained its power in part through the unself-consciousness with which it was held. Their conception of the naturalness of their own racial identities blinded them to the contradictions of learning whiteness, though rarely as directly as in the story of "The Little White Girl," from black women. Within even the most sentimental white southern mammy stories lay a deep recognition of mammy as a third term in the segregated South, the adult who stood between the child and the world, the black who stood between the white home and the culture of segregation.[38]

Motherhood in Black and White

Mammy, then, was a liminal figure in the stark binaries of the culture of segregation. Black women domestics physically crossed the color line on a daily basis, traveling from "Colored Town" to "White Town," wearing the uniforms or cast-off clothing often provided by white employers, and moving through the intimate spaces of white southern homes. And the white South even officially recognized this passing, allowed because it served white needs, with signs in places like parks that read "No Negroes Allowed Except Servants." Yet as black domestic workers physically transgressed the racialized spaces of segregation, mammies also symbolically crossed the line between the Old South with its plantation household, integration, and plantation mistress, and the New South with its white home, segregation, and middle-class white womanhood. All mammies were in an important sense white fictions of black womanhood. As markers of both whiteness and class status and as the conduits through which these identities were reproduced within white children, mammies reinforced the fiction of continuity that legitimated the new southern white middle class. Beyond her race and class functions, however, mammy played an essential role in the reconstruction of white southern gender relations as well.

Crossing both time and space, the black mammy supported another crucial New South fiction, the southern lady—an image of white purity and gendered passivity celebrated by white southern male writers from radical racist Thomas Dixon to the liberal W. J. Cash. Mammy was the key to the paradox of white women empowered by an image of weakness. And although in celebrations of their children's mammies, white women claimed that these black "mothers" were secondary to white mothers as the protectors, nurturers, and teachers of white children, stories whites wrote about their own childhoods asserted the primacy of mammies. White southerners associated black women with all the sentimental values of middle-class womanhood—mammies nurtured children, loved unconditionally, and lived for others. White women, then, could leave the home and still be ladies not only because African American domestic workers performed the labor there but because they also absorbed the celebrated yet constricting gender conventions associated with motherhood. Because mammy crossed the line between the Old South and the New, white southerners could insist that the new middle-class mother and even single white women played the same "lady" role as the plantation mistress. Because mammy crossed the line between the increasingly segregated places of whiteness and blackness, white southern women could cross the gender line between the white home and the larger world without directly challenging the symbol of the southern lady. Mammy's racial passing, then, allowed white women a kind of gendered passing as well.[39]

As the historian Drew Faust has argued, elite white women survived the war with an intense desire to reconstruct their old southern world. By the late nineteenth century, southern whites had already weathered the buffetings of Reconstruction, financial panics, and the Populist movement. These experiences, combined with the impact of a growing consumer culture largely imported from the Northeast and a rising African American middle class, had only intensified many white women's longings for the seeming stability of the past. As Mildred Rutherford proclaimed in 1912 and as many white southerners in varying degrees wanted to believe, the New South was only "the Old South remade." Lost Cause narratives provided a context within which white women could assert their agency in the cause of the Old South, and yet their attempts to rebuild white southern gender relations and especially the passive, subservient conventions of the southern lady were riddled with contradictions. White southern women actively working to construct an image of themselves as women who needed male guidance and protection undermined the very image of the lady they were hoping to save.[40]

But here the old black mammy waddled to the rescue. She played the symbolic role of the woman, she covered the contradictions, and she linked the new white woman to those southern ladies of old. With the mammy in the home, white women could be ladies and yet exercise the privileges and authority granted by white skin. The image of the mammy and the culture of segregation's absolutist white supremacy contradicted any conception of white women as inferior in their gender. Some white women, then, were able to narrow the gender differences between white men and women and yet leave the image of the lady with, as Rutherford declared, her power in the white home intact even as she stood on a platform speaking loudly to a packed ballroom.[41]

Certainly the domestic labor of African American women enabled white women, from elite suffragists to mothers with mill jobs, to turn their attention at least partially away from child rearing and homemaking. Mildred Rutherford could run the Lucy Cobb Institute and still devote considerable time to her UDC activities because she had a staff of African American women feeding and nurturing "her girls," the schools' boarding students. And that perhaps most famous of all southern white women, Margaret Mitchell, enjoyed African American "help" while both writing her novel and later answering her fan mail and defending her international copyrights. No doubt many other middle-class white women found time for temperance, suffrage, anti-suffrage, and UDC work because African American women labored in their homes. Whites' construction of the mammy image, even more than black women's physical labor in the white home, however, seemed to ease the constrictions of conventional white southern womanhood. For mammy's symbolic labor seemed to liberate white women even more effectively than did her actual work. Because mammy was a woman, white women could act with the legitimation of their racial identities as long as they acted in support of white supremacy.[42]

In her work for the UDC and in anti-suffrage activities, Mildred Rutherford often denounced both the "New Negro" and the "New Woman" from the same podium. And yet her own activities, her sought-after speeches praising that antebellum golden age of romanticized southern race relations, often took her far from the home "in which white women found their strength." In a 1915 speech before the Georgia House of Representatives, Rutherford declared that in "the glare of public life" the woman has become "an unsexed mongrel, shorn of her true power and vainly beating against the air in dissatisfaction with herself." The "woman politician" was not an "object of adoration . . . nor has suffrage brought improvement to the homes." The southern "lady," Rutherford claimed, already possessed a more important strength—she just needed to realize where her advantage lay: "Politics are not refining, not uplifting, and Southern men would save their women from politics." Politics, after all, had never recovered from the "black" days of Reconstruction. "But some," Rutherford cried, "are tired of the pedestal that privileges confer, not content with laws already favorable to them, but long for the limelight, for hustings, for things unfeminine." And the "influence that women possessed," rooted in white women's race, created a pedestal with privileges enough to provide a podium as far from the home as the state legislature.[43]

A similar call for racial empowerment occurred at the other end of the white southern debate over votes for women. Belle Kearney, Rebecca Felton, and other white southern suffragists gained support for their once-unpopular cause within the South by switching their arguments from gendered to racial terms. White women, they began to argue publicly in the early twentieth century, deserved the vote not because of their gender but because of their race. As the Louisiana suffragist Kate Gordon wrote to the pioneering Kentucky suffragist Laura Clay in 1907, "We know, after our experience in Mississippi, that there are many politicians who, while they would fight to the death the idea of women voting purely on the merits of the question, would gladly welcome us as a measure to insure white supremacy. My old point of choice between nigger or [white] woman, and glad to take the woman, has more truth than poetry in it." Legislators needed to make white women's role in upholding white supremacy easier by making legally visible the undisputed fact of white women's superiority to African American men. On the issue of white supremacy, then, anti-suffragists and suffragists differed little.[44]

But the suffragist and later senator Rebecca Felton was also unusually perceptive about the need for white women to have greater gendered as well as racial power. In 1891 the Georgia Agricultural Society accepted her proposal for a program called the "Wife's Farm" designed both to alleviate farmers' growing indebtedness and to increase women's power over the farm family's productive assets. In Felton's plan, farm men would join the "Before Breakfast Club," spending that time working crops chosen by the farm wife for family use and planted on land set aside as her farm. But Felton's solution never really gained much ground in equalizing gender roles on southern farms. Her proposal, relying on a repudiation of consumption and a restructuring of the gender relations within farm families, failed on both accounts.[45]

Felton became less and less concerned with challenging gendered hierarchies directly, then, as her earlier efforts failed. In her newspaper column "The Country Home: Women on the Farm," which ran in the *Atlanta Journal* for twenty-eight years, she continued to appeal to the inherent rights of women on the farm and even occasionally proclaimed the common needs of white and black rural women. Felton also used this platform to argue against the popular anti-suffrage conception of women's "influence," which held women responsible for their children's future and yet did not give them the power in the form of the vote to actually effect change. Felton's unique arguments for woman suffrage always demanded both the gendered and racialized empowerment of white women:

Freedom belongs to the white woman as her inherent right. Whatever belongs to the freedom of these United States belongs to the white woman . . . Whatever was won by these noble men of the Revolution was inherited alike by sons and daughters. Fifty years from now this country will hold up its hands in holy horror . . . that any man or set of men in America should assume to themselves the authority to deny to free-born white women the ballot, which is the badge and synonym of freedom!

Outside her dedicated newspaper audience of farm women, however, Felton's arguments about race resonated much more powerfully within white southern society than her support for a more direct restructuring of white gender relations. Felton first became widely known not for the wife's farm but for her 1897 statement at the annual meeting of the Georgia Agricultural Society: "if it takes lynching to protect women's dearest possession from drunken, ravening beasts, then I say lynch a thousand a week if it becomes necessary." In another speech given in the early 1900s, entitled "The Inheritance of the Anglo-Saxon," she argued that "the antagonism of color is fresh and virile—never abates—never subsides. It is the one political problem that defies time . . ." Yet Felton's racial politics were less a turning away from gender reform than a shift in the point of attack—the women she wanted to empower were also whites who came not only from a "womanhood like our mothers did" but also from a "race who shirked no dangers, nor cowered in fear."[46]

Felton described a "country home" as not only threatened by an image of the black man as rapist but also nurtured by the image of the black woman as mammy, more devoted to the white family than to her own. Besides her account of learning her "manners" at the wedding with Mammy Agnes, Felton liked to tell another mammy story. But unlike that tale of youthful disgrace, in "Southern Womanhood in Wartimes" Felton told a story of her own adult triumph. Mammy Agnes had married, and since her new husband's owners would not sell him, Felton sold Agnes so she could live with her husband. Yet Felton claimed that her mammy soon returned and begged to be bought back, her loyalty to her white family stronger than her commitment to her own. Agnes undoubtedly saw this situation differently. Perhaps her new marriage did not work out or her new owners were cruel. That Felton repeated the tale half a century after it occurred as a story of her own domestic empowerment, her control over her family both slave and free, illustrated just the kind of racial and gendered authority that representations of mammies could provide for white women.[47]

Within the culture of segregation that mammy supported, across generations and the political divide of suffrage, then, middle-class white women found a common power through their whiteness. Holding a firm belief in their own racial superiority within white society, they acted as whites more forcefully than as women. And most of them were unwilling to admit that white womanhood had changed at all. Rebecca Latimer Felton explained that the "new woman" was "often criticized" but insisted that suffragists belonged "to a womanhood like our mothers did, which was never bought and sold for a European title, or made a millionaire's plaything to be treated like a pet cat . . . These women of our blood stood side by side with their mates when it was considered treason . . ." Mildred Rutherford also loudly insisted that the white women of today were the same as those of the glorious southern past. Only Belle Kearney seemed able to admit that white women had changed: "The women of the South have not sought work because they loved it; they have not gone before the public because it was desirable for themselves; they have not arrived at a wish for political equality with men simply by process of reasoning; all this has been thrust upon them by a changed social and economic environment. It is the result of the evolution of events set in motion by the bombardment of Fort Sumter." Kearney's deterministic assumptions, however, absolved women of choice and agency. The times, not the white women, had changed.[48]

But even self-consciously "new women" often praised their mammies as their liberators. Lucy Stanton, a white painter born in Atlanta in 1875 who studied and worked in Paris and New York before settling in Athens, Georgia, credited her mammy Chloe with awakening her artistic abilities. She remembered her first creations as the animals she made as a child out of clay from the creek bed to act out Chloe's stories. Two years older than Stanton, Ellen Glasgow, too, credited her mammy with awakening her artistic ambitions: "all the fairies and ghosts and talking animals that Mammy would evoke from her secret magic, when the time came to tell stories." For Glasgow, as far back as she could remember, before she could write, she had "played at making stories with Mammy" and "created Little Willie and his many adventures." When her mammy left her to go to work for another family—Glasgow did not seem to know whether her nurse desired to leave or whether her parents sent her away—Little Willie left her too. Glasgow decided to write books so she could keep her stories with her. And Glasgow,

like Stanton, lived only marginally within the conventions of white southern womanhood: "Only on the surface of things have I ever trod the beaten
path. So long as I could keep from hurting anyone else, I have lived, as completely as it was possible, the life of my choice. I have been free." Though
less overtly racist than most white southerners, "new women" like Stanton
and Glasgow seemed unable to imagine an alternative to white supremacy.
They too needed their mammies, even if in their stories black women's
actions help young white girls take the first steps in structuring an alternative white womanhood. Perhaps even more surprisingly, Lillian Smith, one
of the first white southerners to attack publicly the culture of segregation,
participated in her own version of southern mammy worship. Claiming her
love for her mammy as "one of the profound relationships of my life," Smith
described the greatest violence of segregation as learning that her mammy
"was not worthy of the passionate love I felt for her but must be given instead
a half-smiled-at affection similar to that which one feels for one's dog."[49]

Margaret Mitchell made herself famous by depicting the story of yet
another southern black mammy and her anything but weak and often very
unladylike mistress Scarlett. In the 1936 epic *Gone With the Wind*, Mammy
is introduced on the first page. Large, elderly, and intelligent, with the eyes
of an elephant, she is both "pure African" and yet "devoted to her last drop
of blood" to her white folks, the O'Haras. Certainly no ordinary slave,
Mammy is the household disciplinarian, Scarlett's mother Ellen's right
hand, and the boss of both the three O'Hara daughters and the other serving
slaves. Her personal code of behavior and her white family pride, Mitchell
insists, surpass even her owners'. And Mammy is continuity. Reared in Scarlett's French grandmother's very own room and previously Ellen's mammy
too, Mammy moved from Savannah to the Georgia up-country when her
mistress married. Though of course she loves her white charges, Mammy's
job is to train Scarlett and her sisters in the womanhood proper for girls of
their class and racial privilege, and the mischevious Scarlett becomes the
main recipient of her fused outpouring of chastening and love. In *Gone
With the Wind*, Margaret Mitchell created a mammy figure that quoted
decades of white southern mammy worship and became the archetypal
black mammy.[50]

But midway into the novel Mitchell reverses the direction of the relationship between Mammy and Scarlett. In the beginning Mammy bosses
Scarlett, the age difference overriding the racial divide between them. And
though Scarlett sometimes gets her own way, Mammy holds great authority

and her will cannot be easily or directly challenged. Scarlett, whose coming of age coincides not with her first marriage nor even with the birth of her first child, learns the burdens of adulthood on that eventful day when Melanie screams in childbirth, Atlanta burns, Rhett deserts the refugees on the road to Tara, and her mother dies. The war puts an end to Scarlett's childhood. Yet at a Tara now devoid of the quietly commanding presence of Ellen O'Hara, there is still Mammy, Tara's mammy, her mother's mammy, her own mammy. Mammy enters the room, her face heavy with the "uncomprehending sadness of a monkey's face." And the old relationship flickers: "[Mammy's] eyes lighted up at the sight of Scarlett, her white teeth gleamed . . . and Scarlett ran to her, laying her head on the broad, sagging breasts which had held so many heads, black and white." The integrated refuge of childhood returns: "Here was something of the old stability, thought Scarlett, something of the old life that was unchanging." But Mammy's first words break this spell. As the animal metaphors piled up around the figure of Mammy release their burdens, Scarlett realizes that Mammy, despite her size, has never been a pillar—she has only been strong as an extension of Ellen, as the "martinet" of a white woman: "Oh, Miss Scarlett, now dat Miss Ellen's in de grabe, whut is we gwine ter do? . . . effen Ah wuz jes' daid longside Miss Ellen! Ah kain make out without Miss Ellen. Ain't nuthin' lef' now but mizry an' trouble. Jes' weery loads, honey, jes' weery loads."

This scene, then, marks the reversal of Mammy's and Scarlett's relation-ship. Scarlett, constructed by Mitchell as now doubly motherless, then picks up those burdens, those "weery loads," herself. But this encounter between Mammy and Scarlett marks other transitions as well. Scarlett shifts from dependency to an adult agency not imaginable for white women before the war, taking over Tara from her spiritually defeated father and assuming the burden of providing for her sisters, her sister-in-law Melanie, the white children, and those few "loyal" slaves. In *Gone With the Wind*, Mammy performs the same conflations of the Old South and the New, the plantation household and the postwar home, as her counterparts do in other white southern mammy stories. But with the men gone, in body or in will, the triumph of the white woman is here undisputed—Mammy wrings her hands, Mammy becomes a dependent, and Mammy plays the woman.[51]

The figure of the mammy, then, both eased and marked the contradic-tion at the heart of that new home-based white womanhood, its dependence on a gendered influence and yet possession of a racial authority, its masking of the new with a conscious celebration of the old. "Mammy" enabled the seeming paradox of white women empowered by an image of weakness but also made that paradox visible, as Mildred Rutherford revealed without even naming the threat, in that same 1916 speech where she had celebrated the home-power of white women:

> As you are, so is your child, and as you think, so will your husband think, [laughter, applause] that is, if you are the right kind of mother and wife and hold the confidence of your husband and children. Your children are to be the future leaders of this land. Are you training these children yourself or are you relegating that power to someone else?[52]

Glimpses of white ambivalence about the power of the mammy, about the contradictions between her celebration, the middle-class conception of female influence, and white supremacy, occasionally appeared. If the image of the "black beast rapist" hemmed white women in, as the historian Jacquelyn Dowd Hall has argued, with "fear of a nameless horror," the mammy let them out of the home in the unnamed liberation of their whiteness to be temperance organizers, suffragists, UDC activists, artists, and writers. White womanhood was as much a racial construction as a gendered one.[53]

But the mammy also revealed the contradictions central to the culture of segregation, the form that middle-class development took in the South and in which white women reconstructed southern womanhood. For whites' dependence upon the African American domestic worker both for her physical labor—her nursing and nurturing of white children and cleaning and feeding of white families—and for her image's symbolic labor—the mammy's masking of the discontinuity between the culture of the Old South and the New—belied any conception of her as inferior. The mammy figure revealed, perhaps more than any other construction of the culture of segregation, a desperate symbolic as well as physical dependence on the very people whose full humanity white southerners denied and the centrality of blackness to the making of whiteness. Whites admitted their physical needs when they conducted sanitation campaigns aimed at the "colored towns" from which their mammies came. The subscription appeal for the Black Mammy Institute put this problem rather bluntly: "The LIFE of both races is affected physically and morally by the quality of service rendered necessary in the home."[54]

Yet the symbolic dependence, never squarely confronted, was even more terrifying. As E. E. Brock, editor of the *Waco* (Texas) *Tribune*, told Elisabeth Freeman, a northern white woman who was in Waco in 1916 to investigate a lynching, only white southerners really understood African Americans: "He told me he was raised with them, had a colored mammy, nursed at her breast, etc. 'Then' I said, 'you are part colored.' At this he became very angry." Perhaps white men told fewer mammy stories because of the problematic nature of any acknowledged intimacy between black women and white men, no matter their age. Freeman's remark, then, doubly angered Brock, questioning his own racial identity and thus superiority as well as hinting at the always denied fact of miscegenation. Lillian Smith connected "the three traumatic relationships not common outside the South" that Freeman's remark so slyly invoked and called them the "Three Ghost Stories." These unrecognized relationships, in Smith's analysis, haunted many white southerners: the connection between white men and African American women; that between white fathers and their African American children; and that between white children and their African American caretakers. White southerners could express extreme discomfort when faced with the full implications of their own mammy stories. Without mammy, in a complicated layering of ways, southern whiteness was meaningless. Though not in the sentimentalized narratives they imagined, middle-class white southerners were the children of black and white mothers.[55]

White Self, White South

More than racial identity was at stake in the white home, however. In late nineteenth-century America, a changing political economy undermined older forms of male power. The South did not escape this failing of patriarchal authority. In fact, in many ways the loss of control over slaves, the wartime destruction of households, a generation of white men's loss of life, limb, and will, and African American male suffrage uniquely threatened southern masculinity. But the South also experienced the unhinging of the old meanings, the loosening of past anchors of masculine identities that accompanied growing cities, rising consumption, increasingly national markets, and expanding wage labor throughout the nation. Here, however, the problem was less the suspected effeminacy of white collar occupations and urban life and the antidote was more complicated than the strenuous life. And far from directly challenging their men, many white southern women who had lived through the war and Reconstruction hoped to build them up. White supremacy could offer both white southern men and women a firm basis of authority, grounded in a new culture of segregation.[56]

Mammy became the canvas upon which white women painted their new authority in the same way that another white image of blackness, the "black beast rapist," worked for white men. White southerners could not seem to imagine the white home without surrounding it with images of blackness. The mammy craze coincided, at least during its peak, with white obsession with this opposing symbol, not of nurture but of terror. The white home as the symbolic site of southern whites' gender and racial identities existed in opposition to a darkness both inside and out. But as segregation expanded and left the white home an integrated space within an increasingly racially separated world, the relationships between white southerners and black women domestics became crucial to the reproduction of white supremacy.

To create an alternative to a white womanhood founded in white supremacy, then, required constructing an alternative to the white home as well. Lucy Stanton tried to put back together the home she had lost in her childhood, trading her paintings to relatives for the furnishings they had purchased from the estate and painting a picture of her mammy Chloe Henderson that she never offered for sale. This reconstruction, however, took place within an entirely different space—a house that Stanton designed using Henry Adams's Boston dwelling as a model, a house where she was in charge, and a house that included a place for her painting. The white home had for Stanton been a problematic place to found a female autonomy: "No harm comes to a good girl from contact with men in coeducational colleges or from living and working in ateliers in Paris and like experiences. There she is on her metal . . . It is when in the shelter of her family, off her guard, and listening perhaps to their advice and entreaty that she comes to harm, There she perchance sells her birthright for peace; there she lays down her ideals for others of their choosing . . ." A woman could be destroyed within her home as easily as within the larger world.[57]

Eight years younger than Stanton, the writer Frances Newman attempted to create an alternative home in Atlanta by making a family with a nephew for whom she served as guardian and her mammy Susan Long.

Newman lived with Long virtually all of her life. Having Long in the home enabled Newman to travel to New York, Paris, and an artists' colony in Peterborough, New York. And yet even as an adult Newman wrote to Susan Long, "Louis [the nephew] and I are your family, and . . . we both love you more than anybody in the world . . . I never realize how much I love you until I am away from you like this." And Newman credited Long less with teaching her to be white than with teaching her how not to be:

> I think she must be mostly responsible for my lack of a southern lady's tra-
> ditional illusions. When I was a little girl, she used to tell me about slavery
> times, and I thought Miss——, her old mistress, was a woman and the devil
> was a man, and that was the only difference between them. If you grow up
> hearing of mistress's sons who set dogs on a little girl three years old to see
> her run, who beat the slaves, and who didn't tell them they were free, you
> can't admire the antebellum south completely.

When a critic arrived to interview her about her novels, Newman declared. "You really must meet 'mammy,' for no one could know me without knowing my 'mammy.' "[58]

But how could they keep their mammies, resist the culture of segregation, and create an alternative to the racially empowered conventions of white womanhood? Though even in adulthood Stanton had a painted mammy and Newman a real one, neither of these women succeeded in developing a white southern womanhood that others could emulate. Stanton had to move out of her house and live in a tiny studio she had built behind it in order to bring in the money she had difficulty making from her art. Her beloved, often beautiful, and rarely caricatured pictures of African Americans made up a large part of her uncommissioned work but seldom sold. And if as an artist, her difference was tolerated by the white community of Athens, Georgia, as a model of independent womanhood in her own lifetime she was erased. Newman died mysteriously and tragically in a New York City hotel room at the age of forty-five. And even in her little-known novels *The Hard Boiled Virgin* and *Dead Lovers Are Faithful Lovers*, she proved unable to imagine a white womanhood that she could praise instead of expose. Her heroines proved unable to get past the whiteness, what Newman calls "Southernness," that founded their identities.[59]

As the search for alternative homes continued into the next generation, many of those men and women born around 1900 who grew up within the culture of segregation would live to see it crack. Katharine Lumpkin, too, was preoccupied with white womanhood and homes. She wrote a master's thesis at Columbia on the social activities of white southern women in which she noted that few worked in the professions although many were active in clubs and associations. The problem, Lumpkin argued, quoting Edward K. Graham's 1913 speech to the Southern Association of College Women, was that colleges trained white women for only two functions, "home-getter" and "home-keeper." Graham believed that "the colleges are giving the public what it wants . . . [the South] has standardized its women's colleges to its ideas of what it wants its women to be." Lumpkin, however, disagreed, and left the region to earn her Ph.D. in sociology at the University of Wisconsin. And yet instead of getting or keeping her own home she studied the activities of others, developing a home-rating scale for social workers as her dissertation project. That first and famous critic of segregation as culture, Lillian Smith, also constructed a series of alternative homes for herself upon the top of Old Screamer Mountain in northern Georgia. Beginning with a camp run by young white women for young white girls, Smith spent much of the rest of her life with her partner Paula Snelling in their mountain home. While Lumpkin had only known her father's memories of a mammy, however, Smith's understanding of the meaning of mammy was deeper and much more complex.[60]

For Lillian Smith the loss of mammy marked the beginning of the twisting of love and desire that segregation inflicted on those who had created it. Learning the truth about "my old mammy" she remembered as the cruelest moment of her life:

> I knew but I never believed it, that the deepest respect I felt for her, the tenderness, the love, was a childish thing which every normal child outgrows, that such love begins with one's toys and is discarded with them, and that somehow—though it seemed impossible to my agonized heart— I, too, must outgrow these feelings. I learned to use a soft voice to oil my words of superiority. I learned to cheapen with tears and sentimental talk of "my old mammy" one of the profound relationships of my life.

With the end of childhood, whites learned the meaning of segregation. African Americans could not really be loved. Integrated feelings, integrated living, then, must be packed up with the baby clothes, pulled out and nostalgically caressed perhaps but never taken seriously, not incorporated into adult white ways of being.[61]

Ellen Glasgow, too, remembered the loss of her mammy as the loss of her childhood, as the end of the happiest period of her life. Glasgow, like William Alexander Percy, loved cemeteries. But instead of a dying aristocratic culture, for her cemeteries conjured a blissful girlhood, images of being loved by both her mother and mammy: "There was Hollywood, where I played over graves while Mother and Mammy planted flowers." But even more than her mother, cemeteries reminded her of time spent with her mammy, of even being taken into her world, of "the old colored cemetery, which was fast falling to ruin," and of "the circle of [her] friends in every shade of white, black, or yellow." But this easy integration "had melted away." Cemeteries, then, were always about things that were gone. For Glasgow they recalled the happy integrated days of childhood. But children must outgrow their mammies.[62]

And most white southerners did. Most gave up their mammies, trading the real African American women who had nurtured them for sentimental mammy stories, mammy monuments, literary representations like Scarlett's mammy, and even mammy-sponsored biscuits and flour. But as Margaret Mitchell clearly conveyed in *Gone With the Wind*, while the mammy crossed lines of time, space, race, and gender, her movements also emphasized the edges. Mammy, then, did not just transgress and blur boundaries, the line between what Smith called "White Town" and "Colored Town," the line between the Old South and the New. She also marked them. Giving up mammy highlighted the passage from childhood to adulthood. And this story of development conflated the growth of the individual white child with the growth of the modern white region.

Segregation was the way of adult white southerners who learned to love and then separate from mammy in an integrated island of time, childhood, and space, the white home. To be a mature white southerner meant to leave a love for and intimacy with African Americans behind. And this individual development reenacted the larger regional drama as well. For the "Old South remade" had to continue in a world not of its making. The region had also, as the Lost Cause narratives had illustrated, been forced to give up its "happy darkies," its easy integration. As the Lost Cause made integration and the "family white and black" the past of southern culture, the white home made integration and "me and my mammy" the past of the individual. Regional and individual mammies must be left behind.

Within the culture of segregation, then, the reunion of self and other merged with the reunion of white and black and nostalgia for the lost oneness of childhood merged with nostalgia for the racial innocence of the white child's love for her black mammy. To become an adult white southerner, to become a region of the present and future instead of the past, southern whites believed they must give up their childhood dreams of racial integration. But in heaven anything was possible:

> Sometime to heaven I hope to go,
> And I know my mammy will be "at de do',"
> And her dear old arms around me will twine
> And her old black face with glory will shine.[63]

Only there could southern whites hope to achieve the reunion, the unity of blackness and whiteness that they so desperately feared and yet desired.

Southern African Americans, however, probably doubted that any southern whites would ever make it to that pearly door. In his 1933 autobiography, the writer and activist James Weldon Johnson told a decidedly different mammy story. The breast upon which he laid his baby head was not broad and it was not black. James Weldon Johnson's mammy, he claimed, was white.[64]

CHAPTER FOUR

Bounding Consumption

"FOR COLORED" AND "FOR WHITE"

Ours is a world of inexorable divisions . . . Segregation has made of our eating and drinking, our buying and selling, our labor and housing, our rents, our railroads . . . our recreations . . . a problem of race as well as of maintenance.

EDGAR GARDNER MURPHY[1]

As the advertising industry, which is dedicated to the creation of masks, makes clear, that which cannot gain authority from tradition may borrow it with a mask. Masking is a play upon possibility and ours is a society in which possibilities are many . . . Said a very dark Southern friend of mine to a white businessman who complained of his recalcitrance in a bargaining situation, "I know, you thought I was colored, didn't you." . . . the "darky" act makes brothers of us all.

RALPH ELLISON[2]

"NOW A MAN DROVE two hundred miles from Jefferson before he found wilderness to hunt in," William Faulkner wrote in 1942. "Now the land lay open from the cradling hills on the East to the rampart of the levee on the West, standing horseman-tall with cotton for the world's looms . . . the land in which neon flashed past them from the little countless towns and countless shining this-year's automobiles sped past them on the broad plumb-ruled highways . . . the land across which there came now no scream of panther but instead the long hooting of locomotives . . ." The voices of animals and not machines, he implied, permeated the old geography of unity on which the annual bear hunt had occurred: "It was of men, not white nor black nor red but men, hunters . . ." But the multicolored masculine spaces of the frontier where plantations were wrested from and yet coexisted with the wilderness were disappearing. The ceaseless "puny marks of man" had vanquished the dialectic of wildness and order. In *Go Down, Moses*,

Faulkner mourns the passing of a racially mixed space of often racially mixed men, the hunt's pungent and tangible racial utopia, the "best game of all."[3]

Although Faulkner dedicated his novel to his own "Mammy Caroline Barr," women and civilization complicate and make painful the racial ease of his wilderness. In Go Down, Moses, an archetypal white child, Carothers, finds a kind of innocent racial mixing in both his white and his "Mammy" Molly Beauchamp's homes. But the bear hunt, unlike childhood, does not have to be individually outgrown. Adult white men do not have to participate in mammy worship to revisit a space of idealized racial mixing that stories of the hunt continue to provide.

Posing his racial utopia within a romanticized remnant of the frontier myth instead of a fictionalized golden age of plantation glory, Faulkner writes a story with villains different from the standard Lost Cause antagonists. He replaces "damn Yankees," "black betrayal," and the "dark days of Reconstruction" with the swarming "men myriad and nameless" of literary modernism, figures armed not with black votes but with plows, axes, neon, automobiles, and trains. The victim this time is not the old plantation idyll but the "doomed wilderness," "the land where [even] the old bear had earned a name." A new kind of settlement meant that the region was collectively outgrowing what the hunt had allowed men to save. A new kind of settlement meant a new racial order. While the coincidence of Faulkner's domestic servant Caroline Barr's death with the completion of the novel probably prompted its dedication, Faulkner ironically crowned his nuanced exploration of one white southern fiction of racial mixing by dedicating it to another, even more influential one.[4]

Yet that was not the whole story. Against the powerful fictions of continuity—of the Lost Cause and the mammy—that grounded modern white racial identity, Faulkner asserted throughout his writings a persuasive counternarrative of geographic and cultural change. In Go Down, Moses, the "long hooting" of locomotives and the shine of new automobiles and neon herald the booming early twentieth-century growth of southern towns. Recent historical scholarship has revealed the extent of the movement of Faulkner's "men myriad and nameless" and women too of both races into the region's growing villages and towns. Ex-planters and ambitious farmers joined ex-sharecroppers, lawyers, ministers, merchants, and the operators of cotton, textile, and other mills to form a new white southern middle class.

By 1900, the historian Edward L. Ayers has determined, one in six southerners, by 1910 over seven million people, lived in the region's towns and cities.
Faulkner also explored the less visible social changes dialectically linked to
the rapid transformation of the region's geography. By 1909, the Compsons
of Faulkner's *The Sound and the Fury* had sold the last of their plantation
lands, "the old Compson mile," to launch their children through education
and marriage into this new southern world. Fittingly, the new owners made
the old pasture into a golf course.

The new and growing commercial and thus semi-public spaces that
came with the towns — from that golf course to the stations that serviced those
automobiles and the stores that neon named — provided places of racial mixing less romantic and more conflict-ridden than Faulkner's narrative of masculine adventure in the wilderness. And these places of consumption were,
unlike the idealized images of Lost Cause, the mammy-graced white home,
or the romance of the hunt, the spaces of the southern future. Far from a
racial utopia and less often the subject of literary celebration, the multiplying spaces of consumption within the growing towns and cities of the late
nineteenth- and early twentieth-century South became key sites for the
white southern middle class's creation of and African American resistance
to the culture of segregation. And the first battlegrounds were the hooting
cause of the bear hunt's destruction, the trains.[5]

The railroad lines invaded the region like kudzu, tangling the most
rural southern reaches of piney woods and mountain coves into a strong and
living web. From the end of Reconstruction through the dawning of the
twentieth century, southerners built railroads more rapidly than Americans
in any other region. As early as 1890, Ayers has written, "nine out of every ten
southerners lived in a railroad county." But what this network connected
also changed. In the black belts the plantation houses with their circling
slave cabins were left to ruin or became the country quarters of the wealthy
now living in towns. Instead of those old necklaces of quarters, the less uniform and often more ramshackle dwellings of black and white tenant farmers now dotted the far reaches of the farm lands. For both southern and
nonsouthern whites, the physical deterioration of the old antebellum mansions signaled the transformation of the region's cultural geography. "Most
of the ancestral homes have been abandoned by their owners for residence
in the cities," a reporter for *Lippincott's* wrote in an article on "Life in the
Cotton Belt" in 1897; "the white-columned porticos of the favorite colonial

architecture now moldering in decay, the wide and once hospitable front halls resounding only to the rough banter and quarrels of negro tenants and their children."[6]

Across the South, cities grew and towns took root where the steel vines crossed. A white southerner in 1901 recounted the attractions of town life to a national industrial commission investigating agriculture: "cheap coal, cheap lights, convenient water supply offer inducements; society and amusements draw the young: the chance to speculate, to make a sudden rise in fortunes, to get into the swim attracts others . . . All these things, and many more of the same sort have acted and reacted between the town and the country, and the country has become permeated with tendencies to town life and efforts to imitate." These new, increasingly less rural, more closely settled places, then, asserted an influence far beyond even the growing proportion of the southern population leaving the farms. Villages, towns, and cities became the hothouses of the new culture of segregation. Cross-race interactions there had not had time to groove paths that whites could use and blacks could stand. Families were not entangled. People were not known.[7]

Segregation grew, however, in a compost of the old racial order, the paradoxically personalized but state-backed racial power that grounded the slave regime. Surviving the near-fatal wounds of emancipation and Reconstruction, this racial culture became the foundation of rural southern life through the early twentieth century. The mammy myth proved crucial here, providing a way for white middle-class southerners to anchor a new cultural authority within the relationships between white men and women and African American domestic servants patterned in the old racial order. Yet in the late nineteenth century, the forms if not the fact of modern white supremacy remained unsettled. The debate about the temporal and geographic origins of segregation has missed a key dialectical point. The choice was between segregation and the greater fluidity and relative integration of the more personalized relations of white racial power of the 1870s and 1880s. But the choice was also between the conventions of separation already in place in many southern cities by the 1880s and African Americans' total exclusion. All three options—segregation, the continuation of personalized relations of racial power, and exclusion—were in varying degrees tried and to varying degrees survived in southern society until World War II. Segregation, however, became the foundation of southern society and the central metaphor of southern life because it balanced white demand for a racially figured power, the spread of the new national ways of buying and selling that had originated in the Northeast, and African Americans' insistence that freedom yield tangible benefits over slavery. Segregation provided a way to order the more impersonal social relations and potentially more subversive consuming practices of the new southern town life. White southerners nurtured their new racist culture to contain the centrifugal forces of a much less isolated, less rural world.[8]

The expansion of consumer culture both drew the region into the nation and played an essential role in the re-creation of racial identities between 1890 and 1940. Advertising created an increasingly national market in part through the circulation of black imagery that figured the implied consumer as white. Yet consumer culture created spaces—from railroads to general stores and gas stations to the restaurants, movie theaters, and more specialized stores of the growing towns—in which African Americans could challenge segregation, both explicitly and implicitly. Whites first encountered the very visible disjuncture between the consumer as white and the consuming southern black in the image of the middle-class African American riding first class on the train. As whites broadened segregation, removing this troubling figure from sight, however, consumption also expanded, both in terms of class and in terms of space. Mass consumption both depended upon and created a new geography of shopping. In this complex layering of places, whites interacted with African Americans as consumers, as both indirect and direct violators of both localized and regional rituals of racial deference. The difficulty of racial control over the new spaces of consumption, in turn, provoked an even more formulaic insistence on "For Colored" and "For White."

Training the Ground of Difference

In the turn-of-the-century South, the small-town train station often sat apart. While the courthouse stood tall in the sky and central, fixing a town as an axle pierces a wheel, the train station hung low, attempting dignity while hugging the ground. As structures, southern train stations wore disguises: their physical presences yelled *stop* while their function whispered *go*.[9]

Once inside, the attempt to deny motion continued. If southerners had to travel, then state laws and local customs decreed that would-be passen-

gers would have to buy tickets, wait, use the restroom, and then depart in
clearly racially marked spaces. Even southern children knew these codes, as
white southerner Katharine Lumpkin, born in 1897, vividly remembered:

> As soon as I could read, I would carefully spell out the notices in public
> places. I wished to be certain we were where we ought to be. Our station
> waiting rooms— "For White." Our railroad coaches—"For White." There
> was no true occasion for a child's anxiety lest we make a mistake. It was all
> so plainly marked. (Said the law, it seems, ". . . in letters at least two inches
> high.")

Station doors, ticket windows, waiting rooms, and toilet facilities—
white southerners determinedly labeled all of them "Colored" and "White."
But much more than a "child's anxiety" was at stake. When as a young college student in the mid-1920s Lumpkin boarded a train with a southern co-
worker in the YWCA movement—an African American co-worker—she
felt for the first time the threat of that two-inch lettering, how it marked and
labeled the racial worth of southern people and places, "how deadly serious
the white South was in its signs and separations, . . . its single-mindedness of
aim."[10]

A growing southern African American middle class seemed keenly
aware of just what was at stake in the 1880s and 1890s as they made the
rapidly expanding railroads and streetcars the battleground upon which
whites enacted the forms of the new segregated culture. Train stations were
not new even then—railroads had expanded into the region, albeit tenta-
tively, before the Civil War. But by the end of nineteenth century, those
long low buildings connected an exponentially greater number of spaces
with both freight and passenger service. As importantly, a small but visible
number of African Americans had acquired the money to get on those trains
and ride.[11]

In 1884 at the age of twenty-two, the ex-slave Ida B. Wells boarded a
train in Memphis to travel to the school in Shelby, Tennessee, where, as the
oldest daughter, she taught to support her recently orphaned siblings. Sitting in the "ladies' coach" as usual, Wells was surprised when the white conductor announced he could not take her ticket there. When he later
returned and demanded that she move to the other second-class car, Wells
refused. The other car, she insisted, was a smoker. Annoyed at her refusal,

the conductor grabbed her arm and tried to drag her from her seat. Wells fought back, sinking her teeth into the back of his hand and bracing her feet firmly against the seat in front of her. Nursing his injury, the conductor fled, seeking reinforcements among the baggage handlers. Three white men then successfully forced Wells from her seat to the loud accompaniment of the white passengers who stood upon the cushions to gain a better view and shouted and applauded. As the train was just making its first stop, Wells announced to the white mob that she would get off the train rather than allow them to drag her into the dirty and crowded smoker. Though her linen duster hung in tatters, Wells had managed to hold onto her ticket. When she finally got back to Memphis, she engaged a lawyer. Ida B. Wells had decided to sue.[12]

Wells's struggle on the train was certainly not unusual in the 1880s. After the U.S. Supreme Court repealed the Civil Rights Act in 1883, whites across the South attempted to draw the color line on southern streetcars and railroads. The companies that owned these transportation routes often resisted, wary of the effort and expense involved in providing separate cars and policing racial separation. And like Wells, many southern African Americans resisted segregation in individual ways that sometimes ended in violence. From the 1880s through the 1900s, southern transportation routes were spaces of racial conflict.[13]

But Wells's persistence and her victory, however short-lived, were unique. After months of dissembling and delay, she discovered that the Chesapeake and Ohio and Southwestern Railroad Company had bought off her African American lawyer. Wells then hired a white lawyer—no other black lawyers practiced in Memphis—and won her case in the circuit court under Judge Pierce, an ex-Union soldier. The *Memphis Daily Appeal* headlined the victory on Christmas Day in 1884: "A Darkey Damsel Obtains a Verdict for Damages against the Chesapeake and Ohio Railroad—What It Cost to Put a Colored School Teacher in a Smoking Car—Verdict for $500." Wells had won the first case brought to a southern state court since the repeal in 1883 of the Civil Rights Act.

The railroad, of course, appealed. The Tennessee Supreme Court concluded in 1887, "We think it is evident that the purpose of the defendant in error was to harass with a view to this suit, and that her persistence was not in good faith to obtain a comfortable seat for a short ride." The white judges saw Wells as desiring "social equality," not clean and smoke-free travel.

Southern African Americans, then, were not to enjoy comfortable seats on trains even when they could afford the higher first-class fare. The battle over the racial ordering of modern transportation was on.[14]

Railroads became the focus of late nineteenth-century racial conflict because their connecting lines broke down local southern racial settlements often violently pieced together in the years during and after Reconstruction. Trains moved beyond the reach of personalized local relations of class and racial authority. Most often, travelers found themselves in close proximity to people they did not know, from fellow passengers to line employees, moving through places with which they were not familiar. Visible cues became increasingly important as markers of identity, as ways to categorize others, as railroads spread traveling pockets of anonymous social relations, more akin to the nation's largest urban centers, across the most isolated areas of the region. The problem of black middle-class riders in first-class cars, then, was less that whites feared "racial pollution" than that the visible dress and deportment of these travelers belied any notion of southern blacks' racial inferiority. Railroads did not just regionalize transportation. For whites, they also made clear the need for a state- and region-wide racial order.[15]

Many African Americans followed Wells in filing suit against railroads for discrimination. A handful even won. Young middle-class blacks became increasingly assertive, and one Georgia newspaper rallied black resistance: "When a conductor orders a colored passenger from the first class car it's a bluff, and if the passenger goes to the forward or smoking car, that ends it; should he refuse, it ends it also, for the trainman will reflect seriously before he lays on violent hands, for he knows that such a rash proceeding makes him amenable to the law." Ida B. Wells had not been so lucky, but other southern blacks testified to how they had called the trainmen's "bluff" and argued repeatedly that they simply wanted the first-class accommodations to which the tickets they had purchased entitled them. The marketplace, they asserted, would not join the polling place as a potential arena of racial exclusion. Southern middle-class African Americans were determined to have unmediated access to the increasing variety of products, from first-class train travel to ready-made clothes and moving pictures, that their money enabled them to buy.[16]

For southern whites, however, more was at stake than comfortable plushy cushions and clean-carpeted aisles. Whiteness itself was being defined in late nineteenth-century first-class train cars. When middle-class blacks entered the semi-public spaces of railroads, they placed their better attire and manners in direct juxtaposition with whites' own class signifiers. Because many whites found it difficult to imagine African Americans as anything other than poor and uneducated, finely dressed blacks riding in first-class cars attracted their particular ire. A white conductor told the well-dressed sixteen-year-old Mary Church, "This is first class enough for you." And many whites looked considerably worse for the public comparison with better-off blacks. Greater mobility made the poorest whites more visible to the rising white middle class as well. Katharine Lumpkin, whose own nomadic white southern childhood resulted from her father's employment with the railroad, remembered her shock at her first sight of extremely impoverished whites in the South Carolina sand hills. Class and race, then, became more visibly unhinged as railroads disrupted local isolation. Confusion reigned.[17]

Beneath white concern about racial disorder in a changing southern society lay a fear of the increasing possibility of making a mistake in identifying strangers. The more varied ingredients of white racial anxiety simmered in a stock of white concerns about racial purity. Though the account would have easily ended in violence had the gender roles been reversed, a Tennessee newspaper in 1889 chose to dramatize humorously the dangers of racial uncertainty within first-class cars. When "a bright and good-looking colored girl (or rather an almost white colored girl)" got on board a train in Nashville, a "flashily dressed white gentleman," usually known as the "car masher," flirtatiously sought her company. Wooing his "lady friend" with lunch and witty conversation, he did not realize his mistake until after she got off. Much to the "masher's" dismay, "none enjoyed the episode more than the ladies on the train." White southerners might have laughed, but the story's joke served as a warning about the dangers inherent in the first-class train car's world of anonymous yet intimate social relations and confused appearances. Possessing the middle-class markers of proper clothing and speech and made mobile by the spread of modern transportation networks, the figure of the mulatto became much more threatening. Though white anxiety translated into humor in this case of an "almost white" woman, white "ladies" undoubtedly would not have found funny an "almost white" man. And in an increasingly anonymous world where class and race status depended upon appearances, racial disorder endangered the very meaning of white racial identity.[18]

White southerners devised what Katharine Lumpkin called those "deadly signs and separations" to reproduce a white supremacy that had become detached from the personalized relations of local power. Segregation made racial identity visible in a rational and systematic way, despite the anonymity of social relations within train cars. Racialized spaces could counter the confusion of appearances created by the increased visibility of a well-dressed, well-spoken black middle class. An African American became, as W. E. B. Du Bois described, someone who "must ride Jim Crow in Georgia." The individual's appearance then little mattered. "Colored" inferior cars meant "colored" inferior people. Systemized spatial relations replaced the need to know others personally in order to categorize them. On a childhood visit to Columbia, South Carolina, in 1892, the white southerner John Andrew Rice recalled his first sighting of the new racial order: "The main entrance to the town was the depot, and here was something new, something that marked the town as different from the country and the country depots . . . : two doors to two waiting rooms and on these two doors arresting signs, 'White' and 'Colored.' " By Katharine Lumpkin's childhood a decade later, as a result of state laws the "town" signs had spread across the countryside, and segregation became "all so plainly marked." The railroads, as the historian Edward Ayers has claimed, "took a piece of the city with them wherever they went." Segregation was modern.[19]

The white Georgia writer Flannery O'Connor explores the ways railroads bridged boundaries of urban and rural, white and black, in her short story "The Artificial Nigger." It describes an old white man from a rural all-white northeastern Georgia county taking his grandson to the city. "The thing to do with a boy," Mr. Head says "sagely" to another white passenger on the train, "is to show him all there is to show. Don't hold nothing back." Soon the boy, dressed in his first and only and ill-fitting suit on his first train ride, spies a "huge coffee-colored man . . . in a light suit and a yellow satin tie with a ruby pin." The man comes "slowly forward," punctuated by the deliberate stabbings of "a black walking stick" and adorned by refracted light from "a sapphire ring" on a "brown hand" and two "coffee-colored," yellow-and-green-dressed women companions. But the boy does not recognize the "true" identity of the wealthy passenger. As his grandfather derides him, the boy turns his brimming hatred toward "his first nigger," this finely dressed passenger who with a confusing color and wealth has made a fool of him.

Yet even as the train highlights the boy's rural confusion, it also creates for him a new form of racial order. Visiting the dining car, "the most elegant car in the train," he draws assurance from the busy waiters, their "very black" skins accentuated by their white suits, their work serving whites overriding their somewhat saucy manner. Most clearly, however, in the dining car the boy encounters segregation. The large, almost-black man encountered earlier now sits eating with the two women behind a "saffron-colored curtain." As his grandfather explains, "they rope them off." Though Mr. Head and his grandson cannot even afford to eat on the train, the thin yellow fabric upholds their superiority, their belonging, their whiteness against the black man's roped-off wealth. The boy arrives in the city knowing "niggers" as people who serve whites or inhabit spaces whose separateness and difference are clearly, visibly marked. He, like the nonfictional Katharine Lumpkin, has learned the code.[20]

Segregation, then, could never reattach racial and class identities, could not make middle-class blacks poorly clothed, poorly educated, and poorly spoken and thus more easily identified by whites of all classes as inferior. Instead, systemized racial separation on railroads and streetcars worked to create and extend white supremacy in other ways. Most obviously, segregation reduced cross-racial contact. But segregated transportation facilities offered another marker of racial identity as well. People who moved within spaces marked "colored" were African American, and the difference—the inferiority of the black spaces—marked the difference—the inferiority of the black and even "almost white" people. John Vachon captured this interaction of built environment and racial identity in a 1939 photograph of African American men waiting behind the railroad station at Manchester, Georgia. The "colored men's" toilet as well as the "colored waiting room" faces outside the station, consigning congregating blacks to the muddy and inferior back of the building. Whites' determined racial labeling of railroad, streetcar, and later bus station waiting rooms, dining facilities, and toilets, then, served notice to black passengers of the limits of travel. The stationary points that bounded such journeys would remind everyone that the color bar, unlike town limits and county lines, could never be crossed. From the perspective of southern whites, racial order had been restored.[21]

Thus by the early twentieth century, transportation systems provided both cultural movement and cultural order. Trains and streetcars gave passage to urban commercial and social relations but not alternative racial identities. Boundaries between town and country faded even as the color bar grew, adding the tight adolescent muscles of law to the baby fat of convention. W. E. B. Du Bois emphasizes this contradictory nature of southern transportation in his 1921 exploration of black life in America, *Darkwater: Voices From Within the Veil.* Taking the uninitiated on a literary trip through the intricacies of southern segregated travel, Du Bois describes in great detail how inferior facilities and service worked to ease white anxiety about better-off blacks' contradictory race and class status. Middle-class African Americans, when possible, simply stayed at home.[22]

"Did you ever see a Jim Crow waiting room?" Du Bois begins. "Usually there is no heat in winter and no air in summer; with undisturbed loafers and train hands and broken disreputable settees." And then the traveler must endure the "torture" of buying a ticket. At an unattended window marked "colored" in quality and with a sign, an African American has to "stand and stand and wait and wait until every white person at the 'other window' is waited on." When the agent finally decides to serve the black passenger, he harasses and contradicts, "hurries and confuses the ignorant, gives many persons the wrong change, compels some to purchase their tickets on the train at a higher price, and sends you and me out onto the platform, burning with indignation and hatred!"[23]

Once on the train, in Du Bois's description, the accommodations for black travelers only get worse. The Jim Crow car always joins the train next to the baggage car and the engine, always stops "beyond the platform covering in the rain or sun or dust," and never includes a step to help passengers on board. Often the car is "a smoker cut in two," and black passengers have to face the discomfort of having white smokers pass through the "colored" section, "with swagger and noise and stares." The compartment always encompasses "a half or a quarter or an eighth of the oldest car in service on the road," its plush "caked with dirt," its floor "grimy," its windows muddy. While the conductor lounges across two "colored seats," his services are for whites only. Often "an impertinent white newsboy" also occupies two more of the limited seats, from which he nags black passengers "to the point of rage to buy cheap candy, Coca-Cola, and worthless, if not vulgar books." Dining cars either do not serve African Americans or provide them with meals in some "dirty and ill-attended hole in the wall." As for restroom facilities, Du Bois can only scream "don't!" Finally he admonishes those still brave enough to travel about the ultimate risk, changing trains. In unforeseeable places local welcoming committees often include sheriffs and quarrelsome white persons who hate a " 'darky dressed up.' " Still, writing from a

Georgia home surrounded by the many colors of spring and humanity, Du Bois turns to his host with thoughts of the liberating possibilities of tourism: " 'No,' said the little lady in the corner (she looked like an ivory cameo and her dress flowed on her like a caress), 'we don't travel much.' "[24]

White southerners wanted railroad lines in the South to perform like those long low train stations, to both provide and deny movement. And for Du Bois, southern whites succeeded: "There is not in the world a more disgraceful denial of human brotherhood than the 'Jim Crow' car of the southern United States." Whites and blacks might set out for the same destination, but en route their difference would be continually reenacted and confirmed.[25]

While many white southerners demanded that the new racial order of the railroad enforce an old white supremacy, the white owners of southern railroad and streetcar lines sought profits. This contradiction between market incentives and the desire to encode white racial supremacy within the changing features of the region permeated the emerging culture of segregation. Whites could never achieve the tight and absolute racial ordering of these expanding spaces of transportation despite their efforts. As a white midwestern journalist following the newly erected color line through the spaces of southern transportation in 1906 and 1907, Ray Stannard Baker neither felt the indignity of the African American Du Bois's journeys nor the certainty of the white Lumpkin's childhood. The streetcar, Baker found, was "an excellent place for observing the points of human contact between the races": "In almost no other relationship do the races come together, physically, on anything like a common footing. In their homes and in ordinary employment, they meet as master and servant; but in the street cars they touch as free citizens, each paying for the right to ride, the white not in a place of command, the Negro without an obligation of servitude." Streetcar relationships were, for Baker, symbolic of the new conditions. But Baker found there an uncertainty that surprised him. The sign in the Atlanta cars read "white people will seat from the front of the car toward the back and colored people from the rear toward the front." Yet no boundary existed, and the cars marked no imaginary race line with colored curtains or signs. Baker found "this very absence of a clear demarcation" in many cross-racial interactions within the region: "The color line is drawn, but neither race knows just where it is. Indeed, it can hardly be definitely drawn in many relationships, because it is constantly changing. This uncertainty is a fertile source of friction and bitterness." Baker found the streetcars, and, he implied, most southern spaces, places of racial uncertainty despite the new laws and the new signs.[26]

Though as a child she had noticed the racial "twilight zone between" on southern streetcars, Katharine Lumpkin still had faith in the strength of segregation's racial order. The white conductor, after all, held the power to sharpen the blurred boundary, to use his office and his stick to draw that temporary line. But by the 1920s the adult Lumpkin too understood the contradictions within the seemingly absolute racial order of segregated southern transportation. A train trip with a black YWCA co-worker began without incident: "We entered the railroad station—but through different doors: hers, 'For Colored,' mine, 'For White.' Presumably I was used to this. I had done it all my life." And the two women's physical separation continued as they bought tickets and rested in waiting rooms. But Lumpkin's epiphany occurred as they both left the station: "Only on the platform was there no physical separation . . . So we paced the platform side by side." This coming back together, both understood, was "unacceptable"; but for Lumpkin the arbitrariness and oppressiveness of the separation, which she sensed her co-worker had long known, became clear for the first time. The railroad platform, then, seemed to "baffle" southern white "ingenuity." Only there was any concession made to the necessity of movement. The African American sociologist Bertram Doyle did find evidence of one small-town Georgia train station in the 1930s in which "a fence to separate the races extended from the station almost to the tracks." But in most places no structure had been devised to separate white and black as they crossed the distance between the building and the train. And the disorder of this racial order persisted.[27]

The Farm Security Administration photographer Marion Post Wolcott portrayed the ambiguity of this walk from the main building to the passenger cars in a series of 1940 photographs of a railroad station in northwestern Florida. The series was a part of the FSA's project to document 1930s America in general and the southern United States in particular. Director Roy Stryker had decided to shift coverage from general rural poverty and specific New Deal programs to southern small-town life. Wolcott and other FSA photographers built an extensive visual record of the geography of segregated transportation across the region, documenting black and white waiting rooms, station entrances, and toilets. But in this series, Wolcott emphasized that movement, both metaphoric and material, could never be completely contained. A white woman might have to stop in that no-race's land, that distance unordered by segregation, to let an African American woman cuddling a child make her way. State laws could never account completely for the minutiae of individual cross-racial contacts. Train stations and their younger cousins, bus terminals, remained places of uncomfortable unpredictability within the culture of segregation's attempts at racial fixity, places of movement despite, in the period between 1890 and 1940, the signs.[28]

This unpredictability was the contradictory heart of a system that promoted both travel and stasis; it made the spaces of southern transportation places of racial conflict throughout the history of segregation. The historian Robin D. G. Kelley has demonstrated that southern streetcars continued to be arenas of racial struggle over semi-public space long after Baker's 1908 observations about the particularity and the relative freedom of the contact there. In Birmingham, Alabama, in the late 1930s and early 1940s, African Americans, in this case a more working-class-oriented group than those more middle-class pioneers of the transportation struggle, continued to push at the shifting racial boundaries within the city's buses. Continuing individual and collective protests included moving the detachable race signs inside buses, deliberately sitting in the front seats reserved for whites, and talking explicitly and loudly about racial equality within earshot of whites. African Americans dramatized the contradictions at the intersection of segregation's racialized spaces and the market, moving, muddling, and vocally crossing the color line. Kelley has suggested that the metaphor of the "theater" illuminates the doubled character of buses as sites of both performance and conflict, as theaters of art and of war. Yet common carriers were not the only "theaters" in town.[29]

As the sociologist Bertram Doyle had suggested as early as 1937, "What you see on the railroad is characteristic of the whole structure of the southern states. The Negro occupies a position of inferiority and servility, of which he is constantly reminded when traveling, by restriction, by discriminating laws, and by the attitude of his white neighbors." Between the old southern racial order and the new order of segregation, then, a key shift occurred in the location of white supremacy. African Americans, as Doyle realized, might or might not appear inferior and servile. Instead, in places where cross-racial contact had a tendency to be both anonymous and visible, whites forced blacks to "occupy a position of inferiority and servility." Segregation attempted to counter a world in which people increasingly moved beyond the local and thus the known by creating racial identity anonymously as well, through spatially grounded signifiers of black difference and white belonging. With the color line, whites literalized the metaphor of keeping blacks "in their place." Whether an individual white was superior to an individual black did not matter so much in a world in which the qualities of the spaces within which cross-race contact occurred materially spelled out the racial hierarchy. That yellow curtain alone, a visual marker of black spatial difference, was enough to assert a poor white man's racial superiority.[30]

Lillian Smith sensed these spatial struggles, the way in the first four decades of the twentieth century the entire small-town South served as a theater of racial representation:

> Every little southern town is a fine stage-set for Southern tradition to use as it teaches its children the twisting turning dance of segregation. Few words are needed for there are signs everywhere. *White . . . colored . . . white . . . colored . . .* over doors of railroad and bus stations, over doors of public toilets, over doors of theaters, over drinking fountains . . . And there are the invisible lines that turn and bend and cut the town into segments. Invisible, but electrically charged with taboo. Places you go, places you don't go. White town, colored town; white streets, colored streets; front door, back door. Places you sit. Places you cannot sit . . . These ceremonials in honor of white supremacy.[31]

Segregation materially and metaphorically grounded the South's new racial order. This geography seemed fixed to Smith, a white southerner born in 1897 who grew up with the culture of segregation. Yet the signs "For Colored" and "For White" proclaimed an order they could never command. "Invisible" yet electric lines twisted and snapped and sprang like live wires in the rain of black resistance and whites' contradictory desires for cultural stasis and economic change.

And the movement of those color lines, like the motion of the train, echoed an equally dangerous movement of cultural meanings down those tracks from the North. Trains did not just transport pockets of anonymous social relations. They also carried an expanding culture of consumption that multiplied the sites in which racial difference could break down, adding the potentially transgressive spaces of movie theaters and chain stores. Such standardized products as national network radio programs and automobiles made racial containment and regional distinction even more problematic. The problem for the white southern elite, planters-turned-store owners and other members of a growing white middle class, was how to reconstruct a powerful and collective definition of whiteness within this new semi-public commercial sphere, which depended for its products upon northern manufacturers and marketers and for its profitability upon both white and black buyers.[32]

Transportation facilities revealed the racial fluidity of southern spaces of consumption. While the Farm Security Administration photographs in their absolute numbers provide evidence that a national consumer culture had penetrated even the smallest dirt crossroads by the late 1930s, white southerners in the 1890s began making segregation their culture in large part because they felt threatened by the convergence of a small and yet growing African American middle class and the new northern ways of buying, selling, and living within the growing southern cities. Consumer culture made the disjuncture of race and class in the figure of the middle-class black more visible at a time when southern whites already felt threatened. Reconciliation with the North, the Populist movement, the depth of the 1893 financial panic in the already impoverished region, and the growing indigenous white campaign for woman suffrage shifted other categories of white identity, making a seeming racial stability that much more essential to southern whites. While the Lost Cause and the mammy functioned for the white middle class as fictions of continuity that laid the groundwork for the new racial order, these narratives contributed only the fading memory of wartime valor to the whiteness of poor white southerners and did nothing to counter the spectacle of the well-dressed black consumer.[33]

Train stations, those often-disguised buildings, then, sat at another crucial borderland as well. With their function as nodes of transport for both goods and people and as nodes of connection between northern cities and southern small towns, railroad stations also bridged the transition between the older agrarian-dominated economy and the growing influence of industrial production and mass consumption in the region. As southerners, including farmers, increasingly purchased rather than produced even food items, changes in the nature, variety, and marketing of goods became a very visible marker of the region's encounter with modernity. Consumer culture spread a new world of goods, a revolution in representation, and an associated proliferation of identities across the nation. With transportation facilities—railroads, streetcars, and eventually buses—southern whites found an early

solution to the problem of fixing racial identity in the modern world by marking spaces as racially superior or inferior instead of people. The solutions for
the racial ordering of other emerging spaces of consumption would be more
complicated. At the intersection of regions, races, and world views, railroad
stations needed to hang solid and low to reinforce the boundaries.[34]

Dixie Brand

Seeking to reinforce the regional divide against the impact of this economic
and cultural change, in 1930 twelve self-identified southern intellectuals
cast themselves as twentieth-century apostles and the South as Christ and
proclaimed their region the last moral place in America. The most famous
of the twelve white men—Donald Davidson, Robert Penn Warren, Allen
Tate, and John Crowe Ransom—came together at Vanderbilt University
around the poetry magazine *The Fugitive*, published in Nashville between
1922 and 1925. In their manifesto *I'll Take My Stand*, the Agrarians denounced the hollowness of a land where the end justified the means and
where that end in turn was a consumption that they believed had become as
"brutal and hurried" as had the machine-paced labor that helped produce
it. "Turning to consumption, as the grand end which justifies the evil of
modern labor, we find we have been deceived," John Crowe Ransom proclaimed in his unsigned introduction to the collection. "We have more time
in which to consume, and many more products to be consumed. But the
tempo of our labors communicates itself to our satisfactions." Under "industrialism," leisure had become work, art instrumentalist, the self the creation
of experts, and life a scrambling attempt to cope with incessant change.

    And consumption, they claimed, was forced upon white southerners as
a result of industrialism's inevitable overproduction. "The producers," and
the Agrarians always implied they were white northerners, "disguised as the
pure idealists of progress, must coerce and wheedle the public into being
loyal and steady consumers, in order to keep the machine running." "The
most significant development of [American] industrialism," these white
southerners insisted, was "the use of modern advertising—along with its
twin, personal salesmanship." Advertising persuaded "the consumer to want
exactly what the applied sciences . . . furnish[ed]." It was "the great effort of
a false economy of life to approve itself." More a metaphor than a coherent

plan for economic and social reorganization, Agrarianism stressed individual and localized control of both production and consumption. The South would provide the counterweight to the "eternal flux," the "infinite series," of "our urbanized, antiprovincial, progressive, and mobile American life." "The culture of the soil," these white intellectuals insisted, was "the best."[35]

Their Adam and Eve, the Agrarians grudgingly admitted, had already been tempted. Their garden of ethics in the modern world, the rural and small-town South, they cried, was itself being seduced, was beginning to trade the unified lives of its "humanistic agrarianism" for the glittering baubles of industrialism, its potential to save the nation for the twentieth century's thieves, those gaudy beads of "Progress." "It would be childish and dangerous," claimed the Agrarian Stark Young, "for the South to be stampeded and betrayed out of its own character by the noise, force, and glittering narrowness of the industrialism and progress spreading everywhere . . ." And the Agrarian John Donald Wade provided a parable of the fall. His "The Life and Death of Cousin Lucius" tells the story of the child of planters who came of age after the Civil War.

Following his father's postwar efforts to rebuild their Georgia town, Cousin Lucius attempted to chart a "compromise between farming and industrialism," between the ways of the Old South and the new North, which he embodied in his work as a farmer and a banker. By the first two decades of the twentieth century, the town was prospering. But Lucius felt something had been lost: "the [white] people were going too fast . . . villagers, they were trying to keep the pace of people they considered, but whom he could not consider, the best people in the great cities." "Shooting fiercely about in automobiles," the white townspeople "would swim with him, they would set up a golf club, but they would not read . . . because they were too busy going to the movies." When in 1919 their peach crop failed—at Lucius's urging they had learned to practice diversified farming—"the new god who was so mobile that he had lost his stability" had won. But Lucius could not blame them because "they had wanted too much." He had seen them toil "to feed and clothe a boisterous nation which had become rankly rich," but in return had offered only the false promise of consumer goods, a shine that hid the rottenness at the apple's core.[36]

Agrarian stalwarts published a second manifesto, *Who Owns America?*, in 1936; it incorporated the contributions of like-minded white nonsoutherners who called themselves distributists and wanted to reverse the movement of the American economy toward larger units of production and greater consumption. Americans already accustomed to popular images of the region as moonlight and magnolias proved unready to view the same place as a new moral economy. Still, the Agrarians and their new distributist allies made greater reference to the ways in which "monopoly capitalism," "the imperial Eastern Big-Business economy"—what they had more vaguely called "industrialism" in *I'll Take My Stand*—included the spread of mass consumption as well as production, the extension of market relations into all aspects of southern life.

Ransom spelled out how he felt consumption had seduced southern white farmers. "The mistake which farmers in America have made," he claimed, was "having been taken in by the brilliant (if wayward) spectacle of the business or money economy so that they concluded to rely on money farming alone" rather than to balance it with "subsistence farming." The spectacle, though Ransom does not here elaborate, was the enchanting, exotic sparkle of the things that money could buy. But "passionate partisans of labor," Ransom's vague reference to communists and socialists, also fell prey to consumption's false promises: "they suppose that bigger wages, or a larger share in the spoils of production, is all the compensation for servility that can be thought of; or that it does not really matter how the laborer has to labor if it enables him to ride in a car after working hours." How exactly the hot, backbreaking labor of southern subsistence farming, even when the farmer owned the land, could be made attractive to the majority of white and black southerners in 1936, Ransom never convincingly articulated.[37]

Calling for a regulated market and trying to move beyond Agrarian nostalgia, Allen Tate, in "Notes on Liberty and Property," distinguished carefully between "paper" and "real" property rights of not just small farmers but also small factory owners and small merchants. A little grocery store "with six chain stores surrounding it," like a farm forced into commodity production, did not offer the same independence and control as these productive units had offered their past owners. The problem here, however, was that small grocery stores benefitted from and in much of the South at least depended upon the same shifts. The same move away from home production and toward market production and consumption that increased the indebtedness of small farmers increased the profits of store owners. With Ransom's balance of subsistence farming and money farming, chain stores or not, southerners would need many fewer grocery stores.

While the Agrarians may have been, as Ransom claimed, "fully prepared to concede bathtubs," drawing the line between necessity and want, need and desire, for the proliferation of consumer goods lay beyond even this second manifesto's more detailed plans. Their metaphorical opposition of North and South simplified the degree of change within their native region and muddled their critique of what was being lost within modern America with old southern myths and the new racial denial of segregation. A gentle rebuke that white southerners had simply "wanted too much" did not convince many within those pinched years of the Depression. Published the same year, Margaret Mitchell's *Gone With the Wind* proved more predictive of the region's future. Whatever the Old South had to say could pleasurably be consumed, and Mitchell's heroine matched any Yankee in her grasping and striving.[38]

The serpent, then, as even many Agrarians grudgingly admitted, had long been in their Eden as well. Those railroads transported city goods and city desires as well as more fluid social relations. Despite the Agrarians' own need to use the South as "a pastoral rebuke" to the nation, many white southerners welcomed the proliferation of goods and were enchanted by what Ransom derided, "the brilliant (if wayward) spectacle of the business or money era." In "Greensboro, or What You Will," an essay published in 1924 in Richmond's *Reviewer*, the white journalist Gerald W. Johnson captured the magic of mass-produced abundance for white southern cotton mill workers. On a Saturday afternoon, of course, "when the mill villages in the outskirts of town pour their populations into Greensboro," shops laid their myriad wares before the groaning and "inadequate" sidewalk. "A window advertised a sale of silks," the bolts fixed "on high," the fabric "cascad[ing] to the floor in shimmering streams." Behind glass, "a riot of color blended with artful carelessness, a debauch of loveliness, voluptuous, enticing, exquisite," looked out at the street. With their three children the mill couple stood, impeding the human flow, taking in the spectacle. They were not, Johnson insisted "enraptured, but calming and judiciously admiring."

And yet for the woman who broadens in Johnson's essay into a metaphor for Greensboro itself, there was something more: "Languidly chewing gum and inspecting rich brocades woven for mistresses of empires and broad seas, she [now both the woman and the city] is perhaps justly an object of derision. But I pray you pardon me if I do join in your mirth, for I am somehow not in the mood for laughter. I have seen the gleam in her eyes." Neither the Agrarians' denial nor a cynical dismissal, Johnson implied, would diminish the attraction, for both the mill worker and Greensboro, of this abundant spectacle. Why should not white southerners, like other Americans, have silks and bathtubs? As the young liberal New Dealers who prepared the 1938 "Report to the President on the Economic Conditions of the South" said of even the poorest white and black southerners, "the people of the South need to buy, they want to buy, and they would buy if they had the money." Greensboro, as Johnson had insisted, the industrializing, modernizing small southern city, needed to be understood. Greensboro was the future.[39]

But as the turn-of-the-century conflicts over first-class railroad accommodations revealed, other southerners wanted to buy as well. Middle-class African Americans like Du Bois and Wells left autobiographical evidence of their consuming desires. Du Bois's description of his trip through the perils of segregated train travel had begun with the tasteful appointments of his Georgia host's middle-class home and ended with her stylish dress. In 1932 the African American economist Paul K. Edwards published his detailed statistical study of southern urban black consumers. White businessmen, he complained, viewed all African Americans as "appendages" of the poorest segment of the white market. Black professionals, small business owners and young doctors and lawyers, were community leaders and thus expected "to own automobiles, electrical appliances, and luxuries far above their simple economic level." Black consumers existed for the better and non-necessity items, no matter how much advertisers refused to pitch to them.[40]

But long before 1932, when Edwards perceptively insisted that "the custom of social segregation in the South" had created "differences in the social lives of the two races" that explained the need to consider separately the "Negro market," non-middle-class African Americans had shared that gleam in the eye with those Greensboro mill workers. The song "John Henry," written by African American crews constructing railroads in West Virginia, reveals that a black working class enjoyed the pleasures of access to the new consumer abundance:

> Where did you get that pretty little dress?
> That hat you wear so fine?
> Got my dress from a railroad man,
> Hat from a man in the mine.

As the men composing and singing the song articulated in the voice of the women they hoped to win with their purchases, "bigger wages or a larger share in the spoils of production," readily dismissed by Ransom in 1936 as the false promise of a car ride, seemed well worth having and a significant improvement over their former bondage. From their perspective, the supposedly moral benefits of agrarian life translated into the meager pay of farm labor. The cash wages of railroad work gave them access to the new world of consumer goods, then dresses and hats for the women, and later, maybe even that car. Although "a railroad man" would have trouble voting, he would find it easy to spend his money. White businessmen would remain to varying degrees dependent upon black customers and rarely found it profitable to exclude blacks from the emerging spaces of consumer culture. Segregation as culture emerged in part from white's need to create a racial order that would make an expanding marketplace both for colored and for white.[41]

If the Agrarians denied the South's place in the national economy, other white southerners demanded its inclusion even as they paid homage to the plantation myth. "One of the most significant inventions of the New South was the Old South," as C. Vann Woodward has suggested. Nostalgia complemented progress. White southerners like Henry Grady and Joel Chandler Harris personally embodied this evolving interdependence of the South as a part and yet outside of the nation: "oftener than not this archaic romanticism, this idealizing of the past, proceeded from the mouths of the most active propagandists for the New Order," Woodward has written.

The Lost Cause, the first white southern use of the South as metaphor, enabled the very changes its image of the southern past condemned. In much the same way, then, the Agrarians' self-conscious southern stance would not have been possible without the changes they deplored—the integration of the region within the national economy and the resulting national ties developed by many well-educated and well-off white southerners. "Southernness," which Stark Young admitted was a regional whiteness, did not even have to mean geographic residence: "Provincialism does not at all imply living in the place where you base your beliefs and choices. It is a state of mind or persuasion. It is a source . . . you need not, for instance, live in the South, but you feel your roots are there." From this perspective, southern whiteness became simply one among many identities in the fractured, mobile, and consuming world that twentieth-century American whites could now choose, albeit the construction Young preferred.[42]

The Agrarians, then, began too late to critique the false promises of "industrialism." The South's inclusion or exclusion within the national economy was decided even before the late nineteenth-century campaigns to mandate the segregation of common carriers. Trains erased the boundaries of local economies as readily as they eroded local adjustments in race relations. The Agrarians' lack of popular support stemmed not from their moral blindness to racial oppression—that fault was common enough—but from their inability to account for the economic and social change that had already occurred. They failed to see the ways in which the new racial order of segregation offered its own mediation between the region and the nation. In 1930, Stark Young decreed, "We can accept the machine, but create our own attitude toward it. There is no reason why southern people, however industrialized, should bolt the whole mess as it stands." But by 1930 white southerners had already created an attitude "toward the machine" as both tool and metaphor of modernism: segregation.[43]

Segregation provided that additional compensation for servility even if the payment was not exactly what Ransom had argued. What the historian David Roediger had called "the wages of whiteness" in relation to the northern white working class in the South took the form of a very visible hierarchy of racial worth. Being white by the dawn of the twentieth century meant enjoying the better seats on the train. And segregation's ritualistic enactment of African American inferiority expanded with mass culture—that combination of industrial production and increasing mass consumption—in which it was born. In fact, by 1930 white southerners felt so secure within the new racial order of segregation that white supremacy, often politely expressed as interest in "the Negro question," received much less public attention. The resurrected Ku Klux Klan that peaked in the 1920s, after all, had orchestrated a much broader range of hatreds than white supremacy, from anti-Catholicism and anti-Semitism to the reinforcement of traditional gender roles. Segregation as culture enabled the Agrarians to ignore the many southern African Americans who often lived the very agrarian lives the intellectuals so praised. Not just "modern mechanized labor," as the Agrarians claimed, but agricultural toil in the form of sharecropping, renting, and day laboring bore the "marks of slavishness," traces of the very slave labor from which it came. Segregation both enabled the spread of consumption and provided racial identity as an order and value other than profit. The culture of segregation became the means of the region's integration within modern America and yet difference from it. It provided a way to embrace modernism and also contain it, a way to allow greater fluidity for other identities even while attempting to hold race fast.[44]

What southern African Americans wanted, the Agrarians could not even conceive of asking. The best the twelve whites could muster was Robert Penn Warren's contribution, "The Briar Patch," which, with its resonance of the sentimentality of Joel Chandler Harris's Brer Rabbit stories, asked whites to find a place for blacks in the new plantationless world. Warren called, in effect, for an anachronism, for the construction of a new hierarchical, multi-layered southern social order. Treating southern African Americans more as components of landscapes than as people, the other Agrarians, however, conflated southern blacks with the racialized spaces of segregation with which whites attempted to bound them.[45]

Southern boosters, businessmen rather than intellectuals, understood more clearly than the Agrarians that segregation could provide a way for "the South changing [to] be the South still." Far from Robert Penn Warren's call to find a place for southern African Americans in the modern world, small-town and urban white business owners emphasized that a space "For Colored" had already been made. "Seeing Atlanta By the Photographic Route," an early twentieth-century souvenir and promotional pamphlet, named the Georgia capital the "metropolis" of the "ultra-modern" New South. Perhaps a desire to deny the racial violence and rioting of 1906 colored the publication, which emphasized that "beautiful, hustling, sunny Atlanta [could] be a charming hostess on occasion," assuming of course that the visitors were white. The city's black population disappeared in a "skyline . . . jagged with the silhouettes of tall buildings" and "bristl[ing] with factory chimneys," in wide boulevards bounded by castlelike homes, prim churches, and the pompous buildings of educational and cultural institutions. An absence of African Americans in the photographs implied an absence of racial problems.[46]

But other southern towns spoke more directly. In the early twentieth century, Bedford City, Virginia, called the "descendants of the former slaves of inhabitants of the county" a "completely foreign element" that lived "completely separated from the Caucasian race, making no attempt to obtrude themselves upon the whites." By 1912, the *Virginia Real Estate Journal* advertised Richmond's segregation as one of its most attractive features: "Separate schools for whites and blacks, separate churches, hotels, railroad coaches, and in fact, no intermingling of the races socially, though relations otherwise are amicable and friendly." Segregation, then, reinforced white supremacy, a value other than profit, and yet enabled economic development.[47]

And unlike the Atlanta pamphlet, most town booster and tourist materials explicitly claimed the African American, as both "darky" attraction and industrious servant, as a vital white southern asset. The souvenir booklet "Savannah: Indelible Photographs," printed in 1892, presents images of the city's buildings and monuments with two exceptions. "Two Angels" pictures two African American boys without shirts as another of Savannah's tourist sights. Another image of an African American man and woman hoeing, "Sweet Potato Field," emphasizes with its caption blacks' place as and in southern landscape, as unskilled, subservient laborers. Tourist materials for St. Augustine, Florida, also presented southern blackness as servant and sight. "Constitution Monument" pictures a Washington Monument–like obelisk at the base of which sits an African American nurse and, in a fancy carriage, her white charge. But "The Waiters of the Ponce De Leon" foregrounds black servility much more directly. As if to underscore their limited masculinity and subservience to whites, the photographer posed the tuxedoed group of black waiters at the "Ladies Entrance" of the grand hotel. And all late nineteenth- and early twentieth-century St. Augustine tourist literature promoted the old slave market, often photographed with African Americans posed in front of or within the open-sided building, as one of the city's main attractions. Early twentieth-century souvenir books for Miami and Richmond duplicated these types of images as well.[48]

By the 1930s a generic *Souvenir Folder of Dixieland,* unable to focus on a particular city, presented instead romanticized images of southern landscapes and African American labor. The only black people not "working" here are the children. In pictures captioned "Lollypops and 'Chocolate drops' in Dixieland" and "A Watermelon Feast in Dixieland," their eating, playing, and grooming become a real-life and free minstrel show for the entertainment of any white willing to drive down the scenic highways, photographs of which were included as well. Even African American children, represented as cute, comic, and ignorant, could be profitably sold.[49]

But white southerners did not just commodify southern blackness in their town booster and tourist publications. The same pamphlets promoted old plantation houses and Confederate memorials along with those factories and tall buildings, the Old South as well as the New. Though white bodies were never explicitly commodified, this literature collectively manufactured a southernness, whether Atlanta's "ultra modern South" or Natchez's "where the Old South Lives Again," that could be experienced, known, and consumed. By 1930, DixieBrand meant a regional identity made or marketed as southern, not a metaphor of moral rebuke to

Top: A. B. Frost's rendering of Uncle Remus and the boy, commissioned for the 1895 edition of Joel Chandler Harris's first book, *Uncle Remus: His Songs and His Sayings*, originally published in 1880. *Lower Left:* Illustration by Howard Weeden for her poem "When Mammy Dies," published in Weeden, *Bandanna Ballads* (New York: Doubleday and McClure Company, 1899), 30-31. Joel Chandler Harris praised Weeden's work for presenting "unimpeachable evidence of what they [Negros] were." In the common but not often so transparently circular arguments of white southerners, the work of a young white woman, born after emancipation, was offered by Harris and accepted by many whites as proof of the superiority of "before the war" southern African Americans. *Lower Right:* Illustration by Howard Weeden for her poem "Eventide," published in *Bandanna Ballads*, 26-27. *(Hargrett Rare Book and Manuscript Library, University of Georgia)*

Above: Tansill's Punch Cigar Advertisement. The humor of this trade card depended upon an assumed white audience's relief at discovering that no matter how well African Americans mimicked their white "superiors" in both dress and leisure activities, the face remained transparent and conveyed the "truth." "Beauty on the Street," however, opened up as many questions about identity in a consumer society as it answered. *(Warshaw Collection of Business Americana, Archives Center, NMAH, Smithsonian Institution)* *Below:* Gold Dust Washing Powder Advertisement. Advertisers to the new mass market in the early twentieth century explicitly figured the consumer as white. Spokesservants like the Gold Dust Twins and the better-known Aunt Jemima implied that, like African Americans, consumer products would perform multiple tasks, insuring through their service both the physical and cultural comfort of their white masters. *(Warshaw Collection of Business Americana, Archives Center, NMAH, Smithsonian Institution)*

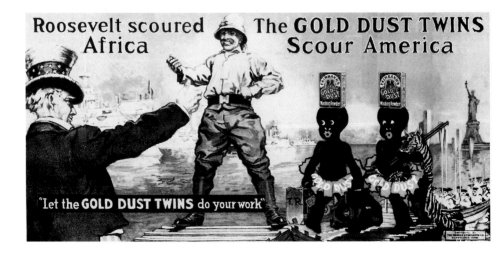

Above: "At the Time of the Louisville Flood," Louisville, Kentucky, 1936-37. This photograph captures visually how whiteness became central to a modern American nationalist consumer identity through the ideological and psychological erasure of African Americans despite their self-evident—even determining—presence in American life. *(Margaret Bourke-White/Life Magazine, © Time Inc.)* **Below:** Ben Shahn, "A Medicine Show and Audience," Huntingdon, Tennessee, 1935. This photograph of a medicine show promoting patent medicine demonstrates the ambiguity of associating blackness (and "Indianness") with the product and whiteness with the consumer in the South, given its integrated mass of potential consumers. *(Farm Security Administration, Library of Congress)*

Above: Marion Post Wolcott, "An Advertisement on the Side of a Drug Store," Wendell, North Carolina, 1939. Two African American boys duck to yield the sidewalk in a commercial district to a white woman, her baby, and her child. Racial separation in the South, despite the seeming solidity of the segregation signs, laws, and customs, was more a white fantasy than a fact. *Below:* Marion Post Wolcott, "A Street Corner," Starke, Florida, 1940. In southern small-town commercial districts in the 1930s, integrated crowds of shoppers were common, especially on Saturdays. *(Farm Security Administration, Library of Congress)*

Above: Photo from the pamphlet "The Facts in the Case of the Horrible Murder of Little Myrtle Vance, and Its Fearful Expiation, at Paris, Texas, February 1, 1893," published in Paris, Texas, in 1893. The lynching of Henry Smith in Paris was the first modern spectacle lynching, a blatantly public, commercially promoted murder of an African American by southern whites. *Below:* Elisabeth Freeman, an undercover investigator for the NAACP who posed as a suffragist to investigate the 1916 murder of Jessie Washington in Waco, Texas, bought a set of photographs of this spectacle lynching. On a tip from the mayor, a local photographer named Gildersleeve captured the atrocities from the windows of City Hall, where he had set up his camera equipment in anticipation. This photograph captures the "unknown" members of the mob in the act of setting Washington on fire. *(NAACP Collections, Library of Congress)*

This photo of the charred body of Jesse Washington, also acquired by Freeman, circulated as a souvenir postcard that Gildersleeve sold in Waco for ten cents to those participants and spectators unable to acquire pieces of the body itself or of the chain or the tree. (*NAACP Collections, Library of Congress*)

The sculptor Gutzon Borglum carving the head of Robert E. Lee into the granite face of Stone Mountain, in 1924. The sculptor's design for the memorial, which was proposed by the United Daughters of the Confederacy, featured Lee riding at the head of a vast grey army carved into the curve of the mountaintop. A less grandiose but more affordable triptych featuring Lee, Jefferson Davis, and Stonewall Jackson was eventually completed after the 1954 Brown decision revived white southern interest in the project. *(Special Collections Department, Robert W. Woodruff Library, Emory University)*

The "slave choir" singing in front of a replica of Tara at the Junior League charity ball held as part of the festivities for the December 1939 premiere of the film version of *Gone With the Wind*. Martin Luther King, Jr., in the front, makes his first appearance here in the national spotlight. The African American stars of the film were not invited to any of the official premiere events. *(Courtesy of the Atlanta History Center)*

the nation. Not just for potential intellectuals, investors, or tourists, self-conscious white southernness came in many less lofty and pretentious packages than Agrarian pieties. Those native white folks who saw small farms as hard work, not nostalgia, could demonstrate their own regional and racial loyalties through the purchase of Robert E. Lee flour, the nationally popular and yet regionally produced Coca-Cola, and even the UDC-endorsed "Library for Southern Homes." The book and film versions of Margaret Mitchell's *Gone With the Wind* made white southernness a national bestseller. In the twentieth-century South, a complex and contradictory relationship evolved between an expansive segregation's racially coded spaces and an increasingly national mass culture's regionally and racially figured products. The expansion of consumer culture generated cultural meaning on two distinct and yet interlocking planes: buying and selling within the region versus buying and selling the "region" itself.[50]

In 1895 white southern boosters spread their vision of a new southern civilization, a fusion of racial order and economic progress, formally before the nation. This inaugural event, appropriately enough, occurred in that ultra-modern city, Atlanta, the home of the late New South champion Henry Grady. The 1895 Cotton States and International Exposition presented the official joining of the South's new culture of segregation with the North's expansive, increasingly consumer-oriented commercial culture (the 1884 World's Industrial and Cotton Exposition, held in New Orleans, served as a trial run, but by 1895 racial violence had blunted African American militancy). In the previous ten years a growing and more urban-oriented white middle class had begun to see segregation as a system that would both address the disturbing divergence of race and class identities signified by the consuming "New Negro" and enable the economic development that would pull the region out of financial depression. The Atlanta fair powerfully linked regional racial views to more national conceptions of progress. Yet many details of both the new systemized racial separation and the new consumer culture's place within the region remained unsettled. The compromises worked out there, however, served as an official template for the southern future. Crafted in the image of the Atlanta businessmen who financed the exposition, the more nationally oriented businesses that sent exhibits, and the federal government which provided crucial funds, the fair presented the South that the Agrarians would come to loathe.[51]

As the historian Robert Rydell has argued, the "Atlanta Compromise" occurred long before Booker T. Washington made his famous speech.

Prominent black Atlantans like the Bishops Wesley J. Gaines and Abram L. Grant by early 1894 had persuaded the white fair directors, led by the exposition's president, the cotton mill operator and banker Charles A. Collier, to include a Negro department among the other displays. African American exhibitors had been excluded from participating in the Chicago World's Columbian Exposition of 1893, and Frederick Douglass and Ida B. Wells had passed out pamphlets in protest. If to whites the fair had been "a reaffirmation of the nation's unity, self-confidence, and triumphant progress," then for blacks the Columbian Exposition had signaled a reworking and expansion of exclusion. But New Orleans had set a different precedent. The African American leader Bishop Henry A. Turner had called the creation of the "Colored Department" there "so marvelous, so Utopian, that we could scarcely believe it was true." Atlanta, the white directors realized, had to continue this limited inclusion, and use the exposition to demonstrate to northern investors that segregation had created a place for southern blacks, transforming the "negro problem" into an economic asset.[52]

In soliciting federal funds for the exposition, the white directors asked three black delegates to join them in speaking before the House Appropriations Committee. Booker T. Washington followed Bishops Gaines and Grant and stressed that the fair offered an opportunity for the federal government to show its concern for both the region and its blacks. His goal, he emphasized, was to teach his fellow African Americans to avoid politics and seek instead the rewards of "industry, thrift, intelligence and property," through which they would earn white respect. The three southern black speakers convinced the committee of the sincerity of the fair's racial message, that as trained laborers blacks were not a hindrance to the region's economic development but an asset. Congress appropriated the funds but added a condition that the fair include a separate "Negro Building" instead of the planned inclusion of a "Negro department" within the "Government Building." A year later the compromise became national policy as *Plessy v. Ferguson* made "separate but equal" the law. At the fair's opening ceremonies before a segregated audience, Booker T. Washington simply gave the "Atlanta Compromise" its memorable rhetorical expression: "in all things that are purely social we can be as separate as fingers, yet one as the hand in all things essential to mutual progress."[53]

But segregation did not prove nearly so eloquent in practice. All public buildings were open to African American visitors, but they were not allowed to purchase refreshments except in the Negro Building. Private exhibitors barred blacks from their restaurant facilities as well and often denied them entrance to their buildings altogether. Ticket takers at the gates proved rude, reportedly trying to dissuade African Americans from even entering. In fact, the streetcars that carried people to the fair set the tone, forcing blacks into separate and inferior seating. Even the opening-day ceremonies featuring Washington's speech entertained a segregated audience at the fair's large auditorium. The congregation of Atlanta's black Big Bethel Church protested the "[l]ack of space for the colored exhibit, jim-crow cars, and convict labor at the grounds." A local African American paper reported:

> The Fair is a big fake . . . for Negroes have not even a dog's show inside the Exposition gates unless it is in the Negro Building. Many people have written, asking whether the exposition is worth coming to see . . . If they wish to feel that they are inferior to other American citizens, if they want to pay double fare on the surface cars and also be insulted, if they want to see on all sides: "For Whites Only," or "No Niggers or dogs allowed," if they want to be humiliated and have their man and womanhood crushed out, then come.

The Georgia governor was perhaps more truthful than he intended when he invited "all mankind to visit us and witness both the problem and the process."[54]

In fact souvenir books proved a more reliable index to race relations at the fair than Washington's speech. *Official Views: Cotton States and International Exposition* presents no image of African American participation except the exterior of the Negro Building, an image of racial identity as geography, of new black spaces rather than new black people. The only African American pictured in the program plays the same old subservient role, a groundskeeper sweeping the street in front of the building being photographed. And the careful order of the grounds visible in the views, built and maintained by convict labor, says more about the reality of African American work in the South than the careful order of the Negro Building's industrial displays. The exposition directors, then, encouraged black attendance at a "Negro Day" for the same reason they included a Negro Building and Washington's speech. Washington's less threatening image of the "New Negro," embodied both within the Negro Building and in the form of segregated African American visitors, would serve as one of the fair's attractions. But black fair visitors would also pay to attend, becoming a double source of

revenue, both subject and object of the exposition's display. The messiness
of the fair's attempt to systemize racial separation flowed both from its muddled orgins and from a fundamental contradiction, the tension between
African American as racial subject and racial object, as consumers and commodities, that would characterize segregation as culture.[55]

But the fair also held other racial attractions. The problem with Booker
T. Washington's image of black and white southerners as fingers on a hand
was that black fingers served whites not only as tools for achieving a "common progress" but also as fetishized objects of entertainment. While the
gruesome southern practice of lynching actually made black fingers into
coveted commodities, lovingly preserved and displayed in jars, northerners
practiced a less deadly form of appropriation in which racial images performed as minstrel entertainment and advertisements for the new consumer
products. Not just African American labor but the commercialization of
their racist representation could be turned into white profit. And this use of
blackness too appeared at the fair, on the midway where the market's
excesses escaped the containment of official display and its erotic spectacle
promised pleasure in exchange for mere coins.[56]

Though fair officials may have believed that the "Old Plantation"
demonstrated to visitors that African Americans could be "easily controlled," the concession in fact made little pretense of instruction. "Old
Plantation" promised "Young bucks and thickliped African maidens 'happy
as a big sunflower' danc[ing] the old-time breakdowns, joined in by 'all de
niggahs' with weird guttural sounds to the accompaniment of 'de scrapin' of
'de fiddle' and 'de old bangjo.' " Its popularity owed as much to its manager's
previous career as a minstrel performer as to its re-creation of the plantations that had once dotted the middle Georgia black belt. Most importantly,
Old Plantation's seductive portrayal of southern blacks as racial products
denied them any subjectivity as free laborers, as the separate-but-equal
southerners that Washington had envisioned but that the realities of convict
labor and unequal facilities had already narrowed. Washington brilliantly
understood the ultimate contradiction between the expansive marketplace
and white supremacy. He knew that when black exclusion hurt whites economically, profit would sometimes triumph over white supremacy: "No
race that has anything to contribute to the markets of the world is long, in
any degree, ostracized." Washington, like other black leaders, felt the racist
portrayals of "happy darkies" would fade in the face of economic and racial

uplift. He did not foresee that racist representations would prove as profitable as racial bondage and that the emancipation of images would be almost as difficult as the freeing of slaves. The "Negro" indeed had a "place" at the Atlanta fair, albeit a multiple and contradictory one, a geography of limited subjectivity and spectacular objectification that segregation both created and sought to contain.[57]

Segregation Signs: Racial Order in the National Market

Though she did not attend the Atlanta Exposition, "Aunt Jemima" was no stranger to world's fairs. At the 1893 Columbian Exposition, where Ida B. Wells protested African American exclusion, a women named Nancy Green, herself an ex-slave working as a domestic for a wealthy Chicago family, impersonated the then four-year-old trademark. Outside a gigantic flour barrel–shaped exhibit hall constructed by her owner, now the milling company instead of a master, Aunt Jemima served, entertained, and sold her products to the fair's overwhelmingly white visitors. Encompassing the multiplication of racial objects at the century's end within Aunt Jemima's broad and smiling embrace, this performance in Chicago was much more complicated than making pancakes from that ready-made mix. Green played an advertising image that both mimicked minstrel show performances inspired by Harriet Beecher Stowe's character Aunt Chloe and resonated with new southern constructions of the old black mammy. Aunt Jemima was at least a representation of a representation of a representation, and her connections to any slave who actually labored for antebellum whites grew dim in the multiple layers of her popular culture rather than domestic duties. Her popularity resulted not only from her pancakes but also from her wide capacity to embody the black as entertainment, labor, and product. Mammies had important cultural work to do in the nation as well as the region.[58]

Aunt Jemima demonstrated the racial foundations of an expansive consumer culture's increasingly national market. Her particular performance of the mammy, her life as a trademark, began when the pancake mix's inventor, Chris Rutt, attended an 1889 blackface minstrel show by the duo Baker and Farrell in St. Joseph, Missouri. Rutt appropriated the title character of the pair's most popular song, "Aunt Jemima," and her lithographed image on their posters to name and symbolize his product.

Aunt Jemima, however, had lived in earlier songs, and this character's musical evolution traced the doubling and circuitous routes by which representations of southern African Americans entered an increasingly national and commercial popular culture. In her first appearance, on the cover of an 1855 minstrel song by Samuel S. Sanford entitled "Aunt Jemima's Plaster," she also sold a product, her own home concoction good for catching thieves, stopping growth, training cats, and even managing lovers. But this Aunt Jemima also profited from her invention's sales. The comedy here turned on the "unnatural" figure of this self-supporting spinster. Aunt Jemima, as depicted on the cover illustration and implied in verse, was white. By 1875, Aunt Jemima had changed color and learned to speak in dialect. With thick white lips and a grinning dark face, a bandanna-bound head, and broad, aproned hips, she graced the cover, and her song described not her livelihood but her "friends" and their drunken and superstitious adventures with talking animals. In 1899 she debuted in a ragtime march called "Aunt Jemima's Cakewalk" in which society "darkies," not "de cheap coons," came "from ebby where" to participate in a dance contest. A 1909 "Jemima: A Sneezing Coon Song," trying to capture some of her increasingly famous trademarked image's popularity, portrayed her cooking cakes and ignoring a suitor. Other songs in the first two decades of the twentieth century took Aunt Jemima on picnics, gave her bandannas for her birthday, and, of course, featured her fried chicken, biscuits, and pancakes. Though the image had changed from comic ridicule of black (or blackfaced) ignorance to nostalgia for the old southern, servant-graced home and a longing for return, the entertainment always depended upon an image of racial and gendered yet asexual subservience, the mammy.[59]

While Aunt Jemima grew directly out of a minstrel character and song, late nineteenth-century advertisers drew most of their imagery from less specific black types. Catalogs for minstrel costumes served as dictionaries of popular black representations as well as promotional vehicles. Philip Ostermeyer's turn-of-the-century collection of wigs covered all the well-known blackface figures, from "Uncle Tom" and "Mammy Negress" to "Topsey" and the "Zulu Man." The minstrelsy tradition's well-known and popular stock of blackface characters, then, provided an expansive and increasingly

visually oriented advertising industry with a readily accessible pictorial vocabulary. Minstrelsy had originated in an antebellum matrix of northern
dramatists, showmen, peddlers, and patent medicine hawkers engaging in
the increasingly blurred enterprises of selling and entertaining. Even before
the Emancipation Proclamation had freed the bodies of African American
southerners, these northern white men had begun the recommodification
of African American images. While northern wage laborers found humor in
blackfaced minstrels' mocking of a stereotyped slave life, sentimental anti-
slavery advocates mourned the plight of Harriet Beecher Stowe's Uncle
Tom. And northerners of both the middle and working classes bought remedies at patent medicine shows that often included "darky" acts. P. T.
Barnum, that master mixer of an older carnival tradition with a new commercialization of popular entertainment, first became known as he toured
the country in 1835 exhibiting the elderly black woman Joice Heth. In perhaps the first instance of the profitability of representing a figure that would
become the mammy, he claimed Heth was George Washington's 161-year-
old slave nurse and quickly netted earnings far above the $1,000 with which
he bought her.[60]

The blackfaced minstrel performer, the figure of the " 'darky' enter-
tainer," as Ralph Ellison first argued persuasively, was not black but white.
Beginning in the 1840s, the mask of burnt cork and later face paint allowed
white men to cross the racial divide and play with images of blackness for
the entertainment of first a northern white male working-class audience and
later a broader white market of men and women, middle- and working-class
people from across the nation. African Americans came to symbolize not
just slavery, the opposite of white freedom, but also the more rural, premodern innocence whites had left behind. Minstrelsy entertained not just
through ridicule but also through nostalgia. And the blackface actor, particularly when performing a slave character, participated in the same elaboration of white longing as the happy slave figure of the plantation romance.
The popularity of minstrelsy, the scholar Eric Lott has argued, grew out of
this theatrical genre's encapsulation of both white desire for and fear and
loathing of African Americans. The minstrel act gave this tension a visible
and bodily form as blacked-up white men strode jauntily and even erotically
across the color line, playing black men and even cross-dressing as black
women. As spectacle, minstrelsy separated black identities from African
American bodies, making representations of blackness a commodity in the

North even as black bodies remained a commodity in the South. In this way, minstrelsy contributed to the antebellum creation of a self-consciously white working class, as the historian David Roediger has argued. Later, as both its audience and its use broadened beyond the genre of the minstrel drama, blackface became essential to the creation of a more self-consciously white American identity as well.[61]

Minstrelsy, then, mediated between slavery and late nineteenth-century mass culture. It placed stylized black racial imagery at the center of commercial popular culture. Selling stereotyped representations of blackness became crucial to the proliferation of mass entertainment forms in the late nineteenth century, from world's fairs to amusement parks to the movies. Fairs blurred scientific and educational figurations of nonwhite races with minstrel idioms as fairgoers surveyed in a day both official exhibits and midway attractions. Photography eased other boundaries, performing an early erasure of blackface minstrelsy's explicit performances of race. With a camera, white photographers hung their representations of blackness not on the white bodies of minstrel performers but upon their own black subjects. Capturing images, then, meant less any transparent relation the lens provided than the white photographer's direction of the identities nonwhite figures performed. Although never a complete welding of white-produced representation and the black object and subject of the photograph, as the scholar Alan Trachtenberg has noted in reference to an 1850s series of daguerreotypes of slaves, the attempt achieved a chilling effect absent in blackface minstrelsy's explicit and playful displacements. Stereographic views, the most widely circulated photographic images of African Americans in the late nineteenth century, excised black subjectivity altogether by depicting black characters playing blackfaced whites.[62]

Movies blended the perception of transparency generated by photography with the explicitly theatrical effects of whites playing black characters. Although D. W. Griffith's *Birth of a Nation*, released in 1915, became the most popular, earlier one- and two-reel films like *Butterflies and Orange Blossoms*, *In the Boarding House*, and *The Bridge Across* worked the same tension. These films continued the minstrelsy humor that always depended in part upon the gap between the black role and the white, blackfaced actor and at the same time began to shorten this distance, echoing photography's "transparency" in a new fusion of actor and character. These developments—the union of education and entertainment and the splitting apart of bodies and identities—made the circulation of black representa-

tions a very profitable enterprise by the early twentieth century. African
American images joined the bodies of Native Americans and other people
of color from around the globe as commodities. Across lines of region, ethnicity, religion, and gender, these cultural productions created a mass and
increasingly national audience as white.[63]

Advertisers quickly put these increasingly commodified white images of
blackness to work selling other commodities. These racial representations
figured the expansive identity of the consumer, increasingly seen as a member of a mass detached from specific localities and even gender and class
identities, racially as well. The consumer, like the audiences for racialized
entertainments, became more self-consciously white. This process accelerated as advances in the technology for reproducing pictures made the circulation of visual imagery increasingly affordable. In the late 1870s and
1880s, lithographers, printers, and businessmen developed trade cards, a
new genre of advertisement, to combine visual imagery with pitches for
products. Circulated by wholesalers and manufacturers, country stores and
urban merchants, trade or ad cards appropriated minstrel figurations of
racial types—African Americans especially but also Native Americans and
Asians—for the promotion of branded products and stores. A card for Fleischmann's Yeast used a combination of racialized representations as three
white girls gather in the center to look at a kitten dressed as a baby while a
black girl and an Asian girl gaze longingly from the margins holding their
own inferior dolls.[64]

Many early trade cards made no pretense of connecting the product
and the advertising copy to the visual imagery used to catch the potential
consumer's attention. Often businesses chose stock images available from
lithographers and printers to save the expense of hiring commercial artists to
do custom work. Thus the same image of two black children tickling an
elderly black man asleep on a cotton bale advertised Rabineau the baby
photographer and Trumby and Rehn, "Manufacturers of Fine Furniture."
Pluto, a young black child wearing a hood and staring out of a background
of flame with whitened eyes at once cute, comic, and solemn, promoted
both the Pomeroy Coal Company and McFerren, Shallcross and Company
meats. Also exploiting this racialized sentimentality, a black boy in a long
gown and bonnet and holding a puppy advertised both Piqua Patent pillows,
bolsters, and sectional mattresses as well as Topsey Tablets. Advertisers
hoped this sentimental racism would attract the attention of middle-class
white women who increasingly controlled household spending. Most early

cards, then, made little or no connection between the promoted product or establishment and the eye-catching images.[65]

Other images of African American children on trade cards were more comically ridiculing than sentimental. Advertisements for Union Pacific Tea used a distorted image of a black child's face, large-eared, thick-lipped, and white-eyed, in four different emotional expressions. I. M. Demming promoted its Alden Fruit Vinegar with a picture of a young African American boy, the whites of his eyes glaring, his exaggerated white teeth sunk into a huge ear of corn as his dog stands guard. The implication, of course, was that the boy must have stolen the enticing, golden ears from a white man's crop. African American children, however, often appeared in association with animals. In a bizarre image used by Walker, Stratman, and Company to advertise its "Pure Bone Fertilizers," an ear of corn sprouts black arms and legs and a black child's head. Sitting in a tree, this corn boy blows a horn draped with a flag while bears dance before the ripened cornfield, his own implied place of birth. He heralds the wonderful crop that the fertilizer will bring, his unity with nature conveyed by his command of the bears and his grotesque hybridity. An ad for Elson, Salisbury, and Company also featured a black boy cavorting with animals. Dressed in an outlandish parody of gentlemen's attire, he rides a bucking pig while chased by a yelping dog to sell the company's rubber goods.[66]

Perhaps the most popular commercial black imagery used in trade card advertising, however, depicted African American adults absurdly trying to mimic their white "superiors." In black and white pictures, mismatched patterns and awkward pairings signaled blacks' inability to achieve that increasingly crucial marker of middle-class status, respectable and proper attire. Color lithographs went further, painting African American clothing in boldly bright and clashing color. To heighten the comedy, these outrageously dressed figures participate in activities seen as the province of leisured, elite whites. In an ad for Sunny South cigarettes, a young black woman, her exaggerated mouth gaping in surprise and pain, pulls up her clashingly striped skirt to hold her hurt foot. She has hit herself, breaking the mallet, instead of striking the ball, while playing croquet in a scene labeled "Cape May." Playing upon conceptions of place, the ad invited viewers to laugh at an ignorant black woman attempting to enjoy the pastimes of a fashionable Victorian seaside resort. A trade card for George W. Boos coffee depicts a black man, his striped top hat and chained pocket watch flying, his polka-dotted pants flailing, as he absurdly tries to ice skate. In checkerboard-patterned pants, another grinning and wall-eyed black man awkwardly rides an English-saddled, grinning, and equally wall-eyed horse in a card for Vacuum harness oil and J. G. Crippen, a New York hardware dealer. "People," Vacuum claims, "cannot exist without It," excluding from humanity this figure who is too ignorant to understand the necessity of well-oiled tack.

Intended to be humorously entertaining, these advertisements addressed white fears of upwardly mobile blacks by insisting that African Americans could never integrate into middle-class society. The New Negro's unhinging of race and class identities, then, demanded a comic containment in the North as well as on southern trains. Even if respectability was increasingly a matter of appearances, of money, passing could never occur. Race would reveal itself in mismatched clothes and ineptness at croquet. Which blood would tell of those "almost white" blacks, advertisements did not say. But light-skinned, racially mixed people of ambiguous identity did not appear on trade cards. Even color advertisements figured racial identities in black and white.[67]

In a more explicit play upon white fears of the confusion of appearances, a trade card for Tansill's Punch, "America's Finest Five Cent Cigar," pictures a rear view of "Beauty on the Street." Attired in respectable clothing, well corseted, and topped with a tasteful hat, the woman lifts her skirt and holds her parasol in one hand and a purse and her dog's leash in the other. Flipping the card over, however, viewers learned their mistake. "Beauty's" "Front View" reveals the woman's coarse, even masculine, black face. On closer examination perhaps the woman has lifted her skirt too high to be a proper lady. "Beauty" soothed fears that in an increasingly anonymous world people were not what they seemed, assuring white readers that in the face, transparency still reigned. But the card also exudes a veiled eroticism, a masculine attraction to a well-turned ankle, the seductiveness of the racialized, feminine other. And the coarseness of "Beauty's" face suggests too the homoerotic performances of minstrelsy, in which white men played not just black men but black women as well. "Beauty's" insistence upon the certainty of racial knowing only reveals other late nineteenth-century anxieties and minstrel borrowings, white men's cross-race sexual attractions. The attempt to figure absolute racial difference often exposed other boundaries.[68]

Other trade cards played upon African Americans' awkward misuse of modern technology. Despite the abolition of slavery, blacks, trade cards insisted, would never really be a part of the modern world in which white consumers bought the advertised products. A trade card for Glenwood Ranges and Parlor Stoves of Massachusetts depicts an elderly black man in striped attire jumping back from a ringing telephone with the dialect caption, "Sartin shoo Dis Chile Dun Gone Rung Up De Debble." An ad for Mitchell's Kidney Plasters also finds humor in another outlandishly dressed, bald black man's attempt to use the telephone. A mule stands at the end of a second phone as the man, looking perplexed, shouts, "Bless my stars! He must be a foreigner and can't understand." White consumers, of course, saw which figure was the real ass.

A trade card for Harrington and Company Merchant Tailors again shows a group of garishly dressed blacks, their checkered and striped pants above their ankles, having their picture taken in a lush tropical setting somewhere between Dixie and Africa, graced with a sharecropperlike cabin, its chimney smoking. Someone, a head hidden under the camera's drape and the ambiguity multiplying the meanings, is photographing them. Is the pants-clad mystery man an imperialist adventurer capturing the "natives," another ignorant black man trying to succeed at a career beyond his racial place, or a white man making a buck off more humorously aspiring blacks seeking that late nineteenth-century middle-class marker of respectability, the family portrait? No matter, the advertisement conveyed. All possibilities figured blacks as locked in a timeless past, crosswise with modern things. Despite the comedy implied, however, trade cards like the minstrel show images from which they borrowed, conveyed longing as well as ridicule. Whites laughed, but in their transference of an imagined past simplicity to blacks, they revealed a nagging nostalgic sense that something had been lost.[69]

Other trade cards too played up the theme of a blackness out of its place. A lithographer's sample of a card labeled "Comic Series H, 1000 for $0.75 postpaid" depicts a large-nosed, big-lipped black man dressed as a fireman. Another card for a Wisconsin dry goods store uses a well-known minstrel character, the ridiculous black politician. In high-waisted pants and suspenders, waving an oversized umbrella over his big-eared, large-mouthed, bug-eyed head, the "political orator" shouts a little late and in dialect, "Separate De Noaf Fom De Souf! 'Nevah!' " But an early trade card for Harry Smith Hatter took the opposite approach, crossing the caricatured big-lipped, wide- and wall-eyed minstrel with the scantily clad figure of anti-civilization, the spear-toting native. "Strolling the Sands" suggested that Africa with its pyramids and exotic palms was exactly where African Americans belonged.[70]

As advertising became a more sophisticated and professionalized industry in the late nineteenth and early twentieth centuries, advertisers developed trade cards in which the racial imagery related directly to the ad copy and the product. Transitional pictures simply depicted blacks holding or embodying the product. African American children dressed in contrasting patterns hold F. H. Brinkman's Four Heart Brand's box and trademark as they ride a seesaw made out of the crackers. Purina Mills of St. Louis combined the connection to product with the African scene, again signified by almost naked black men and spindly palms. In this trade card a foregrounded "African" boy wears the Purina Breakfast box like a suit and with Western spoon and dish in hand proclaims, "I Like the Best!" Purina almost makes him civilized. Arbuckle Brothers took this approach one step further, connecting its trade cards' racial imagery to a "history" lesson and the lesson to the product. Its Ariosa Coffee "set the standard," and thus its wise drinkers would always appreciate another opportunity, in these compact two-dimensional versions of a world exposition, for more information. Official display and midway combine as "American Negroes" and "Central Africa" elide work and play. In an almost mock-serious tone, one side describes while the other side illustrates the banjo playing, cakewalking, and possum hunting of America's own "Child of nature," "the most entertaining, interesting, and happy of beings." The African "child" requires only different activities—river running, elephant and hippo hunting, and dancing—and perhaps a little more bravery to face the dangers that whites were too smart to suffer and so had created civilization. More common, however, were trade cards that depict blacks holding products from Magnolia Ham to Java and Mocha Coffee.[71]

Other advertisers chose brand names that signified blackness and allowed for an easy incorporation of racial imagery within product pitches. A card for Nigger Head Tobacco uses all the common tropes as a black man with exaggerated facial features and mismatched, outrageously patterned clothes speaks in dialect and tries to shoot a target with a bow and arrow, hitting a bull and an Indian instead. "Nigger Head" and "Niggerhead" became common product names, used for canned fruits and vegetables, stove polish, teas, tobacco, oysters, and clams, from 1905 through the 1920s. "Nigger-hair Chewing Tobacco" claimed to be as thick and tightly packed as its namesake. "Korn Kinks" breakfast cereal was only slightly more subtle, promoting its "delicious malted flakes" with dialect tales of little "Kornelia Kinks" and her mop-headed adventures.[72]

As the nineteenth century closed, blacks embodied products both more subtly and more literally. Advertising pitches moved away from minstrelsy's theatrical exaggerations even as minstrel types left the stage as banks, dolls, and other toys, their flamboyance intact, for white homes. An "Automatic Window Attraction" sold by *Harman's Journal* in March 1898 blurred the boundaries between black representations as entertainment, as advertisements, and as commodities. "Topsey," the advertisement directed at merchants suggested, worked "for any line of business": "A cunning, comical little darkey girl. Quick right and left eye movement, which runs for six hours with each winding. Adjustable arms and legs. Cute little feet and toes. Sitting figure. Checked gingham sunbonnet and dress, white pantalettes, lace trimming. Nearly life size head." But Topsey did not just attract attention to herself. She also displayed "an endless variety of merchandise . . . in a catchy manner." Demonstrating what her sellers must have seen as the most irresistible use of the versatile Topsey, the advertisement pictures her holding a "chinese doll." Merchants, however, would have to construct their own doubled spectacle of white consumption and desire. The company did not furnish the Oriental baby. Only the black girl was for sale.[73]

Representations of blacks, then, did not just promote and sell other products. In the late nineteenth century black-figured items, from mammy dolls to jolly nigger banks, became profitable commodities themselves. Again, Aunt Jemima, like the black mammy to which through anti-slavery literature and minstrel show mediations she distantly referred, had multiple duties. As talented as Topsey, she worked simultaneously as a servant cooking pancakes at stores and fairs, an advertising image selling pancakes across the nation, and a rag doll serving for a few cents and a boxtop a multitude of white children. Jemima's career as a product herself began two years after Nancy Green impersonated the trademark at the 1893 Chicago fair. The pancake mammy appeared as an instantly popular paper doll that children could cut out of the mix's carton. Aunt Jemima's owners also created a promotional flour scoop with her red-turbaned head as the handle. In 1905, however, Davis Milling Company introduced what would become the most popular Aunt Jemima–figured product, the rag doll. Anyone with one box top trademark and five cents could acquire an Aunt Jemima doll, and the company boasted that "literally every city child owned one." An Aunt Jemima pancake mix advertisement in the October 1918 *Ladies' Home Journal* offered her friends for sale as well: "Send for these jolly rag dolls . . . send four tops and only fifteen cents for Aunt Jemima and Uncle Mose, and two cunning pickaninnies. In bright colors, ready to cut out and stuff." Whether African American children ever ordered the dolls was unclear, but Aunt Jemima Mills, as the Davis Milling Company later became known, clearly envisioned its market as white. Not every child could have a servant but all but the poorest could have her very own pancake mammy.[74]

Black-figured products also allowed white children to enjoy blackface comedy, the minstrel show at home. In their 1890s catalog, Marshall Field's offered mechanical toys called "the Cake Walker" and "the Mechanical Nurse" that petted and cooked and danced and spun. Figured in blackface, a cast-iron mechanical bank from the 1880s swallowed any money inserted into its grinning, thick-red-lipped, white-toothed mouth. In the 1920s a fascinating mechanical toy named "Jazz-a-bo Jim" featured a black man "in conventionally fantastic attire stand[ing] on a miniature cabin and automatically danc[ing]." Spinning another 1920s tin toy called the "golliwog" caused a white clown to hit a black clown over the head with a huge hammer. Black-figured commodities waited silently and smiling to entertain and assure their white owners. Whether playfully socializing children or humoring adults, Aunt Jemima and her friends signified and magnified whiteness with their uncomplicated subservience. And as importantly, black-figured commodities advertised themselves.[75]

This association of black figures with white service, from minstrel characters' performances to Aunt Jemima's smiling supply of pancakes, also permeated an expanding advertising industry's increasingly sophisticated and subtle productions. Trade cards peaked in the 1880s, although more local merchants and manufacturers continued to use them through the first two decades of the twentieth century. Larger concerns shifted much of their promotion into the new mass circulation magazines. Many early advertisements in national magazines picked up a trade card theme closely related to the use of brand names like "Niggerhead" that signified blackness. In these cards for products like Bixby's Blacking, Bluing, and Ink, and Diamond Dyes' Fast Stocking Black, racial representations did not wear or hold but transferred their most visible racial marker, their color and its steadfastness, to brand name products, which also often had racial names. A card for Coates Black Thread offered not just an image but a story, as a white woman talks with her servant: "Come in Topsey out of the rain. You'll get wet—Oh! It Won't hurt me Missy. I'm like Coates Black Thread. Da Color won't come off by wetting." An 1895 advertisement in the *Ladies' Home Journal* sounded a similar theme. Using an image of a white policeman catching a black boy, Nubian Dress Linings insist they are "Absolutely Fast Black" and that "the black is positively unchangeable." An attractive striped-shirted young black boy, his skin as shiny black as his product, promotes Black Satin Stove Polish in Cans in a 1905 *Delineator* ad. And a 1895 "Onyx" Black Hosiery ad, again in the *Ladies' Home Journal,* depicts a crowd of "pickaninnies" with the caption "Onyx Blacks—We never change color."[76]

Advertisements in mass circulation magazines built upon trade cards' movement away from black-figured spectacle toward black-figured embodiments of products. Soap advertisements in particular became early innovators in the use of whites' conceptions of blacks' racial characteristics to explain rather than attract attention to products. In the late nineteenth century Kirkman's Wonder Soap began featuring a mammy complete with head rag standing over a washtub, one hand upon a naked black boy getting in the water on the right while her other hand holds the white soap bar above a naked white boy getting out on the left. The image illustrates the story underneath about "two little nigger boys" who hated to bathe. Unlike white mothers, however, their mother scrubs not to remove dirt but to change their color. Only Kirkman soap, of course, could turn "pickaninnies" into white boys: "Sweet and clean her sons became—It's true, as I'm a workman—And both are now completely white. Washed by this soap of Kirkman." Despite the advertisement's comic intent, the implication here—that racial identity lay less than skin deep and could be washed away—was unusually subversive. More common were pitches that praised products as almost able to perform the impossible, like Henry's Carbolic Salve, which "would almost make a nigger white." A Procter and Gamble advertisement claimed that Ivory soap "came like a ray/ Of light across our darkened way./ And now we're civil, kind, and good,/ And keep the laws as people should./ We wear our linen, lawn, and lace,/ As well as folks with paler face./ And now I take, where'er we go,/ This cake of Ivory Soap to show/ What civilized my squaw and me,/ And made us clean and fair to see." Yet the illustration depicts a distinctly blackfaced Indian family. Cleanliness was as much about racial as middle-class status. Even fine soap, the image jokes, could only accomplish so much.[77]

Most companies played upon the older and much less transgressive trade card themes of colorfastness and associations of blackness and dirt, whiteness and cleanliness. N. K. Fairbank and Company began using these types of images in its early trade cards, which often featured, like Kirkman, two black boys in a washtub and promises that its White Star laundry soap would not fade "fast colors." The first cards for its Gold Dust all-purpose washing powder again featured what Fairbank called "the original twins, the universal favorites." But in other ads those black twins get up out of the tub and start working, doing dishes, scrubbing pots, cleaning floors, and washing clothes. Fairbank built here upon another crucial trade card figure, the black servant, who from Aunt Jemima to Tom, Topsey, Sambo, and Dinah as well as countless unnamed maids, butlers, and nurses performed the work that the whites, either explicitly within the image or implicitly beyond its frame, directed and observed. A typical example pictures a black domestic interacting with two white children with the caption "Dinah Keeps the children quiet with Libby, McNeill, and Libby's Cooked Corned Beef." But in their Gold Dust advertisements Fairbank moved beyond the working servant and subtly elided the service of the product with the service of the black figures promoting it. A doubling and magnification of a racially figured subservience occurred in these ads as the twins worked for the washing powder, both as trademarks and as representations of servant labor, and the washing powder then worked for the consumer. A 1902 ad captioned "the Passing of the Washboard" emphasizes these translations as cleaned white shirts dance between the black twins and the soap that has done the work. Use Gold Dust, Fairbank proclaimed, and "Let the Gold Dust twins do your work."[78]

As the Gold Dust Twins cleaned into the twentieth century, their image gradually changed from blackface-influenced caricature to a more sentimental racist cuteness to a final cartoonish simplicity of form. But unlike other advertising servants, from a Topsey pushing Coates Thread and a Dinah praising the Universal Clothes Wringer to an unnamed black male cook listing the savory qualities of Armour's Star Hams, the twins rarely spoke. Their one direct address continued the slippage between black domestic service and the service of the readily available Gold Dust Powder: "If you have not yet availed yourself of our services, lose no time, but summon us through your nearest grocer and 'let us do your work.' Your servants, The

Gold Dust Twins." Aunt Jemima's magazine advertisements, not the Gold Dust Twins, made the speaking servant the "spokesservant," a nationally known image.[79]

The "spokesservant" drew from two earlier idioms, the visual vocabulary that figured African Americans as servants and an iconography of romanticized images of African Americans at work, which drew in turn from literary depictions of the happy slave. Advertisements often featured comic or nostalgic depictions of laboring blacks. Pace, Talbot and Company Tobacco used a drawing of a relaxed and smiling, barefoot black man driving a mule. An ad for Sapolio Soap shows a strong black woman on her knees cleaning a floor while white women dust and straighten above her. Walker, Stratman and Company fertilizers used a more humorous image of a black woman dancing in a field with a sack full of cotton, grown with their fertilizer, upon her head. The spokesservant pulled together this kind of imagery, with the Gold Dust Twins' doubling of subservience in a trademarked form that spoke to white consumers. With the growth of mass circulation magazines like Ladies' Home Journal, "spokesservants" like Aunt Jemima, Uncle Ben, and Rastus the Cream of Wheat man became nationally known figures.[80]

But Aunt Jemima was again unique, serving to her owners, white consumers, and by implication the nation her companionable help and her specially blended self-rising cakes. In her early ads, she simply said, "I'se In Town, Honey," implying that all whites could now have a mammy or at least a mammy-cooked breakfast. Aunt Jemima's owners, like those of the Gold Dust Twins, offered a spokesservant and a branded product that promised convenience to white middle-class homes increasingly without real servants. The national rise of Aunt Jemima in particular and the spokesservant in general, then, occurred as fewer white families outside the South could find or afford domestic help and as African American women made up a sharply increasing percentage of the dwindling number of domestic servants. For those southerners and many northerners who continued to employ domestic workers, Aunt Jemima embodied everything that a servant should be. Competent and capable and yet subservient and inferior, Aunt Jemima brought the romance of the old plantation into the most modern of white American homes. Serving up a white-figured blackness on her broad, black body and a soothing nostalgia with her pancakes, Aunt Jemima mammied the nation.[81]

A 1920 advertisement called "When the Robert E. Lee Stopped at Aunt

Jemima's Cabin" made her national service explicit. Drawing upon a biographic pamphlet published after her service in front of that giant flour barrel at the 1893 Chicago world's fair, the ad told the story of the birth of Aunt Jemima's pancake mix from the perspective of an elderly Confederate veteran. This old general had always remembered the place where he had eaten his best meal. During the war he and his orderly had become separated from the rest of the Confederate troops and were almost captured by Union forces. On their third day without food, in proper fairy-tale fashion, they stumbled across a cabin: "Ah can't express mah feelings of that mawnin when out o' that cabin came the sound of a mammy's voice and we heahd'er say sometin' about huh chilluns havin' an evahlastin' appetite fo' pancakes . . . The mammy seemed to guess ouah story." The Confederate and the mammy, of course, recognized each other immediately. "Hahrdly befoah we knew it she had us down at the table with big stacks o' pancakes in front of us. Just pancakes—that's all she had—but such pancakes they wuh! We leahrned aftwhahrds that the mammy was Aunt Jemima; befoah she was cook in the family of one Cun'l Higbee who owned a fine plantation . . ." Twenty years later, the general returned aboard the sidewheeler *Robert E. Lee* to see if Aunt Jemima, that embodiment of both the Old South and the "old-time Negro," remained in her cabin. The advertisement then staged, in the phrase of the historian Nina Silber, another "romance of reunion." The old general this time paid Aunt Jemima in gold pieces, and his generosity suggested he was paying her for not only her past and present pancakes but for the whole of her antebellum unpaid labor. Any past injustices, which Jemima of course had been too big to notice, were absolved in this exchange of coin. And the advertisement subtly linked the old southern white general and the old southern black mammy in other ways as well. Both spoke in dialect—Jemima's famous "I'se in town, honey" echoing the general's "fo' huh pancakes." Neither, however, could turn her recipe into a profitable national product.[82]

Shifting out of the dialect speech, the "legend" then insisted that a border state businessman accompanied the general on a second return visit to persuade Aunt Jemima to sell her secrets and to come to the Missouri flour mill to observe the preparation of a mix form. The pancakes had to travel north to become national products. Blacks, the ad emphasized, served southern whites, as in their varying ways New South boosters, the Atlanta fair, and Booker T. Washington had all suggested. And southern whites then in turn "served" northern whites, sharing their racial harmony and good

food with the rest of the nation in exchange for northern economic exper-
tise. Aunt Jemima had lost her comic minstrel trappings and become a nostalgic figure instead, the archetypal southern black mammy. She had also
regained a limited subjectivity, authoring her pancakes and their translation
into a national commodity and finally receiving payment. Yet this move
became doubly problematic. The advertisers had simply allowed their white
representation of blackness, a kaleidoscope of minstrelsy's mocking impersonations and a new southern white nostalgia and desire, to speak. As in the
white southern home, the black mammy promised wholeness, but the
image created a paradoxical unity, a joining of a white self with a black other
it had created. Past sectional animosities and present racial tensions dissolved in a steaming stack of Aunt Jemima's pancakes.[83]

The Gold Dust Twins, devoid of Aunt Jemima's deep southern resonances, could claim a more explicit national service and a global job as
well. In the same pamphlet where they affectionately signed themselves
"your servant," the twins' international motto appeared: "This earth will be
clean from zone to zone/ when the Gold Dust Twins are better known." In a
1910 billboard the N. K. Fairbank Company made this claim with the force
of foot-high letters: "Roosevelt Scoured Africa. The Gold Dust Twins Scour
America." Two black children could do the work at home, then, that ex-
President Theodore Roosevelt was famously performing abroad. But much
like the 1920 Aunt Jemima legend, this image granted its black figures a limited subjectivity while simultaneously containing this authorship within the
advertisement's frame. Following the light within the image, the white consumer's eye focused on the towering and golden figure of Roosevelt, toward
which an equally gigantic, left-foregrounded image of Uncle Sam reaches
out a hand in honor. The twins loom large as well, but they are of course following Roosevelt, playing the roles of both house-cleaning American pickaninnies and loyal African porters. The first twin carries Roosevelt's bags
while the second twin carries a gun. The gun too is Roosevelt's, and a huge
tiger carcass lies across its barrel, further subverting any chance of the twin's
making use of the weapon. Roosevelt's triumphant homecoming emphasizes that his job, written in the past tense, was done, while the twins' scour-
ing, unlike manly white adventure, can never be completed.

While white men worked for America, then, the Gold Dust Twins performed another double duty. The image depicted them serving the white
man in the figure of Roosevelt while the caption proclaimed they cleaned

the nation, materially and also increasingly metaphorically in the form of temperance and other Progressive era reforms, white women's responsibility. White women could command their dark servants at home while white men commanded dark natives abroad. Hovering high in the background, the Statue of Liberty looks not at the twins but directly out of the frame at the white consumer. Americans were people who could command the service of both blacks and consumer products. Advertising, both by picturing subservient blacks with products and celebrating whites as sovereign consumers, implicitly and explicitly figured the national consumer as white.[84]

By the late nineteenth century, most American whites, across a vast continent of differences, agreed that the freed people would not be included as subjects within the nation. There were many official watersheds—the 1877 compromise that ended Reconstruction, the Supreme Court's 1883 decision that judged the Civil Rights Act unconstitutional, and the 1896 *Plessy v. Ferguson* decision that federally sanctioned the practice of "separate but equal." But what kind of objects would these "free" African Americans be?

In the South many whites continued to see blacks as laborers. But freedom brought a significant change in whites' perception of black labor, alienating it as a commodity from black bodies. The mammy figure was perhaps the most powerful example, and for southern whites this figure acquired cultural values completely removed from black women's performance of domestic labor in white homes. And segregation welded old racial hierarchies to a rapidly changing world where some African Americans would prosper enough to achieve an economic status that transcended their supposed inferiority. Though he misjudged the extent to which economically successful blacks would threaten rather than make allies of many white southerners, Booker T. Washington understood that the payoff for blacks would be a greater access to consumer products. His "emblem of civilization" at Tuskegee, he claimed, in a 1900 article in *Century* magazine, was the humble toothbrush. Cleanliness and hygiene, Washington knew, signified middle-class status. But as advertisers spelled out with reference to some brands of soap, that toothbrush also promised the potential to wash out the stain of race.[85]

In the North the circulation of representations of blacks became another peculiar but profitable institution with many varieties of form. White-figured black images were hung both on the bodies of blackfaced white entertainers and on blackfaced African American ones and sold from

minstrel stages, in stereographic views, and at fairs. It was not surprising that
African Americans, long schooled at putting on masks for whites, proved
adept at performing these newest white impersonations of blacks as well.
But the use of black imagery in advertisements obliterated the problematic
subjectivities of the white and black actors who played minstrel characters.
Lithographed and printed images worked only for their white masters.
"Spokesservants" served their products, their companies, and all white
consumers who bought their products. Advertisers' black-figured iconography helped create an increasingly national market for branded and
mass-produced consumer products by constructing the consumer as white.
And this market, in turn, helped organize the one commonality that all
white consumers shared regardless of their class, regional, religious, or gender positions: their racial privilege. Whiteness became the homogenizing
ground of the American mass market.

An 1894–1895 calendar produced by Nestle's Baby Food summarized
this new figuration of national belonging. "Coming Events Cast their Shadows Before. To Insure a Successful Future 'Give the Babies Nestle's Food'"
scrolls above and below a row of babies swaddled in sacks hung on a line,
their futures symbolized by the objects on the shelf above. While the white
boys get to wear the hats of bankers, scholars, clergymen, soldiers, and kings,
white girls can at least claim the trappings of ladies and musicians. Only
over the black baby, turned away from the white consumer's gaze, does a
question mark shadow the future. Not even Nestle's, which replaced the
black mammy in nursing white children, could work miracles. African
Americans, after all, would not grow up to be American consumers.[86]

Shopping Between Slavery and Freedom: General Stores

Despite the fact that the new mass-produced commodities and advertising campaigns were often created in the North, then, white southerners
between 1890 and 1940 had little cause to complain about the figurations of
blackness that appeared in pictures on labels, names of products, images on
trade cards and signs, and advertisements in magazines. Instead, the problems of the southern white purveyors of the new mass culture ran almost in

the opposite direction. Creating a mass audience through racial othering, constructing the consumer as white, was much more problematic in the South where African Americans made up a large part of the possible market for any mass product from soap to sodas to movies. For commercial enterprises to be successful, outside of the largest southern cities where African Americans were able to develop their own commercial districts, these businesses often depended upon African American customers. Besides Coca-Cola, white southerners created and marketed few of the new mass products. Instead, southern whites attempted to assert control over the growing places of consumption within the region. In 1909 the white southern minister and reformer Edgar Gardner Murphy perceptively outlined the connectedness of an expansive consumption and racial ordering: "Ours is a world of inexorable divisions. Segregation has made of our eating and drinking, our buying and selling . . . a problem of race as well as maintenance." Murphy, however, got the causation backward. Racial separation followed those train tracks from the cities into the countryside, promising a new, standardized racial order even as more localized race relations and markets were transformed. The answer to the problem of consumption in the South, then, was segregation.[87]

But even before the 1890s when white racial "moderates" proposed segregation as the answer to the region's "Negro Problem," country stores were already exposing even the most rural southerners to the quick and glittery promises of the North's consumer culture. General stores, like train stations, wore disguises. Often staked by northern manufacturers and distributors who loaned money to promising young white men who had located the right railroad stop or crossroads, country stores masqueraded as indigenous southern economic development. At the center of life in the turn-of-the-century South, general stores were more than places for picking up local gossip, kerosene, and lard or for chewing tobacco and local politics around spattered stoves. With all their folksy charm, in the years immediately after the Civil War and especially by the 1890s, country stores were the entry points into the region for the new northern ways of selling, the stage upon which many southerners first encountered the new branded items with their colorful packaging, collectible trade cards, and eye-catching outdoor signs.[88]

Soap and patent medicines were the first heavily advertised products widely available across the region. The historian Susan Atherton Hanson undertook a detailed examination of store inventories in Maryland and Virginia and found branded soap available as early as 1879. Popular early brands sold at country stores included Fairy, Venus, Rosadora, Pear's, P and G Blue, and White Clover. Manufacturers and distributors hastened the conversion from homemade to store-bought soaps by offering trade cards and colorful booklets to those southerners who purchased the products from enticing countertop displays. As early as 1875, brightly hued patent medicine advertisements began to cover southern trees, barns, and the stores themselves, promising relief from every pain. Storekeepers made large profits in the late nineteenth century selling Dr. McLean's Strengthening Cordial, Lydia E. Pinkham's famous formulas, Thedford's Black Draught, McElree's Wine of Cardui, Jones' Mountain Herbs, Peruna, Electric Bitters, Carter's Little Liver Pills, King of Malaria, and Fletcher's Castoria for health complaints ranging from women's "private ailments" to fevers, constipation, and colic. Branded hair pomade also appeared on store shelves, claiming to give every African American woman long and fluffy strands in place of her string-wound rolls of hair.[89]

Although the Pure Food and Drug Act cut patent medicine sales in the twentieth century, by the 1890s many more branded products had joined the general store's ever broadening array of goods. Wholesalers and storekeepers pushed rural customers into purchasing the more profitable prepackaged products in household sizes. Laundry products especially accelerated the substitution of homemade goods with store-bought items. Another important category was tobacco, and the branding of tobacco plugs began as early as 1870. Popular early names included Johnny Reb, Rebel Girl, Rebel Boy, Confederate, Sunny Hours, Stud Horse, Blood Hound, and Good and Tough. With the rise of the Populists, Free Silver and Legal Tender appeared. As fewer manufacturers began to dominate the market, Brown Mule, RJR, and Seal of North Carolina pushed out competitors. Bull Durham became the most popular pipe tobacco, promoted with gifts to storekeepers and customers of razors, clocks, hammocks, striped couches, and soaps. Prepackaged foodstuffs like crackers, sardines, and oysters were commonly sold by the late nineteenth century. Flour sacks and barrels bore the images of banjos, possums, Egyptian obelisks, and smiling black men, promoting brands like Homeland, Mama's Pride, Spread Eagle, White Lily, and Sunny Side. By 1900, branded food and household convenience products including Campbell's Soup, Libby's Potted Meats, and Argo Starch dominated store inventories.[90]

General stores, of course, did not just display the clashingly colored and enticingly packaged branded items. They also sold them, often to the region's poorest consumers. But one aspect of southern life endured across the rapidly changing region between 1890 and 1940. In *Light in August,* William Faulkner stages what must have been a frequent collision between the scarcity experienced by many southerners and the abundance embodied by the general store.

For "money and excitement," Lucas Bunch has left, Lena Grove insists, not her but the place, despite the fact that she is pregnant. To stay would only be to put off the going. It is the sort of small southern sawmill town a person would leave, its rural past, modern present, and rusting and desolate future visible at a glance. Lena is the white, orphaned daughter of share-croppers, alone except for the coming child, and when her lover does not send for her she sets out to walk from Alabama to Mississippi after him. But along the way she finds money herself when a middle-aged farm woman taking pity gives Lena the egg money earned by long trading of the fragile commodities for tiny hard coins. When the farm woman's husband carries the then heavy Lena in his wagon to the country store to catch a ride into the town proper, she finds excitement too. Lena has taken little of the woman's food, though she did take her handkerchief-knotted wealth: " 'I et polite,' she thinks, her hands lying upon the bundle, knowing the hidden coins, remembering the single cup of coffee, the decorous morsel of strange bread; thinking with a sort of serene pride: 'Like a lady I et. Like a lady traveling. But now I can buy sardines too if I should so wish.' " "Travers[ing] the ranked battery of maneyes," she enters the store: " 'I'm a-going to do it,' she thinks, even while ordering the cheese and crackers; 'I'm a-going to do it,' saying aloud: 'And a box of sardines.' " And she eats her extravagant purchases "slowly, steadily, sucking the rich sardine oil from her fingers with slow and complete relish." Lena with her sardines embodies both the sensuality and pleasure of consumption and the strictures against a decadent and wasteful indulgence. This juxtaposition permeated experiences of shopping across both time and space in the region between 1890 and 1940.[91]

For many, the sights, smells, and imagined tastes of the shelves piled high and the floor overrun with the multihued and shiny goods and the pungently enticing foods presented a temptation difficult to bear. But most southerners did not find themselves the recipients of a stranger's hoarded coin. From the Reconstruction era through the Great Depression, money was scarce. The country store became the central economic institution across the region at the turn of the century and in the most rural areas through 1940 by inventing a way for people to shop locally without money. Country merchants were able to sell the new branded products because they supplied credit along with sardines, soap, and tobacco. Southern storekeepers, then, sat at the juncture of the urban North and the rural South, occupying the dual roles of banker and merchant as well.

As banker, the storekeeper ended most consuming fantasies like Lena's by saying no to the extension of credit for the purchase of items deemed beyond the customer's means. Despite the northern manufacturers' and distributors' motto of "a store within reach of every cabin in the South," there was little chance of burying the region in a hedonistic wash of buying run amuck. Both white and black southerners could only purchase on their general store accounts what the storekeeper approved. And for many African American and white tenants and sharecroppers, consumption was doubly mediated. Not only the storekeepers but the owners of the farms they worked controlled their buying, although in many localities the same white man often served as storekeeper, creditor, and landowner. Tenants and croppers always needed the boss's approval and often his literary abilities to write up store orders the merchants would accept. Successful storekeepers, depending not just on current sales but also on future payment, managed the encounter between scarcity and abundance, need and desire, with a delicate and practiced hand. Though many storekeepers had not been planters, through the general store a new way of business reinforced an older localized white male authority. At least through the early twentieth century, trains broke down some local southern social relations even as they supplied the goods that helped merchants reconstitute others.[92]

General stores also solved the problem of inscribing racial difference within consumption by combining the old racial inferiority of plantations and paternalism within the new consuming world. Storekeepers to a large degree controlled what African American southerners bought with their limited credit and rarer cash. African American storekeepers were rare, and even in predominantly black areas white men often tended the stores. These white merchants in conjunction with the white landholders who wrote up store orders for their tenants marked the color line in poor-quality goods. A black man who needed clothing received a shirt "good enough for a darky to wear" while a black family low on provisions could have only the lowest grade of flour. Storekeepers also controlled the rituals of deference through which blacks were forced to make their purchases. African Americans often had to wait until all whites were served to take whatever grade of cornmeal, molasses, or sidemeat clerks would give them. The pioneering African American economist Paul K. Edwards reported in 1932 that African Americans often demanded brand-name products in order to acquire quality goods.

Even so, country stores were places of racial mixing, and southern African Americans faced less discrimination there than at the courthouse or polling place. In many parts of the rural South, the fact that whites and blacks purchased many of the same items in the same stores subverted an ideology of absolute white supremacy. The personal authority of the storekeeper, then, eased the contradictions through his control over both his white and black customers' buying.[93]

General stores became the central institution in the economic and cultural transformations of the late nineteenth- and early twentieth-century South. They inserted the new branded consumer products and their associated advertising directly into the old white ways of local communities. Stores competed with churches as places of socializing and often won. Both white and black women and men shopped frequently in country stores, and children marked their coming of age by being allowed to go on an errand to the store alone. The seats around the stove, however—though not usually the benches on the porch—seemed at certain times reserved for white men. Though never tolerated as equals, black men could sometimes listen while sitting on a barrel or crate apart from the central group.

The cyclical visits of the various drummers were often such times of male communion. Salesmen for the wholesale houses who traveled from the large border cities throughout the rural South, the drummers told bawdy stories of their alleged frolics with farmers' daughters in other towns as well as their exploits with more experienced city women. These salesmen turned stove-side storytelling into a subtle form of information gathering and product advertising. Many used their real or imagined pasts as Confederate soldiers to persuade both the merchant and his customers, often veterans or the sons of veterans themselves, to purchase products. According to the historian Thomas D. Clark, "[i]f a drummer lacked the technique of maneuvering the Confederate army and his line of goods into a strategic position to mow down a cornfield full of Yankees and stubborn sales resistance," then he had to rely on vigorous political and religious discussions. Another popular technique, the telling of "Negro" and "Irish" dialect stories picked up by the drummer in the border state cities where the wholesale houses had their headquarters, welded local southern storytelling traditions to the particular racialized images of the newly expansive advertising. General stores housed not only a complicated inventory of goods but a complex geography of human relations as well, providing an embodiment of consumer abundance, integrated shopping, and segregated socializing all under the same small roof.[94]

Yet African American consumers coexisted uneasily with representations of blacks within advertising and their echoes in white drummers' stories. Both idioms figured southern African Americans as objects and not subjects of consuming desires. And drummers did not just promote sales by word of mouth. They also blanketed store walls with their signs, gave storekeepers trade cards to hand out with purchases, and shipped goods in eye-catching and message-laden displays. Southern country stores served as the most important places for advertising in the rural South. In late-1930s photographs taken for the Farm Security Administration, they sit covered with advertisements, both inside and out. In a 1938 Russell Lee photo, the white owner of a general store stands slicing bologna in front of a shelf displaying, among other products, boxes of Aunt Jemima cornmeal. But racist advertisements and stereotypical black "spokesservants" crafted in the Northeast often competed in general stores with more homegrown racist horrors. Displays of souvenir body parts and picture postcards from lynchings were especially popular. A store in Center, Texas, even printed a trade card in 1908 with a lynching poem and photograph. Thus storekeepers created their own black-figured displays as well, and some stores took on the character of informal museums, displaying blackness and other local oddities along with their goods.[95]

Thus even as they sold goods to African American customers, storekeepers participated in the sale and display of racial otherness that was so central to the creation of mass products at the national level. In the country store, however, the storekeeper's doubled role as merchant and banker mediated these contradictions. For the competition in the country store trade was not so much between stores as between the wholesale houses fighting over shelf space on the one hand and the customers struggling to gain credit at the counter on the other. Customers, for the most part, had few convenient shopping options. African American tenants and croppers usually had to make their purchases where their landlord dictated at whatever terms offered. Especially in the twentieth century, better-off southern whites could shop with cash in the larger villages and towns while better-off blacks by definition lived in more urban areas. But in rural regions general stores with their often integrated clienteles flourished through the late 1930s, despite such countermoves as a call for racial separation in stores that formed a part of a campaign for total rural segregation waged between 1913 and 1915 by editor Clarence Poe and his popular *Progressive Farmer* magazine. In FSA photographs from the late 1930s, country or general stores remain sites of integrated shopping and overlapping if segregated socializing. A Jack Delano shot of a store in Fort Bragg, North Carolina, suggests that the only things that had changed in southern stores were a larger inventory of prepackaged foodstuffs and the rules of personal hygiene. A sign over the black and white shoppers commands, "if you have to spit on the floor, go home to do it." The country storekeepers had the power and incentive to mediate as well as promote consumption, and thus their stores remained racially mixed sites of advertising, socializing, and wonder.[96]

Carson McCullers's *Ballad of the Sad Cafe*, originally published in *Harper's Bazaar* in 1936, portrays just what a store could bring to the rural South beyond branded soap, flour, and tobacco. "Miss Amelia," a rare white woman storekeeper who in typical fashion has inherited the trade from a relative, her father, dabbles in commercial ventures from landholding to moonshining and by the village's account is wealthy. Originally her store "carried mostly feed, guano, and staples such as meal and snuff" and catered to an all-white mill village and the African Americans who lived on its fringes. But as its function as a place of socializing began to eclipse its function as a purveyor of general merchandise, Miss Amelia's place became more of a cafe instead. White men drink her bootleg whiskey, women a Nehi and even a swallow of the harder stuff, and children a penny-a-glass drink called Cherry Juice that Miss Amelia also mixes up herself. Besides the dinners cheaper crackers and candy are also available.[97]

Miss Amelia's place soon becomes "the warm center of the town," and its attraction goes beyond its "decorations," "brightness," and "warmth." "This deeper reason," "a certain pride that had not hitherto been known in these parts," has to do with the "cheapness of human life" in that isolated village: "There were always plenty of people clustered around a mill—but it was seldom that every family had enough meal, garments, and fatback to go the rounds. Life could become one long dim scramble just to get the things

needed to keep alive . . . often after you have sweated and tried and things
are not better for you, there comes a feeling deep down in the soul that you
are not worth much." But the cafe brings "a new pride" to the town for the
cost of the spare pennies that all the villagers can lay aside from time to
time: "There, for a few hours at least, the deep and bitter knowing that you
are not worth much in this world could be laid low." Of course, this pride is
not readily available to the blacks who, denied mill employment, live in an
even deeper poverty than the whites. Forced to take their purchases outside
the cafe for enjoyment, they are also denied belonging to the community
that grows up around its commerce. But for the mill families what the store
brings to town becomes more than Lena Grove's "excitement and money."
Before, white people have met at the church or the mill, but they "were
then unused to gathering together for the sake of pleasure." When the cafe
closes, there is "absolutely nothing to do in the town . . . the soul rots with
boredom." McCullers illuminates how stores founded identities and communities even as they supplied goods.[98]

The country store welded the colorful carnivalesque messages of early
advertising with the close-knit communities of the rural South and brought
a sensuous and pleasurable abundance, visible and at least partially ac-
quirable, to most rural southerners. Unlike the national advertisers, white
storekeepers considered blacks profitable customers. But African Americans
held a marginal place at best in the new consuming communities that lit up
white rural life around the country stores where both races shopped. In the
general store, the local racial and class authority of the storekeeper largely
maintained the racial order. Storekeepers had everything to gain and nothing
to lose in asserting a flexible, nonexclusionary, and yet white-commanded
shopping community. Black-figured advertising was not irrelevant in promoting white desire for consumer goods but in the often poor rural South,
desire for more needed little stimulation. General stores mediated the
effects of the new northern consumer culture upon the region by associating its embodiment of the new abundance of both goods and entertainment
with local white community life.

But by the late nineteenth century both white and black rural southerners had access to another shopping alternative, one that paradoxically both
brought that abundance home and also disembodied it, the mail-order catalog. Called the "Farmer's Friend," "the Nation's largest supply house," "a
Consumer Guide," "a city shopping district at your fingertips," and the

"world's largest country store," by the late nineteenth century the catalogs of the Chicago-based Montgomery Ward and Sears and Roebuck made their way into many southern homes. A white Georgia farm woman mentioned its presence in her 1906 rural home with little fanfare, noting in her diary that she had used her telephone to place an order for her white neighbor. The thick books' beguiling pictures and enticing descriptions of goods made images of one thousand general store inventories readily available, no doubt stretching many southerners' consuming imaginations and desires. Customers could thumb through and gawk at the offerings at will, unconstrained by the country store's complicated social geographies and crowded interior and by the eyes of merchants, clerks, and friends. Mail-order catalogs multiplied consuming possibilities for southerners and, along with the U.S. Post Office's 1898 institution of rural free delivery (RFD), made shopping a more private affair.[99]

In the South mail order both erased the problem of integrated shopping and created racial contradictions. Sears's and Montgomery Ward's catalogs forced consumption back into what whites conceived as the already racially ordered spaces of the home where an even more local white male power, the rule of the father, could mediate other family members' consuming desires. In practice, however, purchases were as often made under the direction of white women as men, and the desire to own the pictured goods was held in check as much by the lack of cash as by any gendered exercise of control. Though catalog customers did not reveal their racial identities, African Americans with any access to cash must have enjoyed the opportunity to purchase needed goods without enduring local store rituals of racial deference and white storekeepers' belief that the poorest-quality products were all they deserved. And mail order enabled white and black southerners with money to choose from an exponentially greater array of products, beyond the bounds of the storekeeper and his family's particular tastes and the weight of other community members' most frequent choices. Catalogs brought an individuality to consumption, lifting some southerners above the local geographies of power and identity that positioned shopping at the general store where almost everyone was known. The disembodiment of the products—the goods now flattened, their smells erased, their glitter muted by the two-dimensional pages—mirrored the detachment of shopping from the country store's localized community of consumption. Catalog shoppers had entered a much more national if much less tangible market indeed.[100]

The new mail-order firms understood that potential customers might experience anxiety conducting what had been very personal relations of exchange with faraway and faceless companies. Addressing his customers as "personal friends," Montgomery Ward wrote his catalog's copy himself in an "amateur, folksy vernacular" designed to arrest the fears and stimulate the purchases of mail-order shoppers. Pioneering the promise of "satisfaction guaranteed or your money back," he offered a display of trust in his customers that he hoped they would reciprocate. Richard Sears began his early catalogs with a personal letter designed to set would-be consumers at ease: "Don't be afraid that you will make a mistake. We receive hundred of orders every day from young and old who never sent away for goods . . . Tell us what you want, in your own way, written in any language, no matter whether good or poor writing, and your goods will be promptly sent to you." Sears also mimicked the general stores' groundedness into local communities with the national expansion of its 1905 "Iowaization" scheme. Under this plan, pioneered in the Midwest, current customers were urged to send Sears the names of family and friends who had not yet received the Sears catalog. The company then paid each customer who sent in a name a premium if the new catalog recipient ordered any goods. In return, Sears received both new customers and local endorsers. Sears and Montgomery Ward attempted to counter consumers' fears of the unknown, even as they conjured new wants.[101]

Yet by disembodying consumer desire, mail order created new possibilities for consuming transgressions. Country storekeepers fought back by asserting their local power and attempting to heighten fears of outsiders. Before the initiation of RFD in 1898, storekeepers who were also postmasters refused to sell money orders, write up purchase requests, or sell stamps to customers who still owed on store accounts. After 1898 Sears countered by advising catalog shoppers who lived on rural routes to "just give the letter and the money to the mail carrier and he will get the money order at the post office and mail it in the letter for you." After the passage of the new parcel post laws in 1913 and 1920, catalog customers did not even have to go to the post office, often inside country stores, to pick up medium-sized packages.[102]

Some storekeepers gave in and contented themselves with the profit made by lending customers money at interest to make mail-order purchases. Other southern merchants, along with their midwestern colleagues, resorted to more desperate measures like sponsoring bonfires and handing out prizes to those who turned in the catalogs for burning. Exploiting the very disembodiment that enabled catalogs to be the personal friends of very different customers across the nation, local storekeepers circulated rumors that Sears and Ward were blacks and that they sold by mail because "these fellows could not afford to show their faces as retailers." Sears published photographs to prove the whiteness of its founders while Ward countered with reward offers for the name of the person who had started the rumor that he was a mulatto. Although local southern merchants' actions had little effect on catalog sales, they did reveal the racial anxieties that permeated the continuing expansion of consumption. Catalogs placed the consuming practices of blacks beyond local white knowledge and control. Few southern African Americans had the means to buy much from catalogs. But the possibility that some distant merchant might make money off local blacks or that an African American might try to be uppity by purchasing products similar to or better than the things owned by his white neighbors excited white fears and sometimes white violence. Money and white supremacy were both at stake. Outside of the localized geography of shopping at the general store, southern whites found the potential racial contradictions of consumption much more difficult to control. Markets, mail-order catalogs proved, could, like trains, cross the boundaries of the local racial settlements, but securing white identity in these expanding sites of consumption would prove much more difficult than labeling the spaces of transportation "for colored" and "for white."[103]

Segregation Signs:
Racial Disorder in the Southern Market

On a cool afternoon in 1935 in the small town of Huntingdon, Tennessee, a not yet unusual public spectacle took place. A pitchman for an unnamed but no doubt magically healing elixir set up his medicine show off the town's Main Street in an alleyway by a warehouse. Besides his bottles and vials he had the usual accompaniments, three worn assistants arrayed in once crowd-catching but now frayed attire. Medicine shows, much like the pitchman himself, had seen better days. Modern versions of the peddlers, those nineteenth-century icons of salesmanship, the pitchmen then plied their trade only in marginal towns, beyond the reach of the Federal Pure Food and Drug Act and the New Deal reformers pushing for its strengthening. "The thing about pitching medicine is to make a fuss, and in any bunch of men you draw, half are going to have aches and pains," claimed a patent medicine salesman in a Federal Writers Project (FWP) interview. And in the photographs of Farm Security Administration photographer Ben Shahn, this pitchman in Huntingdon is certainly making a fuss.[104]

In these images Shahn conveys a stark vision of the overlapping interdependence of market and racial identities in such selling, and the ambiguity of peddling blackness to an integrated mass of potential customers. For the pitchman's assistants, in the well-grooved minstrel borrowings of the medicine show tradition, are an Indian-faced white man, a blackfaced black man, and a display dummy much like the advertised "Topsey" in everything except his striped and shabby dress. The blackfaced black man's facial expressions seem to project his lack of enthusiasm for the performance, his sense that the dummy would do just as well in wearing the white-created blackness the pitchman required. The photographs do not show either the Indian or black versions of white racial fantasies speaking, and the men's stiff postures and stillness within the busy photographs' frames heighten an elision between the real men and the dummy's masquerades. An exotic Indian wisdom and the boundary-crossing appeal of a black man portraying a white man performing a black, himself replaced at times by a dummy double, are offered to stimulate consumption of the unnamed elixir. In one frame, a sort of live and bedraggled trade card, the pitchman explicitly links the transformative fantasies associated with both racial masquerade and patent medicines by holding the product in one hand and the dummy in the other. In a border state in the twilight of the peddling era, a pitchman sells a potion on the edge of legality by attempting to orchestrate yet another white staging of racial desire.[105]

In his FWP interview, a patent medicine salesman had emphasized his lack of responsibility, that "people believe what they want to believe." Despite the tired tawdriness of the Tennessee show, the pitchman there too, like the national advertisers, must have at some point thought that this display was what the people, understood as white, wanted. The most interesting aspect of the Shahn photographs, however, is that they depict an integrated audience, despite the edgy spaces and body language that slightly divided some men from others. How African Americans in such situations responded to the manipulations of racial representations is difficult to determine. Did they just come for the medicine show entertainment, described by the pitchman Nevada Ned in a 1929 *Saturday Evening Post* interview as including anything from "full evenings of drama, vaudeville, musical comedy, Wild West shows, minstrels, magic, burlesque, dog and pony circuses" to "Punch and Judy, pantomime, movies, menagerie, bands, parades, and pie-eating contests"? Certainly African Americans, like white southerners, purchased patent medicines. One of Nevada Ned's more profitable ventures, he claimed, was selling liver pads to blacks in Wilmington, North Carolina.[106]

But how did African Americans respond to the use of black-figured imagery in the advertising used to sell less exotic products? Paul K. Edwards's 1932 study insisted that most African Americans in southern cities rarely saw advertisements other than the ones for patent medicines, race records, and toiletries specifically designed for black use. In a detailed examination of a small sample of African Americans in Richmond and Nashville divided evenly by gender and class, Edwards found that about half would not purchase Aunt Jemima pancake flour after viewing an advertisement featuring the bandanna-clad pancake mammy and her cabin. Black consumers also disliked the black-figured advertising used by Cream of Wheat and Fairbank's Gold Dust Powder. In particular, informants did not like "those original twins," calling them "disgusting," "a caricature," and "ridiculous," "not a true picture of Negroes and used to get attention of whites." Middle-class African Americans in particular were outraged at the presentation of African Americans in national advertisements.

In 1930 Nannie Burroughs, a black leader from Washington, D.C., put her opinion more emphatically in the *Philadelphia Tribune*: "The Gold Dust Twins, Aunt Jemima, and Amos and Andy have piled up millions for two business concerns and two white men. Aunt Jemima and the Gold Dust Twins cook and wash dishes while Amos and Andy broadcast subtle and mischievous propaganda against Negro business. They tell the world that when it comes to business the Negro is a huge joke and a successful failure." By then most whites had already seen countless black-figured advertisements on trade cards handed out at general stores, on labels and packaging, on store displays, and in newspapers and magazines for over four decades. And despite Edwards's findings, African Americans must have seen them at general stores too, in the white homes where many African American women worked as domestics, and in the national magazines. Yet for blacks facing a rising tide of discriminatory laws and lingering racial violence, the racist caricatures in advertising must have seemed relatively tame. Created by and for whites, the racial messages of advertising contradicted many white southerners' experience of consumption, a tension that only increased as the center of the geography of southern consumption shifted toward town.[107]

As the twentieth century progressed, southern towns and cities grew, and many white and black southerners no longer lived in a locally inscribed world centered on a general store where everyone was known. Commerce increasingly depended more on cash than on white storekeepers' extensions of credit. Face-to-face selling in a more competitive cash market could be as anonymous and difficult to contain as catalog buying. And the contradictions between using a white-produced blackness to sell products and the need for black customers became both more acute and more visible. The small-town, small-city South, then, sat on a continuum between general stores where all parties were known and the very different anonymities of the old peddlers and the new mail-order houses. And white southerners continued to pass segregation laws and paint signs. The market's disruptions, it seemed, took racial as well as economic form.[108]

Though the day of the week was not recorded, the Tennessee medicine show probably happened on a Saturday afternoon, when the pitchman would be sure to catch the most folks in town. No women appear in the crowds Shahn photographed, perhaps because this method of selling retained something of minstrelsy's bawdy origins. But the ritual of Saturday afternoon shopping belonged to all southerners as black and white, middle-class and poor, men and women crowded into towns. Described both critically and fondly, by reporters, writers of memoirs, and scholars, Saturday afternoons in commercial districts were the most integrated times and spaces in southern life.[109]

The white journalist Rebecca Latimer Felton ranted about just this mixing in her *Atlanta Journal* column in 1901: "Between politics and the Bible there is no lack of discussion in the Saturday gatherings . . . The towns fairly swarm with idle men and boys [of both races] on Saturday afternoons, and the 'colored ladies' are not far off, if there is any money in the pockets of these idlers, or if their credit is good enough to obtain an 'order' on a store for dry goods and sundries." Perhaps not wanting to criticize the white farm women who were her column's most loyal readers, she did not mention the white women who no doubt were also there enjoying Saturday afternoons in town. Revealing her sense of the racial threat represented, Felton continued, "Last Saturday night a disorderly gang [of black men] passed along our road firing pistol and making outcries . . . rousing us from sound sleep to ask what good these Saturday gatherings are doing for the country?" A reader of Felton's column, a white farm woman named Magnolia LeGuin, voiced a similar anxiety about the racial mixing that occurred in towns. In 1908, on her twelve-year-old son Askew's first visit to the town of Barnesville, Georgia, she recorded in her diary that he had fought a young black boy: "The little negro asked him [Askew] if he was a *white* boy." She and her husband had laughed at a postcard Askew wrote about the incident. But her comments also revealed a guilty unease behind the joke: "I guess the negro said it with impudence, or at least Askew thought so, 'tho Askew is tolerably dark and there are *white* negroes in cities." In the early twentieth century for many whites, the town, even more than the localized world anchored in the general store, seemed a place of racial and consuming seductions.[110]

By the 1930s, however, going to town had become routinized for most southerners of both races, and the new racial order of segregation had expanded to order systematically the spaces of consumption that in many places had outgrown the limits of personal authority and local customs. The white sociologist John Dollard, investigating a black belt Mississippi town in 1935 and 1936, described this shopping and socializing in a more even tone: "Saturday is by all odds the big day of the week. In the summer the stores are open all afternoon and evening . . . The country Negroes mill through the streets and talk excitedly, buying and enjoying the stimulation of the town crowds. The country whites are paler and less vivacious [than the town whites]; there are not so many of them, but still a considerable number." The African American sociologist Charles S. Johnson discovered in the late 1930s a similar mixing of blacks and whites in southern cities and towns. In his 1931 novel *Sanctuary*, William Faulkner adds rich detail to the sociologists' accounts in his fictional description of racial mixing and small-town shopping:

> [I]t was Saturday . . . To the left [the street] went on into the square, the opening between two buildings black with a slow, continuous throng, like two streams of ants, above which the cupola of the courthouse rose from a clump of locusts and oaks . . . Empty wagons still passed him and he passed still more women on foot, black and white, unmistakable by the

> unease of their garments as well as by their method of walking, believing
> town dwellers would take them for town dwellers too, not even fooling one
> another . . . The adjacent alleys were choked with tethered wagons . . . The
> square was lined two-deep with ranked cars, while the owners of them and
> of the wagons thronged in slow overalls and khaki, in mail-order scarves
> and parasols, in and out of stores . . .

As Faulkner's account reveals, automobiles had joined the wagons, becoming the last eraser of local boundaries and accelerating the magical process by which on Saturdays the countryside seemed to empty out into the towns.[111]

The commercial geography of 1930s southern towns, the business districts that served many white and black southerners, closely matched in content if not exact layout the "Southerntown" Dollard had described: "A square block of buildings and the four streets around it make up the business district." Businesses there included department stores and drugstores where white customers could "receive courteous curb service . . . and the cold shock of a 'coke' in the throat" without leaving the car. Other enterprises included white law offices serving both white and black patrons and a small hotel and restaurant. Stores serving only African Americans but rarely owned by them lined another street. Somewhat isolated from the other commerce, "a small industrial section devoted to ginning cotton and pressing cotton seed" sat at the edge of the commercial district. A movie theater, "white downstairs and colored in the gallery, with separate entrances" completed the town.[112]

But while the white northerner Dollard stressed the separations, the African American Johnson emphasized the racial mixing. "Negroes," he claimed, were "served in all the business establishments of the towns visited for this study, except in cafés, barbershops, beauty parlors, and some amusement places. Grocery and dry-goods stores depend as much on the Negro buying public as on the white . . ." Despite northern manufacturers' and advertisers' conception of the abstract consumer as white, then, southern consumers came in a multitude of hues. The elaboration of state laws and codes that began with the late nineteenth-century battles over railroads, Johnson found, had created "no uniform pattern of segregation and discrimination" in "private commercial establishments": "Legal codes do not deny Negroes access to such establishments except where eating is involved, nor

guarantee him the privileges usually accorded the white public . . . The
policies of stores vary widely, as do the relations between [white] clerks and
Negro patrons. One generalization can be made: In the interracial situation
in trade relations there is constant uncertainty." Commerce depended,
then, upon a great deal of white denial over the contradictions between
market incentives and segregation's linkage of white supremacy to superior
white spaces.[113]

Farm Security Administration photographs captured this tension
between segregation's claims of absolute racial ordering and the racial
messiness of consumer culture in places that depended upon both white
and black customers. In the late 1930s, after the director Roy Stryker shifted
the project's focus to southern town life, photographers took hundreds of
pictures of the shopping districts of small towns and small cities across the
region. Marion Post Wolcott's 1939 photographs of Saturday afternoons in
Clarkesdale and Belzoni, Mississippi, and Greensboro, Georgia, depict
integrated crowds. In Clarkesdale a heterogeneous group of black and white
men, women, and children mix under store awnings and seep out onto the
sidewalk at a downtown street corner. In Belzoni, across from the A & P and
in front of Turner's Rexall Drugs, a crowd of blacks sit, stand, and visit,
backed by a small knot of young white men, while three white women lean
on the window front to the right. In Lexington, Mississippi, whites sell
apples from the edge of the courthouse lawn across from a street of stores as
whites and blacks walk by on the sidewalk. In Yanceyville, North Carolina,
on a 1939 Saturday afternoon, white and black men lounge outside W. H.
Hooper and Son Groceries, Feed Stuff, Meat, and Country Produce, while
a white woman and child look on from inside a parked car. Racial separation was difficult to maintain on the crowded sidewalks and squares and
under store porches during these ritualistic Saturday afternoon trips to
town.[114]

Wolcott's set of Greensboro images provide even more detail. A closeup
frames two small groups of black women, men, and children socializing on
benches under the authoritative glare of a policeman painted onto the
bricks of the Hunter's drugstore building and commanding "Drink Coca-
Cola, Pure as Sunlight—Go Refreshed." A second shot opens up to set the
benches on an alley off a busy commercial street filled with white and black
shoppers. In another of Wolcott's images of Saturday afternoon in Greensboro, a white woman with her child encounters two young black women as

all three shop at a grocery store for their weekly provisions. And white men, women, and children mix with African American men, women, and children under the awning of the "Home-Owned" "Western Auto Associate Store" in Starke, Florida, in a December 1940 Wolcott photograph. When Jack Delano visited Greensboro, Georgia, over two years after Wolcott, he repeated Wolcott's closeup and wider view approach and photographed different corners with similarly integrated crowds. Delano also shot white and black shoppers outside J. H. Dolven Company's store in Siloam, Georgia, on a Saturday afternoon while Dorothea Lange photographed a white woman selling appliquéd embroideries on a Saturday sidewalk shared with multihued southerners. Certainly, whites and blacks must have connected. Two black boys swerve to make way for a white women carrying a baby and leading a child as a drugstore advertisement touts both Philco radios and Livor-Kaps in a Wolcott photograph taken in Wendell, North Carolina, in November 1939. For many white and black southerners, then, Saturday afternoons in town replaced the consuming communities centered around the general stores. Cyclically reconstituted, overlapping and yet segregated gatherings of family and friends occupied a shared geography of consumption that belied any absolute racial difference.[115]

Despite the culture of segregation, whites and blacks mixed in the shopping districts of 1930s small towns. Signs blared "For Colored" and "For White" on the very streets in which blacks and whites mingled. The intimacy of touching lips to water, for example, attracted the particular attention of white southerners. In a 1938 photograph by John Vachon a black boy finishes his drink at a fountain on the side lawn of the courthouse in Halifax, North Carolina, as the huge sign affixed to an adjacent tree proclaims his race. At Bethlehem-Fairfield Shipyards in Baltimore, a drinking fountain is again racially marked, this time white. At a tobacco warehouse in Lumberton, North Carolina, the fountains and the racial signs stand side by side, and the black man and the white boy drinking indicate their racial identities even as they quench their thirsts. Of course, no sales were at stake here — water was free. Public restrooms offered a space for performing the most private activities and like water fountains offered nothing for sale. Their signs, the condition of their facilities, and the convenience of access shouted out the racial worth of their users. At a bus station in Durham, North Carolina, the "White Ladies Only" restroom faces out on a busy commercial street, its sign signifying not only race but the associated difference whites asserted within womanhood. "Colored Women," no doubt, had to hunt down an alleyway or go behind the station.[116]

Consuming food combined a similar touching of the product to lips and the intimate routines of human maintenance. Because they made public the decidedly home-centered rituals of eating, cafes, restaurants, and diners usually served only one race. Jack Delano took a May 1940 photograph of an exception, "A cafe near the tobacco market" in Durham, North Carolina, where customers pass through separate, clearly marked "white" and "colored" doors to similarly marked tables inside, proclaiming the centrality of racial difference to Durham life for all to see. More typical was "Bryant's Place" for "Hot Fish" in Memphis, Tennessee, its window advertising "for colored" in a 1937 Dorothea Lange photograph. Unusual was the "Choke 'Em Down Lunch Room" in Belle Glade, Florida, built precariously on pilings over a marsh, its sign advertising hot and cold lunches, cold drinks, and "whites and colored served" in a 1939 Wolcott image. Whether the dining space inside the tiny shack was segregated, Wolcott's photograph does not reveal.[117]

Watching movies was a close and sedentary social experience, and theaters were carefully ordered, usually, as Dollard described, with whites downstairs and African Americans in the "too hot or too cold" balcony. Like the cafe in Durham, theaters also had separate entrances, a well-lighted and inviting front door for whites, a side alley and often dark doorway for blacks. Delano shot the white front and black side entrances of a theater in Greensboro, Georgia. In some places, however, whites designated only part of the balcony, always the worst seats, for "colored." Always black southerners had to share their space, as on trains, with whites who wanted to act outside the boundaries of acceptable white middle-class behavior. A domestic interviewed in Marked Tree, Arkansas, by Charles Johnson complained, "when they fill up the downstairs some of the white fellows come up and set with the colored . . . Sometimes they come up with their girlfriends. It's just like it is always—the white can come on your side, but you don't go on theirs." In a later trend theaters opened with seating reserved entirely for blacks. Wolcott shot the "Rex Theater for colored people," its outside decorated with Joe Louis fight posters, in Leland, Mississippi, in 1939. Dorothea Lange had photographed the same business two years earlier. But Marion Post Wolcott constructed a compelling image of the interdependence of segregation and consumption when she took a photograph captioned "Negro

man entering a movie" in the Delta town of Belzoni, Mississippi, in October 1939. Climbing above the "for white men only" restroom between the
segregation sign and the Dr. Pepper advertisement, the black man can
watch the same movie and drink the same soda as a white patron as long as
he declares his race and, by white implication as well as the shabby sur-
roundings, his inferiority as he enjoys his purchases.[118]

But perhaps whites were so intent on racially ordering the relatively
sedentary experiences like eating and watching movies because they understood just how resistant to racial segregation, despite the racially figured
products and advertisements shipped down from the North, the new commercial spaces of consumption would prove to be. Shopping, like boarding
the train, required movement. But segregating shopping proved more difficult than racially ordering trains, streetcars, buses, cafes, and theaters.
Inside shops racial identity could not be secured with segregation signs,
which allowed for customers of both races while grounding black inferiority
in inferior spaces. Certainly whites' desire for absolute racial difference
could have been met by excluding African Americans from white stores—a
solution practiced by most restaurants and often required by law—and by
limiting black purchases of consumer items considered too fine for "colored" consumers. To some degree these policies were pursued, but very few
white southern businesses could afford to exclude a paying customer no
matter their color, especially when the next store down the street would
probably make the sale anyway. Within this most intimate geography of
southern white consumption, then, the collective white need for superiority
clashed headlong with white individuals' desire for greater income, and
money often won.[119]

What occurred within the interiors of southern stores revealed even
more clearly the racial contradictions of integrated shopping within a
regional culture of segregation and a national culture of white consumption. In a 1940 Jack Delano photograph taken in Stem, North Carolina, and
entitled "the 'gossip corner,' " a white woman and a black woman stand
together talking inside the grocery of Mrs. N. L. Clements while another
black woman looks on from the sidewalk. A John Collier series taken inside
a drugstore in Haymarket, Virginia, presents a more detailed representation
of the racial geography of shopping. In a shot taken through the store's glass
doorway, a black woman, her black male companion's arm, and the white
woman behind the counter form a prickly triangle. Framed above and to
the right by advertisements for "Refreshing" Coca-Cola and "The Farmer's

Laxative, Push you Can Depend on, Dr. Caldwell's Syrup Pepsin," the white woman cocks her head listening toward the black arm holding an unidentifiable package for purchase. Another frame depicts the same white woman waiting on a bald round white man dressed in the wrinkled light linen suit of a planter.

The testimonies collected by African American sociologists working alone or in conjunction with white sociologists prove even more revealing. Whites expected certain deference in public encounters, an interaction "on terms of superior and inferior" that became a general code of black shopping behavior: "In places of business, the Negro should stand back and wait until the white has been served before receiving any attention and in entering or leaving he should not precede a white but should stand back and hold the door for him. On the streets and sidewalks the Negro should 'give way' to the white person." Yet because complete segregation existed in the commercial enterprises of few southern communities, southern shopping proved resistant to whites' attempts at racial ordering. Store clerks in businesses with large numbers of black customers often served shoppers in turn, sometimes making whites wait until African Americans had been served. And sites of shopping—the buildings that housed dry goods, drug, clothing, and shoe stores and five-and-dimes—never wore segregation signs.[120]

Fierce price competition between grocery stores enabled many African Americans not dependent on landowner store orders to find better treatment in these sites of consumption. Johnson found that African Americans in the town of Cleveland, Mississippi, preferred to shop at stores owned and operated by Chinese instead of the grocery chains, enjoying there greater "freedom" and escape from "the traditional observances." These stores, he implied, had replaced country stores as centers of socializing as well: "On Saturday migrant farmers may be seen loitering . . . sitting around on the counters and benches enjoying unrestrained conversation. They wait on themselves even to the extent of going behind the counters for articles. There is no particular racial etiquette to observe."

In southern cities, however, Johnson found that many African Americans made the opposite choice, preferring chain stores where clerks were "most likely to place all relations on an economic basis and extend all services to all customers regardless of race." An African American porter at a chain grocery in Houston put the situation bluntly: "We carry packages for everybody, whether they are colored or white. We take them as they come." Chain stores, African Americans insisted, did not resort to the galling practice of selling black customers inferior foodstuffs, often especially set aside for this purpose. A black professional from Richmond summed up the economic incentives that blurred the color line within southern grocery stores: "Of course none of them want to give you the same service they give white people, but competition for Negro trade is so keen that every store has to make some pretense of fair play."[121]

The overlapping nature of the services offered by southern drugstores, their doubled character as places both for purchasing medicines and toiletries and for consuming refreshments, made the racial geographies there more complex and resistant to change. By the 1930s soda fountains in drugstores had become important white sites for youthful socializing. As a result, African Americans were rarely free to linger within these stores. While they could purchase anything offered for sale, ice cream and sodas for which they often had to bring their own buckets or dishes could only be consumed in the back of the store or outside. African Americans could enjoy what Dollard called the "cool shock" of Coca-Cola, but only beyond the spaces marked by the comfortable white familiarity of the drugstore soda fountains.[122]

The most contradictory places among southern sites of consumption, however, were clothing and department stores. Foodstuffs, medicines, sodas, and ice cream were quickly consumed, and their purchases did not so readily mark the bodies of consumers. Clothing, more than other consumer goods, conveyed a lasting meaning and incited white fears of upwardly mobile African Americans and the unhinging of class and racial identities that such "New Negroes" signified. After all, at the turn of the century many whites had found the most galling aspect of African Americans' presence in first-class railroad cars their fine and fashionable dress. And early advertisers clothed their black figures in mismatched and gaudy attire that caught white consumers' attention while confirming their superiority. But in southern apparel stores whites' conceptions of blacks ran headlong into African Americans' own consuming desires. A white mailman's wife expressed the persistence of white anxiety over black dress in the 1930s. Spying the child of an African American professional entering a store, she exclaimed within earshot of a white sociologist, "it's a shame how these nigguhs can dress their children up. They fix them up better than we can afford to fix ours!"[123]

Having little control over what types of clothing African Americans with the means could purchase, white merchants and clerks attempted to assert racial difference at least within the shopping ritual itself. Blacks often could not try on clothing, hats, gloves, or even shoes. At best, some establishments permitted African Americans to try on hats only with a cloth over their heads and dresses, skirts, shirts, and pants only over other clothing. Some shoe stores allowed blacks to try on shoes but would not provide assistance. Other businesses insisted that they discriminated equally, denying unclean whites as well as African Americans, who were of course all assumed to be unclean, the right to handle clothing items.

But blacks again used their value as paying customers to seek less racially discriminating service. Many walked out of shops, often after expressing anger at poor service, and sought needed items in stores with less discrimination, often those owned by nonsouthern whites or African Americans. And clothing had a way of moving beyond whatever racial conventions southern white merchants and clerks strung feebly in place. In Natchez, Mississippi, a white sociologist overheard white salespeople admitting unwittingly that clothing could cross the color line. A black customer had attempted to return a coat. After one white clerk refused to accept the now tainted item, a white assistant manager intervened. The first clerk then said to the other white saleslady, "this is perfectly terrible; I think it is awful. We can't put this coat back in stock." The second clerk replied, "I know it. Who wants a nigger coat? . . . Some little white girl will probably come in and buy it and not know it is a nigger coat." Segregation signs could not racially divide clothing. Whites lived with the contradictions that in an age of mass production and widespread consumption identical hats, shoes, dresses, and pants implied.[124]

Cars even more than clothing crossed the spaces whites attempted with laws and signs to label "For Colored" and "For White." By the 1930s both white and black southerners owned automobiles at rates that matched the national averages. Despite John Crowe Ransom's warnings about the false promises of consumption, many southerners apparently believed a "ride in a car after working hours" was a reward worth pursuing. Cars broke down the distances that had enabled the last country stores to hang on in isolated areas despite the increasing competition of the town trade. Yet by adding pumps many country stores stayed in business selling gas, oil, and service to both locals and town folks passing through. Gasoline pumps graced country stores in FSA photographs of Bynum, North Carolina; Jarreau, Louisiana; Diascond, Virginia; and Penfield, Georgia. Like country stores, country gas stations wore a thick coat of advertising. In a 1938 photograph by John Vachon of a filling station in Enfield, North Carolina, garlands proclaiming Gulfpride motor oil compete with Coca-Cola and BC headache powder signs for the attention of consumers. Other rural filling stations had no store trade but absorbed the store's place at the center of rural communities. And a degree of integration was there, too, sometimes the norm, under the eye of watchful white owners. In a 1940 Jack Delano shot of a filling station in Stem, North Carolina, two black men share a bench with a white man. Local customs, related to the amount of "colored trade" the station depended upon, determined whether African Americans would receive the same service—checking oil, water, and air—and use of facilities as white customers. Automobiles were for a time serviced by the very institutions they would help render obsolete.[125]

Gas stations, however, seemed to come in two extremes. National chains brought with them a rigidly stylized architecture and nationalized rules of management. Often there was no place in the plans for segregated restroom facilities on the one hand or segregated service on the other. At the pumps, first come, first served became the norm and white and black customers, except those with the oldest makes of cars, usually got the same level of service.[126]

Despite the expense and the fact that in the face of the Depression some southern railroad lines relaxed rigid enforcement of the color line and even occasionally abandoned separate cars, many African Americans purchased automobiles. Cars, they claimed, allowed them to escape the indignities of traveling Jim Crow and gave them freedom, despite the segregation of travel facilities like tourist cabins and cafes. On the road race held no sway. The law granted African Americans behind the wheel the same right to their side of the street as whites. And while many white landlords and country merchants complained about black tenant farmers' extravagance in buying automobiles, white opposition gave additional support to the black belief that cars conferred an ease of movement free from white restriction. African Americans of all classes had no trouble finding whites who would sell them vehicles. In 1939 Wolcott photographed a used car lot in Clarksdale, Mississippi, set up to attract speakers flush with wages at the end of the cotton season. The image depicts a white man showing two well-dressed black men the engine of an automobile. Like clothes, cars were highly visible consumer items. Many whites, according to Dollard, cursed African

Americans who could purchase better automobiles. What could segregation signs do in the face of such movement? What was the meaning of inferiority when a southern black could simply get into his better car and ride?[127]

Because white southern store owners needed African American customers, many southern commercial districts remained racially integrated despite the labels "for colored" and "for white." The signs of segregation were as much admissions of weakness as labels of power. African American southerners could not vote, but despite white efforts to keep them down they could spend. Neither the new marketplaces nor the new products provided liberation, but whites and African Americans consumed the same products and often shopped for the same goods in the same places. And even if the level of service offered was markedly different, white salespeople often had to serve black customers. These very public contradictions subverted whites' dependence upon segregation as the signifier of absolute racial difference. As Lillian Smith wrote about the early twentieth-century South in which she grew to adulthood, "there were signs everywhere. White . . . colored . . . white . . . colored . . . over doors of railroad and bus stations, over doors of public toilets, over doors of theaters, over drinking fountains . . ." White southerners needed what Smith called "these ceremonials in honor of white supremacy" because the southern spaces of consumption remained racially ambiguous despite the signs.[128]

And this racial ambiguity ran in two directions, both of which undermined southern whites' attempts to found an alleged superiority in racialized spaces. Too rigid attempts to segregate the southern spaces of consumption spurred the growth of black businesses in the largest cities as early as the late nineteenth century. African Americans formed business associations like the National Negro Business League and worked through churches, women's clubs, and fraternal organizations to encourage blacks to buy black. Even storytelling traditions were employed to shame holdouts into patronizing African American businesses. A story of a black man "who had worked up a nice trade selling ice to both whites and blacks" circulated in the early twentieth century:

> The white man began selling ice too, since the colored man was doing so well he thought he would go in there and get him some customers. So when the white woman saw the colored woman had changed to the white

man—the white woman was still buying from the colored man—she said, "Now why did you stop buying from John, he was so courteous and nice, and we did business with him a long time?" Well I tell you truth, Miz George . . . that white man's ice is just colder than that nigger's ice."

The point, of course, was that African Americans who gave their business to white-owned enterprises supported white supremacy.[129]

But black businesses were not without their racial contradictions. A grocery store in Athens, Georgia, advertised in 1901 that "we'll treat you white." The African American community in Dollard's "Southerntown" resented a local African American woman's use of a mammy dummy, complete with dark skin and a bandanna, to advertise her candy business. By the 1944 publication of *An American Dilemma*, however, the social scientist Gunnar Myrdal insisted that all but the smallest African American communities had the opportunity to patronize black-owned businesses. Segregation had helped build up a black middle class relatively independent from southern whites. The black sociologist Charles S. Johnson asserted that in the early 1940s it was "possible for one who knows the devious paths of this 'ultraviolet' world to travel through the south without encountering the blunt and menacing reminders of the race system." "Ultraviolet" proved an apt term for the growing spaces of black autonomy that the culture of segregation both encouraged and helped render invisible to white eyes.[130]

Where complete segregation had been the white rule, in enterprises engaged in intimate, body-oriented services from barbershops to funeral homes to hospitals, the contradictions could be as bold as the segregation signs. State health codes often demanded that white undertakers handle only white bodies, creating a secure and often profitable business for African American morticians. The police in one southern town mistakenly delivered the body of a white criminal to a black undertaker. The dead man had blackened his face in disguise. More serious were the early-1920s battles over the staffing of the first U.S. veterans' hospital for African Americans in Tuskegee, Alabama. Before beginning construction, the federal government had promised Tuskegee whites that whites would control and partially staff the hospital. But as the staffing plans became public, African Americans learned that white nurses, prevented under Alabama law from touching black patients, would draw professional salaries while poorly paid black "maids" would perform the actual care. Thinking in terms of badly needed jobs, southern whites seemed to have no qualms about the close association of white women and black men in the veterans' hospital. But African American leaders like Booker T. Washington's successor at the Tuskegee Institute, Robert Russa Moton, played publicly upon these transgressions of the color line. By 1924, Tuskegee Veterans Hospital had an entirely black staff. Necessitated by segregation, the hospital became another space of southern black autonomy.[131]

But the racial ambiguity of segregation signs also ran in the opposite direction, erasing lines of racial difference as well. An expansive and only partially segregated consumption implied sameness. In the stores, whites with the will could assert some authority, enforcing black deference within the rituals of shopping. But whites could never completely control what African Americans were buying. A white girl could purchase that "nigger coat," but even more likely with increases in mass production and consumption, whites and blacks could meet the other wearing the same hat or dress, drinking the same soda, or driving the same car. The fact that national advertisers figured consumers in the abstract as white only increased white southern anxiety over African American buying. Even the white sociologist Dollard admitted that middle-class southern whites meeting middle-class African Americans experienced the shock of sameness.[132]

Segregation also served, in the case of lighter-skinned African Americans, to blur further the very problem of confused appearances it had been created to solve. For southern whites were slow to mark a "white" person black. As an informant told an interviewer in the 1930s, "they are pretty careful before they call a person a Negro. I look somewhat like a foreigner, so I can get by without a great deal of trouble." Just as inferior spaces meant inferior people, the white spaces marked off by segregation signs carried their own assumptions of belonging. Light-skinned African Americans like Walter White, James Weldon Johnson, and John Hope often had to insist that they belonged in "colored" sections. Charles Johnson recounted a well-known Negro poet's attempts to ride Jim Crow in Georgia. After asking him twice to move, the confused conductor "examined the man's hair and hands, but without helpful clues in his association of speech and dress, had to take the word of the passenger." Shifting into an ingratiating manner, the conductor then "explained that he had to watch for white men who came into the colored coach to 'meddle the girls.' " Separation, he implied, protected African Americans. Yet the conductor's own actions eased the very passing across the border he was required to patrol.[133]

The shock of racial sameness, it seemed, always brought southern whites back to sex. Dollard quoted a "professional southerner" whose blood boiled "when he went North, to see Negroes riding streetcars side by side with whites, to see them eating in the same restaurants, to see Negro men and white women together." It would, he insisted, upset any white southerner. Perhaps unconsciously, this "professional" had reduced southern white identity to the segregation of travel, consumption, and sex. Prostitution, however, was one business that whites never marked for colored or for white. An African American told the black sociologist Allison Davis, "If a decent culled girl here ain't got a white man, it sho ain't her fault, 'cause anybody can go and pick one up. They jus' hangin' 'round like flies 'round molasses, waiting for somebody to give 'em a sign." Some white women, too, engaged in this most intimate violation of the culture of segregation. And sexual relations across the color line and the mixed-race children that resulted certainly erased difference despite white denial. But traveling, eating, and shopping were more publicly visible activities thus subject to racial ordering both by law and by custom.

The problem was that most southern whites could not control the symbolically significant circulation of mass-produced consumer goods. How could a white feel above an African American who drove a newer automobile or wore a nicer suit or dress? As a black man bluntly stated in a 1913 letter to the *Progressive Farmer*, "seeing that you white folks think you are so much better than the 'nigger,' you ought to be superior to him in every respect."[134]

Segregation signs, then, provided evidence of the vanity and ultimately, the futility, of the culture of segregation. Many southern whites believed that a permanent racial order and their own everlasting superiority had been achieved. Racialized spaces were meant to capture and identify blacks, not set them free from white control. But whites themselves had paradoxically created the color line as permeable, as transgressable by their own desires. And other white southerners had once been confident. Now their wisteria- and kudzu-covered mansions stood deaf and mute, mouthlike porticoes and steps rotted off, eyelike, once-elegant windows shuttered or broken. FSA photographers found them inhabited by poor African American tenants. Other cameras captured an Italian Renaissance–style mansion converted into the greasy, dirt-covered home of the Tuscaloosa Auto Parts and Wrecking Company, and another once-proud plantation house transformed into a bejungled carcass reaching vainly toward the sky. In the 1930s such haughtiness in mere segregation signs betrayed the weakness of their ordering claims. Whites, then, had only violence to hide the emptiness of their allegedly greater worth, their assertion that "niggers" were "all right in their place" difficult to pin down in a world where spaces were rapidly changing. Maybe Faulkner was right about the hunt. There was a certainty to violence, a seductive seeming solidness in blood's warm and sticky rush. But the bear was gone. White southerners instead chose a different symbol, a different prey, and indeed a very different game.[135]

CHAPTER FIVE

Deadly Amusements

SPECTACLE LYNCHINGS AND THE
CONTRADICTIONS OF SEGREGATION AS CULTURE

*This effort to keep the white group solid led directly to mob law.
Every white man [and woman] became a recognized official to keep Negroes
"in their places." Negro baiting and even lynching became a form of amusement.*

W. E. B. DU BOIS[1]

*We are very near an answer to our question—how may the [white]
Southerner take hold of his Tradition? The answer is by violence.*

ALLEN TATE[2]

D ESPITE THE parchment paper pronouncements of separate but equal and the bright block-lettered signs loudly proclaiming "For Colored" and "For White," at the heart of the culture of segregation lay a profound ambiguity. Separation, after all, did not necessarily mean racial inferiority. It could also signify the creation of relatively autonomous black spaces, even autonomous black bodies. In fact, even as African Americans fought disenfranchisement and legal segregation in the courts across the South, many black southerners sought to separate themselves as fully as possible from the white southerners who had been their former masters. Segregation certainly meant shabby or nonexistent waiting rooms and train cars where African American passengers were jumbled together with smoking whites and engine soot. W. E. B. Du Bois made the intended indignity clear in revising his 1925 article on Georgia for *The Nation* while traveling through the state:

"I am in the hot, crowded, and dirty Jim Crow car where I belong . . . I am not comfortable." Yet segregation also created spaces for black doctors, black colleges, and increasingly black business districts—from Auburn Avenue in Atlanta to Beale Street in Memphis—as southern African Americans moved into growing southern cities. The creation of a separate white southern world, a culture of segregation, implied that somewhere there existed a separate black one. As whites strove to create an all-encompassing system of separation, then, they also risked aiding African Americans in the very struggle for more autonomy that white supremacy sought to deny.[3]

The culture of segregation was always a process, never a finished product. Despite the dizzying multiplication of the spaces of consumption, white southerners sought to found their own racial identity within the maintenance of an absolute color bar. Yet black southerners continued to fight separation and exclusion, pushing against each new boundary. And despite Du Bois's discomfort in the Jim Crow car, the expansion of transportation systems across the region rapidly increased spatial mobility, for black as well as white southerners. As threatening to whites as the development of a separate black world were the ways changes in leisure, consumption, and travel threatened to blur the edges of those carefully constructed white and black spaces. Indeed, southern whites found what the film historian Miriam Hansen has described as "the simultaneous liberation and commodification of sexuality that crucially defined the development of American consumer culture" particularly dangerous and yet also titillating. And threats came from within as well. The shift from an agrarian toward a more industrialized and urban economy and increasing activism among white industrial workers as well as Populists made class lines more visible. Southern white women, too, demonstrated a growing interest in reform and joined the temperance and suffrage movements in large numbers. Would a whiteness founded in a culture of segregation, then, be able to hold white southerners together?

Though Allen Tate referred to an older, antebellum southern white tradition in his essay for the Agrarian manifesto *I'll Take My Stand*, he was right about the methods white southerners were using to defeat perceived threats to the racial line they had drawn in the sand. And as Tate participated in yet another recycling of Lost Cause themes of past southern glory and pastoral utopia, he surely would have appreciated the long history of the answer at which he arrived. Unfortunately, white southerners' best-known acts of violence, lynchings, became increasingly bound up between 1890 and 1940 in the very practices of a modern culture of consumption that Tate hoped his region in 1930 would use violence to reject.[4]

It was an uneasy landscape, the early twentieth-century South, a small-town, small-city world of ice companies and beauty parlors, soda fountains and gas stations. It was a world where people who went to church some days watched or participated in the torture of their neighbors on others. In the decades following 1890, many lynchings no longer occurred in places untouched by the technological advances of the larger world. Lynchers drove cars, spectators used cameras, out-of-town visitors arrived on specially chartered excursion trains, and the towns and counties in which these horrifying events happened had newspapers, telegraph offices, and even radio stations that announced times and locations of these upcoming violent spectacles. Although after the peak decades of the 1890s the number of lynchings decreased even in the South, the cultural impact of the practice became more powerful. More people participated in, read about, saw pictures of, and collected souvenirs from lynchings even as fewer mob murders occurred. In the twentieth century white southerners transformed a deadly and often quiet form of vigilante "justice" into a modern spectacle of enduring power.[5]

Yet not all southern lynchings fit this new and evolving pattern. More often, small groups of white men hunted down and shot or hanged their African American victims after an argument over the year-end sharecroppers' settle or to send a message to other timber or turpentine camp laborers not to demand any better. These lynchings in the night claimed many more victims than the open-air spectacles of torture that drew such large crowds. And white violence against southern blacks was not limited only to lynchings—white men continued in more private settings to rape black women and assault African Americans for "reasons" ranging from black resistance and economic success to white hatred, jealousy, and fear.[6] "Private violence," as W. J. Cash explained in 1941, stemmed from the same circumstances that made spectacle lynchings "socially defensible" from a southern white perspective: "to smash a sassy Negro, to kill him, to do the same to a 'nigger lover'—this was to assert the white man's prerogative as pointedly, to move as certainly to get a black man back in his place, as to lynch." Southern whites did not need Tate to encourage them to use violence to secure what he conceived as their more "private, self-contained, and essentially spiritual" way of life—it had been a chosen method of empowerment since colonial Jamestown.[7]

But something was new about lynchings in public, attended by thousands, captured in papers by reporters who witnessed the tortures, and photographed for those spectators who wanted a souvenir and yet failed to get a coveted finger, toe, or fragment of bone. More was at stake than putting African American southerners brutally in their place, as Cash understood, for "private violence" succeeded in limiting and often eliminating African American political activity and achieving significant white control of black labor. Explanations of the practice of lynching in the twentieth century, however, have focused on the persistence of the "barbaric" practice of the past rather than its transformation, in the case of spectacle lynchings, into a peculiarly modern ritual.[8]

Southern whites, according to both contemporary observers like H. L. Mencken and Arthur Raper and present-day scholars like James McGovern and Joel Williamson, lynched African American men and occasionally women in the absence of "modernity"—because they lacked a "modern" economy, a "modern" white male sexuality, or even a "modern" theater.[9] Even Jacquelyn Dowd Hall, in the best analysis of lynching to date, saw the region's extreme racism as existing in conflict with southern modernizing efforts. And while the historians Fitzhugh Brundage and Edward L. Ayers have convincingly argued that lynching was central to the New South and particularly the structuring of its labor markets in areas experiencing rapid increases in their African American populations, they have focused mainly on the more common private lynchings and their role in the New South economy.[10]

African American anti-lynching activists, too—some of whom had barely escaped lynching themselves—saw lynching as central to the New South, and they examined the function of violence in structuring a changing southern economy and culture. From Ida B. Wells, who founded both the study of lynching and anti-lynching activism, to Frederick Douglass, W. E. B. Du Bois, Mary Church Terrell, James Weldon Johnson, and especially Walter White, they understood that whites' practice of ritualized violence, what Terrell called "this wild and diabolical carnival of blood," was central not only to the white economy but to white identity as well. Yet even the liberal W. J. Cash condemned Walter White as an extremist for denouncing the "rape complex" as a "fraud." African American activists were more often simply ignored.[11]

A practice dependent on modern transportation and printing technologies, increasingly intertwined with the practices of an emerging consumer culture, was not some frontier residue and soon-to-be-lost small obstacle to "Progress," then, but a part of the southern present and future, a key medium for resolving the contradictions within the culture of segregation in which these brutal spectacles took place. "Lynch carnivals," as a popular book on the subject written in the 1930s described them, were rituals increasingly bound up with the way southern whites shaped the practices of modern consumption to their own ends, communal spectacles of torture that helped ease white fears of a raceless consumer society even as they helped structure segregation, the policy that would regulate this new southern world. Publicly resolving the race, gender, and class ambiguities at the very center of the culture of segregation, spectacle lynchings brutally conjured a collective, all-powerful whiteness even as they made the color line seem modern, civilized, and sane. Spectacle lynchings were about making racial difference in the new South, about ensuring the separation of all southern life into whiteness and blackness even as the very material things that made up southern life were rapidly changing. Racial violence was modern.[12]

The Genealogy of Lynchings as Modern Spectacle

Despite the roots of an expanding consumer culture outside the South, white southerners made an important contribution to the rapidly evolving forms of leisure in twentieth-century America: they modernized and perfected violence, in the form of the spectator lynching, as entertainment, as what Du Bois had chillingly described as a new and yet grisly form of white southern amusement. And like all cultural forms, over time lynching spectacles evolved a well-known structure, a sequence and pace of events that southerners came to understand as standard. The well-choreographed spectacle opened with a chase or a jail attack, followed rapidly by the public identification of the captured African American by the alleged white victim or the victim's relatives, announcement of the upcoming event to draw the crowd, and selection and preparation of the site. The main event then began with a period of mutilation—often including emasculation—and torture to extract confessions and entertain the crowd, and built to a climax of slow burning, hanging, and/or shooting to complete the killing. The finale consisted of frenzied souvenir gathering and display of the body and the collected parts.[13]

To be sure, in a perverse twist on regional exceptionalism, lynchings of all kinds became fixed in southerners' as well as nonsoutherners' imaginations as the dominant form of southern white violence against blacks. And certainly news of midnight shootings and hangings by small groups of white men circulated among both white and black southerners even when not reported in local papers. Hearing that "the white folks" quietly shot his classmate's brother, Richard Wright recalled the impact all "white death" had on young African American men: "the white brutality that I had not seen was a more effective control of my behavior than that which I knew. The actual experience would have let me see the realistic outlines of what was really happening, but as long as it remained something terrible and yet remote, something whose horror and blood might descend upon me at any moment, I was compelled to give my entire imagination over to it . . ." Since southern blacks rarely attended public lynchings, their knowledge of all these extralegal killings remained paradoxically distant and perhaps fantastic even as their very effective networks of communication publicized the brutality that struck close at hand.

Yet as the twentieth century progressed—or perhaps regressed—spectacle lynchings became the most widely known form of white violence against southern blacks even as less public lynchings claimed many more victims. Cash declared that by 1900, the white South had developed a lynching habit. As Walter White lamented, however, by the 1920s interest in the practice of lynching had spread far beyond the region in which mob murders were most likely to occur: "mobbism has degenerated to the point where an uncomfortably large percentage of American citizens can read in their newspapers of the slow roasting alive of a human being in Mississippi and turn, promptly and with little thought, to the comic strip or sporting page. Thus has lynching become an almost integral part of our national folkways." The distance was not far, then, between titillation and disgust, a white southern amusement, an African American tragedy, and a new national pas-time.[14]

But just how did a practice of quiet vigilante justice become a modern public spectacle, a narrative of astonished interest more than horrified con-cern, a national folkway? Consumer culture, spreading from the Northeast across the country in the late nineteenth and early twentieth centuries, cre-ated the possibility of a new kind of public, a much more heterogeneous group of shoppers, diners, travelers, vaudeville and movie patrons, sports fans, and visitors to local, regional, and national fairs. In the North, as the historian David Nasaw has argued, segregation absolutely excluded African Americans from an emerging world of urban public amusements, denying them access to fair midways, amusement and baseball parks, and vaudeville and movie theaters. Yet segregation alone did not meld these new heteroge-neous crowds into a white public. The spectacle of African American other-ness was also required. Thus whites of all classes, genders, and ethnicities could gawk at the "Dahomeys" in a fair exhibit of "Darkest Africa," "buy three balls for five" to "dunk the nigger" at Coney Island, and cheer on a black man's lynchers in *Birth of a Nation*.[15]

In the North, then, segregation and the spectacle of black otherness made a mass audience for the new purveyors of commercial entertainments and other new mass products. For southern whites, however, the problem of creating a new white public was both more difficult and, they believed, more necessary. There segregation and spectacle lynching made what Du Bois referred to as a new white "amusement" but also a new southern order. Segregation as culture strengthened racial boundaries without denying southern whites and blacks who could afford consumer products access to them, allowing white-owned businesses to sell African Americans Coca-Cola and movies and yet protect white supremacy too. For southern blacks must, while enjoying their purchases, swallow their pride along with their soda. They could only publicly consume goods within spaces marked, whether "For Colored" or not, as clearly inferior. Yet making a spectacle of lynching disrupted the commonality of even this spatially divided experi-ence of consumption. Only whites, whether they endorsed the violence or not, could experience the "amusement" of a black man burned. Only African Americans could be extralegally and publicly tortured and killed. In a grisly dialectic, then, consumer culture created spectacle lynchings, and spectacle lynchings became a southern way of enabling the spread of con-sumption as a white privilege. The violence both helped create a white consuming public and the structure of segregation where consumption could take place without threatening white supremacy.[16]

Newspaper reporters and men around the stove at the crossroads store, telegraph operators and women at the local meeting of the United Daughters of the Confederacy, law "enforcement" officials and trainmen who jumped from the car to tell the news at each stop—all helped shape the stories of specific events into a dominant narrative of southern spectacle lynchings that evolved in the decades between 1890 and 1940. But widely circulated newspaper stories, as Walter White understood, were central to the power of these new "amusements." While thousands of white southerners witnessed and participated in lynchings as the twentieth century unfolded, the majority of Americans—white and black, northern and southern—learned about these events from newspapers and to a lesser extent books, pamphlets, and radio announcements. In many cases these accounts were written by reporters who personally witnessed the spectacle, but the experience for their readers or listeners was mediated, a representation at least once removed from actual involvement. And even those spectators who attended the lynching or later viewed the body or examined a display of "souvenirs" were affected as well by the narratives constructed by reporters to describe and explain these events. Beginning in the 1890s, no matter the specific characteristics, representations of spectacle lynchings increasingly fell into a ritualistic pattern as the narratives constructed by witnesses, participants, and journalists assumed a standardized form. Spectacle lynchings, then, became more powerful even as they occurred less frequently because the rapidly multiplying stories of these public tortures became virtually interchangeable.[17]

Thus the modernization of the practice—the incorporation of cars and trains, radios, phones, and cameras—matched the standardization of the representations. As a dominant narrative evolved and circulated more widely, innovations added in a particular lynching were easily spotted and picked up by subsequent mobs. The grisly dialectic began in the 1890s as newspaper coverage grew, crowds increased, and lynch mobs adapted the rituals of public executions to the needs of vigilantism and racial control. As James Elbert Cutler found in the first academic investigation of lynchings, published in 1905, before 1890 magazines ignored the subject entirely while local newspapers printed small, sparse accounts. Three events in the early 1890s, however, initiated the early development of spectacle lynchings as practice and as narrative. First, the lynching on March 14, 1891, of eleven Italian immigrants accused of aiding in the murder of the New Orleans police chief brought international attention to mob murder in the South as the Italian government condemned the action and demanded indemnities. Before the fervor over these murders had faded, another public lynching in Louisiana occurred: a large crowd of whites tortured and burned an African American named Tump Hampton in St. Tammany Parish on May 30 of the same year. Significantly, publicity generated by the Italians' murder spilled over in this case onto the lynching of a black southerner. The founding event in the history of spectacle lynchings, however, was the final murder in the gruesome triad, the 1893 lynching of Henry Smith in Paris, Texas, for the alleged rape and murder of three-year-old Myrtle Vance.[18]

The 1893 murder of Smith was the first blatantly public, actively promoted lynching of a southern black by a large crowd of southern whites. Adding three key features—the specially chartered excursion train, the publicly sold photograph, and the widely circulated, unabashed retelling of the event by one of the lynchers—the killing of Smith modernized and made more powerful the loosely organized, more spontaneous practice of lynching that had previously prevailed. In what one commentator aptly termed a "neglected feature of railroading," from 1893 on railroad companies could be counted on to arrange special trains to transport spectators and lynchers to previously announced lynching sites. On some occasions these trains were actually advertised in local papers; with railroad passenger service, even small towns could turn out large crowds. Even after automobiles cut into the railroads' "lynch carnival" business, a 1938 commentator found that "modern trainmen, schooled in the doctrine of service," helped "in an informative way" by relaying news of upcoming lynchings to train passengers and townspeople "all along the rail lines."[19]

As crucial as the innovation in transportation, however, was the publication, after Henry Smith's lynching, of the first full account, from the discovery of the alleged crime to the frenzied souvenir gathering at the end: *The Facts in the Case of the Horrible Murder of Little Myrtle Vance, and Its Fearful Expiation, at Paris, Texas, February 1, 1893.* This widely distributed pamphlet is perhaps the most detailed account of a lynching ever written from a lyncher's point of view. It included a photograph of Smith's torture, probably also sold separately. This pamphlet initiated a new genre of lynching narrative, the author as eyewitness and in this case also participant.

More important, however, this anonymous lyncher as reporter implicated the entire white community in the public torture and murder that had
recently occurred: "From the first it was a clear case of temporary insanity of
a whole populace, the moral and social shock for the time eclipsing every
vestige of temperance in dealing with the culprit." And "populace" did not
mean simply white men. Though the photographer focused on the scaffold,
emblazoned with a large sign that proclaimed "JUSTICE," on which Smith
was being tortured, the size of the crowd prevented him from getting very
close to the action. The shot, more a picture of the mob than the mob's victim, depicts a mass of spectators including white women and children.
From the earliest spectacle lynchings, then, white women actively participated in these events as more than the passive alleged victims that fueled
white men's fury. The story of lynching as the entire white community in
action, using savagery to protect "Southern" civilization, was born.[20]

But even in 1893 there was another if extremely vulnerable space from
which to narrate these events. In March of 1892 Ida B. Wells lived through the
lynchings of three of her closest friends—Thomas Moss, Calvin McDowell,
and Henry Stewart, the African American owners of a new and successful
enterprise where the streetcar turned on the outskirts of Memphis, the People's Grocery Company of the colored suburb of the Curve. A quarrel
between white and black boys over a game of marbles had escalated into a
fight between white and black grocers. The black grocers were arrested.
Then a white mob let in by law officers took the three men from their cells,
loaded them on a switch engine that ran on a track behind the jail, drove
them north of the city limits of sleeping Memphis, and shot them to death.
Though no spectators witnessed the event, the good citizens of Memphis
were not forgotten, for somehow one of the morning papers knew enough to
hold up its edition and subscribers were able to read the details of the murders as they sipped a late cup of coffee.[21]

Ida B. Wells, however, also owned a paper. And as a white mob helped
itself to food and drink at the People's Grocery, her *Memphis Free Speech*
attempted to set the record straight. Over the next three months the paper
agitated against the violence and told African Americans to leave a city in
which they could get no justice. Wells was convinced that her friends had
been lynched because the success of their business hurt the Curve's other
grocery, a white-owned establishment. She began a closer investigation of
the lynchings, which had been only briefly recorded in the local and
regional white papers. In late May 1892, she editorialized:

Eight Negroes lynched since the last issue of the *Free Speech*. Three were charged with killing white men and five with raping white women. Nobody in this section believes the old thread-bare lie that Negro men assault white women. If Southern white men are not careful they will over-reach themselves and a conclusion will be reached which will be very damaging to the moral reputation of their women.[22]

Out of town at a convention, Wells escaped her own lynching, but Memphis whites silenced her southern voice as effectively. In a flurry of city elite-led speech making, marching, and threatening, the *Free Speech's* office and type were destroyed. By 1893, however, when Henry Smith was lynched for the alleged rape and murder of "Little Myrtle Vance," Wells had already started her campaign to expose the fallacy of the rape myth as a justification for lynching from her new position at the *New York Age*.[23]

Lynching as practice and as story—the newspaper narratives that reported and even created racial violence in the region—never went unchallenged, then, by African Americans and a few brave liberal and radical whites. In fact, even as the dominant narrative of spectacle lynchings developed, anti-lynching activists worked to subvert the story, believing that by exposing the false accounts of events and empty justifications, they would expose the immorality and end the violence. And the lynchings they and later white liberals described became a hybrid sort of spectacle lynching as well: the stories they told of real or imagined lynchings circulated publicly and bumped against the narrative most white southerners had learned to tell so well. Thus the violence occurred and the story was written within a never-ending dialectic—the pushing and pulling at the boundaries of the racialized yet shifting spaces of segregation as culture.

The Lynching of Sam Hose

If the lynching of Henry Smith marked the beginning of the transformation of the practice from quiet vigilante justice to modern public spectacle, the lynching of Sam Hose in Newnan, Georgia, in 1899 made an isolated event into a new and horrifying pattern. The alleged crimes, the chase, and the lynching occurred in and around places like Palmetto, Newnan, and Griffin—small southern towns like any others yet within forty miles of Atlanta. Easy access to train and telegraph lines ensured that the lynching of Hose would be an "event" not just in the rural Georgia Piedmont but in the self-proclaimed capital of the New South as well. The Hose murder, then, added a key innovation: local and regional newspapers took over the publicity, promotion, and sale of the event and began the development of a standardized, sensationalized narrative pattern that would dominate reporting of spectacle lynchings through the 1940s.[24]

"DETERMINED MOB AFTER HOSE; HE WILL BE LYNCHED IF CAUGHT" began the story in the *Atlanta Constitution* on April 14, 1899. The best men were in the mob, unmasked white men and proud, the cream of "a half dozen counties," "lawyers, doctors, merchant farmers, and every creed and class of men." "Driven . . . almost to a frenzy" and vowing "never to give up the chase," these citizens, however, remained "perfectly cool" and would, the Atlanta papers assured readers, do what had to be done "as thoroughly and as orderly as though nothing unusual was involved." From the first, local and regional papers never doubted that the African American would be tracked down by the mob and killed, and the large black letters in the papers gave an eerie certainty to an act of violence that had previously been both anticipated and feared. After all, the entire white community was behind these best men, not really a mob, the *Journal* stressed, but more of a crowd. Sam Hose's alleged crimes had "closed the store doors in the towns and stopped the plows in the country," as white men, women, and children sought "the fiendish beast."

The white folks in Palmetto believed that on the previous night Sam Hose, a laborer on Alfred Cranford's farm, had split open to the eyeballs the skull of the respected white farmer with an ax and then injured his children and raped his wife within reach of the bleeding corpse. As one of those lawyers or doctors or merchants, boastfully unmasked and yet unwilling to be identified, calmly told a reporter, "whatever death is most torturous, most horrifying to a brute, shall be meted out"; "let him burn slowly for hours." Apparently no death was too horrifying for the lynch "crowd" or for the large numbers of white spectators whom newspaper announcements and specially chartered trains from Atlanta were certain to bring as soon as Hose was captured and the telegraph lines could transmit the appointed time and place. Hose's fate had already been decided by the papers ten days beforehand, and as mobs of white men sifted the countryside, ransacking black houses, black farms, and black sections, the days grew hotter, the reading audience larger, and chances that the torture and killing of a black man would provide white amusement more certain. On April 23, a Sunday after-noon, in Newnan, Georgia, it was done.[25]

But the finale was ten days away when the Atlanta papers began devel-oping the story, and they needed more than the repetitive details of the chase to hook their audiences. Mrs. Cranford, the wife of the murdered man and the alleged rape victim, provided the most exciting copy in those early days, but the reporters' attempts to use her as both subject and source of the story exposed the gendered tensions at the center of spectacle lynch-ings. Granting interviews with reporters from both the *Journal* and the *Con-stitution*, she demanded an active role in planning the lynching, expressing a desire to witness Hose's torture and death and her preference for a slow burning. Mrs. Cranford, then, was the voice of the crime that set the elabo-rate ritual in motion, a witness to her husband's brutal murder and yet a sur-vivor, a white who had easily outsmarted a black man determined not to leave without money by giving him a Confederate bill and convincing him of its worth. She was, in fact, the source of all that was known about the attack on her family.[26]

Yet could a white woman play so important and public a role in a ritual that both brought out and created the white community, that made white-ness? With their desire for authenticity and gore, the newspapers after all had put their spotlights on Mrs. Cranford. She had only claimed the power, possible through her sudden "fame," to shape the story. But the papers were determined to put Mrs. Cranford back on the pedestal. No longer simply a good and common farm wife but now a woman of "refined parentage," Mrs. Cranford, they sympathized, was a lady doubly savaged by the "black beast rapist." The woman who had despite her horror upheld white supremacy by outsmarting her black assailant with a worthless bill was now described as "the horrified and hysterical wife." Proclaiming that "death would have been mercy," the reporters related details of the rape that she alone could have given them. Just as white women both helped in the chase and cheered on the "best men," although it was Mrs. Cranford's account of the crimes that initiated the spectacle lynching, the papers transformed her from active participant to passive victim. In the end, Hose was murdered in Newnan. And Mrs. Cranford's desire to see the lynching, for the spectacle to take place near her home in Palmetto, was ignored.[27]

As the unfolding narrative of the spectacle lynching moved forward from the crime, the story of Hose's capture provided a somewhat lighter interlude between Mrs. Cranford's gruesome descriptions of rape and murder and the anticipated climactic horror of Hose's torture and death. His captors claimed they caught him going to a cakewalk after recognizing him as a "strange negro" near his mother's house outside Marshallville. In one account Hose constructed his own disguise, while in another white men applied the lampblack to conceal his distinguishing copper color and increase their chances of delivering him safely to the sheriff for the promised reward. Either way white readers could find amusement in the picture of a black man in blackface as images of blacked-up black minstrels performing the cakewalk merged with the very different form of entertainment in which Hose would soon star. In this early spectacle lynching, it seemed, the minstrel act bridged the distance between the faithful, laughing slave and the "black beast rapist." Before he could be the beast, Hose played a more familiar role, the joking black fool.[28]

The small group of white men who had captured Hose took him to Griffin on the regular Macon-to-Atlanta train early Sunday morning. Again the papers played up the festive atmosphere. The railroad, eager to please and keep this special traffic separate from the other passengers, provided an excursion train to take Hose and the fast-growing mob from Griffin to Palmetto. En route the reporters cornered their star, and Hose confessed the murder but insisted he had not raped the white woman. His version of events, however, little mattered. He was checked with the sheriff like a package for the official receipt that entitled his captors to a reward. The mob soon stole him back from the sheriff, and the papers reported that "it was marvelous how the news spread and thousands came here to satisfy their curiosity and to take part in the lynching." Other trains too converged on Palmetto for the lynching, and officials of the Atlanta and West Point Railroad estimated they sold one thousand tickets and that stowaways stole five hundred spaces more. The show, it seemed, was on.[29]

But eyewitness descriptions of the main event, the torture, burning, and souvenir gathering for which the large white crowd had assembled, threatened to unhinge the lynchers' role as enforcers of white supremacy. While the papers insisted that the mob escorting the captured Hose was an orderly, determined "crowd," reports did stress that at every step these good citizens feared some crazed outsider would shoot the prize and deny them their fun. Afraid, ironically, that Hose would be killed, they lynched him at Newnan, still ten miles from Palmetto, that Sunday just after church let out. Receiving word quickly by telegram, the papers had special correspondents at the scene, and in the Monday editions reporters as eyewitnesses detailed the cutting off of Hose's ears, his castration, and his very slow burning. Again the papers went to great lengths to "civilize" the mob, though at least one got Hose's name wrong: "the crowd that burned Holt—it could hardly be called a mob, so orderly was its action—has made no mistake . . . the crowd was cool and went about its work carefully and almost with a system." Another paper pronounced "absolute order and decorum." An ex-governor of the state, W. Y. Atkinson, bragged that though he had not prevented the lynching he had at least succeeded in persuading them to move the spectacle out of Newnan's town square and away from the white women and children. "The crowd was a marvel of coolness and determination and . . . was remarkably orderly," said Atkinson. The reporters even went so far as to praise the courage of the victim, who, they wrote, did not flinch as he marched to the stake or cry out as his legs slowly burned. "I stood as close to the flames and the writhing figure in their midst as the heat would permit," wrote the Journal's reporter. He described Hose "battling in the flames with the wildest superhuman energy": "now he was twisting around the tree, now biting at the back of the pine, jumping and springing and twisting and fighting for every inch of life, kicking the embers with his dangling legs, blood vessels bursting, eyes protruding, but not a word, not a tear, but, oh God, the horror of his face . . ." The stronger the victim, the greater the glory of the mob that defeated him. The "superhuman" Hose became both more and less than a man.[30]

Certain images, however, threatened to break through the narrative of a calm avenging white civilization—images of "frenzied men" and "delirious delight," of an old white-haired man screaming "God bless every man that had a hand in this" and "thank God for vengeance," and of a mingling of white and black blood as men rushing to cut off pieces of Hose's body cut the hands of their friends instead. The barbarism of the trophy-gathering in particular exploded any claim of white deliberateness and calm. Mob members had collected some body parts, the choice ears and penis and fingers cut off before the fire, and many spectators afterward turned "souvenir seekers," rushing in to push back the still-hot coals and hack up the body, cutting out the heart and other internal organs, fighting rival onlookers for the most cherished prizes. The Journal reported that "men scrambled and fell over each other in their mad haste to secure something that would be a memento to the horrible tragedy. And everything that had any bearing on the occasion was grabbed and pocketed, even the ashes were picked up in handkerchiefs and carried away in triumph. Men left the scene bearing huge chunks of burned wood, limbs of the tree which was made the stake, pieces of bone, and revolting and bloody segments of skull." A market for souvenirs quickly developed, as spectators too far away from the burning bargained with luckier men and purchased at "inflated prices" their own keepsakes of that glorious day. In the process of giving its readers the sensationalized details of the spectacle, the papers blurred if not obliterated the fine distinction between a ritual of civilization taming savagery and actual savagery itself. If indeed "the whole male community seemed to be a unit," what that unit accomplished did not seem as clear as many southern whites wanted to think.[31]

After there was nothing left to collect, the crowd broke up and went home, and those souvenirs also traveled, ending up in dusty mason jars in crossroads stores, on the mantles of farmhouses, in the homes of some of those best men. At least one of these bloody relics made it back to Atlanta. Although W. E. B. Du Bois did not write his alternative narrative of the aftermath of Hose's lynching until decades afterward, this "souvenir" certainly extended the reach of the horrifying spectacle:

> a Negro in central Georgia, Sam Hose, had killed his landlord's wife. I wrote out a careful and reasoned statement concerning the evident facts and started down to the Atlanta *Constitution* office, carrying in my pocket a letter of introduction to Joel Chandler Harris. I did not get there. On the way the news met me: Sam Hose had been lynched, and they said his knuckles were on exhibition at a grocery store farther down Mitchell Street, along the way I was walking. I turned back to the University. I began to turn aside from my work. I did not meet Joel Chandler Harris nor the editor of the *Constitution*.[32]

The Atlanta shopkeeper or perhaps an enterprising seller of Hose's knuckles must have taken the special excursion train to be back in Atlanta from Newnan so quickly. The Hose lynching signaled a turning point for Du Bois, a transformation in his own thinking on the "race problem" generally and racial violence in particular. The display of Sam Hose's knuckles, he claimed, irrevocably changed his life. Having recently reconstructed the African American experience for an international exhibition, Du Bois was robbed of access to the newspaper of his own city and brought to his knees by a white southerner's own display of the meaning of blackness. Perhaps if Du Bois had reached the *Constitution*, its editors would have at least spelled Hose's name correctly. Yet while Hose lived on in a kind of gruesomely pickled and dried immortality, Du Bois later regained his voice and directed it even more loudly at the horrors of white supremacy. He forgot the facts of the case but he always remembered the fingers.[33]

The Lynching of Jesse Washington

Though seventeen years had passed, the lynching of Jesse Washington in the City Hall square of Waco, Texas, in 1916 mimicked the pace and structure of events in the Hose lynching, at least as constructed by the Atlanta newspapers. Though early reports did not so assuredly predict a lynching beforehand, the Waco papers presented the details of Mrs. Lucy Fryar's murder and rape in the standard sensationalized pattern set in the pamphlet about the lynching of Smith. The doctor reported that she had been surprised by her attacker, killed by the first blow, and ravished while dead. And yet one report followed the dominant narrative and stressed how the highly respected white woman had struggled valiantly against her violator. In the lynching narrative, even the corpse of the white woman recoiled from the black man's lust. The *Waco Semi-Weekly Tribune* provided a "Chronology of the Crime"; though the law-breaking referred to was the rape and murder of Mrs. Lucy Fryar, this summary of events culminating in an eighteen-year-old African American's lynching provided as accurate an outline of the ritual of southern spectacle lynchings as had ever been published. The local Waco papers in 1916, then, told much the same story, revealing similar tensions between sensationalism and newspaper sales, white supremacy and civilization.[34]

But Waco was a small modern city, sixteen years inside the twentieth century, and a far cry from the dusty, slow farm town of Newnan in 1899. Much had happened in the South and in the nation in those seventeen years. The Leo Frank case had subverted the color line by making a Jewish factory supervisor the victim of a public, widely promoted and reported lynching. Yet the class conflict that fueled this 1915 lynching in Atlanta remained within the spaces of the culture of segregation: it was an argument about whether whiteness would be defined by local farmers, mill workers, and small merchants or by an emerging professional and corporate class with ties outside the region. In 1915, the hugely popular film *Birth of a Nation* at least symbolically resolved this conflict within whiteness; D. W. Griffith reworked the spectacle lynching into a gripping film scene and appropriated its power to advance a national rather than southern white unity. The political scientist Michael Rogin has argued that "the nation was born in Gus's castration," as "the passivity forced upon the defeated South"—and here he might have added, upon Leo Frank's lynchers' more recent crisis of masculine authority as well—was "now enforced on Gus," made to stand as the archetypal southern black man. Making a spectacle of lynching, *Birth* both provided a ground for the national unity necessary in the Great War and created the modern film industry.[35]

The 1916 lynching of Jesse Washington, then, was a transitional event in the history of spectacle lynchings. The time and place changed the tone of the event—at Waco no one could deny that violence was modern even as after *Birth*, the presidency of Virginia-born Woodrow Wilson, and the Great War the practice of spectacle lynching would never be the same. White supremacy had long been a national concern, but as *Birth* captured on film, by Wilson's presidency North and South again formed a truly unified nation. The southern whiteness that the culture of segregation made took on a double and sometimes contradictory duty, as both a space of national reunion and a ground for the region's continuing difference.

There were ice trucks at the Waco fire. The leader of the mob was a big white man, a driver for the Big Four Ice Company, and trucks were good to stand on for a latecoming spectator hoping to see over all the other people. Waco, a town with 40,000 inhabitants, sixty-three churches, and ten colleges and universities in 1916, could get up quite an audience. No special trains were necessary here to create the festive atmosphere lent these occasions by large, milling crowds. Since Hose, lynching towns had advertised; in a twisted form of town boosterism they used the standard methods of promoting commerce. But in Waco telephones helped tremendously, speeding the circulation of news by neighborly word of mouth. In the city with the ice trucks the Raleigh Hotel, too, advertised, billing its lodgings as "ten stories of comfort and safety, sleep where life is safe, absolutely fire proof," where "Waco welcomes *You*." The focus of all this attention, a black man named Jesse Washington, unfortunately did not have a room there, and the estimated 15,000 white folks—men, women, and children—who welcomed him instead to Waco's jail, courtroom, and finally City Hall Square found his body very flammable indeed. The burning alive of Jesse Washington in 1916 was a peculiarly modern ritual. As the *Houston Chronicle* recounted with shame, "they did such a thing in the cultured, reputable city of Waco."[36]

In other places participants in such events had sometimes later bragged to journalists and investigators, and as in the Hose case reporters had even been eyewitnesses themselves. But an investigator sent by the recently organized NAACP, a white woman named Elisabeth Freeman, found no one in Waco willing to describe his or her role in the torture. The newspapers largely omitted the gruesome details, even though their correspondents covering the trial must have been at the scene. The only exception was the *Waco Times Herald*, which could not help admitting that "fingers, ears, pieces of clothing, toes, and other parts of the negro's body were cut off by members of the mob that had crowded to the scene as if by magic when the word that the negro had been taken in charge by the mob was heralded over the city." People from farming settlements outside Waco, in fact, had been arriving as early as Sunday afternoon for Washington's quickly scheduled Monday morning trial. Prominent Waco businessmen had driven out to Robinson, the village nearest the Fryar farm, and arranged a deal with the murdered woman's friends and relatives to let the trial proceed unhindered. In exchange these good men promised that the Robinson folks would get to carry out the little-doubted death sentence. Everyone was certain that young Jesse Washington was guilty. Even Freeman reported in an undated letter scribbled hastily to NAACP secretary Roy Nash from Waco that "the boy committed the foulest crime. He premeditated the crime—killed the woman in cold blood—raped the dead body—went back to his work [and] finished the day in the fields—came back and put up his mules and went home. When arrested he frankly admitted his guilt, was coarse and bestal [sic] in the telling." She claimed that the leading African American citizens, too, were "stung and disgraced" by Washington's actions, and the *Waco Semi-Weekly Tribune* even reported—most likely falsely—many blacks among the spectators who witnessed Washington's burning.[37]

Many prominent town citizens had reportedly watched if not participated in the lynching. One paper reported that "from the windows of city buildings hundreds look[ed] out upon the activities of the scene below." Mayor Dollins was perhaps the most prominent Wacoan with this bird's-eye view. The tree the mob chose to hold Washington, luckily for the mayor, was right under his office window, ten feet from the building, and from his box seat he must have seen the mob cut off Washington's ear as a prelude to the obligatory castration. Later, Waco citizens told Freeman that the fire had damaged the tree's beautiful foliage. Only a young manicurist whose window at work also looked out on City Hall Square had been willing to go on record with her description of the horrible scene. As the NAACP investigator recorded, "it was generally known that something was going to happen, and when they heard the noise everybody rushed to the windows, and that child saw them unsex the body . . . [and] others say . . . that they were carrying the proof around in a handkerchief showing it as a souvenir . . ."[38]

A photographer, too, tried his hand at the souvenir business. Freeman discovered that Gildersleeve—he put his name on the photographs—was tipped off by telephone and arrived in time to set up his camera even before the mob lit the fire. "It was a cooked business between the Mayor and himself. The getting of the pictures was a certain amount of rake-off." Quickly printing the photos as postcards, he sold them for ten cents apiece to those unfortunate enough to have missed acquiring their own portion of Washington's body. Ten cents, after all, was significantly cheaper than the five dollars that by day's end Washington's teeth were reportedly fetching and less even than the links of the chain that were trading for a quarter. No one, it seemed, was selling the more coveted body parts. The only important difference in the case of the burning alive of Jesse Washington in Waco in 1916 was that Freeman got the pictures. But Gildersleeve charged Freeman, posing as a suffrage activist, five times his regular price.[39]

The photographs filled in with graphic visuality what the papers with their nods to politeness and decency and the "cultured and reputable city" had largely left out. The pictures gave witness to the new, multistoried buildings, City Hall Square spilling over with Wacoans, and the setting of a black man on fire. They showed the body burning, burnt and charred beyond human resemblance, and the white boys smiling with the ash. Freeman specifically asked only for pictures of City Hall, the courthouse, and the judge, claiming as a motive her desire to show folks up north that Waco was a nice and friendly place. The mayor and sheriff hesitated and hemmed and hawed over her request, reluctant to circulate the pictures further by giving them to outsiders. As even the on-the-take mayor and the sheriff sunk in the politics of his own reelection came to see, these images would subvert the story they wanted told about Waco once they had circulated beyond the approving context of the souvenir-seeking crowd. But they relented and granted Freeman the pictures. Erasing the fine line between civilized ritual and savage spectacle, the photographs appeared widely in the weeks afterward, provoking regional and national condemnation and challenging the often recycled story of the white community in action. Despite *Birth of a Nation*'s declaration of national reunion, the narrative of white unity would not hold.[40]

The sheriff's and the mayor's changes of heart about the photographs, however, were not the only evidence of cracks within the standard white southern lynching story. The unnamed reporter at the *Waco Semi-Weekly Tribune* began well, describing how Washington was seized in the courthouse and making the necessary nod to law officers who had valiantly performed their duty yet somehow misplaced their guns: "once the huge mass of humanity moved, it moved in such a compact formation that nothing could stop it." The paper described the crowd as made of men, women, and children, "all classes of people and among them many negroes." But soon a slip appeared: "Not all approved, but they looked on because they had never seen anything of the kind. No hand was raised to stop the movement, no word spoken to halt the progress of those who carried the negro to his death." Evidently not all 15,000 Texans enjoyed the murder of a man who within days would have been legally executed. In a similar fashion, another local reporter admitted that "many turned away," suggesting that not everyone in Waco wanted to watch such barbarism. By the end of its story, however, the first Waco paper had resurrected the old refrain: "This is the story of the execution of this Negro by the citizens of this county. No one section was implicated more than another. They were here from all parts, and all parts and Waco participated equally." Compelled to assert the unity of the white community, then, newspapers inadvertently included blacks among the citizenry, thereby undermining precisely the point they wanted to make. The act of trying to clarify the boundary between white and black revealed the very fluidity of the color line.[41]

Nonlocal papers also focused on the white crowd in motion and ignored the effects of such blatant white barbarity on southern African Americans, but their accounts displayed a decidedly different moral. The *Houston Chronicle and Herald* put the matter baldly: "The Chronicle leaves him [Washington] entirely out of consideration. It is not him, nor his race, that has been affected; it is the hundreds of whites who participated, the thousands who looked on, the millions who will read." Calling lynching an "American institution," the *San Francisco Bulletin* concluded that "the strangest delusion in connection with lynching is that it is the victim who suffers most. In reality it is the community who is lynched." Commenting on the call to "civilize" Mexico popular among Texan whites, the *Bulletin* implied that "civilization" might be safer there. Even the African American paper the *Chicago Defender* implied that "white culture" was in great danger if it stood "for such bestial cruelty." Only the local *Waco Morning News* editorially took up for the town, but it too saw white Wacoans as the prime victims. Asking who would cast the first stone, the paper presented the Texas city as a victim of national self-righteousness. The culture of segregation conflated "civilization" with white space, and the order of Waco's City Hall Square had been undeniably violated that May morning. The *News* did not understand how much it gave away when it claimed "Civilization is but skin deep."[42]

With Washington's lynching in 1916, then, replaying the familiar ritual of white supremacy, reconstructing the master narrative, was much more complicated than in the 1899 lynching of Hose. Regional papers had abandoned altogether that story of the white community upholding civilization. Instead they deployed varying degrees of outrage over the spectacle's destruction of the very whiteness it was supposed to save. National anti-lynching agitation increased after the Washington lynching under the leadership of the NAACP, and Congress considered the Dyer Anti-Lynching Act in 1919 and 1920. Northern big-city papers, too, expressed a clearer condemnation.[43]

But interpretations of the meanings of these events had never been their main attractions. As NAACP official Walter White stated thirteen years after Waco, many white newspaper readers around the nation could encounter the spectacle with "little thought" and perhaps a small amount of titillation. Even locally the question was less one of agreement than of interest. As the *Waco Semi-Weekly Tribune* had put it, "once the huge mass of humanity moved, it moved in such a compact formation that nothing could stop it . . . Not all approved, but they looked on because they had never seen anything of the kind. No hand was raised to stop the movement, no word spoken to halt the progress of those who carried the negro to his death." Some southern whites had always publicly condemned lynching. Their numbers grew as the twentieth century progressed. But it was white participation, not white agreement, that empowered lynching as modern spectacle, creating a white consuming public and easing white divisions of gender and class. And participation—in a continuum, certainly, of moral repugnance and responsibility—ranged from performing the tortures to watching the murder to looking at the pictures. As the film critic Dana B. Polan has explained, spectacle condensed sense and understanding into sight and "jettison[ed] a need for narrative myths . . . Contradiction itself [became] a new coherence, the modern seduction." Du Bois had boldly stated that even the deadly spectacle of African American otherness had become an amusement. And the amusement, the cultural power of spectacle lynchings, lay not in the assignment of cause and blame, the tallying of rights and wrongs, but in the looking.[44]

As the Smith, Hose, and Washington lynchings demonstrated, then, innovations like trains and cars, telegraphs and telephones, and cheaper newspapers and photographs could expand and strengthen the power of each incident as easily as they increased white condemnation. And *Birth of a Nation,* shown widely from its release through the end of the decade, merged the twentieth-century spectacle lynching with Reconstruction era violence, producing a spectacle of lynching for the entire nation. The symbolic reunion of North and South that *Birth* captured so vividly and to such popular acclaim echoed the political reconciliation evident in the election of the southerner Woodrow Wilson to the presidency in 1912 and the segregation of Washington, D.C., during his first term. The North, then, had accepted southern whites' version of Reconstruction as black space and installed the culture of segregation at the very center of the nation. With America's entrance into the Great War in 1917, Wilson realized what George Creel, his chair of the Committee on Public Information, bluntly stated: the need to "weld the people of the United States into one white hot mass instinct." The president borrowed *Birth of a Nation* imagery to celebrate another American ride to the rescue, the entrance of America into the war. In both the movies and in life, the spectacle of African American otherness created white unity and gave birth to the modern nation. Whether most Americans rationally agreed with *Birth's* interpretation of the Civil War and Reconstruction little mattered. As Wilson understood, the film "wrote history in lightning" because of the pleasure of the looking.[45]

The two regions' elites, then, had come together in whiteness, in their desire for a system of difference that would withstand the corrosive effects of modernity and defend against the breakdown of all social categories. The color line at the foundation of the southern culture of segregation was no longer mediated even by a lingering regional animosity. But the practice of

lynching continued, as southern elites without business connections outside the region and southern whites without business connections at all continued to murder African Americans, not in contradiction to but because of
other white southern elites' and nonsoutherners' increasing opposition. As
lynching became more about conjuring "southernness"—understood as
white—than about "whiteness"—understood as American—the form and
narration of the spectacle necessarily changed.

The Lynching of Claude Neal

The lynching of Claude Neal in Marianna, Florida, in 1934 signaled the
end of the gruesome southern practice of spectacle lynchings. The lynching of Matthew Williams in 1931 in Salisbury, Maryland, had served as a
practice run for Neal. Sending Johns Hopkins professor Broadus Mitchell to
investigate the "gaudy show," H. L. Mencken sarcastically commented on
and editorially condemned the entire Eastern Shore from the *Evening Sun*
in Baltimore. A crowd of over two hundred white men—Mencken called
them "town boomers"—took Williams from a hospital and hanged him
from a tree by the courthouse for the enjoyment of a thousand spectators.
And there were a few other gruesome murders of black men and women
after 1934—the burning to death of two black men with gasoline blow-
torches in the town square of Duck Hill, Mississippi, in 1937 stood out for its
barbarity across the entire history of southern white racial violence. But the
Neal lynching, unfolding against the background of the case of the Scottsboro men, was different. Local whites pointed to the nationally publicized
trials and appeals of these nine young African Americans accused of raping
two white women on a train as evidence of how justice was thwarted when
citizens let "the law take its course." But the NAACP learned a very different
lesson from its struggles with the International Labor Defense, a popular
front organization, over control of the Scottsboro men's defense. The correct publicity could transform an event into a tool for achieving the organization's larger goal, the passage of a federal anti-lynching bill, and from the
Neal lynching forward the NAACP worked to capture the cultural power
inherent in sensationalized, gruesomely voyeuristic stories and even more
grisly pictures for the anti-lynching crusade. Though Neal was lynched in
an isolated backwoods area of northern Florida instead of in broad daylight

in the center of a southern city, the NAACP made the torture and murder of Claude Neal into a spectacle. It uncovered the details, constructed the story, and provided the meaning, telling the nation a tale of white southern injustice rather than of the still-persuasive black beast rapist. And they told it well.[46]

The local, regional, and national press, however, certainly did not ignore the lynching. In fact, the *Marianna* (Florida) *Daily Times-Courier* and the *Dothan* (Alabama) *Eagle* announced the "lynch party" in their October 26 morning editions, at least twelve hours in advance of Neal's torture and murder. The Associated Press issued a series of dispatches from the area around Marianna beginning with an October 26 morning report, and newspapers from the *Richmond Times-Dispatch* to the *Bismarck* (North Dakota) *Tribune* announced "Mob Holds Negro; Invitations Issued for a Lynch Party." But the details of the lynching, which occurred at the hands of the approximately one hundred white men who had taken turns torturing Neal over ten hours, did not appear in the press. The local and state law officials had made a show of trying to prevent the lynching, and no one from the press admitted being a witness to the event.[47]

The NAACP, however, was determined to make use of the case to strengthen its hand in the ongoing fight for the Costigan-Wagner Anti-Lynching Bill. Within eight days of the lynching, it sent an undercover investigator, Howard Kester of the Committee on Economic and Racial Justice, a white liberal southerner in his early thirties, to Marianna, instructing him "to get all the gruesome details possible together with any photographs of the body, crowd, etc . . . " On November 7 Kester wrote Walter White, then secretary of the NAACP, that the night before a member of the mob had related "with the greatest delight" all the specifics of Neal's prolonged torture. By November 30 the NAACP had published Kester's report, and at last the details of perhaps the most chillingly brutal lynching to date were available for public and nauseating consumption.[48]

The NAACP's *Lynching of Claude Neal* was widely circulated—Mencken sent it out to his Christian friends with a Christmas card attached—and over 15,000 copies were distributed and sold. And yet Kester's description varied little from turn-of-the-century narratives of lynchings published by local and regional white papers in praise of the practice. The key differences were his inclusion of a picture taken of the naked and mutilated body, the kind of photograph usually sold as a souvenir but never published in a newspaper, and his arrangement of the narrative's parts. Kester began not with

Neal's alleged crimes, mentioning only that he had been arrested for the murder of Lola Cannidy, but with the mob, "car loads of men" cast as savages hunting down a black man already in custody and threatening his also jailed mother and aunt. The mob played the role of the villain, then, less because of what Kester said about them than because he had not yet proclaimed Neal guilty of rape. And Kester's accounts of the shortcomings of law enforcement officials had also been present in narratives justifying lynchings, though perhaps with less detailed evidence. But most strikingly, Kester moved next to recount the lynching itself, still without having described in voyeuristic detail the black man's alleged crimes. And although later, in a concluding section on the historic, social, and economic context of the Marianna area, he would describe it as otherwise, here he placed the northern section of Florida and southeastern Alabama squarely within 1930s America, a place where newspapers, telephone calls, and even a radio station in Dothan, Alabama, advertised that a "lynching party" would be held "to which all whites were invited." The scheduled "modern Twentieth Century lynching" of Neal, he claimed, drew between three and seven thousand whites to the "ringside seats" at the murdered white woman's home.[49]

Kester did make three subtle innovations in the dominant lynching narrative, however, providing more detail in one central plot section, clarifying necessary ambiguities in another, and extending the story past a frenzied souvenir-gathering aftermath. Though the torturing of lynch mob victims had been described before, no other report surpassed the NAACP's unblinking account of Neal's castration, framed as the words of a bragging eyewitness: "they cut off his penis. He was made to eat it. Then they cut off his testicles and made him eat them and say he liked it." And Kester's arrangement of the Neal story fully utilized these details, transforming the eye-for-an-eye narrative structure in which one violated body demanded another more violated one, a black man's body for a white woman's contaminated soul, into a tale of competing bodies as metaphors for competing truths. Lola Cannidy's clothed and only beaten and still not raped corpse could never overcome, then, the horror of Neal's mutilated remains, scattered across the countryside and shattering the narrative frame, entering the future as alcohol-preserved fingers in a jar.

In addition, Kester clarified the ambiguities that surrounded white women in the lynching narrative. For the story demanded women's participation—identifying their or their relatives' rapists, relating the specifics of their own or other women's torments, and calling for the most brutal deaths for the black men they accused. And yet it also depicted their victimization—the living torture of raped "ladies" whispered better off dead and the shocked and speechless horror of a murdered woman's relatives. Kester presented white women unflatteringly detached from their pedestals. He reported how an unidentified woman at the Cannidy house drove a butcher's knife through the heart of Neal's corpse, brought to the door by some lynchers in a car. His report also described Lola's sister shouting that no possible punishment could ever fit the crime. Most importantly, however, Kester described how Lola herself, about to marry a white man, wanted to end her sexual relationship with Neal and threatened him with lynching. This alternative female image contrasted sharply with the picture of violated ladyhood drawn by the local papers. And whether or not Kester had evidence to back up his account of Lola Cannidy's and Claude Neal's affair, the NAACP engaged in the same kinds of exaggeration that had become standard in the lynching narrative. NAACP activists by the 1930s were as little interested in the truth as the white southerners who defended lynching. Their agenda was a moral, not a historical one—they wanted to save not facts but lives.

Finally, Kester added a postscript to his narrative, describing the lives of African Americans in the days between and after Cannidy's and Neal's murders. Playing "Uncle Tom" and "Sambo," terrified local black men desperately tried to distance themselves from Neal's publicly predicted fate. But a riot broke out after Neal's death anyway, as the thousands of spectators who went to the wrong location and were thus deprived of the promised entertainment roamed the town looking for other victims. In Kester's version, instead of an implied return to white order beyond the narrative frame, the lynching ended with another charge by those rampaging and revenging white men. As the riot exploded, so did white unity. Kester ended his narrative and began his analysis with the image of whites protecting, sometimes with shotguns pointed at other whites, their cherished black butlers and maids.

Lynching as a story of the entire white community in action, using savagery to protect southern "civilization," was dead. And Walter White, then secretary of the NAACP, followed up on the success of the Neal pamphlet by attempting to create yet another lynching spectacle. The NAACP was a silent sponsor along with a distinguished list of published patrons of "An Art Commentary on Lynching," an exhibit of paintings, prints, and drawings about lynchings at the Arthur U. Newton Galleries in New York City.

Almost three thousand people saw the exhibition of thirty-nine works—
some directly inspired by the killing of Neal—on display from February 15
through March 2, 1935. Copies of the catalog, with moving forewords written by Sherwood Anderson and Erskine Caldwell and reproductions of five
of the works, circulated widely. The NAACP and other organizations also
began using photographs and grisly descriptions of lynched black men on
petitions circulated for signatures in support of federal anti-lynching legislation and on postcards mailed out to raise funds. The lynching spectacle,
then, had given way to the growing anti-lynching crusade's attempt to make
a spectacle of lynching. Lynching may have remained a white southern pastime, but it became a much more private sport. If the nation wanted to look
at or read about the mutilated and murdered bodies of black men, it would
have to sign the petition.[50]

And yet since the spectacle itself was enough to create a white public,
the NAACP's capture of the lynching narrative, its impact on national interpretations of lynching's meaning, did not disrupt the cultural work of the
spectacle. Whites were not blacks, and blacks were still humans who could
be tortured and killed with impunity. No doubt for some whites the slippage
between titillation, self-righteousness, and disgust remained. White southern elites blamed "crackers," and northern whites pointed a finger at white
southern barbarity. Having reunited in their common racial identity, northern and southern whites argued, then, about whether lynching protected or
damaged whiteness while glossing over the plight of the African American
victims. And by continuing and expanding the circulation of the stories,
even anti-lynching activists' use of lynchings as spectacle helped maintain
the power of the practice as a cultural form and aided in the cultural work
these narratives performed. That they had no other option demonstrated the
power of the spectacle in setting the boundaries of racial meaning.

After the Neal lynching, spectacle lynchings seldom happened, and
lynchings that became spectacles—the 1955 lynching of Emmet Till was
perhaps the best known—were overwhelmingly condemned. W. J. Cash
was right about the continuing need of white southerners to reassure themselves with yet another reenactment of the old white supremacy ritual.
What he failed to understand, however, was that southern whites no longer
needed to "dirty" their towns with actual lynchings. The spectacle circulated in detailed written accounts of tortures, pickled and dried body parts, a
radio announcement, an Edison recording, a film, and even a gruesome
picture postcard sent and saved: these artifacts increasingly did the cultural

work of othering southern African Americans, of making whiteness across gender and class lines, for them. And from the perspectives of anti-lynching activists, the African American public that supplied the victims, and small-town boosters alike, this shift was progress. Yet the image of the "black beast rapist," providing a foundation for the culture of segregation beyond the reach of rational discussion, remained. The modern twentieth-century lynching had become the white South's own ritual of transgression, and by the late 1930s representations of lynchings worked almost as well as lynchings themselves.[51]

The Meaning of the Spectacle

At a country picnic in 1896, a young white boy hurried up to the booth to trade his sweaty nickel for a rare chance to hear that marvelous modern wonder, the Edison talking machine:

> With the tubes in my ears, the Pitchman was now adjusting the needle on the machine . . . My excitement increased, my heart was pounding so I could hardly hold the tubes in my ears with my shaking hands . . . "All Right Men. Bring Them Out. Let's Hear What They Have to Say," were the first words I understood coming from a talking machine . . . The sounds of shuffling feet, swearing men, rattle of chains, falling wood, brush, and fagots, then a voice—shrill, strident, angry, called out "Who will apply the torch?" "I will," came a chorus of high-pitched, angry voices . . . [I heard] the crackle of flames as it ate its way into the dry tinder . . . My eyes and mouth were dry. I tried to wet my lips, but my tongue, too, was parched. Perspiration dripped from my hands. I stood immobile, unable to move. Now the voice of the Pitchman saying, "That's all gentleman—who's next?" . . . [and] sensing what my trouble was, said, "Too much cake, too much lemonade. You know how boys are at a picnic."[52]

Perhaps little Mell Barrett would have been as sick and excited if he had actually witnessed the lynching of these unidentified men, burned to death by a mob after being forced to confess to rape and after pleading desperately for mercy. A place in a giant rushing crowd and the slow building, perfect pacing, and almost delicate choreography of a lynching such as Hose's three years later might have counteracted the uniquely nauseating stench of burn-ing flesh. Through the recording and the quick working of a young boy's imagination, however, as his physical reactions revealed, Barrett was there. Representations of lynchings, multiplying and increasing their power with the spread of consumer culture, made the line between individual and col-lective experience much more permeable than the line between the races. As Richard Wright knew well, a person did not have to experience the violence directly to feel its effects. And despite the chasm that separated African Americans' mediated experience of the terror and white Americans' mediated experience of the titillation, in both cases contact with a represen-tation of the event was enough. To the newspaper story, the warning or brag-ging word overheard, and the remembered sight of fingers floating in alcohol in a jar were added as the decades passed those more modern ways of spreading knowledge: the radio announcement, the Edison recording, and even the gruesome picture postcard sent and saved.[53]

Lynching was the brutal underside of the modern South, the terrifying and yet for whites also perversely titillating practice and increasingly medi-ated narrative that made the culture of segregation work and even seem sane. As participants, spectators, investigators, and present-day scholars have all to varying degrees argued, lynchings, particularly the blatantly public spectacles, worked by ritualistically uniting white southerners, by embody-ing the community in action. Thus the "whole populace," the "whole male community as a unit," "the citizens of this county," and "all the white peo-ple" lynched Smith, Hose, Washington, and Neal. Even the naming of lynchings revealed their communal nature, as lynchers and anti-lynching activists alike called them after the cities and towns, the white communities that had performed them. But even as early as Hose, cracks appeared in white southerners' stories of lynching as the unified assertion of white su-premacy. Lynchings conjured whiteness, then, through their spectacle of a violent African American otherness as much as through the narratives of white unity they generated. And that spectacle eased the contradictions at the heart of segregation, enacting the whiteness segregation simultaneously created and undermined.[54]

The culture of segregation made race dependent on space, and the color bar became less a line than the ground on which southern people were allowed to drink and buy and stand. The ritualized lynchings of the twentieth-century South were in part the controlled inversion of this practice of racial separation, the southern version of the medieval ritual of "woman on top" in which boundary crossing served as boundary control and the ambivalance and contradictory nature of the proceedings expanded their power. In these spectacles, a transgression of segregated spaces occurred that eased without eliminating the subtle contradictions between the practice of segregation and the ideology of absolute white supremacy upon which it was based. As separation of the races became the foundation for white racial identity, black homes, businesses, churches, and bodies threatened to provide a ground of black autonomy that could challenge white supremacy. Yet lynchings denied that any space was black space, even the very bodies of African Americans were subject to invasion by whites. And public violence asserted this right in a way that was much more visible than the many undoubtedly frequent but much more privately horrible rapes and murders. These "lynch carnivals," then, were not about a lingering frontier past but about strengthening the culture of segregation, creating a new southern future in which an expanding consumer culture created and maintained rather than blurred and transformed racial difference. Lynchings ensured that a black man or woman was not just, as Du Bois had stated, "a person who must ride Jim Crow in Georgia," but also someone who could be publicly tortured and killed, prevented even from being a person.[55]

And lynchings reversed the decommodification of black bodies begun with emancipation. In spectacle lynchings, blacks themselves became consumer items; the sites of their murders became new spaces of consumption. After the lynchings of Smith, Hose, and Washington, markets in the gruesome souvenirs sprang up within minutes of the victim's death, and professional and amateur photographers alike rushed eagerly to the scene to capture the lynchers posing with the body. In other cases, stereographs of lynched black men were made and sold for three-dimensional viewing. Spectators occasionally even broke into black-owned general stores and passed out soda, cake, and crackers as refreshments.[56] In one rare case, a lynch mob in Texas skinned a black victim called "Big Nose" George and made the tanned "leather" into a medical instrument bag, razor strops, a pair of women's shoes, and a tobacco pouch. The Rawlins National Bank proudly displayed the shoes for years in the front window. As H. L. Mencken ironically asked, referring to a much more typical collection of body parts, in his coverage of the 1931 lynching of Matthews Williams: "What has become of these souvenirs the *Marylander and Herald* [the local paper] does not say. No doubt they now adorn the parlor mantlepiece of some humble but public spirited Salisbury home, between the engrossed sea shell from Ocean City and the family Peruna bottle. I can only hope that they are not deposited eventually with the Maryland Historical Society."

Even if no historical society ever received such family heirlooms, Mencken was hardly exaggerating. Souvenirs were often publicly displayed. In the Hose lynching, townspeople considered it a supreme act of friendship when a man offered to split Hose's finger with his neighbor. Claiming all spaces and all consumption as white, lynchings closed off any access, however contingently, to the transformative possibilities of consumer products and consuming spaces by changing blacks themselves into the objects of white desire. This much, these lynchings said, could never be changed: blacks were humans who could be treated as nonhuman, and no amount of care on their part to follow the "rules" could in the end ensure their safety. Segregation seemed, on the other hand, if discriminatory, at least to offer places of relative safety and security, to allow at least the minimal right to exist to the new black bodies and spaces of freedom, a right that public spectacles of violence absolutely denied. Lynching was among other things the horror that made that oppressive system of segregation seem tame. Encountering Hose's knuckles, Du Bois confronted the very center of southern whiteness itself.[57]

But lynchings as a cultural form transgressed the color bar in another way as well. For the lynching narrative joined whiteness and blackness symbolically and bodily as the ritual built to a climax of torture and death. Cutting between the scene of Gus's castration and a Klan ceremony performed with the alleged rape victim Flora's blood, Griffith's original print of *Birth of a Nation* only made more explicit the mixing of white and black blood that was reported in the Hose lynching as white men rushing to cut souvenirs off the still live body sometimes stabbed each other instead. Spectacle lynchings, as the literary critic Robin Wiegman has argued, "enact[ed] a grotesquely symbolic—if not literal—sexual encounter between the white mob and its victim." Certainly this mixing of whiteness and blackness occurred only temporarily. And yet representations of lynchings suspended this moment in time, as pictures or pieces of mutilated bodies became souvenirs much like sexy photographs of or gifts from cherished lovers. Whiteness and blackness merged and civilization became savagery to defeat savages; in the end blackness was destroyed, and whiteness was all. Souvenirs of spectacle lynchings warned southern African Americans that violations of the color line could occur in both directions, that integrated spaces could prove deadly. Whites' transgressions, then, reinforced separation even as they cut out any authority black spaces threatened to provide. The lynching act publicly revisited the biracial origins of southern culture only to deny in its narrative what it furiously displayed in its spectacle. After the "carnival," the white order of the culture of segregation was restored.[58]

Yet the sexuality at the center of spectacle lynchings, the castration of the black beast rapist in exchange for the violated white "virgin," proved that the "ritual of transgression" involved gender as well. Beyond reversing the decommodification of black bodies, the spectacle lynching also reversed the desexualization that also began with emancipation. The black man who during Reconstruction could no longer be stripped and beaten by a white man had demanded the removal of his female relatives from the spaces of white male control. By the end of the nineteenth century, however, he could be stripped and killed, becoming a sexual victim himself. The lynching narrative would never have been so powerful a ritual of subversion if the spectacle had not been invented within the late nineteenth-century context of changing southern white gender relations examined in Chapter 2. As historian Nancy Maclean has argued about the lynching of Leo Frank, "charged issues of sexuality and power between the sexes . . . [acted] as a trigger" for the mob's brutal actions.[59]

In fact, categories of gender and race would not stay fixed within these violent rituals, a slippage Griffith made explicit in the original cut of *Birth of a Nation* but perhaps even more visible in Jean Toomer's 1923 poem "Portrait in Georgia," which transforms a white woman into a lynched black man:

> Hair—braided chestnut,
>> coiled like a lyncher's rope,
> Eyes—fagots,
> Lips—old scars, or the first red blisters,
> Breath—the last sweet scent of cane,
> And her slim body, white as the ash
>> of black flesh after flame.[60]

In his *Light in August* (1932), William Faulkner too explores this violent conflation of womanhood and blackness through the culmination of the racially ambiguous Joe Christmas's fantasy of "womanshenegro" in his murder of his white lover Joanna Burden and his lynching and castration as a black man at the hands of the white Percy Grimm. These writers, then, only made more apparent a transformation working in less artistic lynching narratives as well. In the Hose and Neal lynchings, as in others, the white men seem to fall into a strange love of their victims, praising the supermasculinity displayed by these black men through their calm courage in facing torture and death. White women refused to sit passively on their pedestals: Mrs. Cranford demanded that Hose be burned before her eyes, women in the crowd cheered the slow roasting of Washington, and a female relative of Lola Cannidy drove a butcher's knife through Neal's heart. And Toomer evoked the contestation of bodies, the mutilation and killing of the black man's body in return for the violated one of the white woman, visible in these lynchings as well.[61]

Ida B. Wells was the first investigator to delve beneath southern whites' loudly proclaimed connection of lynching to the "black beast rapist," and her 1892 suggestion that white women's sexual desires played an important role has been largely neglected. Twenty-four years later, Sheriff Fleming of Waco, the law enforcement official who did little to stop the 1916 lynching of Jesse Washington, tried to assure the voting public of his manliness, bragging about his "virility" in campaign ads. But it was not until 1941 that W. J. Cash first connected lynching to a crisis of masculinity. Cash provided one of the first examinations of a threatened white male authority as the overthrow of slavery's racial order also endangered its sexual order:

> For the abolition of slavery, in destroying the rigid fixity of the black at the bottom of the scale, in throwing open to him at least the legal opportunity to advance, had inevitably opened to the mind of every [white] Southerner a vista at the end of which stood the overthrow of this taboo. If it was given to the black man to advance at all, who could say (once more the logic of the doctrine of his inherent inferiority would not hold) that he would not one day advance the whole way and lay claim to complete equality, including, specifically, the ever crucial right of marriage. What [white] Southerners felt, therefore, was that any assertion of any kind on the part of the Negro constituted in a perfectly real manner an attack on the Southern [white] woman.[62]

Cash implied that white male power challenged by black men's political and economic advances translated into white male sexuality threatened by black male sexuality. Rape of white women signaled metaphorically white men's fear of the loss of ability to provide for white women and physically their fear, given their treatment of black women, of the loss of white racial purity.[63]

In his examination of Thomas Dixon, popular author of *The Leopard's Spots* and *The Clansman*, on which *Birth of a Nation* was based, the historian Joel Williamson has made Cash's argument much more explicit, describing a crisis of white male sexuality as southern white men worked themselves into a corner within which black and white women became unavailable sexually. Fear of the white women who held families and communities together after the war competed with white men's romanticization of their brave deeds. Beginning in the Reconstruction era as white men increasingly glorified white women, the pedestal rose too high for the satisfaction of white male sexual desires. At the same time, with the emancipation of female slaves, white men found themselves less and less able to take their sexual desires to the quarters. Lynching, then, relieved these tensions and transferred the supersexual powers of the white-constructed "black beast rapist" to the sexually diminished white man even as it diminished the feared power of the white woman who now needed white male protection. White women and black men were conflated as fear of and the desire to protect the white woman became fear of and the desire to destroy the black man.[64]

And yet more than elite white manhood was at stake. Lynching helped reconcile the ambiguity of gender difference at the heart of a society in which the primary boundary was the color line. The gender lines within the whiteness made by the culture of segregation were less than clearly drawn, no matter the amount of effort both white men and women expended in the praise of the "lady on her pedestal." For white supremacy always carried with it the possibility of strengthening the white woman as it emasculated, often literally, the black man. Toomer's poem can as easily be read as an empowering exchange in which the white woman, not the white man, takes her existence from the last breath of the burned black man. White women, after all, shared a racial power that contradicted the supposed inferiority of their gender. And fear of the "black beast rapist" exploded not in the 1870s, when African American men were more recently released from the reportedly "civilizing influence of slavery," but in the 1890s, as whites began building segregation as culture upon segregation as policy. The historian Jacquelyn Hall has emphasized, "it may be no accident that the vision of the black man as a threatening beast flourished during the first phase of the southern women's rights movement, a fantasy of transgression against boundary-transgressing women. Certainly the rebelliousness of that feminine generation was circumscribed by the feeling that women were hedged about by a 'nameless horror.' "[65]

Spectacle lynchings did sometimes incorporate warnings aimed at unconventional women. When the lynch mob dragged Washington's corpse through the streets of Waco in 1916, some of his charred limbs fell off. The NAACP's investigator discovered that these reminders of the white community's power to define acceptable sexual behavior, instead of being sold as souvenirs, were placed on the stoop of a "disrespectable" woman's home in the reservation district. And yet white women often directed the very rituals by which white men recaptured their own masculinity through the castration of the black male. After all, as in the Hose lynching, the black man's supersexual image was often the result of their testimony. White women like Rebecca Felton, perhaps the region's most popular white woman journalist, were empowered by the lynching narrative. Felton owed much of her region-wide fame to her demand in a speech before hundreds at an 1897 meeting of the State Agricultural Society of Georgia that "if it takes lynching to protect [white] woman's dearest possession from drunken, ravening human beasts, then I say lynch a thousand a week."[66]

The spectacle lynching began in a setting that emphasized a sharp gender difference, with the white woman endangered by a "black beast rapist." For no matter the actual crime, as Wells had argued as early as 1892, no matter that the evidence was inconclusive that Hose, Washington, or Neal committed sexual assault, rape provided the justification. Yet the act of the torture and murder itself brought white men and women together symbolically and physically just as it had merged whiteness and blackness. White women often participated as announcers of the upcoming event, as spectators, and as gatherers of wood and other fuel. They directed the actions of large numbers of white men by alleging rape, attempted rape, or even an attempted stare, and by demanding tortures and egging mobs on. In one case a woman even stood on a car and repeatedly yelled "roast the nigger" when it seemed the mob might show mercy. Not just the white man was empowered when the black man was literally and symbolically deprived of his masculinity. The lynching narrative moved white women toward masculinity even as it subtly shifted white men away from the maleness, embodied in the black beast, that they were trying to capture through castration. Thus spectacle lynchings operated upon gender ideologies in very contradictory ways. Replicating a process at work in the larger southern world, the lynching narrative simultaneously empowered white women as it emasculated black men and limited white women as it signified their need for protection.[67]

The lynching narrative, then, conferred a power that white women accepted ambivalently. No doubt some white women used it. The NAACP reported that Lola Cannidy attempted to break up with Claude Neal by threatening him with lynching. Yet white women were never allowed to assume the major roles in the spectacle, to participate directly in the torture. The southern suffrage movement too had pursued a strategy that sought white women's political power in the name of their racial identities, as a way to strengthen whiteness, and had almost totally failed. Only the Association of Southern Women for the Prevention of Lynching (ASWPL), led by Jessie Daniel Ames, seemed to walk the tightrope between racial strength and gender weakness well, mobilizing this very contradiction in the 1930s and 1940s to help decrease racial violence. Donning a veil of white womanhood—emphasizing and even exaggerating gender difference—white women nevertheless argued privately that even "southern ladies" did not need the protection of the mob. When lynchings seemed imminent in their towns or counties, members of the ASWPL called sheriffs and mayors and quietly reminded them that as women they could not actively intercede with the mob but that as whites they were voters too. The activist Lillian Smith hinted at southern white women's contradictory experience of whiteness and womanhood in her autobiographical work *Killers of the Dream:*

> One day, sometime in your childhood or adolescence, a Negro was lynched in your county or the one next to yours. A human being was burned or hanged from a tree and you knew it happened. But no one publicly condemned it and always the murderers went free. And afterward, maybe weeks or months or years afterward, you sat casually in the drugstore with one of the murderers and drank the Coke he casually paid for. A "nice white girl" could do that but she would have been run out of town or perhaps killed had she drunk a Coke with the young Negro doctor who was devoting his life to the service of his people.[68]

White women's access to the power of whiteness could be effective against lynching, then, but not against the system of segregation that helped create their racial identities in the first place. In the end, both the racialized spaces of consumer culture and male power were restored.[69]

Finally, lynching as the controlled inversion of segregation also helped ease the class tensions within white supremacy. For poor whites, too, experienced a racial power that contradicted the inferiority of their class position. No matter the economic strength of southern progressives, of the mill owners and professionals, or of the new southern middle class that created segregation as policy. Any white man and some white women, too, could "burn a nigger." And white southern elites, even when they wanted to, could not stop other whites from lynching without threatening the system of segregation, itself based on white supremacy, that had helped secure their rise above their fellow farmers in the first place. But as sociologist Arthur Raper found in his 1933 study of lynchings, the "best men" seldom condemned the practice:

> Not infrequently more unanimity can be had on a lynching than on any other subject. Lynching tends to minimize social and class distinctions between white plantation owners and white tenants, mill owners and textile workers . . . This prejudice against the Negro forms a common meeting place for whites.

Only in the Neal case did published accounts question that all whites supported the spectacle. The culture of segregation created a cross-class construction of whiteness, and the mass of white spectators and mob members provided its physical embodiment. For tenants and mill hands, being able to commit unpunished acts of violence created an illusion of individual power, of control over their destinies, however, that their deteriorating place in the southern economy belied.[70]

By the end of World War I, increasing numbers of white elites, especially in cities, had developed important ties beyond the region and had become concerned about outside condemnation of the practice. In addition, lynchings often created race riots, and certainly the same racial tensions fueled both. Many of the buildings, houses, and businesses burned by rioters in Wilmington in 1898, in Atlanta in 1906, and in the widespread racial violence in 1919 after the end of the war did not belong to these poorer whites. And Leo Frank had brought home the danger of calling the white masses into motion—they could turn on their white employers, a task no doubt made considerably easier by Frank's Jewish otherness, instead of their African American neighbors.[71]

Between 1890 and 1940, however, a profound shift occurred within the class tensions that spectacle lynchings ritualistically resolved. The practice had in part originated in the late nineteenth century as white elites tried to consolidate their power in the postbellum economic order by pulling less wealthy whites away from possible Populist allies, the black tenants who lived the same difficult rural lives. By the time of World War I, however, as national reconciliation between northern and southern whites peaked in a recognition of their common racial identity, the class dynamic within southern whiteness reversed. Small-town and rural southern whites continued to lynch in defiance of wealthier and often more urban and nationally oriented members of their race. The lynching of Leo Frank, an early example of this shift despite its urban context, had essentially been an argument about which southern whites would shape this collective racial identity. In the 1920s and 1930s, lynching asserted its practitioners' southern distinctiveness, their own definition of whiteness, in opposition to a more urban, national version. Though spectacle lynchings could not occur without the complicity of mayors, law enforcement officials, and local businessmen, mob leaders were less likely to come from these groups, which increasingly voiced a public appeal for the rule of law. In the Neal case, law enforcement officials did make some effort to avert the lynching, and despite making a secret deal with the lynchers, Marianna businessmen did not publicly lead or support the mob. In addition, especially by the 1930s, southern big-city newspapers always condemned the practice. Their concern, however, passed over the African American victims to focus on injury to white "civilization," as demonstrated by Mencken's attack on the lynchers of Salisbury, Maryland, in 1931 and the *Atlanta Constitution*'s condemnation of the 1934 Neal lynching.[72]

Somehow the violence had to be controlled, then, without upsetting poorer whites' support for the culture of segregation. And here again a growing consumer culture making less violence better known and thus more powerful reinforced the culture of segregation by reconciling its ideological contradictions. Whites could now consume a lynching without consuming a black man, alleviating the danger of a lynching spilling over into an anarchy that destroyed valuable property. A lynching somewhere else could create a white public and yet not hurt local town boosting or challenge local class hierarchies. In growing urban eras, police forces increasingly stepped in to stop extralegal violence and protect property. For many white southerners, representations of lynchings had become better than lynchings themselves.

But not for all. Though the circulation of the lynching narrative—especially with the NAACP's escalation of the anti-lynching campaign—helped eliminate spectacle lynchings, in more isolated places like Glendora and Poplarville, Mississippi, whites continued to assert what they thought was their racial right to kill African Americans, albeit more privately. Private lynchings continued and may even have increased in the 1930s as some rural white southerners saw the violence as an act of southern patriotism. For some whites, then, images of lynchings did not work quite as effectively as lynchings themselves in reconciling the class differences within the whiteness empowered by the culture of segregation.[73]

Spectacle lynchings symbolically and physically subverted segregation, separation as culture, in order to strengthen it. These grisly rituals ensured that the whiteness segregation created remained unbroken within by gender and class divisions and unchallenged without by a black autonomy nurtured on the ground of separation. But as some white southern elites increasingly saw their own interests connected culturally and economically to a North whose conception of justice did not as routinely include extralegal violence, lynchings could no longer conjure southern unity across a growing class divide. The contradictions between more dominant American conceptions of "civilization" and southern whites' claims of superiority cracked whiteness in a way that lynching, as the cause, could not seal. For some whites, then, lynching, "smashing a sassy Negro," became a badge of southern distinctiveness as well as racial identity. The federal government and the moralistic North could not again tell these southern whites how to manage their own affairs. By the 1930s, violence became one way to mediate between the desire for Americanization, a connection to the larger nation, and the fear of losing the white southern self.

But perhaps most frighteningly, the lynching narrative worked as a ritual of inversion that created white unity within the nation as well as the region. Resolving the contradictions of a nationalism based on racial identity—a national white supremacy—the white South could always be condemned by the North as excess, as lack, thereby providing the mask underneath which the inequities of American whiteness could be ignored. The fact that northern African Americans could look south and see a much more explicit oppression must have dampened their confidence in demanding greater rights at home. As NAACP director James Weldon Johnson declared so eloquently, "lynching in the United States has resolved itself into a problem of saving black America's body and white America's soul." Despite the moral as well as racial ambiguity with which William Faulkner surrounds Joe Christmas, perhaps the most famous fictional victim of a lynch mob, then, many whites continued to see the "black beast rapist," their own simple and therefore defeatable devil, their own collective construction of evil. On the black side of Calvary, however, African American and white liberal anti-lynching activists offered a vastly different interpretation of southern white atrocities, attempting to make the Christlike natures as well as the racial identity of lynching victims transparently clear. Only the African American body hung on that charred cross. For whites it meant damnation, the perhaps permanent loss, as Johnson understood, of a large part of America's soul.[74]

CHAPTER SIX

Stone Mountains

LILLIAN SMITH, MARGARET MITCHELL, AND WHITENESS DIVIDED

This isn't the first time the world's been upside down before and it won't be the last. It's happened before and it will happen again. And when it does happen, everyone loses everything and everyone is equal.

MARGARET MITCHELL[1]

There are a lot of people in America today still trying to buy a new world with old Confederate bills . . . It is just possible that old answers which seemed "true" in the tight, rigid frame of the southern past are based on assumptions that are no longer valid. It is just possible that the white man is no longer the center of the universe.

LILLIAN SMITH[2]

IT RISES, gray and ringing, 683 feet of solid granite, straight up from the rippling land of northern Georgia. The foothills surrounding the stone only quote its majesty and make its sudden presence, its hovering bald bulk visible as the pilgrim tops a rise in approach, that much more sublime. Scientists have estimated that at its slow rate of erosion, Stone Mountain will stand its eternal vigil little changed as modern civilization and perhaps even humanity itself disintegrate into dust. Nature has crafted a rock immense, singular, and enduring upon the landscape a mere sixteen miles from Atlanta, that center of the New South.

By the second decade of the twentieth century, white southerners had begun to feel like Stone Mountain, fixed in their place within the nation and yet firm in their regional distinctiveness, secure in their separation from southern blacks and yet strong in their racial power. If the grandiose visions of the Atlanta attorney William H. Terrell and the United Daughters of the

Confederacy leader Caroline Helen Jemison Plane in 1914 had ever been realized, the Stone Mountain Confederate Monument, nature itself transformed into a memorial of white origins, would have stood with the election to the presidency of the southerner Woodrow Wilson, the unprecedented popularity of the film *Birth of a Nation*, and the segregation of Washington, D.C., as symbols of the modern white South's triumphant coming of age.[3]

Yet a world war and the technological and financial obstacles to carving a mountain into a panoramic relief of the Robert E. Lee–led Confederate army intervened. Although the Stone Mountain Confederate Memorial Association (SMCMA), incorporated in April 1916, had hired the internationally known sculptor Gutzon Borglum and secured a deed to the straightest face of the granite dome, work on the mountain did not begin until 1923. Conceived in the context of a national monument building craze, an effort in part to ground in stone the courageous struggles of the Civil War generation and provide their offspring with the lesser but still arguably heroic role of memorialists, the Stone Mountain Monument took shape instead within a new era. Most veterans had passed away by the early 1920s, and the memorialists, children during the Civil War and Reconstruction, now watched their sons and daughters, born as the century turned, grow to adulthood in a significantly different post–World War I world. The South had fought on the winning side in this conflict, and America's increased international stature brought greater opportunity even to the nation's poorest region. Race riots and widespread racial violence had followed African Americans' accelerated migration north, and in the immediate aftermath of this Great War whites across the nation moved much as white southerners had done after Reconstruction to destroy blacks' wartime hopes for expanded freedom. A greater sharing of the "Negro Problem" as well as the wealth further reduced already less significant sectional tensions. This made white southerners, especially an increasingly town- and city-oriented and educated middle class, more secure within their regional culture of segregation and the nation.[4]

For this white southern middle class, especially the generation born around 1900, southern whiteness was less an identity to create and empower within an internal dynamic of white versus black and an external dialect of southern versus northern. The solidification of the culture of segregation, in fact, created the space, narrow at first and yet widening under the pressure of national depression in the next decade, within which middle-class whites could begin to disagree about the nature of their regional identity. For many of these whites, race had become curiously disembodied as segregation left them with little contact with southern blacks outside the increasingly sentimentalized rituals of domestic service. Their whiteness took its form from these unquestioned interracial interactions but also from stories of the regional past transmitted orally by older relatives and formalized into plantation and Civil War fiction and history. Even more importantly, however, for a generation longing to prove its difference and even modernity, whiteness emerged from the racialized spaces and shopping rituals of an expansive consumer culture and from the images of blackness for sale there.

Increasingly in the 1920s, then, more town- and city-oriented middle-class whites lived only with black fictions of their own making. Black identity fixed in segregation seemed as enduring as Stone Mountain, leaving a separate whiteness available for more experimentation and expansion. But the unfinished memorial, its appearance like watered granite in the wavering humid heat of a Georgia summer, served as an apt metaphor for the weak strength of the hegemonic regional racial identity from which it had sprung. Conceived as a symbol of the solid white South, the mountain as monument proved strangely ephemeral as factions within the association squabbled, blasting competing designs from the face and leaving Robert E. Lee's head floating strangely disembodied above his shallowly etched torso and horse. The culture of segregation attempted to secure and fuse regional and racial identities by crafting both literal and metaphorical geographic anchors, and yet success generated the first fissures, the tiny cracks within that would eventually yield to the continual external resistance of black southerners.[5]

Raised entirely within the culture of segregation their parents had made, the white generation of 1900 overflowed with individuals who would make their mark on the region and even the nation. William Faulkner, Allen Tate, Guy B. Johnson, Robert Penn Warren, Arthur Raper, Katharine Lumpkin, Nell Battle Lewis, Julia Collier Harris, Margaret Mitchell, and Lillian Smith were perhaps only the most widely known. Strangely neglected within cultural studies of the period, however, Mitchell and Smith shared much in common as they probed the boundaries of middle-class white southern womanhood and achieved more celebrity than critical fame. Their effects upon the culture of segregation within which they grew to adulthood and the middle-class white identity grounded there, however, could not have been more different. Margaret Mitchell's 1936 best-seller *Gone With the Wind* synthesized, completed, and moved beyond white narratives of a plantation garden, war, and the "dark days of Reconstruction," capturing this southern "past" for both the middle-class southern present and white women in particular. Translated into film by David O. Selznick, the movie version made this white southern narrative of origins into the nation's past as well. While Lillian Smith did not publish *Strange Fruit*, her best-selling novel of interracial love in a small southern town, until 1944, she spoke out with increasing and unparalleled white directness in the late 1930s against the culture of segregation and the damaging effects of racial separation on southern whites themselves. Her 1949 meditation on segregation, *Killers of the Dream*, only made her critique of regional racial identity more explicit. If Margaret Mitchell reempowered regional distinctiveness even as she contributed to a common American whiteness, Lillian Smith attacked white racial identity and its foundation in segregation with both compelling argument and enormous courage.[6]

Segregated Youth

Born in 1897, the eighth of ten children, Smith spent her earliest years in the small town of Jasper, Florida, near the state border with Georgia. Her father virtually embodied that late nineteenth-century American ideal, the self-made man. Having come from a family of small Georgia farmers, he not only built his own turpentine, timber, and naval stores business but also completed his class ascension by marrying the daughter of a Georgia rice planter. By Lillian's birth, Calvin Warren Smith also owned an interest in the local waterworks and electric company and held important positions in the religious and educational institutions of Jasper. And Smith had the requisite Confederate grandfather, even if he had been born in New York and only later moved south, married, became a planter, and "fought valiantly" for his adopted region. But Smith had little interest in romanticizing the exploits of her ancestors. In a documentary about her life she stated simply, "I have never been one of the people to indulge in a great deal of nostalgia." Yet young Lillian's comfortably middle-class childhood ended when her father went bankrupt and lost his lumber and turpentine mills as Europe entered World War I. After Smith finished high school in 1915, the family

left Jasper and moved to their summer home in the mountains near Clayton, Georgia, a property held in her mother's name and thus saved.[7]

Although she never knew the financial hardship Smith experienced in
her youth, Margaret Mitchell grew to adulthood with a father forever
shaped by the long heroic shadow of his father's military and business successes and his own trials establishing a law practice through the 1890s
depression. Born in 1900 into one of Atlanta's first and wealthiest families,
Mitchell nevertheless grew up in a home made literally cold by her father's
miserliness. Unlike Smith, stories of her mother dominated Mitchell's later
recollections of her childhood: "My earliest memories are of my mother
and the woman's suffrage movement." Mitchell's descriptions of May Belle
Stephens Mitchell stressed her reform and charity activities and the selfless-
ness such work entailed: "The first time I was ever permitted to stay up later
than six o'clock was on the tremendous occasion of a suffrage rally which
was to be presided over by Carrie Chapman Catt . . . The cook went home
sick, all the relatives had gone to the meeting, and there was no one to look
after me." Mitchell got her first view of her mother the activist:

> Mother tied a Votes-for-Women banner around my fat stomach, put me
> under her arm, took me to the meeting hissing blood curdling threats if I
> did not behave, [and] set me on the platform between the silver pitcher
> and the water glasses while she made an impassioned speech. I was so
> enchanted at my eminence that I behaved perfectly, even blowing kisses to
> gentlemen in the front row. I was kissed by Mrs. Catt (if it was she), and
> called the youngest suffragette in Georgia and the future of our cause. I
> was intolerable for days afterward and, only after being spanked, was per-
> mitted to witness a [suffrage] parade . . .

And yet such stories reveal Mitchell's unspeakable sense that the duty to
society, encompassing young Margaret as well, twisted into a selfishness that
made a mother deny her own child. Her sharing of her mother's spotlight,
her pride, ended in punishment. While Smith recounted warm memories
despite the difficulties of joining her younger siblings in the bankrupt family's struggle back from ruin, Mitchell remembered a narrow and aloof
father constantly worried about money despite her family's wealth and an
equally distant although much more broad-minded mother simultaneously
bounded by and yet active as a reformer of middle-class conventions of
womanhood.[8]

For Mitchell, family always extended beyond the bond of parents and siblings. Visits with relatives became happily remembered occasions spent swapping stories that strung together the family's and the region's past. While Smith described a family opened up to the larger world by the frequent letters home from her older sister serving as a missionary in China, Mitchell recounted in peppered prose her own family's focus backward on the past: "I heard so much when I was little about the fighting and the hard times after the war that I firmly believed Mother and Father had been through it all instead of being born long afterward. In fact I was about ten years old before I learned the war hadn't ended shortly before I was born . . ." The accounts of older relatives who had witnessed the region's violent transformation firsthand, however, made the war real for young Margaret as well:

> On Sunday afternoons when we went calling on the older generation of relatives, those who had been active in the Sixties, I sat on the bony knees of veterans and the fat slippery laps of great aunts and heard them talk about the times when Little Alex [Alexander Hamilton Stephens, vice president of the Confederate States] was visiting them and about how much fried chicken Father Ryan could put away and how nice thick wrapping paper felt when put between the skin and the corset in the cold days of the blockade when woolen goods were so scarce. And how Grandpa Mitchell walked nearly fifty miles to Sharpsburg with his skull cracked in two places from a bullet. They didn't talk of these happenings as history nor as remarkable events but just as part of their lives and not especially epic parts. And they gradually became part of my life.[9]

This difference would shape their sharply divergent writing and thinking about their region as adults, but in girlhood and adolescence Mitchell and Smith shared everything from male nicknames—Margaret was Jimmy and Lillian Bill—to an early and earnest passion for writing. Both women came of age during the Great War and spent their young adulthood in the period through the early 1920s as self-conscious and rebellious flappers, adopting short hair and skirts and cussing and calling themselves bohemians. And Mitchell and Smith both rejected the strong religious beliefs of their families. Smith captured the general feeling of a generation succinctly if self-righteously: "I had been religious as a child; was brought up in the

Methodist church; just sort of took it for granted. But at 15 or 16 I began to rebel; to ask questions; it was in the air, you know; it was my generation who did the rebelling. So, by the time I went to China, I was an 'agnostic' and took no part in the church." Mitchell abandoned the strict Catholicism of her parents in her single troubled year at Smith College. But their roles as dutiful daughters would prove much less easily left behind.[10]

If childhood provided the fluidity to play at being boys, adulthood necessitated choices, and both Mitchell and Smith had difficulty negotiating the shifting terrain of white southern middle-class womanhood as they attempted to plot adult female independence. Raised in staunchly middle-class homes despite the sharp divergence after 1915 in the Smith and Mitchell family finances, both absorbed all the contradictory messages of their early twentieth-century gender identities: the strong, self-reliant, intelligent, capable, and yet nurturing mother and community reformer versus the passive, gentle, and subservient wife. Although white middle-class womanhood in the South in particular allowed women to assert mastery over African American domestic servants as well as white children, this agency received community sanction only when enacted in the name of others.

Mitchell and Smith both found it difficult to fit their ambitions within this form and yet neither could imagine and craft a mature femininity that did not place their creative desires as secondary to family and community responsibilities. Significantly, Smith also had to earn a living. But both refused to close off the gender fluidity of their childhoods, claiming as young women the self-conscious and tomboyish rebellions of the flapper figure toward the dutiful Victorian wife. Mitchell and Smith carried the stylistic and pleasurable resistance further than most bob-haired women, enacting the playful yet serious masquerade of donning conspicuously male attire. A closeup photo of Smith in 1927 portrayed the young camp director clad in a stiff and mannish white oxford shirt cinched tightly around her neck with a dark necktie. A scrapbook of 1920s photos from her parents' Camp Laurel Falls, where Smith worked summers, depicted women counselors in decidedly martial attire, from army-like riding outfits to navy-inspired sailor shirts. Mitchell enjoyed a similar cross-dressing as part of her job as an *Atlanta Journal Magazine* reporter. "Stunt articles" required the petite reporter to dress as a storm trooper, a window washer atop an Atlanta skyscraper, and a downtown construction worker.[11]

Despite such visible impersonation of male characters, however, neither woman proved able to place creative ambitions above the demands of family. Both interrupted their education and then writing to care for needy parents, siblings, and other relatives. In Mitchell's case, taking on house-keeping for her father and brother after her mother's death became in a way part of her very rebellion. In an act the dramatic gesture of which must have appealed to a daughter who filled her childhood writing and staging plays, May Belle Mitchell wrote from her deathbed, warning Margaret against just such a sacrifice. Yet May Belle, revealing perhaps her own ambivalent feelings about adult womanhood, muddled the message:

> I expect to see you again, but if I do not I must warn you of the one mistake that a woman of your temperament might fall into. Give of yourself with both hands and overflowing heart, but give only the excess after you have lived your own life.

If she had stopped here, she would have transmitted to her daughter a frank and feminist warning. But May Belle, perhaps recoiling from the implications of her own words, continued:

> This is badly put. What I mean is that your life and energies belong first to yourself, your husband and your children. Anything left over after you have served these, give and give generously, but be sure there is no stinting of love and attention at home. Your father loves you dearly, but do not let the thought of being with him keep you from marrying if you wish to do so. He has lived his life; live yours as best you can . . . Care for your father when he is old, as I cared for my mother. But never let his or anyone else's life interfere with your real life.

May Belle's "real life" for her daughter meant first and foremost the young woman's completion of her education at Smith College. Yet Mitchell, unhappy at Smith, used the fact of her mother's death and her father's and brother's prodding—they had never approved of such a "radical" education anyway—to do exactly what her mother feared as well as directed. May Belle's inability to endorse female ambition explicitly, couching it instead in a language of the family her daughter would create versus the family into which she was born, made Mitchell's choices as well as rebellions that much more unclear. After her second marriage to John Marsh in 1925, Mitchell would continue to put her writing grumblingly aside to nurse and even entertain family and friends as well as participate in community service.[12]

Smith proved much less explicit about her own relationship to her mother in her youth but also articulated a sense of conflict between her own choices and a heavy sense of responsibility to her family. She wrote of her parents as fragile both psychically and financially after her father's bankruptcy, and repeatedly she gave up her own goals to help them earn a precarious living. After one year on scholarship at the tiny Piedmont College in Demorest, Georgia, Smith suspended her education to spend the next winter helping her parents manage a Florida hotel. She then studied at Baltimore's Peabody Conservatory for a year as part of her plan for a career in music, followed by a year teaching in a small Georgia mountain school to help support her parents. For the next three years she was back at Peabody, but she still gave her summers to her parents, cleaning cabins and managing activities at the summer hotel that supported them.

In 1922, Smith left home to teach music in a missionary school for Chinese girls in Huchon, China. Although fearful of the unsettled political situation there and disgusted by the blatant racism of her fellow Western teachers, she was enchanted by the landscape and culture, and she found a longed-for sense of autonomy and liberation in China. Again, however, she put aside her own desires and rushed home in 1925 when her father needed her help running the summer camp for girls he had started with Smith's brother Frank on the family's mountain property. Still clinging to her ambition for a career in music, she took a winter job teaching at a college near Clayton. This time the death of another brother's wife changed her plans: Smith dropped this position to care for her brother's small daughter at his home in Fort Pierce, Florida. When one of her dead sister-in-law's relatives pronounced Smith "too young, too radical, [and] too 'progressive' " to serve as surrogate mother and took over this role shortly after Smith's arrival, she helped her brother instead with his job as city manager. Later she remembered ruefully, "By this time my life actually did not seem my own; I was just carrying out other people's directives."[13]

Paradoxically, both Mitchell's and Smith's inability to resist the pull of family responsibilities led to their liberation. In 1925 Smith very reluctantly took over the camp for her father. She possessed, she insisted later, "little interest in it"; although she "swam, played tennis, [and] danced," she "was not the athletic type." Disappointed with the camp's competitiveness and "authoritarianism," she set about trying to establish the creative and partici-

patory pedagogical methods she had learned in China and in the winter of
1927–1928 at Columbia University's Teachers College as well as more programs in art, music, dance, and drama. Her father's failing health and her
growing interest in the camp led her to purchase Laurel Falls in 1928. Running the business shifted Smith's attention from music to her childhood passion, writing, as she spent winters producing camp newsletters, catalogs,
and promotional materials. The time spent with the children, as the scholar
Margaret Rose Gladney has argued, gave Smith "emotional access to her
own childhood and awareness of the socialization process." She would use
this knowledge to examine her own coming of age in particular and the
making of white southerners more generally, in the intricately interwoven
tasks of crafting an independent and nonracist female agency and writer's
voice. The camp became a female-centered world over which Smith, rare
among career women in the 1920s, had extensive control.[14]

Mitchell, on the other hand, had married disastrously in 1923, but the
short-lived union, rather than confining her, instead opened a path for her
out of homemaking. Her husband Red Upshaw's inability to hold down a
job coupled with her father's miserliness—the couple lived in the Mitchell
home—sent Mitchell herself out into the labor market. Although her father
vehemently denounced her pursuit of a career in journalism, Mitchell convinced herself that she and her husband needed the money. In December
1922, she landed a job as a reporter for the *Atlanta Journal*'s Sunday magazine section, where she covered the society news—essentially the social
activities of her family's friends—and wrote feature stories. Here Mitchell
earned validation of and praise for her writing. Being a reporter allowed her
to go places white southern ladies did not go and talk to people beyond
"respectability," from bootleggers to prostitutes to murderers. Mitchell
worked hard, writing a major article every week and often filling the magazine's gossip and "lovelorn" columns as well. She also did copyediting and
paste-up work and wrote book reviews. Her boss Angus Perkerson gave her
the highest praise he could muster. "She wrote," he claimed, "like a man."

One of her early "stunt" stories placed her high above the center of
Atlanta clad in size forty overalls hanging out the side of a skyscraper. In
the flurry of newspaper and magazine coverage surrounding the beginning
of the carving at Stone Mountain, her employer desperately sought a new
angle. His answer was to juxtapose the tiny, attractive Mitchell with the
large body and by implication ego of the monument's sculptor. Mitchell
wrote, "One doesn't feel so very good when one is shoved out of a window of

a skyscraper, especially when one has never been shoved out of any window before. A dizzy whirl of buildings, windows, a glimpse of the sky, anxious faces at windows, all jumbled up for an instant of eternity, a feeling of nausea, then a bump completed the first swing in the air and brought me up against the side of the building with an awful wallop." The photo, of course, depicted Mitchell sitting in the Stone Mountain sculptor Gutzon Borglum's by then famous swing.[15]

The White Maturity of Stone

Gutzon Borglum had been making headlines in Atlanta since 1915, when Helen Plane and the Atlanta chapter of the UDC called him to the city to survey Stone Mountain and discuss their memorial plans. He quickly dismissed the organization's decision to carve a hundred-foot-high face of Lee seventy feet above the ground on the sheer northern face of the site. Seeing the immense block of faultless granite, Borglum shocked the Daughters by telling them their head of Lee would look like a postage stamp stuck on a barn door. Ironically, the sculptor had achieved national fame in 1915 for his towering bust of Lincoln carved for the Rotunda of the United States Capitol. Stone Mountain, however, gave Borglum what he called "a Vision." Instead of the tiny Lee head he saw an image of thousands of Confederate soldiers marching across the steep dome of the mountainside led, of course, by a fully figured Lee riding his horse Traveler. Borglum described his ambitious plan for the *New York Times Magazine* in 1916 as "cutting a great frieze representing a moving mass of troops across its face in full or high relief, in such a manner . . . as to give the impression that they were in full relief and moving over the surface of the mountain. To the spectator, suddenly coming upon the mountain, in a dusk or soft light at a proper distance, the general appearance will be that of the natural mountain over which, silently, this great grey army moves." Newspapers and magazines compared the proposed memorial without irony to the Sphinx, the pyramids, and other ancient wonders of other lost worlds, all of which it would both outlast and dwarf. The mountain would be made into the world's largest monument. Borglum had transformed the UDC's modest plan into the "eighth wonder of the world."[16]

From the first, efforts to convert the eternity the planners saw in the

mountain to an actual carved memorial proved difficult. The UDC envisioned the memorial in sectionalist terms, as a lasting tribute to the "heroes
in gray." The group's Georgia state historian, Mildred L. Rutherford,
repeated the mantra of states' rights and the justice of the cause "not lost."
Borglum seemed more intent on his own rather than the Confederacy's
glory. In December 1922 he discussed the project with the editor of the
Atlanta Journal Magazine and Mitchell's new boss Angus Perkerson: "The
memorial as I plan it will without doubt be the greatest monument ever
built. The single figures will dwarf other pieces of sculpture, and the entire
effect of an army marching across the mountain in review before their leaders will be bigger than anything of the sort ever before attempted." For Borglum, "my memorial" meant the artist's own as well as the Confederacy's
eternity. Yet a theme of sectional reconciliation came through even Borglum's bloated egotism. When asked how he could reconcile his love for
Lincoln with his work on the Confederate memorial, the midwesterner
answered that he shared as well "the deepest respect for the great men of the
other side." More guarded when talking to his employers the SMCMA, Borglum modestly argued again for a national rather than a sectional message.
The project interested him, he insisted, because the Stone Mountain
Memorial was "the first effort in America to build a monument to a nation,
to a movement of a hundred thousand or ten hundred thousand people."[17]

The SMCMA walked a difficult line, making both sectional and
national arguments to appeal to both the nation and the most ardent Lost
Cause supporters in an effort to raise the funding. Politicians from across the
country supported the effort, and in keeping with a national movement
to reclaim Confederate military leaders and especially Lee, praised the
planned "colossal" carvings of these great "American men." Even President
Warren G. Harding complimented the Borglum design and promised "the
people of the South" the aid and cooperation of "Americans everywhere"
while stressing the message of reconciliation: "It will be one of the world's
finest testimonies, one of history's most complete avowals, that unity and
understanding may be brought even into the scene where faction, hatred,
and hostility have once reigned supreme."[18]

In praising a gigantic carving of a Confederate army as a symbol of
the nation, these white men continued a theme of sectional reconciliation through a common white male martial ideal that had begun with the
Spanish-American War in the late nineteenth century and received new life

through the film spectacle of *Birth of a Nation*. By January 21, 1925, the U.S. Congress as well as the new president Calvin Coolidge had sanctioned the project by authorizing the U.S. Mint's coinage of five million silver half dollars designed by Borglum to raise funds and commemorate the carved soldiers, "custodians of imperishable glory." The SMCMA commissioned and sold songs and poems validating the place of Confederate heroes within the nation as well.

White women, too, found their wartime courage and suffering memorialized in the proposed second phase of the project, a vast hall in their honor carved into the heart of the mountain below the sculpted army. The womb-like space, a hall of records as well as a place of contemplation, would celebrate white women's roles as the mothers and wives of soldiers and as the initial planners of the monument and keepers of the Confederate past. Less dramatic and visible than the mountain carving, the women's hall would nevertheless tell the women's own story of southern origins and create a new, monumental domesticity.

On January 19, 1924, the SMCMA ceremonially unveiled the head of Lee, and a stream of articles in popular national magazines as well as successful lecture tours by Borglum kept the country informed of the progress. Travel writers described even the unfinished carving as a tourist attraction. A letter to the *Atlanta Constitution* from a sympathetic northerner reprinted under the caption "The Memorial's Cash Value" predicted that the mountain would make Atlanta the tourist "mecca of American and of other peoples for all times." In December 1925 *Forbes Magazine* even hailed the project as the creation of a truly American art, the nation's "answer to the ancient charge that the country is too absorbed in the pursuit of wealth to be interested in the more enduring things of the spirit."[19]

Yet by 1925 the Stone Mountain monument, planned to make the Lee-led Confederate army the very symbol of sectional reconciliation and American international grandeur, joined the 1925 Scopes trial in Dayton, Tennessee, with which it competed for attention that year, as a very different kind of symbol. The national press characterized the infighting among Borglum, the UDC, the SMCMA, and the mountain's owner, Samuel Venable, as an example of old-fashioned political machine patronage in the same league as the old-fashioned religion on display at the "monkey trial." That the allegations against the SMCMA of corruption, theft, and mismanagement of funds involved charges of Ku Klux Klan involvement only made the story better copy. After all, after the Atlanta lynching of Leo Frank in 1915, the Klan had marked its reorganization with a late-night ceremony atop Stone Mountain itself. Borglum was dismissed; with his flair for the dramatic, he smashed his clay models with an ax left picturesquely at the scene and fled the state. His supporters claimed he feared attack by the Klan but did not reveal that the sculptor was a member of that white supremacist organization as well. Next, the SMCMA, led by Hollins Randolph, sued Borglum for destruction of property. In keeping with his national interpretation of the memorial, Borglum suggested in response that a national committee take over the work of Randolph's SMCMA board. The UDC and Venable attacked the SMCMA for embezzlement and mismanagement of the hundreds of thousands of dollars donated for the project. Through the political allegiances of their editors, the Atlanta newspapers too became involved in the battle, adding journalistic fuel to the mountain monument's fire. Quickly hiring another sculptor, the board tried to bury the controversy and continue the fund-raising. By April 1928, Augustus Lukeman had blasted Borglum's carving off the mountain and unveiled his own head of Lee atop a half-carved horse.[20]

The momentum and national enthusiasm in the project, however, had waned. The Great Depression came early to the South, following the boll weevil east in the late 1920s. And southern whiteness had other less expensive anchors, as narratives of a past pastorale, a heroic and principled war, and those eternally nurturing mammies mingled with the present graphics of segregated consumption and the spectacle of lynching. The SMCMA eventually went bankrupt, and Lee floated vaguely above the ghostly Traveler until work resumed on the project in the 1960s. Borglum went on to plan and carve the much more explicitly national monument on Mount Rushmore, South Dakota. Confederate military leaders, perhaps, could no longer serve as central symbols of an increasingly modern nation's past. Southern and American whiteness needed a more complicated narrative rather than a singular mountain-sized spectacle. Having resigned from her job at the Atlanta Journal Magazine for health reasons, however, Margaret Mitchell had already begun creating the novel that would succeed where the Stone Mountain Memorial, nature itself transformed into a symbol of white supremacy, had so humiliatingly failed.[21]

Cracks in the Mountain

By the 1920s, some white members of the generation of 1900 had turned from rebellions against hair and dress length and Prohibition to more probing investigations of their own culture of segregation. Racial separation had become so naturalized for whites that after the Great War a group of white moderates in Atlanta formed the Commission on Inter-racial Cooperation (CIC) to initiate cooperation between middle-class African Americans and whites in the cause of "racial progress." Middle-class whites and working-class African Americans, of course, had continued despite segregation to interact as white employers and black employees, particularly domestic servants and agricultural workers. But as the African American secretary of the Kentucky Interracial Commission, a state branch of CIC, stated in a brief and widely circulated history of "the Interracial Movement in the South," the white founders of CIC had asked "a number of representative colored men" and later "the South's leading women" to come together in adoption of "a platform upon which all could stand." The group sought legal justice and the end of lynching but saw its main task as the promotion of the "contact necessary in the solution of any problem." Another press release of the CIC, in an indirect attack on both more racist organizations like the KKK and more activist groups like the NAACP, clarified its own "policy of cooperation between the more thoughtful of both races" as "the antithesis of antagonism and polemic discussion." Yet while the CIC sought improvement in southern race relations, the committee never questioned the racial separation at the heart of both modern southern society and modern white racial identity: "Mutual helpfulness between whites and blacks should be encouraged; the better element of both races striving by precept and example to impress the interdependence of peoples living side by side, yet apart." The CIC hoped to bring back to visibility the very middle-class African American on the train, albeit in a limited and white-controlled way, that southern whites had created segregation in large part to deny.[22]

Despite the mild and moderate nature of its protest, then, the CIC opened up a space for the beginning of white questioning of the culture of segregation. While CIC drew most of its white leaders from the generation that preceded Lillian Smith's and Margaret Mitchell's contemporaries, young white southerners sometimes cited their participation as college students in YWCA and YMCA CIC-related activities as the beginning of their racial conversion.

Katharine Lumpkin perhaps best illustrated this route to a critique of segregation. Working as a traveling YWCA secretary in the mid-1920s, Lumpkin was instrumental in the integration of YWCA and YMCA administration and leadership programs. Having instituted a plan through which white and African American YWCA traveling secretaries would cover their territory and its college branches and programs jointly instead of separately, Lumpkin expressed the practical difficulty of putting this integration into practice to a co-worker: "I tell myself it is beginning with the determination to see oneself as only one-half of a proposition." She found it difficult to change her habit of thinking and organizing alone: "and yet we must uproot that at least enough to make room for the fact that we are two instead of one—and yet we must work as nearly as possible as a unit . . . It is one of the manifestations of what a race situation does to society." Reflecting back on her 1920s YWCA activism in 1943, Lumpkin wrote that "something happened to not a few of us. [We saw the] whole problem of the future of the bi-racial South and how changes may come, if they cannot be affected merely by occasional individuals shifting to a new position on . . . race." These young white and black students moved beyond the limited vision of their CIC supporters.[23]

While Smith herself participated in some YWCA activities in Baltimore, she absorbed its brand of progressive evangelicalism more from her missionary sister and her own later experiences in China than through any specific working with an interracial movement. She wrote years later that her racial epiphany occurred as she experienced the contradictions of her fellow American and British missionaries' racial behavior abroad. Living in a small Chinese city, these ten or twelve whites practiced an absolute segregation of their social activities from the young Chinese women and girls they had traveled halfway around the world to serve: "I saw white supremacy over there . . . and the further away from home I was, the worse it looked of course. I had taken it for granted in Jasper . . . I was stirred intellectually by what I saw in China. I was at a distance; I could analyze, criticize, look at, rebel . . . And I did." Yet Smith also admitted that upon her return home to help her father run the camp, she did not work against segregation: "I myself was not prejudiced. I think I thought that was enough. I was decent; I did not bother about the others." Smith saw herself as an artist—an accomplished musician and a beginning writer. She spent her time avidly reading psychoanalytic and psychological theory and working to transform her camp into a creative and nurturing female-centered world.[24]

Although she too devoured psychoanalytic theory, Margaret Mitchell took her youthful flapper antics in a decidedly different direction, one shared by more of the rebellious generation than the unusual insights into whiteness of Lumpkin and Smith. A "little magazine," the *Double Dealer*, launched in New Orleans in 1921, began the attack on the by then traditional white southern use of the past, and railed against this "storied realm of dreams, lassitude, pleasure, chivalry and the Nigger." The Fugitive poets in Nashville followed in 1922, denouncing "the high caste Brahmins of the Old South," and "the treacly lamentations of the old school." As Allen Tate later recalled, their very name reflected their sense of themselves as rebels: "a Fugitive was quite simply a Poet, the Wanderer . . . the Outcast, the man who carries the secret wisdom around the world." These whites posed themselves against the plantation romance and its Reconstruction fall. The historian Darden Asbury Pyron has summarized well their "paradigm of regional history": "instead of dreams and fantasy, they called for realism and sociology; instead of lassitude, for hard work; instead of pleasure, for diligence and self-advancement; instead of chivalry, for the values of the bourgeoisie and the middling sorts. And instead of slavery and the Nigger? They focused on the culture of the White Folk." And this perspective characterized to some degree whites as different as Tate and Wilbur J. Cash, Lumpkin and Caroline Gordon, William Faulkner and Arthur Raper, Margaret Mitchell and Lillian Smith. Although they rarely questioned segregation, the white generation of 1900 challenged the very interpretation of the past that grounded and legitimated both the culture of segregation and their own identities as middle-class white southerners.[25]

While the Scopes trial and the conspicuous failure of the Stone Mountain Memorial project provoked national criticism of the region, a sort of cynical new sectionalism, by 1930 debate among white southerners became visible as well. The 1930 manifesto *I'll Take My Stand* initiated the first heatedly public debate about the meaning and future of southern whiteness since George Washington Cable's lonely stand in the late 1880s and early 1890s. Despite their differences, however, the Agrarians and the regionalists, a loose amalgamation of sociologists and sociologically inclined academics

led by Howard W. Odum and centered in Chapel Hill, shared a critical attitude toward the function of the mythical Old South within the contemporary scene. The Agrarians criticized the deadening effects of the new
southern hypocrisy and demanded that white southerners enact the values
they romanticized and praised as "lost." Allen Tate attempted to clarify his
position in less sectional terms in a 1936 speech: "the way we make our living must dictate the way of life, that our way of getting a living is not good
enough for us if we are driven by it to pretend that it is something else, that
we cannot pretend to be landed gentlemen two days of the week if we are
middle-class capitalists the five others." The regionalists, on the other hand,
blasted the deadening effects of the Old South romance itself and believed
that the South needed more rather than less economic development to ease
the region's extreme poverty. They too believed that most southerners' "way
of getting a living" was "not good enough" but for very different, more mate-
rialist reasons, because many had insufficient income to provide even the
minimum standard of living required for human health.[26]

The regionalists took a different public road, then, and yet arrived on a
very similar white mountain. The race question for them became a subset
of the class structure of the region. That most African Americans were poor
few whites or blacks doubted. And Odum, Guy B. Johnson, and a few other
sociologically minded white southerners consciously buried racial issues in
order to gain public support for programs that would benefit poor blacks as
well as whites. But however strategically, segregation again shaped white
southerners' vision, achieving its intended effect of hiding especially middle-
class African Americans from view. The Agrarian-versus-regionalist debate
became important to the racial future of the region, then, less because of
what either side advocated than because they argued publicly at all. By the
early 1930s the factions bickering over the Stone Mountain Memorial represented the "Solid South" more accurately than the granite mountain.[27]

A Strong White Wind

Margaret Mitchell fit squarely into this context of white southern questioning of the romanticized past, the study of "the white folk" in place of slavery
and "the nigger." Sometime in 1926, before the Stone Mountain project col-

lapsed from corruption and disagreement in 1928 and before the Agrarians launched their debate in 1930, Mitchell had already begun writing the novel that would more firmly fuse previous white southern use of the past with the middle-class southern whiteness of the present. Under the cover of health problems and the responsibilities of her second marriage, she had retired from the *Atlanta Journal* and could now devote all her time to the creative writing that had been her ambition since childhood.

Choosing to tell her story from the perspective of a young white woman coming of age as white southerners fought the war and Reconstruction, Mitchell did not fall prey to the dilemma that limited authors like Tate who often substituted a more modern nostalgia for a unified selfhood for the old Lost Cause. Her heroine Scarlett never lives "the homogeneous life" of Tate's "traditional men," never achieves the transparent unity of livelihood and morality he read back into slavery. Reconstruction does not become the fall for Mitchell's heroine: Scarlett never had any unified sense of self to lose. And Mitchell, in keeping with her flapper youth, denounced the mere mention of magnolias as "old and hackneyed," scorned "Professional Southerners," and blasted "the sweet, sentimental novel of the Thomas Nelson Page type." Like her ancestors in upcountry Georgia, she insisted, the characters in her novel were just not "lavender-and-lace-moonlight-on-the-magnolias people."[28]

In a 1942 letter to the journalist and writer Virginius Dabney, Mitchell made her conception of her novel's relationship to the plantation romance explicitly clear. She complimented Dabney's recognition of her critique of the Old South myth in a chapter, "The South That Never Was," of his recent book, *Below the Potomac*. "Practically all my characters except the Virginia Wilkses," Mitchell wrote, "were of sturdy yeoman stock." She continued:

> Since my novel was published, I have been embarrassed on many occasions by finding myself included among writers who pictured the South as a land of white-columned mansions whose wealthy owners had thousands of slaves and drank thousands of juleps. I have been surprised, too, for North Georgia certainly was no such country—if it ever existed anywhere—and I took pains to describe North Georgia as it was. But people believe what they like to believe and the mythical Old South has too strong a hold on their imaginations to be altered by the mere reading of a 1,037-page book.

She jokingly invited Dabney to join a club she had organized with friends, "The Association of Southerners Whose Granpappies Did Not Live in Houses With White Columns."[29]

Mitchell clearly saw her book as revisionary, a casting into novel form of the substitution of hard-boiled fact for white southern tradition that had first entered the region as white journalists like Gerald W. Johnson, Mitchell's own friends Julian and Julia Collier Harris, and Nell Battle Lewis followed the example set by H. L. Mencken. The sociologists of the regionalist school followed a similar formula. Mitchell emphasized repeatedly that she had historically documented every detail of her novel. While she stated that she did this checking because she "didn't want to get caught out on anything that any Confederate Veteran could nail me on, or any historian either," her tone of almost pleasant astonishment when less conspicuously rebellious southern readers praised the novel revealed that she had at least half-expected otherwise.

Like other young doubting white southerners, Mitchell focused on white culture and its class structure. Unlike most of them, she also dealt with white middle-class mechanisms of gender as well. *Gone With the Wind*'s characters, from Scarlett O'Hara and her father Gerald before her to the renegade aristocrat Rhett Butler and the hard-working small farmer Will Benteen, are white southerners on the make, hustling and scrambling and striving. Scarlett's epiphany as she lies in the dirt of a ravished slave garden behind the ruined Twelve Oaks summarizes Mitchell's critique of her contemporaries' backward vision as well: "What was past was past. The lazy luxury of the old days was gone, never to return. There was no going back. She was going forward." To ensure that readers made the connections, Mitchell denounces in a distant and omniscient narrator's voice the bitter, backward-looking women clinging to dead men and memories. Yet the very stiltedness of the prose in this denial as well as Scarlett's reference to that old "lazy luxury" reveal an ambivalence about the romanticized southern past buried deep within the novel.[30]

Mitchell never acknowledged explicitly how much her work salvaged and completed the romanticized Old South even as it criticized the myth. In her usual style of polite empathy, she thanked in letters all readers, friends, and reviewers who praised her book and did not publicly denounce the association of her novel with the Old South myth until the making of the Selznick movie in the late 1930s. Yet not just "Professional Southerners" but more perceptive readers connected *Gone With the Wind* to the mythic southern past. Julian Harris, a friend and fellow journalist, the son of Joel Chandler Harris, and with his wife Julia Collier Harris the recipient of a Pulitzer Prize for their 1920s exposure of the Klan, wrote Mitchell that she had "cut to the heart of events and at the same time interpreted the soul of the Southern tradition." The historian Henry Steele Commager noted that the novel was both an "old-fashioned southern romance" and yet something more, "a dramatic re-creation of life itself." A fellow white southern writer and Pulitzer Prize winner, Julia Peterkin, praised the book as "the best novel that has ever come out of the South," and wrote that Mitchell had crafted an "authentic account of the fortunes of a community of Southern plantation owners" and of how their "mistaken ideas and ideals" had contained the seeds of their own destruction.

While Mitchell loved these comments, her novel is not nearly so historically authentic as she and these critics claimed. What Mitchell brilliantly managed to do was both expose the Old South's faults and weld whites' mythic sense of the past and its nostalgic power to the white southern present and future. *Gone With the Wind* encapsulates even as it finishes the plantation romance, cementing finally the genealogy of modern southern whiteness, itself a middle-class production, in the service of the new racial culture of segregation. Mitchell highlights the class cracks in the Old South image within a new historical narrative that fuses that flawed aristocracy to a contemporary white southern middle class that corrected its deficiencies.[31]

For what Mitchell brilliantly did in her novel was read the white middle-class present back into the romanticized antebellum southern past. Instead of an educated and leisurely aristocrat, the grasping and striving immigrant Gerald O'Hara sits at the center of Mitchell's antebellum upcountry world. While certainly Mitchell's nuanced portrait of white class difference and fluidity before, during, and after the Civil War corrects some of the plantation romance's sentimental distortions, it also feeds the racial lie of the culture of segregation back into the southern past. Bondage disappears as an economic and social system, and instead slaves become the ornamental markers and even enforcers of white class status. Rarely if ever engaging in productive work on the plantation, the novel's black characters, Mammy, Pork, Prissy, and Sam, instead perform personal services for their owners and occasionally for the Confederacy. It is not cotton production, however sentimentally and songfully portrayed, that makes Gerald O'Hara a planter; it is his acquisition of his first slave (the valet Pork) and his Charleston wife Ellen. Prissy can neither deliver a baby nor even care for a cow. And although Pork and Mammy, as the plantation romance dictated, hide the silver and at least one sow from the Yankees, Mitchell proved either unwilling or incapable of moving her black characters beyond these stilted conventions.

Even Mammy's apparent strength is revealed after Ellen's death to be solely the blackfaced proxy of her mistress's. Scarlett muses about the stupidity of both the slaves and the northerners who desire to free them as she takes account of the desperation and ruin at Tara. But the failures of the "worthless darkies" become Scarlett's successes. Scarlett only praises the loyalty and goodness of the slave/ex-slave in comparison to the despised northern invaders and as a way to make the standard plantation romance speech about how southern whites know and love blacks better than white northerners. The character of the slave/ex-slave, denied even the faintest glimmer of agency, exists in Mitchell's novel only to magnify and reflect the identities of her white southern characters.[32]

The old plantation romance, making the singing slave one of its most persistent tropes, had at least acknowledged—even as it sanitized and sentimentalized—African American contributions to the region's economy and culture. More explicitly racist writers like Thomas Dixon—Mitchell claimed to have been "practically raised on [his] books"—had granted a few of his African American characters a beastly and violent agency in "the horrors of Reconstruction." But even Mitchell's "black beast rapist" character becomes a mere extension of white will. Given a large white man dressed in rags as a partner, the small black man only attempts to rob, not rape Scarlett after the white man yells. She has probably hidden the lumber money in her dress. The entire Klan-led white lynching machinery rolls into action without even explicitly granting Scarlett's black attacker the status of attemped rapist. And although the ex-slave Sam grapples with Scarlett's assailant, Scarlett herself runs over the white man, figured as the real agent of the violence, with her fleeing wagon.

Far from providing a climactic moment, the Ku Klux Klan's ride to the rescue and the lynching of both black and white robbers-branded-rapists do not receive the dramatic re-creation Mitchell lavished on the battle for Atlanta. They exist in the novel only in the retelling. Mitchell instead focuses on a decidedly domestic interior and the elaborate charade the respectable southern white women, their white ex-convict protector Archie, and Rhett Butler concoct and play before the Union soldiers to save the lives of their Klansmen. Mitchell confessed in a 1935 letter to her editor that she had added the Klan ride to correct "a very definite sag of interest over a range of six chapters," a section decidedly without "pictures" in which she had originally disposed of Scarlett's second husband Frank Kennedy with an attack of pneumonia. She claimed she did not like her revision much better. Certainly, Mitchell's Klan ride adds drama mainly through its quotation of past dramatizations of hooded avengers and lynching spectacles. The scene serves as Mitchell intended and also provides an opportunity for Rhett to win back the gratitude of "respectable" white southern society. It serves no racial role in the novel because Mitchell constructs no racial drama.[33]

Mitchell, then, like her segregated society, acknowledged no black contribution to the region at all. Her developed slave/ex-slave characters, mere ciphers of her more aristocratic whites, fail like their former owners to make the transition into the Appomattox-dictated southern future. Although Mitchell follows convention and paints Reconstruction as a horror, her prose lapses into a formulaic account in her distinct narrator's voice of blacks on top backed by Yankee arms and emancipation as a holiday for lazy, thieving, saucy ex-slaves. White southerners, she insists, are the victims, and with no available legal redress, white southern men by necessity form the Klan to protect white women as older, local ex-slaves say they are tired of freedom and beg for their old masters to take them home. That mainstream critics—Commager praised Mitchell for demonstrating that Reconstruction was worse than the war and J. Donald Adams noted approvingly that Mitchell made northerners "feel shame at that black page of our history"—accepted Mitchell's account of Reconstruction proved how much white southern interpretations of the period had become the national standard. But Mitchell did not need Reconstruction as her fall to banish white southerners from their Old South garden and black southerners from the New South home. African Americans are not capable in the novel of anything so grand as the destruction of a civilization. And despite the abuse Mitchell heaps upon "the damn Yankees" for their occupation of the region, even their guilt is secondary. The internal flaws of old southern whites are the ultimate cause of their destruction.[34]

The white southern middle class alone, those pragmatic and forward-looking folks, and not northern whites or southern blacks, will bear the burden and rebuild the region. Although Sherman has looted and burned their plantations, most of the planters Mitchell peoples the "County" with have, as she emphasizes repeatedly, built rather than inherited their status. And losing their slaves has only destroyed those southern whites who were already weak. As "Old Miss," the matriarch of the neighboring Fontaine family, who as a child survived a Creek attack describes to Scarlett most of their planter neighbors: "There never was anything to those folks but money and darkies, and now that the money and darkies are gone, those folks will be Cracker in another generation." Old Miss claims her people survive because they are pragmatic and able to sway in the strong wind of any trouble, silent and smiling and hard working through the storm. When trouble passes, she asserts, the Fontaines emerge resilient, and climb back to the top by stepping upon whoever is ahead of them. And this, she tells Scarlett, is the secret, the way to survive, the triumph of those who live in the present and look to the future over those who perish—whining nostalgically about the past.[35]

What makes *Gone With the Wind* the elaboration of the new southern white middle-class order, then, is that Mitchell places the drama of the war's aftermath wholly within the space of southern whiteness. Instead of the old story of racial conflict that whites invented to sanitize sectional animosity and ground sectional reconciliation, Mitchell writes of southern whites in a desperate struggle for survival with their very own values, with the identities that alone ground their sense of themselves. In place of a sectional marriage or a lynching, Mitchell connects the antebellum and postbellum sections of her novel with a decidedly middle-class scene, a homecoming. Following the road to Tara with weak Melanie, her newborn baby, and the silly Prissy, Scarlett softly hums the faint phrase of a song about carrying a weary load just a little longer, until the very repetition becomes the force that propels her forward. The phrase highlights the chapter, carrying its dramatic force as well, for the song's identity, like Scarlett's transformation, reveals itself only over time. The moment comes that Scarlett has longed for, when she will be able to lay the horrors of the battle for Atlanta and the birth of Melanie's baby on Mammy as at least a substitute for Ellen. Mammy then says, in dialect of course, the same phrase of the song: "Jes' weery loads, honey, jes' weery loads." With her head on Mammy's breast, Mitchell's heroine remembers the rest of the verse: "No matter, 'twill never be light!" Suddenly she sees Mammy and herself and the world completely and irrevocably changed. She marks the end of her childhood and her region's and the beginning of her responsibility. She makes her speech about the deadness of the past, and shouts that she will never be hungry again. Finally, she realizes only her love for Tara remains unchanged and that the land, the red earth, her home, is hers alone to save. In *Gone With the Wind*, Mitchell transforms the old tale of racial conflict into a very different battle, the fight between the pragmatic, modern white South and white southerners' powerful nostalgia for the antebellum past.[36]

Significantly, Mitchell claimed the passage from the road out of the burning Atlanta through Scarlett's assumption of the load of Tara was one of the few sections that she composed easily, that needed no rewriting or revision. For this passage reveals the racial unconscious at the heart of her novel, of racial thefts erased even as they are acknowledged. Mammy makes Scarlett remember the song, a song Scarlett recalls singing with Rhett but that she has forgotten hearing Prissy sing in Atlanta as the northern army advanced toward the city and Melanie went into labor. Although not identified in the text, the verses were drawn by Mitchell from a minstrel song, Stephen Foster's "My Old Kentucky Home," a blackfaced translation of white nostalgia for the past into the figure of the slave/ex-slave. Scarlett's racial taking, that she alone and not her black servants has carried the load, mirrors the collective racial taking the song makes manifest, of slavery with its theft of black labor sentimentalized in minstrelsy with its theft of black music and black representation. The novel here as elsewhere paints over the African American burden and makes it white: white suffering of violence during Reconstruction, white struggles to feed families and find loved ones, black loads transformed into white.[37]

In fact, Mitchell so completely erases black southerners—creating characters that are at least representations of representations—that the internal logic of Gone With the Wind provides no possibility of black subjectivity at all. Mitchell herself never described having close relationships with African American servants as a child; she never claimed a mammy. Mitchell did not, as had many white southerners before her, read a childhood love for an image of black servants back into a romanticized slave past. Braggingly, she wrote a friend soon after she took up housekeeping for her father and brother that a black servant thought her "the meanest white woman God ever made." In her later letters she often seemed to move in the opposite direction, writing her "faithful maid" Bessie Jordan back into her novel itself. At best Mitchell knew slave identity at a double remove from experience, and even then only through white eyes, in the stories of her oldest relatives, who remembered their own and an earlier generation's stories of a life half a century destroyed, and in the fiction and history that formalized and legitimated white tradition. Just how incapable Mitchell was of even beginning to imagine slave identity became clear in her hints that she had modeled the lazy and stupid character Prissy on herself. She manipulated symbols so removed from life that color, as in the case of the darkness of Rhett Butler, became a way to create nuanced divisions completely within whiteness.[38]

When Rhett makes the central speech in the novel to Scarlett, then, in a summation and extension of the words of "Old Miss," no possibility exists that the social and economic fluidity he describes, a transgression of cultural categories at the very foundation of middle-class identity, extends to race as well: "This isn't the first time the world's been upside down and it won't be the last. It happened before and it'll happen again. And when it does happen, everyone loses everything and everyone is equal" and they all start again. Equality in tribulation applies to old white divisions of class. Cathleen Calvert, once Scarlett's chief competition for the county's prettiest belle, has become trash, lower than the poor white overseer she has married. Will Benteen, the poor white who serves after the war as Tara's manager and marries Scarlett's sister Suellen, transforms himself into a gentleman through his hard work and good sense.

And as Rhett knows and Scarlett at least acts upon, survival sets old white gender divisions aside as well. Before the scene with Mammy when she assumes the burden of responsibility for Tara, Scarlett rebels at the conventions of southern ladyhood. Afterward she brashly plays the man in her desperate pursuit to save her plantation home. Ashley comments that she "carried the load of three men," and later when Scarlett understands the fact herself, that on her plantation Tara "she had done a man's work and done it well," she sets her mind to entering the lumber business. Her second husband stands stunned in amazement as his new wife behaves and works like a man. And even though Scarlett's manly activities running her business bring out the Klan, she does not have to suffer the usual penalty for unwomanly behavior; she is not raped. But even white women publicly marked as fallen can transcend their status when the world turns upside down. Belle Watling earns the approval of the grandest lady in the novel, Miss Melanie Wilkes, when this madam and the prostitutes who work for her save Melanie's husband Ashley and the other Klansmen from the federal soldiers. Only one identity cannot be performed and twisted and bent to meet the contingencies of survival. In the novel as in the culture of segregation within which Mitchell crafted it, race is the one absolute.[39]

The continuity critique of the Old South myth, then, the revisionism of Mitchell and others who placed the immigrant and native farmer origins of the supposed planter "aristocracy" on display, served the middle-class present in two ways. White class continuity linked Mitchell's own middle-class present to the old plantation elite even as it deflated white southern aristocratic pretensions. And the implication of white class fluidity, both antebellum and postbellum, connected the middle-class present to workers and farmers who had yet to enjoy the fruits of the new southern prosperity but, as Mitchell's novel suggested, could move up in the class structure if they possessed that essential "gumption" and "sap." *Gone With the Wind* opened up *Birth of a Nation*'s myth of a white manly nation in terms of gender even as it asserted a particular class indentity. White women and even fallen ones, crackers and even ex-convicts, white southerners and even Yankees, could all, by letting go of the deadening effects of nostalgia, by letting "tomorrow" be "another day," survive and claim a middle-class home.[40]

Yet Mitchell reserved one important ambivalence even as she crafted the narrative that legitimated the middle-class whiteness of the culture of segregation. She makes her heroine rebellious against the gender conventions of her antebellum childhood. She depicts her as strong, forward-looking, entrepreneurial, and shrewd. But Scarlett is lonely. Rhett again provides the perspective that encompasses the novel's white social whole when he tells Scarlett that white Atlantans will never forgive her for depriving them of the pleasure of pity, for not allowing them to feel sorry for her. The white southern middle-class present, for Scarlett as for Mitchell herself, has little space for women who act for self and not for family. Mitchell proves as incapable of creating a mature, independent, and yet also sexual womanhood in her novel as she did in her life. Scarlett, in fact, is raped in the novel, but by a white man, her husband Rhett Butler, and Mitchell makes her like it.

Mitchell found herself unable either to claim or to deny her creative ambitions and her authorship of her masterpiece—she claimed she had written her novel because her husband suggested it and because her health problems kept her bedridden, and yet she vigorously defended her craft and outlined in detail her struggles as a writer in letter after letter. In writing her novel, she fell back on the muddled compromise of her own mother's life and last letter, the equation of female self and home. Scarlett can break any gender convention to save Tara, and insists quite perceptively that if she acted the lady, if she remained within her sphere, she would have lost that very place, her home. But Rhett understands her ambition, that she likes to run her businesses and care for herself. Scarlett's flight home to Tara at the novel's end is not a flight into the plantation past. It is not the land's income-producing capability but its geography of identity, its place as a symbol of lost childhood and family and comfort and meaning and the measure of white female agency handed out in its name that draws her back. Unable, once the equality of the world upside down has ended, to craft an independent self, Scarlett retreats into the perceived safety of the middle-class home.[41]

Doubting that racial and class power were enough for independent womanhood and yet unable to break with her culture, Mitchell could not imagine anywhere else to go. In 1938 she wrote her friend and fellow southern author Clifford Dowdey and his wife:

> I couldn't live any other place in the world except the South. I suppose, being adaptable, I *could* live anywhere, but I would probably not be very happy. I believe that I see more clearly than most people (because of my experiences during the last two years) just what living in the South means. There are more rules here to be followed than any place in the world if one is to live in peace and happiness. Having always been a person who was perfectly willing to pay for everything I got, I am more than willing to pay for the happiness I get from my residence in Georgia.

To another southern author, Evelyn Harris, who had just published her first book, Mitchell wrote, "many people cannot understand how you can love your section and yet be honestly critical of it." This ambivalence about the southern past in general and white southern womanhood in particular provided the central tension of Mitchell's life and her novel. But Margaret Mitchell never understood the whole price. In the only personal racial conflict the author ever mentioned, the refusal of her history teacher Miss Ware at Smith to transfer Mitchell out a class with one of Smith's few black students, Mitchell years later could still see the situation only in white. Her teacher, she decided, was a hypocrite. Had she ever "undressed and nursed a Negro woman or sat on a drunk Negro man's head to keep him from being shot by the police?" Her teacher, she raged, still smarted from the fact that her good New England family, living in Atlanta after the war as "teachers of Negroes," had not found acceptance among socially prominent southern whites. That this teacher at the very least saw two students and two sides to the problem never would have occurred to Mitchell and many white southerners. Lillian Smith was one of the few.[42]

Seeing the Land of Difference

The year Margaret Mitchell published *Gone With the Wind*, 1936, was an important year for Lillian Smith as well, although her own celebrity as a best-selling author was eight years in the future. Smith had begun her own southern novel, *Strange Fruit*. But as importantly for her development as one of the most outspoken white southern critics of segregation, she founded, with Paula Snelling, her longtime partner and associate camp director, a "little magazine." In the same spirit in which Mitchell attacked those "Professional Southerners" and "the gentle Confederate novel," Smith and Snelling denounced "that sterile fetishism of the Old South." Their journal would "expose rather than gloss over vapidness, dishonesty, cruelty, [and] stupidity" and publish anything "artistic, vital, and significant" about the South. They would favor "individuality of viewpoint and distinctiveness of style" and replace "different, therefore wrong" with "difference, therefore right." Smith and Snelling named their magazine *Pseudopodia*, a coinage they defined in their first issue as "a temporary and tender projection of the nucleus or inner-self, upon the success of whose gropings the nucleus is entirely dependent for its progress and sustenance." Chosen in fun and because they wanted to encourage writers like themselves whose pieces had elsewhere been rejected, the name in fact defined the role of the magazine in the development of Smith's writing and her incomprehensibly courageous and pioneering 1930s attacks on the culture of segregation.[43]

The magazine, which began, as Snelling recalled, "with three ideas in mind: to find the creative forces at work in the South, to tell 'the honest truth' about everything (impossible of course); [and] to write . . . beautifully," became "the most important and interesting liberal voice in the South." Fellow journalists as important as Lewis Gannett, the editor of the *New York Herald Tribune*, sent in subscriptions and praise. Published between 1936 and 1945 and variously named *Pseudopodia, North Georgia Review*, and *South Today*, Smith and Snelling's journal soon went beyond the critique of the Old South myth that occupied their contemporaries from Mitchell to W. J. Cash.

Telling the "honest truth" led them into places few other white southerners dared publicly to go in the harsh and threatening racial light of the late-1930s South. Again and again they attacked the Agrarians, who, in Snelling's words, promoted a "retrograde Amnesia" and evaded the "central truth" of the region, segregation. In 1937 Smith wrote a critique of recent Civil War and Reconstruction scholarship worthy of W. E. B. Du Bois, whose *Black Reconstruction* she held up as a standard. "An intelligent Negro reading [Paul Buck's *Road to Reunion*]," she argued, "would not share the author's bubbling pleasure in 'the miracle' of reunion for from his vantage point the miracle must seem curiously like a bad conjure done on him." On the theme of sectional reconciliation in general, Smith was just as cynical: "Indeed we have had the privilege of witnessing the North embrace with a great sob of pity the South while the two mingled tears in a kind of ante-bellum love feast—a social phenomenon which probably reached its climax last year leaving us about where we were save for the worries of Miss Mitchell and Macmillan over their income taxes."[44]

Mitchell and Smith had met some time in April or early May of 1936. Mitchell's book had not yet been published, and she played the role of the shy first-time female novelist in a way that surely infuriated the new editor who had seen her own fiction rejected. When she wrote after the interview, Smith requested a piece for the magazine and asked Mitchell to come up to the mountain for one of the "house parties" she and Snelling threw in lieu of paying their contributors. Mitchell's letter declining both the request for an article and the invitation contained some of her greatest dissembling. No, she wrote, Smith herself should write the piece from the interview: "I know you can do it better than I. I really meant it when I told you it took me weeks to write a page . . . I can't think of a thing interesting to write. I have no idea why I happened to write the book, for I wrote it many years ago. Certainly I had no particular urge to write it as I loathe writing." Although Mitchell wrote others about her craft and her creative ability and had been writing all her life, she chose to represent herself to Smith as an amateur. And Smith returned the favor by publishing the interview depicting Mitchell as a "modest" beginner with "no theories of style" in the journal's summer issue, followed by a damning review of Mitchell's novel in the fall.[45]

In "One More Sigh for the Good Old South," Smith wrote that *Gone With the Wind* was yet another interpretation of the region in the "nostalgic terms of old Planter-ideology." "Scarlett's amorous and monetary adventures," she claimed, seem "hardly more than a sentimental effusion enameled with box-office candor and debunking bluster." Yet Smith's critique proved very contradictory. Mitchell had an "admirable," "precise," and "comprehensive" understanding of the history of the period and crafted a background of "authentic detail," at the same time lacking a "comprehension of historical realities." The novelist crafted an "atmosphere of contemporaneity (despite the hoop shirts and stays)" "in the nature of a *tour de force*" but did not understand "the social-economic-intellectual assumptions" of her characters. Condescendingly, Smith took Mitchell to task for not reading Freud and for misunderstanding the "inner life of her characters." Mitchell, as passionate about reading psychoanalytic theory as Smith and perhaps more knowledgeable about fictional point of view, probably laughed. Smith completely missed both Mitchell's critique of the Old South myth and her ambivalence about white southern womanhood. Groping for what about the work made the future uncompromising critic of segregation so uncomfortable, Smith skipped entirely its deplorable racial politics. For her part, Mitchell never liked Smith's work either and wrote on the articles about Smith she clipped and saved over the years comments like "radical" and "a fine specimen of Lillian's double-talk."[46]

In 1936, then, Smith was still working out the stance that would take her far beyond her contemporaries' critique within whiteness. From the first, however, Smith's and Snelling's magazine boldly broke the color bar in southern journalism. While the editors never issued any self-righteous proclamations to the effect, they published white and black authors side by side without marking the racial difference of the nonwhites. As Smith later recalled, "We were going to have Negro contributors and they were going to be called Miss and Mr. No southern magazine [or] . . . southern newspaper had done so up to this time." Manuscripts from African American writers poured in as a result, and Smith and Snelling published W. E. B. Du Bois, James Weldon Johnson, Pauli Murray, and Sterling A. Brown as well as whites like W. J. Cash, Hortense Powdermaker, and Arthur Raper. Their journal became a pioneering example of integration within the region, a crucially expansive intellectual space, even as Smith and Snelling began to formulate what would become one of the most explicit internal attacks on southern whiteness and segregation.[47]

Smith and Snelling seemed to learn a great deal from their own contributors. Their house parties gave them a chance to interact socially with these writers, and beginning in 1936, the two women began to have "biracial groups" up to the camp "for tea and for supper." Smith increasingly took stronger stands on white southern racial attitudes in her editorials, enti-

tled "Dope With Lime," and in her other nonfiction writings. "Dope With
Lime" referred to a southern habit of drinking the native refreshment Coca-
Cola, called "Dope," with lime juice to cut the sweetness, and it suited the
column, in which Smith often laced what the scholar Margaret Rose Gladney has called a "running commentary on southern life and letters" with a
"sprinkling of acid." By the late 1930s she fully questioned her own position:
"there are few of us from middle-class and upper-class families whose living
has not come directly or indirectly from the exploitation of others, be they
Negroes, tenant farmers, laborers, or our own neighbors." Later she recalled
that she and Snelling started the magazine with "a literary point of view."

> For years, we were not especially interested in Negroes; this was just one of
> our many interests . . . we were primarily interested in the white South but
> we soon saw that there is no really "white South"; it is and always has been
> a White and Black South, made of furtive, secret, open, evil and good rela-
> tionships between the two peoples who live down here; made also of
> the secret, furtive, open, evil and good relationships of the two sexes.
> We began to see this as we went along. It was exploration for us, sheer dis-
> covery.

Attempting to tell the honest truth about everything, Smith soon found, led
a white southerner inevitably to the question of race.[48]

In an article entitled "Wanted: Lessons in Hate," Smith translated into
Freudian language her commentary on the growth of fascism and an understanding of race much like that of Joel Chandler Harris's Uncle Remus in
the 1880 story "Why the Negro Is Black." "That the world today prefers a
demonology composed of alien races and nations and political systems," she
wrote as war loomed in Europe, "in place of the devils and ghosts of our
ancestors is a mere genuflection to the scientific age." Blacks in the South
had "through an evil twist of circumstances" been "disguised by strange
masks of alien ideologies into fake devils." Like other white American liberals, having recognized white racism, she could only conceive of it as foreign.

Yet while the Freudian theory that permeated her nonfiction helped
liberate Smith from the racial blindness imposed by the culture of segregation, in her private life with Paula Snelling Freud's theories about sexuality constrained her. As the historian Bruce Clayton has argued, "she had
absorbed his categories and assumptions." Her later writings suggested that

she accepted Freud's argument in *Three Essays on the Theory of Sexuality* that homosexuality was an arrested, immature, and abnormal form of desire, often related to a person's failure to work through their narcissistic attraction to their own body. She certainly would have found no counter to this conception of homosexuality in the 1920s and 1930s South. Freud at least had not argued that this sexual orientation was immoral.[49]

Smith had met Snelling in 1921, but they did not become close until at least 1928, after Smith had experienced two failed affairs with older men and had ended an intense relationship with another young female camp counselor with whom she had shared an apartment in New York while attending Columbia. That their relationship eventually became sexual, at least in terms of desire, was apparent in personal letters that escaped two fires at the camp, one an apparent accident, although it may have been purposefully set to destroy some of Smith's and Snelling's correspondence, and the other set by vandals. Tired and exhausted, writing home from New York to Paula in Clayton in 1944, Smith pleaded: "But I could do with a little loving for a change. Oh, darling, if our full spirits and bodies could effect the marriage that our minds have always had . . . I'd love to feel your lips on mine . . . and I can imagine other feelings too." Her ambivalence about her love for Snelling, however, ran deep: "I am sorry that my letters are burned, that is my ambivalence. My shame about something different and completely good. It has been that shame that has destroyed the keen edge of a pattern of love that was creative and good." But despite the damning effect on her private life and her fiction, Smith's sexual denials and desires were the tools that enabled her to see more clearly than any of her white contemporaries the cost of segregation as culture to both white and black southerners.[50]

In narrating the development of her own pioneering stance, Smith compiled notes for several biographers—she had "too many selves," she insisted, to write an autobiography. She always set her racial epiphany in China, in the experiences she had with power and separation and longing there. While she left their interconnectedness implicit, Smith repeatedly made three overlapping assertions about her life as a missionary. Most important, she claimed that in China she first saw white supremacy and segregation clearly, that there she began to question the social structures within which she had been raised: "Everywhere one found white arrogance, white colonialism in all its manifestations . . . Always, always, we British and Americans segregated the Chinese—even the Christian Chinese from our 'fun.' " Having crossed the world to teach them and pray with them, "we didn't play tennis or swim with them." Did not the best of white southern thinking about the "Negro Problem" at home stem from a similar missionary reworking of an old paternalism, a desire to uplift the inferior and fortunate even while marking through separation white superiority and difference?

In the context of describing how she started writing seriously, Smith made two other important claims about her China experience. In 1930, attempting a "little story about the Ivy Hill community," the black settlement next to the camp, Smith soon abandoned the effort with a sense that the piece was not deeply conceived or imagined. She "realized that I would have to write about my own personal life, or the people I had known well — however much I might change things." Turning to her life in China as a young teacher, she wrote a novel she named *Walls*. By 1934 it had been rejected by several publishers, Smith believed, because the "candor" she "showed in talking about the relationships between women and women and women and girls" was "hair-raising." Significantly, Smith recalled that her China years were full of "secret, furtive, passionate, relationships," "such passionate and forbidden relationships" that Smith later could barely even find the words to say she had written about love between Western women and their Chinese pupils. Finally, Smith revealed that she had participated in a deeply important relationship with a woman there. If *Walls* was about her own life, making the connections explicit between Smith's three statements about her China experience suggests that one of these same love affairs between young Western and Chinese women was Smith's own.[51]

Smith began the novel that would become the 1944 best-seller *Strange Fruit* in 1936, the year Mitchell published *Gone With the Wind*. She was "deeply disturbed," she claimed, "at the South's facility, sheer talent for failing to see the South we all live in," a starting point not unlike Mitchell's own. "I was thinking, too," she continued, "in terms of my own personal life." She shaped the story around the "old Romeo and Juliet theme," with its strands of "caste" and "hidden sex life." *Strange Fruit*, Smith always insisted, which recounts the long but doomed love affair of an educated young black woman, Nonnie Anderson, and the white son of the town doctor, Tracy Deen, is not a racial novel. Its theme is not lynching — the murder of the retarded black man Henry, falsely accused of murdering Deen, is just the outcome of the forbidden love at the center of the plot. Nonnie's brother Ed, visiting his small Georgia hometown from the North, has actually killed

Tracy in rage after discovering the affair. Smith later wrote to a prominent psychoanalyst that "the story was in its deepest sense my own story, of course; the legend of my life . . . I did not even realize myself the urgency of the color problem until I was two-thirds through with the book. My own book converted me to the importance, the urgency and, indeed, the universality of this 'problem.' "

Her novel, Smith claimed, was a "fantasy" and all its characters "myself or a mirror in which I looked at myself." Smith originally conceived *Strange Fruit*, then, with her own forbidden desires in mind. The young white woman Laura Deen's budding and barely articulated attraction to an older white woman, Laura's ambition to be an artist, her brother Tracy's vague longing for a world in which he can live with Nonnie, and Nonnie's own idealistic innocence and her belief that her love will triumph—these longings correlated with Smith's narrations of her own life. By translating her same-sex relationships, whether in China or at home in Clayton, into a heterosexual cross-racial relationship set in a town much like Jasper, Smith perhaps hoped to translate "her personal life" into a novel that could actually be published.[52]

By the time she wrote Walter White in 1942 that the theme of her novel was "the effect upon not only lives but minds and emotions which the concept of race in the South has," her transcription of gender into race, the substitution of a black woman and a white man for two white women lovers, had transformed the subject of her book and her life. Because of her "shame about something different and good," Smith never publicly acknowledged her relationship with Snelling. By 1940 she had aimed her activism at another "wall" between humans, one unlike sexual identity whose name was only too often spoken in the region. In the fight for racial justice, Smith could be both a white pioneer and yet, stepping into the long protest tradition of African Americans and especially the black intellectuals she had met while editing the little magazine, not fight the world alone. She continued, however, to see the connections between the barriers in her own life and the color line. Trying to persuade Snelling to write the story of their relationship, Smith wrote in 1952, "However esoteric or strange or special, you should put down your own feelings about you and me and life . . . What this relationship has meant. *It* might be *the* masterpiece, not my poor attempts to tell the world how to be good."[53]

The synergy of her evolving novel and her editing and writing for the journal made Lillian Smith into the South's most publicly vocal white critic of racial segregation, even as she built her own higher wall around her personal life. By the early 1940s, she filled her periodical, retitled *South Today*, with bold editorials and articles decrying segregation and white supremacy, to the detriment of the creative writing that was her passion and to the horror of her fellow white liberal editors like Virginius Dabney and Ralph McGill. In 1940 she praised the Southern Conference for Human Welfare, of which she was a member, for the absence of segregation at its Chattanooga meeting: "When southern whites and Negroes gather together to confer about their mutual problems in democratic publicity and ease and friendliness and no Jim Crow stalks the aisles something has happened of a significance in excess of literal fact." "Are We Not All Confused?," an editorial published in the spring 1942 issue, stressed that white children were "trained in childhood to believe in their whiteness" and that "no white child ever [forgot] in his heart the sweet power of being superior." In her 1942 piece "Buying a New World With Old Confederate Bills," Smith held a mirror up to an ugly world involved in yet another global war: "It is just possible that old answers which seemed 'true' in the tight, rigid frame of the southern past are based on assumptions that are no longer valid. It is just possible that the white man is no longer the center of the universe."[54]

By the time her novel made her a celebrity, she had already braved the possible loss of her camp and even her life by frankly describing the destructiveness and immorality of segregation. A southern representative for *Time* and *Life* magazines "wrote her a very insulting letter after he read an article I wrote against segregation, asking just when I intended to let my little camp girls have sexual intercourse with my colored workers." Smith's fears about what publicity concerning her private life might do to her camp lay elsewhere as well. She voiced her protest against her nation as best she could, given her "unspeakable" relationship: "so I suspect they like moderates better than my kind of people, whatever 'kind' I and 'my people' are." Not satisfied, she defined that too. "I was trying to persuade you," Smith wrote to the Blue Ridge Conference, a gathering of YWCA and YMCA members in 1944, "to look at our racial problem as the 'white man's problem'—as a problem which involves our whole personality and our entire life. I am not a 'radical.' Radicals hate. I am not a 'revolutionary' . . . I am simply a southerner, like you, who is trying to be human."[55]

And in her autobiographical collection of essays *Killers of the Dream* Smith imagined and struggled to mark out in words what for southern whites was supposed to be unimaginable, a route out of the southern white identity founded in segregation, a path to this humanity. The old story of "white self, white South" had twinned narratives of personal and regional history. An "integrated" childhood, founded in sentimental "memories" of loving mammies, guiding "uncles," and black best friends, mirrored white fantasies of a plantation garden with its family white and black. This childhood of "integration," of course, could not last. The trauma of learning racial difference—individually in a conflict with "Mammy" or a black "friend" or collectively through the Civil War and Reconstruction—doomed a youthful "idealism." Both individuals and regions must, in fact, grow up. Being an adult meant leaving "beloved darkies" behind. Being an adult meant accepting segregation, both as an individual and as a region.[56]

But what Smith managed to do at the levels of both history and psychology was reverse the direction of this story of self and South. Smith wrote instead of a segregated and conflicted childhood and of deep and persistent racial trauma. White children, she claimed, were forever damaged by the contradictory messages they received about racial difference, by the fact that they were encouraged to look down patronizingly on people that they were also encouraged to love. In place of a nostalgia-producing moment of loss, Smith proposed an epiphany of racial knowing, a moment of gain. In this instant—and she gives her personal example of the adopted "white" black girl—the white child sees the absurdity of racial division. A better future becomes possible, in which both the white individual and the white region could finally put aside the deep, deforming pain of racial violence and separation. Adulthood, in Smith's new Freudian-inspired narration of white self, white South, was about tearing down bars and walls and boundaries, was about integration. That Smith herself could not erase her own internalized line of sexual division any more than she could individually obliterate the lines of southern racial segregation has not made her narrative out of whiteness any less powerful or any less true.[57]

Mitchell's novel became the Stone Mountain of the region's culture of segregation, the narrative that both completed the plantation romance and translated it into a new story of origins, of the white middle class and especially its women, who would "tote the weery load" alone but would also triumph. Transforming the narrative power into spectacle, Selznick's film

version made the Old South the entire white nation's past and the story of
Scarlett and her Tara a spectacle of survival for a Depression-weary world.
The Stone Mountain Memorial itself would not be completed until 1970,
when the southern culture of segregation, having long replaced the Con-
federacy remembered there in granite, was enduring and resisting its own
Reconstruction.[58]

But Lillian Smith had stood on a different mountain, her own aptly
named Old Screamer, and looked not at the past or even the present but at
the future. And Smith proved far more prophetic than the white southern
male liberals who attacked her viciously in private and occasionally in print.
Virginius Dabney, in response to her public criticism of his refusal to
denounce segregation in his "Negro Question" editorials in the *Richmond
Times Dispatch*, wrote her angrily in August 1942, "I can only wonder that
living as you do in Georgia, you can imagine that a head on collision with
the overwhelming preponderance of Southern White opinion can end in
anything but disaster for race relations." Less than three weeks later, Dabney
felt compelled to write again more strongly: "I can see how anyone might
say that the Negro ought to be relieved of the onus of segregation, but I find it
difficult to imagine that this will happen in our generation." And yet Smith's
shout from the mountain was not a voice crying alone in the wilderness. Segregation, by law at least, did end within Smith's lifetime, and her own deep
courage helped destroy this one great wall within humanity. But Smith had
also imagined segregation as a culture larger than law, as southern and even
American whiteness itself, as all the categories that excluded others and
ordered power. Integration, she understood, was the only future.[59]

At the festivities surrounding the Atlanta premiere of the motion
picture version of *Gone With the Wind*, the black characters Margaret
Mitchell felt so essential to creating the proper "Southern atmosphere" —
from Hattie McDaniel, who would become the first African American to
win an Oscar for her performance as Mammy, of course, to Butterfly
McQueen, who had starred in some of the most important productions of
the Harlem Renaissance — were barred from the week of events. The premiere and the Junior League Charity Ball that preceded it that December of
1939 were conspicuously segregated. And if atmosphere was needed, local
blacks could be recruited with less fanfare and awkwardness to provide the
"authentic" southern context. At the sold-out charity event, many of these
black extras sang in the "slave choir" before a replication of the white-
columned Tara of the movie. Mitchell found Selznick's plantation houses

so unlike those of the Georgia upcountry setting of her novel that she complained repeatedly, despite her effort to stay out of the filming. The motion picture version, she worried, leaned too heavily on the tired old images of magnolias and singing slaves. And the eyes of the world were on Atlanta. Dressed as a slave in a widely circulated photograph of the choir was the young Martin Luther King, Jr. How he felt about his first appearance in the national spotlight, no white southerner thought to ask.[60]

American Whiteness

[T]he end is in the beginning and lies far ahead . . .
It is a question of who shall determine the direction of events.

RALPH ELLISON[1]

I T   I S   P E R H A P S more than ironic to end a book about the American South
with an attempt to crack open and probe the body, the mind, the very meaning of the region that has become such a central cultural category for the
nation. But Lillian Smith, her uncanny sight surviving even as cancer
wracked her own body in the early 1960s, again has managed to mark the
way. "I am deeply disturbed," Smith wrote in the materials she was collecting for a biographer, "at the [white] South's facility, sheer talent, for failing
to see the South we all live in." In twentieth-century America, the South's
regional identity has been central not just to Smith's local but to our
national racial politics. If white Americans have created their color-blind
conceptions of national identity through, in Toni Morrison's phrase, "playing in the dark," it is important here to highlight the most common place of
the play. The American South has most often provided the metaphorical
and actual settings, the playgrounds of the American racial drama, the loca-

tions of American racial meanings. The region has been central to the erasure of the whiteness of American identity precisely because its dramas have
been so graphic, so violent, so perversely pleasing. White Americans generally have failed to see the ways they imaginatively "live" in a metaphorical
South, even as their relationship to the region has danced between the poles
of attraction and revulsion.[2]

Rarely has any fusion of spectacle and narrative so pleased the nation as
David O. Selznick's 1939 screen version of Margaret Mitchell's novel *Gone
With the Wind*. White America, despite the scandal of Rhett Butler's bitter last line, gave much more than a damn. Selznick's film stripped away
Mitchell's nuanced siting of her story within the local social history and
geography of Clayton County, Georgia. Universalizing—expanding for all
white Americans—her modern narration of southern history as the autobiography of a middle-class and modern regional whiteness, Selznick crafted
a panoramic and technicolored national romance, a story of nation making.
Like Mitchell, he fetishized authenticity to ground the fantasy, and his production company publicized its struggles to document the details of dialect
and custom and even to properly dye red the California dirt. *Gone With the
Wind* was D. W. Griffith's 1915 *Birth of a Nation* dressed and topped for the
mid-century American ball.[3]

But *Gone With the Wind* also narrated a bolder and bigger and more
confident American dream, the creation of not just Griffith's modern national collective but a modern individual American. The American arche-
type had been the self-made man, such as the obscure farmer who, in the
implied background of Mitchell's story, struggled out of poverty to build up
his Clayton County plantation. But better than the self-made man was the
twice-made man, the white southerner who, losing it all in the Civil War
and Reconstruction, could again, despite the failings of the postbellum
world, build yet another self and another fortune. Both old and new, he
could ground his expansive authority in both personality and precedent,
new world will and old world culture. Through the rise and fall of his
finances, the twice-made man could embody all class lives and conflicts and
absorb the individual economic identities of Americans and their resolution
into a new middle-class self. And nurtured in an "integrated family," in
Ralph Ellison's fine phrasing, "the curdled milk" of his black mammy's
breast forever on his lips as she was forever in his "home," this new man
could sanitize biracial origins and make them safe for the modern (white)
American whole. Better than the self-made man was *Gone With the Wind*'s

twice-made man, and Mitchell, joining yet another contradiction into a new modernist mélange, made him in the figure of Scarlett O'Hara, a woman.[4]

Film, welding the power of both narrative and spectacle, animated and made "real" such magical transformations. But the festive pageant marking the premiere of *Gone With the Wind* in Atlanta in 1939, the translation of the romance back into life, ironically highlighted the nature of the performance that was both assumed and thus ignored on the screen. The city auditorium stage with its movie-copied facade was not the movie's Tara, which was itself not a Piedmont plantation just south of Atlanta. The wealthy white deb chosen to play Scarlett was not Vivien Leigh, who was not herself a southern belle transformed by war and poverty into a new man-woman. Most important for the immediate future of America, however, little Martin Luther King, Jr., was a middle-class black boy growing up in the relatively secure black community of midcentury Atlanta, Georgia, not the contented and childlike "happy darky" he portrayed on the stage, who was in turn not a true southern slave. Margaret Mitchell saw and yet failed to see the possibilities embodied in a young black child like Martin King. Heaping praise on the problematic inclusion of both African American actors in the film and black Atlantans as both representational and real servants in the festivities, the local black middle-class paper the *Daily World* saw and yet failed to see the segregation signs in both the movie and the pageant. And at their local theaters across the country, white Americans, both southern and otherwise, saw and yet failed to see the South. *Gone With the Wind* was not "the South we all live in," not in 1939, not in 1963 as an adult King marched on Washington, not now.[5]

The 1939 Atlanta pageant of *Gone With the Wind* stood as the pinnacle of the process of race making I have called the culture of segregation. The spectacle embodied the contemporary universalization of southern segregation on the one hand and yet its national exposure on the other. For the pageant was a triple mediation: a very public staging of *Gone With the Wind*'s performance of "history" as a narration of the origins of modern southern whiteness. These excessive replications, in effect fantasies of fantasies, resulted in caricatures. But while these full-color, larger-than-life exaggerations played well as entertainment, they were seriously flawed as social order. And the seen and not-seen danger here threatened both the part and the whole. The culture of segregation created and staged racial difference for modern America as well as for the modern South. The history of both the post–World War II region and the nation would be the story of the transformation of this increasingly untenable performance as its old persuasive power dissolved into caricature. The civil rights movement would force white southerners and other white Americans to see differently, at least for a moment, the South that white southerners lived in. Whether in return white Americans have or will ever fully understand the metaphoric South in which they "live," that reservoir of many cherished American self-perceptions, remains, even at the end of the twentieth century, uncertain.

Between 1890 and 1940, I have argued here, the culture of segregation turned the entire South into a theater of racial difference, a minstrel show writ large upon the land. A black middle class was rising, with its unhinging of black race and class identities, and hierarchies of personalized power were being subverted in the move to a more urban, less locally grounded, mass society. These threats made the ritualistic enactment of racial difference vital to the maintenance of white supremacy in the twentieth century. And southern whites commanded this performance of segregation for both a local and a national audience, to maintain both white privilege at home and a sense of southern distinctiveness within the nation. Segregation, in turn, helped middle-class white southerners at least mediate the effects of the incorporation of the southern economy into America's expansive and modernizing capitalism.

Since southern black inferiority and white supremacy could not, despite whites' desires, be assumed, southern whites created a modern social order in which this difference would instead be continually performed. For whites, this performance, in turn, made reality conform to the script. African Americans were inferior because they were excluded from the white spaces of the franchise, the jury, and political officeholding. They were inferior because they attended inferior schools and held inferior jobs. As the right to consume became central to changing conceptions of American citizenship and as some educated African Americans became professionals despite discrimination and oppression, African Americans were also and perhaps most publicly inferior because they sat in inferior waiting rooms, used inferior restrooms, sat in inferior cars or seats, or just stood. African Americans were inferior because they entered through inferior doors marked "Colored," relieved their needs in inferior restrooms marked "Colored," and watched movies from inferior balconies marked "Colored." Eating, a particularly intimate yet increasingly public activity, was especially controlled. African Americans dined at blocked-off, racially marked, and inferior tables, or, as was often the case with department stores that otherwise welcomed their dollars, they did not eat at all.

But the growing interdependence of racial making and consumer buying, despite the seeming entrenchment of a racial ordering proclaimed in literal black and white in the segregation signs, proved by the late 1950s to be the most vulnerable point in the culture of segregation. Particularly in southern towns and smaller southern cities, African American consumers could play upon the contradictions between making race and making money and wring concessions from local white southern merchants and from the growing numbers of national chain stores. The difficulty lay in transforming these private, individualized concessions into publicly visible, collective recognition of the importance of African American consumption to white profits. Claiming a right rather than seeking a privilege meant challenging whites' ability to command black performance. For southern African Americans visibly to violate the rituals, to refuse to play the role of blackness that white southerners continually assigned, was to invite the threat of violent retribution that the spectacle lynching periodically and very publicly staged.

By the 1930s, however, southern whites had lost a great deal of control over national interpretations of that spectacle. With the publication and circulation of its report on the lynching of Claude Neal, the NAACP had persuasively and broadly countered white southern narratives of the meaning of this violence. Lynching, in this changing national context, stood more readily as proof of white southern barbarity. And increasing numbers of more urban and suburban middle-class white southerners too had difficulty excusing such violent frenzy as a reluctant act in the maintenance of white supremacy. If southern whites were never more white and southern than when they were participating in a lynch mob, by the 1930s that same experience made them considerably less than modern white Americans. The violence against African Americans that had previously helped publicly fuse white unity now paradoxically pulled open buried fissures of class and gender. More nationally oriented, middle-class, town- and city-dwelling whites increasingly found themselves unable to condone, for reasons of both public relations and principle, the deadly entertainments that their more rural, more agricultural and working-class-oriented white brethren continued to support. Some white southern middle-class women, in particular, emboldened by suffrage and a thriving associational life, organized in the Association of Southern Women for the Prevention of Lynching a regional network that forced white southern men to face their gendered justifications of white violence. Southern whites could still employ the lynching spectacle, but divided among themselves and resisted by a growing civil rights movement, they could no longer dominate the national interpretation of their violent acts.[6]

This loss of control only escalated as World War II remade the universe in which Americans conceived of themselves both regionally and racially. The fight against fascism cemented the growing unwillingness of many white Americans to accept some white southerners' blatant acts of torture and murder. Migrating Americans encountered the diversity of both their nation and their world. African American movement north, the Great Migration, peaked as southern blacks sought the job opportunities created by the wartime economy. White and black northerners ventured south in large numbers for military training, and many carried home an unprecedented sense of the oppressive weight of the white southern racial order. African American men, both northern and southern, fought in large numbers on both fronts, and newsreels, newspapers, and national magazines circulated another black masculine spectacle, the Negro armed and in U.S. uniform, the Negro as soldier. The NAACP once again geared up its increasingly sophisticated public relations machine and promoted nationally "the Double V Campaign," victory against racism both abroad and at home. Anything seemed possible as the organization's stunning 1944 legal victory over the white political primary in *Smith v. Allwright* held out the promise of the first meaningful southern black franchise in the twentieth century.[7]

Progressive promise, then, saturated the changed landscape of post–World War II America. Militant leftists and communists, through the popular front coalitions of the 1930s, had made American and particularly southern racism the primary target of their propaganda. Positioning racial oppression as an integral part of American class inequality and a product of American capitalism, they successfully prodded more moderate liberals, for reasons of both expediency and concern, into bolder stances on civil rights. The United Nations institutionalized wartime idealism, at least at the level of rhetoric, and pushed its promise of human rights for all against the backdrop of Asian and African decolonialization. This unprecedented global American commitment, in turn, linked for the first time the success of American foreign policy to the international progress of human rights. Swedish sociologist Gunnar Myrdal published his Carnegie Corporation–supported and instantly classic *An American Dilemma: The Negro Problem and American Democracy*, which proclaimed American (understood as white) racism the last obstacle to the attainment of a democratic American utopia.[8]

In the political arena, President Franklin D. Roosevelt's successor, Harry Truman, attempted to reassert federal government control over the process and promise of liberal reform. FDR, aided by the nation's preoccupation with waging a global war, had managed to walk a precarious electoral color line. Offering unprecedented presidential gestures that always fell short of decisive action, Roosevelt managed to wrest much of the rising black northern vote from its traditional Republican mooring even while retaining the support of the traditional Democratic white South. The election of 1948, however, both highlighted the contradictions inherent in this strategic attempt to build both a regionally and racially integrated party and put African American civil rights on the national political agenda for the first time since Reconstruction. The meaning of race in America had, as after emancipation, once again become a visibly and narrowly political as well as a broadly cultural problem.[9]

Acting on the advice of administrative assistant Clark Clifford, President Truman boldly announced in his 1948 State of the Union address a then-ambitious civil rights plan. Under the assumption that Congress would pass none of his proposals, Truman called for abolishing the poll tax, making lynching a federal crime, and limiting discrimination in employment. This strategy, Clifford had argued, would gain Truman the grateful swing votes of northern blacks without losing the traditional white southern Democratic vote. Southern whites, in a virtually one-party region, after all, had nowhere else to go. Truman's aim was to seize the liberal reform banner from former New Dealer and Roosevelt vice president Henry Wallace, who had launched his own campaign under the leftist Progressive Party. Outraged, shocked, and betrayed, however, southern Democrats quickly organized the States' Rights Democratic Party, branded the Dixiecrats, and nominated Strom Thurmond as their presidential candidate. With the strong Republican candidate Thomas Dewey, the campaign had become a hotly contested four-way race.

Ignoring the Dixiecrats and delaying any action on civil rights, Truman strategically turned his attack leftward. Wallace took a much bolder civil rights stance. His refusal to speak before segregated audiences, even in southern localities where integrated meetings were illegal, generated tremendous publicity for his campaign. The president hammered Wallace not for his integrationism, however, but with a vicious red-baiting that prefigured the McCarthy era to come. As the campaign continued and northern African American voters demanded not mere proposals but concrete federal action, Truman signed executive orders preventing racial discrimination in the federal bureaucracy and the armed forces. In the end, Truman squeaked to victory over Dewey by claiming the northern black vote while holding enough support from white southerners. However reluctantly, Harry Truman had become the first civil rights president by "integrating" the Democratic Party.

But African American expectations, he and his presidential successors would discover, had a way in the postwar era of moving far beyond and outside of the narrow confines of national party control. Truman's strategic maneuvering empowered a growing black electorate that wanted not individual political patronage but the complete recognition of all African Americans' civil rights, and African American activists in organizations like the NAACP's Legal Defense Fund kept up the pressure on the federal government. In the late 1940s and early 1950s, the Federal Bureau of Investigation continued to list the mere participation in integrated meetings as proof of communist subversion. House Un-American Activities Committee investigations as well as the general climate of anti-communist hysteria destroyed leftist initiatives in the South like "Operation Dixie," the southern organizing campaign of the Congress of Industrial Organizations (CIO). Yet black voters in the North had made the civil rights of all African Americans the primary focus of mainstream liberal efforts at reform.

As conceptions of American identity acquired increasingly global significance, cold war liberalism evolved within a context of an often too superficial federal government support for African American civil rights at home and for colonized peoples abroad. But in the early 1950s, the forced consensus of the McCarthy era temporarily suppressed the contradictions between black demands for remedial action and the explosive tensions that even limited federal gestures in the direction of expanding civil rights generated in southern whites. The uneasy peace ended abruptly in 1954 as the NAACP's quiet legal strategy, aimed at dismantling the legal foundations of segregation, achieved its most important victory. White southerners fittingly called it Black Monday, the day the U.S. Supreme Court handed down its *Brown v. Board of Education* decision, which declared racial segregation in public schools unconstitutional. "We conclude," the Court stated in clear and simple language, "that in the field of public education, the doctrine of 'separate but equal' has no place. Separate educational facilities are inherently unequal . . . Any language in *Plessy v. Ferguson* contrary to this finding is rejected."[10]

But *Brown*, despite the 1955 *Brown II* decision detailing strategies for implementation, did not outline concretely how and when this desegregation of America's public schools would be accomplished. The decision did focus national attention on the distinctive outlines of segregation in the South. The NAACP filed desegregation briefs with many school districts across the region in the year after the decision, and courageous black families prepared their children to cross the deeply material as well as psychological segregation line. Yet *Brown*'s uncompromisingly radical rhetoric galvanized not just civil rights supporters but also civil rights opponents, ironically reuniting many white southerners increasingly divided by class and by the growing differences between rural and suburban white southern life.

Southern whites banded together in White Citizens' Councils and launched an organized segregationist opposition that became known as "massive resistance." Southern state legislators threatened to shut down public school systems altogether and in some cases did. Many white parents faced with the integration of public schools formed the organizations that eventually created "white flight" schools, the segregated academies where racial separation, whatever the educational offerings, could still stand. And when federal courts, in the late 1960s, finally began to apply their remedies to segregated school systems outside the South, northern whites often resisted, minus the reconstituted "Confederate patriotism," as massively as had white southerners. Pairing opposition to busing with accelerating rounds of urban and then suburban flight and resettlement, white Americans have succeeded in maintaining segregation in public education even as class sizes rise, physical plants crumble, and the skill levels of graduating students fall. Today, over four decades after *Brown*, American public schools stand more segregated by race and divided by class than at any time in our history.[11]

White Americans, however, proved much less ambivalent about protecting black lives than about providing equal education. Events surrounding the 1955 lynching of Emmett Till were more important than *Brown* in

prefiguring what would be the successes of the growing civil rights movement and the not very distant destruction of the peculiarly southern culture
of segregation. With the Till case, African Americans did not just write a
counternarrative. Building what activists had learned in cases like the lynching of Claude Neal and making use of the new technology of television,
they staged a counter-spectacle in a new, national, real time.

A fourteen-year-old black boy from Chicago, Emmett Till had been
sent to Leflore County, Mississippi, by his mother, Mamie Bradley, to spend
a summer vacation with his southern relatives. With adolescent bragging
and bravado, he often told his Mississippi cousins and friends that a young
white woman in a photograph he carried was his girlfriend. On August 24,
less than two weeks after he had arrived, Till and his cousins drove from his
uncle's house in the country the three miles into the tiny town of Money.
Not to be outdone by his boasts that evening, the local boys bet Till would
not pursue a southern white woman. Accepting the challenge, Till entered
that muddled middle, a small white-owned store that catered mostly to the
local black grocery trade. He then made some move—whether a comment
or a whistle or just a look witnesses disagree—in the direction of twenty-one-
year-old Carolyn Bryant, who with her sister-in-law Juanita Milam was
minding the store for her husband Roy Bryant. The northern boy and his
southern friends, a cousin later decided, were speaking in different tongues,
and Till obviously took realistically a verbal jousting that for them was a language game. The Chicago boy never understood the line he had crossed or
the danger he was in, a point that was confirmed by as unlikely a source as
Till's murderers, Roy Bryant and J. W. Milam, who confessed to a reporter
for four thousand dollars long after they had been acquitted at their local
trial.[12]

But what made Till more than just another black man murdered was
the way his mother made the lynching into a different kind of spectacle
through her choreography of the Chicago funeral. By publicly naming the
white men who had come to his home and taken the boy, Mose Wright,
Till's great-uncle, bravely opened the possibility of bringing the boy's murderers to court. But the national publicity began with Till's funeral, which
was held outside the South and before the trial. Reporters not just from the
newspapers but from the increasingly important national television networks poured into Chicago. And in a black northern neighborhood, in a
black church, a black mother wrote her own ritual in answer to the white
southern lynching story. Mamie Bradley insisted on an open-casket funeral,

"so the world can see what they did to my boy." Television cameras captured
the mass of black mourners who filed with the deliberate slowness of a dirge
past Till's corpse to emerge hysterical or grimly determined on the other
side. To make sure that no one missed the spectacle, Mamie Bradley
allowed *Jet* magazine to publish a closeup of her boy's face. The image
depicted a misshapen head all the more horrible for the coroner's efforts to
make the mangled corpse back into the boy.[13]

The Till spectacle, then, demonstrated that white southern violence
had not just a black and white southern but a black and white national audience as well. Television crossed the lines of region as well as race much
more immediately than did publications like the NAACP's 1934 Neal
report. The local trial took place in a national context colored by that public
counter-performance of Till's funeral. Bradley had drawn and enacted her
own line across both space and time, suggesting that to view the tortured
head that marked this boundary and to remain unchanged was to leave
morality behind.

Americans across the nation thus watched the trial haunted by the horror of the dead boy's face. They saw the bragging and confident defendants,
the segregated courtroom, and the all-white male jury. They heard U.S.
Representative Charles Diggs of Michigan describe his humiliating treatment at the courthouse as a local judge called him "boy" and roped him off
with the black reporters, and they watched this scene repeat itself as white
officials also mistreated Till's mother. Americans with televisions witnessed
reporters at the scene describe how the defense attorney in closing had
admonished the jury: "every last Anglo-Saxon one of you has the courage to
free these men." And this national audience also watched the acquitted
murderers kiss their wives surrounded by the joyous celebration of other
whites attending the trial. Americans saw a local white southern performance, naked and stripped of the niceties of New South boosterism, bare of
the inflections so often spun by southern politicians and businessmen for
that larger national audience.[14]

For television not only crossed but also marked that regional divide.
Fusing graphically brutal spectacle and story in a much more instantaneous
and much less mediated way than film, television made visible civil rights
activists' sense of the difference between the South and the rest of the
nation. As a result, television shaped a new collective out of many of its
viewers. "Nonsouthern" whites were Americans who would not tolerate
such violence, who understood the deadly irony that such barbarity could

never protect "civilization." Unlike the *Brown* decision, the Till lynching divided rather than united southern whites, splitting apart those who
were invested morally and practically in national opinion from those·who
were not.

To move inside the South and still direct the drama, however, African
Americans would have to find a way besides waiting for a lynching to initiate their counter-performance. They needed a less deadly method of refus-
ing to play the blackface roles assigned southern blacks but a strategy that
would still make visible the ever-present danger for those who refused. And
in Montgomery, Alabama, in 1955 and 1956, when the tired Rosa Parks
refused to give up her seat and local African Americans started the bus boycott that the then twenty-six-year-old Martin Luther King would come to
lead, southern blacks would learn these lessons too.

The outlines of the movement African Americans created to win their civil
rights in the South have become familiar, even legendary, to many Americans now. But we have too often ignored the deep ways in which southern
blacks matched their strategies to the particularly public and performative
nature of the southern culture of segregation. Fusing nonviolence and mass
action, civil rights activists in the South rewrote the drama of racial meaning. In marches, boycotts, and sit-ins, on picket lines, freedom rides, and
voter registration lines, southern blacks peacefully, lovingly refused to play
their parts as scripted in the play of segregation. And they made this stand in
defiance of the white violence that always, whether visibly or not, compelled the performance. Adept at wearing masks, African Americans picked
up that of the stoic and performed their control in an act of willed passivity
that paradoxically belied whites' assumptions of their "natural" deference.
Blending Gandhian philosophy with an indigenous black tradition rooted
in earlier protests like the 1917 Silent Protest Parade, this nonviolence in
turn pushed the system of segregation to its inevitably brutal conclusion. As
the Till murder demonstrated, making white racial violence graphically visible tended to redivide southern whites even as civil rights activism united
them. And television and newspapers publicized the brutality nationally,
circulating white violence representationally in a way that limited white
southerners' ability to employ the violence physically. Media coverage,
immediate and moving, galvanized both the attention and the support from

outside the region that offered civil rights workers some small measure of protection.[15]

African Americans joined by too few white liberals completed the task of making a spectacle of not just lynching but the general, pervasively violent context of segregation. They created a different unity, a liberal, cross-racial coalition of Americans outraged by such acts. Coloring in the nightmares that underlay southern white fantasies, activists moved in a way that both paralleled in its use of representations of violence and yet opposed in its peacefulness the spectacle white southerners had once made of lynching. Civil rights workers filled the romanticized landscapes of postwar America's small towns and small cities with the bodies of black adults and black children, exposing the absurdity of a white superiority that used billy clubs, bats, dogs, and firehoses to enforce a supposedly natural racial order. The civil rights movement transformed the blackface performance of black inferiority into a ritualized enactment of black subjectivity and moral supremacy.

African Americans had finally found a way to counter the black mammy and the black whore, the Uncle Remus and the rapist, with more modern and more persuasive images: white customers pouring ketchup and abuse on black college students at lunch counters, police dogs biting black children in public parks, and firehose torrents rolling black bodies down city sidewalks. At times, the price was beyond measure—perhaps most horrifyingly when Sunday school students in Birmingham, Alabama, were blown to bits in their church instead of being saved. But the violence, the loss of life, had always been there. In the fight against lynching, civil rights activists had simply learned to make the deaths count for their integrationist politics. In Montgomery, Birmingham, Albany, and Selma, white southerners, the new play insisted, were responsible for this barbarity and mayhem. And for once, in a televised, cold war American context, southern blacks found a sizable, integrated, and concerned national and international audience.

Between the mid-1950s and the late 1960s, then, the civil rights movement destroyed the southern culture of segregation by staging mass actions that compelled federal government enforcement of the Reconstruction amendments at last. The Civil Rights Act of 1964 outlawed segregation in all arenas of southern public and commercial life, and across the region the signs "For Colored" and "For White" came down. The Voting Rights Act of

1965 placed voter registration in still-resisting Deep South states in the hands of federal authorities, and African Americans finally had free and clear access to the ballot. The vote, in turn, gave southern blacks a potentially powerful tool for expressing their own conceptions of their identities and their own desires. By the late 1970s, the southern culture of segregation as anchored in the public and continual performance of black inferiority no longer existed, and racial identities there were crafted and resisted in specifically political as well as broadly cultural terms. Many neighborhoods and schools and almost all churches remained segregated, and in isolated small towns in Deep South states the public performance of segregation continued without the laws or the signs. But the South was no longer distinct in its regional racial order, no better and no worse than the rest of an often racist and often segregated American nation.

It is important, I think, and not simply the substitution of one romance for another, to acknowledge the sweeping success of the civil rights movement in overturning the southern culture of segregation and in marginalizing a distinctly southern whiteness. Of course, the movement did not create a racial utopia in the region. That space of collective racial innocence has never existed in American history, only in American fantasy. And integration, true equality, a mutual respect for the shifting play of difference and commonality among all Americans, can only be created from a space of historical reckoning, not historical evacuation. White Americans never have been and never will be racially innocent. To deny the vast accomplishments of the civil rights movement, however, is to succumb to a numbing fatalism in which its real achievements are forgotten or taken for granted and no better future can even be conceived. To deny the success of the movement is to disarm ourselves politically and culturally in the fight against a growing right that has no difficulty seeing and targeting this "progress." The fact that race relations remain a specifically political problem alone signifies a significant shift. Despite continual inequality, African Americans in the South can now join as citizens the debate about who they are and want to be.

But the brutal fact remains that the civil rights movement, which desegregated the South, did not succeed in transforming the rest of the nation. Despite widespread segregation by convention, the racial order there was different. From the start it had been less a problem of racialized masses than one of a racially inflected division of classes. Outside the South, therefore, much more complex patternings of collective identities often emerged. Strong ethnic affiliations fractured whiteness even as other peoples of color complicated conceptions of blackness. Less starkly oppressive, less grounded in a public performance of positioning, and less violent, the American racial order operated for the most part outside legal groundings and direct government backing, dividing and segregating people in much more subtle ways. In the North, the movement's performative tactics found no clear drama to subvert, no transparently white spaces to seize, and no embodiments of evil like Bull Connor to attack.

Economic inequality, not a more starkly material violence, now grounds racial meaning in both the North and the South. Within that southern culture of segregation, activists had attacked that vulnerable muddled middle, that space of consumption where making race could and sometimes did contradict making money. But outside the region, the dynamic of economic development, late twentieth-century capitalism, produced racial inequality in a complex relation to class inequality. To challenge the American racial problem would require more than Myrdal's change of white heart. Activists would have to attack a much more powerful narrative than even the white southern drama of segregation. The violence that they would have to stage would not be the violence of segregation that grounded southern whiteness but the violence of expropriated labor and class inequality that grounded American capitalism.

Before white Americans can even begin to uncover the deep links between class exploitation, disempowerment, and racial privilege, however, they would have to face the reality of "the South" they have all lived in. All of us, white and black, northern and southern, would have to think of "the South," the "race problem," and the "burden of history," not as the weight of some other, of a dark and distant place and time, but as a burden that we still carry and as a history that we have not agreed to face or acknowledge as a source of our subjectivities. We would have to remember that "the South," the romance, the place of not now, the space of safety and mooring for whatever we imagine we have lost, lies not south of anywhere but inside us. We would have to look clear-eyed and straight at "the South" we all live in, that space of "safety" and also always of horror. We would have to pull apart the interwoven ways in which "the South" as metaphor founds much of late twentieth-century "knowing," from nonsouthern white self-righteousness to the "morality" of the American state to even a growing black middle class's nostalgia for segregation. We would have to see "the South" we all live in.

We would have to place the region back within instead of against history. We would have to see ourselves.[16]

This book revisits segregation, then, not to spin the common fantasy of safety in "purity" but to reimagine integration. I want to recapture the civil rights movement's fervor and commitment and faith in humanity's ability to effect progressive change. I want to replace that old and facile liberal lie, that integration will be easy once the "southern problem" is fixed because only they—ironically African Americans are once again paired here with white southerners—will have to change. Assuming African Americans want to or will easily become (white) Americans is not what I mean by integration. As Ralph Ellison reminds us, it is always "a question of who shall determine the direction of events." A newly imagined integration would incorporate black autonomy, authority, and subjectivity, even as it enlarges the spaces and possibilities of both American and African American identities. A newly imagined integration would not tolerate economic, gender, or sexual inequality. But now is the time to act because "the South we all live in," like everything else in this postmodern age, has begun to fragment. A newly imagined integration might even halt this transformation of "the South" into "the City" and the related new cycle of race baiting, demonization, and dehumanization of the poor African Americans who live there. The space of racial excess, of racial knowing, will not just disappear, and in our time we are reconstituting this "South" all over America as our urban core becomes a new space of longing and blackface and horror.

In their culture of segregation, white southerners, despite their best and most violent efforts to separate and to contain southern blacks, recognized at some unconscious level and deeply feared an interdependence, a grayness, an area of "racial" sameness. And these commonalities between black and white southerners grew out of, were forged within, their common history. We need to remember that difference is created within, not before, our communities; that difference is created within, and not before, our histories; that difference is created within, and not before, ourselves. To borrow—that perhaps quintessential American cultural move—a phrase from James Baldwin, "there isn't any other tale to tell, it's the only light we've got in all this darkness."[17]

Would America be American without its white people? No. It would be something better, the fulfillment of what we postpone by calling a dream.

Acknowledgments

THE FOLLOWING PEOPLE have taught me much about life as well as history and I am deeply thankful for their generosity: Carol Anderson, Joel Anderson, Ed Ayers, Numan Bartley, Mia Bay, Michelle Brattain, Porter Bellieu, Marilyn Brownstein, Vic Chesnutt, Tina Chesnutt, Bruce Clayton, Paul Clemens, Nicki Combs, Pete Daniel, Sam Elworthy, Robbie Ethridge, Drew Gilpin Faust, Amy Forbes, Laurie Fowler, Nancy Fraser, Gael, Frederick, and K Gardner, Dee Garrison, John Gingerich, Jacquelyn Dowd Hall, Dan Henry, Red and Rosina Hinesley, Beatrix Hoffman, Eric Jaffe, Karen Parker Lears, Suzanne Lebsock, Chrissy Mahoney, Bill McFeely, Nancy MacLean, Michael Merrill, Susan Rupp Mims, Dawson Mims, Ginny Muller, Eve Oishi, Nell Irvin Painter, Tammy Procter, James Roark, John Salmond, Scott Sandage, Bryant Simon, Diane Sommerville, Claire Swann, Fran Thomas, Rachel Weil, Deborah Gray White, LeeAnn Whites, Nick Yasinski, Jeff Young, and Eli Zaretsky. Ted Koditschek and Paul Gaston deserve special thanks for their spirited criticisms of my manuscript at crucial stages. Bill Muller helped with the intricacies of the book contract.

I am grateful to the following institutions for providing the support which makes writing possible: Rutgers University, the Smithsonian Institution, the Center for the Critical Study of Contemporary Culture, Emory University, the Mellon Foundation, and the University of Missouri—Columbia. I would like to thank the archivists and librarians at the Atlanta History Center, Emory University, the Southern Historical Collection at the University of North Carolina—Chapel Hill, the University of Georgia, the Smithsonian Institution's Archives Center, the Library of Congress, Princeton University, and the Schomburg Center for Research in Black Culture.

Without Jackson Lears and Jan Lewis, this book would not have been written. Without Jean Friedman and Emory Thomas, I would not be a historian. John Inscoe took my investigations of southern history seriously enough to publish them, and I thank him for the thrill of first seeing my words in print. This project originated in the comradeship of conversations with Eliza McFeely and Lynn Mahoney, and for their early and continuing criticisms, support, and friendship I remain indebted. Beth Loffreda has taught me more than I can say about feminism, narrative, and courage, and I thank her.

Linda Reeder and David Tager have given me friendship and support for which I will always be grateful. A special thanks to my family—Joan Berry Hale, Lester Hale, Joanna Hale, Tres Hale, Jim Fischer, Grace Keen Berry, Lois Dubia, and especially, David M. Levitt, who inspired me—for their support and love. I got my passion for history from my grandfather Guy Orrie Berry and yet did not know enough in his lifetime to tell him. I am also indebted to Ed Ayers, Abby Ayers, Nelson Lichtenstein, John Mason, Amy Murrell, Peter Onuf, Kris Onuf, Mark Smith, and the rest of the softball gang, and, especially, Ann Lane and Steve Innes for making Charlottesville home.

Finally, I must thank my editor Peter Dimock for making this book far better than it would have been without him, for his faith both in the language and in me, and for his friendship.

Charlottesville, VA
October 1997

Notes

1. W. E. B. Du Bois, "The Souls of White Folk," in *Darkwater: Voices From Within the Veil* (1921; rpt., Millwood, NY: Kraus-Thompson, 1975).

2. Historically, *black* in American culture has often meant *nonwhite* or what we would today call *people of color*. There are important ways in which people of color are seen as racially identical with blackness and in other ways are not, but these distinctions in the way whites view people of color — as well as the differing ways in which people of color have viewed themselves and whites — are beyond the scope of this book. The Civil War, Reconstruction, and the creation of segregation as culture are key moments in the creation of modern American identity, and as the American South becomes the key site for these events and the ways in which they are subsequently remembered and reimagined, I use the terms that dominate racial thinking there, *white* and *black*.

See Winthrop Jordan, *White Over Black: American Attitudes Toward the Negro, 1550–1812* (Chapel Hill: University of North Carolina Press, 1968), for the pre-nineteenth-century history of whiteness. I am not arguing that whiteness does not have this history. Instead, I am emphasizing that mass racial identity, what we understand as the meaning of race today, is the modern, twentieth-century product of segregation. I am building here on Joel Williamson's profound observation that the Civil War not only freed the slaves, it freed American racism as well. See Joel Williamson, *The Crucible of Race: Black-White Relations in the American South Since Emancipation* (New York: Oxford University Press, 1984).

3. On Reconstruction, see W. E. B. Du Bois, *Black Reconstruction in America, 1860–1880* (1935; rpt., New York: Atheneum, 1969); Eric Foner, *Reconstruction: America's Unfinished Revolution, 1863–1877* (New York: Harper and Row, 1988); and Leon F. Litwack, *Been in the Storm So Long: The Aftermath of Slavery* (New York: Vintage, 1980). On the late nineteenth-century South, see C. Vann Woodward, *Origins of the New South, 1877–1913* (Baton Rouge: Louisiana State University Press, 1951); and Edward L. Ayers, *Promise of the New South* (New York: Oxford, 1992). On postbellum regional antagonisms and reconciliation, see the excellent Nina Silber, *The Romance of Reunion: Northerners and the South, 1865–1900* (Chapel Hill: University of North Carolina Press, 1994).

4. On theories of spatial practice and cultural geography, see Edward T. Hall, *The Hidden Dimension* (New York: Anchor Books, 1966); Henri Lefebvre, *The Production of*

Space, trans. Donald Nicholson-Smith (Cambridge, MA: Basil Blackwell, 1984); and Neil Smith, *Uneven Development: Nature, Capital, and the Production of Space* (Cambridge, MA: Basil Blackwell, 1984).

5.   On modernity, see Marshall Berman, *All That Is Solid Melts Into Air: The Experience of Modernity* (New York: Simon and Schuster, 1982); and David Harvey, *The Condition of Postmodernity: An Enquiry into the Origins of Cultural Change* (Cambridge, MA: Basil Blackwell, 1989).

6.   I have been influenced here by Eric Lott, *Love and Theft: Blackface Minstrelsy and the American Working Class* (New York: Verso, 1991); and Miriam Hansen, *Babel and Babylon: Spectatorship in American Silent Film* (Cambridge: Cambridge University Press, 1991).

7.   James Baldwin, *Notes of a Native Son* (1955; rpt., Boston: Beacon, 1984), xv, quote, ix–xvi. On the origins of minstrelsy in the Northeast in the 1840s and 1850s, see Lott, *Love and Theft.*

8.   W. E. B. Du Bois, *The Souls of Black Folk*, in *W. E. B. Du Bois: Writings* (New York: Library of America, 1986), 3. On segregation, see C. Vann Woodward, *The Strange Career of Jim Crow* (1955; rpt., New York: Oxford University Press, 1974); and John T. Cell, *The Highest Stage of White Supremacy: The Origins of Segregation in South Africa and the American South* (Cambridge: Cambridge University Press, 1982).

9.   Toni Morrison, *Jazz* (New York: Knopf, 1992), and *Playing in the Dark: Whiteness and the Literary Imagination* (New York: Vintage, 1993); and William Faulkner, *Absalom, Absalom!* (1936; rpt., New York: Vintage, 1990).

CHAPTER ONE: *No Easy Place or Time*

1.   W. E. B. Du Bois, *The Souls of Black Folk* (1903), in *W. E. B. Du Bois: Writings* (New York: Library of America, 1986), 545.

2.   James Baldwin, "Sonny's Blues," quoted in Gerald Early, *Tuxedo Junction: Essays in American Culture* (New York: Ecco Press, 1989), 307.

3.   The argument of this book will have been successful to the extent that the reader understands it as an American narrative of the making of whiteness and therefore inescapably written from within an impoverished public historical language—from within whiteness itself, as it were. American culture still conspicuously lacks, at its core and as its common tongue, what it so obviously and desperately requires: in Toni Morrison's words, a language with which "to convert a racist house into a race-specific yet non-racist home." This book's characterizations of the American social experience of segregation, especially that of black people and its persistence as collective memory, will reflect the inadequacy of our public American language even as this book attempts to help clear a place for the language Morrison calls for. See Morrison's essay "Home" in *The House That Race Built: Black Americans, U.S. Terrain*, edited by Wahneema Lubiano (New York: Pantheon Books, 1997).

4. The former slaves are quoted in Lawrence Levine, *Black Culture and Black Consciousness: Afro-American Folk Thought From Slavery to Freedom* (New York: Oxford University Press, 1977), 137. On emancipation, in addition to Levine, see Leon F. Litwack, *Been in the Storm So Long: The Aftermath of Slavery* (New York: Vintage, 1980); Vincent Harding, *There Is a River: The Black Struggle for Freedom in America* (New York: Vintage, 1983), 195–241; and the pioneering W. E. B. Du Bois, *Black Reconstruction in America, 1860–1880* (1935; rpt., New York: Atheneum, 1969), 55–127.

5. Levine, *Black Culture*, 137; Litwack, *Aftermath*, 169, 171.

6. Litwack, *Aftermath*, 183, 171.

7. Paraphrase of song quoted in Litwack, *Aftermath*, 171. See also Levine, *Black Culture*, 136–89; Sterling Stuckey, *Slave Culture: Nationalist Theory and the Foundations of Black America* (New York: Oxford, 1987), 3–97; Eugene D. Genovese, *Roll, Jordan, Roll: The World the Slaves Made Together* (New York: Vintage, 1976); Mechal Sobel, *The World They Made Together: Black and White Values in Eighteenth Century Virginia* (Princeton: Princeton University Press, 1987); and David Brion Davis, *The Problem of Slavery in the Age of Revolution, 1770–1823* (Ithaca, NY: Cornell University Press, 1975).

8. Litwack, *Aftermath*, xiii, 3–220. See also the excellent Joel Williamson, *The Crucible of Race: Black-White Relations in the American South Since Emancipation* (New York: Oxford University Press, 1984).

9. Wright is quoted in Kevin K. Gaines, *Uplifting the Race: Black Leadership, Politics, and Culture in the Twentieth Century* (Chapel Hill: University of North Carolina, 1996), 19.

10. Levine, *Black Culture*, 80, italics mine.

11. Zora Neale Hurston, *Mules and Men* (1935; rpt., New York: Harper Perennial, 1990), 2–3. See also Ralph Ellison, "Change the Joke and Slip the Yoke" (1958), in *Shadow and Act* (1964; rpt., New York: Vintage, 1995), 45–59.

12. Ellison, "Change the Joke." Harriet A. Jacobs, *Incidents in the Life of a Slave Girl* (1861; rpt., Cambridge: Harvard University Press, 1987); and Frederick Douglass, *Narrative of the Life of Frederick Douglass, An American Slave, Written by Himself* (1845; rpt., Cambridge, MA: Harvard University Press, 1988). On plantation novels, see William Taylor, *Cavalier and Yankee: The Old South and the American National Character* (New York: Braziller, 1961), 177–201. On minstrel shows, see Alexander Saxton, *The Rise and Fall of the White Republic: Class Politics and Mass Culture in Nineteenth Century America* (New York: Verso, 1990); David R. Roediger, *The Wages of Whiteness: Race and the Making of the American Working Class* (New York: Verso, 1991); and Eric Lott, *Love and Theft: Blackface Minstrelsy and the American Working Class* (New York: Oxford University Press, 1993). On the minstrel show as a metaphor for black life in America, see the pioneering Nathan Huggins, "White/Black Faces—Black Masks," in *The Harlem Renaissance* (New York: Oxford University Press, 1971), 244–301.

13. Levine, *Black Culture*, 138–89. On the few free people of color who lived in the South, see Ira Berlin, *Slaves Without Masters: The Free Negro in the Antebellum South* (New York: Norton, 1976); Michael P. Johnson and James L. Roark, *Black Mas-*

ters: A Free Family of Color in the Old South (New York: Norton, 1984); Adele Logan Alexander, *Ambiguous Lives: Free Women of Color in Rural Georgia, 1789–1879* (Fayetteville: University of Arkansas Press, 1991); and Suzanne Lebsock, *The Free Women of Petersburg: Status and Culture in a Southern Town, 1784–1860* (New York: Norton, 1985). On escape and slave resistance and rebellion, see Harding, *There Is a River,* 52–116, 140–71.

14. The northern teachers are quoted in Levine, *Black Culture,* 142. James D. Anderson, *The Education of Blacks in the South, 1860–1935* (Chapel Hill: University of North Carolina Press, 1988).

15. On Reconstruction, see Du Bois, *Black Reconstruction;* and Eric Foner, *Reconstruction: America's Unfinished Revolution, 1863–1877* (New York: Harper and Row, 1988).

16. The quotes are from Levine, *Black Culture,* 148, 150. Hurston, *Mules and Men,* 2–3.

17. Quoted in Gaines, *Uplifting the Race,* 83–84. Throughout this chapter I am indebted to Gaines's excellent analysis of the turn-of-the-century black middle class in general and black intellectuals in particular.

18. Gaines, *Uplifting the Race;* E. Franklin Frazier, *Black Bourgeoisie: Rise of a New Middle Class* (New York: Free Press, 1957); and Willard B. Gatewood, *Aristocrats of Color: The Black Elite, 1880–1920* (Bloomington: University of Indiana Press, 1990). On Frederick Douglass, see William McFeely, *Frederick Douglass* (New York: Norton, 1991).

19. W. E. B. Du Bois, "The Souls of White Folk," in *Darkwater: Voices From Within the Veil* (1921), reprinted in Eric J. Sundquist, ed., *The Oxford W. E. B. Du Bois Reader* (New York: Oxford University Press, 1996), 497. On Du Bois, see Eric J. Sundquist, *To Wake the Nations: Race in the Making of American Literature* (Cambridge, MA: Harvard University Press, 1993), 457–626; David Levering Lewis, *W. E. B. Du Bois: Biography of a Race, 1868–1919* (New York: Henry Holt, 1993); and Kwame Anthony Appiah, *In My Father's House: Africa and the Philosophy of Culture* (New York: Oxford University Press, 1992), 28–46. On growing class division, see Gerald David Jaynes, *Branches Without Roots: Genesis of the Black Working Class in the American South, 1862–1882* (New York: Oxford University Press, 1986).

20. Williamson, *Crucible,* 44–78. For more on Pollard, see Chapter 2.

21. Gaines, *Uplifting the Race.*

22. Du Bois, *Souls of Black Folk,* 364–65.

23. Albert Murray, *The Omni-Americans: New Perspectives on Black Experience and American Culture* (New York: Outerbridge and Dienstfrey, 1970), 22. On *Plessy,* see Sundquist, *To Wake the Nations,* 233–49.

24. Du Bois, *Souls of Black Folk,* 359. On progressive reform and racial essentialism, see C. Vann Woodward, *Origins of the New South, 1877–1913* (Baton Rouge: Louisiana State University Press, 1951), 369–95; and George M. Fredrickson, *The Black Image in the White Mind: The Debate on Afro-American Character and Destiny, 1817–1914* (1971; rpt., Hanover, NH: Wesleyan University Press, 1987), 228–55, 283–319.

25. Gaines, *Uplifting the Race,* 62–63, 90–91, 100–27; Williamson, *Crucible,* 55–57, 70–77; Wilson Jeremiah Moses, ed., *Classical Black Nationalism: From the Amer-*

ican Revolution to Marcus Garvey (New York: New York University Press, 1996), and *The Golden Age of Black Nationalism, 1850–1925* (Hamden, CT: Archon Books, 1978).

26. Booker T. Washington, *Up From Slavery* (1901; rpt., New York: University Books, 1993), 1; Gaines, *Uplifting the Race,* 62–63, 90–97; Louis Harlan, *Booker T. Washington: The Making of a Black Leader* (New York: Oxford University Press, 1972), and *Booker T. Washington: The Wizard of Tuskegee, 1901–1915* (New York: Oxford University Press, 1983).

27. Booker T. Washington, *The Story of the Negro: The Rise of the Race from Slavery,* vol. 2 (New York: T. Fisher Unwin, 1909), 394–95, 395, 394, 392.

28. On Washington's "darky" jokes, see Louis Harlan, ed., *Booker T. Washington Papers,* vol. 4 (Urbana: University of Illinois Press, 1975), 330–32.

29. Washington, *Up From Slavery,* 219, and *Story of the Negro,* 399; Harlan, *Wizard;* and Gaines, *Uplifting the Race,* 37–39, 58. For a persuasive critique of the kind of industrial education Washington made famous, see Anderson, *Education of Blacks.*

30. Du Bois, *Souls of Black Folk,* 365. For more on Booker T. Washington's "Atlanta Compromise" speech, see Chapter 4.

31. Henry McNeal Turner, "The American Negro and His Fatherland," an 1895 essay collected in Moses, *Classical Black Nationalism,* 221–27. Turner is quoted in Ann Douglas, *Terrible Honesty: Mongrel Manhattan in the 1920s* (New York: Noonday Press, 1995), 255. See also Gaines, *Uplifting the Race,* 84; and Edwin S. Redkey, *Black Exodus: Black Nationalists and Back to Africa Movements* (New Haven: Yale University Press, 1969).

32. Turner, " 'His Fatherland," quotes 222, 223, 221; Moses, *Classical Black Nationalism,* 21–35.

33. Marcus Garvey, "The Negro's Greatest Enemy," a 1923 essay collected in Thomas Wagstaff, ed., *Black Power: The Radical Response to White America* (Beverly Hills: Glencoe Press, 1969), 76–86, quotes, 76, 78, 79. Moses, *Classical Black Nationalism,* 31–35, 241–50.

34. Garvey, "Enemy," 79–80.

35. Garvey, "Enemy," 76; Moses, *Classical Black Nationalism,* 31–35, 241–50; Gaines, *Uplifting the Race.*

36. On black migration, see William Cohen, *At Freedom's Edge: Black Mobility and the Southern Quest for Racial Control, 1861–1915* (Baton Rouge: Louisiana State University Press, 1991); the excellent Nell Irvin Painter, *Exodusters* (New York: Norton, 1992); and Gaines, *Uplifting the Race,* 88–93, quote from the *Chicago Defender,* 235.

37. Zora Neale Hurston, *Dust Tracks on a Road* (1942; rpt., New York: Harper Perennial, 1991), 144–48; Countee Cullen, "Heritage," in *Color* (New York: Harper and Row, 1925); and Appiah, "The Invention of Africa," in *My Father's House,* 3–27. On the contradictions within nationalism and the nation as an "imagined community," see Benedict Anderson, *Imagined Communities: Reflections on the Origin and Spread of Nationalism* (New York: Verso, 1993).

38. Du Bois, *Souls of Black Folk,* quote, 545, and 363–71; Du Bois, "Little Portraits of Africa" (1924), in Sundquist, *Du Bois Reader,* 645–47, quote, 646; and Du Bois, "The Conservation of the Races" (1897), in Moses, *Classical Black Nationalism,* 228–40,

quotes, 231, 235, 236. See also Sterling Stuckey, "Black Americans and African Consciousness: Du Bois, Woodson, and the Spell of Africa," in *Going Through the Storm: The Influence of African American Art in History* (New York: Oxford University Press, 1994), 120–40; and Appiah, "Illusions of Race," in *My Father's House*, 28–46.

39.   Du Bois, "Of the Meaning of Progress," in *Souls of Black Folk*, 405–14.

40.   Frances E. W. Harper, *Iola Leroy* (1892), in William L. Andrews, *The African-American Novel in the Age of Reaction* (New York: Mentor Books, 1992); Hazel Carby, "Of Lasting Service for the Race," in *Reconstructing Womanhood: The Emergence of the Afro-American Woman Novelist* (New York: Oxford University Press, 1987), 62–94; Du Bois, "Of the Meaning of Progress" and "The Talented Tenth," in Booker T. Washington, ed., *The Negro Problem: A Series of Articles by Representative Negroes of Today* (New York: James Pott, 1903), 33–75. Any research into African American women must begin with Paula Giddings, *When and Where I Enter: The Impact of Black Women on Race and Sex in America* (New York: Bantam, 1985); and Darlene Clark Hine, ed., *Black Women in United States History*, 16 vols. (Brooklyn: Carlson, 1990).

41.   Harper's speech is quoted in Carby, *Reconstructing Womanhood*, 69. On gender relations among African Americans in the post–Civil War era, see, on middle-class blacks, Gaines, *Uplifting the Race*; Glenda Gilmore, *Gender and Jim Crow: Women and the Politics of White Supremacy in North Carolina, 1896–1920* (Chapel Hill: University of North Carolina Press, 1996); and Giddings, *When and Where I Enter*; and on working-class blacks, Jacqueline Jones, *Labor of Love, Labor of Sorrow: Black Women, Work, and the Family, From Slavery to the Present* (New York: Vintage, 1986); and Herbert G. Gutman, *The Black Family in Slavery and Freedom, 1750–1925* (New York: Vintage, 1976). For the mammy-versus-jezebel duality, see Deborah Gray White, *Ar'n't I a Woman* (New York: Norton, 1985), 27–61. For more on the mammy figure, see Chapter 3.

42.   Anna Julia Cooper, *A Voice From the South* (Xenia, OH: Aldine, 1892), i. On Cooper, see Carby, *Reconstructing Womanhood*, 95–107; and Gaines, *Uplifting the Race*, 128–51. See also Stephanie J. Shaw, *What a Woman Ought to Be and to Do: Black Professional Women Workers During the Jim Crow Era* (Chicago: University of Chicago Press, 1996); and Beverly Guy-Sheftall, *Daughters of Sorrow: Attitudes Toward Black Women, 1880–1920* (Brooklyn: Carlson, 1990), vol. 11 of the *Black Women in United States History* series.

43.   Mary Church Terrell, *A Colored Woman in a White World* (1940; rpt., New York: Arno Press, 1980), 15–16; and Beverly Washington Jones, *Quest for Equality: The Life and Writings of Mary Eliza Church Terrell, 1863–1954* (Brooklyn: Carlson, 1990), vol. 13 of the *Black Women in United States History* series.

44.   Cooper, *Voice From the South*, 91–97, quotes, 91, 96. See Chapter 4 for Du Bois's use of a train trip to analyze black identity.

45.   Cooper, *Voice*, quotes, 80, 81; Carby, *Reconstructing Womanhood*, 102–03.

46.   Dunbar-Nelson is quoted in Gaines, *Uplifting the Race*, 227. Harper is quoted in Carby, *Reconstructing Womanhood*, 70.

47.   Cooper, *Voice*, 28, iii, 31.

48.   Alain Locke, *The New Negro* (1925; rpt., New York: Atheneum, 1992), 7; Huggins, *Harlem Renaissance*; Nathan I. Huggins, ed., *Voices of the Harlem Renaissance*

(New York: Oxford University Press, 1995); and David Levering Lewis, *When Harlem Was in Vogue* (New York: Vintage, 1982).

49.   James Weldon Johnson, *Along This Way* (1933; rpt., New York: Penguin Books, 1990), 318–21, 380–82; and Douglas, *Terrible Honesty*, 325–28.

50.   Pamphlet quoted in Douglas, *Terrible Honesty*, 326. Locke, *New Negro*, 3,5.

51.   Huggins, *Harlem Renaissance*; Lewis, *When Harlem Was in Vogue*; Douglas, *Terrible Honesty*, 303–45, Johnson quote, 313; and Johnson, "Harlem: The Culture Capital," in *New Negro*, 301–11.

52.   Johnson, "Harlem," 301; Langston Hughes, "I Too," in *New Negro*, 145; Huggins, *Harlem Renaissance*. For the long counter-history produced by African American scholars in response to the distortions of historical facts and the general erasure of any black subjectivity in white-authored histories, see W. E. B. Du Bois, "The Propaganda of History," including his annotated bibliography, in *Black Reconstruction*, 711–37; Carter G. Woodson, *The Education of the Negro Prior to 1861* (New York, 1915; rpt., New York: Arno Press, 1968), and *The Negro in Our History* (Washington, D.C.: The Associated Publishers, 1924); John Hope Franklin, *From Slavery to Freedom: A History of Negro Americans* (New York: Knopf, 1972), and *Race and History: Selected Essays, 1938–1988* (Baton Rouge: Louisiana State University Press, 1989). To see this counter-history unfold, see the issues of the *Journal of Negro History* and the *Bulletin of Negro History*. Correspondence with Nell Irvin Painter has been especially helpful in my thinking here.

53.   For the term "miscegenated culture," see Douglas, *Terrible Honesty*, 303–45, Bert Williams quote, 329.

54.   Nella Larsen, *Quicksand and Passing* (1928; rpt., New Brunswick: Rutgers University Press, 1988), and the introduction by Deborah E. McDowell, ix–xxxv; Carby, *Reconstructing Womanhood*, 89–90; and William L. Andrews, "Introduction," in James Weldon Johnson, *The Autobiography of an Ex-Colored Man* (1912; rpt., New York: Penguin Books, 1990), vii–xxvii.

55.   Johnson, *Autobiography*, 1; Andrews, "Introduction," vii–xxvii. The same tensions pervaded movie-making. See Thomas Cripps, " 'Race Movies' as Voices of the Black Bourgeoisie: *The Scar of Shame* (1927)," in John E. O'Connor and Martin A. Jackson, *American History/ American Film: Interpreting the Hollywood Image* (New York: Continuum, 1988), 39–55.

56.   Johnson, *Autobiography*, 58, 139.

57.   Zora Neale Hurston, *Their Eyes Were Watching God* (1937; rpt., New York: Harper Perennial, 1990); Ralph Ellison, *Invisible Man* (New York: Random House, 1952). Two fine examples of the vast literature on the civil rights movement are Taylor Branch, *Parting the Waters: America in the King Years, 1954–1963* (New York: Simon and Schuster, 1988); and Clayborne Carson, *In Struggle: SNCC and the Black Awakening of the 1960s* (Cambridge, MA: Harvard University Press, 1981).

58.   Ralph Ellison, "The World and the Jug," 107–43, quote, 115, and "Change the Joke," 45–59, both in *Shadow and Act*.

CHAPTER TWO: *Lost Causes and Reclaimed Spaces*

1. Thomas Nelson Page, *Red Rock: A Chronicle of Reconstruction* (New York: Scribner, 1898), vii, viii.

2. William Faulkner, *The Unvanquished* (1938; rpt., New York: Vintage International, 1991), 94, 199, 223.

3. Allen Tate, "Remarks on the Southern Religion," in Twelve Southerners, *I'll Take My Stand* (1930; rpt., Baton Rouge: Louisiana State University Press, 1991), 174; Robert Penn Warren, "Literature as a Symptom," in Herbert Agar and Allen Tate, eds., *Who Owns America* (Boston: Houghton Mifflin, 1936), 271. For a very similar assertion that the past was in the present, see Ben Robertson, *Red Hills and Cotton: An Upcountry Memory* (1942; rpt., Columbia: University of South Carolina Press, 1960), 26, 28. On the creation of legitimating narratives of origins, see Edward W. Said, *Beginnings: Intention and Method* (New York: Basic Books, 1975); and J. F. Lyotard, *The Postmodern Condition* (Minneapolis: University of Minnesota Press, 1984), 18–20. I have found Lyotard's conception of "narrative knowledge" (18), of "the preeminence of the narrative form in the formulation of traditional knowledge" (19), useful in understanding whites' use of stories of the racial past in creating the racial future. On the construction of memory and tradition, see Eric Hobsbawm, "Mass-Producing Traditions: Europe, 1870–1914," in Eric Hobsbawm and Terence Ranger, eds., *The Invention of Tradition* (Cambridge: Cambridge University Press, 1983), 263–307; Edward Shils, *Tradition* (Chicago: University of Chicago Press, 1981), 1–62; and Barry Schwartz, "The Reconstruction of Abraham Lincoln," in *Collective Remembering* (London: Sage, 1990), 81–107. For the reconstruction and redefinition of the Civil War in the years immediately following it, before my analysis begins, see Charles Royster, *The Destuctive War: William Tecumseh Sherman, Stonewall Jackson, and the Americans* (New York: Vintage, 1993), and LeeAnn Whites, *The Civil War as a Crisis in Gender: Augusta, Georgia, 1860–1890* (Athens: University of Georgia Press, 1995), especially ch. 6. Although I will not continue to place "Old South" in quotes, the term refers not to antebellum history but to how late nineteenth- and early twentieth-century white southerners, often joined by white northerners, imagined that time and place before the Civil War.

4. George W. Cable, "The Freedman's Case in Equity," *Century Magazine* 29 (January 1885): 409–18, quote, 416; "The Silent South," *Century Magazine* 30 (September 1885): 674–91; *The Negro Question* (New York: Scribner, 1890); and *The Silent South* (New York: Scribner, 1885). See also George Washington Cable, *The Negro Question: A Selection of the Writings on Civil Rights in the South*, ed. Arlin Turner (New York: Doubleday, 1958); Lucy Leffingwell Cable Bickle, *George W. Cable: His Life and Letters* (New York: Scribner, 1928); Louis D. Rubin, *George W. Cable: The Life and Times of a Southern Heretic* (New York: Pegasus, 1969); Edmund Wilson, *Patriotic Gore: Studies in the Literature of the American Civil War* (New York: Farrar, Straus and Giroux, 1962), 549–604; Paul M. Gaston, *The New South Creed: A Study in Southern Mythmaking* (New York: Knopf, 1970), 127–30; and David L. Chappell, *Inside Agitators: White Southerners and the Civil Rights Movement* (Baltimore: Johns Hopkins University Press, 1994), 10–17.

5. Cable, "Freedman's Case," 416; On the origins of segregation as policy, see C. Vann Woodward, *The Strange Career of Jim Crow* (New York: Oxford University Press, 1965); and John T. Cell, *The Highest Stage of White Supremacy: The Origins of Segregation in South Africa and the American South* (Cambridge: Cambridge University Press, 1982).

6. Cable, "Silent South," 686; "Freedman's Case," 415; *Negro Question*, 10–11.

7. Henry Grady, "In Plain Black and White. A Reply to Mr. Cable," *Century Magazine* 29 (April 1885), 917; Cable, *Negro Question*, 21, 22; "Freedman's Case," 417, 415.

8. Cable, *Negro Question*, 24; "Silent South," 683; Chappell, *Inside Agitators*, 15. For an antebellum example of "upstanding" free blacks seeking to differentiate themselves from the slave masses, see Michael P. Johnson and James L. Roark, *Black Masters: A Free Family of Color in the Old South* (New York: Norton, 1984).

9. Cable, "Silent South," 679. George Fredrickson, *The Black Image in the White Mind: The Debate on Afro-American Character and Destiny, 1817–1914* (1971; rpt., Hanover, NH: Wesleyan University Press, 1987), 198–255.

10. The most helpful texts in the vast literature of the Lost Cause are Gaines M. Foster, *Ghosts of the Confederacy: Defeat, the Lost Cause, and the Emergence of the New South* (New York: Oxford University Press, 1987); Rollin G. Osterweis, *The Myth of the Lost Cause, 1865–1900* (Hamden, CT: Archon Books, 1973); and Charles Reagan Wilson, *Baptized in Blood: The Religion of the Lost Cause* (Athens: University of Georgia Press, 1980), all of which conceive the "Lost Cause" as the strictly white southern celebration of the Confederate cause. Hereafter, the term "Lost Cause" will not appear in quotes.

11. Cable, "Freedman's Case," 410, 415; "Silent South," 674; W. E. B. Du Bois, *Black Reconstruction in America* (1935; rpt., New York: Atheneum, 1962), 726, 723. Du Bois had written praising Reconstruction as early as 1910, in "Reconstruction and Its Benefits," *American Historical Review* (July 1910): 781–99. Jackson Lears, *No Place of Grace: Antimodernism and the Transformation of American Culture* (New York: Pantheon, 1981). On the *Plessy* case, see Eric J. Sundquist, *To Wake the Nations: Race in the Making of American Literature* (Cambridge: Harvard University Press, 1994), 233–49; Otto H. Olsen, *The Thin Disguise: Plessy v. Ferguson, A Documentary Presentation* (New York: Humanities Press, 1967); C. Vann Woodward, "The National Decision Against Equality," in *American Counterpoint: Slavery and Racism in the North–South Dialogue* (Boston: Little, Brown, 1971); Barton J. Bledstein, "Case Law in *Plessy v. Ferguson*," *Journal of Negro History* 47 (July 1962): 192–98; and Charles Lofgren, *The Plessy Case: A Legal-Historical Interpretation* (New York: Oxford University Press, 1987).

12. Charles W. Chesnutt, *The Marrow of Tradition* (1901) in William L. Andrews, ed., *The African-American Novel in the Age of Reaction: Three Classics* (New York: Mentor Books, 1992), 257, 256.

13. W. E. B. Du Bois, *Darkwater: Voices From Within the Veil* (1921; rpt., Millwood, NY: Kraus-Thompson, 1970), 228–30; "The Superior Race," *Smart Set* 70 (April 1923): 55–60, reprinted in David Levering Lewis, ed., *W. E. B. Du Bois, A Reader* (New York: Henry Holt, 1995), 470–77, quote, 476; and "Georgia, Invisible Empire State, *Nation* 120 (21 January 1925): 63–67. For more on the segregation of public and

semi-public, commercial facilities as central to modern southern racial identities, see Chapter 4.

14. Chesnutt, *Marrow*, 468; Cable, *Lovers of Louisiana* (1918), quoted in Wilson, *Patriotic Gore*, 603; and Richard Gray, *Writing the South: Ideas of an American Region* (New York: Cambridge University Press, 1986), 89–90.

15. Page, *Red Rock*, viii; and *Bred in the Bone* (New York: Scribner, 1904), 4–5. Du Bois, *Black Reconstruction*, 715. See also Page, *In Ole Virginia; or Marse Chan and Other Stories* (New York: Scribner, 1887); *Pastime Stories* (New York: Scribner, 1898); and *The Old Gentleman of the Black Stock* (New York: Scribner, 1900). Writing realistic fiction from the late nineteenth century into the 1930s, Ellen Glasgow provides the only consistent exception to the tendency of white southern writers to romanticize the past. See especially her 1900 novel *Voice of the People*. Glasgow set the pattern for a later generation, avoiding race relations and African Americans as topics of her fiction and using black servants more as atmosphere than as subjects. See C. Vann Woodward, *Origins of the New South* (Baton Rouge: Louisiana State University Press, 1951), 142–74, 434–36. See Chapter 6 for the "generation of 1900."

16. Albion Tourgee, "The South as a Field for Fiction," *Forum* 6 (December 1888): 404–18, quote, 406–07; Lucinda MacKethan, "Plantation Fiction, 1865–1900," in Louis D. Rubin et al., *The History of Southern Literature* (Baton Rouge: Louisiana State University Press, 1985), 209–18; Francis Pendleton Gaines, *The Southern Plantation: A Study in the Development and the Accuracy of a Tradition* (New York: Columbia University Press, 1925); Woodward, *Origins of the New South*, 142–74; Gray, *Writing the South*, 75–121; Nina Silber, *The Romance of Reunion* (Chapel Hill: University of North Carolina Press, 1994); and Wilson, *Patriotic Gore*. On black images as products and in advertising, see Chapter 4.

17. Gaston, *New South Creed*, 167–84, quote, 170; Joel Chandler Harris, *Uncle Remus: His Songs and His Sayings* (1880; rpt., New York: D. Appleton, 1917), viii, vii; Julia Collier Harris, *The Life and Letters of Joel Chandler Harris* (New York: Houghton Mifflin, 1918), 142–98; Page, *In Ole Virginia*; Margaret Mitchell, *Gone With the Wind* (1936; rpt., New York: Warner Books, 1993); David Selznick, producer, *Gone With the Wind* (motion picture, 1939); and Wilson, *Patriotic Gore*, 604–16. See also Irwin Russell, "Christmas Night in the Quarters," a poem published in 1878 and an important early example of the use of the slave character as a symbol of the Old South. On the symbolism of slavery in postbellum American culture, see Pete Daniel, "The Metamorphosis of Slavery, 1865–1900," *Journal of American History* 66 (June 1979): 88–99; and William L. Van Deburg, *Slavery and Race in American Popular Culture* (Madison: University of Wisconsin Press, 1984).

18. Gray, *Writing the South*, 89–90; and Page, *Red Rock*, vii, 29. For the erasure of the issue of slavery from the meaning of the war, see Whites, *Civil War as a Crisis in Gender*, 160–224. On peonage and convict labor, see Pete Daniel, *The Shadow of Slavery: Peonage in the South, 1901–1969* (Urbana: University of Illinois Press, 1972); and Edward L. Ayers, *Vengeance and Justice: Crime and Punishment in the Nineteenth Century American South* (New York: Oxford University Press, 1984). On racial violence, see Chapter 5. Page also wrote nonfiction books that stressed the racial ease and plantation pastorale of

the Old South. See *The Old South: Essays Social and Political* (New York: Scribner, 1892); *Social Life in Old Virginia Before the War* (New York: Scribner, 1898); and *The Negro: The Southerner's Problem* (New York: Scribner, 1904).

19. Woodward, *Origins of the New South*, 142–74, quote, 158; Gaston, *New South Creed*, 125, 167–84; Whites, *Civil War as a Crisis in Gender*, 199–224; MacKethan, "Plantation Fiction," 212–16; Julia C. Harris, *Joel Chandler Harris*, 1–35; John David Smith and John Inscoe, *Ulrich Bonnell Philips: A Southern Historian and His Critics* (Westport, CT: Greenwood Press, 1990); Foster, *Ghosts of the Confederacy*, 79–114, 163; and *The Confederate Veteran*. On the work of nostalgia, see Christopher Lasch, *The True and Only Heaven: Progress and Its Critics* (New York: Norton, 1991), 82–119.

20. Joel C. Harris, *On the Plantation: A Story of a Georgia Boy's Adventures During the War* (1892; rpt., Athens: University of Georgia Press, 1989); Edwin Mims, "Thomas Nelson Page," *Atlantic Monthly* (1907), 113, quoted in Woodward, *Origins of the New South*, 167; Page, *Old South*; and Belle Kearney, *A Slaveholder's Daughter* (New York: Abbey Press, 1900).

21. Julia C. Harris, *Joel Chandler Harris*, 1–53; Hugh T. Keenan, ed., *Dearest Chums and Partners: Joel Chandler Harris's Letters to His Children* (Athens: University of Georgia Press, 1993); and Bruce Bickley, Jr., *Critical Essays on Joel Chandler Harris* (Boston: G. K. Hall, 1981). See also the Joel Chandler Harris Papers, Robert W. Woodruff Library, Emory University, Atlanta (hereafter JCH-EU).

22. Harris, *Uncle Remus*, 3–172, quotes, 164, 16, 163. Other Harris collections of Uncle Remus tales include *Nights with Uncle Remus: Myths and Legends of the Old Plantation* (Boston: James R. Osgood, 1883); *Uncle Remus and His Friends: Old Plantation Stories, Songs and Ballads, with Sketches of Negro Character* (Boston: Houghton Mifflin, 1892); *Told By Uncle Remus; New Stories of the Old Plantation* (New York: McClure, Phillips, 1905); *Uncle Remus and Brer Rabbit* (New York: Frederick A. Stokes, 1906); *Uncle Remus and the Little Boy* (Boston: Small, Maynard, 1910); and *Uncle Remus Returns* (Boston: Houghton Mifflin, 1918). Other partially subversive black characters created by Harris include the mammy figure Aunt Minerva Ann in *The Chronicles of Aunt Minerva Ann* (New York: Scribner, 1899) and Free Joe, a free black living in the antebellum South, in *Free Joe and Other Georgian Sketches* (New York: Scribner, 1887).

23. Harris, *Uncle Remus*, 98–99; Silber, *Romance of Reunion*, 93–158; Joel Chandler Harris, "Plantation Music," *The Critic* 3 (15 December 1883): 506. Harris expressed similar sentiments in the introduction to *Uncle Remus*, vii–xvii. Page, *In Ole Virginia*, and *Red Rock*.

24. Scholars disagree strongly about the racial identities of the voices within Harris's work and about how much Harris authored and how much he took from conversations with African Americans. See Bernard Wolfe, "Uncle Remus and the Malevolent Rabbit: 'Takes a Limber-Toe Gemmun fer ter Jump Jim Crow,' " 70–84; Robert Bone, "The Oral Tradition," 130–45; Florence E. Baer, "Joel Chandler Harris: An 'Accidental' Folklorist," 185–95; and Joseph M. Griska, Jr., " 'In Stead of a "Gift of Gab" ': Some New Perspectives on Joel Chandler Harris Biography," 210–25, all in Bickley, *Critical Essays*. Charles Chesnutt understood the subversive potential of the Remus-type narrator perhaps better than Harris did himself and modeled his own narrator Uncle Julius on Har-

ris's creation. Julius first appeared in print in "The Goophered Grapevine," *Atlantic Monthly* (1887), which was reprinted in *The Conjure Woman* (1899; rpt., Durham: Duke University Press, 1993). See MacKethan, "Plantation Fiction," 216–17.

25. Harris, "The Fourth of July," in *Uncle Remus: His Songs and His Sayings*, 262–65, quote, 263.

26. Ibid., 262–65, quotes, 263, 264, 264–65. "Uncle Remus and the Savannah Darkey," 220–22, depicts Remus making fun of a well-dressed black servant from Savannah visiting northern Georgia with his employer. On the controversy about whether the racial subversiveness that floats within Harris's works was intentionally crafted by him or was instead a trace of the black voices from which he took his material, see note 22 and more recently, James A. Miller, "The Other Fellow," a review of R. Bruce Bickley's *Joel Chandler Harris*, in *Nation* 244 (9 May 1987): 614–17. On the racial complexity of Mark Twain's work, especially the 1894 novel *Pudd'nhead Wilson*, see Sundquist, *To Wake the Nations*, 225–70, which inexplicably leaves a serious examination of Harris out of its account of "race in the making of American literature."

27. Joel Chandler Harris, "Why the Negro is Black," in *Uncle Remus: His Songs and Sayings*, 163–65; and "The Adventures of Simon and Susanna," in Richard Chase, ed., *Complete Tales of Uncle Remus* (Boston: Houghton Mifflin, 1955), 459. Remus, in mythology, was the "black" twin of Romulus, the legendary founder of Rome and murderer of Remus. The brothers were the secret sons of the god Mars.

28. Wayne Mixon, "The Ultimate Irrelevance of Race: Joel Chandler Harris and Uncle Remus in Their Time," *Journal of Southern History* 56 (August 1990): 457–80. On Harris's work as editor of the *Atlanta Constitution* from 1876 to 1900, see Julia Collier Harris, *Joel Chandler Harris, Editor and Essayist: Miscellaneous Literary, Political, and Social Writings* (Chapel Hill: University of North Carolina, 1931), especially Part II, "Joel Chandler Harris and the Negro Question," 95–178, a series of excerpts from his editorials on race. Harris occasionally signed his letters "Uncle Remus." See Harris, Atlanta, 21 July 1884, to R. U. Johnson, *Century Magazine*, New York City, Box 1, JCH-EU. Others often wrote to him or about him as Uncle Remus instead of as Harris. See the letters addressed to "Uncle Remus": Walter Hines Page, New York City, n.d., 22 October 1900, 18 December 1900, 11 November 1908, to Harris, Atlanta, Box 1; Thomas Nelson Page, Richmond, 28 December 1885, to Harris, Atlanta, Box 4; and Theodore Roosevelt, White House, Washington, D.C., 24 October 1907, to Harris, Atlanta, Box 4; all in JCH-EU. Joel Chandler Harris, Atlanta, 21 October 1894, to Charles Scribner's Sons, New York, Charles Scribner's Sons Archive, Princeton University Library, Princeton, NJ; and Harris, Atlanta, 2 November 1907, to Andrew Carnegie, New York City, Box 4, JCH-EU; Walter Hines Page quoted in Julia Harris, *Joel Chandler Harris*, 164; and "Joel Chandler Harris Talks of Himself," *Atlanta Daily News*, 10 October 1900, 5. Even Harris's obituaries called him Uncle Remus. See, for example, "Calm Death Comes to 'Uncle Remus,'" *Washington Herald*, 4 July 1908. See also Robert Bone, "The Oral Tradition," 130–45; and Darwin T. Turner, "Daddy Joel Harris and His Old-Time Darkies," 113–29, in Bickley, *Critical Essays*. On Harris's conception of his identity as a creative writer as "the other fellow," see Harris, Atlanta, 19 March 1899, to Lillian and Mildred Harris, Washington, GA, JCH-EU. On his conception of his relation to Uncle Remus, see Harris,

Atlanta, 4 August 1881, to Samuel Clemens, Box 4, JCH-EU: "I understand that my relations toward Uncle Remus are similar to those that exist between an almanac-maker and the calendar." On his sense of "invention" versus "drawing on the oral stories," see Harris, Atlanta, 24 December 1886, to R. W. Gilder, *Century Magazine*, New York City, Box 1, JCH-EU.

29. Harris, Atlanta, 26 May 1887, to R. W. Gilder, New York City, Box 1, JCH-EU: "Beg him [the illustrator E. W. Kemble] also to give the old negro man some dignity." Harris, *Told By Uncle Remus*, 59; and Wolfe, "Uncle Remus and the Malevolent Rabbit," 84. On the way Harris's Remus books worked within northern culture to make southern blacks seem more like foreign exotics and external to the nation, see Silber, *Romance of Reunion*, 138–41.

30. Julia Porcher Wickham, "My Children's Mammy—An Appreciation," *Confederate Veteran* 34 (November 1926): 414.

31. Ray Stannard Baker, *Following the Color Line: American Negro Citizenship in the Progressive Era* (1908; rpt., New York: Harper and Row, 1964), 44. On classifications of turn-of-the-century white racism, see Joel Williamson, *The Crucible of Race: Black-White Relations in the American South Since Emancipation* (New York: Oxford University Press, 1984), 2–7; and Fredrickson, *Black Image*, 198–319. Confederate patriotic societies like the UDC and UCV were dominated by middle-class memberships by the early twentieth century. See Foster, *Ghosts of the Confederacy*, 79–103, 163–79. On Joel Chandler Harris's and Thomas Nelson Page's class backgrounds, see Julia C. Harris, *Joel Chandler Harris*, 1–35, and Wilson, *Patriotic Gore*, 604–16. On celebration of the specifically female version of the blurred slave/ex-slave figure, the "mammy," see Chapter 3.

32. Miss Mary M. Solari, "Monument to Faithful Slaves," *Confederate Veteran* 13 (March 1905): 123–24, quote, 123; Mrs. W. Carleton Adams, "Slave Monument Question," *Confederate Veteran* 12 (November 1904): 525. On the 1923 mammy monument, see Cheryl Thurber, "The Development of the Mammy Image and Mythology," in Virginia Bernhard, Betty Brandon, Elizabeth Fox-Genovese, and Theda Perdue, eds., *Southern Women: Histories and Identities* (Columbia: University of Missouri Press, 1992). On the Uncle Tom Memorial, see "Monument, 'Uncle Tom' Natchitoches Parish, Louisiana," April 1933, U.S. Department of Agriculture photograph collection, S-16927C. For this reference, I would like to thank Pete Daniel.

33. Solari, "Monument," 123; and Adams, "Monument Question," 525. On African American women's opposition to the proposed national mammy monument, see Mary Church Terrell, "The Black Mammy Monument," *The Star*, 10 February 1923, Terrell Papers, quoted in Tera Hunter, "Household Workers in the Making: Afro-American Women in Atlanta and the New South, 1861–1920" (Ph.D. dissertation, Yale University, 1991), 252. On white southern monument building in general, see Foster, *Ghosts of the Confederacy*, 40–44, 129–30, 158, 167–68, 175–78, 273; and Catherine W. Bishir, "Landmarks of Power: Building a Southern Past, 1885–1915," *Southern Cultures* 1 (Inaugural Issue, 1993): 9–13.

34. Sumner A. Cunningham, "Give the Old Slave a Home," *Confederate Veteran* 1 (March 1893): 80; and "Pensions for Faithful Negroes," *Confederate Veteran* 29 (August 1921): 284. See also "U.C.V. to Honor Wartime Slave," *New York Age*, 18 January 1914;

"Eleven Former Slaves Dined by Owner's Sons," *New York Age*, 13 May 1915; "South Still Honors 'Old-Time' Negro," *Philadelphia Public Ledger*, 2 May 1915; " 'Black Mammy' Day Observed," *St. Louis Republic*, 14 October 1915; "Black Mammy," *Christian Science Monitor*, 21 October 1918; "Homes for Ex-Slaves," *Indianapolis Freeman*, 2 February 1915; "Home for Ex-Slaves Helped by Atlantans," *Atlanta Constitution*, 19 April 1918; "Slaves Who Deserve Pensions," *Montgomery Advertiser*, 12 July 1913; "Will Tallahassee Heed?" *Palatka* (Florida) *Advocate*, 2 October 1915; and "Negro Confederate Buried with Honors," *Atlanta Constitution*, 19 October 1915, all in Slavery and Race Problem Files, Microfilm Reels for 1913–1918, Tuskegee Institute Clipping File. See also Robert Timmons, "Aged Ex-Slaves Gather at Home of Old Master," in *The Possibilities of the Negro in Symposium* (Atlanta, 1904), 69–73.

35.   Mildred L. Rutherford, "The Wrongs of History Righted," speech given in Savannah, GA, 13 November 1914, 61, 62; "Thirteen Periods of United States History, speech given in New Orleans, 21 November 1912, 34. Both are published in Rutherford, *Four Addresses* (Birmingham, AL: Mildred Rutherford Historical Circle, 1916). Advertising copy for The Lucy Cobb Institute, *Miss Rutherford's Scrap Book*, 1942, clipping in Box 1, Mildred L. Rutherford Collection, Hargrett Rare Book and Manuscript Library, University of Georgia, Athens (hereafter MLR-UGA). Rutherford served this school for girls in Athens, Georgia, as principal, president, and director in the years 1880–1895, 1917–1922, and 1925–1926. See Grace Elizabeth Hale, " 'Some Women Have Never Been Reconstructed': Mildred Lewis Rutherford, Lucy M. Stanton, and the Racial Politics of White Southern Womanhood, 1900–1930," in John Inscoe, ed., *Georgia in Black and White: Explorations in Race Relations of a Southern State, 1865–1950* (Athens: University of Georgia Press, 1994). Rutherford's other publications include *The South Must Have Her Rightful Place in History* (Athens, GA: the author, 1923); *A Measuring Rod to Test Books and Reference Books in Schools, Colleges and Libraries* (Athens, GA: the author, 1919); *Georgia: The Thirteenth Colony* (Athens, GA: McGregor, 1926); *What the South May Claim* (Athens, GA: McGregor, 1916); *Facts and Figures vs. Myths and Misrepresentations: Henry Wirz and the Andersonville Prison* (Athens, GA: the author, 1921); *The Civilization of the Old South: What Made It; What Destroyed It; What Has Replaced It* (Athens, GA: the author, 1916); *Where the South Leads and Where Georgia Leads* (Athens, GA: McGregor, 1917); *The History of the Stone Mountain Memorial* (n.p.: United Daughters of the Confederacy, 1924); and *The South in the Building of the Nation; Thirteen Periods of United States History* (Athens, GA: the author, 1913). Rutherford also published her own historical journal, called *Miss Rutherford's Historical Scrap Book* (1923–1925), *Miss Rutherford's Historical Scraps* (1926), and *Miss Rutherford's Historical Notes* (1927), all published by the McGregor Company, Athens, GA. See also Chapter 3.

36.   Mildred L. Rutherford, Athens, GA, n.d., to Mrs. Oscar McKenzie, president of the UDC Georgia Division, in Box 2, MLR-UGA. Ulrich B. Phillips, *American Negro Slavery* (1918; rpt., Baton Rouge: Louisiana State University Press, 1966), 309–41, quote, 327; "The Economics of the Plantation," *South Atlantic Quarterly* 2 (July 1903): 231–36; "The Economics of Slave Labor in the South," in Julian A. C. Chandler et al., eds., *The South in the Building of the Nation* (Richmond: Southern Historical Publication Soci-

ety, 1909), vol. 5, 121–24; "The Plantation as a Civilizing Factor," *Sewanee Review* 12 (July 1904): 257–67, quote, 264. Page, *Red Rock*, 30. For Du Bois's famous statement about the doubled vision of African Americans, see *The Souls of Black Folk*, in *Du Bois: Writings* (1903; rpt., New York: Library of America, 1986), 364–65. His review of *American Negro Slavery* was published in *American Political Science Review* 12 (November 1918): 722–26. On Phillips, see Daniel Joseph Singal, *The War Within: From Victorian to Modernist Thought in the South, 1919–1945* (Chapel Hill: University of North Carolina Press, 1982), 37–57; and John David Smith and John C. Inscoe, *Ulrich Bonnell Phillips: A Southern Historian and His Critics* (New York: Greenwood Press, 1990). See also John David Smith, "*American Negro Slavery*: The Triumph of the New Proslavery Argument," in *An Old Creed for the New South* (Westport, CT: Greenwood Press, 1985), 239–83, 7–10, and 13, n. 18 on the blurred line between academic and professional historians in the late nineteenth and early twentieth centuries. Like Smith, I am interested in "writers who identified slavery as a topic of historical significance," but I also include writers of fiction in this category. On the professionalization of historical work, see Peter Novack, *That Noble Dream: The "Objectivity Question" and the American Historical Profession* (New York: Cambridge University Press, 1988).

37.   Phillips, *American Negro Slavery*, first quote, 313, n. 1, third quote, 383–84; and "Plantation as a Civilizing Factor," fourth quote, 263. The second quote is from Phillips, Tulane University, New Orleans, 21 January 1911, to John M. Parker, Esquire, New Orleans, Box 1, Ulrich Bonnell Phillips Collection, Southern Historical Collection, University of North Carolina at Chapel Hill (hereafter UBP-UNC). For Phillips's sense of the great differences between academic and amateur historians, see Phillips, University of Wisconsin, Madison, 23 February 1903, 3 March 1903, 25 March 1903, and 10 April 1903, to Lucien H. Boggs, Savannah; Phillips, University of Wisconsin, Madison, 2 May 1903, 4 May 1903, 5 May 1903, and 9 May 1903, to George J. Baldwin, Savannah; Carl Russell Fish, University of Wisconsin, Madison, 27 April 1922, to Phillips, University of Michigan, Ann Arbor; Phillips, Ann Arbor, 19 May 1922, to Carl Russell Fish, Madison; Armida Moses Jennings, United Daughters of the Confederacy, Chairman, Committee on University Prize Award, Lynchburg, VA, 3 November 1924, to Phillips, University of Michigan, Ann Arbor; and Phillips, Ann Arbor, 4 November 1924, to Mrs. Jennings, Lynchburg; all in Box 1, UBP-UNC.

38.   Phillips, *American Negro Slavery*, 228–401, quote, 514; and "Plantations with Slave Labor and Free," *American Historical Review* 30 (July 1925): 738–53. Northern and southern white critics with the notable exceptions of Frederick Bancroft, W. E. B. Du Bois, and Carter G. Woodson praised *American Negro Slavery*. See Smith, "The New Proslavery Argument," 262–72. Phillips was born in 1877. For more on his life, see Merton L. Dillon, *Ulrich Bonnell Phillips: Historian of the Old South* (Baton Rouge: Louisiana State University Press, 1985); and John Herbert Roper, *U.B. Phillips: A Southern Mind* (Macon, GA: Mercer University Press, 1984). Page, *Red Rock*, vii–viii.

39.   Theodore Langdon Van Norden, Katonah, NY, 15 June 1929, to Phillips, Box 1, UBP-UNC. Anonymous review in the *Baltimore Sun*, 3 August 1918; and Bruce, 11 March 1919, to Phillips, Phillips Collection, Yale University; both quoted in Smith, "The New Proslavery Argument," 268–69. Universal Pictures Corporation, Universal City,

CA, 10 August 1926, to Phillips, University of Michigan, Ann Arbor; and William H. Carpenter, Secretary, Columbia University Press, New York, 16 October 1907, to Phillips, New Orleans; both in Box 1, UBP-UNC. On sectionalism within the practice of history, see Novick, *That Noble Dream*, 76–80, 181, 226, 357.

40.   Smith, "New Proslavery Argument," 10.

41.   Phillips, *American Negro Slavery*, 313 (quotes), 326–30.

42.   Phillips, *American Negro Slavery*, 317, 327, 329; and "The Plantation Product of Men," *Proceedings of the Second Annual Session of the Georgia Historical Association* (Atlanta: Georgia Historical Association, 1918), 14.

43.   For the phrase "the hell that is called Reconstruction," see William H. Carpenter, New York, 16 October 1907, to Ulrich B. Phillips, New Orleans, Box 1, UBP-UNC. Carpenter quotes back to Phillips here a phrase Phillips has written to him.

44.   Editor of *Century Magazine* to Jubal Early, 23 April 1884, quoted in Foster, *Ghosts of the Confederacy*, 69; and H. O. Nelsen, "An Almost Forgotten Shrine," *Confederate Veteran* 20 (February 1912): 59. The "Battles and Leaders of the Civil War" series appeared in *Century Magazine* from November 1884 to March 1888. Conciliatory accounts of the Civil War include Rebecca Latimer Felton, *Country Life in Georgia in the Days of My Youth* (Atlanta: Index Printing Company, 1919), 80–94; and Harris, *On the Plantation*. On accounts by white southerners born around 1900, after the publication of the series, of the partisan lessons learned from parents or other relatives who had experienced the war, see Margaret Mitchell, Atlanta, 28 April 1928, to Julia Collier Harris, Chattanooga, in Richard Harwell, ed., *Margaret Mitchell's Gone With the Wind Letters, 1936–1949* (New York: Macmillan, 1976), 2–6; Katharine Lumpkin, *The Making of a Southerner* (1946; rpt., Athens: University of Georgia Press, 1991), 3–46, 111–50; and William Alexander Percy, *Lanterns of the Levee: Recollections of a Planter's Son* (1941; rpt., Baton Rouge: Louisiana State University Press, 1994), 25–75. On growing northern respect for Confederate soldiers and officers and sectional reconciliation, see Foster, *Ghosts of the Confederacy*, 63–75, quote, 196; Silber, *Romance of Reunion*, 12, 118–19, 152–56, 172–82; and Gray, *Writing the South*, 75–87. On sectional reconciliation and the Spanish-American war, see Nell Irvin Painter, *Standing at Armageddon: The United States, 1877–1919* (New York: Norton, 1987), 141–69.

45.   David R. Roediger, *The Wages of Whiteness: Race and the Making of the American Working Class* (New York: Verso, 1991), 167–81; David Montgomery, *The Fall of the House of Labor: The Workplace, the State and American Labor Activism* (Cambridge, MA: Harvard University Press, 1987), 25; Silber, *Romance of Reunion*, 159–96; Whites, *Civil War as a Crisis in Gender*; Marjorie Spruill Wheeler, *New Women of the New South* (New York: Oxford University Press, 1993); Fredrickson, *Black Image in the White Mind*, 283–319; Painter, *Standing at Armageddon*, 141–69, 216–52; and Richard Slotkin, *The Fatal Environment: The Myth of the Frontier in the Age of Industrialization* (New York: Atheneum, 1985), 301–24.

46.   Foster, *Ghosts of the Confederacy*; and Royster, *The Destructive War*.

47.   The *Century* series was later reprinted as a book. See *Battles and Leaders of the Civil War* (New York: Yoseloff, 1956).

48. "Time to Call Off Dixie," *Confederate Veteran* 5 (March 1897): 113; Ruther-
ford, *Civilization of the Old South*; and *South in the Building of the Nation*; and U. B.
Phillips, "The Central Theme of Southern History," *American Historical Review* 34
(October 1928): 30–43.

49. On marriage as a key trope of sectional reconciliation, see Silber, *Romance of
Reunion*, 39–65. Perhaps the earliest Reconstruction novel, Albion W. Tourgee's *A Fool's
Errand*, published in 1879, attempted to tell the northern public the true story of the era
from the perspective of a transplanted white northern family. The novel, popular in the
North, was compared to *Uncle Tom's Cabin*. Recounting in great detail white southerners' violent attacks on the freedpeople, Reconstruction government officials, and their
white sympathizers, Albion did not romanticize or sensationalize the period. His unique
contribution to sectional reconciliation lay instead in an empathetic expression of the
dominant white southern perspective and in his belief in the federal government's efforts
as a "fool's errand." In 1896, Tourgee would argue the case of Homer Plessy before the
U.S. Supreme Court, challenging not the equality of separate facilities but the right of
the state to racially label its citizens. See Sundquist, *To Wake the Nations*, 233–49; and
Wilson, *Patriotic Gore*, 529–48.

50. Harris, "A Story of the War," 201–12; and Thomas Nelson Page, "Meh Lady: A
Story of the War," in *In Ole Virginia*, 78–139; Foster, *Ghosts of the Confederacy*, 46, 60,
115–26, 136, 141, 194; Silber, *Romance of Reunion*, 125–58; and MacKethan, "Plantation
Fiction," 209–18.

51. Harris, *Uncle Remus*, 201–12, quotes, 210, 202, 208. Sally B. Hamner, "Mammy
Susan's Story," *Confederate Veteran* 1 (September 1893): 270–71; Julia B. Reed, "Blue-
coats at Liberty Hall," *Confederate Veteran* 7 (July 1899): 303–5; Captain James Dinkins,
"My Old Black Mammy," *Confederate Veteran* (January 1926): 20–22; and Chapman J.
Milling, "Ilium in Flames," *Confederate Veteran* 36 (May 1928): 179–83.

52. Joel C. Harris, *Uncle Remus* (Savannah: The Beehive Press, 1992), 204, 212. I
disagree strongly here with Mixon, "Ultimate Irrelevance of Race," 469, and Tumlin,
ed., *Uncle Remus*, xxii, on Remus's shooting of the northern soldier. Mixon claims that
the historical record documents a few similar incidents and that Remus is too old to follow the Union army. Tumlin argues that Remus's act is redeemed by his "sense of obligation to his would-be liberator" and that he stays on the plantation in part to care for the
man he has wounded. These explanations are plausible, and Remus's cold chills about
the irony of his situation do add a small measure of awareness of the slave's point of view
entirely missing in other white war stories. But the shooting nevertheless confirms what
white southerners desperately wanted to believe.

53. Harris, *On the Plantation*, quotes, 227, 229; and John C. Inscoe, "The Confederate Home Front Sanitized: Joel Chandler Harris' *On the Plantation* and Sectional
Reconciliation," *Georgia Historical Quarterly* 76 (Fall 1992): 652–74. On Harris's own
fatherlessness—his mother was deserted by her itinerant laborer lover and left her family
to raise Joel alone—and his apprenticeship as a printer's assistant on the same Turnwold
plantation that appears in the novel, see Julia C. Harris, *Joel Chandler Harris*, 1–35.
Other Harris war stories appear in *Stories of Georgia* (New York: American Book, 1896);

Tales of the Homefront in Peace and War (Boston: Houghton Mifflin, 1898); and *On the Wings of Occasions: Being the Authorized Version of Certain Curious Episodes of the Late Civil War, including the Hitherto Suppressed Narrative of the Kidnapping of President Lincoln* (New York: Doubleday, Page, 1900). The phrase "love and theft" is from Eric Lott, *Love and Theft: Blackface Minstrelsy and the American Working Class* (New York: Oxford University Press, 1993).

54. Harris, *On the Plantation*, 28–35, 113, 122–26, 206–22, 223–33, quotes, 232, 233, 230, 230–31, 230. Other white southern writings that erase the importance of emancipation include Page, *Red Rock*; Harris, *Gabriel Tolliver: A Story of Reconstruction* (New York: McClure, Phillips, 1902); Mitchell, *Gone With the Wind*; and Faulkner, *The Unvanquished*. See also G. B. Garwood, "The 'Coon' Was Exchanged," *Confederate Veteran* 13 (March 1905): 124.

55. Thomas Dixon, *The Clansman: A Historical Romance of the Ku Klux Klan* (1905; rpt., Lexington: University Press of Kentucky, 1970). Other white southern fictional accounts of Reconstruction include the much less racist Harris, *Gabriel Tolliver*, and the unfocused and formulaic Page, *Red Rock*. On the historiography of Reconstruction, see Du Bois, "The Propaganda of History," in *Black Reconstruction*, 711–29, which covers a broad range of historical writing; and Eric Foner, *Reconstruction: America's Unfinished Revolution, 1863–1877* (New York: Harper and Row, 1988), xix–xxvii, which focuses on professional historians.

56. Chapman J. Milling, "Illium in Flames," *Confederate Veteran* 26 (May 1928): 179–83; A. J. Emerson, "Stonewall Jackson: A Homily," *Confederate Veteran* 20 (February 1912): 58–59; Julia B. Reed, "Bluecoats at Liberty Hall," *Confederate Veteran* 7 (July 1899): 303–305; Margaret Heard Dohme, "Alexander Hamilton Stephens," *Confederate Veteran* 40 (March 1932): 91–94; Page, *In Ole Virginia*, 10; and F. Hopkinson Smith, *Colonel Carter of Cartersville* (Boston: Houghton Mifflin, 1891), 61–62. Clarence Cason, *Ninety Degrees in the Shade* (1935; rpt., Westport, CT: Negro University Press, 1970), 124–27.

57. Cason, *Ninety Degrees*, 120–24. See Chapter 3.

58. On racism and imperialism, see Benedict Anderson, *Imagined Communities: Reflections on the Origin and Spread of Nationalism* (New York: Verso, 1993), 83–112, 141–54.

59. E. A. Pollard, *The Lost Cause: A New Southern History of the War of the Confederates* (New York: G. W. Carleton, 1866); and *The Lost Cause Regained* (New York: G. W. Carleton, 1868), quotes, 13, 165, 129; Phillips, "Central Theme of Southern History," 40–41; Osterweis, *Myth of the Lost Cause*, 11–15.

60. Pollard's books were quite popular in the South from their earliest publication, but their interpretation of Reconstruction as race war did not become generally accepted until the late nineteenth century. White southern autobiographies and memoirs that describe Reconstruction in these terms include Kearney, *Slaveholder's Daughter*, 10–19, quote, 11; and Myrta Lockett Avary, *Dixie After the War* (New York: Doubleday, Page, 1906). Later accounts include Percy, *Lanterns on the Levee*, 68–70; Lumpkin, *Making of a Southerner*, 47–108; Cason, *Ninety Degrees in the Shade*, 20–24; and W. J. Cash, *The Mind of the South* (1941; rpt., New York: Vintage, 1991), 103–44, a

work that blended historical and personal observations. White southern fictional accounts of Reconstruction include Page, *Red Rock*; Harris, *Gabriel Tolliver*; Thomas Dixon, *The Leopard's Spots* (1902; rpt., Ridgewood, NJ, 1967); *Clansman*, Mitchell, *Gone With the Wind*; and Faulkner, *The Unvanquished*. William H. Carpenter, New York, to Ulrich B. Phillips, New Orleans, 16 October 1907, Box 1, UBP-UNC.

For professional historians' revisions of this history of Reconstruction presented in white southern fiction and memoir, see Foner, *Reconstruction*; and Du Bois, *Black Reconstruction*.

61. Page, *Red Rock*, 41, 61–62.

62. Kearney, *Slaveholder's Daughter*, 10–19, quote, 12; Harris, *Gabriel Tolliver*, 113–16.

63. William Faulkner, "Raid," *Saturday Evening Post*, 3 November 1934, republished in *The Unvanquished*, 77–118, quote, 92–93.

64. Dixon, *Leopard's Spots* and *Clansman*; Dixon, Wellington, KS, 4 April 1902, to Wallace Hugh Cathcart, Cleaveland, Box 1, Thomas Dixon Papers, Woodruff Library, Emory University (hereafter TD-EU). On Dixon's life, see Thomas D. Clark's introduction to the 1970 edition of *The Clansman*, x–xv; and Williamson, *Crucible*, 140–76.

65. Dixon, Sioux City, IA, 7 February 1904, to Walter Hines Page, no location, Box 1, TD-EU. On *The Clansman* and Griffith's film *Birth of a Nation*, see Michael Rogin, " 'The Sword Became a Flashing Vision': D. W. Griffith's *Birth of a Nation*," in *Ronald Reagan, the Movie, and Other Episodes in Political Demonology* (Berkeley: University of California Press, 1987), 190–235. See also Chapter 5.

66. Page, *Red Rock*, 49–50, 60; and "Meh Lady: A Story of the War," in Page, *In Ole Virginia*, 78–139; Rutherford, *Four Addresses*, 37–45; Mrs. Adelaide Stuart Dimitry, "The Battle of the Handkerchiefs," an excerpt from *War-Time Sketches* (New Orleans), published in *Miss Rutherford's Scrapbook* 3 (December 1925): 29–30; Mitchell, *Gone With the Wind*; Matthew Page Andrews, ed., *The Women of the South in War Times* (Baltimore: Norman, Remington, 1923); and Hale, " 'Some Women Have Never Been Reconstructed.' " Nina Silber has argued that the portrayal of white women as strong and even manly by northern writers immediately after the war was a part of a process by which northerners emasculated white southern men. By the late nineteenth century, however, white southern women often portrayed themselves in a similar manner. See Silber, *Romance of Reunion*, 13–65; and Whites, *The Civil War as a Crisis in Gender*, 160–98.

67. John W. Burgess, *Reconstruction and the Constitution, 1866–1876* (New York, 1902), 218; Foner, *Reconstruction*, xix–xx, quote, xx; E. Merton Coulter, *William G. Brownlow, Fighting Parson of the Southern Highlands* (Chapel Hill: University of North Carolina Press, 1937), 352; and William A. Dunning, *Reconstruction, Political and Economic 1865–1877* (New York, 1907). See the excellent discussion of the early historiography of the period in Du Bois, *Black Reconstruction*, 711–29.

68. Du Bois, *Black Reconstruction*, 711–29; quotes, 725, 714, 723. See also A. A. Taylor, "Historians of the Reconstruction," *Journal of Negro History* 23 (January 1938), 16–34.

69.   Du Bois, *Black Reconstruction*, 728.

70.   Faulkner, *Go Down, Moses* (1942; rpt., New York: Vintage, 1990), quotes, 104, 101; Cable, *Negro Question*, 22. Faulkner's character Quentin Compson, in *Absalom, Absalom!* (New York: Random House, 1936) and *The Sound and the Fury* (New York: Random House, 1929), cannot live with the limits of his failed mastery and thus kills himself. In Faulkner's Civil War novel *The Unvanquished*, a black adolescent provides a precedent for Beauchamp. Ringo, the black playmate grown into a much smarter and more resourceful "Confederate" than his white master Bayard, works with his elderly white mistress to ensure the survival of the white family and their hundreds of poor white neighbors. See also the complex reading of *Go Down, Moses* in Eric J. Sundquist, *Faulkner: The House Divided* (Baltimore: Johns Hopkins University Press, 1983), 131–60.

71.   Mitchell, *Gone With the Wind*. See Chapter 3 and especially Chapter 6 for a more detailed reading of Mitchell's novel. For the crucial gendered aspects of the blackening of Reconstruction, see Chapter 3.

72.   Ben Robertson, *Red Hills and Cotton: An Upcountry Memoir* (1942; rpt., Columbia: University of South Carolina Press, 1960), 29; Cash, *Mind of the South*, 66, 83–85, 106–20, 167–73, 297–319; and Allen Tate, "Remarks on the Southern Religion," 174.

CHAPTER THREE: *Domestic Reconstruction*

1.   Ray Stannard Baker, *Following the Color Line: American Negro Citizenship in the Progressive Era* (1908; rpt., New York: Harper and Row, 1964), 44. In this chapter, "mammy" is always the representation created by whites and never refers to how African American women understood or represented themselves.

2.   Margaret Mitchell, *Gone With the Wind* (1936; rpt., New York: Warner Books, 1993), 408–9.

3.   Mildred Lewis Rutherford, "The South in the Building of a Nation," in *Four Addresses* (Birmingham, AL: Mildred Rutherford Historical Circle, 1916), 3. Sources on Rutherford include the Mildred L. Rutherford Collection, Hargrett Rare Book and Manuscript Library, University of Georgia, Athens (hereafter MLR-UGA); Grace Elizabeth Hale, " 'Some Women Have Never Been Reconstructed': Mildred Lewis Rutherford, Lucy M. Stanton, and the Racial Politics of White Southern Womanhood, 1900–1930," in John C. Inscoe, ed., *Georgia in Black and White: Explorations in the Race Relations of a Southern State, 1865–1950* (Athens: University of Georgia Press, 1994); and Margaret Anne Womack, "Mildred Lewis Rutherford, Exponent of Southern Culture" (M.A. thesis, University of Georgia, 1946), especially 73–81, 86, 146. Celebratory biographies of Rutherford include Virginia Clare, *Thunder and Stars* (Atlanta: Ogelthorpe University Press, 1941); and Hazelle Beard Tuthill, "Mildred Lewis Rutherford" (M.A. thesis, University of South Carolina, 1929). I have taken my description of Rutherford's physical appearance from the picture on the cover of *Four Addresses*. For an alternative

view of Rutherford, see Fred Arthur Bailey, "Mildred Lewis Rutherford and the Patrician Cult of the New South," *Georgia Historical Quarterly* 78 (Fall 1994): 509–35.

4. Rutherford, *Four Addresses*, 14, 4. For the greatness of southern white women, see Mildred L. Rutherford, *Where the South Leads* (Athens: McGregor, 1917), 1, 24, 28–30; *What the South May Claim* (Athens: McGregor, 1917), 5, 7, 23–24; and *Four Addresses*, 37–39. For southern white women as the keepers of culture and kinship, see Nancy Press, "Private Faces, Public Lives: The Women of the Downtown Group of Charleston, South Carolina," in Holly F. Matthews, ed., *Women in the South: An Anthropological Perspective* (Athens: University of Georgia Press, 1989), 95–109. For southern white women and the writing of southern history, see Chapter 2. All published speeches and writings of Mildred L. Rutherford are in the Georgia Collection, University of Georgia Library, Athens, Georgia.

5. See Chapter 2 for a detailed description of the racial arguments embedded within white southern historical narratives.

6. Baker, *Color Line*, 44; John C. Cell, *The Highest Stage of White Supremacy: The Origins of Segregation in South Africa and the American South* (Cambridge: Cambridge University Press, 1982), ix–xiv, 1–20; U. B. Phillips, "The Central Theme of Southern History," *American Historical Review* 34 (October 1928): 30–43, quote, 30–31; and masthead, *Confederate Veteran* 14 (March 1906). Published from 1893 to 1932, the *Veteran* was the official publication for the United Confederate Veterans, the United Daughters of the Confederacy, the Confederated Southern Memorial Association, and the Sons of Confederate Veterans. See Louis H. Manarin, ed., *Cumulative Index: The Confederate Veteran Magazine, 1893–1932* (Wilmington, NC: Broadfoot, 1986), vol. 1, xi. On changing racial attitudes within a national context, see George M. Fredrickson, *The Black Image in the White Mind: The Debate on Afro-American Character and Destiny, 1817–1914* (1971; rpt., Hanover, NH: Wesleyan Press, 1987). On changing racial attitudes within a southern context, see Joel Williamson, *The Crucible of Race: Black-White Relations in the American South Since Emancipation* (New York: Oxford University Press, 1984). See also Evelyn Nankano Glenn, "From Servitude to Service Work: Historical Continuities in the Racial Division of Paid Work," *Signs* (Autumn 1992). On a consumer-oriented domesticity among the planter elite in the antebellum period, see the excellent Jeffrey R. Young, "Domesticating Slavery: The Ideological Formation of the Master Class in the Deep South, From Colonization to 1837" (Ph.D. dissertation, Emory University, 1996). The crucial difference is that in the postwar South, domestic consumption spread across class lines to all but the poorest southerners.

7. Frances Newman, *Dead Lovers Are Faithful Lovers* (New York: Boni and Liveright, 1928), 177. On the plantation household as the dominant institution of antebellum southern society, see Elizabeth Fox-Genovese, *Within the Plantation Household: Black and White Women of the Old South* (Chapel Hill: University of North Carolina Press, 1988), 37–99. On the southern households and the place of white women in southern society from Reconstruction through 1900, see the pioneering work in Jean E. Friedman, *The Enclosed Garden: Women and Community in the Evangelical South, 1830–1900* (Chapel Hill: University of North Carolina Press, 1985), 92–130. See also Nell Irvin

Painter, "The Journal of Ella Gertrude Clanton Thomas: An Educated White Woman in the Eras of Slavery, War, and Reconstruction," in Virginia Ingraham Burr, ed., *The Secret Eve: The Journal of Ella Gertrude Clanton Thomas, 1848–1889* (Chapel Hill: University of North Carolina Press, 1990), 1–67.

8.   Though slaves were forced members of these households and had few opportunities to participate in market activities, Ted Ownby has found evidence of slaves' participation in buying and selling. See "Mississippi Slavery and the Meanings of Consumer Goods," paper given at the Rutgers Center for Historical Analysis workshop on "Mass Consumption and the Construction of Race in America," 18 September 1992. On the transformation of southern households, see Drew Gilpin Faust, "Altars of Sacrifice: Confederate Women and the Narratives of War," *Journal of American History* 76 (March 1990):1200–28; Fox-Genovese, *Plantation Household*, 37–99; Gavin Wright, *The Political Economy of the Cotton South: Households, Markets, and Wealth in the Nineteenth Century* (New York: Norton, 1978), 164–84, and *Old South, New South: Revolutions in the Southern Economy Since the Civil War* (New York: Norton, 1986), 1–123; and Steven Hahn, *The Roots of Southern Populism: Yeoman Farmers and the Transformation of the Georgia Upcountry, 1850–1890* (New York: Oxford University Press, 1982), 137–203. The shift away from production and toward consumption, especially in terms of textiles, began before the Civil War. Thus the war did not initiate but only deepened this important trend. See Lacy K. Ford, *Origins of Southern Radicalism: The South Carolina Low Country, 1800–1860* (New York: Oxford University Press, 1988), 219–77; and Hahn, *Roots of Southern Populism*.

An early twentieth-century study gave strong evidence of increasing consumption by tenants. See W. Fitzhugh Brundage, "A Portrait of Southern Sharecropping: The 1911–1912 Georgia Plantation Survey of Robert Preston Brooks," *Georgia Historical Quarterly* 77 (Summer 1993): 367–81. On the rise of general stores and their late nineteenth- and early twentieth-century domination of southern economic life, see Susan Atherton Hanson, "Home Sweet Home: Industrialization's Impact on Rural Households, 1865–1925" (Ph.D. dissertation, University of Maryland, 1986); Thomas D. Clark, *Pills, Petticoats, and Plows: The Southern Country Store* (Indianapolis: Bobbs-Merrill, 1944); Edward L. Ayers, *The Promise of the New South: Life After Reconstruction* (New York: Oxford University Press, 1993), 13–21, 24–29, 81–103; and Thomas J. Schlereth, "Country Stores, County Fairs, and Mail Order Catalogues: Consumption in Rural America," in Simon J. Bonner, ed., *Consuming Visions: Accumulation and Display of Goods in America, 1880–1920* (New York: Norton, 1989), 339–75.

9.   Sources on Rebecca Latimer Felton include the Rebecca Latimer Felton Collection, Hargrett Rare Book and Manuscript Collection, University of Georgia (hereafter RLF-UGA); LeeAnn Whites, "Rebecca Latimer Felton and the Wife's Farm: The Class and Racial Politics of Gender Reform," *Georgia Historical Quarterly* 76 (Summer 1992): 354–72, and "Rebecca Latimer Felton and the Problem of 'Protection' in the New South," in Nancy Hewitt and Suzanne Lebsock, eds., *Visible Women* (Chicago: University of Chicago Press, 1993); John E. Talmadge, *Rebecca Latimer Felton: Nine Stormy Decades* (Athens: University of Georgia Press, 1960); Josephine Bone Floyd, "Rebecca Latimer Felton, Political Independent," *Georgia Historical Quarterly* 30 (March 1946):

14–34, and "Rebecca Latimer Felton, Champion of Woman's Rights," *Georgia Historical Quarterly* 30 (June 1946): 81–104; Marjorie Spruill Wheeler, *New Women of the New South: The Leaders of the Woman Suffrage Movement in the Southern States* (New York: Oxford University Press, 1993), 41–43, 48, 54, 66–67, 81, 88–110, 162, 173, 190–91; Williamson, *Crucible*, 124–30; and Felton's own memoir, *Country Life in the Days of My Youth* (Atlanta: the author, 1919). Quotes are from *Country Life*, 33.

10.   Mary I. Stanton, "Two Master Farmers of the Seventies," manuscript in her niece Lucy M. Stanton's papers, Hargrett Rare Book and Manuscript Collection, University of Georgia, Athens. Lucy Stanton's nephew W. Stanton Forbes had the manuscript published. See *Georgia Review* (Spring 1962): 23–34, quotes, 28, 34, 28. For the overall tendency to construct *Gemeinschaft* from the perspective of *Gesellschaft*, see T. J. Jackson Lears, "Packaging the Folk: Tradition and Amnesia in American Advertising," in Jane S. Becker and Barbara Franco, eds., *Folk Roots, New Roots: Folklore in American Life* (Lexington, MA, 1988), 103–40.

11.   *Proceedings of the Convention of Southern Governors, Held in the City of Richmond, Virginia on April 12 and 13, 1893* (Richmond: published by the governors of Arkansas, Alabama, Louisiana, Maryland, Mississippi, North Carolina, South Carolina, and Virginia, 1893), 9. This pamphlet is in the Arkansas Box, Warshaw Collection, National Museum of American History, Smithsonian Institution, Washington, D.C. See also town-boosting publications throughout the southern state files within the Warshaw Collection. Edward L. Ayers has calculated that five million southerners moved from rural areas to towns between 1880 and 1910. See Ayers, *Promise of the New South*, 55–80, 467. On southern urban development, see also Don H. Doyle, *New Men, New Cities, New South: Atlanta, Nashville, Charleston, Mobile, 1860–1910* (Chapel Hill: University of North Carolina Press, 1990), 1–21; Blaine A. Brownwell and David R. Goldfield, eds., *The City in Southern History: The Growth of Urban Civilization in the South* (Port Washington, NY: Kennikat, 1977); David R. Goldfield, *Cotton Fields and Skyscrapers: Southern City and Region, 1607–1980* (Baton Rouge: Louisiana State University Press, 1982); and Lawrence Larsen, *The Rise of the Urban South* (Lexington: University Press of Kentucky, 1985). On the general development of the suburbs in America, see Clifford Edward Clark, Jr., *The American Family Home, 1800–1960* (Chapel Hill: University of North Carolina Press, 1986), 37–130; and Kenneth Jackson, *Crabgrass Frontier: The Suburbanization of America* (New York: Oxford University Press, 1985).

12.   Burton J. Bledstein, *The Culture of Professionalism: The Middle Class and the Development of Higher Education in America* (New York: Norton, 1976); Stuart M. Blumin, *The Emergence of the Middle Class: Social Experience in the American City, 1760–1900* (New York: Cambridge University Press, 1989); David Brion Davis, *The Problem of Slavery in the Age of Revolution, 1770–1823* (Ithaca, NY: Cornell University Press, 1975); and William Taylor, *Cavalier and Yankee: The Old South and American National Character* (New York: Braziller, 1961).

Historians have linked the division of the household into the private family space of the home and public productive space outside it as well as the separation of domesticity from political economy to the rise of industrial capitalism. In the South, this process of spatial change occurred in conjunction with market-driven agriculture and the spread of northern consumer products, via the general store network, throughout the region. Southern industry rapidly expanded throughout the period from 1890 to 1940, but agriculture dominated the southern economy through World War II. For more on the spread of consumption throughout the South, see Chapter 4.

See Leonore Davidoff and Catherine Hall, *Family Fortunes: Men and Women of the English Middle Class, 1780–1850* (Chicago: University of Chicago Press, 1987), for an excellent book on middle-class development that examines the economic, social, and cultural processes at work as the middle class moved toward hegemony in Great Britain. For a comparable but more narrowly focused analysis of middle-class formation in America, see Mary Ryan, *Cradle of the Middle Class: The Family in Oneida County, New York, 1790–1865* (New York: Cambridge University Press, 1981).

On the relations between market expansion, middle-class formation, and the renegotiation of public and private boundaries, see Jürgen Habermas, *Structural Transformation of the Public Sphere,* trans. by Thomas Burger with Frederick Lawrence (Cambridge, MA: MIT Press, 1989); and Habermas's many critics, especially Bruce Robbins, ed., *The Phantom Public Sphere* (Minneapolis: University of Minnesota Press, 1993). See also David Roediger, *The Wages of Whiteness* (New York: Verso, 1991); David Montgomery, *Beyond Equality: Labor and the Radical Republicans, 1862–1872* (New York: Knopf, 1967); Harriet Beecher Stowe, *Uncle Tom's Cabin* (Boston, 1852); Walter Benn Michaels, *The Gold Standard and the Logic of Naturalism: American Literature at the Turn of the Century* (Berkeley: University of California Press, 1987), 101–6; and Eric Lott, *Love and Theft: Blackface Minstrelsy and the American Working Class* (New York: Oxford University Press, 1993).

13.   Ryan, *Cradle of the Middle Class;* Dolores Hayden, *The Grand Domestic Revolution: A History of Feminist Designs for American Homes, Neighborhoods, and Cities* (Cambridge, MA: MIT Press, 1982), 1, 11–13; Jeanne Boydston, *Home and Work: Housework, Wages, and the Ideology of Labor in the Early Republic* (New York: Oxford University Press, 1990); Ann Douglas, *The Feminization of American Culture* (New York: Doubleday, 1988); Kathryn Kish Sklar, *Catharine Beecher: A Study in American Domesticity* (New Haven: Yale University Press, 1973); Carol Smith-Rosenberg, *Disorderly Conduct: Visions of Gender in Victorian America* (New York: Oxford University Press, 1986); and Karen Halttunen, *Confidence Men and Painted Women: A Study of Middle Class Culture in America, 1830–1870* (New Haven: Yale University Press, 1982).

14.   Gavin Wright, *Old South, New South;* Mary Ryan, *Women in Public: Between Banners and Ballots, 1825–1880* (Baltimore: Johns Hopkins University Press, 1990); Friedman, *Enclosed Garden.* Friedman, examining an earlier period, sees family and kin relations as surviving the Civil War and reinforcing traditional gender conventions. I argue that by the 1890s, antebellum gender relations often survived only as a consciously created appearance. In addition to the argument here, see Hale, " 'Some Women Have Never Been Reconstructed.' " Drew Gilpin Faust, looking at the period from 1860 through Reconstruction, has found a similar attempt to consciously re-create the role of the southern "lady." See "Altars of Sacrifice," and *Mothers of Invention: Women of the Slaveholding South in the American Civil War* (Chapel Hill: University of North Carolina Press, 1996), 220–33. See also LeeAnn Whites, *The Civil War as a Crisis in Gender:*

Augusta, Georgia, 1860–1890 (Athens: University of Georgia Press, 1995). By the early twentieth century, then, traditional southern white womanhood was a case of form over substance, as Ann Firor Scott argues in *The Southern Lady: From Pedestal to Politics, 1830–1930* (Chicago: University of Chicago Press, 1970). White women, as much as white men, however, were responsible for this gap between representations of the lady and southern white women's activities.

In emphasizing the shifting southern economy, I am not arguing for total absence of production within domestic spaces but its relative reduction.

15. Katharine Lumpkin, *The Making of a Southerner* (1946; rpt., Athens: University of Georgia Press, 1991), 131. Historians have long waged an argument about planter hegemony in the post–Civil War South and the continuity versus difference of southern elites. Planters who persisted, who held on to their economic and political power, however, became increasingly middle class and commercially oriented. Even in cases where the same families maintained power, then, they possessed a different world view. Economic and cultural changes operated dialectically, and by the late nineteenth century white southern elites lived and worked within a very different economy and culture. For a persuasive argument in favor of difference, see Wright, *Old South, New South*, 17–80. For the argument in favor of continuity, see Jonathan Weiner, *Social Origin of the New South* (Baton Rouge: Louisiana State University Press, 1978).

16. Ellen Glasgow, *The Woman Within* (New York: Harcourt, Brace, 1954, but book begun in 1934 and finished by 1943), 218; Belle Kearney, *A Slaveholder's Daughter* (New York: Abbey Press, 1900), 43–45, quotes, 2, 43; and William Alexander Percy, *Lanterns on the Levee: Recollections of a Planter's Son* (1941; rpt., Baton Rouge: Louisiana State University Press, 1994), 344–48, quote, 346.

17. On black domestic service in the postbellum period, see David M. Katzman, *Seven Days a Week: Women and Domestic Service in Industrializing America* (New York: Oxford University Press, 1978); Trudier Harris, *From Mammies to Militants: Domestics in Black American Literature* (Philadelphia: Temple University Press, 1982); Susan Tucker, *Telling Memories Among Southern Women: Domestic Workers and Their Employers in the Segregated South* (New York: Schocken, 1988); Tera Hunter, "Household Workers in the Making: Afro-American Women in Atlanta and the New South, 1861–1920" (Ph.D. dissertation, Yale University, 1991); Elizabeth Ross Haynes, "Negroes in Domestic Service in the U.S.," *Journal of Negro History* 8 (October 1923): 25–33; and Heather Biola, "The Black Washerwoman in Southern Tradition," in Darlene Clark Hine, ed., *The Black Woman in United States History*, vol. 9 (Brooklyn: Carlson, 1990). On domestics in the Washington, D.C., area between 1900 and 1920, see Elizabeth Clark-Lewis, *This Work Had an End: The Transition from Live In to Day Work* (Memphis: Southern Women: The Intersection of Race, Class, and Gender, Working Paper 2, 1985), and *Living In, Living Out: African American Domestics in Washington, D.C., 1910–1940* (Washington, D.C.: Smithsonian Institution, 1994). On the mammy image, see Cheryl Thurber, "The Development of the Mammy Image and Mythology," in Virginia Bernhard, Betty Brandon, Elizabeth Fox-Genovese, and Theda Perdue, eds., *Southern Women: Histories and Identities* (Columbia: University of Missouri Press, 1992), 87–108; Kenneth Goings, *Mammy and Uncle Mose: Black Collectibles and American Stereotyp-*

ing (Bloomington: Indiana University Press, 1994); Patricia Morton, *Disfigured Images: The Historical Assault on Afro-American Women* (New York: Greenwood Press, 1991); Patricia Morton, " 'My Ol' Black Mammy' in American Historiography," in Caroline Matheny Dillman, ed., *Southern Women* (New York: Hemisphere, 1988); Patricia A. Turner, *Ceramic Uncles and Celluloid Mammies: Black Images and Their Influence on Culture* (New York: Anchor Books, 1994); K. Sue Jewell, *From Mammy to Miss America and Beyond* (London: Routledge, 1993); and Alice Walker, "Giving the Party: Aunt Jemima, Mammy, and the Goddess Within," *MS*, May/June 1994, 22–25.

18.   Lillian Smith, *Killers of the Dream* (1949; rpt., New York: Norton, 1978), 25–40, quotes, 27, 34–35. Sources on Smith include the Lillian Smith Collection (hereafter LS-UGA) and the Paula Snelling Collection, Hargrett Rare Book and Manuscript Collection, University of Georgia, Athens; see especially biographic papers and notes about *Killers* prepared by Smith, in Box 1, LS-UGA. See also Pat Bryan Brewer, "Lillian Smith: Thorn in the Flesh of Crackerdom" (Ph.D. dissertation, University of Georgia, 1982); Roseanne V. Camacho, "Race, Region, and Gender in a Reassessment of Lillian Smith," in Bernhard, Brandon, Fox-Genovese, and Perdue, eds., *Southern Women: Histories and Identities*, 157–76; Bruce Clayton, "Lillian Smith: Cassandra in Dixie," *Georgia Historical Quarterly* 78 (Spring 1994): 92–114; Margaret Rose Gladney, *How Am I to Be Heard? Letters of Lillian Smith* (Chapel Hill: University of North Carolina Press, 1993); Fred Hobson, *Tell About the South: The Southern Rage to Explain* (Baton Rouge: Louisiana State University Press, 1983), 307–22; Anne C. Loveland, *Lillian Smith: A Southerner Confronting the South* (Baton Rouge: Louisiana State University Press, 1986); Kathleen Atkinson Miller, "Out of the Chrysalis: Lillian Smith and the Transformation of the South" (Ph.D. dissertation, Emory University, 1984); and Jo Ann Robinson, "Lillian Smith: Reflections on Race and Sex," *Southern Exposure* 4 (Fall 1977): 43–48. Smith was born in 1897. For more on Smith, see Chapter 6.

19.   Smith, *Killers of the Dream*, 35, 36–37, 38.

20.   Lumpkin, *Making of a Southerner*, 130.

21.   Ibid., 121–47. Katharine Lumpkin, 23 May 1944, to Groff Conklin, Washington, D.C.; and Katharine Lumpkin, 16 July 1943, to Milton Rugoff, New York, Box 1; and "Plans for Work," application for 1944 Alfred A. Knopf literary fellowship, Box 4. For biographical information, see "Vita," Box 7, and "Accomplishments," 1944 Knopf fellowship, Box 7, all in Katharine DuPre Lumpkin Collection, Southern Historical Collection, University of North Carolina at Chapel Hill (hereafter KDL-UNC). Lumpkin was born in Macon, Georgia, in 1897 but spent much of her childhood in South Carolina.

22.   Lumpkin, *Making of a Southerner*, quotes, 132, 132, 133. On learning race in the white home, see also Lillian Smith's review of *The Making of a Southerner*, "The Crippling Effect of White Supremacy," *New York Herald Tribune*, 2 February 1947, clipping in Box 4, KDL-UNC. For the role of the category of gender in placing people within society, in making them social beings, see Gayle Rubin, "The Traffic in Women: Notes on the 'Political Economy' of Sex," in Rayna R. Raiter, ed., *Toward an Anthropology of Women* (New York: Monthly Review Press, 1975.) Within the culture of segregation, race became the primary category of social identity and performed part of the function that Rubin assigns to gender.

23. Kearney, *Slaveholder's Daughter*, quotes, 92, 30. Belle Kearney was born in Mississippi in 1863 and became a well-known temperance activist and suffragist. See also Wheeler, *New Women*, xvi, xviii, 9, 41, 43–45, 48, 54, 60–64, 69–79, 84–85, 89–91, 97, 99, 102–4, 107–9, 112, 119–22, 125, 143, 162–63, 191–94, 216, 218. On white southerners' unconscious use of arguments that implied the cultural constructedness of race to support the extension of segregation, see Chapter 2.

24. Glasgow, *Woman Within*, 10–11. On Glasgow, see Anne Goodwyn Jones, *Tomorrow Is Another Day: The Woman Writer in the South* (Baton Rouge: Louisiana State University Press, 1981), 225–70; Blair Rouse, ed., *Letters of Ellen Glasgow* (New York: Harcourt, Brace, 1958); M. Thomas Inge, ed., *Ellen Glasgow: The Centennial Essays* (Charlottesville: University Press of Virginia, 1976); and Louis D. Rubin, Jr., *No Place on Earth: Ellen Glasgow, James Branch Cabell, and Richmond-in-Virginia* (Austin: University of Texas Press, 1959).

25. Smith, *Killers of the Dream*, 28, 25–40, 114–55; Lumpkin, *Making of a Southerner*, 155, 36; and Kearney, *Slaveholder's Daughter*, 3.

26. Mammies appear in a wide variety of white-authored southern fiction written between 1890 and 1940. See, for example, Katherine Anne Porter's short stories "The Old Order" and "The Last Leaf," in *The Leaning Tower and Other Stories* (New York: Harcourt, Brace and World, 1944); Mark Twain, *Pudd'nhead Wilson and "Those Extraordinary Twins,"* Sidney E. Berger, ed. (1894; rpt., New York: Norton, 1980); Thomas Nelson Page, *Red Rock* (New York: Scribner, 1898); and Mitchell, *Gone With the Wind*. For a domestic servant more animal-like than motherly, an exception that figures the mammy more like the black beast rapist, see Thomas Dixon, *The Leopard's Spots* (New York: Doubleday, Page, 1902), and *The Clansman* (1905; rpt., Lexington: University of Kentucky Press, 1970).

"Monumental Industrial Institute in Memory of 'The Old Black Mammy,' " pamphlet in Black Mammy Institute File, Hargrett Rare Book and Manuscript Collection, University of Georgia, Athens; Thurber, "Mammy Image," 87–108; Francis Pendleton Gaines, *A Study in the Development and Accuracy of a Tradition* (New York: Columbia University Press, 1925), 10–17; Jessie W. Pankhurst, "The Role of the Black Mammy in the Plantation Household," *Journal of Negro History* 23 (July 1938): 349–50; and Eugene D. Genovese, *Roll, Jordan, Roll: The World the Slaves Made* (New York: Vintage: 1974), 353. For examples of mammies used in advertising and on menus, see "African Americans," Box 4, and "Restaurants," Box 1, Warshaw Collection of Business Americana, Smithsonian Institution, National Museum of American History. Chapter 4 examines the mammy image in advertising and consumer items. For African American women's opposition to the UDC monument, see Mary Church Terrell, "The Black Mammy Monument," *The Star*, 10 February 1923, Terrell Papers, quoted in Hunter, "Household Workers," 252. For a white woman's opposition to the mammy movement, see L. H. Hammond, *Southern Women and Racial Adjustment* (Lynchburg, VA: J. F. Slater Fund Occasional Paper, no. 19, 1917).

For a rare glimpse of an African American woman's view of nursing white children, see A Negro Nurse, "More Slavery in the South," *Independent* 72 (25 January 1912): 196–200. African American historians also present African American views of domestic service. Despite her own replication of white romanticization of the mammy, Pankhurst emphasized that mammy was "an acceptable symbol to whites and an unacceptable one to Negroes" ("Role of the Black Mammy," 350). See also Carter G. Woodson, "The Negro Washerwoman, A Vanishing Figure," *Journal of Negro History* 15 (July 1930): 269–77, in which Woodson argues that "the Negroes of this country resent any such thing as the mention of the Plantation Black Mammy," and "What Is a Good Negro?" *Voice of the Negro* 1 (December 1904): 618–19.

27.   Howard Weeden, "Me and Mammy," *Confederate Veteran* 34 (November 1926): 415. See also the following works by Howard Weeden: *Shadows on the Wall* (New York: Doubleday and McClure, 1898); *Bandanna Ballads* (New York: Doubleday and McClure, 1899), which is "dedicated to the memory of all the faithful mammies who ever sung southern [white] babes to rest," and includes the poems "When Mammy Dies" and "Mother and Mammy," as well as many sentimentalized portraits of mammy figures; *Songs of the Old South* (New York: Doubleday, Page, 1901), which includes more portraits and three poems about mammies, "When Angels Call," "Hush," and "The Arabian Nights"; and *Old Voices* (New York: Doubleday, Page, 1904), which is dedicated "for the love of unforgotten times," and includes more portraits and the poems "A Toilet" and "The Angel of the Dark." On Weeden herself, see Mary Brabson Littleton, "Howard Weeden, Poetess and Artist," *Confederate Veteran* 14 (April 1906): 162–63 (this article includes a reproduction of one of Weeden's mammy paintings); and Frances C. Roberts and Sarah Huff Fisher, *Shadows on the Wall: The Life and Works of Howard Weeden* (Northport, AL; Colonial Press, 1962). Joel Chandler Harris, a great admirer of her work, wrote the introduction to *Ballads* and sent his daughters a copy at their school. See Harris, Atlanta, to Lillian and Mildred Harris, Washington, GA, 19 November 1898, Box 4, JCH-EU. See also Hugh T. Keenan, ed., *Dearest Chums and Partners: Joel Chandler Harris's Letters to His Children: A Domestic Biography* (Athens: University of Georgia Press, 1993), 239, 241. Thurber, "Mammy Image," 102–3. For other mammy poems, see Estelle T. Oltrogge, "My Old Black Mammy," *Confederate Veteran* 25 (January 1917): 45; and anonymous, "Mammy—and Memory," *Confederate Veteran* 28 (February 1920): 55.

28.   Captain James Dinkins, "My Old Black Mammy," *Confederate Veteran* 34 (January 1926): 21; and Reverend G. L. Tucker, "Faithful to the Old Mammy," *Confederate Veteran* 20 (December 1912): 582. Examples of the genre written by white women include Julia Porcher Wickham, "My Children's Mammy," *Confederate Veteran* 34 (November 1926): 414; anonymous, "In Memory of a Faithful Servant," *Confederate Veteran* 24 (October 1916), in which the author describes herself as a mother; and Virginia B. Sherrard, "Recollections of My Mammy," *Southern Workman* 30 (February 1901): 86–87. Thomas Nelson Page discusses the mammy figure in *The Old South: Essays Social and Political* (New York: Scribner, 1892), 156, 165–66.

For a general discussion of whites' images of older, African American wage workers as "befo' de war niggers" and as "white folks' niggers" and of the celebration of ex-slaves, see Chapter 2. Recent scholarship has found mammy to be a post–Civil War construction. See Deborah Gray White, *Ar'n't I a Woman: Female Slaves in the Plantation South* (New York: Norton, 1985), 46–61; Jane Turner Censer, *North Carolina Planters and*

Their Children, 1800–1860 (Baton Rouge: Louisiana State University Press, 1984); and Catherine Clinton, *The Plantation Mistress: Women's World in the Old South* (New York: Pantheon, 1982), 201–2.

Thurber argues that the peak period of mammy glorification was between 1906 and 1912 and that by the late 1920s there was little mention of the mammy. I have found, however, continued romanticization of the mammy in white southern autobiographical writing through the 1970s. See, for example, many of the white women's accounts recorded in the 1970s and 1980s in Tucker, *Telling Memories*. Adrienne Rich, in *Of Woman Born: Motherhood as Example and Institution* (New York: Bantam, 1976), 253, recalls her childhood in segregated Baltimore: "I had from birth not only a white, but a black mother. This relationship, so little explored, so unexpressed, still charges the relationships of Black and White women . . . we have been mothers and daughters to each other . . ." Here Rich echoes Smith's more detailed and Freudian analysis of some white children's two mothers in Smith, *Killers of the Dream*, 25–40, 114–58.

29. Mildred Rutherford, *Mannie Brown That School Girl* (Buffalo: Peter Paul, 1896); and Wickham, "My Children's Mammy," 413. On the education of southern girls, see Florence Elliot Cook, "Growing Up White, Genteel, and Female in a Changing South" (Ph.D. dissertation, University of California, Berkeley, 1992). On manners and the American middle class, see Halttunen, *Confidence Men and Painted Women*.

30. Felton, *Country Life*, 48. Perhaps the African American woman was upset because the white child was eating food that otherwise would have reached the inhabitants of the quarters.

31. Wickham, "My Children's Mammy," 413; Felton, *Country Life*, 38, 48. See also John Dollard, *Caste and Class in a Southern Town* (1937; rpt., New York: Doubleday Anchor, 1957), 106–9.

32. Wickham, "My Children's Mammy," 413, 415; anonymous, "In Memory of a Faithful Servant," 476; G. L. Tucker, "Faithful to the 'Old Mammy,' " 582; Dinkins, "My Old Black Mammy," 21–22; anonymous, "Burial of 'Aunt' Mary Marlow," *Confederate Veteran* 14 (March 1906).

33. William Faulkner, *Go Down, Moses* (1942; rpt., New York: Vintage International, 1990), frontispiece. For Faulkner and his relationship to Caroline Barr, see Joel Williamson, *William Faulkner and Southern History* (New York: Oxford University Press, 1993), 153–54, 163, 230, 262, 265, 270, 327, 344. Faulkner's famous fictional mammy Dilsey, modeled on Mammy Barr, appeared in his 1929 novel *The Sound and the Fury*.

34. Anonymous, "In Memory of a Faithful Servant," 476. Margaret Heard Dohme, "Alexander Hamilton Stephens," *Confederate Veteran* 40 (March 1932): 91–94. In this story a white woman goes to a family's ex-slave to learn about her white ancestors' connections to Stephens. Dinkins, "My Old Black Mammy," 20.

35. Arthur Raper, *The Tragedy of Lynching* (Chapel Hill: University of North Carolina Press, 1933), 262; Jacquelyn Dowd Hall et al., *Like a Family: The Making of a Southern Cotton Mill World* (New York: Norton, 1989), 157. On white women hiring African American women to perform domestic work on small farms, see the unique portrait of this world provided by Charles A. Le Guin, ed., *A Home-Concealed Woman: The*

Diaries of Magnolia Wynn Le Guin, 1901–1913 (Athens: University of Georgia Press, 1990).

36. Sara Haardt, *The Making of a Lady* (New York: Doubleday, Doran, 1931). The story also circulated widely in Bucklin Moon, ed., *Primer For White Folks* (Garden City, NY: Doubleday, Doran, 1945), 184–93, quotes, 187, 191. Haardt later married journalist and critic H. L. Mencken. The twinning of white and black girls in this fictional story matches the twinning Lillian Smith described between herself and the "black" adopted child.

37. Zora Neale Hurston, *Their Eyes Were Watching God* (1937; rpt., New York: Harper Perennial, 1991), 37.

38. Percy, *Lanterns on the Levee*, 299. On whites seeing African American women in simplified, dualistic terms, see White, "Jezebel and Mammy: The Mythology of Female Slavery," in *Ar'n't I a Woman*, 27–61; and Morton, *Disfigured Images*.

39. Thomas Dixon, *The Clansman: An Historical Romance of the Ku Klux Klan* (1905; rpt., Lexington: University Press of Kentucky, 1970); and W. J. Cash, *The Mind of the South* (1941; rpt., New York: Vintage Books, 1991), 84–87. See also Dixon's notes for the title page of his novel *The One Woman: A Story of Modern Utopia*; and "The Dixon Lecture Program," a listing of his current lectures including "The New Woman," a speech that he summarizes "The woman who rules the future will be the high priestess of humanity in the religion of a home life . . . ," in Box 1, Thomas Dixon Collection, Robert W. Woodruff Library, Emory University, Atlanta. For accounts written about the mammy from the perspective of white mothers, see Sally B. Hamner, "Mammy Susan's Story," *Confederate Veteran* 1 (September 1893): 270–71; and Wickham, "My Children's Mammy." Accounts written from the perspective of white children were much more common. See Weeden, "Mammy and Me"; Dinkins, "My Old Black Mammy"; Smith, *Killers of the Dream*; and Felton, *Country Life*. For gender and the Lost Cause, see Chapter 2. On the southern lady and the problem of image versus reality, see Scott, *Southern Lady*. My arguments here draw upon the theoretical insights of Marjorie Garber, *Vested Interests: Cross-Dressing and Cultural Anxiety* (New York: Harper Perennial, 1993); Eve Kosofsky Sedgwick, *Between Men: English Literature and Male Homosocial Desire* (New York: Columbia University Press, 1985); and Mary Poovey, *Uneven Developments: The Ideological Work of Gender in Mid-Victorian England* (Chicago: University of Chicago Press, 1988).

40. Faust, "Altars," and "The Garb of Gender"; Hale, " 'Some Women Have Never Been Reconstructed' "; and Whites, *Civil War as a Crisis in Gender*.

41. Mildred Rutherford's speech before the 1912 national convention of the UDC in Washington, D.C., is published in her *Four Addresses* (Birmingham: Mildred Rutherford Historical Circle, 1916), 14. See also Hale, " 'Some Women Have Never Been Reconstructed.' "

42. MLR-UGA; Lucy Cobb Institute Papers, Hargrett Rare Book and Manuscript Collection, University of Georgia, Athens; and Phyllis Barrow, "The Lucy Cobb Institute" (Ph.D. dissertation, University of Georgia, 1951). On Margaret Mitchell's longtime servant Bessie Berry, see Margaret Mitchell, Atlanta, 18 September 1936, to Mrs. Her-

schel Brickell, Ridgefield, CT, and Margaret Mitchell, Atlanta, 14 October 1940, to Mrs. Alfred Lunt, New York, in Richard Harwell, ed., *Margaret Mitchell's Gone With the Wind Letters, 1936–1949* (New York: Macmillan, 1976), 62–63, 315–17; and Margaret Mitchell, Atlanta, 10 December 1937, to Katharine Brown, New York, Box 75, in Margaret Mitchell Collection, Hargrett Rare Book and Manuscript Collection, University of Georgia (hereafter MM-UGA). See also Darden Asbury Pyron, *Southern Daughter: The Life of Margaret Mitchell* (New York: Harper Perennial, 1992), 285, 289, 292, 400, 426, 444, 451, 518, 536–38, 599. Pyron quotes a letter Berry wrote to Medora Perkerson, 6 July 1936: "I was with Miss Mitchell at the time this wonderful book started" (289). For more on Mitchell, see Chapter 6.

43. Rutherford, *Four Addresses*, 4; "With the Influence She Possesses, Why Should a Woman Want the Vote?" *Athens Daily Herald*, 7 August 1915; and *Athens Daily Herald*, 23 June 1914. For other articles and speeches against suffrage and praising slavery, see *Four Addresses; The Civilization of the Old South: What Made It; What Destroyed It; What Has Replaced It* (Athens, GA: the author, 1916); *Georgia: The Thirteenth Colony* (Athens, GA: McGregor, 1926); *Facts and Figures vs. Myths and Misrepresentations: Henry Wirz and the Andersonville Prison* (Athens: the author, 1921); "What Would Our Grandmothers Do If Faced With the Problems of the Present Days?" *Athens Banner*, 26 July 1913; and *Athens Daily Herald*, 1 April 1915. For Rutherford's use of Lost Cause narratives to argue for white women's post–Civil War superiority to white men, see Chapter 1. For a more detailed examination of Rutherford's gendered white supremacy, see Hale, " 'Some Women Have Never Been Reconstructed.' "

On the anti-suffrage movement, see Elna Green, "The Ideology of Southern (White) Antisuffragism: White Supremacy vs. White Monopoly" (unpublished paper in author's possession); Jane Jerome Camhi, *Women Against Women: American Anti-Suffragism, 1880–1920* (New York: Carlsen, 1994); and Thomas J. Jablonsky, *The Home, Heaven, and Mother Party: Female Anti-Suffragists in the United States, 1868–1920* (New York: Carlsen, 1994).

44. Kate Gordon to Laura Clay, 5 December, 1907, Clay papers, quoted in Wheeler, *New Women*, 100. See especially her chapter "Southern Suffragists and 'the Negro Problem,' " 100–32. Wheeler stresses the strategic reasons for southern suffragists' capitulation to racism and asserts that "the patronizing but protective attitude toward blacks characteristic of their class was, in fact, enlightened compared to the attitudes of most white Southerners in this period" (131). For the purpose of my argument, however, the distinction between strategic and "real" racism is unimportant. White women across the spectrum on the issue of women's rights were racist in that they used representations of African Americans to empower themselves. This symbolic oppression of African Americans (not to mention the much more direct oppression of paying their African American domestic workers impossibly low wages) was not as bad, for example, as lynching southern blacks, although white women often participated in this practice too. White women in general, however, were important creators of a culture in which the most violent forms of oppression could and did occur. For a discussion of white women and lynching, see Chapter 5.

45. Rebecca Felton, "Southern Chivalry: The Wife's Farm—The Husband's Pledge!," RLF-UGA. I am indebted here to LeeAnn Whites, "Rebecca Latimer Felton and the Wife's Farm."

46. Rebecca Latimer Felton, "Shooting Wives and Sweethearts," 21 June 1901, and "How Much Responsible," 4 January 1904, both published in the column "The Country Home: Women on the Farm," *Atlanta Semi-Weekly Journal*; "Crime in Georgia and the Courts," *Atlanta Tri-Weekly Journal*, 18 November 1924; and "The Subjection of Women and the Enfranchisement of Women," quotes, 13, 14, 14 May 1915, all in RLF-UGA. Felton, Cartersville, GA, to the *Atlanta Constitution*, 19 December 1898; and "The Inheritance of the Anglo-Saxon," no date given but internal evidence suggests early 1900s, 20, both in RLF-UGA. See also Diane Miller Sommerville, "The Rape Myth in the Old South Reconsidered," *Journal of Southern History* 61 (August 1995).

47. "Southern Women in Wartimes," RLF-UGA.

48. Felton, "Subjection of Women," 14; Rutherford, *Four Addresses*, 14; and Kearney, *Slaveholder's Daughter*, 112.

49. On Lucy M. Stanton, see the Lucy M. Stanton Collection, Hargrett Rare Book and Manuscript Collection, University of Georgia (hereafter LMS-UGA); the Lucy M. Stanton Collection, Robert W. Woodruff Library, Emory University, especially their extensive collection of Stanton paintings; W. Stanton Forbes, *Lucy M. Stanton, Artist* (Atlanta: Special Collections Department, Robert W. Woodruff Library, Emory University, 1975); and Grace Elizabeth Hale, " 'In Terms of Paint': Lucy Stanton's Representations of the South, 1890–1931," *Georgia Historical Quarterly* 77 (Fall 1993): 577–92, and " 'Some Women Have Never Been Reconstructed.' " On Stanton's Mammy Chloe, see Forbes, *Stanton*, 1–19; and oral history transcripts, LMS-UGA. Chloe's last name was Henderson, but this fact is not mentioned in the Stanton materials. After Stanton's mother died in 1888, the Stanton home was dismantled and Stanton and her sister were sent to boarding school. Chloe Henderson went to work for Joel Chandler Harris across the street. In his letters to his children, where she is frequently discussed, she is identified as Chloe Henderson. See Keenan, *Joel Chandler Harris's Letters*, 39, 47, 64–65, 84, 90, 92, 107, 113, 118, 120, 128, 129 (photograph), 140, 151–52, 172, 189, 197, 200, 208, 216, 219, 221, 225–27, 261, 270. Glasgow, *Woman Within*, 29–35, quotes, 33, 36. Smith, *Killers of the Dream*, 28–29, quotes.

50. Mitchell, *Gone With the Wind*, 5, 24, 25. My arguments here are based on Mitchell's novel, not on the equally popular David Selznick film that Mitchell refused repeatedly to act as a consultant to. Some examples of the many letters in which she refuses to consult for or help in any way with the film are Margaret Mitchell, Atlanta, 6 October 1936, 19 October 1936, 17 November 1936, 18 November 1936, to Katharine Brown, story editor, Selznick International Pictures Inc., New York, Box 75, MM-UGA. Mitchell discusses the character of Mammy in *Gone With the Wind* in several letters: Margaret Mitchell, Atlanta, 4 March 1937, to Jason H. Murphy, Ellicottville, NY; and 8 April 1937, to Herschel Brickell, New York, in Harwell, *Letters*, 126–27, 137–39. For more about Mitchell and the differences between Mitchell's novel and the film, see Chapter 6 and the Epilogue. Little has been written about the character of Mammy. None of the articles in two recent collections on the book and novel focus on her. See Darden Asbury

Pyron, *Recasting: Gone With the Wind in American Culture* (Miami: University Presses of Florida, 1983); and Richard Harwell, ed., *Gone With the Wind as Book and Film* (Columbia: University of South Carolina Press, 1983).

51. Mitchell, *Gone With the Wind*, 408–9.

52. Rutherford, *Four Addresses*, 4. These ideas were not confined to the South; they pervaded the pages of northern-based women's magazines like *Good Housekeeping* in this period as well. The racial dimensions of "influence," however, were uniquely southern.

53. Jacquelyn Dowd Hall, " 'The Mind That Burns in Each Body': Women, Rape, and Racial Violence," in Ann Snitow, Christine Stansell, and Sharon Thompson, eds., *Powers of Desire: The Politics of Sexuality* (New York: Monthly Review Press, 1983), 328–49, especially 337. For another perspective of the gendering of racial power and the racializing of gender identities, see Nancy MacLean, *Behind the Mask of Chivalry: The Making of the Second Ku Klux Klan* (New York: Oxford University Press, 1994).

54. "Monumental Industrial Institute in Memory of 'The Old Black Mammy,' " pamphlet in Black Mammy Institute File, Hargrett Rare Book and Manuscript Library, University of Georgia, Athens; June O. Patton, "Moonlight and Magnolias in Southern Education: The Black Mammy Memorial Institute," *Journal of Negro History* 65 (Spring 1980): 149–55; and Hunter, "Household Workers," 188–230. See also "Findings," Women Members of the Texas State Inter-racial Committee, Dallas, TX, 21 March 1922, NAACP Papers, Part 7B, microfilm reel 31.

55. Elisabeth Freeman, report on Waco lynching, NAACP Papers, Part 7A, Library of Congress, Group 1, Box C-370 and microfilm reel 19. Smith, "Three Ghost Stories," in *Killers of the Dream*, 116, 114–37.

56. On masculinity in the North, see E. Anthony Rotundo, *American Manhood: Transformation in Masculinity from the Revolution* (New York: Basic Books, 1993); "Learning About Manhood: Gender Ideals and the Middle Class Family in Nineteenth Century America," in J. A. Mangan and James Walvin, eds., *Manliness and Morality: Middle Class Masculinity in Britain and America, 1800–1940* (New York: St. Martin's Press, 1987), 35–51; and "Body and Soul: Changing Ideals of American Middle-Class Manhood, 1770–1920," *Journal of Social History* 16 (1983): 23–38. On southern white masculinity, see Ted Ownby, *Subduing Satan: Religion, Recreation, and Manhood in the Rural South, 1865–1920* (Chapel Hill: University of North Carolina Press, 1990). On the southern crisis of masculinity from the Civil War to the late nineteenth century, see Faust, "Altars of Sacrifice"; Suzanne Lebsock, "On Feminism, Slavery, and the Experience of Defeat," in *The Free Women of Petersburg: Status and Culture in a Southern Town, 1784–1860* (New York: Norton, 1984), 237–49; LeeAnn Whites, "The Civil War as a Crisis in Gender," in Catherine Clinton and Nina Silber, eds., *Divided Houses: Gender and the Civil War* (New York: Oxford University Press, 1992), 3–21; Whites, *Civil War as a Crisis in Gender*; and Stephanie McCurry, *Masters of Small Worlds: Yeoman Households, Gender Relations, and the Political Culture of the Antebellum South Carolina Low Country* (New York: Oxford University Press, 1995). On the origins of the image of "black beast rapist," see Diane Miller Sommerville, "The Rape Myth Reconsidered: The Intersection of Race, Gender, and Class Through the Reconstruction South" (Ph.D. disserta-

tion, Rutgers University, 1995). On the image's role within the culture of segregation, see Chapter 5.

57.   Stanton Diary, 1910, LMS-UGA.

58.   The best source on Frances Newman is Anne Goodwyn Jones, *Tomorrow Is Another Day*, 271–312. The quotes are from Frances Newman to Susan Long, May 1927; and Frances Newman to Hudson Strode, 2 September 1927, in *Frances Newman's Letters* (New York: Horace Liveright, 1929), 254, 273; and Winifred Rothermel, "Aristocratic Writer, Daughter of the South, Taken By Death in Gotham," *Birmingham News–Age-Herald*, 28 October 1928, 4, quoted in Jones, *Tomorrow Is Another Day*, 279.

59.   On the white community's attitude toward Stanton, see Francis Forbes Heyn, interview with the author, 2 November 1990, New Orleans; Paul Hodgeson, interview with the author, 25 October 1990, Athens, GA; and Susan Barrow Tate, interview with the author, 9 October 1990, Athens, GA; all in the author's possession. See also Hale, " 'Some Women Have Never Been Reconstructed.' " Many of Stanton's paintings of African Americans are in the Stanton Collection at Emory University. Color reproductions are available in Hale, " 'In Terms of Paint.' " On Newman, see Jones, *Tomorrow Is Another Day*, 298–310; Frances Newman, *The Hard Boiled Virgin* (New York: Boni and Liveright, 1926), and *Dead Lovers*.

60.   See Box 3, KDL-UNC, for Lumpkin's thesis and dissertation. See the Laurel Falls Camp Collection, LS-UGA; and the Paula Smith Collection, Hargrett Rare Book and Manuscript Collection, University of Georgia, Athens, for Smith's life at camp and with Paula. Given the complexity and contradictions of white and black women's racial and gender identities in general and their relationships within white homes in particular, it is not surprising that many of the first white critics of segregation were white women like Lillian Smith and Katharine Lumpkin and that some of the first civil rights activists were African American women like Rosa Parks who had worked as domestic servants. For more on Smith and Lumpkin and their pioneering white attacks on segregation, see Chapter 6.

61.   Smith, *Killers of the Dream*, 29.

62.   Glasgow, *Woman Within*, 20–31, quotes, 20, 30.

63.   Estelle T. Oltrogge, "My Old Black Mammy," *Confederate Veteran* 25 (January 1917): 45. This is the last stanza of the poem.

64.   James Weldon Johnson, *All Along This Way: The Autobiography of James Weldon Johnson* (1933; rpt., New York: Penguin Books, 1990), 9–10.

CHAPTER FOUR: *Bounding Consumption*

1.   Edgar Gardner Murphy, *The Basis of Ascendancy* (New York: Longmans, 1909), 122, 138.

2.   Ralph Ellison, "Change the Joke and Slip the Yoke," *Partisan Review* (Spring 1958), reprinted in *Shadow and Act* (1964; rpt., New York: Vintage International, 1995), 54–55.

3. William Faulkner, *Go Down, Moses* (1942; rpt., New York: Vintage International, 1990), 324–25, 184, 326, 184.

4. Ibid., frontispiece, 185. Joel Williamson, *William Faulkner and Southern History* (New York: Oxford University Press, 1993), 264–66, 414–18; Eric J. Sundquist, *Faulkner: The House Divided* (Baltimore: Johns Hopkins University Press, 1983), 131–59. On the hunt, see Ted Ownby, *Subduing Satan: Religion, Recreation, and Manhood in the Rural South, 1865–1920* (Chapel Hill: University of North Carolina Press, 1990), 21–37; and Stuart A. Marks, *Southern Hunting in Black and White: Nature, History, and Ritual in a Carolina Community* (Princeton: Princeton University Press, 1991).

5. Faulkner, *Go Down, Moses*, 325, 185; Edward L. Ayers, *The Promise of the New South: Life After Reconstruction* (New York: Oxford University Press, 1992), 20, 55; William Faulkner, *The Sound and the Fury* (1929; rpt., New York: Modern Library, 1956), 10. Faulkner also explores the social and cultural transformation of southern life resulting from the move to town in *The Hamlet* (1940; rpt., New York: Vintage Books, 1956). Of course, Faulkner also peopled his Old South with "New Men," upwardly mobile planters like Thomas Sutpen, who live among and yet differ from the more established and more traditional planters.

6. Ayers, *Promise of the New South*, 9, 3–20, 25; Francis A. Doughty, "Life in the Cotton Belt," *Lippincott's* 59 (May 1897): 687. For other evidence of the decaying rural antebellum mansion as the most haunting symbol in the first half of the twentieth century of the changing South, see Faulkner's frequent use of these once-grand homes as setting and sometimes almost as characters in *Sanctuary* (1931; rpt., New York: Vintage International, 1993), *Light in August* (1932; rpt., New York: Modern Library, 1968), and *The Hamlet*. In the late 1930s and 1940s, many of the Farm Security Administration (FSA) photographers sent into the Deep South took pictures of these structures, often indicating in their captions that they were now inhabited by African American tenant families. See, for example, Jack Delano, "The old Branch home, on the Athens road, now occupied by a Negro family," LC-USF34-46193-D, Greensboro, GA, October 1941; Arthur Rothstein, "The old home of the Pettways which is now occupied by Negroes," LC-USF34-25380-D, and "John Miller and his family who are living in the old Pettway mansion," LC-USF34-25381-D, Gee's Bend, AL, April 1937; Russell Lee, "Entrance to the old Trepanier plantation house. This house is now occupied by Negroes," LC-USF34-31351-D, Norco, LA, September 1938; Walker Evans, "An abandoned plantation house," LC-USF342-8233-A, "Antebellum plantation house," LC-USF342-8052-A and LC-USF342-8050-A, Vicksburg, MS, March 1936, and "An abandoned plantation house," LC-USF33-9049-M2, Monticello, GA, March 1936; Dorothea Lange, "An antebellum plantation house," LC-USF34-17937-E, Green County, GA, July 1937; Marion Post Wolcott, "An abandoned plantation house," LC-USF34-51286-D, Green County, GA, May 1939; Jack Delano, "The old plantation house of Elisha Jarrell which now belongs to the FSA," LC-USF341-44252-A, White Plains, GA, May 1941, and "A deserted old plantation house that belonged to Rayburn Sanders, LC-USF34-44201-D, Penfield, GA, May 1941; Marion Post Wolcott, "The old Butler place . . . ," LC-USF34-51364-D, Social Circle, GA, May 1939, and "An old home built about 1850, called 'Silver Place,' " LC-USF34-51802-D, Alabama, March 1939. Prints of all FSA photographs are located in

the Prints and Photographs Division, Library of Congress. Further references will cite only LC numbers.

7.   Harry Hammond, *Report of the Industrial Commission on Agriculture and Agricultural Labor*, vol. 10 (Washington, D.C.: Government Printing Office, 1901), 820.

8.   C. Vann Woodward, *The Strange Career of Jim Crow* (1955; rpt., rev. ed., New York: Oxford University Press, 1974), 67–147, and *Origins of the New South, 1877–1913* (Baton Rouge: Louisiana State University Press, 1951), 353–56. For the argument in favor of continuity and against the 1890s as the key decade in the construction of a new racial order, see Howard N. Rabinowitz, *Race Relations in the Urban South, 1865–1890* (Urbana: University of Illinois Press, 1980), and "More Than the Woodward Thesis: Assessing *The Strange Career of Jim Crow*," *Journal of American History* 75 (December 1988): 842–56. The weight of recent scholarship supports Woodward's version of segregation's origins and thus the 1880s as a period of relative racial fluidity. See Ayers, *Promise of the New South*; Joel Williamson, *The Crucible of Race: Black-White Relations in the American South Since Emancipation* (New York: Oxford University Press, 1984); Dewey W. Grantham, Jr., *Southern Progressivism: The Reconciliation of Progress and Tradition* (Knoxville: University of Tennessee Press, 1983), especially 126–27; Joseph H. Cartwright, *The Triumph of Jim Crow: Tennessee Race Relations in the 1880s* (Knoxville: University of Tennessee Press, 1976); and Glenda E. Gilmore, *Gender and Jim Crow: Women and the Politics of White Supremacy in North Carolina* (Chapel Hill: University of North Carolina Press, 1996). On race relations within the national context, see the classic George M. Fredrickson, *The Black Image in the White Mind: The Debate on Afro-American Character and Destiny, 1817–1914* (1971; rpt., Hanover, NH: Wesleyan University Press, 1987).

9.   On southern train stations, see the trade literature, especially *Railroad Magazine*, published from the 1890s onward, and photographs and drawings of southern stations in the Division of Transportation, National Museum of American History, Smithsonian Institution (hereafter, RR-NMAH). See also Jeffrey Richards and John M. MacKenzie, *The Railway Station: A Social History* (Oxford: Clarendon Press, 1986). Taking an international perspective, these authors argue that though stations were "extraordinary agent[s] of social mixing," they were also "designed to avoid these encounters across class and racial boundaries as much as possible" (137). I am indebted to the excellent Ayers, *Promise of the New South*, 3–33, 132–59, throughout my discussion of southern railroads.

10.   Katharine DuPre Lumpkin, *The Making of a Southerner* (1947; rpt., Athens: University of Georgia Press, 1991), 133, 215. See also Box 4 and Box 7, Katharine DuPre Lumpkin Collection, Southern Historical Society, University of North Carolina, Chapel Hill (KDL-UNC), for biographical materials on Lumpkin, and her *The South in Progress* (New York: International Publishers, 1940), 99–102. See the photographs of Jim Crow cars; the blue Pullman blanket (worn passenger blankets were dyed blue for use by African American porters); and the fiction about railroad travel in *Railroad Magazine* and *Saturday Evening Post*, which often included descriptions of segregation, all in RR-NMAH.

11.   On the growing African American middle class, see E. Franklin Frazier, *Black*

Bourgeoisie: Rise of a New Middle Class (New York: Free Press, 1957); and Paul K. Edwards, *The Southern Urban Negro as a Consumer* (1932; rpt., New York: Negro Universities Press, 1969), 1–45. On the growth of railroads in the South, see John F. Stover, *The Railroads of the South, 1865–1900* (Chapel Hill: University of North Carolina Press, 1955); and Maury Klein, *History of the Louisville and Nashville Railroad* (New York: Macmillan, 1972).

12.   Ida B. Wells, *Crusade for Justice: The Autobiography of Ida B. Wells* (Chicago: University of Chicago Press, 1970), 18–20.

13.   C. Vann Woodward, *Origins of the New South*, 216, and *Strange Career*, 23–24, 27–28, 38–40, 97, 140, 169; and Ayers, *Promise of the New South*, 16–20, 136–46. Other sources on railroad and streetcar struggles include August Meir and Elliot Rudwick, "The Boycott Movement against Jim Crow Streetcars in the South, 1900–1906," in August Meir and Elliot Rudwick, eds., *Along the Color Line: Explorations in the Black Experience* (Urbana: University of Illinois Press, 1977), 267–89; Roger A. Fischer, "A Pioneer Protest: The New Orleans Street-Car Controversy of 1867," *Journal of Negro History* 53 (July 1968): 219–33; Neil McMillen, *Dark Journey: Black Mississippians in the Age of Jim Crow* (Urbana: University of Illinois Press, 1989), 293–95; Lester C. Lamon, *Black Tennesseans, 1900–1930* (Knoxville: University of Tennessee Press, 1977), 20–36; John Dittmer, *Black Georgia in the Progressive Era, 1900–1920* (Urbana: University of Illinois Press, 1977), 16–19; George C. Wright, *Life Behind a Veil: Blacks in Louisville, Kentucky, 1865–1930* (Baton Rouge: Louisiana State University Press, 1985), 52–55, 191–92, 248–49. On the whites' denial of black mobility, see William Cohen, *At Freedom's Edge: Black Mobility and the Southern Quest for Racial Control, 1861–1915* (Baton Rouge: Louisiana State University Press, 1987).

14.   Wells, *Crusade for Justice*, 19–20, 20, n. 5.

15.   Ayers, *Promise of the New South*, 136–46. On the importance of the visual in middle-class identity of the late nineteenth century, see Karen Halttunen, *Confidence Men and Painted Women: A Study of Middle Class Culture in Victorian America, 1830–1870* (New Haven: Yale University Press, 1982); T. J. Jackson Lears, *No Place of Grace: Antimodernism and the Transformation of American Culture, 1880–1920* (New York: Pantheon, 1981), 1–47; and Henry Adams, *Mont-Saint-Michel and Chartres* (1904; rpt., New York: Anchor Books, 1959).

16.   *Savannah Tribune*, 7 May 1887, in Horace Calvin Wingo, "Race Relations in Georgia, 1872–1908" (Ph.D. dissertation, University of Georgia, 1969), 130; Mary Church Terrell, *A Colored Woman in a White World* (1940; rpt., New York: Arno Press, 1980), 296–98; Stephen J. Riegel, "The Persistent Career of Jim Crow: Lower Federal Courts and the 'Separate but Equal' Doctrine, 1865–1896," *American Journal of Legal History* 28 (January 1984): 25–27; Ayers, *Promise of the New South*, 141–42; Rabinowitz, *Race Relations*, 334–35.

17.   Stereotypes of poorly dressed and poorly spoken African Americans were key figures in the development of an increasingly national and commercial popular culture. On the national context of whites' imagination of the black other, see Ellison, "Change the Joke"; Eric Lott, *Love and Theft: Blackface Minstrelsy and the American Working Class* (New York: Oxford University Press, 1993); Harriet Beecher Stowe, *Uncle Tom's*

Cabin (Boston, 1952); David Roediger, *The Wages of Whiteness: Race and the Making of the American Working Class* (New York: Verso, 1991); Alexander Saxton, *The Rise and Fall of the White Republic: Class Politics and Mass Culture in Nineteenth-Century America* (New York: Verso, 1990); Theodore W. Allen, *The Invention of the White Race: Racial Oppression and Social Control* (New York: Verso, 1994); David Nasaw, *Going Out: The Rise and Fall of Public Amusements* (New York: Basic Books, 1993); Robert W. Rydell, *All the World's a Fair: Visions of Empire at America's International Expositions, 1876–1916* (Chicago: University of Chicago Press, 1984), and *World of Fairs: The Century of Progress Expositions* (Chicago: University of Chicago Press, 1993); and Michael Rogin, " 'The Sword Became a Flashing Vision': D. W. Griffith's *Birth of a Nation*," in *Ronald Reagan, the Movie and Other Episodes in Political Demonology* (Berkeley: University of California Press, 1987), 190–235. On the more specifically southern context, see Chapter 2.

Terrell, *Colored Woman*, 296–98; and Lumpkin, *Making of a Southerner*, 151–73.

18.   *Chattanooga Times* quoted in *Nashville American*, 19 March 1889, quoted in Ayers, *Promise of the New South*, 139. On violence in southern race relations in general and in the case of African American men and white women in particular, see Chapter 5. On the centrality of sexuality to southern racial conflict, see Williamson, *Crucible*, 140–223; and Françoise Lionnet, *Autobiographical Voices: Race, Gender, Self-Portraiture* (Ithaca, NY: Cornell University Press, 1991), 1–29.

19.   W. E. B. DuBois, *Dusk of Dawn: An Essay Toward an Autobiography of the Race Concept* (1941; rpt. in DuBois, *Writings*, New York: Library of America, 1986), 666. John Andrew Rice, *I Came Out of the Eighteenth Century* (New York: Harper, 1942), 41–42; Lumpkin, *Making of a Southerner*, 133; Ayers, *Promise of the New South*, 145, 136–46; John T. Cell, *The Highest Stage of White Supremacy: The Origins of Segregation in South Africa and the American South* (New York: Cambridge University Press, 1982). Cell argues persuasively for the modernity of segregation, but his analysis breaks down in his functionalist assumption that a "power elite" created segregation solely for its own capitalist advancement. Railroad and streetcar owners protested segregation laws as too expensive for their capitalist advancement. See Ayers, *Promise of the New South*, 491, n. 35. I rely on Ayers heavily here, but I focus much more specifically on whites' sense of their own threatened racial identities.

I have not used the capitalized phrase "New South" unless referring to the program put forward by southern boosters like Henry Grady.

20.   Flannery O'Connor, "The Artificial Nigger," in *A Good Man Is Hard to Find* (1955; rpt., New York: Harcourt Brace, 1983), 102–29, quotes, 109, 109–10, 110, 111, 112.

21.   John Vachon, "A Railroad Station," LC-USF33-1172-M4, Manchester, GA, May 1938. Other photographs that provide evidence of segregation in railroad and bus travel include Jack Delano, "At the bus station," LC-USF33-20522-M2, and "A street scene near the bus station," LC-USF33-20522-M5, Durham, NC, May 1940; and Esther Bubley, "People waiting for a bus at the Greyhound bus terminal," LC-USW3-37973-E, LC-USW3-37986-E, LC-USW3-38020-E, and LC-USW3-37975-M, Memphis, September 1943. For more on the segregation of streetcars and buses, see "A Negro Car Line," *Horseless Age* 16 (20 September 1905): 347; and the trade journal *Bus Transportation* (1922–1949), in the Bus and Automobile Section, Segregation File, RR-NMAH. The

FSA photograph collections provide the best evidence of the impact of consumer culture within the region in the 1930s. Photographic evidence is central to my argument because the culture of segregation creates racialized spaces, making new racial signifiers whose power is visible and a new geography of racial difference.

For more on speech and dialect patterns as markers of racial identity, see Sterling A. Brown, "On Dialect Usage," in Charles T. Davis and Henry Louis Gates, Jr., eds., *The Slave's Narrative* (New York: Oxford University Press, 1985), 37–39.

22.   W. E. B. Du Bois, *Darkwater: Voices From Within the Veil* (1921; rpt., Millwood, NY: Kraus-Thompson, 1975), 228–30. For other early twentieth-century descriptions of segregated railroad and streetcar travel, see the series T. Montgomery Gregory, "The 'Jim Crow' Car," *The Crisis* 11 (1915–1916): 87–89, 137–38, 195–98; Ray Stannard Baker, *Following the Color Line: American Negro Citizenship in the Progressive Era* (1908; rpt., New York: Harper and Row, 1964), 30–34; Bertram Wilbur Doyle, *The Etiquette of Race Relations in the South: A Study in Social Control* (1937; rpt., New York: Schocken, 1971), 147–50; and Lumpkin, *Making of a Southerner*, 133–39. For descriptions of segregated trains and streetcars in the 1930s, see George S. Schuyler, "Traveling Jim Crow," *American Mercury* (August 1930): 423–32; Allison B. Davis, Burleigh B. Gardner, and Mary R. Gardner, *Deep South: A Social Anthropology of Caste and Class* (1941; rpt., Chicago: University of Chicago Press, 1969), 261; Charles S. Johnson, *Patterns of Negro Segregation* (New York: Harper, 1943), 44–51; and Gunnar Myrdal, *An American Dilemma: The Negro Problem and Modern Democracy* (1944; rpt., New York: Harper and Row, 1962), 576, 581, 588, 628, 634–35.

23.   Du Bois, *Darkwater*, 228, 229.

24.   Ibid., 229, 230.

25.   Ibid., 230. On Du Bois's attempt to gain from Booker T. Washington the funds and support to sue the Southern Railway, see David Levering Lewis, *W.E.B. Du Bois: Biography of a Race, 1868–1919* (New York: Henry Holt, 1993), 243–44.

26.   Baker, *Following the Color Line*, 30, 31.

27.   Lumpkin, *Making of a Southerner*, 133, 215; Doyle, *Etiquette of Race Relations*, 233, n. 66.

28.   Marion Post Wolcott, "Passengers leaving the railroad station," LC-USF34-54336-E and LC-USF34-54335-E, northwestern Florida, October 1940. See also the photographs cited in note 21. On New Deal documentary photography, see Pete Daniel, Merry Foresta, Maren Strange, and Sally Stein, eds., *Official Images: New Deal Photography* (Washington, D.C.: Smithsonian Institution, 1987); Nicholas Natanson, *The Black Image in the New Deal: The Politics of FSA Photography* (Knoxville: University of Tennessee Press, 1992); and William Stott, *Documentary Expression and Thirties America* (New York: Oxford University Press, 1973). Historians must be sensitive to the ways in which photographs, despite their seeming transparency, are like all historical documents constructed. Photographic theory and the methods of the new historicism in cultural criticism are helpful here. See especially Walter Benjamin, "The Work of Art in the Age of Mechanical Reproduction," in James Curran et al., eds., *Mass Communication and Society* (Beverly Hills: Sage, 1979, 384–408); Alan Trachtenberg, *Reading American Photographs: Images as History, Matthew Brady to Walker Evans* (New York: Hill and Wang,

1989); Miles Orvell, *The Real Thing: Imitation and Authenticity in American Culture, 1880–1940* (Chapel Hill: University of North Carolina Press, 1989); Susan Sontag, *On Photography* (New York: Farrar, Straus and Giroux, 1973); Roland Barthes, *Camera Lucida: Reflections on Photography* (1980; rpt., New York: Hill and Wang, 1993); and Neil Harris, "Iconography and Intellectual History: The Halftone Effect," in *Cultural Excursions: Marketing Appetites and Cultural Tastes in Modern America* (Chicago: University of Chicago Press, 1990), 304–17.

29.   Robin D. G. Kelley, *Race Rebels: Culture, Politics, and the Black Working Class* (New York: Free Press, 1994), 55–75; and Johnson, *Negro Segregation*, 44–51.

30.   Doyle, *Etiquette of Race Relations*, 149–50; O'Connor, "The Artificial Nigger."

31.   Lillian Smith, *Killers of the Dream* (1948; rpt., New York: Norton, 1978), 95–96.

32.   Lumpkin, *Making of a Southerner*, 215. On the racial epiphanies Lumpkin experienced in her work in the first stages of the YWCA and YMCA interracial student movement in the 1920s, see the 1923 and 1924 letters from Lumpkin to other officers and staff of the YMCA and YWCA interracial student movement, especially Katharine D. Lumpkin, Atlanta, 12 March 1923, to Leslie [no last name given], a letter marked "Confidential–Very," all in Box 1, KDL-UNC. See also Chapter 6.

33.   Doyle, *Etiquette of Race Relations*. According to C. Vann Woodward in the introduction to Rabinowitz, *Race Relations*, ix–xi, in 1890, 90 percent of all African Americans lived in the South, and while only 15 percent of southern African Americans lived in cities, they made up one-third of the total southern urban population. Ayers, *Promise of the New South*, 55, 467, stresses that between 1890 and 1910, five million southerners moved to town, and by 1910, a majority of southerners lived in towns and villages. For the national context in this period and the manner in which the new spaces of consumption "created a unique fusion of economic and cultural values" and became "the staging ground for the making and confirming of new relations between goods and people," see Alan Trachtenberg, *The Incorporation of America: Culture and Society in the Gilded Age* (New York: Hill and Wang, 1982).

34.   Sources on consumer culture include Jackson Lears, *Fables of Abundance: A Cultural History of Advertising in America* (New York: Basic Books, 1994); Jackson Lears and Richard Wrightman Fox, *The Culture of Consumption* (New York: Pantheon, 1983); Jackson Lears, "Beyond Veblen: Rethinking Consumer Culture in America," in Simon J. Bonner, ed., *Consuming Visions: Accumulation and Display of Goods in America* (Chicago: University of Chicago Press, 1990), 73–97; Lizabeth Cohen, *Making a New Deal: Industrial Workers in Chicago, 1919–1939* (Cambridge: Cambridge University Press, 1990); Warren Susman, *Culture as History: The Transformation of American Society in the Twentieth Century* (New York: Pantheon, 1984); and Harris, *Cultural Excursions*. On railroads opening up the entire nation as a market for consumer goods, see Thomas J. Schlereth, "Country Stores, County Fairs, and Mail Order Catalogues: Consumption in Rural America," in Bonner, ed., *Consuming Visions*, 339–75.

35.   Twelve Southerners, *I'll Take My Stand* (1930; rpt., Baton Rouge: Louisiana State University Press, 1991), xlii, xxxvii, xlv–xlvi, xlvi, 8, 5, xllvii. The quotes are from the

unsigned "Introduction," xxxvii–xlviii, written by John Crowe Ransom, and from Ransom's contribution, "Reconstructed But Unregenerate," 1–27. For the history of the collection, see Donald Davidson, "*I'll Take My Stand*: A History," *American Review* 5, No. 3 (Summer 1935). See also Daniel Joseph Singal, *The War Within: From Victorian to Modernist Thought in the South, 1919–1945* (Chapel Hill: University of North Carolina Press, 1982), 198–264; Richard H. King, *A Southern Renaissance: The Cultural Awakening of the American South, 1930–1955* (New York: Oxford University Press, 1980), 51–57; and Michael O'Brien, *The Idea of the American South, 1920–1941* (Baltimore: Johns Hopkins University Press, 1979), 117–212. For a thoughtful reassessment of *Stand*, see Jackson Lears, "Still Taking Their Stand," *Nation* (10–17 July 1982): 52–54.

36.   Twelve Southerners, *I'll Take My Stand*, 328, 293, 288–89, 289, 296, 293. The first quote is from Stark Young's contribution to this volume, "Not in Memoriam, But in Defense," 328–59; the rest are from John Donald Wade, "The Life and Death of Cousin Lucius," 265–301. I am indebted here in my analysis of the Agrarians to the penetrating readings of earlier American anti-modernists in Lears, *No Place of Grace.*

37.   Herbert Agar and Allen Tate, eds., *Who Owns America? A New Declaration of Independence* (Boston: Houghton Mifflin, 1936), viii, 179, 188, 190. Quotes are from Herbert Agar, "Introduction," vii–ix, and John Crowe Ransom, "What Does the South Want?," 178–93.

38.   Ibid., 92, 190. Wade, "Cousin Lucius," 296. The Amish, as Tate had conceded in "Remarks on the Southern Religion" in *I'll Take My Stand*, 155–75, were the only communities organized around religious imperatives that seemed able to resist the dynamic of capitalist economic development. Certainly religious fundamentalisms today do not shun such development.

39.   H. Wayne Mixon, *Southern Writers and the New South Movement, 1865–1913* (Chapel Hill: University of North Carolina Press, 1980), 33; Ransom, "What Does the South Want?," 188; Gerald W. Johnson, "Greensboro, or What You Will," *Reviewer* (April 1924), reprinted in Fred Hobson, ed., *South Watching: Selected Essays by Gerald W. Johnson* (Chapel Hill: University of North Carolina Press, 1983), 47, 48, 49–50; and "Report to the President on the Economic Conditions of the South" (Washington, D.C., 1938), 58–60. For Johnson's specific critique of the Agrarians, see "No More Excuses," *Harper's* (February 1931), reprinted in Hobson, ed., *South Watching*, 129–36.

40.   Edwards, *Negro as a Consumer*, vii, 11, 12.

41.   Ayers, *Promise of the New South*, 33; Ransom, "What Does the South Want?," 190; and Edwards, *Negro as a Consumer*.

42.   Eugene D. Genovese, *The Slaveholders' Dilemma: Freedom and Progress in Southern Conservative Thought, 1820–1860* (Columbia: University of South Carolina Press, 1991); Woodward, *Origins of the New South*, 154–55, 157–58, and 145–47; Stark Young, "Not in Memoriam," 344. On the extended life of the pro-slavery argument, see John David Smith, *An Old Creed For the New South: Proslavery Ideology and Historiography, 1865–1918* (Westport, CT: Greenwood Press, 1985). On the Lost Cause, see Chapter 2.

43.   Young, "Not in Memoriam," 355.

44.   Williamson, *Crucible*; Fredrickson, *White Mind*; Cell, *White Supremacy*. On

the second Klan, see Nancy MacLean, *Behind the Mask of Chivalry: The Making of the Second Ku Klux Klan* (New York: Oxford University Press, 1993).

45. Robert Penn Warren, "The Briar Patch," in *I'll Take My Stand*, 246–64. A similar call for the reconstruction of a racially inflected hierarchy, and not the reinstitution of segregation as many commentators have insisted, is at work in the recent Richard J. Herrnstein and Charles Murray, *The Bell Curve: Intellectual and Class Structure in American Life* (New York: Free Press, 1994).

On the economic implications of the shift from agrarian self-sufficiency and production to a more urban domesticity and consumption, see Gavin Wright, *Old South, New South: Revolutions in the Southern Economy Since the Civil War* (New York: Norton, 1986), 1–123. On increasing consumption by sharecroppers and tenants of both races, see "Reports on Georgia Plantation Districts, 1911–1912," in the Robert Preston Brooks Collection, Box 28, Hargrett Rare Book and Manuscript Library, University of Georgia, Athens. The shift away from production and toward consumption began before the Civil War. See Lacy K. Ford, *Origins of Southern Radicalism: The South Carolina Low Country, 1800–1860* (New York: Oxford University Press, 1988), 219–77; and Steven Hahn, *The Roots of Southern Populism: Yeoman Farmers and the Transformation of the Georgia Upcountry, 1850–1890* (New York: Oxford University Press, 1983). I am not arguing here for the complete eradication of subsistence farming but for its continuing decline in relation to total agricultural production. Despite the fact that fewer southerners lived in urban areas between 1890 and 1940, segregation as a form of race relations developed earliest in southern cities and had a profound impact upon the southern future. Southern urban historians, however, continue to neglect the impact of consumer culture upon the region. See Blaine A. Brownell and David R. Goldfield, *The City in Southern History: The Growth of Urban Civilization in the South* (Port Washington, NY: Kennikat, 1977); David R. Goldfield, *Cotton Fields and Skyscrapers: Southern City and Region, 1607–1980* (Baton Rouge: Louisiana State University Press, 1982); Don H. Doyle, *New Men, New Cities, New South: Atlanta, Nashville, Charleston, Mobile, 1860–1910* (Chapel Hill: University of North Carolina Press, 1990); and Lawrence H. Larsen, *The Rise of the Urban South* (Lexington: University Press of Kentucky, 1985).

46. Stark Young, "Not in Memoriam," 359; *Seeing Atlanta, Georgia By the Photographic Route* (Atlanta: P. and V., n.d., but early automobiles visible in some pictures), Georgia Box, Warshaw Collection, Archives Center, National Museum of American History (hereafter Warshaw, NMAH); and Woodward, *Origins of the New South*, 142–74.

47. *Bedford, Virginia, Offers Homes to All* (Bedford City: Bedford Index Print, n.d., but appears to be early 1900s), 8; *Virginia Real Estate Journal* (Richmond: R. B. Chaffin, 1912), both in Virginia Box, Warshaw, NMAH.

48. *Savannah: Indelible Photographs* (no publisher, 1892); *St. Augustine. Photographs in Black* (no publisher, 1892); *Souvenir Album of St. Augustine* (no publisher, n.d.); *Post Card Guide and History of Old St. Augustine* (no publisher, 1912); *Bloomfield's Illustrated Historical Guide, Embracing an Account of St. Augustine, Florida* (St. Augustine: Max Bloomfield, Bookseller, 1884); *Souvenir of Miami and Biscayne Bay* (no publisher, 1902), which also includes a photograph of "A Group of Seminoles" in which Indians are posed as yet another tourist attraction; *Richmond on the James* (Philadelphia:

J. Murray Jordan, 1905); and *Plant System Budget*, vol. 1, no. 11, October 1896; in Alabama, Florida, Georgia, and Virginia Boxes, Warshaw, NMAH. See Clifton Johnson, *Highways and Byways of the South* (New York: Macmillan, 1904), for a travel book that presents both southern African Americans and rural southern whites as tourist attractions. An early twentieth-century advertisement for the Nodark Camera by Popular Photograph Company in *McClure's Magazine*, n.d., p. 32, Afro-Americana, Box 4, Warshaw, NMAH, also depicts an African American man as a tourist attraction worth capturing on film.

49. *Souvenir Folder of Dixieland* (Asheville, NC: Asheville Post Card Co., n.d.), postmarked 2 January 1930.

50. *Natchez Pilgrimage: Where the Old South Still Lives* (no publisher, 1941), Mississippi Box, Warshaw, NMAH. For Robert E. Lee flour, see Dorothea Lange, "A grocery store window," LC-USF34-20227-E, Mebane, NC, July 1939. "Furl that Banner," ad for the "Library of Southern Literature," with Mildred Rutherford's endorsement, "Do you realize the value of these books in your home?," endpaper to *Miss Rutherford's Scrap Book: The South's Greatest Vindication*, vol. 2 (October 1924); see also ads in other 1924 and 1925 issues and *Miss Rutherford's Historical Notes*, 1926 and 1927 issues, for other books endorsed as literature that should be in all white southern homes, all in author's collection.

51. Rydell, *All the World's a Fair*, 72–104; *Official Views: Cotton States and International Exposition, Atlanta, 1895* (St. Louis: C. B. Woodward, 1895), Georgia Box, Warshaw, NMAH; W. Y. Atkinson, "The Atlanta Exposition," *North American Review* 467 (October 1895): 385–93.

52. Turner is quoted in Rydell, *All the World's a Fair*, 80–81; see also 78, 52–53. Wells-Barnett, *Crusade for Justice: The Autobiography of Ida B. Wells* (Chicago: University of Chicago Press, 1970), 115–19; Nasaw, *Going Out*, 47–61, 77–79, 92–93. On southern whites' having solved the "Negro Problem," see Atkinson, "Atlanta Exposition," 392–93.

53. Booker T. Washington, quoted in Rydell, *All the World's a Fair*, 83; see also 83–85. The "Atlanta Compromise" speech was reprinted in Washington's autobiography, *Up From Slavery* (1901; rpt., New York: University Books, 1993), 217–37, quote, 221–22.

54. The church congregation and the black paper are quoted in Rydell, *All the World's a Fair*, 85; and Atkinson, "Atlanta Exposition," 393.

55. *Official Views*; Rydell, *All the World's a Fair*, 80, 85–89.

56. Nasaw, *Going Out*. On lynching and consumption, see Chapter 5.

57. Certainly, the idea of "common progress," the degree to which the profits of economic development within the region would ever be shared between blacks and whites, was also problematic. For more on Washington, see Williamson, *Crucible*, 70–78; and August Meir, *Negro Thought in America, 1880–1915: Racial Ideologies in the Age of Booker T. Washington* (Ann Arbor: University of Michigan Press, 1963). The quotes are from Rydell, *All the World's a Fair*, 87.

58. Patricia A. Turner, *Ceramic Uncles and Celluloid Mammies: Black Images and Their Influence on Culture* (New York: Anchor Books, 1994), 45–50; Kenneth

W. Goings, *Mammy and Uncle Mose: Black Collectibles and American Stereotyping* (Bloomington: Indiana University Press, 1994), 28–32; Marilyn Kern-Foxworth, *Aunt Jemima, Uncle Ben, and Rastus: Blacks in Advertising, Yesterday, Today, and Tomorrow* (Westport, CT: Praeger, 1994), 66–67; and Janice Jorgensen, ed., *The Encyclopedia of Consumer Brands* (Detroit: St. James, 1994), vol. 1, *Consumable Products*, 20–23. The term "Aunt Jemima" will not be put within quotes but always refers to the role as constructed in song and by the companies that owned the trademark and never to the women playing this character. On mammies, see Patricia Morton, *Disfigured Images: The Historical Assault on Afro-American Women* (New York: Greenwood Press, 1991); and Donald Bogle, *Coons, Mulattos, Mammies, and Bucks* (New York: Viking, 1973). See also Chapter 3.

59. M. A. I. Author, "Aunt Jemima's Plaster" (Philadelphia: William H. Shuster, 1855); James Grace, "Old Aunt Jemima" (no location: John F. Perry, 1875); J. W. Johnson and Fred S. Stone, "Aunt Jemima's Ragtime Walk" (Detroit: Broadwell and Wolf, 1899); Jack Mahony and Theodore Morse, "Jemima: A Sneezing Coon Song" (New York: Haviland, 1909); J. Will Callahan and F. Henri Klickmann, "Aunt Jemima's Picnic Day" (Chicago: McKinley Music, 1914); no author given, described as a "plantation melody," "Old Aunt Jemima," in Peter W. Dykema et al., eds., *Twice 55 Plus: Community Songs: The New Brown Book* (Boston: C. C. Birchard, 1919); William Tracey and Maceo Pinkard, "Aunt Jemima's Jubilee" (New York: Fred Fisher, 1921); Bud De Sylva, Bud Green, and Ray Henderson, "Alabamy Bound" (New York: Shapiro, Bernstein, 1925); and Raymond B. Egan and Richard A. Whiting, "Aunt Jemima" (New York: Jerome H. Remick, 1925), all in Box 75, the Sam DeVincent Illustrated Sheet Music Collection, National Museum of American History (hereafter DeVincent, NMAH).

60. Philip Ostermeyer Catalogue, Jersey City, New Jersey, 18–19, Afro-Americana, Box 4, Warshaw, NMAH. P. T. Barnum Collection, NMAH; obituaries, *New York Times*, 8 April 1891, and *New York Tribune*, 8 April 1891; Neil Harris, *Humbug: The Art of P. T. Barnum* (Boston: Little, Brown, 1973). See also Lears, *Fables*, 123–24, 164, 86–87; the sources on the construction of whiteness cited in note 17; Goings, *Black Collectibles*; and Turner, *Black Images*, 9–25, 41–50.

61. Ellison, "Change the Joke"; Lott, *Love and Theft*; Roediger, "White Skins, Black Masks: Minstrelsy and White Working Class Formation Before the Civil War," in *Wages of Whiteness*, 115–31; and Saxton, *White Republic*, 165–82.

62. Rydell, *All the World's a Fair*, 72–104; Nasaw, *Going Out*, 49–61. On the 1850 Zealy daguerreotypes of slaves, see Trachtenberg, *Reading American Photographs*, 53–58. On the power at stake between photographers and their subjects, see Sontag, *On Photography*, 1–22. For stereographs that depict African Americans, see the stereograph collection at the Schomburg Center for Research in Black Culture, New York Public Library, New York City. See Jack Delano, "Mr. Ward and his wife looking at stereographic pictures . . .," LC-USF34-44599-D, Green County, GA, June 1941, for a photograph of a black couple enjoying stereographs in their farm home.

63. On early films that used blackfaced characters, see, for example, the films advertised in *The Biograph*, 28 November 1914, 2; 16 January 1915, 3; 20 January 1915, 2; 30 January 1915, 3; 3 April 1915, 6; all in Motion Pictures, Box 1, Warshaw, NMAH. On early

cinema, see Miriam Hansen, *Babel and Babylon: Spectatorship in American Silent Film* (Cambridge, MA: Harvard University Press, 1991). On *Birth of a Nation*, see Chapter 5.

64.   Fleischmann's Yeast trade card, Yeast, Box Y, Warshaw, NMAH. For an advertisement with specifically Oriental subject, see the Palmolive ad, *Everybody's Magazine* (May 1904): 44; in Afro-Americana, Box 4, Warshaw, NMAH. On Oriental themes in advertising, see Lears, *Fables*, 18, 45, 51–52, 63, 64, 66, 96, 103–4. On the history of trade cards and the development of the advertising industry, see Robert Jay, *The Trade Card in Nineteenth Century America* (Columbia: University of Missouri Press, 1987); Lears, *Fables*, 105–6, 111, 148–52; and Daniel Pope, *The Making of Modern Advertising* (New York: Basic Books, 1983). On the impact of advances in reproducing images on American culture, see Harris, "Iconography and Intellectual History," 304–17. See also Jan Nederveen Pieterse, *White on Black: Images of Africa and Blacks in Western Popular Culture* (New Haven: Yale University Press, 1992); and William L. Van Deburg, *Slavery and Race in American Popular Culture* (Madison: University of Wisconsin Press, 1984). Advertisers did not use photographs in advertisements widely until the Depression, when the switch from custom artwork to photographs was made because photographs had become cheaper. By 1932, half the ads in national magazines used photographs. See Roland Marchand, *Advertising the American Dream: Making Way for Modernity, 1920–1940* (Berkeley: University of California Press, 1984), 149.

65.   For examples of samples of generic racialized black imagery, see Fireman sample and Stone Litho Co. sample, unlabeled picture of a black man reaching for a watermelon, both in Afro-Americana, Box 4. Rabineau trade card, Afro-Americana, Box 4; Trymby and Rehn Furniture trade card, Furniture, Box 7; Pomeroy Coal Company Trade Card, Afro-Americana, Box 4; McFerren, Shallcross and Company trade card, Meat, Box M; and Piqua Patent Pillow and Topsey Tablets trade cards, Afro-Americana, Box 4. See also Rich Novelties trade card, Afro-Americana, Box 3; and B. M. Weed and Co., Pictures and Picture Frames, Afro-Americana Box 4. For other examples of sentimental racist imagery, see the other trade cards for Piqua Patent Pillows and Topsey Tablets; Allen's Root Beer Trade Card, Beverages, Box 1; and R. T. White, product not identified, Afro-Americana, Box 4. All sources are in Warshaw, NMAH. On the origins and popularity of trade cards, see Lears, *Fables*. For use of racialized black images, see Goings, *Black Collectibles*; and Turner, *Black Image*. For the construction of the consumer as female, see Marchand, *Advertising*, 52–87; and Ellen Garvey, *Reading Consumer Culture: Gender, Fiction, and Advertising in American Magazines, 1880s to 1910s* (New York: Oxford University Press, 1995).

66.   Union Pacific Tea Co. Trade Card, Afro-Americana, Box 3; I. M. Demming trade card, Vinegar, Box V.9; Walker, Stratman and Co. trade card, Fertilizer, Box 7.8; and Elson, Salisbury and Co. trade card, Afro-Americana, Box 4; all in Warshaw, NMAH. For a fascinating discussion of a particular genre of commercial black imagery that depicted alligators chasing or eating black children, see Turner, *Black Image*, 31–40.

67.   "Sunny South Cigarettes" trade card, Afro-Americana, Box 4; George W. Boos Coffee trade card, Coffee, Box C.83; Vacuum Harness Oil and J. G. Crippen Hardware trade card, Afro-Americana, Box 4; Dannemiller's Cordova Coffee trade card, Coffee, Box C.84; and Sampson Brothers Clothiers trade card series, Afro-Americana, Box 4;

all in Warshaw, NMAH. See also Halttunen, *Confidence Men*; and Lears, *No Place of Grace*, on the confusion of appearances in white middle-class culture. These types of images were also used to portray Irish Americans in the late nineteenth century.

68.   Tansill's Punch trade card, Afro-Americana, Box 3, Warshaw, NMAH. Lott, *Love and Theft*.

69.   Glenwood Ranges and Parlor Stoves trade card, Stoves, Box S.T-Z; Mitchell's Kidney Plasters trade card, Afro-Americana, Box 4; Harrington and Company Merchants Tailors trade card, Dry Goods, Box D.66; all in Warshaw, NMAH. On nostalgia and advertising, see T. J. Jackson Lears, "Packaging the Folk: Tradition and Amnesia in American Advertising, 1880–1940," in Jane S. Becker and Barbara Franco, eds., *Folk Roots, New Roots: Folklore in American Life* (Lexington, MA: Museum of Our National Heritage, 1988), 103–40.

70.   "Comic Series H," Afro-Americana, Box 4; "Political Orator," Dry Goods Ad Cards, Wisconsin, Box D.88; and "Strolling on the Sands," Harry Smith Hatter, 1877, Afro-Americana, Box 4; all in Warshaw, NMAH.

71.   F. H. Brinkmann's Four Heart Crackers, Afro-Americana, Box 4; "I Likes the Best!," Purina Mills, Food Stuffs, Box 4; "American Negroes" and "Central Africa," Arbuckle Bros., Coffee, Box C.86; "Java and Mocha Coffee," Chase and Sanborn, Afro-Americana, Box 3; and "Magnolia Ham," McFerran, Shallcross, and Co., Box M.29; all in Warshaw, NMAH. For another ad card that implies that a particular product almost makes blacks civilized, see the Great Atlantic and Pacific Tea Company's 1884 trade card "Our Boarding House," Afro-Americana, Box 4, Warshaw, NMAH. See also "Maple Leaf Chewing Gum," Maple Leaf Gum Works, Ohio, Chewing Gum, Box C.56; "Fine Shoes," Edwin C. Burt, Lowell, MA, Afro-Americana, Box 4, also in Warshaw, NMAH. On the professionalization of advertising, see Lears, *Fables of Abundance*, 198–210.

72.   "Nigger Head Tobacco," William S. Kimball and Co., Tobacco, Box H-M; and "Korn Kinks," H. O. Company, Cereal, Box C.41; both in Warshaw, NMAH. See also Kern-Foxworth, *Blacks in Advertising*, 30; and Goings, *Black Collectibles*, 20, 79. Darkie Toothpaste by Hawley and Hazel was still being sold in the 1970s.

73.   "Automatic Window Attractions" advertisement in *Harman's Journal*, March 1898, 11–12; Afro-Americana, Box 4, Warshaw, NMAH. On p. 11 an article describing Easter displays for the "Grocery Department" suggested using "one of the mechanical nigger babies which sell for $6.50." See also unidentified advertisement for "Original Sambo and Dinah": "These lively 'cullud people' are exceedingly popular wherever introduced, both with young and old. They are eleven inches high, and are dressed in bright Southern costumes of the old plantation style . . . They will dance to music, bow, fall down, rise up, etc., without the manager being anywhere near them, and the secret of their movements can be discovered only by the closest examination." In Afro-Americana, Box 3, Warshaw, NMAH.

74.   *Ladies' Home Journal*, October 1918. Goings, *Black Collectibles*, 19–50; Kern-Foxworth, *Blacks in Advertising*, 73–75, 107–8; Turner, *Black Images*, 9–61; and Frances Pendleton Gaines, *The Southern Plantation: A Study in the Development and the Accuracy of a Tradition* (New York: Columbia University Press, 1925), 11–12. On black-figured toys, see Doris Y. Wilkinson, "The Toy Menagerie: Early Images of Blacks in Toys,

Games, and Dolls," in Jessie Carney Smith, ed., *Images of Blacks in American Culture* (Westport, CT: Greenwood Press, 1988).

75. Goings, *Black Collectibles*, 19–50 and plate 4; Kern-Foxworth, *Blacks in Advertising*, 74; and Gaines, *Plantation*, 11–12.

76. S. M. Bixby and Co. Blacking, Blueing, and Ink trade card, Inks, Box 1; Mason's Challenge Blacking trade card, Afro-Americana, Box 4; Diamond Dyes' Fast Black for Wool and Fast Stocking Black, Afro-Americana, Box 4; Nubian Dress Linings ad from the *Ladies' Home Journal*, April 1895, 18, Afro-Americana, Box 3; Black Satin Stove Polish ad in *Delineator*, May 1905, 902, Afro-Americana, Box 4; and "Onyx" Black Hosiery ad in the *Ladies' Home Journal*, April 1895, 30, Afro-Americana, Box 4; all in Warshaw, NMAH. The J and P Coates Black Thread trade card is from Goings, *Black Collectibles*, plate 2.

77. John Kirkman and Son's "Two Little Nigger Boys" advertisement for Wonder Soap, and Procter and Gamble's "Reclaimed" advertisement for Ivory Soap, both in Afro-Americana, Box 4, Warshaw, NMAH. See also Henry's Carbolic Salve, Cosmetics, Box 3, Warshaw, NMAH. For racial imagery in soap trade cards and other advertisements, see the nine boxes in Soap, Warshaw, NMAH. On the cultural meanings of cleanliness, see Ruth Schwartz Cowen, *More Work for Mother: The Ironies of Household Technology from the Open Hearth to the Microwave* (New York: Basic Books, 1983), 51–53; Claudia and Richard Bushman, "The Early History of Cleanliness in America," *Journal of American History* 75 (December 1988): 675–725; and Richard L. Bushman, *The Refinement of America: Persons, Houses, Cities* (New York: Knopf, 1992).

78. See the Fairbank's Soaps and their later specialized Gold Dust Washing Powder trade cards in Soap, Box 2, Warshaw, NMAH. Advertisements that stress the service of the product and the black twins include a December 1899 ad, "Scrubbing Floors," in an unidentified magazine; "The Passing of the Washboard," *The Delineator*, November 1902, 829; and "Three times a day, 1095 times a year," *The Delineator*, December 1901, no page number; all in Soap, Box 2, Warshaw, NMAH. Examples of trade cards with servant themes include Libby, McNeill, and Libby Meats' "Dinah keeps the children quiet"; Imperial Shirts' "Topsy's Delight"; Eureka Poisoned Fly Plate's "Golly, I wish missus would get . . ."; Rising Sun Stove Polish's "A Tale . . ."; and D. White and Sons' "What Brush You Usin Sae?"; all in Afro-Americana, Box 4, Warshaw, NMAH. Examples of other ads that equate the service of the servant pictured with the service of the product are the front cover of the new Columbia Music publication for its sales force, *The Columbia Salesman* (August 1907), which promises that the magazine will serve the salesmen like the black waiter depicted; and Chicago Great Western Railway's advertisement for its "A La Carte Dining Car Service," whose service, like the black waiter pictured, is "unexcelled." The Gold Dust Twins also had minstrel connections and even their own radio show. See Alfred Bryan, Arthur Terker, and Pete Wendling, "There's Something Nice About Everyone 'But' There's Everything Nice About You" (New York: Henry Waterson, 1927), as "featured by the Gold Dust Babes," two white men in blackface drag, Box 68, DeVincent, NMAH.

79. Coates Thread Trade Card in Goings, *Black Collectibles*, plate 2; Universal Clothes Wringer Trade Card, Afro-Americana, Box 3; Armour "Star" Hams and Bacon

advertisement, "The Why of 'The Ham What Am!,' " Afro-Americana, Box 3; in Warshaw, NMAH. Other trade cards using spokesservants include E. R. Durkee and Company trade card, "De Kurn'l done give me a bottle dis yere Durkee's salad Dressin'," Afro-Americana, Box 3; Fleischmann's Yeast trade card, "I can make anything in de bakin line wif . . . ," Afro-Americana, Box 4; in Warshaw, NMAH. For the letter from the twins, see the Gold Dust Twins pamphlet: N. K. Fairbank Company, "Who Are We?" (Chicago: N. K. Fairbank Company, n. d.), in Soap, Box 2, Warshaw, NMAH.

80.   Pace, Talbott and Company trade card; Sapolio Soap Lithograph; Walker, Stratman and Company trade card; Buckeye Forge Pumps trade card; and Cream of Wheat ad, *Today's Housewife*, August 1917; all in Afro-Americana, Box 4, Warshaw, NMAH. Uncle Ben also had minstrel connections. See E. G. Samuel, "Uncle Ben's Lament" (New York: North American Music Co., 1906), Box 75, DeVincent, NMAH. See also Julian Lewis Watkins, *The 100 Greatest Advertisements: Who Wrote Them and What They Did* (New York: Moore, 1949).

81.   Early Aunt Jemima ads include "I'se In Town, Honey," *Ladies' Home Journal*, November 1896, 32; and "The Best Breakfast," *What to Eat* (Minneapolis: Pierce and Pierce, 1897), no page number, in Afro-Americana, Box 4, Warshaw, NMAH. Other advertisements in which a domestic servant serves as mammy to the product include "Honey I's cooked for your granma and your ma . . . ," in E. R. Durkee and Company, *Salads: How to Make and Dress Them* (New York: Durkee, n. d.); Campbell's Soup's "Cook Could you spare me a little, please?," *Modern Priscilla*, October 1914, no page; both in Afro-Americana, Box 4; and Crisco's "Children Will Eat Pastry," *McCall's*, April 1913, 89; in Afro-Americana, Box 3; all in Warshaw, NMAH. On domestic service see Tera Hunter, "Household Workers in the Making: Afro-American Women in Atlanta and the New South, 1861–1920" (Ph.D. dissertation, Yale University, 1990), 1–5; Susan Tucker, *Telling Memories Among Southern Women: Domestic Workers and Their Employers in the Segregated South* (New York: Schocken, 1988), 1–18; and David M. Katzman, *Seven Days a Week: Women and Domestic Service in Industrializing America* (New York: Oxford University Press, 1978). See also Chapter 3.

82.   The ad and its text are reproduced in Goings, *Black Collectibles*, 29–32. Nina Silber, *The Romance of Reunion: Northerners and the South, 1865–1900* (Chapel Hill: University of North Carolina Press, 1993).

83.   Goings, *Black Collectibles*, 29–31. Popular illustrated sheet music also changed its tone by the 1920s, replacing the often bluntly racist "coon songs" linked to minstrel performances with more nostalgic songs that longed for a return to the old southern home. The hundreds of "coon songs" include Jean Havez, "Everybody Works But Father" (New York: Helf and Hager, 1905); William Jerome and Jean Schwartz, "Back to the Woods" (New York: Shapiro Bernstein, 1902); Lew Dockstader and Karl St. Clair, "I Want My Lulu: A Disturbance in Coontown" (New York: W. B. Gray, 1897); and Irving Jones, "St. Patrick's Is a Bad Day for Coons" (New York: Sol Bloom, 1891); all in Box 69, DeVincent, NMAH.

84.   Copy of N. K. Fairbank's 1910 billboard for Gold Dust Washing Powder, "Roosevelt scoured America," Soap, Box 2, Warshaw, NMAH. In another current events–oriented Fairbank's ad, the Gold Dust Twins ride an airplane and are billed as "The Right

Brothers for Cleaning," also in Soap, Box 2, Warshaw, NMAH. On the connections between imperialism abroad and racism at home, see Nell Irvin Painter, *Standing at Armageddon: The United States, 1877–1919* (New York: Norton, 1987), 141–69. On the trope of the native bearer, see Marianne Torgovnick, *Gone Primitive: Savage Intellects, Modern Lives* (Chicago: University of Chicago Press, 1990), 3–41.

85. Booker T. Washington, "Signs of Progress Among the Negroes," *Century Magazine* 3 (January 1900): 472; Woodward, *Origins of the New South*, 211–16; and Ayers, *Promise of the New South*, 326–27.

86. Nestle's Baby Food 1894–1895 calendar, Afro-Americana, Box 4, Warshaw, NMAH.

87. John N. Ingham, "Prejudice, Pride and Profits: African-American Business in the South, 1880–1929" (Wilmington, DE: Hagley Museum and Library unpublished seminar paper 16, 10 March 1994); Edwards, *Negro as a Consumer*, 120–50; Woodward, *Origins of the New South*, 353–54; and Myrdal, *American Dilemma*, 800–5, 815–17. See also the FSA photographs of African American business districts, especially Marion Post Wolcott's series shot on Beale Street, LC-USF33-30637-M3, LC-USF33-30369-M3, LC-USF33-30639-M4, and LC-USF33-30638-M2, Memphis, October 1939. Auburn Avenue in Atlanta was also an important African American business district. See the listings under Georgia for tourist-related enterprises serving African Americans in *The Negro Motorist's Green Book*, 1938 ed., copy in the Segregation File at the Division of Automobiles and Buses, NMAH, from the original at the Schomburg Center for Research in Black Culture, New York Public Library; and Clifford M. Kuhn, Harlon E. Joye, and E. Bernard West, *Living Atlanta: An Oral History of the City, 1914–1948* (Athens: University of Georgia Press, 1990), 10–12, 39, 95, 99–108; and Murphy, *Ascendancy*, 122, 138. See also Murphy, *Problems of the Present South* (New York: Macmillan, 1904); and Maud King Murphy, *Edgar Gardner Murphy* (New York: the author, 1943), which includes a complete biography.

88. Susan Atherton Hanson, "Home, Sweet Home: Industrialization's Impact on Rural Households, 1865–1925" (Ph.D. dissertation, University of Maryland, 1986); Thomas D. Clark, *Pills, Petticoats, and Plows: The Southern Country Store* (1944; rpt. Norman: University of Oklahoma Press, 1989); Ayers, *Promise of the New South*, 13–19, 81–103; Schlereth, "Country Stores, County Fairs, and Mail Order Catalogues," in Bonner, ed., *Consuming Visions*, 339; and Gerald Carson, *The Old Country Store* (New York: Dutton, 1965).

89. Hanson, "Home," 64–70; Clark, *Southern Country Store*, 99–217. On advertising and patent medicines, see Lears, *Fables*, 41–45, 65, 69, 83–101, 141–61, 201–2. On the history of the patent medicine business, see James Harvey Young, *The Toadstool Millionaires: A Social History of Patent Medicine in America Before Federal Regulation* (Princeton: Princeton University Press, 1961).

90. Hanson, "Home," 64–70; Clark, *Southern Country Store*, 118–35.

91. Clark, *Southern Country Store*, 9–10, 33, 113. Faulkner, *Light in August*, 22, 23, 23–24, 26.

92. Clark, *Southern Country Store*, 34, 55–59, 76; Ayers, *Promise of the New South*, 13–19, 81–103; Hanson, "Home, Sweet Home," 7–8, 54–56. On the continuity-versus-

change debate about the persistence of planter power after the Civil War, see Harold D. Woodman, "Economic Reconstruction and the New South," in Jon B. Boles and Evelyn Thomas Nolen, eds., *Interpreting Southern History: Historiographic Essays in Honor of Sanford W. Higginbotham* (Baton Rouge: Louisiana State University Press, 1987), 254–307. In *Promise of the New South*, 458, n. 51, Ayers asserts that by 1895, planter power had greatly eroded.

93. Clark, *Southern Country Store*, 9–10, 35, 55–57; Edwards, *Negro as a Consumer*, 159; Johnson, *Negro Segregation*, 63–65. Photographs of southern country stores taken by the FSA in the late 1930s often depict integrated shopping or socializing. See Russell Lee, "A Negro Woman trading a sack of pecans for groceries," LC-USF34-31759-D, and "A Negro Woman waiting for groceries in a general store," LC-USF34-31757-D, Jarreau, LA, October 1938; Jack Delano, "On the porch of a general store," LC-USF33-20816-M3, Hinesville, GA, April 1941; Dorothea Lange, "A country store located on a dirt road, on a Sunday afternoon," LC-USF34-19911-E, Gordonton, NC, July 1939; Jack Delano, "A general store . . . ," LC-USF34-43438-D, Manchester (vicinity), NC, April 1941; and Marion Post Wolcott, "A part of the interior," LC-USF34-52678-D, "The front of the general store," LC-USF34-52655-D, and "The front of the Whitley general store," LC-USF34-52677-D, Wendell, NC, November 1939. For an account of African Americans only being able to buy at white-owned stores with landowner's store orders, see John Dollard, *Caste and Class in a Southern Town* (1937; rpt., New York: Doubleday Anchor, 1957), 126. For an account of a white man keeping a store in a black section of a small southern town in the 1940s and 1950s, see Melton A. McLaurin, *Separate Pasts: Growing Up White in the Segregated South* (Athens: University of Georgia, 1987). Some African Americans also ran general stores, although they too were rare. See Davis, Gardner, and Gardner, *Deep South*, 258, for an account of poor whites' deferential treatment of an African American store owner from whom they hoped to get credit. See Maya Angelou, *I Know Why the Caged Bird Sings* (New York: Random House, 1969) for a discussion of her grandparents' store in the 1930s.

94. Charles A. Le Guin, ed., *A Home-Concealed Woman: The Diaries of Magnolia Wynn Le Guin, 1901–1913* (Athens: University of Georgia Press, 1990), 29; Clark, *Southern Country Store*, 84–97, quotes, 88, 90; Ownby, *Subduing Satan*, 38–55; and Carson, *Old Country Store*, 162–67. See also Timothy B. Spears, *100 Years on the Road: The Traveling Salesman in American Culture* (New Haven: Yale University Press, 1995).

95. Photographs of general stores covered with advertising include Dorothea Lange, "The daughter of a sharecropper at a country store," LC-USF34-19740-E, Gordonton, NC, July 1939; Russell Lee, "A store front," LC-USF33-11695-M2, Altheime, AK, September 1938; Lee, "A sign in a country store," LC-USF33-11805-M5, Vacherie, LA, September 1938; Lee, "The interior of a general store," LC-USF33-11797-M1, Pilottown, LA, September 1938; Cox (no first name given), "The interior of a general store," LC-USF34-15763-D, Florence, SC, Summer 1938; Walker Evans, "The interior of a general store," LC-USF342-8164-A, Moundville, AL, 1935; and Jack Delano, "Mr. Jackson in his general store," LC-USF34-44483-D, Siloam, GA, June 1941. For the sale of Aunt Jemima products, see Russell Lee, "The owner of the general store slicing bologna," LC-USF34-31747-D, Jarreau, LA, October 1938, which shows these items on the store shelves. Partic-

ularly in rural North Carolina, tobacco and other ads covered over barns and even a privy as well. See, for example, Dorothea Lange, "A hillside farm . . . ," LC-USF34-19995-C, Person County, NC, July 1939; Arthur Rothstein, "U.S. Resettlement administration tenant farm . . . ," LC-USF34-5764-C, Johnston County, NC, December 1936; and John Vachon, "A privy," LC-USF34-8366-C, Greensboro, NC, April 1938. The 1908 postcard is reproduced in Guy C. McElroy, *Facing History: The Black Image in American Art, 1719–1940* (San Francisco: Bedford Arts, 1990), xxxii. Clark, *Southern Country Store*, 18–22.

96. See FSA photos of integration and advertising at general stores cited in notes 91 and 93. Clarence Poe, "Flashlights on the Negro Problem in Southern Farm Life," *Progressive Farmer*, 12 July 1913; "South Carolina Views on Grouping the Races," *Progressive Farmer*, 26 July 1913; "A South-Wide Campaign for Racial Segregation," *Progressive Farmer*, 2 August 1913; "Racial Segregation Necessary to Education and Co-operation," *Progressive Farmer*, 9 August 1913; and "Rural Land Segregation between Whites and Negroes: A Reply to Mr. Stephenson," *South Atlantic Quarterly* 13 (1914): 207–12. Jack Delano, "A general store . . . ," LC-USF34-43438-D, Manchester, NC, April 1941. On integration at a country fair, see Louise Schmier and Denise Montgomery, "The Other Depression: The Black Experience in Georgia Through an FSA Photographer's Lens," *Georgia Historical Quarterly* 78 (Spring 1994): 141. For firsthand accounts by whites of frequent interactions with blacks in the rural South, see William Alexander Percy, *Lanterns on the Levee: Recollections of a Planter's Son* (1941; rpt., Baton Rouge: Louisiana State University Press, 1994), especially ch. 25, "A Bit of Diary," 322–31; LeGuin, *Diaries*, 15–17, 24, 44–45, 71–73, 82–84, 167, 178–79, 183–87, 192, 255–56, 279, 299–300, 314. See also Clark, *Southern Country Store*, 9–10, 18–22, 34–35, 54, 76, 82, 103, 111–42, 189–211; Jack Temple Kirby, "Black and White in the Rural South, 1915–1954," *Agricultural History* (July 1984): 411–22; and "Clarence Poe's Vision of a Segregated 'Great Rural Civilization,'" *South Atlantic Quarterly* 68 (Winter 1969): 27–38.

97. Carson McCullers, *Ballad of the Sad Cafe* (1951; rpt., New York: Bantam Books, 1971).

98. Ibid. 54, 54, 55, 55, 55, 22, 71.

99. LeGuin, *Diary*, 196; Stuart and Elizabeth Ewen, *Channels of Desire: Mass Images and the Shaping of American Consciousness* (New York: McGraw-Hill, 1982), 63–68; Schlereth, "Country Stores, Country Fairs, and Mail Order Catalogues," in Bonner, ed., *Consuming Visions*, 364–72; and Wayne E. Fuller, *RFD: The Changing Face of Rural America* (Bloomington: Indiana University Press, 1964). On Montgomery Ward and Sears, see Frank B. Latham, *A Century of Serving Customers: The Story of Montgomery Ward* (Chicago: Montgomery Ward, 1971); Nina Baker, *Big Catalogue: The Life of Aaron Montgomery Ward* (New York: Harcourt, Brace, 1956), and *Our Silver Anniversary: Being a Brief and Concise History of the Mail-Order or Catalog Business Which Was Invented by Us a Quarter of a Century Ago* (Chicago: Montgomery Ward, 1897). On Sears, see David L. Cohen, *The Good Old Days: A History of American Morals and Manners as Seen through the Sears, Roebuck Catalogs, 1905 to the Present* (New York: Simon and Schuster, 1940); Gordon L. Weil, *Sears, Roebuck, U.S.A.: The Great American Catalog Store and How It Grew* (New York: Stein and Day, 1977); Boris Emmet and John E.

Jeuck, *Catalogues and Counters: A History of Sears, Roebuck and Company* (Chicago: University of Chicago Press, 1950); and Robert Hendrickson, *The Grand Emporiums: The Illustrated History of the Great Department Stores* (New York: Stein and Day, 1979).

100.   Schlereth, "Country Stores, County Fairs, and Mail Order Catalogues," in Bonner, ed., *Consuming Visions*; LeGuin, *Home-Concealed Woman*, 192; Hendrickson, *Grand Emporiums*, 205–06.

101.   S. and E. Ewen, *Channels of Desire*, 63–68, quotes, 64, 65–66; Weil, *Sears, Roebuck, U.S.A.*, 5, 25–27; Cohen, *Good Old Days*; and Hendrickson, *Grand Emporiums*.

102.   Clark, *Southern Country Store*, 72–75; Sears, Roebuck and Co. Catalogue no. 113 (Spring 1904), 1, and no. 126 (Spring 1913), 2, both in NMAH; Fuller, *RFD*, 250–52; Schlereth, "Country Stores, Country Fairs, and Mail Order Catalogues," in Bonner, ed., *Consuming Visions*, 370–71.

103.   S. and E. Ewen, *Channels of Desire*, 67–68; Weil, *Sears, Roebuck, U.S.A.*, 62–64; Hendrickson, *Grand Emporiums*, 236–53. See Dollard, *Caste and Class*, 48–49, for a description of a white northerner living in Mississippi who hated southern whites so much that he made all his purchases from the Sears Roebuck catalog.

104.   Ben Shahn, "A Medicine Show," LC-USF34-6164-M3, "A Medicine Show and Audience," LC-USF34-6165-M5, "A Medicine Show," LC-USF34-6164-M5, "A Medicine Show Puppet," LC-USF34-6167-M4, and "Watching a Medicine Show," LC-USF34-6165-M1, all Huntingdon, TN, 1935. Natanson, *Black Image*, 100–6. For the quotes from the Federal Writers' Project interview with medicine show pitchman Josiah Roberts, see Natanson, *Black Image*, 100, from Ann Banks, ed., *First-Person America* (New York: Random House, 1981), 188–89. I rely here on Natanson's excellent discussion of the Shahn series but with a different emphasis on the racial meanings involved and a skepticism about Natanson's assumptions of photographic transparency. See also Marion Post Wolcott, "Men outside a tobacco warehouse, listening to a patent medicine salesman during a tobacco auction," LC-USF33-30699-M5, Durham, NC, November 1939. On medicine shows see also N. T. Oliver, as told to Wesley Stout, "Med Show," *Saturday Evening Post* 202 (14 September 1929): 12, 13, quoted in Lears, *Fables of Abundance*, 141–42.

105.   See Shahn photographs cited in note 103.

106.   Ibid.; Natanson, *Black Image*, 100–6, quote, 100. Oliver, "Med Show," 12.

107.   Edwards, *Negro as a Consumer*, 151–60, 214–51, quote from Burroughs, 235, quotes about the Gold Dust Twins, 250. See also Melvin Patrick Ely, *The Adventures of Amos and Andy: A Social History of an American Phenomenon* (New York: Free Press, 1991).

108.   On the contradictions between segregation and the profit motive, between the demands of white supremacy and black customers, see Davis, Gardner, and Gardner, *Deep South*, 258–63; Dollard, *Caste and Class*, 126–30; Johnson, *Negro Segregation*, 56–77; Myrdal, *American Dilemma*, 636–39; Doyle, *Etiquette of Race Relations*, 146–56.

109.   Descriptions in sociological studies of racial mixing in the commercial districts of southern towns and cities on Saturdays and at other times include Johnson, *Negro Segregation*, 63–77; Dollard, *Caste and Class*, 4–5; Davis, Gardner, Gardner,

Deep South, 15–16, 22–23, 54–55, 253–80; Myrdal, *American Dilemma*, 627–38. Fictional accounts include Faulkner, *Sanctuary*, 11–13.

110. Mrs. W. H. [Rebecca Latimer] Felton, "The Country Home: Women on the Farm," *Atlanta Journal Semi-Weekly*, 24 May 1901; LeGuin, *Diaries*, 299.

111. Dollard, *Caste and Class*, 4–5; Johnson, *Negro Segregation*, 63–77; Faulkner, *Sanctuary*, 111; Kirby, "Rural South," 420–21.

112. Dollard, *Caste and Class*, 4.

113. Johnson, *Negro Segregation*, 63.

114. Marion Post Wolcott, "Saturday afternoon in the Delta area," LC-USF33-30640-M5, Clarksdale, MS, October 1939; "On the main street," LC-USF34-51879-D and LC-USF34-51878-D, Greensboro, GA, Spring 1939; "Main street on Saturday afternoon," LC-USF33-30592-M1, Belzoni, MS, October 1939; "Selling apples on Main street on Saturday afternoon," LC-USF33-30587-M1, Lexington, MS, October 1939; and "A street scene on Saturday afternoon," LC-USF33-30520-M4, Yanceyville, NC, September 1939. On the administration of the FSA project in general and attitudes among photographers including the one African American, Gordon Parks, toward photographing southern blacks, see Natanson, *Black Image*, 49–84.

115. Natanson, *Black Image*, 49–84; and Marion Post Wolcott, "Grocery store on a Saturday afternoon," LC-USF33-30409-M5, Greensboro, GA, June 1939; "A street corner," LC-USF34-56719-D, Starke, FL, December 1940; and "An advertisement on the side of a drug store," LC-USF34-52631-D, Wendell, NC, November 1939. Jack Delano, "Saturday afternoon," LC-USF34-46401, LC-USF34-46421-D, and LC-USF33-20891-M2, Greensboro, GA, November 1941; "A Saturday afternoon crown in the town," LC-USF34-44171-D and LC-USF34-44651-D, Siloam, GA, May 1941. Dorothea Lange, "Appliquéd embroideries for sale on the street in front of the 10 ct. store on a Saturday afternoon," LC-USF34-20217-E.

116. John Vachon, "A drinking fountain on the county courthouse lawn," LC-USF33-1112-M1, Halifax, NC, April 1938; Arthur Siegel, "A drinking fountain," LC-USW3-26442-D, Bethlehem-Fairfield shipyards, Baltimore, May 1943; and Esther Bubley, "Tobacco sales. Drinking fountains at a Lumberton warehouse," Milton Meltzer Collection, Schomburg Center for Research in Black Culture, New York Public Library; Jack Delano, "A street scene near the bus station," LC-USF33-20522-M5. See also Russell Lee, "Man drinking at a water cooler in the street car terminal," LC-USF33-12327-M5, Oklahoma City, July 1939; John Vachon, "A railroad station," LC-USF33-1172-M4, Manchester, GA, May 1938; and Esther Bubley, "A rest stop for Greyhound bus passengers on the way from Louisville, KY, to Nashville, TN, with separate accommodations for colored passengers," LC-USW3-37919-E, September 1943.

117. Jack Delano, "A cafe near the tobacco market," Durham, NC, May 1940, LC-USF33-20513-M2; Dorothea Lange, "A fish restaurant for Negroes in the section of the city where cotton hoers are recruited," LC-USF34-17593-E, Memphis, June 1937; Marion Post Wolcott, "A lunch room," LC-USF34-50500-D, Belle Glade, FL, January 1939; Johnson, *Negro Segregation*, 59; and Doyle, *Etiquette of Race Relations*, 146–47.

118. Dollard, *Caste and Class*, 4; Jack Delano, "The movie house," LC-USF33-20963-M4 and "The new moving picture theater," LC-USF33-20956-M4, Greensboro,

GA, May 1941; Johnson, *Negro Segregation*, 72–74, quote, 73; Marion Post Wolcott, "The Rex theatre for Negro people," LC-USF34-52508-D, Leland, MS, November 1939; Dorothea Lange, "The Rex theatre for colored people," LC-USF34-17417-E, Leland, MS, June 1937; and Marion Post Wolcott, "Negro man entering movie," LC-USF33-30577-M2, Belzoni, MS, October 1939. On this famous FSA image, see Natanson, *Black Image*, 1–3.

119.   Myrdal, *American Dilemma*, 627–39; Baker, *Following the Color Line*, 34–35; Johnson, *Negro Segregation*, 56–77.

120.   Jack Delano, "The 'gossip corner,'" LC-USF33-20540-M1, Stem, NC, May 1940; and John Collier, "A drugstore," LC-USF34-80516-D, LC-USF34-80523-D; and LC-USF34-80540-D, Haymarket, VA, August 1941. Doyle, *Etiquette of Race Relations*, 146–59, quote, 143; Davis, Gardner, and Gardner, *Deep South*, 15–24, quote, 22–23. For the Commission on Interracial Relations, a region-wide body that developed out of the Atlanta Interracial Committee and its findings in the 1920s that African Americans objected to "For Whites Only" signs and being called "Uncle" or "John" in southern stores, see George Brown Tindall, *The Emergence of the New South, 1913–1945* (Baton Rouge: Louisiana State University Press, 1967), 177–81.

121.   Johnson, *Negro Segregation*, 63–65; Myrdal, *American Dilemma*, 627–39.

122.   Doyle, *Etiquette of Race Relations*, 146–47; Johnson, *Negro Segregation*, 71, 249–51; and Dollard, *Caste and Class*, 4.

123.   Davis, Gardner, and Gardner, *Deep South*, 272; Johnson, *Negro Segregation*, 65–70; Myrdal, *American Dilemma*, 637–38.

124.   Davis, Gardner, and Gardner, *Deep South*, 16; Johnson, *Negro Segregation*, 65–70, 296–97; Dollard, *Caste and Class*, 127; Myrdal, *American Dilemma*, 636–39.

125.   John Crowe Ransom, "What Does the South Want?," 178–93; Marion Post Wolcott, "The post office, general store, and filling station," LC-USF34-52116-D, Bynum, NC, September 1939; Russell Lee, "The general store with a cow eating in the foreground," LC-USF34-31749-D, Jarreau, LA, October 1938; John Vachon, "A general store," LC-USF341-15631-B, Diascond, VA, October 1937; Jack Delano, "Garage and general store," LC-USF34-44619-D, Penfield, GA, June 1941. See also Russell Lee, "Negro children coming out of the store . . . ," LC-USF33-11890-M1, Mix, LA, November 1938; and Dorothea Lange, "A country store . . . ," LC-USF34-19989-C, Gordonton, NC, July 1939. Dorothea Lange, "A country filling station . . . these small independent stations have become the meeting place for farmers in the countryside," LC-USF34-20207-E, Granville County, NC, July 1939; John Vachon, "A filling station," LC-USF33-112-M3, Enfield, NC, April 1938; and Jack Delano, "Men sitting on a bench outside a filling station," LC-USF34-40647-D, Stem, NC, May 1940. All these gas stations were covered with advertising. On automobiles in the rural South, see Kirby, "Rural South," 420–21; Joseph Interrane, "You Can't Go to Town in a Bathtub: Automobile Movement and the Reorganization of American Space, 1900–1930," *Radical History Review* 21 (March 1980): 151–68; Steve Gurr, "Toy, Tool and Token: Views of Early Automobiling in Georgia," *Georgia Historical Quarterly* 77 (Summer 1993): 383–94.

126.   Johnson, *Negro Segregation*, 71–74; Kirby, "Rural South," 420–21.

127.   Marion Post Wolcott, "A used car lot. Big sales start after the cotton picking season to get the money the pickers have earned," LC-USF33-30641-M1 and LC-USF33-30642-M3, Clarksdale, MS, October 1939. On segregation of tourist facilities, see the *Negro Motorist Green Book*; and Marion Post Wolcott, "A highway sign advertising tourist cabins for Negroes," LC-USF34-51945-D, SC, June 1939. Davis, Gardner, and Gardner, *Deep South*, 261; Johnson, *Negro Segregation*, 270–71; Kirby, "Rural South," 420–21; Dollard, *Caste and Class*, 126.

128.   Lillian Smith, *Killers of the Dream* (1949; rpt., New York: Norton, 1978), 95–96. Other sources on Smith include the Lillian Smith Collection (LS-UGA) and the Paula Snelling Collection, Hargrett Rare Book and Manuscript Collection, University of Georgia, Athens, especially biographic papers and notes on the preparation of *Killers of the Dream* in Box 1, LS-UGA; Roseanne V. Camacho, "Race, Region, and Gender in a Reassessment of Lillian Smith," in *Southern Women: Histories and Identities* (Columbia: University of Missouri Press, 1992), 157–76; Bruce Clayton, "Lillian Smith: Cassandra in Dixie," *Georgia Historical Quarterly* 78 (Spring 1994): 92–114; Margaret Rose Gladney, ed., *How Am I to Be Heard? Letters of Lillian Smith* (Chapel Hill: University of North Carolina Press, 1993); Fred Hobson, *Tell About the South: The Southern Rage to Explain* (Baton Rouge: Louisiana State University Press, 1983), 307–22; and Anne C. Loveland, *Lillian Smith: A Southerner Confronting the South* (Baton Rouge: Louisiana State University Press, 1990). See Chapter 6.

129.   Al-Tony Gilmore, "The Black Southerners' Response to the Southern System of Race Relations," in Robert Haws, ed., *The Age of Segregation: Race Relations in the South, 1890–1945* (Jackson: University Press of Mississippi, 1978), 67–88, quote, 81; Baker, *Following the Color Line*, 39–44; Johnson, *Negro Segregation*, 268–310.

130.   *Athens* (Georgia) *Clipper*, 31 August 1901, 1, advertisement for the Newtown Colored Enterprise, a grocery store, photograph of this page of the paper in the Vanishing Georgia Collection, Hargrett Rare Book and Manuscript Library, University of Georgia, Athens; Dollard, *Caste and Class*, 87; Myrdal, *American Dilemma*, 638; Johnson, *Negro Segregation*, 272; Baker, *Following the Color Line*, 39–44.

131.   Johnson, *Negro Segregation*, 77; Myrdal, *American Dilemma*, 627–39; Pete Daniel, "Black Power in the 1920s: The Case of Tuskegee Veterans Hospital," *Journal of Southern History* 36 (August 1970): 368–88.

132.   On the racial contradictions in the soft drink business, see the descriptions of Pepsi-Cola in the 1930s as "nigger Coke" and problems with white southern bottlers and their black customers in Harvey Russell interview, 15 November 1984, Pepsi-Cola Advertising History Collection, NMAH. Dollard, *Caste and Class*, 92–93. On whites' experience of the shock of sameness, see Flannery O'Connor, "Everything That Rises Must Converge," in *Everything That Rises Must Converge* (New York: Noonday Press, 1956), 3–23. In this story an elderly white woman desperately trying to keep up the pretensions of her genteel past gets on a bus and meets an African American woman wearing the same expensive purple hat.

133.   Johnson, *Negro Segregation*, 286; James Weldon Johnson, *All Along This Way* (New York: Viking, 1933); Walter White, *A Man Called White* (New York: Viking, 1948);

and Ridgely Torrence, *The Story of John Hope* (1948; rpt., New York: Arno Press, 1969). On the ease of passing in the almost complete anonymity of New York City in the early twentieth century, see Chapter 1. See also the fictional accounts in James Weldon Johnson, *Autobiography of an Ex-Colored Man* (1912; rpt., New York: Penguin Books, 1990); and Langston Hughes, "Passing," in *The Ways of White Folks* (New York: Knopf, 1934), 49–53.

134.   Dollard, *Caste and Class*, 44; Davis, Gardner, and Gardner, *Deep South*, 31–39, quote, 33; Poe, "Negro Problem in Southern Farm Life," quoting a letter from "A North Carolina Negro."

135.   See FSA photographs cited in note 6. Clarence Cason, *Ninety Degrees in the Shade* (1935; rpt., Westport, CT: Negro Universities Press, 1970), photographs by J. Edward Rice between pp. 8 and 9, pp. 168 and 169. Dollard, *Caste and Class*, 64.

CHAPTER FIVE: *Deadly Amusements*

1.   W. E. B. Du Bois, "Georgia, Invisible Empire State," *Nation* 120 (21 January 1925): 63–67.

2.   Allen Tate, "Remarks on the Southern Religion," in Twelve Southerners, *I'll Take My Stand* (1930; rpt., Baton Rouge: Louisiana State University Press, 1991), 174.

3.   Du Bois, "Georgia," and *The Souls of Black Folk* (1903; rpt., New York: Library of America, 1990), 7–48, 59–67. In 1901, Du Bois, exasperated with segregated facilities, asked for Booker T. Washington's financial help in filing suit against the Southern Railway concerning segregation in interstate travel. See David Levering Lewis, *W. E. B. Du Bois: Biography of a Race, 1868–1919* (New York: Henry Holt, 1993), 243–44. On pre–World War I court victories of the NAACP against segregation, see Walter White, *A Man Called White* (1948; rpt., New York: Arno Press, 1969), 39–58. In 1884, Ida B. Wells was the first African American to file a discrimination suit against a railroad. See Ida B. Wells, *Crusade for Justice: The Autobiography of Ida B. Wells* (Chicago: University of Chicago Press, 1970), 18–20.

On blacks' desire for separation from whites in southern urban areas, see Howard N. Rabinowitz, *Race Relations in the Urban South, 1865–1890* (Urbana: University of Illinois Press, 1980), 125–254, and "More than the Woodward Thesis: Assessing *The Strange Career of Jim Crow*," in *Race, Ethnicity, and Urbanization: Selected Essays* (Columbia: University of Missouri Press, 1994), 23–41. But see C. Vann Woodward, *The Strange Career of Jim Crow* (New York: Oxford University Press, 1974), for a convincing view of a relative degree of integration before 1890. Recent scholarship has supported Woodward's argument and found a rising black middle class striving for a more racially integrated future and white recognition of class commonalities across the color line. See Glenda Gilmore, *Gender and Jim Crow: Women and the Politics of White Supremacy in North Carolina, 1896–1920* (Chapel Hill: University of North Carolina Press, 1996); and John William Graves, "Jim Crow in Arkansas: A Reconsideration of Urban Race Relations in the Post-Reconstruction South," *Journal of Southern History* 55 (August 1989).

On sex and modernism, see Jacquelyn Dowd Hall, *Revolt Against Chivalry: Jesse Daniel Ames and the Women's Campaign Against Lynching* (New York: Columbia University Press, 1974), 147–48; and Joel Williamson, *The Crucible of Race: Black-White Relations in the American South Since Emancipation* (New York: Oxford University Press, 1984), 115–17.

4. Miriam Hansen, *Babel and Babylon: Spectatorship in American Silent Film* (Cambridge, MA: Harvard University Press, 1991), 2. See also Jacquelyn Dowd Hall, "Private Eyes, Public Women: Images of Class and Sex in the Urban South, Atlanta, Georgia, 1913–1915," in Ava Baron, ed., *Work Engendered: Toward a New History of American Labor* (Ithaca, NY: Cornell University Press, 1991), 262–71; Daniel J. Singal, *The War Within: From Victorianism to Modernist Thought in the South, 1919–1945* (Chapel Hill: University of North Carolina Press, 1982), 8.

Ida B. Wells claimed that when African Americans stopped riding the streetcars and trains as they saved money to leave Memphis in the wake of the 1893 lynching of three black grocery store owners, one streetcar company faced bankruptcy. See *Crusade for Justice*, 53–64.

A form of violence with a long history in America, lynchings have nevertheless occurred within vastly different social and economic spaces and asserted widely varying cultural meanings. The term "lynching" covers a variety of practices of mob murder; definitions have changed as investigators focused on different characteristics. Stressing "popular justice," James Elbert Cutler, *Lynch-Law: An Investigation into the History of Lynching in the United States* (1905; rpt., Montclair, NJ: Patterson Smith, 1969), defines lynching as "the practice whereby mobs capture individuals suspected of crime, or take them from the officers of the law, and execute them without any process at law, or break open jails and hang convicted criminals, with impunity" (1). Cutler's work was the first academic investigation of lynching. See also Ray Stannard Baker, "What Is a Lynching?: A Study of Mob Justice, South and North," *McClure's Magazine* 24 (January 1905): 299–314, and *McClure's Magazine* 25 (February 1905): 422–30. By 1929, Walter White had decided that lynching needed no definition; see *Rope and Faggot: A Biography of Judge Lynch* (New York: Knopf, 1929). Arthur Raper, *Tragedy of Lynching* (Chapel Hill: University of North Carolina Press, 1933) and the related Southern Commission on the Study of Lynching, *Lynchings and What They Mean* (Atlanta: The Commission, 1933) followed Walter White's lead and gave no definition. In a popularized account of the practice published in 1938, Frank Shay defined lynching as "an execution without process of the law, by a mob, of any individual suspected or convicted of a crime or accused of an offense against prevailing social customs." See Frank Shay, *Judge Lynch: His First Hundred Years* (New York: Ives Washburn, 1938), 7. But by 1940, confusion reigned, and the NAACP, the Tuskegee Institute (an important collector of data on lynchings), and the Association of Southern Women for the Prevention of Lynching (ASWPL) got together to develop a common definition. They stressed that "the group [conducting the lynching] must have acted under pretext of service to justice, race, or tradition." See Jesse Daniel Ames, *The Changing Character of Lynching: Review of Lynching, 1931–1941 with a Discussion of Recent Events in this Field* (Atlanta: Commission for Interracial Cooperation, 1942), 29–30. The ASWPL, however, came to feel that this definition was too broad. Ames also quotes the definition developed by authors of various federal anti-lynching bills, which stressed death or maiming by a mob, defined as three or more persons acting outside the law (22).

By the late nineteenth century, lynchings both occurred more often in the South and mainly claimed black victims. For an excellent theoretical and historical overview of lynching, see Hall, *Revolt Against Chivalry*, 129–57. For white American conceptions of blackness in general, see George M. Fredrickson, *The Black Image in the White Mind: The Debate on Afro-American Character and Destiny* (1971; rpt., Hanover, NH: University Press of New England, 1987). Sources for lynching statistics include the NAACP's *Thirty Years of Lynching* (1919) and *Supplements* (1919–1928) and Monroe Work, ed., *Negro Year Books*, 11 vols. (Tuskegee, AL, 1912–1956). These sources in turn drew from lists kept by the *Chicago Tribune* beginning 1 January 1894 as well as their own research. See also Ida B. Wells, *A Red Record: Tabulated Statistics and Alleged Causes of Lynchings in the United States, 1892–1893–1894* (Chicago: Donohue and Henneberry, 1895). Cutler also compiled lynching statistics through 1903. See *Lynch-Law*, 155–92. See Hall, *Revolt Against Chivalry*, 134–35, for compilations by region, race, and state.

On the lynching of whites, see "Georgia's Body-Blow at Mob Murder," *Literary Digest*, 4 December 1926, 10, for a premature celebration of the end of lynch law because the leader of a mob that lynched a white man was sentenced to life in prison. In 1903 Cutler convincingly argued that the lynching of whites and blacks took place in very different geographies, the settled community versus the frontier community: "There is no psychic connection between the lynching of a negro in the South and the lynching of a [white] murderer or cattle thief in the West" (*Lynch-Law*, 171). For the declining practice of lynching whites after 1900, see W. Fitzhugh Brundage, *Lynching in the New South, Georgia and Virginia, 1880–1930* (Urbana: University of Illinois Press, 1993), 86–102. Between 1880 and 1930, Brundage counts fifteen lynchings in Virginia and nineteen in Georgia.

5. For the NAACP's extensive case files, see NAACP Papers, Part 7, "The Anti-Lynching Campaign, 1912–1953," Series A, "Anti-Lynching Investigation Files, 1912–1953." These records contain news clippings and lynching studies dating back to 1885, but the case files begin in 1912. See also case studies provided in White, *Rope and Faggot*, 23–39; James Weldon Johnson, "The Practice of Lynching: A Picture, the Problem, and What Shall Be Done About It," *Century Magazine* (November 1927): 65–70; Raper, *Tragedy of Lynching*, 59–440; and Shay, *Judge Lynch*, 153–204. See also W. E. B. Du Bois, *Dusk of Dawn: An Essay Toward an Autobiography of a Race Concept* (1940), reprinted in *W. E. B. Du Bois: Writings* (New York: Library of America, 1986), 602–3, 716–39; and W. J. Cash, *The Mind of the South* (1941; rpt., New York: Vintage 1991), 43–45, 116–23, 170, 299–310, on the changing practice of lynching in the South.

6. On contemporary sources on African American women and the ever-present threat of rape by white men, see W. E. B. Du Bois, "Damnation of Women," in *Darkwater: Voices From Within the Veil* (1920; rpt., Millwood, NJ: Kraus-Thompson, 1975), 163–86; and White, *Rope and Faggot*, 62–66. See also Jacquelyn Dowd Hall, " 'The Mind That Burns in Each Body': Women, Rape, and Racial Violence," in Ann Snitow, Christine Stansell, and Sharon Thompson, eds., *Powers of Desire: The Politics of Sexual-*

ity (New York: Monthly Review Press, 1983): 329–49; Catherine Clinton, "Bloody Terrain: Freedwomen, Sexuality, and Violence During Reconstruction," *Georgia Historical
Quarterly* 76 (Summer 1992): 313–32; and Darlene Clark Hine, "Rape and the Inner
Lives of Southern Black Women: Thoughts on the Culture of Dissemblance," in Virginia Bernhard, Betty Brandon, Elizabeth Fox-Genovese, and Theda Purdue, eds.,
Southern Women: Histories and Identities (Columbia: University of Missouri Press, 1993)
177–90. On violence in general and lynching in particular as a form of labor control and
as a weapon whites used against black economic competitors, see Nell Irvin Painter,
" 'Social Equality': Miscegenation, Labor, and Power," in Numan Bartley, ed., *The Evolution of Southern Culture* (Athens: University of Georgia Press, 1988), 47–67; Wells,
Crusade for Justice, 35–67; and Brundage, *Lynching in the New South*, 57, 62–63, 111–13.
Flogging and tar-and-feathering were also used in this way. See William F. Holmes,
"Whitecapping in Mississippi: Agrarian Violence in the Populist Era," *Journal of South-
ern History* 35 (May 1969): 165–85, and "Moonshining and Collective Violence: Georgia,
1889–1895," *Journal of American History* 67 (December 1980): 589–611.

    7. Cash, *Mind of the South*, 118–19. Tate, "Remarks," 174. General studies of
southern violence include Sheldon Hackney, "Southern Violence," *American Historical
Review* 74 (February 1969): 906–25; and John Hope Franklin, *The Militant South,
1800–1861* (Cambridge, MA: Harvard University Press, 1956). On race relations in colonial America, see Edmund S. Morgan, *American Slavery, American Freedom: The Ordeal
of Colonial Virginia* (New York: Norton, 1975); and Peter H. Wood, *Negroes in Colonial
South Carolina from 1670 through the Stono Rebellion* (New York: Norton, 1975).

    On the intertwined racial and political motives for violence during Reconstruction,
see George C. Rable, *But There Was No Peace: The Role of Violence in the Politics of
Reconstruction* (Athens: University of Georgia Press, 1984). Also see Allen W. Trelease,
White Terror: The Ku Klux Klan Conspiracy and Southern Reconstruction (New York:
Harper & Row, 1971). On the history of lynching before the 1880s, see Cutler, *Lynch-
Law*, 41–154. See also George C. Wright, *Racial Violence in Kentucky, 1865–1940* (Baton
Rouge: Louisiana State University Press, 1990).

    Brundage's *Lynching in the New South*, an excellent social history of lynchings in
Georgia and Virginia, focuses on the composition of mobs in his attempt to find an interpretation of lynchings "broad enough to explain banal lynchings as well as those laden
with symbolism" (15). Delineating different types of lynchings by examining the size and
intent of the mob involved, he describes small mobs, less than fifty participants, as "terrorist"—no pretense of upholding the law—or "private"—bent on punishing some
alleged offense. Posses, a third type of mob, varied widely in size and were distinguished
instead by their overstepping of their "quasi-legal" function. Finally, mass mobs numbered from fifty to thousands of members and punished their victims "with extraordinary
ferocity and, on occasion, great ceremony" (19). For my purposes, Brundage's rigid distinction between mass mobs and posses, mob members and spectators, does not always
hold. The difference between women who gathered wood and cheered on the torture
and the men who lit the fire seems more one of gender than mob member versus spectator. Though there were certainly differences of degrees between those whites who carried out the torture and killing and other whites who taunted and cheered their actions

and scrambled for souvenirs, mob members blended into spectators along a continuum, without sharp divisions. Also, both mass mobs and posses conducted what I have called spectacle lynchings. See my discussion of the lynching of Sam Hose.

For a statistical study of lynching, see Stewart E. Tolnay and E. M. Beck, *A Festival of Violence: An Analysis of Southern Lynchings, 1882–1930* (Urbana: University of Illinois Press, 1995).

8.   Michel Foucault, *Discipline and Punish: The Birth of the Prison*, Alan Sheridan, trans. (New York: Vintage Books, 1979), 3–72. See Michael McKeon, *Origins of the English Novel, 1600–1740* (Baltimore: Johns Hopkins University Press, 1987), 98–100; and Lincoln B. Faller, *Turned to Account: The Forms and Functions of Criminal Biography in Late Seventeenth and Early Eighteenth Century England* (New York: Cambridge University Press, 1987), for an explanation of the ways in which the proliferation of the press changed the spectacle of violence and its effects in the early modern period in England, transforming earlier public tortures and executions like the auto-da-fé, the ritualized practice of the Inquisition. According to Faller, "criminals lived their lives over in readers' imaginations, committed their crimes and met their deaths again and again . . . the res publica—less 'total,' more flexible, inventive, and 'modern'—had more than the criminal's body on which to figure (and refigure) its particular concerns. It also had the 'literary' corpus which, in effect its own creation, it stood in his place . . ." (xi). I argue in this chapter that the proliferation of images, particularly in the form of photographs, transformed the life of the spectacle of lynching in the South in particular and violence in general as greatly again as had the printed word three hundred years earlier.

9.   For the modern economy argument, see Raper, *Tragedy of Lynching*, 3–40; and James R. McGovern, *Anatomy of a Lynching: The Killing of Claude Neal* (Baton Rouge: Louisiana State University Press, 1982), 1–41. For an argument about white male sexuality, see Williamson, *Crucible*, 140–223. H. L. Mencken is quoted in White, *Rope and Faggot*, 9: "lynching often takes the place of the merry-go-round, the theatre, the symphony orchestra, and other diversions common to larger communities." See also Gunnar Myrdal, *An American Dilemma: The Negro Problem and Modern Democracy* (New York: Harper and Row, 1944), 563–64.

10.   Hall, *Revolt against Chivalry*, 129–57. Brundage, *Lynching in the New South*, 15; and Edward L. Ayers, *The Promise of the New South: Life After Reconstruction* (New York: Oxford University Press, 1993), 155–59.

11.   Cash, *Mind of the South*, 115; Ida B. Wells, *On Lynchings: Southern Horrors; A Red Record; Mob Rule in New Orleans* (New York: Arno Press, 1969); Frederick Douglass, *Why Is the Negro Lynched?* (Bridgewater, England: John Whitby and Sons, 1895); W. E. B. Du Bois, "Georgia" and "Jesus Christ in Texas," in *Darkwater*, 123–33; Du Bois, *Dusk of Dawn*, 602–3, 716–39; Du Bois, "Lynchings," *The Crisis* (August 1927); Mary Church Terrell, "Lynching from a Negro's Point of View," *North American Review* 178 (June 1904): 853–68, quote, 865; James Weldon Johnson, *Lynching: America's National Disgrace* (New York: NAACP, 1924), and "The Practice of Lynching," 65–70; and White, *Rope and Faggot*.

12.   Spectacle lynchings of African Americans were in no way the most common form of lynching, but they captured public attention and became a central narrative in

the culture of segregation. A partial list of these lynchings includes the 1893 lynching of Henry Smith in Paris, Texas; the 1899 lynching of Richard Coleman in Maysville, Kentucky; the 1899 lynching of Sam Hose in Newnan, Georgia; the 1904 lynching of Luther Hobert and his wife near Vicksburg, Mississippi; the 1916 lynching of Jesse Washington in Waco, Texas; the 1918 lynching of Jim McIlherron in Estill Springs, Tennessee; the 1921 lynching of Henry Lowery in Nodena, Arkansas; the 1921 lynching of John Lee Eberhart in Oconee County, Georgia; the 1925 lynching of Bertha Lowman and her seventeen- and twenty-one-year-old sons in Aiken, South Carolina; the 1925 lynching of J. P. Ivy in Rocky Ford, Mississippi; the 1930 lynching of George Hughes in Sherman, Texas; the 1931 lynching of Matthew Williams in Salisbury, Maryland; the 1934 lynching of Claude Neal in Marianna, Florida; and the 1937 lynchings of two black men in Duck Hill, Mississippi. See the NAACP case files, Part 7; Johnson, "Practice of Lynching," 65–67; White, *Rope and Faggot*, 23–27, 29–33, 35; White, *Man Called White*, 40–42, 56, 58–59; Du Bois, *Dusk of Dawn*, 602–3, 716–39; Raper, *Tragedy of Lynching*, 319–55; Shay, *Judge Lynch*, 168–204; Brundage, *Lynching in the New South*, 34, 82–84; and Nancy MacLean, *Behind the Mask of Chivalry: The Making of the Second Ku Klux Klan* (New York: Oxford University Press, 1994), 150–51. Ames, *Changing Character of Lynching*, gives only a minimal amount of information about lynchings occurring between 1931 and 1941, but she lists eleven where the lynchers are reported as the entire community and one where several thousand people participated and watched. These lynchings include the last three lynchings listed above. Whites in the South were rarely lynched by large mobs and were not tortured. See Brundage, *Lynching in the New South*, 91–92.

Spectacle lynchings claimed at least three African American victims outside the South: in Marion, Indiana, where two men were lynched, and in Coatesville, Pennsylvania. See White, *Rope and Faggot*, 36–37; Raper, *Tragedy of Lynching*, 387–406; Shay, *Judge Lynch*, 149; and Dennis B. Downey and Raymond M. Hyser, *No Crooked Death: Coatesville, Pennsylvania and the Lynching of Zachariah Walker* (Urbana: University of Illinois Press, 1991).

13. On contributions of early cinema to violence as entertainment, see Hansen, *Babel and Babylon*, 1–20. However, with lynchings, at least for the thousands of white spectators and participants, the violence was unmediated.

Literary critic and historian Trudier Harris found that in the early twentieth century the practice of lynching was changing, shifting from an act of vigilante justice carried out by a few white men in an isolated place to a ritualistic event in which masses of whites responded "in community spirit" to an alleged black offense "with burning, mutilation, gathering trophies, and initiating children." Brundage, *Lynching in the New South*, 36–37, however, has demonstrated that what he calls mass mobs and posses committed a small percentage of the total number of lynchings, and yet southerners had mass mobs in mind when discussing lynchings. See his breakdown of Georgia and Virginia lynchings by type (21). What Harris is responding to, then, is less the actual transformation of the practice and more the increasing standardization and circulation of a dominant narrative of spectacle lynching and its growing cultural power within the region and even the nation. See Trudier Harris, *Exorcising Blackness: Historical and Literary Lynching and Burning Rituals* (Bloomington: Indiana University Press, 1984), 2.

Lynchings existed as both physical practice and as written and photographic representations. I use the term "cultural form" instead of the more often used "text" because I want to stress the dialectic between practice and representation and because I do not want to abandon the world in which African Americans died real, very painful deaths in favor of an analysis that recognizes only the realm of representations, even though my investigation must find its evidence there. For thousands of white southerners and some African American southerners, spectacle lynchings existed as rituals observed and participated in firsthand.

14.   Richard Wright, *Black Boy: A Record of Childhood and Youth* (1937; rpt. Harper and Row, 1989), 190; and White, *Rope and Faggot*, viii. For African Americans as members of lynch mobs and as spectators at lynchings, see Shay, *Judge Lynch*, 82–83; and Brundage, *Lynching in the New South*, 45, 178–79. Cash, *Mind of the South*, 118. For lynching as southern exceptionalism, see Cash, *Mind of the South*, 118; and Brundage, *Lynching in the New South*, 3.

15.   See David Nasaw, *Going Out: The Rise and Fall of Public Amusements* (New York: Basic Books, 1993) 72–79, 92–94. On consumer culture, see Richard Wrightman Fox and T. J. Jackson Lears, *The Culture of Consumption* (New York: Pantheon, 1983); Lizabeth Cohen, *Making a New Deal: Industrial Workers in Chicago, 1919–1939* (Cambridge: Cambridge University Press, 1990), 99–158; and Warren Susman, *Culture as History: The Transformation of American Society in the Twentieth Century* (New York: Pantheon, 1984).

16.   On consumption, see Chapter 4.

17.   On the swift standardization of the lynching ritual, see Williamson, *Crucible*, 184–85. On the cultural power of spectacle lynchings apart from narrative developments and journalistic innovations, see Hall, " 'Mind That Burns,' " 331.

Historians have only the mediations, and our studies, whether we acknowledge it or not, are studies not of lynchings but of representations of lynchings. At best we can study documents constructed at one remove from the actual lynching, and many of our sources are double or triple mediations. Thus, we can never uncover what actually happened, only how a variety of reporters, photographers, newspaper artists, witnesses, and investigators represented the event. I am not arguing that actual lynchings followed a particular script, then, but that representations of them did.

18.   For the history of lynching and its development out of frontier vigilantism, regulator movements, and the violence inherent in slavery, see Cutler, *Lynch-Law*, 41–154; John Ross, "At the Bar of Judge Lynch: Lynching and Lynch Mobs in America" (Ph.D. dissertation, Texas Tech University, 1983), 1–27; and Mary Elizabeth Hines, "Death at the Hands of Persons Unknown: The Geography of Lynching in the Deep South, 1882–1910" (Ph.D. dissertation, Louisiana State University, 1993). On lynching during Reconstruction, see Rable, *No Peace*. See Cutler, *Lynch-Law*, 227–28, and Williamson, *Crucible*, 185–223, on the 1890s. On the New Orleans lynchings, see Richard Gambino, *Vendetta: A True Story of the Worst Lynching in America, the Mass Murder of Italian-Americans in New Orleans in 1891, the Vicious Motivations Behind It, and the Tragic Repercussions That Linger to This Date* (Garden City, NY: Doubleday, 1977). Despite

Cutler's racism, relatively mild for the first decade of the twentieth century (the height of what Williamson called radical racism and Du Bois called the nadir of American race relations), Walter White found him "a careful scholar" (*Rope and Faggot*, 252), and all subsequent investigators of mob violence have relied on his path-breaking research.

19. Sources on the 1893 lynching of Smith include no author given, *The Facts in the Case of the Horrible Murder of Little Myrtle Vance, and Its Fearful Expiation, at Paris, Texas, February 1, 1893* (Paris, TX: P. L. James, 1893); Cutler, *Lynch-Law*, 228; Shay, *Judge Lynch*, 92; Williamson, *Crucible*, 185–87; and Ross, "At the Bar of Judge Lynch," 28. For the quote on modern trainmen, see Shay, *Judge Lynch*, 92.

20. *Facts*, no page numbers. See also the photographs of the Smith lynching in the Pictures of Lynchings file, the Division of Prints and Photographs, Library of Congress. Though the victims of lynch mobs do not often live to tell their stories, at least two accounts of lynchings have been written by men who have escaped from lynch mobs. See Irenas J. Palmer, *The Black Man's Burden; or the Horrors of Southern Lynchings* (Olean, NY, 1902); and James Cameron, *A Time of Terror* (Milwaukee: the author, 1982). See also Raper, *Tragedy of Lynching*, 387–406, on the 1930 lynching in Marion, Indiana, from which Cameron escaped.

21. Wells, *Crusade for Justice*, 47–72. See Paula Giddings, *When and Where I Enter: The Impact of Black Women on Race and Sex in America* (New York: Bantam, 1988), 17–31, 89–94; and Gail Bederman, " 'Civilization,' the Decline of Middle-Class Manliness, and Ida B. Wells's Anti-Lynching Campaign," *Radical History Review* 52 (Winter 1992): 5–30. See also Patricia Ann Schechter, " 'To Tell the Truth Freely': Ida B. Wells and the Politics of Race, Gender, and Reform in America, 1880–1913" (Ph.D. dissertation, Princeton University, 1994).

22. Wells, *Crusade for Justice*, 65–66.

23. Ibid.

24. Newspaper sources on the Hose lynching include the *Atlanta Constitution*, 14 April 1899, 1–2, and 24 April 1899, 1–2; the *Atlanta Journal*, 15 April 1899, 1, 3, and 24 April 1899, 1, 3; the *Macon Telegraph*, 24 April 1899, 1, and 25 April 1899, 6; the *Birmingham News*, 24 April 1899, 1; and the *New York Times*, 25 April 1899, 2. See also Mary Louise Ellis, " 'Rain Down Fire': The Lynching of Sam Hose" (Ph.D. dissertation, Florida State University, 1992); Williamson, *Crucible*, 204; and Brundage, *Lynching in the New South*, 34, 82–83. See Mary Church Terrell, "Lynching," 859–60, for African American anti-lynching activists' efforts to challenge white southerners' descriptions of Hose's crimes. See also the *New York Age*, 22 June 1899.

25. See the newspaper sources cited in note 24. Hose was accused of committing the "Most Atrocious crime in Georgia's Criminal Record." Yet the next article over on the *Constitution*'s front page described a white man's confession that he had murdered his wife at the insistence of his mother by repeatedly pushing her down a well and beating her when she tried to climb out. This brutal murder of a wife by her own husband was only the worst crime in "that section" of Tennessee, and law officers had conscientiously moved him to another county to prevent a lynching. The murderer lamented that he had been unable despite his mother's demands to kill his father as well. Quotes in the

first sentence are from the *Constitution*, 14 April 1899. The rest are from the *Journal*, 15 April 1899.

26. See the newspaper sources cited in note 24.

27. Ibid.

28. For Lost Cause images of blackness, see Chapter 2.

29. *Atlanta Constitution*, 14 April 1899; and *Atlanta Journal*, 15 April 1899. The quote is from the *Constitution*. The *Constitution* claimed he blackened his own face as a disguise. The *Journal* said his white captor applied the lampblack. On the details about the trains from Atlanta, see the *Atlanta Constitution*, 14 April 1899, 2. On minstrel traditions, see Eric Lott, "Love and Theft: The Racial Unconscious of Blackface Minstrelsy," *Representations* 39 (Summer 1992): 23–50; and Alexander Saxton, *The Rise and Fall of the White Republic: Class Politics and Mass Culture in Nineteenth-Century America* (New York: Verso, 1990), 165–82.

30. See the newspaper sources cited in note 24. The first quote is from the *Constitution*. The rest are from the *Journal*.

31. Ibid. On a market for lynching "souvenirs," see the *New York Tribune*, as quoted in Shay, *Judge Lynch*, 109: "those unable to obtain the ghastly relics directly, paid more fortunate possessors extravagant sums for them." All quotes are from the *Journal* except the last one, which is from the *Constitution*. Many opponents of lynching attacked this most obvious contradiction of spectacle lynchings, that southern whites claimed to uphold "civilization" when acting in such an uncivilized manner. See Ida B. Wells, *Southern Horrors: Lynch Law in All Its Phases* (1892), reprinted in *On Lynchings*; Walter Hines Page, "The Last Hold of the Southern Bully," *Forum* 16 (November 1893): 303–14; and Thomas Nelson Page, "The Lynching of Negroes—Its Causes and Its Prevention," *North American Review* 566 (January 1904): 33–48. See also Bederman, "Wells's Anti-Lynching Campaign," 5–30.

32. Du Bois, *Dusk of Dawn*, 602–3.

33. Ibid. From this point on, Du Bois turned away from his academic work and toward activism, leaving his life as a scholar for the editorship of the *Crisis* and a more direct battle with the evils of racism. See Lewis, *Du Bois*, 226–27. On the display in a drugstore in Milledgeville, Georgia, of a finger and an ear in a large bottle labeled, "What's left of the niggers that shot a white man," see Brundage, *Lynching in the New South*, 43. On general stores as places of display and even as informal rural museums, see Thomas J. Schlereth, "Country Stores, County Fairs, and Mail-Order Catalogues: Consumption in Rural America," in Simon J. Bonner, ed., *Consuming Visions: Accumulation and Display of Goods in America, 1880–1920* (New York: Norton, 1989), 353.

34. "Negro Confesses to Terrible Crime at Robinsonville," *Waco Times-Herald*, 9 May 1916; "Negro Burned to a Stake in the Yard of City Hall," *Waco Semi-Weekly Tribune*, 17 May 1916; "Who Will Cast the First Stone?" *Waco Morning News*, 24 May 1916. An NAACP press release, "Waco Horror Stirs to Action," quotes a now unavailable *Times-Herald* article, probably 16 May 1916. All these sources are available in NAACP Papers, Part 7, Series A, the Library of Congress, Group 1, Box C-370, Subject Files, Lynching—Waco, TX, Folders 1-3, and microfilm reel 19. See also "The Waco Horror," special supplement to the *Crisis* 12 (July 1916): 1–8.

35. On the Leo Frank case, see Nancy MacLean, "The Leo Frank Case Reconsidered: Gender and Sexual Politics in the Making of Reactionary Populism," *Journal of American History* 78 (December 1991): 917–48; Leonard Dinnerstein, *The Leo Frank Case* (New York: Columbia University Press, 1966); White, *Man Called White*, 25–26; Shay, *Judge Lynch*, 153–61; and Brundage, *Lynching in the New South*, 91. MacLean argues that economic development, acting "as a solvent of older relations of power and authority," created popular anxieties that both made class hostilities "more volatile and more amenable to reactionary solution." She uses the term "reactionary populism" to describe how anti-elitism could support "a political agenda that enforces the subordination of whole groups of people" (920–21). See also MacLean, *Mask of Chivalry*. The culture of segregation, then, made a collective racial identity that narrowed the possibilities for class politics. Whiteness, I have argued in previous chapters, denied the instrumental expression of class divisions but certainly did not abolish them. On the film *Birth of a Nation*, see Michael Rogin, " 'The Sword Became a Flashing Vision': D. W. Griffith's *The Birth of a Nation*," in *Ronald Reagan, the Movie and Other Episodes in Political Demonology* (Berkeley: University of California Press, 1987), 190–235, quotes, 219, 220. The castration scene was cut out of the film by the censors, but the final version hints at it, prompting viewers to imagine Gus's torture (221).

36. On the Washington lynching, see the series of letters between Elisabeth Freeman, NAACP investigator, Waco, TX, and NAACP head Roy Nash, New York City, dated 21–29 May 1916 and undated (the description of the Waco Hotel is taken from Freeman's stationery letterhead); ten black-and-white photos, some made into postcards, taken by Gildersleeve of the town and of the lynching; "The Waco Lynching," a typed report by Elisabeth Freeman, NAACP investigator sent to Waco; a copy of Jesse Washington's official confession; and the local newspaper clippings cited in note 34. Quote from "The Horror at Waco," *Houston Chronicle and Herald*, 16 May 1916. All of these sources and clippings from nonlocal papers cited in the following notes are in the NAACP Papers, Part 7, Series A, the Library of Congress, Group I, Box C-370, and microfilm reel 19. See also James M. SoRelle, " 'The Waco Horror': The Lynching of Jesse Washington," *Southwestern Historical Quarterly* 86 (April 1983): 517–36.

Freeman claimed that her informants originally admitted 15,000 spectators at the lynching and then reduced this number as they became suspicious. When she left, her informants had reduced the crowd to only 500. See her report, 20. Newspaper accounts gave many different estimates of the crowd size. The photographs, however, show that the crowd was extremely large and numbered in the thousands.

37. Freeman report, 14; NAACP Press Release, "Waco Horror Stirs Action"; *Waco Semi-Weekly Tribune*, 17 May 1916; Freeman report, 4; Elisabeth Freeman, Waco, TX, to Roy Nash, not dated; Freeman report, 2.

38. *Waco Semi-Weekly Herald Tribune*, 17 May 1966; Freeman report, 15, 14.

39. Freeman report, 15, 21.

40. Freeman report, 15, 21. The ten photographs NAACP acquired are in the Lynching Pictures file, NAACP Collection, lot 10647-4, the Division of Prints and Photographs, Library of Congress.

41. *Waco Semi-Weekly Tribune*, 17 May 1916. An NAACP press release quotes the

Waco Times Herald on Washington's torture, but other Waco papers did not provide any details. Freeman reported that the *Waco Morning News* had no stories on the lynching and only reprinted a poem, "Vengeance Is Mine" (Freeman report, 21).

42. *Houston Chronicle and Herald*, "The Horror at Waco," 16 May 1916; *San Francisco Bulletin*, "The Background of Lynching," 16 May 1916. Ignoring the effect on the African American community entirely in the first editorial, the *Bulletin* later nodded to the fact that "negroes are lynched on evidence that would not convict a dog in any pound in Christendom" in a second. Still, even this second editorial, "Does It Pay?," 18 May 1916, emphasized that the welfare of the white Waco community was most importantly at stake. *Chicago Defender*, "Police Jail Husband of Dead Woman . . . ," 10 June 1916; *Waco Morning News*, "Who Will Cast the First Stone?," 24 June 1916.

43. The NAACP stepped up its investigations of lynchings in the 1910s and published its important anti-lynching book, *Thirty Years of Lynching*. On the fight for the Dyer Anti-Lynching Act, see Walter White, *Man Called White*, 42, and Robert L. Zangrando, *The NAACP Crusade Against Lynching* (Philadelphia: Temple University Press, 1980), 51–71. For the most recent and forceful argument that modernization, urbanization, and technological advances were responsible for the decrease in the practice of lynchings, especially after 1934, see McGovern, *Anatomy of a Lynching*. Interestingly, though McGovern compares what he considers the almost complete powerlessness of southern blacks in the 1930s and the situation of Jews in Nazi Germany, he fails to recognize that modernization and technological advances were central to the success of the Holocaust and contributed to the very powerlessness of the Jews he describes. See 151–53.

44. Dana B. Polan, " 'Above All Else to Make You See': Cinema and the Ideology of Spectacle," in Jonathan Arac, *Postmodernism and Politics* (Minneapolis: University of Minnesota Press, 1986), 62, quote, 59. By looking, I mean here a variety of experiences: reading voyeuristic descriptions and seeing photographs of the spectacle, physically watching the murder occur, and seeing preserved "souvenir" body parts. In this sense, reading my reconstruction of the newspapers' eyewitness accounts of the Hose lynching is an example of looking at the spectacle, an experience perhaps not entirely contained by my positioning of myself and my audience as morally repulsed by the murder. We, too, are looking and thus also contributing to the power of the lynching narrative.

45. On the Spanish-American War and expanding American imperialism in the late 1890s as increasing northern acceptance of white southern racism, see Nell Irvin Painter, *Standing at Armageddon: The United States, 1877–1919* (New York: Norton, 1987), 141–69; and Walter LaFeber, *The New Empire: An Interpretation of American Expansion, 1860–1898* (Ithaca, NY: Cornell University Press, 1963), 38–39, 78–79, 305–6, 363. Both regions then came to share "the white man's burden" as the "little brown brother" overseas joined southern African Americans at home.

See Chapter 2 for a discussion of white southerners' racializing of Reconstruction history. On the implementation of segregation in Washington, D.C., see "Jim Crowing Has Begun at Washington," *New York Age*, 7 May 1913; and "Are the Negroes Cowards?," *New York Age*, 8 May 1913; both in Tuskegee Institute News Clipping File, Series 1, Reel 1. George Creel is quoted in Rogin, " 'Sword Became a Flashing Vision,' " 230. This entire paragraph draws heavily from Rogin's excellent analysis of *Birth* within the context of American culture.

46. On the Salisbury lynching, see NAACP Papers, Part 7, Series A, Group 1, Box C-358, and Reel 12; H. L. Mencken, "The Sound and the Fury," *Baltimore Evening Sun*, 14 December 1931; and Broadus Mitchell's report on the lynching for Mencken, in Broadus Mitchell Papers, file 61, box 6, the Southern Historical Collection, University of North Carolina at Chapel Hill. On the Duck Hill, Mississippi, lynching, see NAACP Papers, Part 7, Series A, Group 1, Box C-360, and Reel 13; White, *Man Called White*, 123, 172; and Shay, *Judge Lynch*, 247–48. On the Scottsboro case, see Dan T. Carter, *Scottsboro: A Tragedy of the American South* (Baton Rouge: Louisiana State University Press, 1969); James Goodman, *Stories of Scottsboro* (New York: Pantheon, 1994); White, *Man Called White*, 125–33, and "The Negro and the Communists," *Harper's Magazine* 164 (December 1931): 62–72.

The NAACP had been moving toward greater publicity of individual lynchings before Neal. After the 1916 lynching of Washington, Elisabeth Freeman's report of it circulated widely, both as a speech she gave and as excerpted in an NAACP press release. Details of individual lynchings were also cited in *Thirty Years of Lynching*.

47. The NAACP files contain more information on the Neal lynching than on any other. See NAACP Papers, Part 7, Series A, Group 1, Box C-352, and Reel 9. Local newspaper sources include a series of articles in the *Marianna Daily Times-Courier*, 20–27 October 1934; and the *Dothan* (Alabama) *Eagle*, 26 October 1934. Most large American newspapers carried the story. See also McGovern, *Anatomy of a Lynching*.

48. Walter White, New York City, to Howard "Buck" Kester, Nashville, 31 October 1934 (quote); Howard "Buck" Kester, Nashville, to Walter White, New York City, 1 November 1934; and Howard "Buck" Kester, Marianna, FL, to Walter White, New York City, 7 November 1934, NAACP Papers. See also Kester's report, published by the NAACP as a report by a "southern white university professor whose entire life has been spent in the South and whose family for generations has occupied high rank there." NAACP, *The Lynching of Claude Neal* (New York: NAACP, 1934). The NAACP also publicized the Neal lynching through extensive press reports, examples of which are NAACP, "Florida Officials Ignored NAACP Plea to Halt Advertised Lynching" (n.d. but after 27 October 1934), and "NAACP Investigator Says Secret Interracial Romance Was Basis of Florida Lynching" (n.d. but after 16 November 1934), in NAACP Papers, Part 7, Series A, Group 1, Box C-341, and Reel 4. McGovern, *Anatomy of a Lynching*, 126–30.

49. H. L. Mencken, Baltimore, to Walter White, New York City, 30 November 1934 and 26 December 1934, NAACP Papers. NAACP, *Claude Neal*. The first quote is from p. 1, the rest are from p. 2. For accounts of turn-of-the-century lynchings, see my discussion of the lynching of Sam Hose. On Kester's report, see McGovern, *Anatomy of a Lynching*, 126–30.

50. NAACP, *Claude Neal*, 1–8, quote, 2. On the art exhibit, see NAACP Part 7B, Reels 2 and 3, especially the exhibit catalog, *An Art Commentary on Lynching*. See NAACP Part 11, Series B, Reel 28, for an example of a petition with two photographs of the bodies of lynch mob victims circulated by the NAACP and the American Society for Racial Tolerance. See the Pictures of Lynchings from the NAACP archives, Division of

Prints and Photographs, Library of Congress, for a postcard with a picture of a lynch mob victim circulated to raise funds for the NAACP. For another example of a picture of a lynch mob victim circulated by an unidentified group to protest lynching, see SC-CN-80-0188, photograph of the lynching of Rubin Stacy, Fort Lauderdale, FL, 19 July 1935, Schomburg Center for Research in Black Culture, New York Public Library. On the anti-lynching crusade, see Zangrando, *NAACP Crusade*; Wells, *Crusade for Justice*, 87–200; White, *Man Called White*, 3–173; and Hall, *Revolt Against Chivalry*, 159–266. See also the materials on the Writers' League Against Lynching, an organization that included many prominent white and black writers, in NAACP, Part 7, Series B, Reel 4. Other efforts in the publicity for the anti-lynching crusade included a radio play, "Death at the Hands of Persons Unknown," performed over station WEVD in New York City, 1 August 1939, NAACP, Part 7, Series A, Reel 5.

51.   For an example of a letter written by a southern white to protest northern reformers' antagonism toward the white South, see Josiah Moore, Professor of Psychology and Philosophy, University of South Carolina, Columbia, to Florence Kelley, 3 March 1917, Nicholas Kelley Papers, Box 62, New York Public Library. I am indebted to Beatrix Hoffman for this reference.

Cash, *Mind of the South*, 116–22. The image of the "black beast rapist" has remained powerful in our culture long after the practice of lynching was driven underground and even stopped. See Hall, *Revolt Against Chivalry*, 149; and Robyn Wiegman, "The Anatomy of Lynching," in John C. Fout and Maura Shaw Tantillo, eds., *American Sexual Politics: Sex, Gender, and Race Since the Civil War* (Chicago: University of Chicago Press, 1993), 244–45.

It is interesting to speculate about the relationship between consumer culture and a much older Catholic tradition of reliquaries and sacred body parts. The difference, of course, is that the technology to mass-produce representations of the event both transforms people's experience of it and democratizes the ownership of the "relics."

52.   Mell Marshall Barrett, "Recollections of My Boyhood: The Picnic at Pitman's Mill," 49–50, quoted in Ayers, *Promise of the New South*, 159.

53.   A "graphophone record" was reportedly made of the Smith lynching as well. See Williamson, *Crucible*, 186. The best discussion of the symbolic function of lynching is Hall, *Revolt Against Chivalry*, 129–57. I am indebted to her analysis in the arguments that follow.

54.   Page, "Last Hold," 303–14; Terrell, "Negro's Point of View," 860–61; Cutler, *Lynch-Law*, 269–70, 279; Raper, *Tragedy of Lynching*, 46–47; "A New Public Opinion on Lynching: A Declaration and a Pledge" (Atlanta: Association of Southern Women for the Prevention of Lynching, 1935); Jesse Daniel Ames, "Toward Lynchless America" (Atlanta: Association of Southern Women for the Prevention of Lynching, 1940); Cash, *Mind of the South*, 113–22; Lillian Smith, *Killers of the Dream* (1949; rpt., New York: Norton, 1978), 68, 97–98; and Hall, *Revolt Against Chivalry*, 139–42. See NAACP Papers, Part 7, Series A, Group 1, Boxes C-348 through C-370 and reels 7–19 for lynching case studies filed under the names of the communities where they occurred. In the Neal case, "all the white people" in northwestern Florida and southern Alabama were invited by the local papers and at least one radio station, but in the interests of "safety," "a well orga-

nized orderly mob" actually lynched Neal. See NAACP, *Claude Neal*, 2, and *Marianna Daily Times-Courier*, 27 October 1934.

55. The exploration of the function of popular rituals and what theorist M. M. Bakhtin in *The Dialogic Imagination: Four Essays* (Austin: Texas University Press, 1981) called the carnivalesque in upholding the status quo by allowing for a controlled transgression of boundaries was begun by Natalie Zemon Davis in "Women on Top," a chapter in *Society and Culture in Early Modern France* (Stanford, CA: Stanford University Press, 1975), and expanded in Peter Stallybrass and Allon White, *The Politics and Poetics of Transgression* (Ithaca, NY: Cornell University Press, 1986). The most sophisticated interpreters of Bakhtin emphasize the ambivalent and contradictory nature of the rituals and the fact that they do not always contain the violence. See also Mary Douglas, *Purity and Danger: An Analysis of the Concepts of Pollution and Taboo* (1966; rpt., New York: Routledge, 1991), 7–40, for a discussion of how the categories at the center of a given cultural order are maintained. For a provocative discussion of how sacrificial rituals create the very categories, and of how the process of symbol making itself, the foundation of culture, is rooted in ritualistic violence, see René Girard, *Violence and the Sacred* (Baltimore: Johns Hopkins University Press, 1977). For Girard, "there can be nothing in the whole range of human culture that is not rooted in violent unanimity—nothing that does not find its source in the surrogate victim" (297). The culture of segregation is created in the communal, ritualistic killing of African American men. No one is ever more white than the members of a lynch mob.

In insisting that spectacle lynchings are modern, I am not denying their roots in American frontier and even European charivari practices. My insistence on their modernity is instead an insistence on white responsibility, a foregrounding of the complicity of all white Americans and a recognition that violence is central to our twentieth-century social order. For more here, see the Epilogue.

56. Three examples of lynching stereographs, LC-USZ62-26548, LC-USZ62-2462, and LC-USZ62-26548, are in the Pictures of Lynchings file, Division of Prints and Photographs, Library of Congress. Two show the bodies of lynched black men surrounded by the mob; the other shows a picture of a lynch mob. The stereographs are dated 1882 and 1907. For raids on black-owned stores, see Wells, *Crusade for Justice*, 47–52; and Shay, *Judge Lynch*, 203–4.

57. H. L. Mencken, "The Sound and the Fury," *Baltimore Evening Sun*, 14 December 1931; NAACP, *Claude Neal*; Du Bois, *Dusk of Dawn*, 602–3. Photographs and postcards of lynchings have remained valuable items, selling for high prices among collectors at historical document shows even today. Interview with John Gingrich, August 1993, Lexington, GA, historical document dealer.

58. Rogin, " 'Sword Became a Flashing Vision,' " 220–21. Wiegman, "Anatomy of Lynching," in Fout and Tantillo, eds., *American Sexual Politics*, 224.

59. Nancy MacLean, "Leo Frank," 947. See also her "White Women and Klan Violence in the 1920s: Agency, Complicity, and the Politics of Women's History," *Gender and History* 3 (Autumn 1991): 285–303, and her *Behind the Mask of Chivalry*. Other works situate a southern gender crisis in the immediate post–Civil War era. See Drew Faust, "Altars of Sacrifice: Confederate Women and the Narratives of War," *Journal of*

American History 76 (March 1990): 1200–28; LeeAnn Whites, "The Civil War as a Crisis in Gender," in Catherine Clinton and Nina Silber, eds., *Divided Houses: Gender and the Civil War* (New York: Oxford University Press, 1992), 3–21; and Suzanne Lebsock, *The Free Women of Petersburg: Status and Culture in a Southern Town, 1784–1860* (New York: Norton, 1984), 237–49.

60.   Jean Toomer, *Cane* (1925; rpt., New York: Liveright, 1975), 27.

61.   William Faulkner, *Light in August* (1932; rpt., New York: Modern Library, 1968), 147. See also Joel Williamson, *William Faulkner and Southern History* (New York: Oxford University Press, 1993), 365–98; Rogin, " 'Sword Became a Flashing Vision,' " 219–23; and Wiegman, "Anatomy of Lynching," in Fout and Tantillo, eds., *American Sexual Politics*, 227. On the connections between gender, sexuality, and race in lynchings, see Hall, " 'Mind That Burns,' " 329–49; Smith, *Killers of the Dream*, 161–63; and Wiegman, "Anatomy of Lynching," in Fout and Tantillo, eds., *American Sexual Politics*, 223–45. Wiegman argues that "castration literalizes the association of 'womanshenegro' " (227). Another powerful, fictionalized account of a lynching originally considered factual is James Weldon Johnson, *The Autobiography of an Ex-Colored Man* (1912; rpt., New York: Penguin Books, 1990), 134–38.

62.   Cash, *Mind of the South*, 116.

63.   Cash, *Mind of the South*, 84–87, 113–22. For an early examination of the gender implications of lynching, see Jane Addams, "Respect For the Law," *The Independent*, 3 January 1901; and in response, Ida B. Wells-Barnett, "Lynching and the Excuse for It," *The Independent*, 16 May 1901. Walter White was the first scholar to write explicitly about the connections between lynching and sex; see *Rope and Faggot*, 16, 54–75. Black women, though less vulnerable to sexual assault or being drawn into prostitution for white men than before emancipation, nevertheless were still vulnerable. See my discussion in Chapter 4 about crossroads stores as places where white men preyed on young black women, and where black women prostitutes were picked up by their white clients. On the reconstruction of white gender relations, see Chapter 3.

64.   Williamson, *Crucible*, 115–17, 140–41, 169–76, 183–89, 306–10.

65.   U. B. Phillips, "The Plantation as a Civilizing Factor," *Sewanee Review* 12 (July 1904): 257–67, on slavery as a school for "civilization"; Jean Toomer, *Cane*, 27; Hall, " 'Mind That Burns,' " 337. See also Chapter 3.

66.   Freeman report, 16. On Rebecca Felton, see Chapter 2; John E. Talmadge, *Rebecca Latimer Felton: Nine Stormy Decades* (Athens: University of Georgia Press, 1960); Williamson, *Crucible*, 124–30; and Lee Ann Whites, "Rebecca Latimer Felton and the Wife's Farm: The Class and Racial Politics of Gender Reform," *Georgia Historical Quarterly* 76 (Summer 1992): 354–72. The quote is from Rebecca L. Felton to the *Atlanta Constitution*, 19 December 1898, clipping in Scrapbook 24, 76–77, Rebecca Latimer Felton Papers, University of Georgia. On white women's exploiting of the myth of their own innocence and the guilt of the black man as rapist to satisfy their own sexual desires, see Harris, *Exorcising Blackness*, 26–28.

67.   White southern men's condemnation of lynching on the grounds that it brutalized women hinted at this potential masculinization of white women. See Henry M.

Edmonds, "Let'er Burn Down; the Taxpayers Will Put'er Back!: The Cost of the Mob," *Birmingham Age-Herald*, 8 October 1933.

68. Smith, *Killers of the Dream*, 97–98.

69. NAACP, *Claude Neal*. See Marjorie Spruill Wheeler, *New Women of the New South: The Leaders of the Woman Suffrage Movement in the Southern States* (New York: Oxford University Press, 1993), on southern white women in the suffrage movement. On the ASWPL campaign, see Hall, *Revolt Against Chivalry*, 159–266; and Lewis T. Nordyke, "Ladies and Lynchings," *Survey Graphic*, November 1939. Yet their success must be put in context of the NAACP crusade and other efforts.

70. Raper, *Tragedy of Lynching*, 47. Many scholars and activists argued that lynchings occurred because the white community countenanced them. For a sample, see Johnson, "Practice," 67–70; White, *Rope and Faggot*, viii–ix, and "Georgia's Body Blow at Mob Murder," *Literary Digest*. For an interesting examination of the way in which southern industrialists attempted to submerge class difference in a rhetoric of race and gender divisions, see Dolores Janiewski, "Southern Honor, Southern Dishonor: Managerial Ideology and the Construction of Gender, Race, and Class Relations in Southern Industry," in Baron, ed., *Work Engendered*, 70–91. For middle-class African Americans' call for the elevation of class over racial difference, see Terrell, "Negro's Point of View," 856–58.

71. On southern elites' changing attitudes toward lynching, see Brundage, *Lynching in the New South*, 161–90, 208–59, on Virginia and Georgia; and Robert P. Ingalls, *Urban Vigilantes in the New South: Tampa, 1882–1936* (Gainesville: University Press of Florida, 1993), 163–68, on Florida. On the Wilmington Riot of 1898, see Williamson, *Crucible*, 195–201; and C. Vann Woodward, *Origins of the New South, 1877–1913* (Baton Rouge: Louisiana State University Press, 1951), 350. On the Atlanta race riot, see Ray Stannard Baker, "Following the Color Line," *American Magazine* 63 (April 1907): 564–79, for a nationally read piece that blamed the riot on poor whites; Charles Crowe, "Racial Violence and Social Reform: Origins of the Atlanta Race Riot of 1906," *Journal of Negro History* 53 (July 1968): 234–56; Woodward, *Origins of the New South*, 350–57; and Williamson, *Crucible*, 209–23. On the violence after World War I, see NAACP Press Release, 29 October 1919, NAACP Papers, Part 7, Series A, Group 1, Box-C338 and reel 2; Robert T. Kerlin, *The Voice of the Negro, 1919* (1920; rpt., New York: Arno Press, 1968); and Tera W. Hunter, "Household Workers in the Making: Afro-American Women in Atlanta and the New South" (Ph.D. dissertation, Yale University, 1991), 231–92. On loss of property and other financial losses as a result of lynchings, see Raper, *Tragedy of Lynching*, 41–42; and Edmonds, "Let'er Burn Down."

72. On Leo Frank, see MacLean, "Frank," 917–48. See Mencken, "The Sound and the Fury," and *Atlanta Constitution*, 28 October 1934, for condemnation of lynchings in southern city newspapers. The large southern dailies had taken a stand on their editorial pages against lynching early, except for cases of rape. After 1936, most southern dailies condemned the practice editorially regardless of the crime. The problem was that the news columns often supported the mob. After the 1940s, however, few lynchings made the front page and even fewer were announced in banner headlines. See Ames,

Changing Character of Lynching, 15; and Raper, *Tragedy of Lynching*, 23–24. See also Virginius Dabney, "Dixie Rejects Lynching," *Nation* 145 (November 1937): 582.

73. For the decline of spectacle lynchings, see Ames, *Changing Character of Lynching*, 2, 5; McGovern, *Anatomy of a Lynching*, 140–41, and Brundage, *Lynching in the New South*, 37. Only four lynchings occurred in southern cities—Vicksburg, Jackson, Birmingham, and Tampa—between 1931 and 1935. See Commission on Interracial Cooperation, *The Mob Still Rides: A Review of the Lynching Record*, 1931–35 (Atlanta, n.d.), 15. On the continuation of a much more private practice of lynching past 1940, see Stephen J. Whitfield, *A Death in the Delta: The Story of Emmet Till* (Baltimore: Johns Hopkins University Press, 1991), on the 1955 lynching of Emmet Till near Glendora, MS; and Howard Smead, *Blood Justice: The Lynching of Mack Charles Parker* (New York: Oxford University Press, 1986), on the 1959 lynching of Parker near Poplarville, MS.

74. Woodward, *Origins of the New South*, 353, and *Strange Career of Jim Crow*, 108. James Weldon Johnson is quoted in White, *Rope and Faggot*, 33. On nationalism, see Amy Kaplan, "Romancing the Empire: The Embodiment of American Masculinity in the Popular Historical Novel of the 1890s," *American Literary History* 2 (1990): 659–90; and Benedict Anderson, *Imagined Communities: Reflections on the Origin and Spread of Nationalism* (1983; rpt., New York: Verso, 1993).

CHAPTER SIX: *Stone Mountains*

1. Margaret Mitchell, *Gone With the Wind* (hereafter GWTW) (1936; rpt., New York: Warner Books, 1993), 765.

2. Lillian Smith, "Buying a New World with Old Confederate Bills," *South Today* 7 (Winter 1942–1943): 8, 11.

3. Mildred Lewis Rutherford, "The History of Stone Mountain" (no location: the Georgia Division of the UDC, 1923); handwritten chronology and notes; and Ralph T. Jones, "Man's Brain Cannot Measure the Myriad Ages of Time Needed to Make That Block of Granite. The Monument Now Being Cut Will Remain for Millions of Years," *Atlanta Constitution*, 5 August 1923; all in the Stone Mountain File, Hargrett Rare Book and Manuscript Collection, University of Georgia, Athens (hereafter SM-UGA). See also Historical Note for the Stone Mountain Collection, and the correspondence of the SMCMA, 1915, in Box 1, Stone Mountain Collection, Robert W. Woodruff Library, Emory University, Atlanta (hereafter ST-EU).

4. Gaines M. Foster, *The Ghosts of the Confederacy: Defeat, the Lost Cause, and the Emergence of the New South*, 1865–1913 (New York: Oxford University Press, 1987), 40–45, 128–31, 158, 167–68, 175–78, 273; Catherine W. Bashir, "Landmarks of Power: Building a Southern Past, 1885–1915," *Southern Cultures* 1 (Inaugural Issue): 5–45. For race relations and the Great War, see George Brown Tindall, *The Emergence of the New South*, 1913–1945 (Baton Rouge: Louisiana State University Press, 1967), 33–183; and George M. Fredrickson, *The Black Image in the White Mind: The Debate on Afro-*

American Character and Destiny, 1817–1914 (1971; rpt., Hanover, NH: Wesleyan University Press, 1987), 283–332.

5. Rutherford, "History of Stone Mountain"; and Craig F. Thompson, "The Stone Mountain Fiasco," *Plain Talk*, undated clipping circa 1928; both in SM-UGA.

6. On the cultural context of the 1920s and 1930s South, see W. T. Couch, *Culture in the South* (Chapel Hill: University of North Carolina Press, 1934); Fred C. Hobson, Jr., *Serpent in Eden: H. L. Mencken and the South* (Baton Rouge: Louisiana State University Press, 1974), and *Tell About the South: The Southern Rage to Explain* (Baton Rouge: Louisiana State University Press, 1983), 180–322; Daniel Joseph Singal, *The War Within: From Victorian to Modernist Thought in the South, 1919–1945* (Chapel Hill: University of North Carolina Press, 1982), 115–372; Richard H. King, *A Southern Renaissance: The Cultural Awakening of the American South, 1930–1955* (New York: Oxford University Press, 1980); Michael O'Brien, *The Idea of the American South, 1920–1941* (Baltimore: Johns Hopkins University Press, 1979); and John Egerton, *Speak Now Against the Day: The Generation Before the Civil Rights Movement in the South* (New York: Knopf, 1994). Scholars have examined the male members of the generation of 1900, particularly the literary critics and sociologists associated with the Agrarian-versus-regionalist debate and the writers linked together as a literary renaissance; but women have been neglected, studied separately as a category, or tacked on to arguments constructed around white men. While both Hobson and King examine Lillian Smith, Hobson proves unable to distance himself from Smith's southern white liberal male contemporaries' opinions of her. King provides an insightful reading of her magazine and book-length works, but does not account for her close personal and often intimate relationships with other women. See Autobiographical Materials, Box 1, Lillian Smith Collection, Hargrett Rare Book and Manuscript Library, University of Georgia, Athens (hereafter LS-UGA); and Margaret Rose Gladney, ed., *How Am I to Be Heard? Letters of Lillian Smith* (Chapel Hill: University of North Carolina Press, 1993); Roseanne V. Camacho, "Race, Region, and Gender in a Reassessment of Lillian Smith," in Virginia Bernhard, Betty Brandon, Elizabeth Fox-Genovese, and Theda Perdue, eds., *Southern Women: Histories and Identities* (Columbia: University of Missouri Press, 1992), 157–76; and the excellent Bruce Clayton, "Lillian Smith: Cassandra in Dixie," *Georgia Historical Quarterly* 78 (Spring 1994): 92–114. On Mitchell, see Darden Asbury Pyron, *Southern Daughter: The Life of Margaret Mitchell* (New York: Harper Perennial, 1992); Richard Harwell, ed., *Margaret Mitchell's Gone With the Wind Letters, 1936–1949* (New York: Macmillan, 1976); and Ann Goodwyn Jones, " 'The Bad Little Girl of the Good Old Days': Gender, Sex, and the Southern Social Order," in *Tomorrow Is Another Day: The Woman Writer in the South* (Baton Rouge: Louisiana State University Press, 1981), 313–50. Lillian Smith, *Strange Fruit* (1944; rpt., New York: Harcourt Brace Jovanovich, 1992).

7. "A Few Facts about Lillian Smith"; "Biographical Data: Lillian Smith, 12 December 1956"; and "Miscellaneous information, Lillian Smith," all in Autobiographical Materials, Box 1, LS-UGA; and Gladney, ed., *Letters*, 1–2.

8. The quote is from Finis Farr, *Margaret Mitchell of Atlanta* (1965; rpt., New

York: Avon, 1974), 22–23. Pyron, *Southern Daughter*, 50–62, 260–61; Smith, "Travels and Education," 1–5, and "flashback to my personal life with Mother," both in Autobiographical Materials, Box 1, LS-UGA.

9. Smith, "Travels and Education," 1–5, Autobiographical Materials, Box 1, LS-UGA; Mitchell, Atlanta, 28 April 1936, to Julia Collier Harris, Chattanooga, in Harwell, ed., *Letters*, 3–4; Mitchell, Atlanta, 13 May 1943, to Mr. and Mrs. Clifford Dowdey, New York, in Harwell, ed., *Letters*, 369–70; and Pyron, *Southern Daughter*, 14.

10. Smith, "Travels and Education," 5, in Autobiographical Materials, Box 1, LS-UGA; Pyron, *Southern Daughter*, 121, 127–52; and the very revealing letters Mitchell wrote Allen Edee, a student at Amherst she became friends with while attending Smith, collected in Jane Bonner Peacock, ed., *Margaret Mitchell, Dynamo Going to Waste: Letters to Allen Edee, 1919–1921* (Atlanta: Peachtree Publishers, 1985).

11. Pyron, *Southern Daughter*, 120–23; Medora Field Perkerson, "When Margaret Mitchell Was a Girl Reporter," *Atlanta Journal Magazine*, 7 January 1945, 5–7; Harwell, ed., *Letters*, photographs of Mitchell dressed in men's work clothes on a ladder and on a swing, unnumbered pages between 202 and 203; and photographs of Mitchell dressed to ride in a men's felt hat, jodhpurs, and spats, 1 June 1916, and dressed as a storm trooper, taken at Stone Mountain, 2 April 1922, both in Box 168, MM-UGA. Photograph of Smith as a camp director, c. 1927, in Gladney, ed., *Letters*, 153; and photographs in Paula Snelling photo album, Box 68, LS-UGA. On the transition from Victorian to modern womanhood, see Caroll Smith-Rosenberg, "The Female World of Love and Ritual: Relations Between Women in Nineteenth Century America," *Signs* 1 (Autumn 1975): 1–29; Rosalind Rosenberg, *Beyond Separate Spheres: Intellectual Roots of Modern Feminism* (New Haven: Yale University Press, 1982); Jones, *Tomorrow Is Another Day*, 3–50, 313–62; and Marjorie Spruill Wheeler, *New Women of the New South: The Leaders of the Woman Suffrage Movement in the Southern States* (New York: Oxford University Press, 1993).

12. My analysis of Mitchell here draws heavily on Pyron, *Southern Daughter*, 118–23. May Belle Mitchell's letter dated 22 January 1919 is quoted in Farr, *Margaret Mitchell*, 43–44.

13. Smith, Laurel Falls Camp, Clayton, GA, 4 March 1928, to Calvin W. Smith, no address, in Box 4, LS-UGA; Smith, Baltimore, undated but fall 1917, to Calvin Smith, no location, in Gladney, ed., *Letters*, 18–19. "A Skeleton chronology . . . ," 2, "Chronology," and "Travels and Education," 5–6, all in Autobiographical Materials, Box 1, LS-UGA.

14. "Travels and Education," 6, and "Directing the camp," in Autobiographical Materials, Box 1, LS-UGA. Gladney, ed., *Letters*, 8.

15. Perkerson, "When Margaret Mitchell Was a Girl Reporter"; Pyron, *Southern Daughter*, 170–209. Thompson, "Stone Mountain Fiasco"; and Mary Carter Winter, "Stone Mountain: Its Message and Its Memories" (Atlanta: SMCMA, published for the Children's UDC Medal Contest, February 1924), both in SM-UGA.

16. *New York Times Magazine*, 2 January 1916. James C. Derieux, "A Sculptor Who Rode to Fame on Horseback," *American Magazine*, January 1924, 12–14, 66, 68, 70,

72, quote, 13; Rutherford, "History of Stone Mountain;" and "The Memorial Idea: A Brief Sketch of the Beginnings of the Movement for a Confederate Memorial," *Stone Mountain Magazine*, 20 April 1923, 5, 6, all in SM-UGA.

17.   Angus Perkerson, "World's Biggest Photograph to Be Printed on Face of Stone Mountain," *Atlanta Journal Magazine*, 10 December 1922, 1, 4, quote, 4. Rutherford, "History of the Stone Mountain Memorial," 3–5; Derieux, "A Sculptor," 72; Winter, "Its Message and Its Memories;" and "The Memorial Idea," 6; all in SM-UGA. Thomas L. Connelly, *The Marble Man: Robert E. Lee and His Image in American Society* (New York: Knopf, 1977).

18.   SMCMA, "Custodians of Imperishable Glory" (Atlanta: SMCMA, 1925), 6; Winter, "The Memorial Idea," 6; and Warren G. Harding, Washington, D.C., 16 April 1923, to Hollins N. Randolph, Chairman, SMCMA, Atlanta, reprinted in *Stone Mountain Magazine* 3 (1923): 14; all in SM-UGA.

19.   "Custodians of Imperishable Glory," 2; SMCMA letter to "Banks, Bankers, and the General Public," not dated; SMCMA, "Stone Mountain Belongs to the Nation," not dated but attached to previous letter; SMCMA, "Buy Confederate Memorial Coins: The Nation's Tribute to the South," undated promotional pamphlet; Association for the Information of the American People, "The Confederate Memorial Half-Dollar," undated pamphlet; Rogers Winter, "The Founders Roll," undated pamphlet; SMCMA, "The Children's Founders Roll," undated pamphlet; SMCMA, "A Plan for the Children of the Confederacy . . . ," undated flyer; "The Memorial Song," 15–17, and Herbert Myrick, Springfield, MA, Patriot's Day, 1922, to the *Atlanta Constitution*, reprinted as "The Memorial's Cash Value," in *Stone Mountain Magazine* 1 (20 April 1923): 12; Virginia Milmow, "Stone Mountain: A Song and March" (Atlanta: SMCMA, 1926); Richard Peckham, "Commemorating a Great Lost Cause," *Travel* (October 1924): 21–22; "The World's Most Wonderful Monument," *McClure's Magazine* (January 1924); Forrest Dunne, "A Mountain Speaks for America to a World of Critics," *Forbes Magazine*, 1 (December 1925), 15–16, 67, quote, 15; "Making a Monument Out of a Mountain," *Scientific American* (August 1924); A. J. Hain, "The World's Most Wonderful Memorial: The Great Borglum Sculpture on Stone Mountain, Georgia," *Landmark* (June 1924); and other 1923–1925 clippings, all in SM-UGA.

20.   Thompson, "A Stone Mountain Fiasco"; "Borglum and Tucker are Sought on Warrants Following Destruction of Memorial Models," *Atlanta Constitution*, 26 February 1925; "Stone Mountain Not Given to Daughters of Confederacy, Memorial Historian Shows," *Atlanta Georgian*, 14 March 1925; "Howell's Statement False, Says Hollins N. Randolph in Card to the Public," *Atlanta Journal*, 20 March 1925; Walter Davenport, "The Battle of Stone Mountain," *Liberty*, 16 May 1925, 13–16; and "Notable Work of New Mountain Sculptor," *Atlanta Journal*, 19 April 1925; all in SM-UGA. On the founding of the second Klan at Stone Mountain in 1915, see Kenneth T. Jackson, *The Ku Klux Klan in the City* (New York: Oxford University Press, 1967), 5.

21.   Chronology, SM-UGA; Historical Note and Miscellaneous Printed Material, including information on the 1958 formation by the Georgia legislature of the Stone Mountain Memorial Association, which bought the mountain as a state park, and the

completion and unveiling of the carving in 1970, in Box 26, ST-EU. The racial message of the mountain is apparent in the fact that interest in the project regained momentum in the late 1950s as the region's segregated order came increasingly under attack.

22. Dr. James Bond, "The Interracial Movement in the South," CIC Press Release, Atlanta, February 1923; "Southern Editors on Race Relations, Stand for Mutual Helpfulness, Education, Justice, and Abatement of Mobs," CIC Press Release, Atlanta, 1923; and T. J. Woofter, CIC Atlanta, 14 July 1922, to Walter F. White, NAACP, New York; all in Papers of the NAACP, Part 7B, microfilm reel 31. On the CIC, see Wilma Dykeman and James Stokely, *The Seeds of Change: The Life of Will Alexander* (Chicago: University of Chicago Press, 1962); and Tindall, *Emergence of the New South*, 177–82, 198–99.

23. Katharine Lumpkin, no location, 11 June 1924, to Constance Ball, National Student Council, Box 1; Lumpkin, no location, 16 July 1943, to Milton Rugoff, New York City, Box 1; and Application for a Knopf fellowship, Box 4; all in Katharine Lumpkin Papers, Southern Historical Collection, University of North Carolina, Chapel Hill.

24. Smith, "Travels and Education," 5, 7, in Autobiographical Materials, Box 1, LS-UGA.

25. Tindall, *Emergence of the New South*, 293, 297, 299; Allen Tate, manuscript of "The Fugitive: 1922–1925: A Personal Recollection," 14 April 1942, in Box 1, the Allen Tate Papers, Firestone Library, Princeton University (hereafter AT-PU); and Pyron, *Southern Daughter*, 314. The Fugitives later renamed themselves the Agrarians.

26. Allen Tate, "What Is a Traditional Society?," Phi Beta Kappa Address at University of Virginia, 8 June 1936, in Box 1, AT-PU. Hobson, *Tell About the South*, 180–243; Singal, *War Within*, 115–52, 198–263, 302–38; O'Brien, *Idea of the American South*, 31–96, 117–209; King, *Southern Renaissance*, 39–76; Tindall, *Emergence of the New South*, 575–606; and Daniel T. Rodgers, "Regionalism and the Burdens of Progress," in J. Morgan Kousser and James M. McPherson, eds., *Region, Race, and Reconstruction: Essays in Honor of C. Vann Woodward* (New York: Oxford University Press, 1982), 3–26.

27. Howard W. Odum, *Folk, Region, and Society: Selected Papers of Howard W. Odum*, edited by Katharine Jocher, Guy B. Johnson, George Lee Simpson, Jr., and Rupert B. Vance (Chapel Hill: University of North Carolina Press, 1964); Guy B. Johnson, "Does the South Owe the Negro a New Deal?," *Social Forces* 13 (October 1934): 100–3; and Singal, *War Within*, 115–52, 315–27.

28. Margaret Mitchell, Atlanta, 11 July 1936, to Fanny Butcher, Chicago, in Harwell, ed., *Letters*, 41; Allen Tate, "What Is a Traditional Society?," 1–4, 10–11; Mitchell, Atlanta, 7 December 1939, to Howard Dietz, Metro-Goldwyn-Mayer, New York City, Box 75, Margaret Mitchell Collection, Hargrett Rare Book and Manuscript Collection, University of Georgia (hereafter MM-UGA); and Mitchell, Atlanta, 28 April 1936, to Julia Collier Harris, Chattanooga, TN, in Harwell, ed., *Letters*, 5. Tate failed to consider how men who earned a living from slave labor could have been moral. A unity of livelihood and immorality, perhaps?

29. Mitchell, Atlanta, 23 July 1942, to Virginius Dabney, Richmond, VA, in Harwell, ed., *Letters*, 357–59. Virginius Dabney, *Below the Potomac: A Book About the New South* (New York: D. Appleton-Century, 1942), 1–25.

30. Hobson, *Serpent in Eden*; Pyron, *Southern Daughter*, 308–36; Fred Hobson, ed., *South Watching: Selected Essays by Gerald W. Johnson* (Chapel Hill: University of North Carolina Press, 1983); Darden Asbury Pyron, "Nell Battle Lewis (1896–1955): The Dilemmas of Southern Womanhood," *Social Science Perspectives on the South: An Interdisciplinary Annual* 3 (1984): 77–99; letters between Mitchell and Julian and Julia Collier Harris, 1936–1947, especially Mitchell, Atlanta, 21 April 1936, to Julia Collier Harris, Chattanooga, TN; and Mitchell, Atlanta, 27 January 1947, to Julia Collier Harris, Atlanta; all in Box 35, MM-UGA; Mitchell, Atlanta, 21 May 1936, to Lillian Smith, Clayton, GA, in Box 78, MM-UGA; Mitchell, Atlanta, 18 June 1936, to Harry Stillwell Edwards, Macon, GA, in Harwell, ed., *Letters*, 13–15; and Henry Steele Commager, "The Civil War in Georgia's Red Clay Hills," *New York Herald Tribune Books*, 5 July 1936, 1–2, reprinted in Darden Asbury Pyron, ed., *Recasting: Gone With the Wind in American Culture* (Miami: University Presses of Florida, 1983), 11–16. Mitchell, *GWTW*, 421.

31. Julian Harris, Chattanooga, TN, September 1936, to Mitchell, Atlanta, Box 35, MM-UGA; Commager, "Georgia's Red Clay Hills," 12; Mitchell, Atlanta, 10 July 1936, to Henry Steele Commager, Harwell, ed., *Letters*, 37–40; Mitchell, Atlanta, 25 July 1936, to Julia Peterkin, Forte Motte, SC, in Harwell, ed., *Letters*, 46–48; and Julia Peterkin, "Review of *GWTW*," *Washington Post*, 12 July 1936, reprinted in Richard Harwell, ed., *Gone With the Wind as Book and Film* (Columbia: University of South Carolina Press, 1983), 21–23. Herschel Brickell also praised the novel's accurate portrayal of history in his gushing review in the *New York Post*, 30 June 1936, reprinted in Harwell, ed., *GWTW as Book and Film*, 24–27. Less perceptive reviewers missed *GWTW*'s critique entirely. See, for example, Malcolm Cowley, "Going With the Wind," *New Republic* 16 (September 1936): 161–62, reprinted in Pyron, *Recasting*, 17–20, who called it "an encyclopedia of the plantation legend." For an overview of critical attention to the novel, see Richard Dwyer, "The Case of the Cool Reception," in Pyron, *Recasting*, 21–31. Richard King, "The 'Simple Story's' Ideology: *Gone With the Wind* and the New South Creed," in Pyron, *Recasting*, 167–84, especially 181. On the confluence of "the construction and critique of ideological narratives," see Eve Kosofsky Sedgwick, *Between Men: English Literature and Male Homosocial Desire* (New York: Columbia University Press, 1985), 14–15, 8–11.

32. Mitchell, *GWTW*, 5–34, 44–51, 307–10, 314, 340, 345–428, 702–4, quote, 630. This reading draws on Pyron, *Southern Daughter*, 316–33, who notes that Faulkner's Dilsey, characterized as bronze instead of black and as having Indian ancestry, is the exception; and, to a lesser degree, on Elizabeth Fox-Genovese, "Scarlett O'Hara: The Southern Lady as New Woman," *American Quarterly* 33 (Fall 1981): 391–411. On Scarlett and her mammy, see Chapter 3.

33. On the plantation romance, see Chapter 1. Mitchell, Atlanta, 15 August 1936, to Thomas Dixon, Raleigh, in Harwell, ed., *Letters*, 52; Mitchell, *GWTW*, 780–803; and Mitchell, Atlanta, 27 July 1935, to Harold Latham, New York, quoted in Pyron, *Southern Daughter*, 306.

34. Pyron, *Southern Daughter*, 322; Mitchell, *GWTW*, 637–51, quotes, 639, 646, 647, and 646; Commager, "Georgia's Red Clay Hills," 15; and J. Donald Adams, *New York Times Book Review*, 19 July 1936, quoted in Dwyer, "Cool Reception," 23.

35.   Mitchell, Atlanta, 6 September 1938, to Evelyn Hanna, Thomaston, GA, in Harwell, ed., *Letters*, 225–28; Mitchell, Atlanta, 23 July 1942, to Virginius Dabney, Richmond, in Harwell, ed., *Letters*, 357–59; and Mitchell, *GWTW*, 446, 706–10.

36.   Mitchell, *GWTW*, 397–428, quotes, 409.

37.   Mitchell, Atlanta, 19 January 1937, to Mrs. Alfred L. Lustig, Rhode Island, quoted in Richard Harwell, "A Striking Resemblance to a Masterpiece," in Pyron, *Recasting*, 47; and *GWTW*, 343, 398–421. In *Southern Daughter*, 363–65, Pyron identifies the song as Stephen Foster, "My Old Kentucky Home, Goodnight," *As Sung by Christy's Minstrels* (New York: Firth, Pond, 1892).

38.   Mitchell, Atlanta, to Allen Edee, n.d., in Peacock, *Dynamo*, 97; Mitchell, Atlanta, 13 August 1937, to Katharine Brown, New York City, in Harwell, ed., *Letters*, 163; Mitchell, Atlanta, 11 July 1936, to Dr. Mark Allen Patton, Virden, IL, in Harwell, ed., *Letters*, 43; Mitchell, Atlanta, 3 November 1936, to Miss Sara Helena Wilson, Anniston, Alabama, in Harwell, ed., *Letters*, 84–85; Pyron, *Southern Daughter*, 279–80, 347–50; and Joel Williamson, "How Black Was Rhett Butler?," in Numan V. Bartley, ed., *The Evolution of Southern Culture* (Athens: University of Georgia Press, 1988), 87–107.

39.   Mitchell, *GWTW*, 706–13, 800–12, quotes, 523, 611, 765.

40.   Fox-Genovese, "Southern Lady as New Woman," argues persuasively for Scarlett as a "New Woman," an excellent example of rebellious and yet middle-class white womanhood.

41.   I disagree strongly here with the assumption in Jones, "Bad Little Girl," 313–50, that Scarlett returns to the "old days" at the end of the novel. Pyron, *Southern Daughter*, 308–67; Mitchell, *GWTW*, 671, 670, 1023–24.

42.   Mitchell, Atlanta, 22 August 1938, to Mr. and Mrs. Clifford Dowdey, Norwalk, CT, in Harwell, ed., *Letters*, 222–23; Mitchell, Atlanta, 6 September 1938, to Miss Evelyn Hanna, Thomaston, GA, in Harwell, ed., *Letters*, 227; Jonathan Worth Daniels, notes from his interview with Mitchell before 1938, quoted in Pyron, *Southern Daughter*, 110–11. See Jonathan Daniels, *A Southerner Discovers the South* (1938; rpt., New York: Da Capo, 1970), 290–91, where Daniels recounts this interview and the stories Mitchell told him while referring to her only as "a red-headed woman immaculate and immediate from the beauty parlor."

43.   Smith, "About the Novel, *Strange Fruit*," 2; "Chronology"; "The Magazine," 1–5; all in Autobiographical Materials, Box 1, LS-UGA. Promotional material from the magazine, Box 94, LS-UGA. *Pseudopodia* 1 (Spring 1936): 6; Gladney, ed., *Letters*, 23–26.

44.   Snelling and Gannet quotes in Gladney, ed., *Letters*, 23, 28; Paula Snelling, "Southern Fiction and Chronic Suicide," *North Georgia Review* (Summer 1938): 6; Smith, "Wisdom Crieth in the Streets," *North Georgia Review* (Fall 1937), reprinted in Helen White and Redding S. Sugg, Jr., eds., *From the Mountain: Selections from Pseudopodia, The North Georgia Review, and South Today* (Memphis: Memphis State University Press, 1972), 45, 42; and "About the magazine, 1936–1946," 1–3, 9, and "The Magazine," 4, both in Autobiographical Materials, Box 1, LS-UGA.

45.   Smith, Clayton, GA, 16 May 1936, to Mitchell, Atlanta; and Mitchell, Atlanta, 21 May 1936, to Smith, Clayton; both in Box 78, MM-UGA; and Smith, "Dope with Lime," *Pseudopodia* 1 (Summer 1936).

46. Smith, "One More Sigh for the Good Old South," *Pseudopodia* 1 (Fall 1936), reprinted in White and Sugg, *Mountain*, 28–30; clippings in Folder 60, Lillian Smith, in Box 78, MM-UGA.

47. "The Magazine, 1936–1946," 3, Autobiographical Materials, Box 1, LS-UGA. The Hargrett Rare Book and Manuscript Library, University of Georgia, possesses a complete collection of the journal in the Georgia Room.

48. Gladney, ed., *Letters*, 42; White and Sugg, *Mountain*, 137, n. 1; and Smith, "After All, It's Better to Be Livin' Than Dead," *North Georgia Review* (Autumn 1939): 38. "The Magazine, 1936–1946," 3–4, quote, 3, Autobiographical Materials, Box 1; sample "letter to Negro Women," in which Smith describes the segregated accommodations on the train from Atlanta and advises the women to come in a group by car if possible, Box 3; and Smith, Clayton, GA, 1 October 1943, to Eugene and Bertha Barnett, no location, Box 1; all in LS-UGA.

49. On Joel Chandler Harris and Uncle Remus, see Chapter 1. Smith, "Wanted: Lessons in Hate," *North Georgia Review* 3 (Fall and Winter 1938–1939): 12, 13; Clayton, "Cassandra in Dixie."

50. Gladney, ed., *Letters*, 5–7, ; Smith, Brooklyn, 6 February 1946, to Paula Snelling, Clayton, GA; and Smith, Brooklyn, 19 June 1952, to Paula Snelling, Clayton, in Gladney, ed., *Letters*, 99–101, 136–38.

51. Smith, "Chronology," 2; "Travels and Education," 5; "Flashback to 1925–1935," 5, 7; "Comments to Maggie"; and "1922–1925 China"; all in Autobiographical Materials, Box 1, LS-UGA. Smith, Clayton, GA, 30 October 1965, to Wilma Dykeman Stokely, no location, in Gladney, ed., *Letters*, 331–34. The China novel was lost in the 1955 fire.

52. Clayton, "Cassandra in Dixie," suggests quite persuasively and originally that *Strange Fruit*, as a novel about forbidden relationships, was at least in part a translation of Smith's own "forbidden" relationship into an interracial setting.

53. Smith, Clayton, 14 February 1942, to Walter White, New York City, in Gladney, ed., *Letters*, 54–56, quote, 55. Smith, untitled sheet that begins "As I have often said," Autobiographical Materials, Box 1, LS-UGA; Clayton, "Cassandra in Dixie." See also Smith, Brooklyn, 19 June 1952, to Paula Snelling, Clayton, GA, in Gladney, ed., *Letters*, 136–38, quote, 137. Smith, Clayton, GA, 2 June 1955, to Lawrence S. Kubie, New York City, in Gladney, ed., *Letters*, 166–69, quote, 167; and Lawson M. Sullivan, "What's in a Name: Lillian Smith and Lesbian Identity" (unpublished undergraduate thesis, University of Georgia, 2 December 1990), in the author's possession. Smith, *Strange Fruit*.

54. Smith, "Southern Conference," *North Georgia Review* 5 (Spring 1940): 23; Smith, "Are We Not All Confused," *South Today* 7 (Spring 1942), in White and Sugg, *Mountain*, 105; and Smith, "Buying a New World with Old Confederate Bills," *South Today* 7 (Autumn-Winter 1942–1943): 11.

55. Smith, Clayton, GA, 30 August 1944, to "Family," Box 1; Smith, Clayton, 11 December 1943, to Mary McLeod Bethune, no location, Box 1; "Fall of 1944, mainly," Box 1; Smith, Clayton, GA, 1944, "Addressed to members of the Blue Ridge Conference," Box 59; all in LS-UGA. Smith was threatened by the Klan, the Georgia Bureau of Investigation, and anonymous writers and callers. In 1943, Atlanta officials at the Post

Office along with the Georgia Bureau of Investigation attempted to ban *South Today*. See "About the Magazine," 9, Autobiographical Materials, Box 1; and Smith, Clayton, GA, 17 February 1943, to Mr. Rotnem, Atlanta, Box 94; both in LS-UGA.

56. See Chapters 2 and 3 for the elaboration of the arguments condensed here.

57. Smith, *Killers of the Dream.*

58. Edward D. C. Campbell, Jr., *The Celluloid South: Hollywood and the Southern Myth* (Knoxville: University of Tennessee Press, 1981), 118–40; Jack Temple Kirby, *Media-Made Dixie: The South in the American Imagination* (Baton Rouge: Louisiana State University Press, 1978), 72–74, 168; and Thomas H. Pauly, "*Gone With the Wind* and *The Grapes of Wrath* as Hollywood Histories of the Depression," in Harwell, ed., *GWTW as Book and Film*, 218–28.

59. Virginius Dabney, Richmond, 1 August 1942, to Lillian Smith, Clayton, GA; and Dabney, Richmond, 20 August 1942, to Lillian Smith, Clayton, GA, both in Box 2, LS-UGA.

60. Mitchell, Atlanta, 11 January 1937, to Russell Birdwell, Culver City, CA; Mitchell, Atlanta, 8 March 1937, to Kay Brown, New York City; and Mitchell, Atlanta, 30 January 1939, to David Selznick, Culver City, CA; all in Box 75, MM-UGA. For the controversy within the African American community over Hattie McDaniel's acceptance and performance of the role of Mammy, see Walter White, *A Man Called White* (1948; rpt., New York: Arno Press, 1969), 198–205; and Carlton Jackson, *Hattie: The Life of Hattie McDaniel* (Lanham, NY: Madison Books, 1990).

EPILOGUE

1. Ralph Ellison, *Invisible Man* (New York: Random House, 1951), 9, 266. Conversations with University of Missouri colleagues Carol Anderson and Ted Koditschek have been crucial in shaping my thinking in this conclusion.

2. Lillian Smith Collection, Hargrett Rare Book and Manuscript Library, University of Georgia, Autobiographical Materials, Box 1. Toni Morrison, *Playing in the Dark: Whiteness and the Literary Imagination* (New York: Vintage, 1993).

3. Margaret Mitchell, *Gone With the Wind* (New York: Macmillan, 1936); David O. Selznick, producer, *Gone With the Wind* (motion picture, 1939); and Richard B. Harwell, ed., *Gone With the Wind: The Screenplay, by Sidney Howard* (New York: Macmillan, 1981).

4. Ellison, *Invisible Man*, 404, quote, 101.

5. See the *Atlanta Constitution* and *Atlanta Journal*, daily, including special editions, 12–15 December 1939. "Thousands to See Colorful Parade," and "In Heated Discussion: Resolutions Adopted by Baptist Union," *Atlanta Daily World*, 14 December 1939. I would like to thank Emory University undergraduate Michael Forstadt for these last two references.

6. Jacquelyn Dowd Hall, *Revolt Against Chivalry: Jessie Daniel Ames and the Women's Campaign Against Lynching* (New York: Columbia University Press, 1974).

7. On the impact of World War II on the South, see Numan Bartley, *The New South, 1945–1980* (Baton Rouge: Louisiana State University Press, 1995); Gavin Wright, *Old South, New South: Revolutions in the Southern Economy Since the Civil War* (New York: Basic Books, 1986); Nicholas Lemann, *The Promised Land: The Great Black Migration and How It Changed America* (New York: Vintage, 1992); and Harvard Sitkoff, "Harry Truman and the Election of 1948: The Coming of Age of Civil Rights in American Politics," *Journal of Southern History* 38 (November 1974): 597–616. On whiteness and the southern working class, see Michelle Brattain, "The Politics of Whiteness: Race, Workers, and Culture in the Modern South" (Ph.D. dissertation, Rutgers University, 1996); and Bryant Simon, *A Fabric of Defeat: South Carolina Textile Workers in State and Nation, 1914–1948* (Chapel Hill: University of North Carolina Press, forthcoming).

8. Gunnar Myrdal, *An American Dilemma: The Negro Problem and Modern Democracy* (New York: Harper and Row, 1944). See also David W. Southern, *Gunnar Myrdal and Black-White Relations: The Use and Abuse of An American Dilemma* (Baton Rouge: Louisiana State University Press, 1987).

9. Sitkoff, "Election of 1948," 597–616.

10. *Brown et al. v. Board of Education of Topeka et al.*, in Clayborne Carson et al., eds., *The Eyes on the Prize Civil Rights Reader: Documents, Speeches, and Firsthand Accounts from the Black Freedom Struggle, 1954–1990* (New York: Penguin Books, 1991), 64–73, quote, 72. See also Richard Kluger, *Simple Justice: The History of Brown v. Board of Education and Black America's Struggle for Equality* (New York: Vintage, 1977).

11. Bartley, *New South*, 147–260; Carson, *Eyes on the Prize Reader*, 95–96.

12. On the Till case, see Stephen J. Whitfield, *A Death in the Delta: The Story of Emmett Till* (New York: Free Press, 1988); and Ruth Feldstein, " 'I Wanted the Whole World to See': Race, Gender, and Constructions of Motherhood in the Death of Emmett Till," in Joanne Meyerowitz, *Not June Cleaver: Women and Gender in Postwar America, 1945–1960* (Philadelphia: Temple University Press, 1994), 263–303. On postwar race relations, see Lillian Smith, *Killers of the Dream* (1948; rpt., New York: Norton, 1978); James Baldwin and Margaret Mead, *Rap on Race* (1971; rpt., New York: Dell, 1996); Frantz Fanon, *Black Skin, White Masks*, trans. Charles Markman (New York: Grove Press, 1967); James Baldwin, *The Fire Next Time* (1963; rpt., New York: Vintage, 1993); James Baldwin, *Nobody Knows My Name* (1961; rpt., New York: Vintage, 1993); and Ralph Ellison, *Shadow and Act* (1964; rpt., New York: Vintage, 1995).

13. Ellison, *Shadow and Act*. See also Anne Moody, *Coming of Age in Mississippi* (1968; rpt., New York: Dell, 1976).

14. Whitfield, *Death in the Delta*, 33–69.

15. For the history of the civil rights movement, I have relied on Taylor Branch, *Parting the Waters: America in the King Years, 1954–1963* (New York: Simon and Schuster, 1988); David J. Garrow, *Bearing the Cross: Martin Luther King, Jr., and the Southern Christian Leadership Conference* (New York: Vintage, 1988); Carson, *Eyes on the Prize Reader*; Henry Hampton and Steve Fayer, *Voices of Freedom: An Oral History of the Civil Rights Movement from the 1950s through the 1980s* (New York: Bantam Books, 1990); and Bartley, *New South*.

16. See, for an example here, Henry Louis Gates, Jr., "Parable of the Talents," in

Gates and Cornel West, eds., *The Future of the Race* (New York: Knopf, 1996). For a harsh overview of this nostalgia, which discounts the ways in which middle-class African Americans are participating in a broadly American cultural moment, see Adolf Reed, Jr., "Dangerous Dreams: Black Boomers Wax Nostalgic for the Days of Jim Crow," *Village Voice* 24 (16 April 1996): 24–29.

17. James Baldwin, "Sonny's Blues," quoted in Gerald Early, *Tuxedo Junction: Essays in American Culture* (New York: Ecco Press, 1989), 307.

Bibliography

PRIMARY SOURCES

Libraries, Archives, and Collections

Robert W. Woodruff Library, Emory University, Atlanta
    Thomas Dixon Collection (TD-EU)
    Joel Chandler Harris Collection (JCH-EU)
    Julian LaRose Harris Collection (includes Julia Collier Harris)
    Lucy M. Stanton Paintings and Papers Collection
    Stone Mountain Collection (ST-EU)
Firestone Library, Princeton University, Princeton, New Jersey
    William Faulkner Collection
    Allen Tate Collection (AT-PU)
Hargrett Rare Book and Manuscript Library, University of Georgia, Athens
    Black Mammy Institute File
    Lucy Cobb Institute Collection
    Cox College Collection
    Rebecca Latimer Felton Collection (RLF-UGA)
    Margaret Mitchell Collection (MM-UGA)
    Mildred L. Rutherford Collection (MLR-UGA)
    Lillian Smith Collection (LS-UGA)
    Lucy M. Stanton Collection (LMS-UGA)
    Stone Mountain File (SM-UGA)
    Vanishing Georgia Photograph Collection
Southern Historical Collection, University of North Carolina at Chapel Hill
    Katharine DuPre Lumpkin Collection (KDL-UNC)
    Broadus Mitchell Collection
    Howard W. Odum Collection
    Ulrich Bonnell Phillips Collection (UBP-UNC)
Library of Congress
    Farm Security Administration Photograph Collection
    National Association for the Advancement of Colored People Papers
    Stereograph Collection

National Museum of American History, Smithsonian Institution (NMAH)
    Black Motorists File
    Bus, Train, and Druggist Trade Journals Collection
    Sam DeVincent Illustrated Sheet Music Collection (DeVincent)
    Division of Transportation Collections
    Historic Photograph Collection
    Pepsi Marketing Campaigns Oral History Collection
    Warshaw Collection of Business Americana (Warshaw)
Schomburg Center for Research in Black Culture, New York Public Library
    Photographs of Lynchings Collection
    Photographs of Segregation and Integration Collection
    Stereograph Collection
Tuskegee Institute Clipping File, Microfilm Version

Published Books and Articles

Addams, Jane. "Respect for the Law." *The Independent*, 3 January 1901.

Agar, Herbert, and Allen Tate, eds. *Who Owns America? A New Declaration of Independence*. Boston: Houghton Mifflin, 1936.

Ames, Jesse Daniel. *The Changing Character of Lynching: Review of Lynching, 1931–1941 with a Discussion of Recent Events in This Field*. Atlanta: Commission for Interracial Cooperation, 1942.

Andrews, Matthew Page, ed. *The Women of the South in War Times*. Baltimore: Norman, Remington, 1923.

Angelou, Maya. *I Know Why the Caged Bird Sings*. New York: Random House, 1969.

Avary, Myrta Lockett. *Dixie After the War*. New York: Doubleday, Page, 1900.

Baker, Ray Stannard. "What Is a Lynching?: A Study of Mob Justice, South and North." *McClure's Magazine* 24 (January 1905): 299–314, and (February 1905): 422–30.

———. "Following the Color Line." *American Magazine* 63 (April 1907): 564–79.

———. *Following the Color Line: American Negro Citizenship in the Progressive Era*. 1908. Reprint, New York: Harper and Row, 1964.

"Battles and Leaders of the Civil War" *Century Magazine*, November 1884 to March 1888.

Baugh, Hansell, ed. *Frances Newman's Letters*. New York: Horace Liveright, 1929.

Bickle, Lucy Leffingwell Cable. *George W. Cable: His Life and Letters*. New York: Scribner, 1928.

Cable, George W. "The Freedman's Case in Equity." *Century Magazine* 29 (January 1885): 409–18.

———. "The Silent South." *Century Magazine* 30 (September 1885): 674–91.

———. *The Negro Question*. New York: Scribner, 1890.

————. *The Negro Question: A Selection of the Writings on Civil Rights in the South*, ed. Arlin Turner. New York: Doubleday, 1958.

————. *The Silent South*. New York: Scribner, 1885.

Cameron, James. *A Time of Terror*. Milwaukee: the author, 1982.

Cash, W. J. *The Mind of the South*. 1941. Reprint, New York: Vintage, 1991.

Cason, Clarence. *Ninety Degrees in the Shade*. 1935. Reprint, Westport, CT: Negro Universities Press, 1970.

Chesnutt, Charles W. *The Conjure Woman*. 1899. Reprint, Durham: Duke University Press, 1993.

————. *The Marrow of Tradition*. In *The African-American Novel in the Age of Reaction: Three Classics*, ed. William L. Andrews, 213–468. 1901. Reprint, New York: Mentor Books, 1992.

Commission on Interracial Cooperation. *The Mob Still Rides: A Review of the Lynching Record, 1931–35*. Atlanta: CIC, n.d.

Cooper, Anna Julia. *A Voice from the South*. Xenia, OH: Aldine, 1892.

Couch, W. T. *Culture in the South*. Chapel Hill: University of North Carolina Press, 1934.

Cutler, James Elbert. *Lynch-Law: An Investigation into the History of Lynching in the United States*. 1905. Reprint, Montclair, NJ: Patterson Smith, 1969.

Dabney, Virginius. *Below the Potomac: A Book About the New South*. New York: D. Appleton-Century, 1942.

Daniels, Jonathan. *A Southerner Discovers the South*. 1938. Reprint, New York: Da Capo, 1970.

Davenport, Walter. "The Battle of Stone Mountain." *Liberty* (16 May 1925): 13–16.

Davidson, Donald. "*I'll Take My Stand*: A History." *American Review* 5 (Summer 1935).

Derieux, James C. "A Sculptor Who Rode to Fame on Horseback." *American Magazine* (January 1924): 12–14, 66, 68, 70, 72.

Dixon, Thomas. *The Leopard's Spots*. New York: Doubleday and Page, 1902.

————. *The One Woman: A Story of Modern Utopia*. New York: Doubleday and Page, 1904.

————. *The Clansman: A Historical Romance of the Ku Klux Klan*. 1905. Reprint, Lexington: University of Kentucky Press, 1970.

Doughty, Francis A. "Life in the Cotton Belt." *Lippincott's* 59 (May 1897).

Douglass, Frederick. *Narrative of the Life of Frederick Douglass, An American Slave, Written by Himself*. Reprint, Cambridge, MA: Harvard University Press, 1988.

————. *Why Is the Negro Lynched?*. Bridgewater, England: John Whitby and Sons, 1895.

Du Bois, W. E. B. *The Souls of Black Folk*. 1903. Reprinted in *Du Bois: Writings*. New York: Library of America, 1986.

————. *Darkwater: Voices From Within the Veil*. 1921. Reprint, Millwood, NY: Kraus-Thomson, 1975.

——. "Georgia, Invisible Empire State." *Nation* 120 (21 January 1925): 63–67.

——. "Lynchings." *The Crisis*, August 1927.

——. *Dusk of Dawn: An Essay Toward an Autobiography of a Race Concept*. 1940. Reprinted in *W. E. B. Du Bois: Writings*. New York: Library of America, 1986.

Dunne, Forrest. "A Mountain Speaks for America to a World of Critics." *Forbes Magazine* (1 December 1925): 15–16, 67.

Ellison, Ralph. *Invisible Man*. New York: Random House, 1952.

The Facts in the Case of the Horrible Murder of Little Myrtle Vance, and Its Fearful Expiation, at Paris, Texas, February 1, 1893. Paris, TX: P. L. James, 1893.

Faulkner, William. *The Sound and the Fury*. 1929. Reprint, New York: Modern Library, 1956.

——. *Light in August*. 1932. Reprint, New York: Modern Library, 1968.

——. *Absalom, Absalom!* 1936. Reprint, New York: Modern Library, 1968.

——. *The Unvanquished*. 1938. Reprint, New York: Vintage, 1991.

——. *The Hamlet*. 1940. Reprint, New York: Vintage, 1956.

——. *Go Down, Moses*. 1942. Reprint, New York: Vintage, 1990.

Felton, Rebecca Latimer. *Country Life in Georgia in the Days of My Youth*. Atlanta: Index Printing, 1919.

Foster, Stephen. "My Old Kentucky Home, Goodnight." *As Sung by Christy's Minstrels*. New York: Firth, Pond, 1892.

"Georgia's Body-Blow at Mob Murder." *Literary Digest* (4 December 1926): 10.

Gladney, Margaret Rose, ed. *How Am I to Be Heard? Letters of Lillian Smith*. Chapel Hill: University of North Carolina Press, 1993.

Glasgow, Ellen. *Voice of the People*. 1900. Reprint, New York: Scribner, 1938.

——. *The Woman Within*. New York: Harcourt, Brace, 1954.

Grady, Henry. "In Plain Black and White. A Reply to Mr. Cable." *Century Magazine* 29 (April 1885): 917–18.

Gregory, T. Montgomery. "The 'Jim-Crow' Car." *The Crisis* 11 (1915–1916): 87–89, 137–38, 195–98.

Haardt, Sara. *The Making of a Lady*. New York: Doubleday, Doran, 1931.

Hain, A. J. "The World's Most Wonderful Memorial: The Great Borglum Sculpture on Stone Mountain, Georgia." *Landmark*, June 1924.

Hammond, Harry. *Report of the Industrial Commission on Agriculture and Agricultural Labor*, vol. 10. Washington, D.C.: Government Printing Office, 1901.

Hammond, L. H. *Southern Women and Racial Adjustment*. Lynchburg, VA: J. F. Slater Fund Occasional Paper no. 19, 1917.

Harlen, Louis. *Booker T. Washington Papers*. 14 volumes. Urbana: University of Illinois Press, 1972–1989.

Harper, Frances E. W. *Iola Leroy*. 1892. Reprinted in William L. Andrews, ed., *The African-American Novel in the Age of Reaction*. New York: Mentor Books, 1992.

Harris, Joel Chandler. *Uncle Remus: His Songs and His Sayings.* 1880. Reprint, New York: D. Appleton, 1917.

———. *Nights with Uncle Remus: Myths and Legends of the Old Plantation.* Boston: James R. Osgood, 1883.

———. "Plantation Music." *The Critic* 3 (15 December 1883): 506.

———. *Free Joe and Other Georgian Sketches.* New York: Scribner, 1887.

———. *On the Plantation: A Story of a Georgia Boy's Adventures During the War.* 1892. Reprint, Athens: University of Georgia Press, 1989.

———. *Uncle Remus and His Friends: Old Plantation Stories, Songs and Ballads, with Sketches of Negro Character.* Boston: Houghton Mifflin, 1892.

———. *Stories of Georgia.* New York: American Book, 1896.

———. *Tales of the Homefront in Peace and War.* New York: Houghton Mifflin, 1898.

———. *The Chronicles of Aunt Minerva Ann.* New York: Scribner, 1899.

———. *On the Wings of Occasions: Being the Authorized Version of Certain Curious Episodes of the Late Civil War, including the Hitherto Suppressed Narrative of the Kidnapping of President Lincoln.* New York: Doubleday, Page, 1900.

———. *Gabriel Tolliver: A Story of Reconstruction.* New York: McClure, Phillips, 1902.

———. *Told by Uncle Remus; New Stories of the Old Plantation.* New York: McClure, Phillips, 1905.

———. *Uncle Remus and Brer Rabbit.* New York: Frederick A. Stokes, 1906.

———. *Uncle Remus and the Little Boy.* Boston: Small, Maynard, 1910.

———. *Uncle Remus Returns.* Boston: Houghton Mifflin, 1918.

———. *Complete Tales of Uncle Remus,* ed. Richard Chase. Boston: Houghton Mifflin, 1955.

Harris, Julia Collier. *The Life and Letters of Joel Chandler Harris.* New York: Houghton Mifflin, 1918.

———. *Joel Chandler Harris, Editor and Essayist: Miscellaneous Literary, Political, and Social Writings.* Chapel Hill: University of North Carolina, 1931.

Harwell, Richard, ed. *Margaret Mitchell's Gone With the Wind Letters, 1936–1949.* New York: Macmillan, 1976.

Hobson, Fred, ed. *South Watching: Selected Essays by Gerald W. Johnson.* Chapel Hill: University of North Carolina Press, 1983.

Huggins, Nathan I., ed. *Voices of the Harlem Renaissance.* New York: Oxford University Press, 1995.

Hughes, Langston. *The Ways of White Folks.* New York: Knopf, 1934.

Hurston, Zora Neale. *Their Eyes Were Watching God.* 1937. Reprint, New York: Harper Perennial, 1991.

———. *Dust Tracks on a Road.* 1942. Reprint, New York: Harper Perennial, 1991.

Jacobs, Harriet A. *Incidents in the Life of a Slave Girl.* 1861. Reprint, Cambridge, MA: Harvard University Press, 1987.

Johnson, Guy B. "Does the South Owe the Negro a New Deal?" *Social Forces* 13 (October 1934): 100–3.

Johnson, James Weldon. *The Autobiography of an Ex-Colored Man*. 1912. New York: Viking, 1933. Reprint, New York: Penguin Books, 1990.

———. *Lynching: America's National Disgrace*. New York: NAACP, 1924.

———. "The Practice of Lynching: A Picture, the Problem, and What Shall Be Done About It." *Century Magazine* (November 1927): 65–70.

———. *All Along This Way: The Autobiography of James Weldon Johnson*. 1933. Reprint, New York: Penguin Books, 1990.

Kearney, Belle. *A Slaveholder's Daughter*. New York: Abbey Press, 1900.

Keenan, Hugh T., ed. *Dearest Chums and Partners: Joel Chandler Harris's Letters to His Children*. Athens: University of Georgia Press, 1993.

Larsen, Nella. *Quicksand* and *Passing*. 1928, 1929. Reprint, New Brunswick, NJ: Rutgers University Press, 1988.

Le Guin, Charles A., ed. *A Home-Concealed Woman: The Diaries of Magnolia Wynn Le Guin, 1901–1913*. Athens: University of Georgia Press, 1990.

Lumpkin, Katharine DuPre. *The South in Progress*. New York: International Publishers, 1940.

———. *The Making of a Southerner*. 1947. Reprint, Athens: University of Georgia Press, 1991.

"Making a Monument Out of a Mountain." *Scientific American*, August 1924.

McCullers, Carson. *The Ballad of the Sad Cafe*. 1951. Reprint, New York: Bantam, 1971.

McLaurin, Melton A. *Separate Pasts: Growing Up White in the Segregated South*. Athens: University of Georgia Press, 1987.

"The Memorial Idea: A Brief Sketch of the Beginnings of the Movement for a Confederate Memorial." *Stone Mountain Magazine* 1 (20 April 1923): 5, 6.

Milmow, Virginia. "Stone Mountain: A Song and March." Atlanta: SMCMA, 1926.

Mitchell, Margaret. *Gone With the Wind*. 1936. Reprint, New York: Warner Books, 1993.

Moon, Bucklin, ed. *Primer for White Folks*. Garden City, NY: Doubleday, Doran, 1945.

Moses, Wilson Jeremiah, ed. *Classical Black Nationalism: From the American Revolution to Marcus Garvey*. New York: New York University Press, 1996.

Murphy, Edgar Gardner. *Problems of the Present South*. New York: Macmillan, 1904.

———. *The Basis of Ascendancy*. New York: Longmans, 1909.

Myrick, Herbert. "The Memorial's Cash Value." *Stone Mountain Magazine* 1 (20 April 1923): 12.

NAACP. *Thirty Years of Lynching*. New York: NAACP, 1919.

———. *The Lynching of Claude Neal*. New York: NAACP, 1934.

"A Negro Car Line." *Horseless Age* 16 (20 September 1905): 347.

The Negro Motorist's Green Book. New York: Victor H. Green, 1938.

Newman, Frances. *The Hard Boiled Virgin.* New York: Boni and Liveright, 1926.

———. *Dead Lovers Are Faithful Lovers.* New York: Boni and Liveright, 1928.

O'Connor, Flannery. *A Good Man Is Hard to Find.* 1955. Reprint, New York: Harcourt, Brace, 1983.

———. *Everything That Rises Must Converge.* 1956. Reprint, New York: Noonday Press, 1993.

Odum, Howard W. *Folk, Region, and Society: Selected Papers of Howard W. Odum,* ed. Katharine Jocher, Guy B. Johnson, George Lee Simpson, Jr., and Rupert B. Vance. Chapel Hill: University of North Carolina Press, 1964.

Official Views: Cotton States and International Exposition, Atlanta, 1895. St Louis: C. B. Woodward, 1895.

Our Silver Anniversary: Being a Brief and Concise History of the Mail-Order or Catalogue Business Which Was Invented by Us a Quarter of a Century Ago. Chicago: Montgomery Ward Co., 1897.

Page, Thomas Nelson. *In Ole Virginia; or Marse Chan and Other Stories.* New York: Scribner, 1887.

———. *The Old South: Essays Social and Political.* New York: Scribner, 1892.

———. *Red Rock: A Chronicle of Reconstruction.* New York: Scribner, 1898.

———. *Pastime Stories.* New York: Scribner, 1898.

———. *Social Life in Old Virginia Before the War.* New York: Scribner, 1898.

———. *The Old Gentleman of the Black Stock.* New York: Scribner, 1900.

———. *The Negro: The Southerner's Problem.* New York: Scribner, 1904.

———. *Bred in the Bone.* New York: Scribner, 1904.

———. "The Lynching of Negroes—Its Causes and Its Prevention." *North American Review* 566 (January 1904): 33–48.

Page, Walter Hines. "The Last Hold of the Southern Bully." *Forum* 16 (November 1983): 303–14.

Palmer, Irenas J. *The Black Man's Burden; or the Horrors of Southern Lynchings.* Olean, NY: the author, 1902.

Peacock, Jane Bonner, ed. *Margaret Mitchell, Dynamo Going to Waste: Letters to Allen Edee, 1919–1921.* Atlanta: Peachtree, 1985.

Peckham, Richard. "Commemorating a Great Lost Cause." *Travel,* October 1924, 21–22.

Percy, William Alexander. *Lanterns on the Levee: Recollections of a Planter's Son.* 1941. Reprint, Baton Rouge: Louisiana State University Press, 1994.

Perkerson, Angus. "World's Biggest Photograph to Be Printed on Face of Stone Mountain." *Atlanta Journal Magazine* (10 December 1922): 1, 4.

Perkerson, Medora Field. "When Margaret Mitchell Was a Girl Reporter." *Atlanta Journal Magazine* (7 January 1945): 5–7.

Phillips, Ulrich B. "The Economics of the Plantation." *South Atlantic Quarterly* 2 (July 1903): 231–36.

——. "The Plantation as a Civilizing Factor." *Sewanee Review* 12 (July 1904): 257–67.

——. "The Economics of Slave Labor in the South." In *The South in the Building of the Nation*, ed. Julian A. C. Chandler et al., vol. 5, 121–24. Richmond: Southern Historical Publication Society, 1909.

——. *American Negro Slavery.* 1918. Reprint, Baton Rouge: Louisiana State University Press, 1966.

——. "The Plantation Product of Men." *Proceedings of the Second Annual Session of the Georgia Historical Association.* Atlanta: Georgia Historical Association, 1918.

——. "Plantations with Slave Labor and Free." *American Historical Review* 30 (July 1925): 738–53.

——. "The Central Theme of Southern History." *American Historical Review* 34 (October 1928): 30–43.

Pollard, E. A. *The Lost Cause: A New Southern History of the War of the Confederates.* New York: Carleton, 1866.

——. *The Lost Cause Regained.* New York: Carleton, 1868.

Proceedings of the Convention of Southern Governors, Held in the City of Richmond, Virginia on April 12 and 13, 1893. Richmond: published by the governors of Arkansas, Alabama, Louisiana, Maryland, Mississippi, North Carolina, South Carolina, and Virginia, 1893.

"Report to the President on the Economic Conditions of the South." Washington, D. C., 1938.

Rice, John Andrew. *I Came Out of the Eighteenth Century.* New York: Harper, 1942.

Robertson, Ben. *Red Hills and Cotton: An Upcountry Memoir.* 1942. Reprint, Columbia: University of South Carolina Press, 1960.

Rouse, Blair, ed. *Letters of Ellen Glasgow.* New York: Harcourt, Brace, 1958.

Rutherford, Mildred L. *Mannie Brown That School Girl.* Buffalo, NY: Peter Paul, 1896.

——. *The South in the Building of the Nation: Thirteen Periods of United States History.* Athens, GA: the author, 1913.

——. *Four Addresses.* Birmingham, AL: Mildred Rutherford Historical Circle, 1916.

——. *What the South May Claim.* Athens, GA: McGregor, 1916.

——. *The Civilization of the Old South: What Made It; What Destroyed It; What Has Replaced It.* Athens, GA: the author, 1916.

——. *Where the South Leads and Where Georgia Leads.* Athens, GA: McGregor, 1917.

——. *A Measuring Rod to Test Books and Reference Books in Schools, Colleges and Libraries.* Athens, GA: the author, 1919.

——. *Facts and Figures vs. Myths and Misrepresentations: Henry Wirz and the Andersonville Prison.* Athens, GA: the author, 1921.

——. *The South Must Have Her Rightful Place in History.* Athens, GA: the author, 1923.

——. *The History of the Stone Mountain Memorial*. Atlanta: United Daughters of the Confederacy, 1924.

——. *Georgia: The Thirteenth Colony*. Athens, GA: McGregor, 1926.

Schuyler, George S. "Traveling Jim Crow." *American Mercury* (August 1930): 423–32.

SMCMA. "Custodians of Imperishable Glory." Atlanta: SMCMA, 1925.

Smith, F. Hopkinson. *Colonel Carter of Cartersville*. Boston: Houghton Mifflin, 1891.

Smith, Lillian. "Wanted: Lessons in Hate." *North Georgia Review* 3 (Fall and Winter 1938–1939): 12–13.

——. "After All, It's Better to Be Livin' Than Dead." *North Georgia Review* (Autumn 1939): 38.

——. "Buying a New World with Old Confederate Bills." *South Today* 7 (Winter 1942–1943): 8–11.

——. *Strange Fruit*. 1944. Reprint, New York: Harcourt Brace Jovanovich, 1992.

——. *Killers of the Dream*. 1948. Reprint, New York: Norton, 1978.

Snelling, Paula. "Southern Fiction and Chronic Suicide." *North Georgia Review* (Summer 1938): 6.

Southern Commission on the Study of Lynching. *Lynchings and What They Mean*. Atlanta: SCSL, 1933.

Stanton, Mary I. "Two Master Farmers of the Seventies." *Georgia Review* (Spring 1962): 23–34.

Stowe, Harriet Beecher. *Uncle Tom's Cabin*. Boston, 1852.

Terrell, Mary Church. "Lynching from a Negro's Point of View." *North American Review* 178 (June 1904): 853–68.

——. *A Colored Woman in a White World*. 1940. Reprint, New York: Arno Press, 1980.

——. "The World's Most Wonderful Monument." *McClure's Magazine*, January 1924.

Timmons, Robert. "Aged Ex-Slaves Gather at Home of Old Master." In *The Possibilities of the Negro in Symposium*, 69–73. Atlanta, 1904.

Tourgee, Albion. "The South as a Field for Fiction." *Forum* 6 (December 1888): 404–18.

Twelve Southerners. *I'll Take My Stand*. 1930. Reprint, Baton Rouge: Louisiana State University Press, 1991.

Wagstaff, Thomas, ed. *Black Power: The Radical Response to White America*. Beverly Hills: Glencoe, 1969.

Washington, Booker T. "Signs of Progress Among the Negroes." *Century Magazine* 3 (January 1900): 472.

——. *Up From Slavery*. 1901. Reprint, New York: University Books, 1993.

———. *The Story of the Negro: The Rise of the Race from Slavery*, vol. 2. New York: T. Fisher Unwin, 1909.

———, ed. *The Negro Problem: A Series of Articles by Representative Negroes of Today*. New York: James Pott, 1903.

Weeden, Howard. *Shadows on the Wall*. New York: Doubleday and McClure, 1898.

———. *Bandanna Ballads*. Doubleday and McClure, 1899.

Wells, Ida B. *On Lynchings: Southern Horrors; A Red Record; Mob Rule in New Orleans*. 1892, 1895, 1900. Reprint, New York: Arno Press, 1969.

———. *Crusade for Justice: The Autobiography of Ida B. Wells*. Chicago: University of Chicago Press, 1970.

Wells-Barnett, Ida B. "Lynching and the Excuse for It." *The Independent* (16 May 1901).

———. *Songs of the Old South*. New York: Doubleday, Page, 1901.

———. *Old Voices*. New York: Doubleday, Page, 1904.

White, Helen, and Redding S. Sugg, Jr., eds. *From the Mountain: Selections from Pseudopodia, The North Georgia Review, and South Today*. Memphis: Memphis State University Press, 1972.

White, Walter. "The Negro and the Communists." *Harper's Magazine* 164 (December 1931): 62–72.

———. *A Man Called White*. 1948. Reprint, New York: Arno Press, 1969.

Winter, Mary Carter. "Stone Mountain: Its Message and Its Memories." Atlanta: SMCMA, published for the Children's UDC Medal Contest, February 1924.

Work, Monroe, ed. *Negro Year Books*. 11 vols. Tuskegee, AL: Tuskegee Institute, 1912–1956.

Wright, Richard. *Black Boy: A Record of Childhood and Youth*, 1937. Reprint, New York: Harper and Row, 1989.

Motion Pictures

Birth of a Nation. D. W. Griffith, producer and director. 1915.

Gone With the Wind. David O. Selznick, producer. Victor Fleming, director. 1939.

SECONDARY SOURCES

Published Books and Articles

Alexander, Adele Logan. *Ambiguous Lives: Free Women of Color in Rural Georgia, 1789–1879*. Fayetteville: University of Arkansas Press, 1991.

Allen, Theodore W. *The Invention of the White Race: Racial Oppression and Social Control*. New York: Verso, 1994.

Anderson, Benedict. *Imagined Communities: Reflections on the Origin and Spread of Nationalism*. New York: Verso, 1993.

Anderson, James D. *The Education of Blacks in the South, 1860–1935.* Chapel Hill: University of North Carolina Press, 1988.

Appiah, Kwame Anthony. *In My Father's House: Africa and the Philosophy of Culture.* New York: Oxford University Press, 1992.

Ayers, Edward L. *Vengeance and Justice: Crime and Punishment in the Nineteenth Century American South.* New York: Oxford University Press, 1984.

———. *The Promise of the New South: Life After Reconstruction.* New York: Oxford University Press, 1993.

Bailey, Fred Arthur. "Mildred Lewis Rutherford and the Patrician Cult of the New South." *Georgia Historical Quarterly* 78 (Fall 1994): 509–35.

Baker, Nina. *Big Catalogue: The Life of Aaron Montgomery Ward.* New York: Harcourt, Brace, 1956.

Bakhtin, M. M. *The Dialogic Imagination: Four Essays.* Austin: Texas University Press, 1981.

Barthes, Roland. *Camera Lucida: Reflections on Photography.* 1980. Reprint, New York: Hill and Wang, 1993.

Bashir, Catherine W. "Landmarks of Power: Building a Southern Past, 1885–1915." *Southern Cultures* 1 (Inaugural Issue): 5–45.

Bederman, Gail. " 'Civilization,' the Decline of Middle-Class Manliness, and Ida B. Wells' Anti-Lynching Campaign." *Radical History Review* 52 (Winter 1992): 5–30.

Berlin, Ira. *Slaves Without Masters: The Free Negro in the Antebellum South.* New York: Norton, 1976.

Bickley, Bruce, Jr. *Critical Essays on Joel Chandler Harris.* Boston: G. K. Hall, 1981.

Bledstein, Barton J. "Case Law in *Plessy v. Ferguson.*" *Journal of Negro History* 47 (July 1962): 192–98.

———. *The Culture of Professionalism: The Middle Class and the Development of Higher Education in America.* New York: Norton, 1976.

Blumin, Stuart M. *The Emergence of the Middle Class: Social Experience in the American City, 1760–1900.* New York: Cambridge University Press, 1989.

Bogle, Donald. *Coons, Mulattos, Mammies, and Bucks.* New York: Viking, 1973.

Boles, Jon B., and Evelyn Thomas Nolen, eds. *Interpreting Southern History: Historiographic Essays in Honor of Sanford W. Higginbotham.* Baton Rouge: Louisiana State University Press, 1987.

Boydston, Jeanne. *Home and Work: Housework, Wages, and the Ideology of Labor in the Early Republic.* New York: Oxford University Press, 1990.

Branch, Taylor. *Parting the Waters: America in the King Years, 1954–1963.* New York: Simon and Schuster, 1988.

Brownwell, Blaine A., and David R. Goldfield, eds. *The City in Southern History: The Growth of Urban Civilization in the South.* Port Washington, NY: Kennikat, 1977.

Brundage, Fitzhugh. "A Portrait of Southern Sharecropping: The 1911–1912 Georgia Plantation Survey of Robert Preston Brooks." *Georgia Historical Quarterly* 77 (Summer 1993): 367–81.

——. *Lynching in the New South, Georgia and Virginia, 1880–1930*. Urbana: University of Illinois Press, 1993.

Burgess, John W. *Reconstruction and the Constitution, 1866–1876*. New York, 1902.

Bushman, Claudia, and Richard Bushman. "The Early History of Cleanliness in America." *Journal of American History* 75 (December 1988): 675–725.

Bushman, Richard L. *The Refinement of America: Persons, Houses, Cities*. New York: Knopf, 1992.

Camacho, Roseanne V. "Race, Region, and Gender in a Reassessment of Lillian Smith." In Virginia Bernhard, Betty Brandon, Elizabeth Fox-Genovese, and Theda Perdue, eds., *Southern Women: Histories and Identities*. Columbia: University of Missouri Press, 1992.

Camhi, Jane Jerome. *Women Against Women: American Anti-Suffragism, 1880–1920*. New York: Carlson, 1994.

Campbell, Edward D. C., Jr. *The Celluloid South: Hollywood and the Southern Myth*. Knoxville: University of Tennessee Press, 1981.

Carby, Hazel. *Reconstructing Womanhood: The Emergence of the Afro-American Woman Novelist*. New York: Oxford University Press, 1987.

Carson, Clayborne. *In Struggle: SNCC and the Black Awakening of the 1960s*. Cambridge, MA: Harvard University Press, 1981.

Carson, Gerald. *The Old Country Store*. New York: Dutton, 1965.

Carter, Dan T. *Scottsboro: A Tragedy of the American South*. Baton Rouge: Louisiana State University Press, 1969.

Cartwright, Joseph H. *The Triumph of Jim Crow: Tennessee Race Relations in the 1880s*. Knoxville: University of Tennessee Press, 1976.

Cell, John T. *The Highest Stage of White Supremacy: The Origins of Segregation in South Africa and the American South*. Cambridge: Cambridge University Press, 1982.

Censer, Jane Turner. *North Carolina Planters and Their Children, 1800–1860*. Baton Rouge: Louisiana State University Press, 1984.

Chappell, David L. *Inside Agitators: White Southerners and the Civil Rights Movement*. Baltimore: Johns Hopkins University Press, 1994.

Clare, Virginia. *Thunder and Stars*. Atlanta: Ogelthorpe University Press, 1941.

Clark, Clifford Edward, Jr. *The American Family Home, 1800–1960*. Chapel Hill: University of North Carolina Press, 1986.

Clark, Thomas D. *Pills, Petticoats, and Plows: The Southern Country Store*. Indianapolis: Bobbs-Merrill, 1944.

Clark-Lewis, Elizabeth. *Living In, Living Out: African American Domestics in Washington, D.C., 1910–1940*. Washington, D.C.: Smithsonian Institution, 1994.

Clayton, Bruce. "Lillian Smith: Cassandra in Dixie." *Georgia Historical Quarterly* 78 (Spring 1994): 92–114.

Clinton, Catherine. *The Plantation Mistress: Women's World in the Old South*. New York: Pantheon, 1982.

——. "Bloody Terrain: Freedwomen, Sexuality, and Violence During Reconstruction." *Georgia Historical Quarterly* 76 (Summer 1992): 313–32.

Clinton, Catherine, and Nina Silber, eds. *Divided Houses: Gender and the Civil War*. New York: Oxford University Press, 1992.

Cohen, David L. *The Good Old Days: A History of American Morals and Manners as Seen through the Sears, Roebuck Catalogs, 1905 to the Present*. New York: Simon and Schuster, 1940.

Cohen, Lizabeth. *Making a New Deal: Industrial Workers in Chicago, 1919–1939*. Cambridge: Cambridge University Press, 1990.

Cohen, William. *At Freedom's Edge: Black Mobility and the Southern Quest for Racial Control, 1861–1915*. Baton Rouge: Louisiana State University Press, 1987.

Connelly, Thomas L. *The Marble Man: Robert E. Lee and His Image in American Society*. New York: Knopf, 1977.

Cowen, Ruth Schwartz. *More Work for Mother: The Ironies of Household Technology from the Open Hearth to the Microwave*. New York: Basic Books, 1983.

Cripps, Thomas. " 'Race Movies' as Voices of the Black Bourgeoisie: *The Scar of Shame* (1927)." In John E. O'Connor and Martin A. Jackson, eds., *American History/American Film: Interpreting the Hollywood Image*. New York: Continuum, 1988.

Daniel, Pete. "Black Power in the 1920s: The Case of the Tuskegee Veterans Hospital." *Journal of Southern History* 36 (August 1970): 368–88.

———. *The Shadow of Slavery: Peonage in the South, 1901–1969*. Urbana: University of Illinois Press, 1972.

———. "The Metamorphosis of Slavery, 1865–1900." *Journal of American History* 66 (June 1979): 88–99.

Daniel, Pete, Merry Foresta, Maren Strange, and Sally Stein, eds. *Official Images: New Deal Photography*. Washington, D.C.: Smithsonian Institution, 1987.

Davidoff, Leonore, and Catherine Hall. *Family Fortunes: Men and Women of the English Middle Class, 1780–1850*. Chicago: University of Chicago Press, 1987.

Davis, Allison B., Burleigh B. Gardner, and Mary R. Gardner. *Deep South: A Social Anthropology of Caste and Class*. 1941. Reprint, Chicago: University of Chicago Press, 1969.

Davis, David Brion. *The Problem of Slavery in the Age of Revolution, 1770–1823*. Ithaca, NY: Cornell University Press, 1975.

Davis, Natalie Zemon. *Society and Culture in Early Modern France*. Stanford, CA: Stanford University Press, 1975.

Dillon, Merton L. *Ulrich Bonnell Phillips: Historian of the Old South*. Baton Rouge: Louisiana State University Press, 1985.

Dinnerstein, Leonard. *The Leo Frank Case*. New York: Columbia University Press, 1966.

Dittmer, John. *Black Georgia in the Progressive Era, 1900–1920*. Urbana: University of Illinois Press, 1977.

Dollard, John. *Caste and Class in a Southern Town*. 1937. Reprint, New York: Doubleday Anchor, 1957.

Douglas, Ann. *The Feminization of American Culture*. New York: Doubleday, 1988.

———. *Terrible Honesty: Mongrel Manhattan in the 1920s*. New York: Noonday Press, 1995.

Douglas, Mary. *Purity and Danger: An Analysis of the Concepts of Pollution and Taboo*. 1966. Reprint, New York: Routledge, 1991.

Downey, Dennis B., and Raymond M. Hyser. *No Crooked Death: Coatsville, Pennsylvania and the Lynching of Zachariah Walker*. Urbana: University of Illinois Press, 1991.

Doyle, Bertram Wilbur. *The Etiquette of Race Relations in the South: A Study in Social Control*. 1937. Reprint, New York: Schocken, 1971.

Doyle, Don H. *New Men, New Cities, New South: Atlanta, Nashville, Charleston, Mobile, 1860–1910*. Chapel Hill: University of North Carolina Press, 1990.

Du Bois, W. E. B. *Black Reconstruction in America*. 1935. Reprint, New York: Atheneum, 1962.

Dunning, William A. *Reconstruction, Political and Economic 1865–1877*. New York, 1907.

Dykeman, Wilma, and James Stokely. *The Seeds of Change: The Life of Will Alexander*. Chicago: University of Chicago Press, 1962.

Early, Gerald. *Tuxedo Junction: Essays on American Culture*. New York: Ecco Press, 1989.

Edwards, Paul K. *The Southern Urban Negro as a Consumer*. 1932. Reprint, New York: Negro Universities Press, 1955.

Egerton, John. *Speak Now Against the Day: The Generation Before the Civil Rights Movement in the South*. New York: Vintage, 1994.

Ellison, Ralph. *Shadow and Act*. 1964. Reprint, New York: Vintage, 1995.

——. *Going to the Territory*. 1986. Reprint, New York: Vintage, 1995.

Emmet, Boris, and John E. Jeuck. *Catalogues and Counters: A History of Sears, Roebuck and Company*. Chicago: University of Chicago Press, 1950.

Ewen, Stuart, and Elizabeth Ewen. *Channels of Desire: Mass Images and the Shaping of American Consciousness*. New York: McGraw-Hill, 1982.

Farr, Finis. *Margaret Mitchell of Atlanta*. 1965. Reprint, New York: Avon, 1974.

Faust, Drew Gilpin. "Altars of Sacrifice: Confederate Women and the Narratives of War." *Journal of American History* 76 (March 1990): 1200–28.

Fischer, Roger A. "A Pioneer Protest: The New Orleans Street-Car Controversy of 1867." *Journal of Negro History* 53 (July 1968): 219–33.

Floyd, Josephine Bone. "Rebecca Latimer Felton, Political Independent." *Georgia Historical Quarterly* 30 (March 1946): 14–34.

——. "Rebecca Latimer Felton, Champion of Woman's Rights." *Georgia Historical Quarterly* 30 (June 1946): 81–104.

Foner, Eric. *Reconstruction: America's Unfinished Revolution, 1863–1877*. New York: Harper and Row, 1988.

Forbes, W. Stanton. *Lucy M. Stanton, Artist*. Atlanta: Special Collections Department, Robert W. Woodruff Library, Emory University, 1975.

Ford, Lacy K. *Origins of Southern Radicalism: The South Carolina Low Country, 1800–1860*. New York: Oxford University Press, 1988.

Foster, Gaines M. *The Ghosts of the Confederacy: Defeat, the Lost Cause, and the Emergence of the New South, 1865–1913.* New York: Oxford University Press, 1987.

Foucault, Michel. *Discipline and Punish: The Birth of the Prison,* trans. Alan Sheridan. New York: Vintage Books, 1979.

Fox-Genovese, Elizabeth. "Scarlett O'Hara: The Southern Lady as New Woman." *American Quarterly* 33 (Fall 1981): 391–411.

———. *Within the Plantation Household: Black and White Women of the Old South.* Chapel Hill: University of North Carolina Press, 1988.

Franklin, John Hope. *The Militant South, 1800–1861.* Cambridge, MA: Harvard University Press, 1956.

———. *From Slavery to Freedom: A History of Negro Americans.* New York: Knopf, 1972.

———. *Race and History: Selected Essays, 1938–1988.* Baton Rouge: Louisiana State University Press, 1989.

Frazier, E. Franklin. *Black Bourgeoisie: Rise of a New Middle Class.* New York: Free Press, 1957.

Fredrickson, George M. *The Black Image in the White Mind: The Debate on Afro-American Character and Destiny, 1817–1914.* 1971. Reprint, Hanover, NH: Wesleyan University Press, 1987.

Friedman, Jean E. *The Enclosed Garden: Women and Community in the Evangelical South, 1830–1900.* Chapel Hill: University of North Carolina Press, 1985.

Fuller, Wayne D. *RFD: The Changing Face of Rural America.* Bloomington: Indiana University Press, 1964.

Gaines, Francis Pendleton. *The Southern Plantation: A Study in the Development and the Accuracy of a Tradition.* New York: Columbia University Press, 1925.

Gaines, Kevin K. *Uplifting the Race: Black Leadership, Politics, and Culture in the Twentieth Century.* Chapel Hill: University of North Carolina Press, 1996.

Garber, Marjorie. *Vested Interests: Cross-Dressing and Cultural Anxiety.* New York: Harper Perennial, 1993.

Garvey, Ellen. *Reading Consumer Culture: Gender, Fiction, and Advertising in American Magazines, 1880s to 1910s.* New York: Oxford University Press, 1995.

Gaston, Paul M. *The New South Creed: A Study in Southern Mythmaking.* New York: Knopf, 1970.

Gatewood, Willard B. *Aristocrats of Color: The Black Elite, 1880–1920.* Bloomington: University of Indiana Press, 1990.

Genovese, Eugene D. *Roll, Jordan, Roll: The World the Slaves Made.* New York: Vintage, 1975.

———. *The Slaveholders' Dilemma: Freedom and Progress in Southern Conservative Thought, 1820–1860.* Columbia: University of South Carolina Press, 1991.

Giddings, Paula. *When and Where I Enter: The Impact of Black Women on Race and Sex in America.* New York: Bantam Books, 1988.

Gilmore, Glenda. "Gender and Jim Crow: Sarah Dudley Pettey's Vision of the New South." *North Carolina Historical Review* 68 (July 1991): 261–85.

——. *Gender and Jim Crow: Women and the Politics of White Supremacy in North Carolina, 1896–1920*. Chapel Hill: University of North Carolina Press, 1996.

Girard, René. *Violence and the Sacred*. Baltimore: Johns Hopkins University Press, 1977.

Glenn, Evelyn Nankano. "From Servitude to Service Work: Historical Continuities in the Racial Division of Paid Work." *Signs* (Autumn 1992).

Goings, Kenneth. *Mammy and Uncle Mose: Black Collectibles and American Stereotyping*. Bloomington: Indiana University Press, 1994.

Goldfield, David R. *Cotton Fields and Skyscrapers: Southern City and Region, 1607–1980*. Baton Rouge: Louisiana State University Press, 1982.

Goodman, James. *Stories of Scottsboro*. New York: Pantheon, 1994.

Grantham, Dewey W., Jr. *Southern Progressivism: The Reconciliation of Progress and Tradition*. Knoxville: University of Tennessee Press, 1976.

Graves, John William. "Jim Crow in Arkansas: A Reconsideration of Urban Race Relations in the Post-Reconstruction South." *Journal of Southern History* 55 (August 1989).

Gray, Richard. *Writing the South: Ideas of an American Region*. New York: Cambridge University Press, 1986.

Gutman, Herbert G. *The Black Family in Slavery and Freedom, 1750–1925*. New York: Vintage, 1976.

Habermas, Jürgen. *Structural Transformation of the Public Sphere*, trans. Thomas Burger with Frederick Lawrence. Cambridge, MA: MIT Press, 1989.

Hackney, Sheldon. "Southern Violence." *American Historical Review* 74 (February 1969): 906–25.

Hahn, Steven. *The Roots of Southern Populism: Yeoman Farmers and the Transformation of the Georgia Upcountry, 1850–1890*. New York: Oxford University Press, 1982.

Hale, Grace Elizabeth. " 'In Terms of Paint': Lucy Stanton's Representations of the South, 1890–1931." *Georgia Historical Quarterly* 77 (Fall 1993): 577–92.

——. " 'Some Women Have Never Been Reconstructed': Mildred Lewis Rutherford, Lucy M. Stanton, and the Racial Politics of White Southern Womanhood, 1900–1930." In John Inscoe, ed., *Georgia in Black and White: Explorations in Race Relations of a Southern State, 1865–1950*, 173–201. Athens: University of Georgia Press, 1994.

——. "Deadly Amusements: Spectacle Lynchings and Southern Whiteness, 1890–1940." In Bruce Clayton and John A. Salmond, eds., *Varieties of Southern History*. Westport, CT: Greenwood Press, 1996.

——. " 'For Colored' and 'For White': Bounding Consumption in the South," in Glenda Gilmore, Jane Dailey, and Bryant Simon, eds., *Jumping Jim Crow: The New Political History of the New South*. Princeton: Princeton University Press, 1998.

——. "Granite Stopped Time: The Stone Mountain Memorial and Representations of White Southern Identity." *Georgia Historical Quarterly* 81 (Winter 1997).

Hall, Jacquelyn Dowd. *Revolt Against Chivalry: Jesse Daniel Ames and the Women's Campaign Against Lynching*. New York: Columbia University Press, 1974.

———. " 'The Mind That Burns in Each Body': Women, Rape, and Racial Violence." In Ann Snitow, Christine Stansell, and Sharon Thompson, eds., *Powers of Desire: The Politics of Sexuality*, 328–49. New York: Monthly Review Press, 1983.

———. "Private Eyes, Public Women: Images of Class and Sex in the Urban South, Atlanta, Georgia, 1913–1915." In Ava Baron, ed., *Work Engendered: Toward a New History of American Labor*, 262–71. Ithaca, NY: Cornell University Press, 1991.

———, et al. *Like a Family: The Making of a Southern Cotton Mill World*. New York: Norton, 1989.

Halttunen, Karen. *Confidence Men and Painted Women: A Study of Middle Class Culture in America, 1830–1870*. New Haven: Yale University Press, 1982.

Hansen, Miriam. *Babel and Babylon: Spectatorship in American Silent Film*. Cambridge, MA: Harvard University Press, 1991.

Harding, Vincent. *There Is a River: The Black Struggle for Freedom in America*. New York: Vintage, 1983.

Harlan, Louis. *Booker T. Washington: The Making of a Black Leader*. New York: Oxford University Press, 1972.

———. *Booker T. Washington: The Wizard of Tuskegee, 1901–1915*. New York: Oxford University Press, 1983.

Harris, Neil. *Humbug: The Art of P. T. Barnum*. Boston: Little, Brown, 1973.

———. *Cultural Excursions: Marketing Appetites and Cultural Tastes in Modern America*. Chicago: University of Chicago Press, 1990.

Harris, Trudier. *From Mammies to Militants: Domestics in Black American Literature*. Philadelphia: Temple University Press, 1982.

———. *Exorcising Blackness: Historical and Literary Lynching and Burning Rituals*. Bloomington: Indiana University Press, 1984.

Harwell, Richard, ed. *Gone With the Wind as Book and Film*. Columbia: University of South Carolina Press, 1983.

Haws, Robert, ed. *The Age of Segregation: Race Relations in the South, 1890–1945*. Jackson: University of Mississippi Press, 1978.

Hayden, Dolores. *The Grand Domestic Revolution: A History of Feminist Designs for American Homes, Neighborhoods, and Cities*. Cambridge, MA: MIT Press, 1982.

Hendrickson, Robert. *The Grand Emporiums*. New York: Stein & Day, 1978.

Hine, Darlene Clark. "Rape and the Inner Lives of Southern Black Women: Thoughts on the Culture of Dissemblance." In Virginia Bernhard, Betty Brandon, Elizabeth Fox-Genovese, and Theda Purdue, eds., *Southern Women: Histories and Identities*, 177–90. Columbia: University of Missouri Press, 1993.

———, ed. *Black Women in United States History*. Brooklyn: Carlson, 1990.

Hobsbawm, Eric. "Mass-Producing Traditions: Europe, 1870–1914." In Eric Hobsbawm and Terence Ranger, eds., *The Invention of Tradition*, 263–307. Cambridge: Cambridge University Press, 1983.

Hobson, Fred C., Jr. *Serpent in Eden: H. L. Mencken and the South.* Baton Rouge: Louisiana State University Press, 1974.

———. *Tell About the South: The Southern Rage to Explain.* Baton Rouge: Louisiana State University Press, 1983.

Holmes, William F. "Whitecapping in Mississippi: Agrarian Violence in the Populist Era." *Journal of Southern History* 35 (May 1969): 165–85.

———. "Moonshining and Collective Violence: Georgia, 1889–1895." *Journal of American History* 67 (December 1980): 589–611.

Huggins, Nathan I. *The Harlem Renaissance.* New York: Oxford University Press, 1971.

———. "The Deforming Mirror of Truth: Slavery and the Master Narrative of American History." *Radical History Review* 49 (Winter 1991): 25–48.

Hurston, Zora Neale. *Mules and Men.* 1935. Reprint, New York: Harper Perennial, 1990.

Ingalls, Robert P. *Urban Vigilantes in the New South: Tampa, 1882–1936.* Gainesville: University Press of Florida, 1993.

Inge, M. Thomas, ed. *Ellen Glasgow: The Centennial Essays.* Charlottesville: University Press of Virginia, 1976.

Inscoe, John C. "The Confederate Home Front Sanitized: Joel Chandler Harris's *On the Plantation* and Sectional Reconciliation." *Georgia Historical Quarterly* 76 (Fall 1992): 652–74.

Jablonsky, Thomas J. *The Home, Heaven, and Mother Party: Female Anti-Suffragists in the United States, 1868–1920.* New York: Carlsen, 1994.

Jackson, Kenneth. *Crabgrass Frontier: The Suburbanization of America.* New York: Oxford University Press, 1985.

Jackson, Kenneth T. *The Ku Klux Klan in the City.* New York: Oxford University Press, 1967.

Janiewski, Dolores. "Southern Honor, Southern Dishonor: Managerial Ideology and the Construction of Gender, Race, and Class Relations in Southern Industry." In Ava Baron, ed., *Work Engendered: Toward a New History of American Labor,* 70–91. Ithaca, NY: Cornell University Press, 1991.

Jay, Robert. *The Trade Card in Nineteenth Century America.* Columbia: University of Missouri Press, 1987.

Jaynes, Gerald David. *Branches Without Roots: Genesis of the Black Working Class in the American South, 1862–1882.* New York: Oxford University Press, 1986.

Johnson, Charles S. *Patterns of Negro Segregation.* New York: Harper and Row, 1943.

Johnson, Michael P., and James L. Roark. *Black Masters: A Free Family of Color in the Old South.* New York: Norton, 1984.

Jones, Ann Goodwyn. *Tomorrow Is Another Day: The Woman Writer in the South.* Baton Rouge: Louisiana State University Press, 1981.

Jones, Jacqueline. *Labor of Love, Labor of Sorrow: Black Women, Work, and the Family, From Slavery to the Present.* New York: Vintage, 1986.

Jorgensen, Janice, ed. *The Encyclopedia of Consumer Brands*. Detroit: St. James, 1994.

Kaplan, Amy. "Romancing the Empire: The Embodiment of American Masculinity in the Popular Historical Novel of the 1890s." *American Literary History* 2 (1990): 659–90.

Katzman, David M. *Seven Days a Week: Women and Domestic Service in Industrializing America*. New York: Oxford University Press, 1978.

Kelley, Robin D. G. *Hammer and Hoe: Alabama Communists During the Great Depression*. Chapel Hill: University of North Carolina Press, 1990.

——. *Race Rebels: Culture, Politics, and the Black Working Class*. New York: Free Press, 1995.

Kern-Foxworth, Marilyn. *Aunt Jemima, Uncle Ben, and Rastus: Blacks in Advertising, Yesterday, Today, and Tomorrow*. Westport, CT: Greenwood Press, 1991.

King, Richard H. *A Southern Renaissance: The Cultural Awakening of the American South, 1930–1955*. New York: Oxford University Press, 1980.

Kirby, Jack Temple. "Clarence Poe's Vision of a Segregated 'Great Rural Civilization.' " *South Atlantic Quarterly* 68 (Winter 1969): 27–38.

——. *Media-Made Dixie: The South in the American Imagination*. Baton Rouge: Louisiana State University Press, 1978.

——. "Black and White in the Rural South, 1915–1954." *Agricultural History* (July 1984): 411–22.

Klein, Maury. *History of the Louisville and Nashville Railroad*. New York: Macmillan, 1972.

Kluger, Richard. *Simple Justice: The History of Brown v. Board of Education and Black America's Struggle for Equality*. New York: Vintage, 1977.

Kuhn, Clifford M., Harlon E. Joye, and E. Bernard West. *Living Atlanta: An Oral History of the City, 1914–1948*. Athens: University of Georgia Press, 1990.

LaFeber, Walter. *The New Empire: An Interpretation of American Expansion, 1860–1898*. Ithaca, NY: Cornell University Press, 1963.

Lamon, Lester C. *Black Tennesseans, 1900–1930*. Knoxville: University of Tennessee Press, 1977.

Larsen, Lawrence. *The Rise of the Urban South*. Lexington: University of Kentucky Press, 1985.

Latham, Frank B. *A Century of Serving Customers: The Story of Montgomery Ward*. Chicago: Montgomery Ward, 1971.

Lears, T. J. Jackson. *No Place of Grace: Antimodernism and the Transformation of American Culture, 1880–1920*. New York: Pantheon, 1981.

——. "Packaging the Folk: Tradition and Amnesia in American Advertising." In Jane S. Becker and Barbara Franco, eds., *Folk Roots, New Roots: Folklore in American Life*, 103–40. Lexington, MA: Scottish Rite Masonic Museum and Library, 1988.

——. "Beyond Veblen: Rethinking Consumer Culture in America." In *Consuming Visions: Accumulation and Display of Goods in America*. Chicago: University of Chicago Press, 1990.

——. *Fables of Abundance: A Cultural History of Advertising in America.* New York: Basic Books, 1994.

Lears, Jackson, and Richard Wrightman Fox, eds. *The Culture of Consumption.* New York: Pantheon, 1983.

——. *The Power of Culture.* Chicago: University of Chicago Press, 1993.

Lebsock, Suzanne. *The Free Women of Petersburg: Status and Culture in a Southern Town, 1784–1860.* New York: Norton, 1984.

Levine, Lawrence W. *Black Culture and Black Consciousness: Afro-American Folk Thought from Slavery to Freedom.* New York: Oxford University Press, 1977.

Lewis, David Levering. *W. E. B. Du Bois: Biography of a Race, 1868–1919.* New York: Henry Holt, 1993.

Lewis, David Levering, ed. *W. E. B. Du Bois, A Reader.* New York: Henry Holt, 1995.

——. *When Harlem Was in Vogue.* New York: Vintage, 1982.

Lionnet, Françoise. *Autobiographical Voices: Race, Gender, Self-Portraiture.* Ithaca, NY: Cornell University Press, 1991.

Litwack, Leon F. *Been in the Storm So Long: The Aftermath of Slavery.* New York: Vintage, 1980.

Lofgren, Charles. *The Plessy Case: A Legal-Historical Interpretation.* New York: Oxford University Press, 1987.

Lott, Eric. *Love and Theft: Blackface Minstrelsy and the American Working Class.* New York: Oxford University Press, 1993.

Loveland, Anne C. *Lillian Smith: A Southerner Confronting the South.* Baton Rouge: Louisiana State University Press.

Lyotard, J. F. *The Postmodern Condition.* Minneapolis: University of Minnesota Press, 1984.

MacKethan, Lucinda. "Plantation Fiction, 1865–1900." In Louis D. Rubin et al. eds., *The History of Southern Literature,* 209–18. Baton Rouge: Louisiana State University Press, 1985.

MacLean, Nancy. "White Women and Klan Violence in the 1920s: Agency, Complicity, and the Politics of Women's History." *Gender and History* 3 (Autumn 1991): 285–303.

——. "The Leo Frank Case Reconsidered: Gender and Sexual Politics in the Making of Reactionary Populism." *Journal of American History* 78 (December 1991): 917–48.

——. *Behind the Mask of Chivalry: The Making of the Second Ku Klux Klan.* New York: Oxford University Press, 1994.

Mangan, J. A., and James Walvin, eds. *Manliness and Morality: Middle Class Masculinity in Britain and America, 1800–1940.* New York: St. Martin's Press, 1987.

Marchand, Roland. *Advertising the American Dream: Making Way for Modernity, 1920–1940.* Berkeley: University of California Press, 1984.

Marks, Stuart A. *Southern Hunting in Black and White: Nature, History, and Ritual in a Carolina Community.* Princeton: Princeton University Press, 1991.

McElroy, Guy C. *Facing History: The Black Image in American Art, 1979–1940.* San Francisco: Bedford Arts, 1990.

McFeely, William. *Frederick Douglass.* New York: Norton, 1991.

McGovern, James R. *Anatomy of a Lynching: The Killing of Claude Neal.* Baton Rouge: Louisiana State University Press, 1982.

McMillen, Neil R. *Dark Journey: Black Mississippians in the Age of Jim Crow.* Urbana: University of Illinois Press, 1977.

Meir, August. *Negro Thought in America, 1880–1915: Racial Ideologies in the Age of Booker T. Washington.* Ann Arbor: University of Michigan Press, 1963.

Meir, August, and Elliot Rudwick, eds. *Along the Color Line: Explorations in the Black Experience.* Urbana: University of Illinois Press, 1977.

Michaels, Walter Benn. *The Gold Standard and the Logic of Naturalism: American Literature at the Turn of the Century.* Berkeley: University of California Press, 1987.

Mixon, H. Wayne. *Southern Writers and the New South Movement, 1865–1913.* Chapel Hill: University of North Carolina Press, 1980.

Montgomery, David. *Beyond Equality: Labor and the Radical Republicans, 1862–1872.* New York: Knopf, 1967.

———. *The Fall of the House of Labor: The Workplace, the State and American Labor Activism.* Cambridge, MA: Harvard University Press, 1987.

Morgan, Edmund S. *American Slavery, American Freedom: The Ordeal of Colonial Virginia.* New York: Norton, 1975.

Morton, Patricia. " 'My Ol' Black Mammy' in American Historiography." In Caroline Matheny Dillman, ed., *Southern Women.* New York: Hemisphere, 1988.

———. *Disfigured Images: The Historical Assault on Afro-American Women.* New York: Greenwood Press, 1991.

Moses, Wilson Jeremiah. *The Golden Age of Black Nationalism, 1850–1925.* Hamden, CT: Archon Books, 1978.

Murphy, Maud King. *Edgar Gardner Murphy.* New York: the author, 1943.

Murray, Albert. *The Omni-Americans: New Perspectives on Black Experience and American Culture.* New York: Outerbridge and Dienstfrey, 1970.

Myrdal, Gunnar. *An American Dilemma: The Negro Problem and Modern Democracy.* 1944. Reprint, New York: Harper and Row, 1962.

Nasaw, David. *Going Out: The Rise and Fall of Public Amusements.* New York: Basic Books, 1993.

Natanson, Nicholas. *The Black Image in the New Deal: The Politics of FSA Photography.* Knoxville: University of Tennessee Press, 1992.

Novack, Peter. *That Noble Dream: The 'Objectivity Question' and the American Historical Profession.* New York: Cambridge University Press, 1988.

O'Brien, Michael. *The Idea of the American South, 1920–1941.* Baltimore: Johns Hopkins University Press, 1979.

Olsen, Otto H. *The Thin Disguise: Plessy v. Ferguson, A Documentary Presentation* New York: Humanities Press, 1967.

Orvell, Miles. *The Real Thing: Imitation and Authenticity in American Culture, 1880–1940.* Chapel Hill: University of North Carolina, 1989.

Osterweis, Rollin G. *The Myth of the Lost Cause, 1865–1900.* Hamden, CT: Archon Books, 1973.

Ownby, Ted. *Subduing Satan: Religion, Recreation, and Manhood in the Rural South, 1865–1920.* Chapel Hill: University of North Carolina Press, 1990.

Painter, Nell Irvin. *Standing at Armageddon: The United States, 1877–1919.* New York: Norton, 1987.

——. " 'Social Equality': Miscegenation, Labor, and Power." In Numan Bartley, ed., *The Evolution of Southern Culture,* 47–67. Athens: University of Georgia, 1988.

——. "The Journal of Ella Gertrude Clanton Thomas: An Educated White Woman in the Eras of Slavery, War, and Reconstruction." In Virginia Ingraham Burr, ed., *The Secret Eye: The Journal of Ella Gertrude Clanton Thomas, 1848–1889,* 1–67. Chapel Hill: University of North Carolina Press, 1990.

——. *Exodusters.* New York: Norton, 1992.

Pankhurst, Jessie W. "The Role of the Black Mammy in the Plantation Household." *Journal of Negro History* 23 (July 1938): 349–50.

Patton, June O. "Moonlight and Magnolias in Southern Education: The Black Mammy Memorial Institute." *Journal of Negro History* 65 (Spring 1980): 149–55.

Pieterse, Jan Nederveen. *White on Black: Images of Africa and Blacks in Western Popular Culture.* New Haven: Yale University Press, 1992.

Polan, Dana B. " 'Above All Else to Make You See': Cinema and the Ideology of Spectacle." In Jonathan Arac, ed., *Postmodernism and Politics,* 55–69. Minneapolis: University of Minnesota Press, 1986.

Poovey, Mary. *Uneven Developments: The Ideological Work of Gender in Mid-Victorian England.* Chicago: University of Chicago Press, 1988.

Pope, Daniel. *The Making of Modern Advertising.* New York: Basic Books, 1983.

Press, Nancy. "Private Faces, Public Lives: The Women of the Downtown Group of Charleston, South Carolina." In Holly F. Matthews, ed., *Women in the South: An Anthropological Perspective,* 95–109. Athens: University of Georgia Press, 1989.

Pyron, Darden Asbury. *Recasting: Gone With the Wind in American Culture.* Miami: University Presses of Florida, 1983.

——. "Nell Battle Lewis (1896–1955): The Dilemmas of Southern Womanhood." *Social Science Perspectives on the South: An Interdisciplinary Annual* 3 (1984): 77–99.

——. *Southern Daughter: The Life of Margaret Mitchell.* New York: Harper Perennial, 1992.

Rabinowitz, Howard N. *Race Relations in the Urban South, 1865–1890.* Urbana: University of Illinois Press, 1980.

——. "More than the Woodward Thesis: Assessing *The Strange Career of Jim Crow.*" *Journal of American History* 75 (December 1988): 842–56.

Rable, George C. *But There Was No Peace: The Role of Violence in the Politics of Reconstruction.* Athens: University of Georgia Press, 1984.

Raper, Arthur. *The Tragedy of Lynching*. Chapel Hill: University of North Carolina Press, 1933.

Redkey, Edwin S. *Black Exodus: Black Nationalists and Back to Africa Movements*. New Haven: Yale University Press, 1969.

Rich, Adrienne. *Of Woman Born: Motherhood as Example and Institution*. New York: Norton, 1976.

Richards, Jeffrey, and John M. MacKenzie. *The Railway Station: A Social History*. Oxford: Clarendon Press, 1986.

Riegel, Stephen J. "The Persistent Career of Jim Crow: Lower Federal Courts and the 'Separate But Equal Doctrine,' 1865–1896." *American Journal of Legal History* 28 (January 1984).

Robbins, Bruce, ed. *The Phantom Public Sphere*. Minneapolis: University of Minnesota Press, 1993.

Roberts, Frances C., and Sarah Huff Fisher. *Shadows on the Wall: The Life and Works of Howard Weeden*. Northport, AL: Colonial Press, 1962.

Robinson, Jo Ann. "Lillian Smith: Reflections on Race and Sex." *Southern Exposure* 4 (Fall 1977): 43–48.

Rodgers, Daniel T. "Regionalism and the Burdens of Progress." In Morgan Kousser and James M. McPherson, eds., *Region, Race, and Reconstruction: Essays in Honor of C. Vann Woodward*, 3–26. New York: Oxford University Press, 1982.

Roediger, David R. *The Wages of Whiteness: Race and the Making of the American Working Class*. New York: Verso, 1991.

———. *Towards the Abolition of Whiteness: Essays on Race, Politics, and Working Class History*. New York: Verso, 1994.

Rogin, Michael. " 'The Sword Became a Flashing Vision': D. W. Griffith's *Birth of Nation*." In *Ronald Reagan, the Movie, and Other Episodes in Political Demonology*, 190–235. Berkeley: University of California Press, 1987.

Roper, John Herbert. *U. B. Phillips: A Southern Mind*. Macon, GA: Mercer University Press, 1984.

Rosenberg, Rosalind. *Beyond Separate Spheres: Intellectual Roots of Modern Feminism*. New Haven: Yale University Press, 1982.

Rotundo, E. Anthony. *American Manhood: Transformation in Masculinity from the Revolution*. New York: Basic Books, 1993.

Royster, Charles. *The Destructive War: William Tecumseh Sherman, Stonewall Jackson, and the Americans*. New York: Vintage, 1993.

Rubin, Louis D. *No Place on Earth: Ellen Glasgow, James Branch Cabell, and Richmond-in-Virginia*. Austin: University of Texas Press, 1959.

———. *George W. Cable: The Life and Times of a Southern Heretic*. New York: Pegasus, 1969.

Ryan, Mary. *Cradle of the Middle Class: The Family in Oneida County, New York, 1790–1865*. New York: Cambridge University Press, 1981.

———. *Women in Public: Between Banners and Ballots, 1825–1880*. Baltimore: Johns Hopkins University Press, 1990.

Rydell, Robert W. *All the World's a Fair: Visions of Empire at America's International Expositions, 1876–1916*. Chicago: University of Chicago Press, 1984.

——. *World of Fairs: The Century of Progress Expositions*. Chicago: University of Chicago Press, 1993.

Said, Edward W. *Beginnings: Intention and Method*. New York: Basic Books, 1975.

Saxton, Alexander. *The Rise and Fall of the White Republic: Class Politics and Mass Culture in Nineteenth-Century America*. New York: Verso, 1990.

Schlereth, Thomas J. "Country Stores, County Fairs, and Mail Order Catalogues: Consumption in Rural America." In Simon J. Bonner, ed., *Consuming Visions: Accumulation and Display of Goods in America, 1880–1920*, 339–75. New York: Norton, 1989.

Schwartz, Barry. "The Reconstruction of Abraham Lincoln." In *Collective Remembering*, 81–107. London: Sage, 1990.

Scott, Ann Firor. *The Southern Lady: From Pedestal to Politics, 1830–1930*. Chicago: University of Chicago Press, 1970.

Sedgwick, Eve Kosofsky. *Between Men: English Literature and Male Homosocial Desire*. New York: Columbia University Press, 1985.

Shaw, Stephanie J. *What a Woman Ought to Be and to Do: Black Professional Women Workers During the Jim Crow Era*. Chicago: University of Chicago Press, 1996.

Shay, Frank. *Judge Lynch: His First Hundred Years*. New York: Ives Washburn, 1938.

Shils, Edward. *Tradition*. Chicago: University of Chicago Press, 1981.

Silber, Nina. *The Romance of Reunion: Northerners and the South, 1865–1900*. Chapel Hill: University of North Carolina Press, 1994.

Simon, Bryant. *A Fabric of Defeat: South Carolina Textile Workers in State and Nation, 1914–1948*. Chapel Hill: University of North Carolina Press, 1998.

Singal, Daniel Joseph. *The War Within: From Victorian to Modernist Thought in the South, 1919–1945*. Chapel Hill: University of North Carolina Press, 1982.

Sklar, Kathryn Kish. *Catharine Beecher: A Study in American Domesticity*. New Haven: Yale University Press, 1973.

Slotkin, Richard. *The Fatal Environment: The Myth of the Frontier in the Age of Industrialization*. New York: Atheneum, 1985.

Smead, Howard. *Blood Justice: The Lynching of Mack Charles Parker*. New York: Oxford University Press, 1986.

Smith, Jessie Carney, ed. *Images of Blacks in American Culture*. Westport, CT: Greenwood Press, 1988.

Smith, John David. *An Old Creed for the New South*. Westport, CT: Greenwood Press, 1985.

Smith, John David, and John Inscoe. *Ulrich Bonnell Phillips: A Southern Historian and His Critics*. Westport, CT: Greenwood Press, 1990.

Smith-Rosenberg, Caroll. "The Female World of Love and Ritual: Relations Between Women in Nineteenth Century America." *Signs* 1 (Autumn 1975): 1–29.

——. *Disorderly Conduct: Visions of Gender in Victorian America*. New York: Oxford University Press, 1986.

Sobel, Mechal. *The World They Made Together: Black and White Values in Eighteenth Century Virginia*. Princeton: Princeton University Press, 1987.

Sommerville, Diane Miller. "The Rape Myth in the Old South Reconsidered." *Journal of Southern History* 61 (August 1995): 481–518.

Sontag, Susan. *On Photography*. New York: Farrar, Straus and Giroux, 1973.

SoRelle, James M. " 'The Waco Horror': The Lynching of Jesse Washington." *Southwestern Historical Quarterly* 86 (April 1983): 517–36.

Stallybrass, Peter, and Allon White. *The Politics and Poetics of Transgression*. Ithaca, NY: Cornell University Press, 1986.

Stott, William. *Documentary Expression and Thirties America*. New York: Oxford University Press, 1973.

Stover, John F. *The Railroads of the South, 1865–1900*. Chapel Hill: University of North Carolina Press, 1969.

Stuckey, Sterling. *Slave Culture: Nationalist Theory and the Foundations of Black America*. New York: Oxford University Press, 1987.

——. *Going Through the Storm: The Influence of African American Art in History*. New York: Oxford University Press, 1994.

Sundquist, Eric J. *Faulkner: The House Divided*. Baltimore: Johns Hopkins University Press, 1983.

——. *To Wake the Nations: Race in the Making of American Literature*. Cambridge, MA: Harvard University Press, 1994.

Sundquist, Eric J., ed. *The Oxford W. E. B. Du Bois Reader*. New York: Oxford University Press, 1996.

Susman, Warren. *Culture as History: The Transformation of American Society in the Twentieth Century*. New York: Pantheon, 1984.

Talmadge, John E. *Rebecca Latimer Felton: Nine Stormy Decades*. Athens: University of Georgia Press, 1960.

Taylor, A. A. "Historians of the Reconstruction." *Journal of Negro History* 23 (January 1938): 16–34.

Taylor, William. *Cavalier and Yankee: The Old South and American National Character*. New York: Braziller, 1961.

Thurber, Cheryl. "The Development of the Mammy Image and Mythology." In Virginia Bernhard, Betty Brandon, Elizabeth Fox-Genovese, and Theda Perdue, eds., *Southern Women: Histories and Identities*, 87–108. Columbia: University of Missouri Press, 1992.

Tindall, George Brown. *The Emergence of the New South, 1913–1945*. Baton Rouge: Louisiana State University Press, 1967.

Tolnay, Stewart E., and E. M. Beck. *A Festival of Violence: An Analysis of Southern Lynchings, 1882–1930*. Urbana: University of Illinois Press, 1995.

Torgovnick, Marianne. *Gone Primitive: Savage Intellects, Modern Lives*. Chicago: University of Chicago Press, 1990.

Torrence, Ridgely. *The Story of John Hope*. 1948. Reprint, New York: Arno Press, 1969.

Trachtenberg, Alan. *The Incorporation of America: Culture and Society in the Gilded Age.* New York: Hill and Wang, 1982.

————. *Reading American Photographs: Images as History, Matthew Brady to Walker Evans.* New York: Hill and Wang, 1989.

Trelease, Allen W. *White Terror: The Ku Klux Klan Conspiracy and Southern Reconstruction.* New York: Harper and Row, 1971.

Tucker, Susan. *Telling Memories Among Southern Women: Domestic Workers and Their Employers in the Segregated South.* New York: Schocken, 1988.

Turner, Patricia A. *Ceramic Uncles and Celluloid Mammies: Black Images and Their Influence on Culture.* New York: Anchor Books, 1994.

Van Deburg, William L. *Slavery and Race in American Popular Culture.* Madison: University of Wisconsin Press, 1984.

Watkins, Julian Lewis. *The 100 Greatest Advertisements: Who Wrote Them and What They Did.* New York: Moore, 1949.

Weiner, Jonathan. *Social Origins of the New South.* Baton Rouge: Louisiana State University Press, 1978.

Wells-Barnett, Ida B. *A Red Record: Tabulated Statistics and Alleged Causes of Lynchings in the United States, 1892–1893–1894.* Chicago: Donohue and Henneberry, 1895.

Wheeler, Marjorie Spruill. *New Women of the New South: The Leaders of the Woman Suffrage Movement in the Southern States.* New York: Oxford University Press, 1993.

White, Deborah Gray. *Ar'n't I a Woman: Female Slaves in the Plantation South.* New York: Norton, 1985.

White, Walter. *Rope and Faggot: A Biography of Judge Lynch.* New York: Knopf, 1929.

Whites, LeeAnn. "Rebecca Latimer Felton and the Wife's Farm: The Class and Racial Politics of Gender Reform." *Georgia Historical Quarterly* 76 (Summer 1992): 354–72.

————. "Rebecca Latimer Felton and the Problem of 'Protection' in the New South." In Nancy Hewitt and Suzanne Lebsock, eds., *Visible Women.* Chicago: University of Chicago Press, 1993.

————. *The Civil War as a Crisis in Gender: Augusta, Georgia, 1860–1890.* Athens: University of Georgia Press, 1995.

Whitfield, Stephen J. *A Death in the Delta: The Story of Emmet Till.* Baltimore: Johns Hopkins University Press, 1991.

Wiegman, Robyn. "The Anatomy of Lynching." In John C. Fout and Maura Shaw Tantillo, eds., *American Sexual Politics: Sex, Gender, and Race since the Civil War,* 240–71. Chicago: University of Chicago Press, 1993.

Williamson, Joel. *The Crucible of Race: Black-White Relations in the American South Since Emancipation.* New York: Oxford University Press, 1984.

———. "How Black Was Rhett Butler?" In Numan V. Bartley, ed., *The Evolution of Southern Culture*, 87–107. Athens: University of Georgia Press, 1988.

———. *William Faulkner and Southern History*. New York: Oxford University Press, 1993.

Wilson, Charles Reagan. *Baptized in Blood: The Religion of the Lost Cause*. Athens: University of Georgia Press, 1980.

Wilson, Edmund. *Patriotic Gore: Studies in the Literature of the American Civil War*. New York: Farrar, Straus and Giroux, 1962.

Wood, Peter H. *Black Majority: Negroes in Colonial South Carolina from 1670 through the Stono Rebellion*. New York: Norton, 1975.

Woodward, C. Vann. *Origins of the New South*. Baton Rouge: Louisiana State University Press, 1951.

———. *The Strange Career of Jim Crow*. 1955. Reprint, New York: Oxford University Press, 1974.

———. *American Counterpoint: Slavery and Racism in the North-South Dialogue*. Boston: Little, Brown, 1971.

Wright, Gavin. *The Political Economy of the Cotton South: Households, Markets, and Wealth in the Nineteenth Century*. New York: Norton, 1978.

———. *Old South, New South: Revolutions in the Southern Economy Since the Civil War*. New York: Norton, 1986.

Wright, George C. *Life Behind a Veil: Blacks in Louisville, Kentucky, 1865–1930*. Baton Rouge: Louisiana State University Press, 1987.

———. *Racial Violence in Kentucky, 1865–1940*. Baton Rouge: Louisiana State University Press, 1990.

Young, James Harvey. *The Toadstool Millionaires: A Social History of Patent Medicine in America Before Federal Regulations*. Princeton: Princeton University Press, 1961.

Zangrando, Robert L. *The NAACP Crusade Against Lynching*. Philadelphia: Temple University Press, 1980.

Dissertations and Theses

Brattain, Michelle. "The Politics of Whiteness: Race, Workers, and Culture in the Modern South." Ph.D. dissertation, Rutgers University, 1996.

Brewer, Pat Bryan. "Lillian Smith: Thorn in the Flesh of Crackerdom." Ph.D. dissertation, University of Georgia, 1982.

Cook, Florence Elliot. "Growing Up White, Genteel, and Female in a Changing South." Ph.D. dissertation, University of California, Berkeley, 1992.

Ellis, Mary Louise. " 'Rain Down Fire': The Lynching of Sam Hose." Ph.D. dissertation, Florida State University, 1992.

Finnegan, Terence. " 'At the Hands of Parties Unknown': Lynching in Mississippi and South Carolina, 1881–1940." Ph.D. dissertation, University of Illinois at Urbana-Champaign, 1993.

Hanson, Susan Atherton. "Home Sweet Home: Industrialization's Impact on Rural Households, 1865–1925." Ph.D. dissertation, University of Maryland, 1986.
Hines, Mary Elizabeth. "Death at the Hands of Persons Unknown: The Geography of Lynching in the Deep South, 1882–1910." Ph.D. dissertation, Louisiana State University, 1993.
Hunter, Tera. "Household Workers in the Making: Afro-American Women in Atlanta and the New South, 1861–1920." Ph.D. dissertation, Yale University, 1991.

McCurry, Stephanie. "In Defense of Their World: Gender, Class, and the Yeomanry of the South Carolina Low Country, 1820–1860." Ph.D. dissertation, State University of New York at Binghamton, 1988.
McFeely, Eliza. "Palimpsest of American Identity: Zuni, Anthropology, and American Culture, 1879–1925." Ph.D. dissertation, New York University, 1995.
Miller, Kathleen Atkinson. "Out of the Chrysalis: Lillian Smith and the Transformation of the South." Ph.D. dissertation, Emory University, 1984.

Ross, John. "At the Bar of Judge Lynch: Lynching and Lynch Mobs in America." Ph.D. dissertation, Texas Tech University, 1983.

Schechter, Patricia Ann. " 'To Tell the Truth Freely': Ida B. Wells and the Politics of Race, Gender, and Reform in America, 1880–1913." Ph.D. dissertation, Princeton University, 1994.
Sommerville, Diane Miller. "The Rape Myth Reconsidered: The Intersection of Race, Gender, and Class Through the Reconstruction South." Ph.D. dissertation, Rutgers University, 1995.

Tuthill, Hazelle Beard. "Mildred Lewis Rutherford." M.A. thesis, University of South Carolina, 1929.

Womack, Margaret Anne. "Mildred Lewis Rutherford, Exponent of Southern Culture." M.A. thesis, University of Georgia, 1946.

Permissions Acknowledgments

Robert W. Woodruff Library at Emory University: Nov. 2, 1907, letter from Joel Chandler Harris to Andrew Carnegie. Joel Chandler Harris Collection, Box 4. Feb. 7 1904, letter from Thomas Dixon to Walter Hines Page. Thomas Dixon Collection, Box 1. Reprinted by permission of Special Collections, Robert W. Woodruff Library, Emory University, Atlanta, GA.

Helen H. Tate and the Princeton University Library: Excerpts from material from the Allen Tate Collection. Manuscripts Division, Department of Rare Books and Special Collections, Princeton University Library. Reprinted by permission of Helen H. Tate and the Princeton University Library.

The University of North Carolina at Chapel Hill: Excerpts from material from the Ulrich Bonnell Phillips Papers, #2832, and the Katharine DuPre Lumpkin Papers, #417. Southern Historical Collection, Library of the University of North Carolina at Chapel Hill. Reprinted by permission of The University of North Carolina at Chapel Hill.

Index

Scopes trial, 253, 257
Scottsboro men, 222
Sea Islands, 19
Sears, Richard, 178
Sears and Roebuck, 177, 178, 179
sectional reconciliation, 79
segregation:
    ambiguities and contradictions of, 131,
        133–36, 179–97, 199–200, 205, 242–43
    blacks as bearing cost of, 10
    black side of, 13–41
    Cable's opposition to, 44–48, 49
    class differences and, 46–51
    as culture, xi–xii, 3, 9–10, 40, 44, 50, 144,
        242–43, 283–85
    described and attacked by Smith, 111,
        136, 193, 244
    Faulkner on, 82–83
    general stores and, 168–79
    official watersheds in, 167
    Old South and legitimating of, 44, 48
    outlawing of, 288–89, 293
    as political and social solution, xi, 8, 45,
        87–88, 93, 123–25, 144
    as response to black success, 21–22
    as sales pitch for tourism, 145–46
    "separate but equal" ruling and, 23, 46,
        48
    signs for, 105, 126, 130, 133–34, 135, 136,
        186–87, 191, 193, 284, 293
    transportation and, see railroads
    vulnerable mixed-race aspect of, 9
    of Washington, D.C., 221, 242
    white questioning of, 255–58
Selznick, David O., 52, 244, 277, 282
Senate, U.S., first woman elected to, 89
"separate but equal" ruling, 23, 46, 48, 148,
    167
sexuality, 38
Shahn, Ben, 180, 182
sharecropping, 7
Shaw, Anna, 34
Shelby, Tenn., 126

signs, for segregated facilities, 105, 126,
    130, 133–34, 135, 136, 186–87, 191, 193,
    284, 293
Silber, Nina, 68, 69, 165
Silent Protest Parade, 35–36, 292
"silent South," 45, 48
skin color, 4, 45, 96, 129, 195
slaveholders, black, 4
Slaveholder's Daughter, A (Kearney), 77,
    96
slave narratives, 17
slavery, 4, 88, 102
    class differences and, 91
    cultural heritage of, 19
    labor system vs. race at heart of, 76
    meaning of blackness determined by, 4
    "necessary space" provided by, 15–18, 23
    supposed benefits derived by blacks
        from, 62–63
    Turner on, 27
    see also emancipation
slaves:
    antebellum freeing of, 4
    comic and contented images of, 51–52
    fictional representations of, 51–67
    SMCMA (Stone Mountain Confeder-
        ate Memorial Association), 242, 243,
        252–54
Smith, Bessie, 38
Smith, Calvin Warren, 244
Smith, Henry, 207–8, 209, 221, 228, 229
Smith, John David, 65
Smith, Lillian, 96, 97, 98, 104, 117, 241–79,
    281
    antisegregationist views of, 111, 244, 276
    childhood and family background of,
        244–45, 246–47
    in China, 247, 249, 250, 256, 273–74
    cross-dressing by, 247
    education of, 249, 250
    family ties vs. independence of, 249–50
    girls' camp run by, 117, 249–50, 256–57
    on Gone With the Wind, 270–71

About the Author

Grace Elizabeth Hale is an assistant professor of American history at the University of Virginia. She lives in Charlottesville, Virginia.